The Evolution
of Psychotherapy
The Second Conference

Edited by

Jeffrey K. Zeig, Ph.D.

Brunner/Mazel, *Publishers* • New York

This book is dedicated to

Viktor Frankl, M.D., Ph.D.,
for his monumental contributions to
humanity and for being an
affirming flame, illuminating possibilities
for discovering meaning in life,

and to Ellie Frankl,
the warmth behind the flame.

Library of Congress Cataloging-in-Publication Data
The Evolution of psychotherapy : the second conference / edited by
    Jeffrey K. Zeig.
        p.   cm.
    Includes bibliographical references and indexes.
    ISBN 0-87630-677-6
    1. Psychotherapy—Congresses.   I. Zeig, Jeffrey K.
    [DNLM: 1. Psychotherapy—trends—congresses.   WM 420 E9255]
RC4755.E963   1992
616.89′14—dc20
DNLM/DLC
for Library of Congress   92-9527
                                                            CIP

Published by
BRUNNER/MAZEL, INC.
19 Union Square West
New York, New York 10003

Manufactured in the United States of America

10 9 8 7 6 5 4 3 2 1

About The Milton H. Erickson Foundation

The Milton H. Erickson Foundation, Inc., is a federal nonprofit corporation. It was formed to promote and advance the contributions made to the health sciences by the late Milton H. Erickson, M.D., during his long and distinguished career. The Foundation is dedicated to training health and mental health professionals. Strict eligibility requirements are maintained for attendance at our training events or to receive our educational materials. The Milton H. Erickson Foundation, Inc., does not discriminate on the basis of race, color, national or ethnic origin, handicap, age, or sex. The Board of Directors of The Milton H. Erickson Foundation, Inc., are Jeffrey K. Zeig, Ph.D., Kristina K. Erickson, M.S., M.D., J. Charles Theisen, M.A., M.B.A., J.D., and Elizabeth M. Erickson, B.A.

ELIGIBILITY

Training programs, the newsletter, audiotapes, and videotapes are available to professionals in health-related fields, including physicians, doctoral-level psychologists, podiatrists, and dentists who are qualified for membership in, or are members of, their respective professional organizations (e.g., AMA, APA, ADA). Activities of the Foundation also are open to professionals with graduate degrees from accredited institutions in areas related to mental health (e.g., M.S.W., M.A., or M.S.). Full-time graduate students in accredited programs in the above fields must supply a letter from their department, certifying their student status, if they wish to attend events, subscribe to the newsletter, or purchase tapes.

TRAINING OPPORTUNITIES

The Erickson Foundation organizes International Congresses on Ericksonian Approaches to Hypnosis and Psychotherapy. These meetings were held in Phoenix in 1980, 1983, and 1986. In 1988, the Foundation held its Fourth International Congress in San Francisco on the subject, "Brief Therapy: Myths, Methods and Metaphors." Each was attended by approximately 2,000 professionals.

In the intervening years, the Foundation organizes seminars. The four-day seminars are limited to approximately 450 attendees, and they emphasize skill development in hypnotherapy. The 1981, 1982, and 1984 seminars were held in San Francisco, Dallas, and Los Angeles respectively. In 1989, the Foundation celebrated its 10th Anniversary with a training seminar in Phoenix.

The Milton H. Erickson Foundation organized the Evolution of Psychotherapy Conference in 1985, in Phoenix. It was hailed as a landmark conference in the history of psychotherapy. Faculty included Beck, the late Bruno Bettelheim, the late Murray Bowen, Ellis, M. Goulding, the late Robert Goulding, Haley, the late Ronald D. Laing, Lazarus, Madanes, Marmor, Masterson, May, Minuchin, Moreno, E. Polster, M. Polster, the late Carl Rogers, Rossi, the late Virginia Satir, Szasz, Watzlawick, Whitaker, the late Lewis Wolberg, Wolpe, and Zeig.

Regional workshops are held regularly in various locations. Training programs are announced in the Foundation's newsletter.

The Foundation provides both psychotherapy for clients and training/supervision for professionals. The Foundation is equipped with observation-room and audio-video-recording capabilities. Training and supervision programs for professionals are available. Inquiries regarding services should be made directly to the Foundation.

ERICKSON ARCHIVES

In December 1980, the Foundation began collecting audiotapes, videotapes, and historical material on Dr. Erickson for the Erickson Archives. The goal is to have a central repository of historical material on Erickson. More than 300 hours of videotape and audiotape have been donated to the Foundation. The Erickson Archives are available to interested and qualified professionals who wish to come to Phoenix to independently study the audiotapes and videotapes that are housed at the Foundation. There is a nominal charge for use of the Archives. Please call or write for further details or to make advance arrangements to view the Archives.

PUBLICATIONS OF THE ERICKSON FOUNDATION

The following books are published by Brunner/Mazel Publishers:

A Teaching Seminar with Milton H. Erickson (J. Zeig, Ed., & Commentary) is a transcript, with commentary, of a one-week teaching seminar held for professionals by Dr. Erickson in his home in August 1979.

Ericksonian Approaches to Hypnosis and Psychotherapy (J. Zeig, Ed.) contains the edited proceedings of the First International Erickson Congress. (out of print)

Ericksonian Psychotherapy, Volume I: Structures, Volume II: Clinical Applications (J. Zeig, Ed.) contain the edited proceedings of the Second International Erickson Congress.

The Evolution of Psychotherapy (J. Zeig, Ed.) contains the edited proceedings of the 1985 Evolution of Psychotherapy Conference.

Developing Ericksonian Therapy: State of the Art (J. Zeig & S. Lankton, Eds.) is the edited proceedings of the Third International Erickson Congress.

Brief Therapy: Myths, Methods & Metaphors (J. Zeig & S. Gilligan, Eds.) is the edited proceedings of the Fourth International Erickson Congress.

If you wish to order these volumes, contact Brunner/Mazel Publishers, Inc., 19 Union Square West, New York, NY 10003.

The following book is published by Jossey-Bass, Inc.:

What Is Psychotherapy? (J. Zeig and W. M. Munion, Eds.) is the compilation of innovators' contributions to psychotherapy. *What Is Psychotherapy?* can be purchased from Jossey-Bass, Inc., 350 Sansome Street, San Francisco, CA 94104.

NEWSLETTER

The Milton H. Erickson Foundation publishes a newsletter for professionals three times a year to inform its readers of the activities of the Foundation. Articles and notices that relate to Ericksonian approaches to hypnosis and psychotherapy are included and contributions should be sent to the editor, Michael D. Yapko, Ph.D., The Milton H. Erickson Institute of San Diego, 380 Stevens Avenue, Suite 208, Solana Beach, CA 92075-2068. Business and correspondence about subscription matters should be directed to the Foundation at 3606 North 24th Street, Phoenix, AZ 85016.

THE ERICKSONIAN MONOGRAPHS

The Foundation sponsors *The Ericksonian Monographs*, published on an irregular basis, up to three times a year. Edited by Stephen Lankton, M.S.W., only the highest quality articles on Ericksonian hypnosis and psychotherapy (including technique, theory, and research) are selected for *The Monographs*. Eight issues have been published since 1985. Manuscripts should be sent to Stephen Lankton, M.S.W., P.O. Box 958, Gulf Breeze, FL 32562. For subscription information, contact Brunner/Mazel Publishers.

Contents

———————◆———————

SECTION I. FAMILY THERAPISTS

Acknowledgments

◆

Much of the success of the Second Evolution of Psychotherapy Conference can be attributed to the assistance of many dedicated persons, with special recognition due to Elizabeth Erickson, B.A., Kristina Erickson, M.S., M.D., and J. Charles Theisen, M.S., M.B.A., J.D., members of the Board of Directors of The Milton H. Erickson Foundation, who gave generously of their time and energy in making many executive decisions about the conference.

On behalf of the Board of Directors of the Erickson Foundation, I thank the distinguished keynote speakers, Viktor Frankl, M.D., Ph.D., and Betty Friedan, as well as faculty and cofaculty of the meeting, whose efforts were appreciated by all involved in the conference. The cofaculty included Peter Brown, M.D., Clifford N. Lazarus, Ph.D., Christine A. Padesky, Ph.D., Dott. Matteo Selvini, Molly Sterling, M.A., MFCC, Janet Wolfe, Ph.D., and Marjorie Weishaar, Ph.D.

Also, I greatly appreciate the outstanding jobs done by the moderators at this conference. Deserving of recognition are Ellyn Bader, Ph.D., Joseph Barber, Ph.D., Betty Alice Erickson-Elliott, M.S., Lance Erickson, Ph.D., Brent Geary, M.S., Stephen Gilligan, Ph.D., Carol Lankton, M.A., Stephen Lankton, M.S.W., Camillo Loriedo, M.D., Ruth McClendon, M.S.W., W. Michael Munion, M.A., Bill O'Hanlon, M.S., and Michael Yapko, Ph.D.

Executive Director Linda Carr McThrall and the staff of the Erickson Foundation worked endless hours in handling the registration, publicity, meeting arrangements, and numerous administrative tasks. Led by Ms. McThrall, the following staff members deserve special recognition: Monica Bobak, Assistant Registrar; Theresa Cords, Administrative Assistant; Sylvia Cowen, Bookkeeper; Greg Deniger, Registrar; Dana Deniger, Staff Assistant; Jeannine Elder, Staff Assistant; Sachi Eng, Volunteer Coordinator; Janis Gambill, Administrative Assistant; Alice McAvoy, Staff Assistant; Regina Molina, Staff Assistant; and Lori Weiers, M.S., Staff Assistant.

Volunteers who helped prior to and at the conference deserve commendation, including Brent B. Geary, M.S., Ed Hancock, Ph.D., and Philip McAvoy, M.S.W. In addition, more than 200 student volunteers served as monitors and staffed the registration and continuing education desks.

The Evolution of Psychotherapy Conference was cosponsored by the University of California, Irvine, Department of Psychiatry and Human Behavior, and California State University, Fullerton, Department of Psychology, and their efforts are gratefully acknowledged.

JEFFREY K. ZEIG, Ph.D.
Director
The Milton H. Erickson Foundation

viii

The History of the 1990 Evolution of Psychotherapy Conference

◆

When the first Evolution of Psychotherapy Conference was over in December 1985, we were sure it could never again be emulated. Recreating the essence of that meeting seemed an unlikely possibility.

Organized by The Milton H. Erickson Foundation, the 1985 conference attracted some 7,200 professionals from around the world. The attendees of the first conference gathered in Phoenix, Arizona, to see and hear 26 of the foremost leaders in the field of psychotherapy.

In early 1987, the Erickson Foundation's Board of Directors decided to schedule the second Evolution of Psychotherapy Conference for December 1990. The second event would be held in Anaheim, California.

Letters were sent to the 1985 faculty inviting them to participate in the second conference, and the response was enthusiastic. The momentum from the first meeting was still apparent. While nearly all the original presenters accepted our invitation, we would lose some of the most resonant voices in the field before the December 1990 meeting: Carl Rogers, who died in 1987; Lewis Wolberg and Virginia Satir, who died in 1988; R. D. Laing, who died in 1989; and Bruno Bettelheim and Murray Bowen, who died in 1990. Robert Goulding was unable to attend the second event due to chronic obstructive pulmonary disease. (Dr. Goulding died in February, 1992.)

The first announcement of the December 1990 Evolution of Psychotherapy Conference was made in November 1989. A month later, more than 60 people had registered for the meeting. Throughout 1990, registrations were processed for more than 6,800 professionals and full-time graduate students. Demographically, the second Evolution Conference was similar to the first event. There were about 2,100 doctoral practitioners (M.D.s, Ph.D.s, etc.), and 1,900 master's level professionals, and about 1,800 graduate students. Attendees came from each of the United States and 26 other countries, including four psychologists from the Soviet Union.

The Soviets brought with them a sense of awe for the conference and for the United States. Experiencing life outside the Soviet Union for the first time, these professionals expressed deep appreciation for the opportunity to attend such an historic event. They were able to return to their country with new knowledge, gleaned from the masters whose works they had studied.

The spirit of a smaller world was dimmed by rumors of war in the Middle East. President George Bush announced that if Saddam Hussein had not pulled out of Kuwait by January 15, 1991, the Allied Forces would look toward a "forceful solution." Despite the worry of war, conference attendees expressed gratitude for the chance to meet others from around the world whose backgrounds were diverse but whose goals were similar.

The purpose of both The Evolution of Psychotherapy Conferences is much the same: to develop an accord among schools of thought. The 1985 Conference began that task, and in planning the 1990 event, we kept that goal at the forefront of our minds.

Our goal of conciliation was the basis of creating the conference. The theme, "Psyche-Scapes: Positions and Projections," provided the presenters a medium through which to survey the "landscape" of their disciplines.

The list of faculty was inspiring: Aaron Beck, James Bugental, Albert Ellis, William Glasser, Mary Goulding, Jay Haley, James Hillman, Helen Singer Kaplan, Arnold Lazarus, Alexander Lowen, Cloé Madanes, Judd Marmor, James Masterson, Rollo May, Donald Meichenbaum,

Salvador Minuchin, Mara Selvini Palazzoli, Erving Polster, Miriam Polster, Ernest Rossi, Thomas Szasz, Paul Watzlawick, Carl Whitaker, Joseph Wolpe, and Jeffrey Zeig. Each brought to the conference his or her unique approach to psychotherapy.

Keynote addresses were presented by Viktor Frankl and Betty Friedan. A third keynote address was to have been presented by Norman Cousins, but he died of a heart attack only two weeks before the meeting. Robert Coles, noted child psychiatrist, had to cancel his keynote appearance due to a back problem.

The response to the conference was overwhelmingly positive. After the conference, the Erickson Foundation staff reviewed applications for continuing education credits. Page after page of applications and evaluations indicated that the meeting exceeded attendees' expectations.

The format of the second conference was essentially the same as the first. Attendees could follow one of two tracks: (1) there were three-hour *workshops* where delegates could learn about the presenter's clinical approach in-depth; or (2) they could spend time attending *addresses*, *panels*, and *conversation hours*. Each faculty member presented an *invited address*, which was followed by a *discussion* by another faculty member.

The Milton H. Erickson Foundation, as an approved provider of various continuing education credits, offered CEUs for physicians, psychologists, counselors, social workers, nurses, and other health professionals. The conference was cosponsored by The University of California, Irvine—The Department of Psychiatry and Human Behavior—and by California State University, Fullerton—The Department of Psychology.

The educational flavor of the conference was matched by the entertainment: The Erickson Foundation arranged to have a private party at Disneyland Park. The event, held for five hours one evening, was open only to attendees and their guests. Most of the attractions were open, and park-goers enjoyed the opportunity to go on popular rides without waiting in long lines.

The city of Anaheim was filled with conference attendees. The Foundation contracted with 14 hotels or motels throughout Anaheim.

Due to the proximity of hotels and the Anaheim Convention Center, delegates had easy walks to and from their meetings.

Some 9,000 lunches were served at the Convention Center to attendees who purchased meal packages. Nearly 1,600 people attended the final banquet Saturday night.

The size of the conference created a need for 200 graduate student volunteers. The volunteers monitored rooms, served as assistants to some of the faculty members, and helped attendees with questions. Volunteers also worked with the staff during registration and continuing education validation.

Sessions were held in the Anaheim Convention Center and the Anaheim Hilton and Towers. Registration, exhibits, and luncheons were set up in a 100,000-square-foot exhibit hall at the Convention Center.

There were 34 exhibits at the conference, plus a 3,000-square-foot bookstore managed by Brunner/Mazel Publishers, Inc., and an 800-square-foot booth for tape sales by InfoMedix, Inc.

Additionally, there was a booth set up for the sale of T-shirts and posters as commemorative items from the conference. Profits from the T-shirt and poster sales were used to provide scholarships for graduate students.

Attendees stood in long lines during the Authors' Hour to get autographs of the presenters. Thousands of books, posters, and other media—including at least one baseball—were signed by the faculty.

All the activities—the educational sessions, the party at Disneyland Park, Authors' Hour, exhibits—created memorable moments throughout the week.

In the end, we realized that each Evolution of Psychotherapy Conference has its own essence. Each event has a unique spirit. To emulate the essence is not the point. With the 1990 conference we continued the beginnings of a tradition to bring together the great thinkers—creators—originators—in the field of psychotherapy. Their invited addresses and discussions form the content of these proceedings.

LINDA CARR MCTHRALL
Executive Director
The Milton H. Erickson Foundation

Introduction:
The Evolution of Psychotherapy Revisited

◆

Jeffrey K. Zeig, Ph.D.

I devised The Evolution of Psychotherapy Conferences, held in 1985 and in 1990, with the naive idea of promoting consilience in our field. But psychotherapy is a house divided: There are numerous schools, each has its own leaders and adherents, and each promotes its particular theories and methods. Cross-fertilization with other schools is limited. Purity of position is exalted; eclectic approaches are still considered "second rate."

The 1985 Evolution Conference featured leading contemporary theorists/clinicians, many of whom were meeting for the first time. The Conference also coincided with the 100th anniversary of the birth of psychotherapy.

The first century of psychotherapy was by necessity a period of divergence and proliferation (Zeig, 1987). Perhaps the second 100 years could foster convergence so that effective perspectives and procedures could be harnessed across schools. It was thought that the 1985 Evolution Conference might be a vehicle: Could cross-fertilization occur among renowned experts on the faculty, who, by virtue of the Conference, would have to compare and contrast their approaches? The answer to this question—at least as evidenced by the position of the 1985 faculty compared to their position in 1990—was a resounding "No."

The faculty for the first Evolution Conference was composed of Aaron Beck, Bruno Bettelheim, Murray Bowen, Albert Ellis, Mary Goulding, Robert Goulding, Jay Haley, Ronald Laing, Arnold Lazarus, Cloe Madanes, Judd Marmor, James Masterson, Rollo May, Salvador Minuchin, Zerka Moreno, Erving Polster, Miriam Polster, Carl Rogers, Ernest Rossi, Virginia Satir, Thomas Szasz, Paul Watzawick, Carl Whitaker, Lewis Wolberg, Joseph Wolpe, and Jeffrey Zeig. These experts represented 13 distinct schools. In 1990, these seminal thinkers came together again at the second Evolution Conference with the exception of Bruno Bettelheim, Murray Bowen, R.D. Laing, Carl Rogers, Virginia Satir, and Lewis Wolberg, who had died. Robert Goulding was ill* and Zerka Moreno could not attend. Additional faculty for the 1990 Conference included James Bugental, William Glasser, James Hillman, Helen Singer Kaplan, Alexander Lowen, Donald Meichenbaum, and Mara Selvini Palazzoli. Viktor Frankl and Betty Friedan presented keynote addresses in 1990.

Those from the 1985 faculty who presented in 1990 did not seem profoundly influenced by their interaction with colleagues at the 1985 meeting. Members of the 1990 faculty presented *their* positions on principles and practice with as much vigor as ever. A perusal of the references of these proceedings offers confirmation: Few of the faculty cite the work of faculty members from other schools. (For an exception, see Minuchin, 1987).

As faculty and organizer, I was unable to

---

*Dr. Goulding died February 13, 1992.

attend much of the Conference, but subsequent to the meeting, I listened to the audiotapes of almost all of the panels, demonstrations, workshops, and dialogues. A striking feature of the faculty members' presentations was that rarely was there any acknowledgment of the influence of other members of the faculty.

This position of independence may be prudent and even necessary for pioneers who have added brilliant new facets to our field; however, the front-line clinicians cannot afford the "luxury" of theoretical and technical purity. For those practicing therapy daily, effectiveness takes primacy over the "correctness" of position; multiple perspectives and techniques are required.

I had another reaction when I studied presentations from the 1990 Conference: Each of the experts seemed intrinsically correct about his or her technical/theoretical position. This was startling because many times opinions were dramatically opposed. For example, one expert would indicate that changing cognitions is the preeminent element in therapy. Another would opine that change in social patterns is required. Evidence would be presented adamantly and persuasively. I would finish one program convinced that I had learned the royal road to therapeutic efficacy. Then I would listen to the differing perspective of another expert and be equally convinced that I had discerned therapeutic "truth."

In the introduction to the 1985 proceedings, I tried to offer a communications metamodel to explain why disparate approaches could elicit change (Zeig, 1987). This schema was based on dividing communications (and symptoms—also communications) into 12 elements—four primary elements: behavior, feeling, thought, and sensation; and eight secondary elements: attitudinal, ambiguous, symbolic, relational, qualitative, contextual, biological, and idiosyncratic.

In this chapter, I sketch out a different metamodel. Perhaps the reader can use both metamodels to understand better the process of therapy and the positions of therapy's experts. The present metamodel uses an evolved form of the "Erickson Diamond," which I present in my chapter in these proceedings, entitled, "The Virtues of Our Faults." Here is the revision: The main modification between the

metamodel and the Erickson Diamond (see page 263) is that "The Position of the Therapist," rather than "Utilization," appears as the central facet. The metamodel is more accurate than the version of the Erickson Diamond that appears in my chapter.

The position of the therapist occupies the central portion of the model because of its importance, and because it may account for most of the variance in successful psychotherapy. An explanation of the metamodel begins with a description of the position of the therapist.

The Position of the Therapist

Each therapist brings to the consulting room personal and professional postures that, to a large extent, determine the course of treatment. The personal positions may be even more important than the technical positions in determining treatment outcome.

The Personal Position

I offer an illustrative vignette to introduce the concept of the personal position of the therapist. A patient, who happened to be a therapist, came to my office. As we prepared for the day's

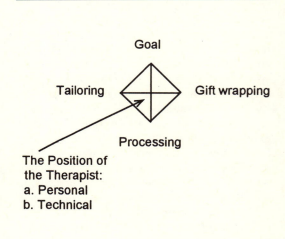

Figure 1. The metamodel of psychotherapy

consultation, he mentioned in passing that he had recently read a professional book that he found valuable. He then proceeded to describe a litany of failures that had happened during the week. Failure was an important issue for this man. He showed an extraordinary amount of natural promise, but had been unable to satisfactorily activate that potential energy.

I interrupted his recital of failures, indicating that I would pose an existential query. I looked at him meaningfully and said, "What are you passionate about?"

Over the next 20 minutes, I repeated the question several times in various ways until he answered, "I'm passionate about knowledge." That made sense to me as it was quite customary for this man to begin a session by obliquely mentioning a book he had read or a seminar he had attended.

Subsequently, I asked the man to hold his hands a few inches from his chest, as if he were holding some playing cards and did not want anyone else to see them. When he complied, I explained, "The distance from your chest to your hands is the distance that you project your passion for knowledge into this room. However, if we explored the topic of failure, you could fill this entire room with failure, so much so that the essence of failure would even seem to linger in the room after you left."

I gave the man a task: Whenever he touched a door knob, whenever he passed the threshold of a room, he was to immediately and covertly project his passion for knowledge into the space that he entered. He was to begin interactions by externalizing his passion for knowledge without ever having to mention it directly. I explained that I had no idea how he would accomplish the task. I reasoned that he had the capacity to project failure into the room, so he must have within himself the mechanism to externalize a passion for knowledge.

I explained further that a projection of his passion for knowledge would be a starting place for the psychotherapy that he conducted. Whatever psychotherapy he did—be it hypnosis, behavioral, psychodynamic—would flow from the headwaters of his passion for knowledge.

This exercise led to an unexpected turn in my own thinking, pressing me to re-examine what I projected in my own consultations. Was I projecting enthusiasm, humor, personal affirmation, positive expectations, intellectual scrutiny, shyness, goal-directedness? Qualities such as these represent the personal position of the therapist.

The personal position of the therapist is an admixture of the therapist's positive and negative characteristics, constituting the "heart" of the therapist. Each therapist projects an essential position into the consulting room, and it is a place, perhaps *the* place, in which therapy begins.

In psychoanalytic schools, the personal position of the therapist could be called "countertransference," a term that is perjorative and laden with negative affect. In traditional psychoanalysis, the therapist is to avoid the projection of residual unconscious conflicts into the therapy situation. Moreover, the therapist is expected to assiduously avoid any projections, which seems an impossible requisite. Therapists project their values onto patients; they project their expectations about therapy. Maladaptive projections must be avoided, but one cannot help but project, just as one cannot avoid manipulation: The goal, then, is to construct and utilize therapeutically helpful projections.

The Technical Position of the Therapist

Each therapist has a technical position, which includes specific "lenses" (input operations) and "muscles" (output operations) that are used to help the patient construct a more fulfilling existence. The lenses and muscles are modified by the exigencies of specialized training and experience; they become set within a range, representing the technical posture of the therapist.

For example, some therapists focus their therapeutic lenses on behavior, others on feelings, and still others on relational patterns. Some use their clinical muscles to intervene with caring tones, others with humor, others with stories. These lenses and muscles combine to become an idiosyncratic integration of natural abilities and acquired characteristics. In the field of psychotherapy, there are widely differing opinions as to the composition of "correct" lenses and muscles required of a therapist. Moreover, there is no standardized baseline: The quarks (essential elements) in one school of therapy are "quirks" to another (Zeig, 1987).

Therapy is more an art than a science: In a science, experts should be able to agree on fundamental units. In psychotherapy, this is not the case. There is discussion, disagreement, and discrepancy at every level. Are the basic units behaviors or feelings? Id or child ego state? Awareness or cognition? Relationship patterns or psyche? Experts and front-line therapists, alike, cannot even agree on the purpose of treatment. Some insist on specific goals. Others argue that therapy is a growth experience and that concrete goals are antithetical to the process.

The lenses and muscles that the therapist acquire are heirlooms. They are learned in the therapist's early training, and are meant to be passed on to generations of students and patients. The heart, lenses, and muscles of the therapist are extremely important because they represent the starting point of treatment. Treatment is influenced by the posture that the therapist assumes as much as it is directed by the posture that the patient takes. The posture of the therapist may be more powerful in determining clinical outcome than the posture of the patient.

Milton H. Erickson is a good example of an effective therapeutic communicator. Erickson developed a number of postures during his long and distinguished career. Erickson championed the concept of *utilization*, for example, (see Zeig, Chapter 12), and he developed his *acuity* so that he could perceive the useful details of his patients' patterns. Further, Erickson used *indirection* and he created *dramatic therapeutic experiences* around which change could constellate. Although these four postures are used by many therapists, Erickson especially developed and harnessed them.

Each therapist develops a constellation of heart, lenses, and muscles that influence the progression of treatment. It might be of value to the reader of this volume to ascertain and delineate the postures of the contributors.

The remainder of the metamodel—including

goal-setting, gift wrapping, tailoring, and processing—is presented in my chapter (pp. 252–269). Special reference is made to use of those aspects in Ericksonian therapy. Next, I will briefly review these additional aspects of the metamodel, presenting them with a more general than specifically Ericksonian slant. Each aspect has a primary question that the clinician can keep in mind.

Setting the Goal

The primary question in goal-setting is, "What do I want to communicate to the patient?" Humanistic therapists might want to communicate to the patients that the purpose of the treatment is to have a growth experience. Family therapists might want patients to improve relational patterns. Symptom-oriented therapists might have narrower goals. Each therapist must have an outcome in mind, whether or not it is openly articulated.

Gift Wrapping

In terms of "gift wrapping," the first question the clinician must ask is, "How do I want to present the goal?" Usually the goal is gift-wrapped within a technique. Techniques can be very specific, for example, conducting a systematic desensitization, and they can be quite general, such as the contact provided by a humanistic therapist. Some schools of therapy have many techniques; others have few. For example, some psychodynamic approaches may proscribe therapist intervention to interpretation, clarification, and confrontation. Other schools, such as Ericksonian approaches, may have a wide variety of techniques, such as hypnosis, reframing, symptom prescription, and so forth.

Gift wrapping can be quite courteous. Patients often "gift wrap" their problems into symptoms. Therapists can respond by gift wrapping solutions within techniques. Therapy thus becomes an exchange of presents (c.f. Ritterman, 1983).

Gift-wrapping a goal is not enough to accomplish competent psychotherapy. Therapy is most effective when it is individualized according to the unique qualities of the patient; a process referred to as "tailoring."

Tailoring

Tailoring centers on the question, "What position does the patient take?" The patient's position consists of both positive and negative components, both strengths and pathologies.

Therapists can proceed by matching the patients' style. For example, the gift wrapping used when a patient is distant and intellectually curious should be different from that applied when a patient is affiliative and artistic.

Tailoring is interactive with the position the therapist takes. Some clinicians posit that the patient is the family or even the interaction pattern among family members, rather than an individual within the system. Tailoring can also influence the choice of gift wrapping. A therapist can gift wrap by using a mechanism that a patient uses to create a problem. For example, a therapist can speak "schizophrenic" to make contact with a psychotic patient, thereby therapeutically harnessing an aspect of the patient's position.

Some schools, the Ericksonian approach for example, put great stock in tailoring. Other schools may deemphasize tailoring, preferring more standardized gift wrapping of interventions.

It is not enough to merely tailor an intervention. Therapists need to create a "process' through which the tailored and gift-wrapped goal is offered.

Process

The "process" question for the clinician to ponder is, "How can I make the therapy into a drama?" Tailored and gift-wrapped goals are best presented dramatically so that the ideas come alive for the patient. Through drama, the therapy becomes a significant emotional event (Massy, 1979). Processing is a matter of timing, in which the therapist sets up, presents, and follows through on the tailored and gift wrapped goal. (For more information, see my chapter in this volume.)

Therapists can merely present a technique, such as assertiveness training, to a patient; however, theatrical, dramatic process may make the technique more memorable.

Some therapists—Salvador Minuchin, Virginia Satir, and Milton Erickson, among others—use drama extensively. These therapists exalt experiential learning. Therapists with a psychoanalytic orientation may deem it unnecessary for therapists to provide much drama at all.

Perspectives on the Metamodel

The metamodel is highly interactive. The goals set by the therapist are in great part determined by the personal and technical positions of the particular clinician. Clinicians who value proactive assertiveness will have different goals than therapists who are of a more laissez-faire nature. Some therapists will value individual differences and spend a lot of time tailoring their techniques. Other therapists may have specific techniques that are mandated for specific patients. Some therapists may be quite theatrical in their presentation, helping their patients in the way that a dramatist helps an actor to experientially learn method acting. Other therapists may be more didactic in their clinical work.

One benefit of the metamodel is that it provides "choice points" for therapists. If the therapist gets stuck, the therapist can change the goal, the tailoring, the processing, and/or the gift wrapping. The clinician also can change his or her own posture. Such flexibility can empower the therapeutic process; it may lead to better results and decrease therapist burnout.

Another advantage of the metamodel is that it provides therapists a way to understand their own predilections. Some clinicians may emphasize tailoring; others may emphasize gift wrapping. It also may have value for training. Some schools will train therapists to use a myriad of techniques, eschewing the necessity for personal development. Other schools elevate the personal development of the therapist, and avoid techniques.

It also is interesting to examine the evolution

of our field with the metamodel in mind. At first, development of the therapist was primary. Analytic candidates were required to have an extensive personal training analysis. Subsequently, there was a proliferation of techniques and efforts to develop the person of the therapist were minimal (for example, with behavioral approaches). Humanistic methods are an exception—much humanistic training is oriented to therapist growth.

Although tailoring and processing have been developed in some schools, such development has been mostly of a rudimentary nature. Much more work is needed to promote these essential aspects of effective treatment.

In summary, any approach to therapy must address the five aspects of the metamodel: the position of the therapist, goal-setting, gift wrapping, the position of the patient, and the processing of interventions. However, some schools may focus on one set of components, while other schools emphasize another group. The metamodel can clarify the reader's understanding of the many perspectives presented in this volume.

REFERENCES

Massey, M. (1979). *The people puzzle: Understanding yourself and others*. Reston, VA: Reston Publishing.

Minuchin, S. (1987). My many voices. In. J. K. Zeig (Ed.), *The evolution of psychotherapy* (pp. 5–14). New York: Brunner/Mazel.

Ritterman, M. (1983). *Using hypnosis in family therapy*. San Francisco: Jossey-Bass.

Zeig, J. K. (Ed.) (1987). *The evolution of psychotherapy* (xv–xxvi). New York: Brunner/Mazel.

Zeig, J. K. (Ed.) (1987). *The evolution of psychotherapy* (pp. xxvii–xxviii). New York: Brunner/Mazel.

Convocation

Exactly five years ago I stood on a similar stage in Phoenix, Arizona, and welcomed attendees to the first Evolution of Psychotherapy Conference, a meeting that celebrated the 100th birthday of psychotherapy. That conference attracted 7,200 delegates, making it the largest meeting ever held devoted solely to the topic of psychotherapy. It was the first comprehensive assembly of leaders of major contemporary schools. With 6,850 delegates from 26 countries, this is the second largest conference on psychotherapy, and we continue the tradition of providing comprehensive representation of major approaches.

In 1985, the faculty included Carl Rogers, Bruno Bettelheim, R. D. Laing, Virginia Satir, Lewis Wolberg, Murray Bowen, and Robert Goulding. Those great voices will not be heard at this conclave. Yet, they are a constant inspiration. Their influence singly, or in combination, is felt on a daily basis in the way we address our patients. Their voices speak through us—as overtones for some, primary themes for others. They are a foundation from which much of our creativity is generated. This conference is dedicated to them.

As architect of the two Evolution Conferences, my idea was to provide a forum through which leaders in our field could interact. Attendees would be able to study the work of the masters at a multidisciplinary assembly. These would not be typical meetings in which family therapists talk to family therapists, transactional analysts speak to transactional analysts, and so on. Early in our evolution, sectarianism was important. A myriad of schools developed, each proclaiming a better philosophy and more effective style of intervention. With the advent of eclecticism, rigid adherence to particular approaches has declined. Most practitioners pride themselves on having diverse tools available to help patients.

Our daily challenge as therapists is an apparently simple one: Help patients bring out their best. And yet, the complexities of that task often seem overwhelming. To complicate the matter, we merely have a modest tool to accomplish our charge; namely, our ability to communicate. We assemble here to learn how to improve that art by studying the work of seminal thinkers in our field.

I hope that as you proceed among the lines of this great psychotherapeutic smorgasbord, you will take the time to sample some previously unfamiliar approaches, and select from the menu things that you can use in your daily practice. The theme of this conference is "PsycheScapes." The meeting is a vehicle through which presenters and attendees can interact to develop the landscape of their method and plant new seeds—developments that will continue to shape the face of modern psychotherapeutic practice.

Another goal in organizing the Evolution Conferences was to honor personal great thinkers. In this way I can fulfill a desire to be a dutiful son honoring the achievement of predecessors. Faculty are, for the most part, the senior experts who have worked diligently to provide new impetus and direction. They deserve to see the effect of their contributions, and your presence here is a token of your appreciation.

Before introducing the speakers, I would like to describe the history of the Evolution Conferences: The Conferences are organized by The Milton H. Erickson Foundation, a nonprofit corporation, which has promoted effective psychotherapy, especially through strategic and hypnotic approaches. The Board of Directors consists of Kristina K. Erickson, M.S., M.D., Elizabeth M. Erickson, J. Charles Theisen, M.B.A., J.D., and myself. The Foundation has been active in organizing meetings since 1980, when we sponsored the First International Congress on Ericksonian Approaches to Hypnosis and Psychotherapy.

In mid-1984, the decision was made to organize the first Evolution Conference. The response was more than we could have dreamed. We originally hoped that the conference would draw 3,000 people, but that meeting, held in Phoenix, sold out in early September, 1985. Even the media recognized the importance of the event. Daily articles appeared in *The New York Times* and the *Los Angeles Times*. A feature article appeared in *Time* magazine. A thought-provoking critique was published in a literary magazine, and republished as a book, *The Lourdes of Arizona*.

There was no way to really know whether or not a sequel to the first conference was warranted. As it turns out, the idea was right. Your attendance today is a testimony to the need for this kind of program.

I am glad that you are here to contribute to the goals of the conference: promoting the evolution of psychotherapy, attending to the commonalities that underlie successful clinical work, and honoring some of the great leaders of our field. I also hope there are ample opportunities for developing personally in the process.

What can you expect at this conference? I think what we have in store is extraordinary. The faculty could not be better. It's gratifying that so many renowned experts have agreed to be here to teach. The topics they have selected to present are engaging and up-to-date. We will cover the gamut of psychological issues relevant to clinical practice. Considering the faculty and the topics, this program is what a friend of mine called an "embarrassment of riches."

On behalf of the Board of Directors of The Milton H. Erickson Foundation, I welcome you. I hope you will find at this meeting some of the important experiences that you are seeking. And, I hope the meeting will be as rewarding and stimulating for the faculty as it will be for attendees.

JEFFREY K. ZEIG, PH.D.
Director
The Milton H. Erickson Foundation

SECTION I

◆

Family Therapists

The Restoried History of Family Therapy

Salvador Minuchin, M.D.

Salvador Minuchin, M.D.
Salvador Minuchin received his M.D. degree from the University of Cordoba in Argentina in 1947. For ten years, he served as Director of the Philadelphia Child Guidance Clinic. Currently, he is Clinical Professor of Child Psychiatry at the University of Pennsylvania School of Medicine and Research Professor of Psychiatry at New York University. He resides in New York, where he directs Family Studies, Inc., and teaches and practices family therapy.

Minuchin developed the structural approach to family therapy. He has written two books and is the coauthor of three, and a volume about his approach has been published. A recipient of the Distinguished Family Therapy Award of the American Association of Marriage and Family Therapy, Minuchin has also received the Distinguished Achievement in Family Therapy Award from the American Family Therapy Association.

Salvador Minuchin describes how the theoretical concepts of family therapy have evolved since their beginnings in the 1950s. Family therapy practice and theory parallel the political ethos of the time. He discusses the philosophy of constructivism, which has received considerable attention in contemporary family therapy, and he places its contribution in context.

Once upon a time, an admiring student gave Milton Erickson a present he cherished. It was a pillow embroidered with the words: "God created man because He loves to tell stories."*

The pillow was too small to have footnotes, so we do not know whether the phrase meant that men are stories that God tells himself or men are the audience God needed to tell stories to; whether women are not stories or are not good listeners; or whether the pillow was embroidered before consciousness raising

transformed men into people, humans, or humankind. Could the message be an anticipation of the social constructivist movement so visible in the family therapy literature today, with a small addendum of Creationism for good measure? Or is it nothing of the sort, but merely an admiring homage to Milton Erickson's talent as a master storyteller?

In any case, the power of story telling is making headlines in the literature of family therapy. As an example, three papers that appeared in *Family Process* during the past year restory the history of family therapy. In this story, the contributions of Ackerman, Bowen, Boszormenyi-Nagy, Fleck, Haley, Lidz, Minuchin, Satir,

---

*After the conference, I received a package from Elizabeth Erickson. Milton's pillow is one of my most treasured possessions now, so the story continues . . .

Whitaker, and Wynne, among others, disappear. A straight and narrow line leads from Bateson to the Milan group and then forward until we meet the constructivist approach. I want to take this story and look at the loss to family therapy, should it become the official history.

The first article is by one of the most elegant writers in the field: Lynn Hoffman (1990), who wrote in the March issue. Using herself as a carrier of history, Ms. Hoffman describes how 25 years ago she "picked up a lens called cybernetics that was lying on the floor of the universe." Through this lens, theories of family therapy described a symptom as part of a homeostatic cycle that stabilized the family. Such cycles were hidden from the family. The therapist was the expert who could see and disrupt those cycles.

Jumping forward 20 years, Ms. Hoffman then describes herself as having (like a number of people in the family field) "fallen in love with constructivism" (p. 2). Maturana, Varela, Van Forster, and Von Glaserfield are the names that populate this literature, along with the family therapists Brad Keeney, Paul Watzlawick, and Paul Dell. Two concepts of this period attract Ms. Hoffman. One is Maturana's view of human beings as closed systems: When two people talk together, "interaction takes place between . . . informationally closed nervous systems" (p. 3). She likes this concept because it challenges the idea of the therapist as an "expert on how the other person ought to be" (p. 3). The second is the "lens" of second-order cybernetics. In this view, with the therapist as part of the system she or he attempts to change, "living systems are not seen as objects that could be programmed from outside, but as self-creating independent entities" (p. 5).

A third concept currently important to Ms. Hoffman is the "lens of gender" and its challenge to a variety of concepts with biases about families built in from patriarchal family organization. All together, these new concepts serve Ms. Hoffman to move away from the instrumental tendencies of her early training and from models of family therapy that have normative biases.

In "The Therapeutic Use of Self in Constructionist/Systemic Therapy," Terry Real (1990) looks at the evolution of concepts of the "sys-temic school of family therapy," acknowledging that other schools may have different evolvements. She presents an interesting historical schema with three phases: The first, the *expanded strategic phase*, occurred at the time of the writing of the Milan team's *Paradox and Counterparadox* in 1978. In this, *instrumental*, phase, the therapist uses himself paradoxically and there is a plethora of techniques: restraining from change, reframing and positive connotation, the prescription at the end of the session, and the structure and function of the team. The second phase, the Batesonian *information-based phase*, appears with the article, "Hypothesizing-Circularity-Neutrality," in 1985, bringing forth a therapy resting not on intervention, but on the creation of new information. The last, the constructivist or *language-based phase*, has as its central tenet the eradication of the idea of objectivity. Human beings are closed systems, and the idea of therapy as conversation becomes the central metaphor.

In "Further Thoughts on Second-Order Family Therapy—This Time It's Personal," Brent Atkinson and Anthony Heath (1990) propose that "second-order cybernetics in no way replaces the validity of first-order cybernetics" (p. 145). Rather, they are related in a complementary fashion. The authors suggest that therapists should shift their personal epistemology in such a way that they become less determined to reorganize the world to suit their individual purposes. In a reply to this paper, Harlene Anderson and Harold Goolishan (1990) suggest that the authors have not gone far enough— that it is "necessary to abandon the core concept of cybernetics" since the issues of power and control, of intervention and of curing, "are all implicit in cybernetic epistemology" (p. 160). They find themselves moving toward what they call a postcybernetic interest in human meaning, narrative, and history. "Change is the evolution of new meaning through the narratives and stories created in the therapeutic conversation and dialogue" (p. 161).

It seems that lurking between the lines in these papers is a straw man, an expert who measures patients against the procrustean bed of his or her own biases dressed as universal norms. A new modality of family therapy, it seems, must be constructed to save families from the misguided intrusiveness of such power-linked expertise.

I know that simply by selecting, I have created a story about these issues that is shaped by my own biases. But the impossibility of objectivity aside, what about these issues that are engaging colleagues so heatedly? Is this simply the squabbling of cousins, or are we dealing with a legitimate theoretical dialogue? Both, I think. So I want to consider these issues as encompassed by two large headings. One is the nature of objectivity in therapy. The other is the right to intervene as experts.

There are a number of feeder streams that run into these two main channels. Are there norms that bracket the nature of people and of families? Are these brackets universals, or are they culturally constructed products of political and ideological constraint? If we become experts, do we ourselves create the fields that we will then discover? Can we influence people at all? Worse, is it not impossible not to influence them? How do we know we are not simply agents of social control? What right have we to constrain diversity, imposing ways of being on others?

I have some agreements with the way these issues are being framed in the theory and practice of family therapy. But I also have some disagreements, and I want to air them, because I am extremely concerned about the preservation of strengths that, I think, are vitiated by the constructivist framing.

Let me introduce, by way of contrast, another group of family therapists who are almost unseen by the family therapy establishment. Within the past decade, some therapists in different parts of the United States, mostly social workers working with welfare populations, have begun to explore the possibility of a different way of working with poor families. Differentiating themselves from traditional social welfare services that depend on institutions that disempower the poor and from the establishment family therapist who works with the family's internal realities, this group forms a new breed of therapist/advocates.

To begin with, these interveners, highly sensitized to issues of social control and of therapeutic paternalism, have shunned the label of family therapist, preferring instead "family-based services." Aware that the reality of poverty in the United States in the 1990s cannot be countered with new and improved stories because it takes human shape on the sidewalks of our cities, these colleagues have developed a new form of clinical intervention. Their services have certain characteristics in common: They emphasize working (1) in the homes of families; (2) at times of crisis (risk of removal of a child, as an alternative to jailing a parent or dismembering a family; (3) with intensive time involvements—the therapist has a very small caseload so he or she can spend as much time as needed with each family, usually carrying a beeper in order to be available at all hours; and (4) within time limits, from two months to six to nine months.

Interested in working with larger systems, this group is knowledgeable about issues having to do with welfare families. These therapists are alert to politics and fiscal changes at state levels. They lobby state legislators. They work through networks, making use of and manipulating the multiple institutions that receive money through the many different channels that fund mandated services to the poor. They are aware of cultural and ethnic differences, sensitive to the exploitation and abuse of poor families by the institutions created to serve them—welfare departments, housing, family courts, and hospitals. And, as I said, they are concerned with the issues of therapeutic paternalism. Their theories and practice are a mixture that includes systems theory, informational approaches, social activism, behavioral and Rogerian approaches, and structural family therapy, among others.

It might seem strange that these two movements, the family-based services and the family therapy establishment, function in parallel, until one remembers that mental health and welfare services are funded by different sources and have always created separate structures.

OBJECTIVITY AND THE RIGHT TO INTERVENE

So we have two types of family therapies. Both are concerned with the nature of reality in therapy, with the dangers of intervening as experts and imposing therapeutic biases, but they function in strikingly different ways. The therapist for the poor is proximal. He or she enters the family and becomes a systems member; learns about patterns, culture, and language; functions as a healer, helper, and teacher, providing information and gathering information in conversations, sharing affects, irrationality, and sweat. The therapist for the rest of us is comfortably distant. This culture-free therapist is an expert on dialogues, targets meaning in restorying, but takes care not to impose or influence meaning. The therapist of the poor, dealing with specific families embedded in society, addresses concrete realities. The culture-free therapist, who knows that reality cannot be grasped, deals with universal constructs. The constructivist therapist promotes increasing complexity in the interior of the family. The therapist for the poor deals with the realities of a family embedded in a network of social institutions that monitor and intervene in the family's life.

I think that these two approaches reflect not only different target populations, but also the sociopolitical movements in which their theories evolved. When family therapy began to develop, in the late 1950s and early 1960s, it was a movement of optimism, of goal-directed intervention and results. Diagnosis could not be an end in itself. Therapy was services and solutions. Do you remember the 1960s with their great sense of searching for better solutions?

Structural family therapy—as well as strategic, experiential, and Bowenian therapies, the therapy of Virginia Satir, and multiple-impact and other therapies—was a product of the 1960s. We became involved in describing and understanding families and in creating and providing interventions to help families in trouble. Structural family therapy focused on family shapes and their different norms of behavior and interaction. So we made maps. Maps oversimplified the complexity of human behavior, but they gave the therapist an Ariadne's thread to use as a guide through the family labyrinth. With the optimism of the period, we may sometimes have mistaken the map for the territory. But I think that the concepts are still valid and are implicit in the practice of all family therapy. The same can be said about the stages of family

development, an idea we took from theories in child development.

The therapist we liked was proximal, inventive, committed, interventive, and optimistic that his or her involvement with the family would solve problems. Let me dwell a little longer on that scenario of hope, 30 years ago. This was the era of the war on poverty. Frank Riessman and others were advancing the idea of the culture of poverty, a partial challenge to the concept of poverty as deficit. Understanding poverty not as an absence of culture, but as a culture in itself, was a more positive concept for that positive decade. This was the era of community mental health centers, like Lincoln Hospital, with Harris Peck championing the idea of the community's taking control of the institutions providing services. Martin and Cynthia Deutsch, Ed Zigler, and Robert Hess were studying cognitive processes of the disadvantaged child and their effects on the learning process, and programs of infant stimulation sprang up all over. Headstart was developed.

In retrospect, it is easy to see how even these adventuresome incursions were governed by the blinders of the time. We were sure there were solutions. If the factors that were hindering poor families were removed, they would be able to break through the cultural barriers. A middle-class optimism was grafted onto the studies of the poor.

I was working at the time in an institution for delinquent boys called Wiltwyck. We began, for the first time, to work with families, and developed some of the concepts and practices I still find useful. But I realize now that in our enthusiastic encounter with systemic thinking, we bracketed the family. We never thought of exploring the nature of the courts that were referring children to us, or the welfare agencies, or the state. We were not aware enough of our participation in the systems we were describing or the way our belonging to a particular group of experts shaped our descriptions.

But in the 1960s, family therapy was marked by the optimism of "Small is beautiful," "Black is beautiful," Spaceship Earth, the new concern with ecology, and systemic concepts. We rejected the counterpositioning of "they and us," saying instead, "We are one." Bateson's ideas mushroomed in this historical period. For a while, "us against them" became, "We are the cosmos."

Laing was another cult figure, a challenger of the representive psychiatric establishment. He was also a member of the group of elders who met with Sartre, trying to focus the flower children movement. His activism in both the flower children's crusade and in the revolt against psychiatric hospitalization was not strange in the context of the period. Both were part of its political atmosphere.

Similarly, the Milan school of family therapy, it seems to me, was a product of its time. Europe had been subjected to years of political repression and American family therapy seemed far too intrusive to a people whose psyche had been occupied.

Paralleling cultural trends important in that period in Europe, the Milan school concerned itself with therapeutic neutrality. In the early 1970s, I went to Heidelberg and, in my American optimism, presented some cases of anorexia, in one of which I had directed the parents of an anorexic girl to make her eat at a lunch session. The German professional audience recoiled and called me "Nazi." A land whose psyche had been occupied by Naziism was supersensitive to the implications of power.

Maturana's concepts may be another example of the influence of the sociopolitical climate on the theories of its time. His concept of biological determinism is not new in the world of science, but it seems interesting that its philosophical correlate that a human being is a closed system gained importance in the atmosphere of fear and social isolation of Pinochet's dictatorship in Chile, where a person needed to close himself or herself off as a way of surviving.

CONSTRUCTIVISM IN THE NINETIES

Let's jump 30 years and enter the present, a different scenario. We are passing through an era of greed and disempowerment, of junk bonds and the Savings and Loan defaults, of a loss of economic power, of diminished pride, of homelessness, of racially motivated murder, of adolescent rape gangs, of riches in the ghettos

in the hands of crack dealers, of AIDS, of Saddam Hussein. We feel powerless in this era, so naturally we question the wisdom of wielding power.

When the constructivists equate expertise with power, however, and develop a new technology of interventions that avoid control, they are only creating a different use of power. Control does not disappear from family therapy when it is renamed "cocreation." All that happens is that the influence of the therapist on the family is made invisible. Safely underground, it may remain unexamined.

Therapy is a temporary arrangement. Hierarchies are mutually organized for a period of time and for a "more or less" specific purpose. Temporary as it is, this arrangement would be a sham if the therapist were not an expert—that is, a person of informed uncertainty—on the human condition, the variety of family systems, family and individual development, processes of change, and the handling of dialogues, metaphors, and stories.

The questions of the constructivists are not new. They are reflected in the early concern in psychodynamics for the meaning and use of transference. They are at the core of Rogerian psychotherapy, of Ericksonian therapy, and of hypnosis in general, and of advocacy movements of all sorts, including the feminist movement, the movement for patient rights, and the self-help groups. In fact, they have held validity for the West throughout recorded history. We can trace them back to the sophists in Greece and Zeno's arrow that never reaches its target, and forward through an argument I witnessed at the last conference at which Bateson appeared, in Kansas. The poet Wendell Barry, who was on the program, insisted on his reality. "I have a land. I walk on my land. I step on a stone. I kick the stone. The stone rolls away," he said. Bateson, he complained, "takes his intellectual shovel, and neatly piles the stone, land, and walking all back inside my brain."

These questions have maintained their validity for millenia, but why have they gained such salience in family therapy today? Do we sidestep expertise because we have seen its miscarriages? Because we are uncertain of intervention as we realize the limitations of knowledge? As we realize our personal limitations?

These are interesting questions, but the bottom line is that the constructivist approach, by bracketing the idiosyncratic story, obscures the social fabric that also constructs it. As it denies the instructive interaction, it makes our social connections invisible. From a social point of view, therefore, this posture is reactionary.

SOCIAL SERVICE IN THE NINETIES

Nowhere is this conclusion clearer than in working with poor families. We have to be aware of the structure and function of the institutions that write the stories of poor families—stories of hopelessness, helplessness, and dependency. If the writing of these stories is made invisible, the stories are told as if they were constructed by the families themselves. This depresses the family members, confuses potential interveners, and makes them both ineffectual. We need to look at this process.

Judicial-system procedures grafted onto the welfare system are a prime example. The party line glorifies the best interests of the child. The actual organization of services abuses and neglects poor children and their families. Consider the language used in a standard training manual for protective-service workers. Assessing a family is called I&R—"Investigation and Reporting." The protective-service workers who actually contact families are minimally trained, mostly on procedures. They are taught to use the language of control, uncontaminated with more human language. When a child is taken away from home, this is not called taking the child away from the home or family dismemberment. It is called "Removal to a Place of Safety." Whatever needs and rights any individual case may entail, the overall language is a language of objects. The language of social service has become the language of the police.

In New York City alone, some 45,000 children are separated from their parents and located in "places of safety." If we include their families and the foster-care families, the affected population must number some 150,000 to 200,000 people. Removals are frequently made on an emergency basis, and the horror stories of young children sleeping in offices until a foster bed can be found are true. Beds in such cases are found whenever it is possible. Therefore, separations of children from parents without any preparation and the separation of siblings in placement are common, although nobody thinks they are right. Because removals are court ordered, procedure involves the transformation of psychological and behavioral data into judicial command. In the best interests of the children, on behalf of family values, the court may prescribe removal of the children, a course on parenting skills, individual psychotherapy for the mother, and when indicated, special programs for detoxification, addiction, sexual offenses and so on. All such programs are assigned and administered for the individual without concern for the family context.

In court, the child and the family are polarized. The family court will assign one lawyer to the mother, another to the child, and a third to the Child Welfare Administration. All three are paid by the state and all three are supposed to operate on behalf of that client—and, that means challenge and attack. The parent talks through a lawyer to "contest" the loss of the child. To speak directly to the judge would require a different language.

Since the governing ideology is to serve poor families, the story of the family court features a concerned society responding to the needs of families and their children. But the procedures that actually touch these families and children control, punish, isolate, and dismember.

Let me introduce you to Marian. Marian is a woman in her 40s with four children. Her grown son is a bank teller, engaged to be married. The three younger children, who were removed to a place of safety, are Anthony, 14, Richard, four, and Nathaniel, two, who has cerebral palsy.

The case came to the attention of the Child Welfare Agency Services when Marian took the baby to a pediatric hospital because he was not gaining weight. The pediatrician ordered the child to be hospitalized immediately. Either Marian did not understand or she did not want the baby hospitalized, so she took Nathaniel home. The pediatrician reported her to Protective Services, and on his recommendation, Nathaniel was removed to a pediatric hospital. Protective Services sent an I&R team which filed a report saying that the apartment was disorderly and there was no food in the refrigerator. A few days later, Protective Services removed the two older children. Anthony was sent to a residential placement and Richard to a foster home in another borough. Six months later, Anthony was returned to Marian, but Richard remained in placement. The court-ordered psychiatric report on her stated that she was disturbed, and although a second psychiatrist diagnosed depression reactive to the loss of her children, the representatives of Child Welfare gave enough weight to the first report to keep Richard in placement, pending mandatory psychotherapy for Marian.

Look at the procedures that touched this family. Marian's children were taken from her, with neither warning nor explanation. Marian was not told their destination, but only that she could contest the removal in court. She knew that Nathaniel was in a hospital in Brooklyn, but it was to be several days before she could learn that Anthony was in a group home on Staten Island and Richard was in a foster home in Brooklyn. She never found out where Richard was living with his first foster mother, and she was not consulted when he was moved to a second foster home. Her life became a desperate struggle to comply with the demands of Protective Services in order to get her child back.

Michel Foucault (1977), who studied power in society, not as it is embodied in people or institutions, but as it is manifested in social transactions, concluded that there is a technology to the way power is allocated that is something apart from the underlying concepts. Penal law, for instance, articulates the concepts that form the basis of judgment and punishment, but prison is what makes the judgment and punishment visible.

So we have two forms of expression. There is the explicit, which is written in the law, and the implicit, which is hidden in the procedures of dispensing punishment. These two forms may or may not be congruent with each other.

In services to poor families, the explicit, "articulated" ideological values are governed by the best interests of the child, by the protection of the child, by family values, by empowering poor families, by helping the destitute and desperate. In their implicit, visible, procedural implementation, services to poor families stress obedience and control. Thus a Marian must

demonstrate her parental love. She is allowed to visit each child for two hours, every two weeks. Traveling for hours to different boroughs will be considered "diligent effort" by the agency and will be a point in her favor. She will have to show compliance by going to the court-ordered course in parenting, without her own or anybody else's children. She knows she must always keep her appointment for the psychotherapy recommended for some unspecified reason having to do with her failure as a mother. However, she will never understand what "they" expect her to do to get her children back, for "they" do not speak in one voice. The story "they" have written is a mystery to the family they have broken.

It happened that I had interviewed Marian several times in the course of a study of foster and biological families. So I went with her to the family court hearing on her request for Richard's return. Before the hearing, I told the Child Welfare Administration's lawyer that I, a psychiatrist, was going to testify on Marian's behalf. He immediately handed me a yellow pad and a pencil and asked me if I would put that in writing. I wrote a statement and signed it. After a five-minute hearing, Richard was returned to his mother. It seemed that in a decision based on a psychiatrist's report, procedure required that another psychiatrist take the responsibility away from the lawyers. By fulfilling the requirements of the ritual, I was able to change the course of this family's life. But notice that even I, playing the deus ex machina with psychiatric credentials, acted as part of this depowering and abusive system. When I persuaded the legal machinery to relinquish Richard, I became responsible for Marian's competence as a mother. Now I, not Marian, am responsible for her future behavior.

In this Kafkaesque world, any restorying of Marian's life will have to include a political understanding of how institutions work and a commitment on the therapist's part to work within the social labyrinth. This is not a construct. This is reality as we experience it. In this world, Zeno's arrow reaches its target. The family-based-services movement is bringing an acknowledgment of reality. It also is bringing a sense of compassion and commitment, a confused array of mixed theories, and an enthusiasm for the exploration of new modalities of intervention. In the face of this social reality, the family therapy movement, in general, and certainly the constructivist branch, is continuing its exploration for a better theoretical understanding of the therapeutic process and is in grave danger of missing the reality of poor families in America.

I think that the strength of the family therapy field lies in the richness of its many roots. In no particular order, and certainly this is not a complete list, these would include the understanding of family organization and family development explored by the structural approach; the concern with the meaning of symptoms and strategies for change brought by the strategic approach; Bateson's thinking about systems; the exploration and acceptance of the irrational cherished by Carl Whitaker; the focus on values and on loyalties of the Boszormenyi-Nagy approach; the focus on human evolution, triangles, reasons, and differentiation to which Bowen dedicated his life; the emphasis on love in Satir's work; Peggy Papp's imaginative work with couples; gender in the work of the feminist group; and the tenacity of Lyman Wynne's work with families of schizophrenics. It would also include R. D. Laing's revolutionary challenge to the psychiatric establishment, the innovations of the Milan school relating time in therapy and the precision of circular questions; Mara Palazzoli's research on the invariant prescrip-

tion; the emphasis on large systems in the work of Don Bloch and Evan Imber Black; the concern for children's context highlighted by Alan Cooklin and Lee Combrinck Graham; the exploration of ethnicity by Monica McGoldrick, Celia Falicov, and others; Andolfi's construction of confrontations; and the use of imagination in externalizations by Michael White.

Of course, the richness that the constructivist movement contributes to our understanding of language, stories, and co-construction is another valuable contribution. However, as presented in current literature, constructivist practice, with some exceptions, binds the therapist to the procrustean bed of talking and meaning, robbing the therapist of human complexity.

REFERENCES

Anderson, H., and Goolishan, H. A. (1990). Beyond cybernetics: Comments on Atkinson and Heath's "Further thoughts on second-order family therapy." *Family Process, 29*, 157–163.

Atkinson, B. J., and Heath, A. W. (1990). Further thoughts on second-order family therapy—this time it's personal. *Family Process, 29*, 145–155.

Foucault, M. (1977). *Discipline and punish: The birth of the prison.* Translated by Alan Sheridan. New York: Pantheon Books.

Hoffman, L. (1990). Constructing realities: An art of lenses. *Family Process, 29*, 1–12.

Real, T. (1990). The therapeutic use of self in constructionist/systemic therapy. *Family Process, 29*, 255–272.

Discussion by Mara Selvini Palazzoli, M.D.

◆

A "discussant" is expected to provide a polemic. But I cannot do it, because I found this presentation masterly. And since my discussion must, unfortunately, be limited, I will synthesize my intervention and divide the address into two parts. First is the historical part, which connects current trends of family therapy with corresponding sociopolitical phases in the United

States and Europe. The second part concerns the present dichotomy between two types of family therapy and Dr. Minuchin's protracted personal experience with what he refers to as the therapy of the poor.

With regard to the first part, I will limit my comments to two points: (1) that which concerns the Milan school and myself at the time of the writing of *Paradox and Counterparadox* and (2) that which concerns constructivism. With regard to Dr. Minuchin's explanation of *Paradox and Counterparadox*, I fully agree with his connecting the distance-keeping mechanism of our way of working with families at that time with the contemporary rejection, in Europe, of everything that was reminiscent of Hitler's and Mussolini's dictatorships. But there was much more than that.

I was a psychoanalyst in my youth. For 17 years, I was almost entirely dedicated to working with anorexic girls. I spent years with each case. I am sure that many of my patients were gentle girls who decided to recover out of pity for me. So when I abandoned psychoanalysis, adopting system theory and inventing paradoxical intervention, I surely was reacting against my depression. When, after two or three sessions with the new method, the first anorexic patient began to eat—and other patients followed by abandoning their symptom—I got a feeling of omnipotence, a sort of manic excitement. I think that it was perfectly understandable: I had suffered too much in those 17 years of commitment—ups and downs, relapses and frustrations. Also, the "spirit of contest" that permeated our work with families could be understood as a sort of game of retaliation or revenge.

Let me now comment on the second point of Dr. Minuchin's historical meditation—constructivism and the hypothetical answer he gives to his own question, "Why has constructivism gained such salience in our time?" I completely agree with that answer, but, in my opinion, there is more. Constructivist family therapists are honest people who do not want to act as experts because they know that, at present, nobody is a real expert in our field. Many of us can be expert in conducting a session, in conversing, in questioning, and so on, but our basic knowledge is intolerably inadequate. Constructivists realize this inadequacy. In my opinion, however, in accordance with the present sociopolitical period of hopelessness he has described, they have resigned themselves to this lack of knowledge.

I can better explain what I mean by telling why I did not accept constructivist family therapy. There were many reasons, of which the most important is that in our center we treat only very difficult families, such as those with chronic schizophrenics and psychotic children. With these families, a systemic constructivist therapy is an inadequate tool. Personally, I was deeply convinced that our ignorance was so great as to be intolerable. But I could not resign myself to ignorance.

IGNORANCE OF WHAT?

We realized we could not be expert on everything since human minds are limited. We could not be expert on every problem and in the psychotherapy of every possible case, such as the treatment of alcoholics, of patients dying of AIDS, of phobics, and so on. Thus we decided to limit ourselves and to treat only families with psychotic children. Having defined the area in which we wanted to diminish our ignorance, we started to look for the existence of recurrent interactive family processes (through time) that are typical of families with a psychotic offspring. Knowledge of these processes could guide us in helping our clients. It was imperative to enjoin ourselves from using paradoxical methods that did not permit a comparison of data and to invent a clinical experimentation that would allow it.

Knowledge is based on comparison. Therefore, in 1979, we began to give all of our families the same series of prescriptions that had proved to be therapeutically powerful. After many years of work, we drew up general models of six stages of schizophrenic and anorexic processes within families. It is imperative to emphasize that our models were not built on storytelling, but on *facts* directly observed in the sessions, and especially on *reactions* that each member of the family had to our prescriptions.

Are these models realities? I do not know. However, I also do not know if the famous double-helix model of Watson and Crick in genetic research (God pardon me for such a disproportionate similitude!) is a reality. But what a help it has been for the evolution of genetic knowledge! What a number of mysteries it has helped to explain! A step forward in knowledge is always marked by a new model that explains more than the previous one and whose validity is provisional.

The models of interactive family processes we have presented in our latest book are coarse and simplistic, notwithstanding the many years we have spent in drawing them out. But they are better than nothing. They are, in our opinion, the first steps toward increasing our knowledge. (Parenthetically, I think that a difference between our models of certain family processes and the maps of structural therapy are the attention we now give to temporal factors.)

With regard to the second part of this important presentation, essentially I will consider the part Dr. Minuchin has based on what he defines as the actual *dichotomy* of two types of family therapies, namely, culture-free therapy and the therapy of the poor.

I remember that a dichotomy (for different reasons) already existed at the time of *Paradox and Counterparadox*. I remember when I began working in the public sector in 1981. It was really a traumatic experience for me, because it turned out that it was not possible to export into the public sector the method we had invented for middle-class families coming to our private center. Everything had to be reinvented, and too many situations were disheartening because we had incorrect tools.

Our situation is different now. We have new models of interactive family processes and a growing experience in reconstructing their historical course. We can overcome the dichotomy and unify our way of working in different fields. We are a team of four. Personally, I work only in our center, but the other three members of our team work part-time in the center and also work with the poor in the public sector. Here, they are importing our method of reconstructing the course of family processes with the help of our models and adapting them to the relational vicissitudes specific for those cases. I am now convinced that to help these people, just as is true in helping schizophrenic or psychotic adolescents, commitment is indispensable. But it is not enough. There is also the problem of knowing *how* to obtain cooperation through a rapid and empathic grasping of the specific roots of their suffering.

People need to be understood in the context of their past and present relational intricacies, which they cannot see clearly by themselves. Neglected children often are instrumentalized by their neglecting parents both to *indict* their families of origin and to *ask* for help.

QUESTION AND ANSWER

Question: I am Dr. L. V., and as a child psychiatrist, I do a lot of work with social control systems, with the courts, and I reluctantly find myself in a position of power. I don't particularly enjoy that, but I recognize that it has been given to me in the same way that the courts gave you, Dr. Minuchin, the power with Marian to get her child returned. How can I use my position to empower other players in the system, and more important, to empower the people that the system directly affects? How can I use my power to empower people like Marian to the courts? The social control systems are more responsive to them.

Dr. Minuchin: It is very difficult to train people to be incompetent. Therapists, psychiatrists, and also counselors are trained for competence. When you are working with people like Marian who has been trained for incompetence, then you are a complementary match. She elicits from you the kind of thing that you do best. We try to train our students to what we call strategic incompetence. You need to declare yourself in need of help. That is a very difficult thing for a psychiatrist to do.

Symbolic Experiential Family Therapy: Model and Methodology

◆

Carl A. Whitaker, M.D.

Carl A. Whitaker, M.D.

Carl Whitaker (M.D., Syracuse University, 1936) has practiced psychotherapy for almost 50 years. For nine years, he was a professor and Chairman of the Department of Psychiatry at Emory University College of Medicine. For almost 20 years, he was Professor of Psychiatry at the University of Wisconsin Medical School. One of the founding fathers of family therapy, Whitaker received the Distinguished Family Therapy Award from the American Association of Marriage and Family Therapy. He is a Life Fellow of the American Psychiatric Association. Whitaker is the coauthor of three books and has edited one, and a number of books have been written about his approach. He has 60 contributions to books to his credit, including introductions, chapters, and forewords, and he has published more than 70 papers. Whitaker is a former president of the American Academy of Psychotherapy.

Carl Whitaker's approach has been named "the experiential school." In this chapter, Whitaker describes essential aspects of his symbolic approach. Typical of his style, the chapter is a symbolic growth-promoting experience for therapists, rather than an objective comment on his method of therapy.

I want to talk about the therapist. I am really not interested in patients. I don't have to worry about patients, so I can be more personal. Thus what I have tried to do in these past 15 years has been a fun experience. It is really a shame it takes so damn long to have the fun of old age. Importantly, these things that drop out of you are not the things you have gathered from somebody else. Rather than taking notes of what you hear today, you take notes on what pops into your head when you are listening. You can listen to the content some other time.

At 4 o'clock in the morning, I had two new titles for this chapter. One was "Parallel Play" and the other was "Glasnost and Perestroika." I want to talk about the therapist, and I want to talk about the therapist's capacity to learn how to play. I want to talk about the capacity for openness and the capacity for restructuring your work as you go along. Needless to say, one of the glories of old age is that I can talk about my life and you are stuck with listening. Sorry about that, but not much. The other nice thing about old age is that you do not much care what people think about you. It takes so many years to get ready to be honest.

I also want to discuss the use of power, which Sal Minuchin talked about in his address.

I would like to set up a way that you can use power and the other thing he talked about, "strategic incompetence." I am really so sorry for him because it is so natural for me I don't have to be strategic about it.

Before we get into anything serious, I want to describe my new beliefs about family therapists, what we are and who we are. First is our character defect, which is a delusion of grandeur. My second belief is that the process of psychotherapy is a process of becoming a foster parent. That means that our power is time-limited and dominated by the larger system, including the culture, the society, and the courts—all these things Minuchin has discussed so beautifully.

My new words make this next belief difficult, and I sort of hesitate. A couple of my esteemed colleagues warned me not to do it. But here goes: I think our job is distorted. I think essentially we are psychological prostitutes. And if we are trained, it is even more serious. Then we learn how to be better actors, better operators in this psychological prostitution game. The problem is we might not be taught not to be promiscuous, and that worries me more than almost anything else, except the thing that Minuchin was talking about. The related question is a haunt: "Do I need somebody to teach me how to handle the pimp?" Whether it is the judge or the social worker who is in charge of protection or the probation worker, all those other people are pressuring us to make sure that we do not do psychotherapy. They want us to be spies. That power is serious.

I want to describe a symbolic experience. I was a little old country boy from the Adirondacks doing an obstetrics residency in the middle of Manhattan. After a year of being a rotating intern, it was my first day as the resident in surgery, and at 4 o'clock that morning, Dr. Richie—the big, fat, wonderful Chief of Surgery—showed up in his nightclothes from his hospital in Manhattan. He had worked all night writing and then got into a cab and came over to our hospital, still in his underclothes. In the operating room, he asked, "What are you doing over on the other side of the patient?" I said, "Well, I'm just beginning." He said, "You get over here. You're going to do the operation." I said, "Please, I have never done an operation." He

said, "It doesn't make any difference, I'm going to be on the stool right behind your shoulder. You won't make a move until I okay it. But you're going to do the operation."

That is one of the horrors in our racket. You are all alone, except for the sweet grandparents outside the one-way mirror. They're just Peeping Toms. The problem of what you do when you are there all by yourself is the horror story. Do you just get more defensive? I think you ought to be pathologically honest. I think you ought to say to the first patient, "You know, this is the first time I've ever been paid for this. So please keep coming back, it will help pay my rent." I am very serious. I don't think that is a joke. I think if you can use that kind of honesty you are five steps along in learning how to be a professional psychological prostitute. And if you don't learn, you are in bigger trouble because you could get AIDS and all sorts of other things.

Now let me relate another symbolic experience I had. It was with a wonderful social worker, Ruth Mellor, who was about 60 years old. She was at the Child Guidance Clinic and she saw the mothers while I saw their little children in the playroom. She said, "Don't ever come to talk to me until you have written the play hour out for yourself."

I suggest you learn about how to develop your own theory and your own understanding of how to be professional by writing before you talk to anyone. Don't contaminate your own thinking and wait until you have been hyped up on your way out of an interview or are ready for a court appearance; write it down for yourself first. Your experience is more critical than the combination you make with someone else. If you have to talk to a supervisor, take a peer with you. Then the two of you can outvote the supervisor; otherwise you become an imitation psychotherapist. Don't you become one. There are so many of them around now that it's terrible.

I had three lucky breaks. My first was that I was trained in surgery so I was never indoctrinated in psychodynamics psychiatry. My second good break was that my entire second year consisted of play therapy with small children. Parallel play is a unique experience. You cannot play with a three-year-old. You can "play parallel" to them. They build blocks and you sit on the floor with them and you build your castles. By the time they are four, you may team up to build a bigger house. I now think that most families come as three-year-olds. The important caution is not to take over. The autistic problem they bring to the first interview can be countered if you don't play in their toy box. If you play beside them in your toy box, they can watch and gradually learn to play with you.

My third break in learning to become a professional was the chance to spend 12 years doing cotherapy with individual chronic schizophrenics. Since this was before the days of tranquilizers and contamination through drugs, I had a very humiliating, very devastating experience. The pathological integrity of the schizophrenic forces an endless plunge into your own solitude.

My work with schizophrenics helped develop the professional assumptions I make in all professional therapy. First, I assume that the therapist and the patient are both participating members of the adult community. We each evolve a social personality. Second, each of us is also a preverbal printout of our own unique infant-growth experience. These are two separate things. Third, there is also evolving an entrenched character. The fourth assumption is that there is an interaction between the *"I-ness"* involved in the infant preverbal experience and the *"We-ness"* learned in the subsequent years of belonging to a family; early on there is the biopsychosocial unit, then later the psychosocial organism, and later still the social family. This combination of We-ness and I-ness, with the emerging character structure and the evolving social living, do, of course, merge. The variability in this two-system interaction is massive. The relative dominance of the I-ness and the We-ness is also overdetermined and establishes our whole life-style.

This life-style can be pictured. The healthy sociopathic family develops a dominant "We" pattern. Time seems to foster a lack of integration and a loss of integrity in both the family and the individuals in it. In contrast, the healthy schizophrenic family establishes a dominate "I" pattern. Schizophrenia seems to foster a process of abnormal integrity and isolationism, and even a denial of the scapegoat dyad. Those families live with an internal chaos, but without anxiety.

Behind the assumptions is a theory that we all are more or less schizophrenic and more or less sociopathic; we are schizophrenic in our sleep and sociopathic in our daytime living.

I am convinced that psychological growth necessitates an equal amount of schizophrenia and sociopathy. I can only be as crazy here as I can be tricky in putting it across. Ordinarily, we work all day long to establish a We-ness. Some call it a therapeutic alliance. We plan and maneuver to facilitate joining. Most of our night life is an equally massive effort to expand and live out our I-ness. We are all schizophrenics in the middle of the night, and we wake up and make believe it was just a man who dreamed he was a moth, not a moth who woke up and now assumes he is actually a man.

Emotional growth is not only the process of developing more competence and security in the verbally duplicitous attachment we have with each other. We all double-talk. The unconditional positive regard is available for the first nine months of the baby's life. Then the baby starts playing peek-a-boo, and from then on becomes trickier and trickier.

Growth is also the full-bodied play into and out of I-ness. Each of us struggles to be ourself, the same self we have avoided and been unfaithful to all our maturing years. If I trace growth inch by inch, it is a process of gradually getting over being unfaithful to yourself. One gradually gets over being a fake with other people. Each of us then carries some sign or emblem that proclaims that here is a person unique in his (or her) oneness and ready to face any other self in defense of that emblem.

PROFESSIONAL PSYCHOTHERAPY

Any life incident can be therapeutic; however, there is a difference between something that is therapeutic and psychotherapy as a process. Being fired, getting married, or inheriting $10,000 from your grandfather can be therapeutic. That is not therapy. It can promote your growth and increase your integrity, your capacity, without having any deliberate process at all. An episode can be symbolically therapeutic if it resonates to the printout of our computer's early programming. Symbolic episodes are unique because they click for us. Many, many things are nonsymbolic. Even massive experiences may be nonsymbolic. For contrast, miniature things also can be symbolic and powerful.

Professional psychotherapy, as I picture it, is the deliberate effort to empower a family that has reached an impasse in its evolution of We-ness or of I-ness. Most psychotherapy is an effort to reempower both the unique pain and isolation of I-ness and the stress induced by the pain of belonging. Styles of psychotherapy can be classified as the effort to reinforce either We-ness or I-ness. These are two separate growth patterns. Patterns modifying We-ness are basically verbal. Patterns modifying I-ness seem to necessitate symbols that either induce anxiety or patient–therapist affect summation. We sometimes call this pattern "acting in." Acting in is more dangerous and needs more and more trickiness in the modern legalistic world and with its lawyers.

Augmented therapeutic transference is one way to describe the process I am trying to describe. I believe that transference rules the world. I hate to think of what President Bush does when he talks to Gorbachev. They are really not individuals representing countries; they are adult children of their parents, siblings of their brothers and sisters, and ex-patients of their nonprofessional therapists.

Transference includes both the patient and the therapist. It is also both negative and positive, and mostly below awareness. This is another part of what I think makes parallel-play work. The process of professional psychotherapy can most efficiently use the power of transference to facilitate the control and the augmentation of joining and individuating, or We-ness and I-ness.

POST-THERAPY GROWTH

Successful psychotherapy creates a greater freedom to utilize endless opportunities for growth by repeated covert transference experiences. I have had a fascinating experience in the past five years or so. Gradually, I have become clear in my thinking. I have become objective about my subjective experience. When I am on stage, I am freer than when I am anywhere else. I actually become a patient to the audience. It doesn't make a bit of difference whether they know it or not. My transference, my investment in myself, and my need for the audience make me more of who I am. I am more ready to free-associate on the stage than anywhere else, except in dreams. It is a weird process, but I think it is one to define successful psychotherapy.

There was a joke I long played with Murray Bowen ("Boy, I'll miss him"). He would say that he didn't believe in transference and I would say, "Murray, that is one of the craziest stories. Three minutes with you and I am transferred up to my ears. If you don't know it, that's too bad." That's one of all therapists' problems. I have never seen any mother who knows how powerful she is. Think about your mother and realize how powerful she is. Yet I have never seen a mother who knew she had that power. It is eerie to think that a mother can have this power and her child knows it, and her husband, who is the oldest child, also knows it. Don't tell anybody that—it's a secret. But the mother doesn't know it. She doesn't know her power. The mothering we do in psychotherapy keeps us from knowing the power we carry. I don't know how to get myself over that misperception. Finally, those people who are able to transfer freely for their own growth experience don't need any response from a transference figure. The transference experiences of joining and then killing the Buddha are both intrapsychic. So nobody needs to know.

SYMBOLIC PSYCHOTHERAPY

Doing psychotherapy of the healthy nonrational psychotic core, the "I-ness," is like relating to an LSD flashback or to the outflung arms of a tiny infant. I can still remember coming around a corner in medical school and there was a mother and her six-month-old baby. The baby just put out her arms to this stranger. That's life being therapeutic. That's life becoming symbolic. These healthy moments may be the only unconditional positives available. Typically, symbolic psychotherapy necessitates a primitive "parent–child" holding quality that empowers the patient to experience chaos as creative and exciting and worth the danger.

Play therapy is the golden path by which to enter the psychotic nonrational self of infancy. Each of us yearns for and is equally terrified by such a plunge.

THE POLITICS OF FAMILY THERAPY

First, there is the power dynamics. We have a sellers' market before the first meeting. The request concerns the family's universal symptom. There is only one symptom in family therapy: Who is going to win? He and his family or she and her family? Actually, there is no such thing as a family. It is a combination of two families. And the question is, like the Israelis and the Arabs: How can you tolerate it? How can you find a way to move into that whole-person to whole-person psychotherapy we call marriage or family building? That stress about the next generation: Are the baby's ears like his mother's? Does she have the same wide eyes that Dad's father has? So the two families fight for the rest of the kid's life. Whom does she look like? To whom does he belong? Does she have the smartness of Uncle Pete? Is he going to be stupid like old Ezra?

This power is offered when you first get the call. The operator says, "There is a lady downstairs to see you." Maybe you get a call from the father saying, "I want some help." This is your power. Listen carefully. Symbolically, you are a female being called by a stranger for a blind date. The potential patient is approaching you in a language that is unique, a language of pain and impotence. "I am in pain and I can't do anything about it." If you respond to that with, "I'll take care of you," you are cutting your own throat. You need to use your power by keeping the initial contact provisional. Our pathology is such that it is almost impossible to avoid being overprotective. That is why I likened the experience to a blind date. When they come in, they are paranoid about you, and you should be more paranoid about them because you are in more danger. They are coming for real, they have power. You are acting a part so you are an actor, and a psychological prostitute needs to be very careful. The questions are, "Why now?"

"Why me?" "What else have you tried?" "What about your previous therapists" professional and nonprofessional?

Someone should write a thesis on the nonprofessional psychotherapist. I will be your first case. I can trace 15 nonprofessional therapists before I ever got up the nerve to go to a professional one. And I only went then because my wife went first. You need to call on a support team before this first blind date. You can even evolve a support team out of the family over the telephone. "Would Aunt Minnie care about you?" "Do you think she would help me be useful to you if we decided to go ahead?" You should expose your impotence, the possibility of failure, and still keep all the decisions about the therapy in your hands. You can even delay the first appointment and say, "I need to think about it a little more," or, "I want to talk to a colleague about what you are asking."

The blind date itself is an experiment in dyadic-relationship diagnosis. If you can make this telephone call a way to assemble the family, you have a big advantage. When the family members get together, you can say, "Grandma, I'm trying to find out how to think differently about how two people live together." Then, "Grandpa, can you tell me how it was between your mother and father? Now I don't want you to tell me about your mother, and don't tell me about your father. But how did they get along? Did they fight and then make up? Did they live back to back? Was she his mother and he her little boy? Was he her mother? How did those two get along?" Next is Grandma. "Grandma, would you tell me about your mother and father and how they made it with each other? What was their twosome like?" Then you go right down the family, father, son, all the kids. Make each of them describe another twosome. "Sonny, will you describe how it was between, well you pick one, your sister and your mother, your sister and your father, your older brother and younger sister? How do they make it? Who did the pairing in the family and how was it done?" And you may be lucky and find some people who can talk about triangles. If Mom and Dad get into a fight, who fixes it? Who starts it? Who can stop it? They begin to get a sense of the dynamics of the system before you get through this first blind date. They also sense that you are talking about whether or not you want to be a therapist for this family.

Then, if you have a good family, you can move to family diagnosis. Fred Ford had a wonderful classification: the family that lives back to back, the one in which the children come first, the family that lives as a unit against the world, and the family in which each member is for himself or herself.

If you are trying to expand this first interview, you can do some parallel play. Using a stimulus from the family after a playful feedback from your fantasy of the moment (e.g., "That reminds me of my Aunt Minnie. When she was mad, she was scary, but when she was good, she was wonderful. Was your aunt like that? Is that what you were trying to tell me?"), you play parallel to what they seem to be implying. If you stay more and more outside of their content, they are left with a symbolic metaphor they cannot negate. The more you stay in your world and keep exposing the head games you play (e.g., "If my mother were like that, I don't think I would have made it through first grade") is very different from, "I understand how you were mad at your mother," or, "I understand why you got sick." That may invade their world. If, instead, you just show them your world, you leave them with the responsibility for changing the world they live with and live by.

DANGER OF CONTENT

Maybe it helps to face with yourself, and with the family members, the fact that every therapy interview is only a place in which to think about living. We should push them to live their own lives so that they get the credit. Anytime we try invading their living, we become like a transference figure in their world and then they can turn us off or leave us responsible for their living. If you don't get into their world, they can't turn you off. You are just a haunt.

At the end of this first interview, I prefer to decline the second interview. It is important to join the family, but we are good at that. Most of us are lousy at individuating. We must teach the family to separate and how to differentiate. And the best way to do this is to model it. I recommend that halfway through the first inter-

view, you get up and walk out, get a cup of coffee, answer your mail, talk to a colleague. And after a while, you come back. They ask, "Where were you? What did you do" You answer, "Nothing." "Well, why did you go?" "I don't know, I just had this sudden feeling that I wanted to be myself."

I heard this crazy, old therapist who thought this was a good trick to help the family realize that the therapist is just working, and doesn't belong to the family. He was afraid that we are always tempted to be an imitation of an adopting mother. He said we need to know that, but I think the family also needs to know. I think one should decline the second appointment. "You know what, I listened to you and I think I understand something about the kind of struggle you are in. I appreciate your pain, but I want to think about this and you to think about the whole thing. Why don't you go home? Don't talk to each other about the interview. Go home and stay in your own head until tomorrow. And then get together and decide whether you want another appointment."

A wonderful trick John Warkington taught me was to tell the family, "You know, you don't have to pay for the first interview unless you come back. If you come back, then you have to pay for the first one, too." Perhaps every interview should be the first and the last. I suspect that the most successful outcomes were in the families I only saw once. Forcing the family members to get together and making them think about the family for one hour gave them enough experience to do something about their setup on their own, in their own way, and without ever letting me know about it. You can retain, at the end of this first interview, the right to decline the alliance until they redecide and call back. When they call back, you try to make sure that you get the people who previously didn't want to come. "If you decide to come back, why doesn't Joe call me, because he is the one who seems less interested in therapy and I am afraid of any loss of power in the family? I need to have everyone together, and he will probably have a better estimate than anyone else."

The second interview is a complete flip. This is where I expose my deliberate incompetence. I don't have to learn it, it is automatic. It is their life, so I carefully and tenderly force them to take the initiative. This is a strange paradox. I start by fighting for my "I position," and now, in the second interview, I force them to establish their "I position." I learned this in a symbolic experience with a woman whose job was teaching children to paint. She had a group of ten little kids, three- or four-year-olds. I spent a couple of hours with her and asked, "How do you do it? All you do is put up easels and give them some paints. What do *you* do?" She said, "I just wander around. If I see something pretty, I say, 'Hey, that's nice.'" "Don't you tell them how or what to paint?" "Never." "Well, don't you advise them or something?" "Oh, no." "Why not?" "Well, they are just trying to learn." "Don't you teach them?" "No, I just sit around and help them learn." "Isn't that the same thing?" She said, "No, no." Then I thought of Tillich's book *Being Is Becoming*. I worried for several years. Finally, I got the other half, "Doing is to keep from being." So as long as you keep doing something, as long as you stay manic, you don't have to face your schizophrenic insides.

That is true of us too, so I sit and say, "You take over. Talk when you want to." "Well, we don't know what to talk about." "I'll wait while you think about it." "What do you think we ought to talk about?" "Well, I don't really know what you have courage to talk about." "We don't know how to be patients." "I'll be glad to wait." "You are going to have to help me." "Okay, I worry about my retirement. I keep wondering what to do." "Hey, we don't care about your retirement." "You don't need to be a patient." "I thought maybe I'd grow a little if you would let me talk about myself." Finally, Dad says, "Look, if we are going to sit around like this, let me tell you about my mother-in-law. Is she gruesome!" "I suppose that means we are going to have a fight now because your wife doesn't think her mother is gruesome." "Oh yes, she agrees that her mother is gruesome." "Well, why didn't you bring her? I might have a wonderful fight with her." "You know, I hadn't thought about that. Could we bring her next time?" "I think it would be great." "Any possibility to get your grandpop to come along, or is he just too retired?" So you keep building the system. You can even add to it by using a speaker phone. "Oh you can't get Pops, he's 2,000 miles away." "Well, why don't you get him on the phone? We could have him

here for the whole hour and he would be part of the entire interview."

By your declining to lead and forcing them to declare their family position, they inch into taking on the anxiety they were terrified of when they came to see you. Now they are facing the anxiety with your supporting them, but not leading them. Change is beginning to occur, although it is minimal.

At the third interview, you encourage them as they begin to take over. "You know, Dad, it took a lot of guts to talk about your wife's mother in front of all the kids. Is she going to get you? How about next week? Do you think she will get back at you next week?" "Maybe Mom can talk about your husband being a little boy to your mother?" "I'm not a little boy to my mother." "I wasn't asking you. I wouldn't expect you to know. But your wife would know, and I wouldn't ask her because I wouldn't want to embarrass her." You can play out your fantasy to keep their pain in semishadow and your hunches offside.

During the third visit, the initiative is still theirs. You may sit there for half an hour while they try to make up their minds or as they inch back and forth, hem and haw, until they gradually begin to move. By the third visit, they may be afraid to lead, but if they are clearly in action and leading and they carry the anxiety, you can begin to do more parallel play with your own fantasy. "I'd have gone crazy if I had been living in the thing you're talking about now. I'd have been in a state hospital, sure as hell, or ended up being a criminal. Maybe I'd have gotten an AK-47. Most people would give up." Or, "Life is a mess." Or, "How did you keep from being suicidal? I had a couple of good attempts. I almost made it the first time. The second time it was touch-and-go. What happened with your first time?" So you parallel play with them. You don't make them confess, you don't invade their world. You try to keep them in their world by letting them peek into your inner world.

FINALLY

The therapeutic alliance is sacred. *Progress is really not important.* I was so tickled when that one dropped out of my head. Progress is not important. The only thing that is important is process. The process you are operating is what is critical. Training and learning perfect the process.

The process of symbolic experiential psychotherapy begins by expanding the anxiety-laden move to include the entire three-generation family unit by offering to be foster parent or coach in the detente between the two parental subsystems.

After an initial trial of labor, the therapist or therapeutic team forces the family to initiate a therapeutic alliance in which the family must reempower itself and the therapist thereafter will catalyze a healthy craziness and the control of all subunits by the family as a whole.

Discussion by Paul Watzlawick, Ph.D.

◆

Needless to say, out of the richness of Dr. Whitaker's presentation, I can only include a very few points in my discussion, and I can imagine that a different discussant probably would include very different points. His style is highly personal, idiosyncratic, and very difficult to describe, and therefore difficult to discuss.

Take his assertion that any life incident can be therapeutic. This is, I think, a very, very important point. It brings us closer to the understanding of the phenomenon of change as such—which has, as far as I know, never been studied. Change is a phenomenon in its own right. I have a persistent fantasy that if that proverbial little green man from Mars came down here and asked us, "How do you humans bring about change?" and we were to present our complicated and contradictory theories about human change, the little green man would scratch his head, or its equivalent, and would ask, "Why haven't you ever studied change in the first place, as it occurs millions of times in human lives without so-called therapy?" How can we take this over into therapy? That is, of course, the big question, and here we get to what I consider an important crossroad. There are those of us who want to systematize, who need a theory, and in that respect, it is probably insignificant whether or not the techniques we use are the cause or the effect of that theory. I think that this is what Dr. Whitaker means by the "We-ness" phenomenon. There are those

outstanding people like Carl Whitaker who "simply know" or "simply do" what brings about change, and I guess this comes close to his concept of the "I-ness." The relationship of those two groups was well expressed by the famous mathematician Gauss, who is supposed to have said one day when confronted with a difficult mathematical problem: "The solution I already had; now I have to find the way by which I arrived at this solution."

In listening to Dr. Whitaker, I am very much reminded of this strange ability to grasp the essence of something. Such people are very rare in our field, but they are absolutely fascinating. Take, for instance, John Rosen, a psychiatrist in Philadelphia whom Dr. Whitaker knew very well, since he and Dr. Malone worked with him. Rosen had this concept of "entering into the psychosis," and he was never quite able to explain what it would mean, but I saw him do it and found it fascinating. I remember one case of an autistic patient, himself an M.D., who had not spoken a word in three years. Within 15 minutes, John Rosen had an animated discussion with this person. His *explanations* were, as I have already hinted at, less impressive. And we all know about Milton Erickson and his fantastic ability to find seemingly miraculous, but terribly simple, ways of arriving at a change. There is also the founder and first director of the Mental Research Institute (MRI), Don Jackson. He was capable of doing therapy within the first ten minutes of the first session. He had a fantastic ability to gain the understanding of the system and exactly what would bring about change. I remember how for many, many Wednesday mornings, we would play to him parts of what I then called the structured family interview. It was an interview technique that, we hoped, would substitute for the *Diagnostic and Statistical Manual of Mental Disorders* (DSM-II). It was supposed to become an interactional kind of diagnostic manual, but it never worked out.

One of the tasks was to ask the parents, in the absence of the children, "How out of all the millions of people in the world did the two of you come together?" In this way, we obtained a brief description of their original meeting. We played these tape recordings of the couple's discussion to Don Jackson. He did not know who they were or how old they were, whether they had children, or why they had come to MRI. But invariably Jackson would give the right diagnosis or description of the problem.

It would not be something as general as saying, "Well, they sound depressed." I remember one case about which Jackson said, "If they have a son, he is probably a delinquent. If they have a daughter, she probably has psychosomatic trouble." He was right every time. I would ask, "Don, how do you do it? How do you arrive at these conclusions?" And he would give some "clarifying" explanation, like, "Well, it was the way the mother just laughed at that point."

Or consider our informants. When we began our Brief Therapy Project at MRI 24 years ago, we wanted to study precisely this phenomenon of bringing about change. We therefore interviewed people we knew who had some kind of innate problem-solving talent. For example, we talked to bartenders, who often have to deal with very unpleasant customers; airline pilots, who have to deal with hysterical or anxious people; and even financial counselors, who try to bring order into some of the most irrational behaviors, namely, those related to the handling of money. I remember a police officer who was known for his ability to defuse very dangerous situations through the use of humor. For instance, one night he was sent to an address where the neighbors had reported that the

members of a family on the third floor seemed to be about to kill each other. When he arrived there and got out of his car, a television set came sailing out of the third floor window and crashed on the pavement in front of him. It occurred to him to pick up the pieces, run upstairs, and ring the bell. When they opened the door, he announced, "TV repair," and the people inside started laughing.

People who laugh are less likely to kill each other. And it is this element of humor that I find so strong in Carl Whitaker's work. In his book *Symbolic Experiential Therapy*, he says, "The object of all techniques is to eliminate techniques." For him, there is more to life than can be observed, especially measured and quantified—which seems to be the main obsession of psychology. The person of the therapist is more important than the therapist's skill. For training, he tries to expand the creative potential. We lesser people can only look up to the great ones like Carl with respect and wonder secretly, "How do they really do it?" And this, I am afraid, is in spite of his brilliant explanations and sublime satire.

QUESTIONS AND ANSWERS

Question: I am attracted to being an intuitive therapist, but having been trained as a scientist, perhaps to my misfortune, sometimes I feel the need for more rigor in my work. Yet I love the idea of just being myself in the session and shooting from the hip, so to speak, using my creative unconscious. I was wondering if you, Dr. Whitaker, trusted your students to do what you did.

Whitaker: You have to learn to be very careful. The next guy may have an AK-47. I don't think you should trust yourself. I don't trust myself. I don't even believe in trust. I think trust is a fake. The question is, are you willing to take a chance? Trust means that something else is going to intervene. If you take a chance, then there isn't any third entity. There's only the other and you. You either take a chance or decline. Other people out there aren't where you want them to be, they are where they happen to be. You need to be very paranoid.

Question: I guess I'm there then. Thank you.

Whitaker: I was going to tell you a wonderful story about a nonprofessional therapist in Chicago who is hired by the police department to answer home calls. He tells about a woman who called the police, saying, "The lady next door is pumping electricity into my house and I can't stand it. Something has to be done." So this character tore out to the house and went up to the door. He showed her his badge and said, "Come with me." He walked her out of her house and to the next door. He banged on the door, showed his police badge, and said, "Stop pumping electricity into this lady's house or I'll send you to jail." Cure.

Question: I'd like to ask you, Dr. Whitaker, to respond to the discussant, Dr. Watzlawick. Are there no theoretical methodologies? Is it all idiosyncratic? That is what I gathered from your discourse and short, wonderful vignettes. Do you have a theory? Is there a model?

Whitaker: The model I have comes from my opportunity of not being trained. I was trained in surgery and then everybody went overseas for World War II. At about that time, I switched to psychiatry. There was nobody left to teach. I was told, "You will teach psychiatry. After all, you have been trained as a surgeon." So my theory grew out of experience. I didn't have anybody who gave me a theory, and being in the child psychiatry unit, I had to teach medical students. I didn't learn how other people did therapy. I inched my way along. Mostly, I found a peer to work with me. So it was two peers, neither of whom knew much and both of whom were trying to learn. Like Paul Watzlawick's description of Gauss' problem with mathematics, I got the solution and now I have to figure out how I got there.

I have an example: Jeff Zeig called me ten years ago and said, "We are going to have this Ericksonian conference. Erickson was going to be the lead speaker, and then he died. Bateson was also to be a lead speaker, and then he died." Then they called me. I thought they were crazy. I don't know anything about hypnosis and I had never done any. Why should I talk to a conference on hypnosis? Jeff said, "Well, we thought

it would be a good idea." So I said, "Yes." After I hung up, I thought, "Whitaker, you are crazy. Why would you agree to a thing like that?" Three weeks later, I found out why. It suddenly occurred to me that the only thing I knew about hypnosis was that we are all hypnotized by our mothers and we never get over it. So that's what I talked about.*

Question: Dr. Whitaker, I really like your work. I've seen you a couple of times doing work in front of an audience with families. My question is: Are you ever concerned about harming the client in any way by any maneuvers or any of the things you may do?

Whitaker: Very much so. I think that the thing that makes me dare to take a chance is when I am in pain. The therapist's pain is the anesthesia for confrontation. If you don't have pain, if you aren't hurting, then you ought to find somebody else to help the two of you get straightened out before you do anything. If you do have pain, you are more free. Courage comes with experience. I can do a lot of tricky things now that I would never have touched five, ten, 15, or 20 years ago.

Question: Dr. Whitaker, as a student, I'd be interested in hearing some of your feelings about and opinions of the different forms of supervision for trainees and interns.

Whitaker: That is a nice question. Ordinarily, I stayed out of the students' work, but I would be a consultant if asked. Later, I made the students cotherapists in my work with my private families, the families I was treating to earn my income. I just told the patients that that was how I worked. If they didn't want the resident there, they could find somebody else for their therapist. The resident would be present at each interview if possible. That's how we did it.

Dr. David Keith, my most esteemed colleague and now a professor at the State Univer-

Editor's Note: Whitaker's fascinating keynote address, "Hypnosis and Depth Therapy of the Family," at the 1980 First International Congress on Ericksonian Approaches to Hypnosis and Psychotherapy is a chapter in *Ericksonian Approaches to Hypnosis and Psychotherapy,* J. Zeig (Ed.). New York: Brunner/Mazel, 1982.

sity of New York in Syracuse, is evolving some new kind of supervision. He is using group supervision. I tried using two or three residents for the supervising hour. They could fight with each other and me. Dave gets a group of five or six and plays this kind of thing. He also becomes the patient and talks about his failures so they get the courage to talk about theirs. Then the seven of them struggle. It's like good group therapy. You start being the mother, and as the children grow, you get to be the oldest sibling, and then the group becomes the therapist and you become the best patient. But that sometimes takes a couple of years. It's a hard way to learn family therapy.

Question: What are your notions of insight in psychotherapy and why do you believe that insight is rarely effective in producing change?

Whitaker: I assume that insight is understanding or knowledge or information input. I have had six years of therapy and 50 years of trying everybody I could find to get help from, including several thousand patients, and I don't think it has made me any more mature. If insight or understanding were useful, all we therapists would be so grown up that it would be ridiculous. Imagine 50 years of having all these children who try to take care of us, their parents. It doesn't seem to make any difference. We are about as screwed up as anybody else. Or you all are. I don't know about me, I'm just all right.

Question: At the risk of being a heretic to you, there is a method to your madness. I think that the parallel play that you describe is very powerful. Could you go further and talk about the time zones to which it takes you, and, therefore, takes them? Your parallel play is going into the past, and then they go into the past or into the future.

Whitaker: When I start parallel play in my head, I go back to my childhood, I go back to my teenager period, or I go back to my dating period. When I can play in my fantasy world, I think that encourages them to play in their fantasy world rather than being haunted by it. I appreciate the question. I think it is a good idea; the whole issue of time is seldom discussed. My fantasy is timeless to them!

Zen and the Art of Therapy

◆

Jay Haley, M.A.

Jay Haley, M. A.

Jay Haley (M.A., 1953, Stanford University) is Codirector of the Family Therapy Institute of Washington, D.C. He is one of the leading exponents of the strategic approach to psychotherapy. Haley served as Director of the Family Experiment Project at the Mental Research Institute and as Director of Family Therapy Research at the Philadelphia Child Guidance Clinic. He has written seven books, is coauthor of two, and has edited five. Additionally, he has made more than 50 contributions to professional journals and books. Haley is the former editor of Family Process *and the first recipient of the Lifetime Achievement Award of the Milton H. Erickson Foundation.*

Haley describes how he was introduced to Zen Buddhism by Alan Watts and then used Zen as a model to understand the paradoxical therapy of Milton H. Erickson, M.D. Haley compares Zen parables with Erickson's cases to illuminate the process of change.

Zen Buddhism is apparently the oldest continuing procedure in which one person sets out to change another. For at least 700 years, Zen masters have responded in a one-to-one relationship with someone who wishes to change. I will attempt to clarify the nature and influence of Zen on the ways of changing people in Western therapy, particularly in relation to the strategic, or directive, approach best represented by Milton Erickson.

For those pursuing the spiritual aspects of therapy, I should emphasize that here the focus is not on the spiritual side of Zen, but on the practical side of the art of changing people. That is, there is an interpersonal setting for spiritual development, which does not "just happen," just as therapeutic change does not "just happen." To achieve satori in Zen, one is not struck by enlight-

enment while sitting under the bo tree. A special relationship with a master is required, and a set of procedures, some of them bizarre, make up the interpersonal setting for spiritual growth. What I am emphasizing here is the materialist situation that frees an individual to develop spiritually. The actions to achieve enlightenment in Zen can be seen as similar to the actions that lead to change in strategic therapy.

The ideas of Zen influenced me in the 1950s when I was developing a therapy approach and doing research on the nature of therapy. For ten years, I was a member of Gregory Bateson's research project on communication where we investigated the paradoxes that occur because of the nature of classification systems. In 1953, the year I joined the project, I attended, with my colleague John Weakland, a series of lectures by Alan Watts on "Eastern Philosophy and Western Psychology." Watts was the Director of the American Academy of Asian Studies at that time. An authority on Zen, he became an informal consultant on our project since we shared the enthusiasm for paradox. Watts became interested in therapy as it related to Zen and later published a book on this topic (Watts, 1961). At that time, little was known about Zen, even in California where many philosophies flourished. Watts described himself as "back-door Zen," since he had not officially trained with a Zen master in Japan. His interests were both personal and intellectual and his fascination with Zen was contagious.

In 1953, the same year we discovered Zen, I took a seminar on hypnosis from Milton Erickson and began to study his therapy. I found the premises of Zen to be just about the only way of explaining Erickson's directive therapy, which at that time was quite deviant in the field. As an apprentice of Erickson, I used ideas from Zen to understand his supervision.

I should make it clear that I am not an authority on Zen and that what I have to say about it is largely confined to its relevance to the field of therapy. There are also many different views, and schools, of Zen, ranging from ritualistic rites and bureaucratic procedures to sheer spontaneity. I am offering a view largely based on the ideas of Watts, which were in some ways deviant (just as Erickson was a deviant in the field of therapy and Gregory Bateson a deviant in the field of anthropology). For example, some authorities on Zen consider extensive meditation to be essential to enlightenment. Therefore, the path to satori can become a life of painful sitting while proctors hit the trainees with sticks if they go to sleep or into trance. Watts considered meditation personally important, but he saw these ritualistic procedures as ordeals imposed on trainees to help them discover that enlightenment occurs in other ways.

PERSPECTIVES ON ZEN

Zen Buddhism had its origins in India and traveled through China before being introduced into Japan in about 1200 when Zen monasteries were established there. A body of literature has grown up on this topic, even though it is the premise of Zen that one cannot achieve enlightenment by reading about it, but only by experiencing it personally. In Zen stories, there is an antiliterature, if not an antiintellectual view. As an example, a woman who was a student of Zen died and left her son a letter in which she said: "There are 80,000 books on Buddhism and if you should read all of them and still not see your own nature you will not understand even this letter. This is my will and testament." Signed, "Your Mother, Not born, Not dead" (Reps, undated, p. 49).

A more typical example is the following Zen story (Reps, undated, p. 59).

The Zen master Mu-nan had only one successor. His name was Shoju. After Shoju had completed his study of Zen, Mu-nan called him into his room. "I am getting old," he said, "and as far as I know, Shoju, you are the only one who will carry on this teaching. Here is a book. It has been passed down from master to master for seven generations. I also have added many points according to my understanding. The book is very valuable, and I am giving it to you to represent your successorship."

"If the book is such an important thing, you had better keep it," Shoju replied. "I received your Zen without writing and am satisfied with it as it is."

"I know that," said Mu-nan. "Even so, this work has been carried from master to master for seven generations, so you may keep it as a symbol of having received the teaching. Here."

The two happened to be talking before a brazier. The instant Shoju felt the book in his hands, he thrust it into the flaming coals. He had no lust for possessions. Mu-nan, who never had been angry before, yelled: "What are you doing?"

Shoju shouted back: "What are you saying?"

This antiliterature view contrasts sharply with the intellectual tradition of Western therapy where something is said to be true only if a reference can be made to a previous authority, or prophet, who had written it. Yet it is reminiscent of the teachings of Milton Erickson. He rarely quoted past authorities and never as evidence that something was true. He did not say that something was so because a previous authority had said it was so. In a pragmatic

American way, he said, "It is so, and if you try it, you will find that out." Although this kind of pragmatism was often misunderstood by clinicians who came from the European tradition of scholarship, it is typical of Zen.

The goal of Zen is satori, or enlightenment, which is assumed to come about in relation to a teacher who, when successful, frees the student from a preoccupation with the past or the future (or with trying to become enlightened). The relevance of Zen to therapy becomes apparent when one observes that Western ideas of psychopathology are extreme versions of the problems of the average person dealt with in Zen. The client in distress is typically said to be preoccupied with the past, with guilts, obsessions, or desires for revenge. Or the client can be overpreoccupied with the future, as with anxieties and phobias about what might happen. He or she struggles to control his or her thinking, wanting to be rid of certain thoughts. Sometimes the client fears death and sometimes the client seeks it, being so depressed about living. Interpersonally, the client is often so attached to a person, either in anger or love, that it is like an addiction. Sometimes the person is fixed on material possessions or compulsively works and never enjoys a nice day. By definition, a symptomatic person keeps repeating behavior that causes distress while protesting that he or she would rather not be doing so and cannot help it. These kinds of foci and fixations are assumed in Zen to be preventing a person from fully experiencing the present moment, which is one way to view enlightenment.

ZEN AND ERICKSON'S THERAPY

In the 1950s when Zen ideas began to enter the clinical field, there could not be a comparison with therapy. The psychodynamic ideology, which was what was available, contained premises so opposite from Zen that the two approaches could not be related. The focus on insight was in sharp contrast to the Zen focus on action. However, one therapist was establishing a therapy with a different set of ideas. Milton Erickson was known as the leading medical hypnotist of that time, and he was practic-

ing a therapeutic approach that was new and was based on an ideology different from that of psychodynamic theory.

When I began to practice therapy in the mid-1950s and sought supervision from him, Erickson was the only therapist I knew about who had a new set of premises relevant to brief therapy. I also realized that one way to understand his directive therapy, which was incomprehensible in the nondirective psychodynamic framework, was to view it within the framework of some of the ideas of Zen. I talked to Erickson about the similarities between his work and the approach of Zen. His response was typical: He gave me case examples. These stories illustrated some of his views on the attempt to live in the present moment. For example, he described a case in which he hypnotized a golfer. The golfer was instructed to live only in the present moment and so focus total attention on one shot at a time. When the man next played golf, he was aware only of each shot. On the 16th hole, he was shooting his best game, but he did not know what his score was or what hole he was on. He was aware of only the present moment and not of the context.

PSYCHOPATHOLOGY IN TERMS OF CLASSIFICATION SYSTEMS

A basic characteristic of human beings is that we are classifying animals. In fact, it appears that we cannot not classify. We must hypothesize about and categorize whatever is, or is not, happening. Past social psychology experiments and current brain research (Gazzanaga, 1985) suggest that we constantly make hypotheses; perhaps there is a nodule of the brain devoted to that. Since we must classify, we are vulnerable to the nature of classification systems. There are several important factors about classification related to the therapy field.

When we create a class, we automatically create other classes. If we create the classification "good," we also produce the class of "bad," as well as those of "not so bad" and "not so good." If something is "high," something must be "low." It is in the nature of classification that one cannot have the figure without the ground to contrast it—in fact, multiple grounds or other classes. Therefore, a person pursuing a class creates the opposite class, even when not wishing to do so, as when pursuing happiness, one creates unhappiness. Lao-tse put it this way, "When everyone recognizes goodness to be good, there is already evil. Thus to be and not to be arise mutually."

Another consequence of a classification system is that paradoxes inevitably are generated. This happens when the class of items conflicts with the item in the class. If a person says, "Disobey me," the responder cannot classify that in a way that allows either obedience or disobedience. The person who disobeys is obeying as instructed. To obey requires disobeying. Paradoxes of this kind are generated by the nature of classification systems (Whitehead & Russell, 1910) and human beings must deal with them. The classification problem has been recognized since Epimenodes said, "If a man says he is lying, is he telling the truth?" Another aspect was emphasized by Korzybski and the general semanticists. Once something is classified, we tend to respond to all the items within the class as identical when they are not. The phobic responds to each phobic situation as identical to every other. As Korzybski liked to point out, "Cow 1 is not Cow 2" (Korzybski, 1941).

Changing a person means changing the person's classification system. Individuals have difficulty changing on their own because they think within that system. The task is given to therapists and to Zen masters to induce change. For example, a person who wishes to stop being constantly preoccupied with particular thoughts or actions tries not to think of them. It is the act of trying not to think of them that creates the class whose items one must think about in order not to think of them. It is like trying not to think of an elephant. A person wishing to be liberated and to behave more freely can try to achieve that by deliberately attempting to be spontaneous. Yet a person who *tries* to be spontaneous must fail, since spontaneous behavior is a class that does not include the item "trying." It is like trying to free-associate when the fact that one is directed to do so means it is not "free," but "purposeful." Similarly, if a person tries to be tranquil, it is like trying to try, since tranquility is a class of behavior

that requires not trying. The more one tries to be tranquil, the less tranquil one becomes. As another aspect of the problem, if one tries to change oneself when the way one classifies is what must be changed, each attempt to change activates the classification framework, which prevents change. Like the self-corrective system of systems theory, the attempt to change is what activates the governors that respond to prevent change.

An inevitable problem in therapy and Zen is how to change a person when to do so means changing how the person classifies the helper who is trying to change that system. By asking for help, the client classifies the relationship between himself or herself and the therapist in a certain way, as being unequal. The goal of therapy is to achieve the point where the client is defined as equal to the therapist in that the client does not need help. The client is to become a peer, rather than a supplicant who asks for help. Yet how can the therapist change the helping relationship to one of equality when every act of help, guidance, giving interpretations, or giving a directive defines the relationship as unequal and the client as being helped by a helper? The acts of helping a person to change mean defining the relationship as not changed. The therapist, or Zen master, must influence the person to change "spontaneously" and so escape the helping relationship. This is the essential paradox of Zen and of therapy. One solution is the example of a student who attempted again and again to answer a Zen master's koan, only to be informed each time that he was wrong. Finally, he simply sat down beside the teacher. That was the answer, since he was behaving as an equal.

Many Zen anecdotes illustrate the problem of changing classification. Reps (undated, p. 11) provides a subtle example.

Just before Ninakawa passed away, the Zen master Ikkyu visited him. "Shall I lead you on?" Ikkyu asked.

Ninakawa replied, "I came here alone and I go alone. What help could you be to me?"

Ikkyu answered: "If you think you really come and go, that is your delusion. Let me show you the path on which there is no coming and no going."

With his words, Ikkyu had revealed the path so clearly that Ninakawa smiled and passed away.

SYSTEMS THEORY AND ZEN

In the 1950s, the cybernetic revolution was influencing the field of therapy by introducing the ideas of self-corrective systems. Erickson had been a participant in the first Macy Conference in the late 1940s and he was familiar with systems theory. The relevance of this to Zen appears with the basic premise of Zen that human beings are trapped on the wheel of life and keep repeating distressing behavior. The more a person attempts to escape from this destiny, the more he or she is caught up in it because the attempts to change cause the system to continue. One goal of Zen is to free the person from the repeating system so that new, spontaneous behavior can occur. Obviously, that is also the goal of therapy. It is the assumption of Zen that the attempt to change, or help, causes the reaction that prevents change or help. Obviously, that is the assumption of a cybernetic, self-corrective system. As any element moves toward changes in the parameters of the system, a reaction occurs that prevents the change. How to change without activating the forces that prevent change is the paradox of both Zen and therapy. It requires an almost trickster approach to free the person from preventing change. As an example, how can one obey a teacher who is instructing one to think independently and not to obey teachers?

As part of the trickster aspect of enlightenment, both Zen masters and Erickson have been accused of being too concerned with interpersonal power and manipulation. In both situations, the need of a teacher to have power and skill in influencing people is simply assumed. As an example, Erickson liked to describe how someone in an audience called out that he could not be hypnotized and he defied Erickson to try. Erickson shifted the issue to whether the person was able to refuse to do what he was told. When the person insisted he could refuse, Erickson told him to come up the right aisle and sit beside him on his left. In defiance, the person came up the left aisle and sat beside him on his right. Erickson continued to induce a trance, assuming that is what the man wanted (Haley, personal communication).

There is a Zen story one cannot read without thinking of Erickson (Reps, undated, p. 8).

The Master Bankei's talks were attended not only by Zen students, but by persons of all ranks and sects. . . . His large audiences angered a priest of the Nichiren sect because the adherents had left to hear about Zen. The self-centered Nichiren priest came to the temple, determined to debate with Bankei.

"Hey, Zen teacher," he called out. "Wait a minute. Whoever respects you will obey what you say, but a man like myself does not respect you. Can you make me obey you?"

"Come up beside me and I will show you," said Bankei.

Proudly, the priest pushed his way through the crowd to the teacher.

Bankei smiled. "Come over to my left side."

The priest obeyed.

"No," said Bankei, "we may talk better if you are on the right side. Step over here."

The priest proudly stepped over to the right.

"You see," observed Bankei, "you are obeying me and I think you are a very gentle person. Now sit down and listen."

One problem in helping a person who seeks help, or a person who seeks enlightenment, is that to help that person one must change his or her way of life of constantly seeking help. I recall Watts telling a story of a Zen master who wished to inform his students that he could not enlighten them by teaching them something new. All the knowledge they needed to become enlightened was within them, so he could only help the students discover what they already knew. He said to a student, "You already know anything I could teach you." The student assumed that this was a wise master withholding, for some educational reason, important truths. The student could not escape from the classification of himself as a student yet that was the goal of the relationship.

ZEN, ERICKSON, AND SELF-MONITORING

In the 1950s, I began to find similarities among Zen, systems theory, and the therapy of Erickson. There was a way to describe human problems and an ideology for therapy that was an alternative to psychodynamic theory and practice. It was also different from the learning theory therapies that developed later. One dissatisfaction with psychodynamic therapy was the growing realization that people were being created who spent their lives monitoring themselves and hypothesizing why they did what they did. The constant preoccupation with exploring one's past and watching out for unconscious conflicts led to an extreme self-consciousness. In the attempt to use self-exploration and awareness as a way to avoid distress, people became preoccupied with their distress and its origins. Supposedly the self-preoccupation was to free people from the past, but such a change was not occurring. After years of therapy, people were habitually monitoring themselves. Even while having sexual relations, they would be wondering why they were enjoying the experience.

In contrast, Milton Erickson came from the tradition of the unconscious as a positive force. One should give up trying to monitor one's unconscious consciously and allow it to direct one's actions. The centipede should not attempt consciously to coordinate its 100 legs. Erickson's goal was to have people respond to their impulses in the present without being concerned about whether or how they were doing so. In the same way, the primary goal in Zen is simply to live rather than to be preoccupied with how one is living. The goal is to recover from self-monitoring. In fact, it is said, "When you are really doing something, you are not there." As an example (Reps, undated, p. 18):

Tanzan and Ekido were once traveling together down a muddy road. A heavy rain was still falling. Coming around a bend, they met a lovely girl in a silk kimono and sash, unable to cross the intersection, "Come on, girl," said Tanzan at once. Lifting her in his arms, he carried her over the mud.

Ekido did not speak again until that night when they reached a lodging temple. Then he no longer could restrain himself. "We monks don't go near females," he told Tanzan, "especially not young and lovely ones. It is dangerous. Why did you do that?"

"I left the girl there," said Tanzan. "Are you still carrying her?"

The goal of therapy is to change someone's actions or to change the ways the person classifies actions and thoughts as bad or good,

painful or pleasant, useful or not useful, and so on. Rational advice does not usually solve such a problem. The change must occur in action, according to Zen. One way is for the master to direct the person in some action and resolve the problem as part of that activity. As a result, Zen is often structured as a joint activity between master and student in some type of art. Often, it is taught through archery, swordsmanship, or the tea ceremony. There is a task, and the student associates with the master as part of the task. In that process, the master is directing what happens, rather than merely reflecting with the student.

As an example, one way to practice Zen is to apprentice to a master swordsman. A student who did that was given the task of cleaning the floors of the master's house. As he swept the floor, the student was surprised by the master's suddenly hitting him with a broom from around a corner. This happened again and again. No matter how the student anticipated where the blow of the broom would come from next, and got set to defend himself, he was hit with the master's broom. At a certain point, the student learned that he was best prepared to defend himself from some surprising direction by being unprepared in any direction. Then he was ready to receive a sword. He had begun the move toward enlightenment in the context of action between teacher and student. Zen masters pride themselves on being responsive in any direction. Watts told me of one who asked another, "What do you know of Zen?" The other immediately threw his fan at the man's face, and the man tilted his head just enough for the fan to fly by, and he laughed. (Once when Watts was visiting my home, my wife asked him, "What is Zen?" Watts happened to be holding a box of matches and he threw it at her. I don't know if she became enlightened, but she became angry.)

This active involvement of master and student in a task contrasts sharply with traditional psychodynamic, nondirective therapy. When I searched for a therapy relevant to Zen, I found that the directive therapy of Erickson included activities he set up between himself and the client, just as Zen master and student related around an activity.

As an example, a mother brought her

50-year-old son to Erickson, saying that he would do nothing and that he constantly bothered her, not even leaving her alone to read a book. Erickson said that the son could use exercise, and he suggested that the mother drive the son out into the desert and push him out of the car. Then she was to drive one mile and sit and read her book in the air-conditioned car while the son walked in the hot sun to catch up with her. The son would have no alternative except to walk. The mother was pleased with this task, but the son was not. After some time walking his mile in the desert, the son asked Erickson if he could not do some other exercise while his mother read her book. When he suggested that he would rather go bowling, Erickson agreed. Erickson pointed out to me that his use of classification in this way was calculated; the son would reject walking in the desert, but when he protested and wanted something else, he would remain within the classification of exercise and choose another exercise (Haley, personal communication). This example is typical of Erickson's way of getting into a relationship of action with a problem client, as is done in Zen.

Traditional therapy was based on a theory of psychopathology. Symptoms, thoughts, and character were classified according to a diagnostic system that was shared by clinicians and differentiated them from other people. A little girl who would not eat was classified as a case of anorexia nervosa, not as a little girl who would not eat. The language of psychopathology set clinicians apart from those who thought of human problems as dilemmas that arise in life. In contrast, a directive therapist prefers to think of problems as temporary, as a fluctuation in normal living that must be corrected. For example, when I was testing families of different kinds, it was necessary to select a normal sample. I found that I could not use clinicians to select normal families because they never found one. They always discovered some psychopathology in a family. It was characteristic of Erickson that he emphasized problems of living rather than pathological states. Instead of describing a child as having a school phobia, he would emphasize the problem as one of avoiding school and he would have a way of dealing

with that. He did not call a woman an agoraphobic, but a person who could leave the house only under special circumstances.

One problem in finding similarities between Zen and therapy is that in Zen there is no psychopathology. There are simply problems on the road to enlightenment. It is particularly significant that in Zen there is a way of classifying and dismissing human dilemmas that clinicians might consider serious psychopathology. In Zen, hallucinations, fantasies, and illusory sensations are called "makyo." It is said (Kapleau, 1989, p. 41), "Makyo are the phenomena—visions, hallucinations, fantasies, revelations, illusory sensations—which one practicing zazen is apt to experience at a particular stage in his sitting.... These phenomena are not inherently bad. They become a serious obstacle to practice only if one is ignorant of their true nature and is ensnared by them." Describing the phenomena further, hallucinations are said to be common, whether verbal or auditory, as are other sensations. "One may experience the sensation of sinking or floating, or may alternately feel hazy and sharply alert.... Penetrating insights may suddenly come.... All these abnormal visions and sensations are merely the symptoms of an impairment arising from a maladjustment of the mind with the breath." The author adds,

Other religions and sects place great store by the experiences which involve visions of God or deities or hearing heavenly voices, performing miracles, receiving divine messages, or becoming purified through various rites and drugs. ... From the Zen point of view all are abnormal states devoid of true religious significance and therefore only makyo. ... To have a beautiful vision of a Buddha does not mean that you are any nearer becoming one yourself, any more than a dream of being a millionaire means that you are any richer when you awake.

The phenomena that could lead to a diagnosis of psychopathology are assumed, in this view of Zen, to be a product of the special situation of the person and will change as that situation changes. That is also the view of a strategic approach to therapy: such phenomena are a response to a situation and not a character defect or a permanent malady.

CHANGE IN ZEN

A strategic approach to therapy has no single method that is applied to all problems. Each case is considered unique and requires a special intervention for that person. Similarly, in Zen there is no method that is used to enlighten everyone who comes. There are standardized procedures, such as meditation, but it is assumed that a unique intervention must be made for enlightenment to be achieved. In a similar way, in a strategic approach to therapy, there might be standardized interviewing, but the directive must fit the unique situation. In Zen, learning and cognition are not considered the path to enlightenment. One is not taught how to live or instructed how to relate to others. In addition, neither strategic therapy nor Zen is based on the theory of repression. Therefore, insight into unconscious dynamics is not considered necessary to change nor is the expressing of emotions a goal. It is assumed that expressing emotions, like expressing anger, leads to more expressions of emotions and so to more anger.

In Zen, change is described as sudden and discontinuous, not as cumulative and step-by-step, as when learning or being educated. Similarly, in strategic therapy, the client is not educated by being taught to behave in a certain way or taught how to be a spouse or a parent. Nor is the Zen student taught how to become enlightened, and, in fact, one discovers that one must give up theories about it to achieve it. The assumption is that when the situation is changed by an intervention, the behavior will be appropriate to that new organization without ritual learning.

One of the characteristics of Erickson's therapy was the use of imagery. Often he would have a client image a scene in the past or in the present and use it to induce change. Such imaging might seem unrelated to Zen practice, where the focus is on reality, but a Zen story describes a wrestler named Great Waves who was of champion caliber in private training, but was so bashful that he lost all public bouts. He went to a Zen master for help (Reps, undated, p. 11).

"Great Waves is your name," the teacher advised, "so stay in this temple tonight. Imagine that you are those billows. You are no longer a wrestler who is afraid. You are those huge waves sweeping everything before them, swallowing all in their path. Do this and you will be the greatest wrestler in the land." The young man did that to the point where, "Before dawn the temple was nothing but the ebb and flow of an immense sea." The next morning, the master said to him, "You are those waves. You will sweep everything before you." And he did.

There is another similarity to Erickson's therapy that could be emphasized. In Zen, there are stories, or analogies, told over the centuries to illustrate the path to enlightenment. Erickson also told stories to illustrate his view of changing people. In both cases, education is accomplished with analogies and metaphors. As an example, Erickson liked to tell of an experience he had when he was 17 years old. He was totally paralyzed by polio and his doctor said he would not live until morning. Erickson asked his mother to arrange a mirror so that he could see the sky outside the window. He wished to enjoy his last sunset.

How similar that is to a parable Buddha told in a sutra (Reps, undated, p. 22).

A man traveling across a field encountered a tiger. He fled, the tiger after him. Coming to a precipice, he caught hold of the root of a wild vine and swung himself down over the edge. The tiger sniffed at him from above. Trembling, the man looked down to where, far below, another tiger was waiting to eat him. Only the vine sustained him.

Two mice, one white and one black, little by little started to gnaw away the vine. The man saw a luscious strawberry near him. Grasping the vine with one hand, he plucked the strawberry with the other. How sweet it tasted!

When we compare Zen with other therapies, we can think of examples where it is difficult to find parallels. We can turn to the Zen metaphor of Gutei's finger (Reps, undated, p. 92).

Gutei raised his finger whenever he was asked a question about Zen. A boy attendant began to imitate him in this way. When anyone asked the boy what his master had preached about, the boy would raise his finger.

Gutei heard about the boy's mischief. He seized

him and cut off his finger. The boy cried and ran away. Gutei called and stopped him. When the boy turned his head to Gutei, Gutei raised up his own finger. In that instant the boy was enlightened.

When one examines different schools of therapy to find a case similar to this painful removal of a finger, it is difficult to do so, particularly in this age of litigation. If one existed, it would be a case of Erickson. One of his classic cases comes to mind (Haley, 1986, p. 197).

A mother came to Erickson saying that her adolescent daughter had stopped going out of the house. She would not go to school or see her friends because she had decided that her feet were too big. The girl would not visit the office and so Erickson visited the home on the pretext that mother was unwell and that he needed to examine her as a physician. When he arrived at the house, he observed that the girl's feet were of normal size. He examined the mother, asking the girl to help him by holding a towel, and he maneuvered the girl so that she was standing beside him. Suddenly, he stepped back and trod on her foot as hard as he could. She yelped in pain. Erickson turned angrily to her and said "If you would grow those things big enough for a man to see, I wouldn't be in this difficulty." That afternoon, the girl told her mother that she was going out and she went to visit friends and returned to school. Apparently, she was enlightened.

In this case and the Zen example, it is assumed that a sudden intervention causes change, that inducing pain can be a necessary part of an intervention in some cases, and that no education or cognitive and rational discussion is needed.

Related to this example is the use of ordeals, which are commonly part of both Zen and Erickson's work. The path to enlightenment is often painful, with an ordeal sometimes arranged by the master and sometimes voluntarily by the student, such as suffering hunger and cold.

With all the similarities between a strategic approach to therapy and Zen, one might wonder if there are differences. There are many, of course. For one, there is often a long-term involvement of years in Zen. Strategic therapy is briefer. Also, a primary difference is the remu-

neration to the therapist. One does not find therapists in yellow robes with begging bowls. They have reconciled financial success and therapy as a calling. There is also no emphasis on meditation in therapy; the activity is conversation and directives. One other difference is that strategic therapy has its origins in hypnosis and practitioners often use trance to achieve their ends. In Zen, if one is meditating and goes into a trance, one is hit with a stick, since trance is not a goal of the interaction with a teacher. However, one might note that Erickson did not encourage meditating trances, but active responses.

There is also no family approach in Zen. Monks typically live with each other, not in families. Interventions by masters do not change families to change the individual. Once enlightened, the Zen monk might marry and live in a family, but the task of Zen is not to change a family constellation.

One important similarity is the use of humor in Zen and in therapy. There are many Zen stories that are amusing, and a characteristic of Erickson's therapy was his humor and practical jokes. Related to humor is the Zen use of koans and Erickson's use of riddles. Both techniques seem designed to help a trainee change perspective and to recover from being rigid and intellectual. When dealing with a client who believed that change was not possible, Erickson would pose a riddle that seemed impossible to solve. Then he would show the obvious solution. One riddle he liked was that of diagramming how to plant ten trees in five straight rows, four trees in each row, without lifting the pen off the paper. When the client tried and failed to do it, Erickson would show how simple the answer was if one can escape from rigid and stereotyped ways of classifying.

In the same way, and apparently for the same purpose, Zen masters build much of their work around koans and such impossible riddles. "What is the sound of one hand clapping?" is an example. One that provokes action rather than tranquil reflection is the koan where the master holds a stick over the trainee's head and says, "If you say this stick is real, I will hit you. If you say it is not real, I will hit you. If you don't say anything, I will hit you." The student must solve that koan or be hit. Such examples make one wonder whether much of Zen might not have been created to cure young Japanese intellectuals of being so self-conscious and rational.

Perhaps the most basic similarity between strategic therapy and Zen is the willingness to make use of the absurd to change logical classification systems. Not only are absurd riddles and koans used, but absurd actions are demanded. With particularly rational and logical clients, Erickson would give them absurd tasks (Haley, personal communication). He would tell an overrational, intellectual person, for example, to go exactly 7.3 miles out into the desert, and there to park the car carefully, get out of it, and find a reason for being there. I have replicated this technique with overly logical scientists by sending them a certain distance up a mountain road to find a reason for being there. When they come back, they are different. Erickson's directive to climb Squaw Peak might have had similar purposes. It should be noted that when Erickson sent clients into the desert, they always went, and always found a reason for being there. When they came back, they were different—less rational and less logical, and perhaps more spiritual.

SUMMARY

In summary, what are the procedures of Zen that are relevant to therapy? In Zen, enlightenment is sought through a relationship with a master who believes that change can be sudden and discontinuous; who becomes personally involved with the student; who joins the student in a task that involves directing him or her; who attempts to escape from intellectualizing about life or monitoring personal behavior; who poses impossible riddles and insists on solutions; who approaches each student as a unique situation; who has a wide range of behavior and many techniques, including a willingness to be absurd; who focuses on the present and not the past; who solves the systemic problem that attempting to change prevents change; and who, within a kindly framework, uses ordeals to force a change. These are also the characteristics of a strategic approach to therapy.

If we take a broad view of the task of changing people, Zen practitioners and therapists have much to offer each other. Clearly, Zen came first, by a few hundred years. However, even though a latecomer, therapy has developed many innovations in recent years. When we take a broader view of enlightenment we see that Erickson was not simply a unique therapist. He was working in a centuries-old tradition of masters sending people out into the desert to discover new ways of spiritual being.

REFERENCES

Gazzanaga, M. S. (1985). *The social brain*, New York: Basic Books.

Haley, J. (1986). *Uncommon therapy*. New York: Norton.

Kapleau, P. (1989). *The three pillars of Zen*, New York: Doubleday.

Korzybski, A. (1941). *Science and sanity* (2nd ed.), New York: The Science Press.

Reps, P. S. (undated). *Zen flesh, Zen bones*, New York: Doubleday.

Watts, A. (1961). *Psychotherapy East and West*, New York: Random House.

Whitehead, A. N., and Russell, B. (1910–1913). *Principia mathematica, (3 vols.)*, Cambridge, England: Cambridge University Press.

Discussion by William Glasser, M.D.

---◆---

I would like to preface my discussion with expressing why I believe we came to this conference. I think we came to find answers to two questions: "What is psychotherapy?" And, "How do you do it?" There is a possible third question that was frequently addressed when I was in my training. I really didn't concern myself too much with it, but I had to acknowledge it; that question was, "Who needs psychotherapy?" There would be long discussions about this person who needs it and that person who doesn't or this person who is a good candidate and that person who is not. At that time, I had a great teacher, Dr. G. L. Harrington, who settled the question for me by saying the answer is, "Anyone who is in your office." He said that although there are probably a lot of other people who need it, anyone who comes to your office certainly does. He advised, "Don't worry about whether or not they are good or bad candidates, just try to help them."

As we attempt to find answers to the first two questions, keep in mind that everyone here is talking about people, almost all of whom are very much like you and me. No one is talking about deeply technical concepts like nuclear physics or the intricacies of viral infections. People may be complicated, but be skeptical if anyone says anything that you cannot understand or uses a great deal of psychological jargon. If you cannot understand what you hear, I think you have to entertain the idea that there may be something wrong with what you are hearing, not with you. If, in our field, we cannot communicate what we believe in ways we can all clearly understand, then that is a flaw in our field, not in the people listening.*

I enjoyed Haley's paper. I read it five or six times, and I think that I know it almost by heart. I enjoy Zen stories; I have for years. They are filled with quick, clean action and instant enlightenment. But I sat in my office and practiced for years and years, and I was never able to achieve the quick, clean action discussed here. What I always struggle with is the opposite of Zen: a muddy, erratic, slow process. And I consider myself a fast counselor, but compared with Zen, I am slow as a snail.

I especially enjoyed the story of Great Waves, the bashful wrestler. It wasn't said why he was bashful. I have a feeling about that. It was partly because he was an inept wrestler. He sat there all night in the temple and the priest

came in the morning and said, "You are now Great Waves. Go out and do it." He went out and did better. Still, my feeling is that he would be better off going to a wrestling master and taking a few lessons if he wanted to continue winning in the ring, because someone eventually would be able to flatten those Great Waves very quickly, which is probably why he was so bashful.

Great Waves wanted to change, but, in my experience, few people come into the office and want to change. Zen is one of the oldest disciplines, but it is not psychotherapy; the Zen masters deal with students who want to change and clients rarely do. Few clients tell me they want to change; what they want is for other people to change. They want better treatment from parents, spouses, children, employers, teachers, judges, and especially correctional officers and others they think "do them" wrong. Some people who have been mistreated as children want the mistreaters to change retroactively. They want to be "unmistreated," as if they are still children, when they are now 38 years old and the "mistreaters" are dead. It is hard to get people to change retroactively, especially when they are dead. I have not figured that one out yet.

Very few of my clients come in and say, as a husband might say, "Please help me change the way I behave so I can treat my wife better and have a better marriage." Most husbands (and wives) tell me in some detail how the problems in their marriage are caused by their spouses. Even more clients come and say, "Fix me." They want me to get rid of their depressions, compulsions, anxieties, addictions, and so on. They rarely say, "Please help me to change so that I can relate to the people I need in such satisfying ways that I can stop choosing depression, headaches, compulsions, anxiety attacks, backaches, sicknesses, irrational fears, and craziness addictions," to name some of the things they want me to fix. What many clients want is for me to cure their mental illness, just as a general practitioner cures a strep infection, which can be done if it is caused by a susceptible bacterium.

They want psychological magic. They do not want to do the hard work of recognizing their own inadequacies and irresponsibilities or to

---

Editor's Note: Haley's address and Glasser's subsequent discussion were presented during the group of events held immediately after the conference convocation.

face the fact that they have chosen to be where they are now, no matter how badly they were treated, and that they have to learn to make better choices. I admit it is hard to learn what needs to be learned, but who among us thinks that life is easy or fair?

In therapy, enlightenment occurs when we finally realize that we cannot control others, and that, from birth to death, the only person one can control is oneself. Occasionally, as we live our lives, we will get glimmers of that enlightenment, and when we do, we will have a good day. I once asked my teacher, Dr. Harrington, "What is life about?" His answer was, "Every once in a while you have a good day." It is only when we actually start doing all the hard things that a human being has to do to live a satisfying life that we have a chance for the enlightenment that is a good day, and even then we often need a little luck. Life is too difficult, too dependent on things we cannot control no matter how hard we try, to have more than an occasional brush with enlightenment.

Anyone who thinks one can reach satori by contemplating something like the sound of one hand clapping has bought a bowl of wishful-thinking sukiyaki. This is not meant to diminish the wisdom of the masters, but it is the students who imbue the masters with all their wisdom, and especially with all their magic. To be a master, I think, is to learn that there is never anything up your sleeve. What they are all trying to teach when they burn a sacred book, cut off a finger, write a cryptic will, or persuade some fool from the audience to dance around them is, "You can't control me or anyone else. And I certainly care enough about you so that I don't want to control you." This, I believe, is what the masters are trying to say. If students get that message, they have a chance to become enlightened. What is characteristic is that masters have learned to deliver that message succinctly. That is their skill, and I certainly admire it.

Succinct and powerful as this message is, however, how many people can get it from the words of a story? Keep in mind what Jack Raper, a Cleveland philosopher whose column was published in the *Cleveland Press*, said, "Keep in mind that the records show that the tortoise only won one race with the hare." So don't bet on tortoises if you want to achieve satori. Maybe I am wrong, maybe satori has been gained through a quick, insightful, safe story, but I'm skeptical. It is too pat, too easy; it is too magical. It tends to cast the therapist in a power role; that is, to me, antithetical to therapy. I have a feeling that these stories are really written by the students, not the masters, because the students want to see their "masters" as powerful. After all, who wants to study with a powerless master? We are all looking for masters who will bestow their power on us. There may even be a few here who are masters, but don't count on it and you won't be disappointed.

If there are any masters here, no one taught them. No one taught Milton Erickson anymore than anyone taught Abraham Lincoln or Thomas Jefferson. And sad to say, most of us will never hear the sound of one hand clapping, as maybe they did. I am willing to accept that Erickson was a master. I wish I had known him. He sounds a great deal like my teacher, D. L. Harrington, who certainly was a master in every way you could describe.

I have a story that is attributed to Milton Erickson.* It exemplifies what I believe about therapy. It may be apocryphal because I never knew him and I never read it, but someone said that this is Erickson's story and it rings true. And it really embodies what I believe is enlightenment.

A woman came to Milton Erickson because she felt she was too fat. She said, "Dr. Erickson, I've searched the world for thinness. I want to be thinner. I've gone to Switzerland and France, to all the spas, every place where people get thin, and no one, Dr. Erickson, has been able to reduce me." Erickson asked, "How much do you weigh?" She replied, "About 190 pounds." He asked, "Well, how much would you like to weigh?" She said, "Maybe about 125–130 pounds. That would be fine." She asked him if he could arrange this, and Dr. Erickson said, "No problem at all." And so the woman felt quite good. Then Erickson said, "My therapy is kind of directive; I tell you what to do and you do it." The woman said, "Fine, I'll do anything reasonable." He said, "Well, the first thing you

---

Editor's Note: The case can be found in *Collected Papers, IV*, pp. 66–70, and in *Uncommon Therapy*, pp. 115–119.

do is go home and start eating. When you get up to 220 pounds, come back." The woman said, "Dr. Erickson, you must be crazy." He said, "Well, it's your privilege to say that, but this is the therapy. Go home and eat up to 220 pounds. You should be able to accomplish that quite quickly." Within a week, the woman was back. She said, "Dr. Erickson, it's not working?" He asked, "What is not working?" She said, "I've lost my appetite completely. I don't want to be 220 pounds. I can't eat!" Well that's the story. That woman received enlightenment.

What was the woman trying to do all these years? Was she trying to lose weight. Of course not. If she lost weight, she would lose power. She wanted to prove that all the great weight doctors, all the gurus who ran all the spas, were worthless. And she had succeeded in proving it for years. Now she had found through her research that there was a great doctor in Phoenix, Ariz. She was out to prove that he was just as inept as the rest of them. Erickson instantly recognized what was going on and taught the woman the basic therapeutic lesson: you cannot control me and I do not want to control you. She learned that lesson when she sat there trying to munch her way to 220 pounds and found it impossible. She didn't want to weigh 220 pounds. And did she really want the control she had with 190 pounds? When she realized how stupid she was, she lost her appetite. This is a powerful story and I use it quite often. What people are looking for in this world, unfortunately, is control; and when they meet a real master, they lose the need to seek this self-destructive control.

Although I am not a strategic therapist, I am a firm believer in the use of humor and funny stories. They are not Asian, but they are filled with satori. I recently heard a story I would like to share. It is a modern tale, but I think you will agree that the heroine of this story received enlightenment—at least for a while. This is the story of a woman who was married to a man who just didn't do the things a husband should do for a wife. He was lazy. She was busy. She worked, took care of the children, mowed the lawn, painted the house, did the washing, ironing, and the cooking; she was a really hard-working woman. And her husband mostly watched television and clutched his bottle of

beer. Finally, she said to him, "Look, honey, I'm working really hard around here, but I need the car for all the things I do and it's barely running. You know about cars. Could you help me with the car? Give it a little tune-up?" He just growled at her, "Who do you think I am, Mr. Goodwrench?" What could she do? A little later, she said, "You know, everything in this house, the washing machine, the iron, the dryer, they're barely working. You could fix things. You used to fix things. You could help me out." He said, "Who do you think I am, Mr. Maytag?" The woman just continued doing all the good things she did and didn't complain anymore.

Then one day, the man came home from work and found his wife very cheerful. She was singing and bustling around the house. He asked, "Why are you so happy?" "Oh," the woman said, "our next-door neighbor stayed home from work today and I was talking to him. I told him all about the car, and he got out his tools, and in no time at all, the car was humming like it never has before. I told him the same things about the washer and dryer. He brought his tools into the house, worked for a couple of hours, and they are probably better than new." Her husband asked, "What did you have to do for him?" The woman said, "He gave me two choices: He said I could either bake him a cake or I could go to bed with him." The husband asked, "What kind of a cake did you bake for him?" And she said, "Who do you think I am, Betty Crocker?"

QUESTIONS AND ANSWERS

Question: This would be for either or both of you, if you care to comment. I've heard it said that we come into the world wanting to be loved, and when we find out we can't have that, we settle for power. Do you feel that is true? Do you have a comment on that?

Glasser: I don't think we come into the world wanting love and that, if we don't find it, we look for power. I think we come into the world wanting power just as much as we want love. And that is what makes the human task so difficult. Lower creatures are different from us in that they may come into the world mostly wanting to survive, and, if they are mammals, also wanting a little love. But they do not want the power we want, so they get along with each other. Human beings, however, come into the world wanting power for the sake of power, and they want it whether or not they have love. This means we cannot help people unless we come to grips with their need for power.

Let me just say one more thing. I work a great deal in public schools, trying to improve the educational system. There are huge numbers of children who don't get much out of school and many even hate it. The reason they hate school is that once past kindergarten, there is little opportunity for a child to gain the sense that he or she has some power in school. Everybody hates a situation in which they have no power, because power, I think, is an innate need built into our genetic structure.

Question: Mr. Haley, you described the man playing golf in an enlightened state who was able to play better than he had ever played, but did not know the score. To me, a person who is enlightened doesn't care what the score is. This illustrates a dilemma with which I have been struggling: If you are enlightened, are you able to live as a civilized person in society since you are living in and experiencing the moment? But I am concerned about the past and the future and perhaps also the concerns of other people.

Haley: I think it is one of the paradoxes of Zen that you have to live for the moment and, at the same time, deal with the future. There are Japanese generals who are said to be enlightened, but they also plan campaigns.

It raises the issue of defining enlightenment. Let me give an example. Some years ago, I was testing a variety of families. I tested Japanese families who spoke only Japanese because I was making some cultural comparisons. I got a family in which the father was a Zen monk. It was interesting to watch them. They began in a proper Japanese way, folding their hands, the wife being very respectful and the man very strong in living from moment to moment.

The test included reaching agreement on items. There were some items the kids liked, some the women liked, and some the men liked.

They had to reach an agreement. As this session progressed, the wife began to take over and began to say what everybody was to have. The monk began to sort of disintegrate before my eyes. Thus I think it is very difficult to be a Zen monk and live in a family. Perhaps that is why most of them live in monasteries. The adjustment to life and the practice of moment-to-moment Zen is, I think, very difficult.

Question: Dr. Glasser, I understood you to say that you didn't feel that change could be accomplished very suddenly. What about in a case of great trauma?

Glasser: The answer to that question has to be "yes" in the sense that anything is possible. But here I'm trying to address the experience of therapists and, in therapy, even when working with people who have suffered trauma, quick change is the exception. People sometimes experience a sudden enlightenment or understanding, but not usually during trauma. More likely, they dig in and cling to behaviors that have never worked and won't work now. Psychotherapy is a learning process in which we learn about ourselves; learn what to do that is different and then try, tentatively, some things that may work a little better; and continue if things do get better. I don't say that this takes years and years, but it usually doesn't happen with the speed with which enlightenment comes in a story. Trauma may cause a few people to pay a little attention to the fact that they need to think about changing, but I don't think it is a major factor in accelerating change.

Question: I have a question for Jay Haley. You mentioned the idea of testing families. I gather you're probably not sitting down with paper and pencil with them. How do you test families, what is the goal, and how does it work?

Haley: At one time, we thought we would be able to differentiate families, particularly clinical families, by some testing situation. Could we differentiate a family with a schizophrenic member from a family with a delinquent member, from a family with a psychosomatic problem, and so on? Back in the 1960s, quite a number of institutes were putting families in testing situations. We had realized we had no tests for families. We had tests for individuals—how they perceive, think, feel, and so on—but we had no way to describe a sequence of family behavior. So we worked out various kinds of test materials, and then rated variables, such as conflict or cooperation, among family members. For example, we did experiments in which they pressed buttons to form coalitions, and we tried to measure the interchange of behavior. We tried to measure how parents communicated a task to a child over the telephone. A variety of tests were developed and these were important in the 1960s.

I assume that universities are doing testing now, but I'm not sure. It turned out to be a dif-ficult task. The methods were not available, nor was the ideology. There were no techniques for measuring sequences between people. An example of a sequence is when a child does something wrong and the father says, "Don't do that." The mother says, "Don't pick on the child." The father says, "He shouldn't do that." The child again does something, and the father says, "Don't do that." The mother says, "Don't pick on the child." You can observe this sequence in a testing room, but you have no measure or experiment to show that it happens. We wanted to show, for example, whether or not the sequence changed after therapy. Those were the kinds of tasks we were struggling with in those days, and I hope that people still are.

Stories of Psychotherapy

◆

Cloé Madanes

Cloé Madanes
*Cloé Madanes is Codirector of the Family Therapy Institute of Wash-
ington, D.C. The author of three books on family therapy, she is
renowned for her innovative directive approaches to psychotherapy and
supervision.*
*Ms. Madanes posits that societal changes should be reflected in
changes in the theory and practice of psychotherapy. She illustrates her
ideas about strategic therapy with case examples. The family should
be viewed as a self-help network, promoting hope and constructive
change.*

I thought it appropriate in a conference on the evolution of psychotherapy to discuss prevalent concepts—some new and some very old—and how the evolution of the therapy that I teach relates to these concepts. Because I think that therapists communicate with each other best by telling stories, I will explain some of the concepts through my favorite stories of therapy.

INSTITUTIONAL HELP VERSUS SELF-HELP

The first concept refers to the shift that has taken place in the past ten years from institutional help to self-help. For decades, we have been dependent on the protection of institutions such as the government, the medical establishment, the corporation, and the school system. But in the last 20 years, it became apparent that we had lost not only the war in Vietnam, but also the war on poverty. Education declined, and we learned to mistrust medicine for its unnecessary operations and prescription of addictive drugs.

Self-help then began to replace institutions and it has become part of American life. Community groups are acting across the nation to prevent crime, to feed the elderly, to build houses, to promote health, and to educate children.

Family therapy originated in the 1950s as part of the development from the individual as the unit for study to the system as the unit. It was difficult to make the transition from focusing on individuals to focusing on relationships among individuals. As we struggled to change our point of view, some concepts from an individual approach were inappropriately transferred to the systems approach. We talked about family therapy as a "cure" for the whole family that was supposed to be "sick" or "pathological." In fact, there is no such thing; only individuals can be sick. Families do not exist as individuals exist, but are merely constructs that refer to relationships. Family members can be loving or hostile, hopeful or pessimistic, tolerant or intolerant, but there is no such thing as a sick or healthy family.

What is the family? Truly, it is the ultimate self-help group. We bring the family to therapy to help us, the therapists, to solve the problems of the individuals who consult us. There is no one who can help or interfere as much with the well-being of a person as those who have ongoing relationships with the person, with a history, a present, and a future.

In the interactional view, we believe that a problem exists because of the context in which it takes place, and the most important context is the relationship with significant others. If these relationships change, the person changes. As the ultimate self-help group, the family is the unit in society for tolerance, compassion, and love. The therapist needs to intervene quickly, reorganizing the natural network of the family, the tribe, and then disengaging, leaving family members to care for and protect one another. The idea that the family is a self-help group became more apparent to me when I was working with cases of abuse, neglect, and incest, where the very existence of the family unit is threatened. In these cases, the therapist needs to find a protector, a strong, responsible person in the extended family or in the community, and transfer responsibility to him or her. For example, if an adolescent has been abused by a father, a responsible uncle or grandmother can be put in charge of supervising the family to make sure that this will not happen again. If a child must be removed from the home, it is usually preferable to find a placement with relatives rather than with strangers. The family is a self-help group where children can help their parents, uncles and aunts can take charge, grandparents are responsible, and everyone can help one another.

A therapist can organize a family as a self-help group in direct or indirect ways, straightforwardly or metaphorically.

CASE EXAMPLES

Case One

An example of a direct approach is the story of a woman who came to therapy because of anxiety attacks and panic that she thought were related to conflicts with her lover. However, she had three adult sons who had disappeared from her life and did not write or call. She did not know whether they were dead or alive. She lived with a daughter who was an alcoholic. The therapist organized the mother to find the sons through contacts with her estranged husband, friends, relatives, and the police. There was a family reconciliation, with everybody coming together at the mother's house and resuming communication. The woman recovered from her anxiety attacks and the daughter found a boyfriend and learned to control her alcoholism.

A therapist needs to reunite family members not only when children abandon their parents, but also when parents try to expel their children, literally or emotionally. In these cases, before one can do anything else in therapy, one has to arrange for the family to contain the children without expulsion. It is important to understand that in the parents' minds, expulsion may not be contradictory to wanting to love and protect the children. Parents with low self-esteem may love their children, and precisely because they do love them, want to give them away to others, that is, to people whom they think will be better parents.

Case Two

Sometimes it is necessary to find ways for parents to benefit from containing their children. A single mother of a ten-year-old boy beat her son brutally. Her boyfriend also beat him. The boy had been placed in foster homes and hospitalized several times. Previous interventions by therapists and the Department of Social Services had failed. The mother said that when she beat her son, she had out-of-body experiences; she could see herself doing it from the ceiling, where she was floating in the air. She could not control her behavior.

After several sessions, during which all attempts to improve the relationship were unsuccessful, the therapist told the woman that our institute was so concerned that we had decided to pay her $10 a day for each day that she or her boyfriend did not hit the boy. She would be paid $70 once a week, at the therapy session. However, if she had hit the boy even once, she would lose all $70 for that week. The therapist told the woman that he believed that she was an honest person and so he would take her word as to whether or not she or the boyfriend had hit the child. The boy's report also would be taken into consideration and obvious marks would be noticed, but basically she would be on an honor system.

The son would be paid $1 a day for every day that his mother did not hit him. He would make $7 a week, but he also would lose the whole amount if his mother hit him even once during the week. Paying the boy for not getting hit would take care of the issue of provocation. In this way, the family's income was practically doubled, since the mother was on public assistance. The contract was in effect for three months, and then it had to be discontinued because of the high cost to the institute. The boy was not abused again. The mother accepted the fact that she could control her behavior, as well as that of her boyfriend. The relationship with her son improved, and she took steps to find a job and improve her life.

Case Three

People in a family can help each other in indirect ways and even outside of their awareness. Siblings often help each other unwittingly. A young woman from a wealthy family came to therapy because she had a serious problem of procrastinating with writing her thesis. She was working on her Ph.D. degree for a prestigious European university, but found excuses to write things other than her dissertation. This was not difficult to do because she worked as a journalist.

I sympathized with her problem and asked her about her family, her friends, her life in Europe, how she got along with her siblings, and so on. The woman said that she had a stepsister in Europe whom she disliked intensely. I changed the subject back to her dissertation and asked how many pages a day she reasonably could expect to write. She said she could write four pages. I told her that there was a solution to her problem, but first she had to promise that she would follow my directive. She was not going to like it, I told her, but I was not going to argue with her. She knew how important it was to obtain her Ph.D. degree and further her career, and she accepted my decision. "Every day that you don't write four pages, I want you to write a $100 check to your sister and mail it to her with a note saying, 'With all my love,' or 'Thinking about you.'"

The woman said that was the last thing in the world she wanted to do and immediately began to negotiate exceptions. I agreed that if there was an international crisis and she had to fly somewhere to report it, that would not count. She was not expected to write on the airplane or while reporting. But she had to keep a log of her jobs and flights, which I would carefully check every time she came to a session. The dissertation was finished within a few months and the sister never was sent a check. However, the woman, puzzled by the directive, visited her sister in Europe and became closer to her.

CHANGING MEMORIES

When a person has had cruel parents, he or she may become isolated and estranged from everyone. A first step towards reintegrating the person into the family is to change the memory of an adult's involvement with his or her parents in the past. This strategy is useful with people who are tormented by low self-esteem because of memories of being victimized by their parents. The strategy is to say that there must have been someone kindly in the person's childhood who has perhaps been forgotten, but who must have existed and whose influence explains the good qualities that the person presents today. One can suggest that perhaps it was a grandmother, an uncle or an aunt, or maybe even a school teacher. Slowly, the person will begin to remember someone and to build upon this memory.

Our childhood memories are not more than a few isolated episodes to which we attribute meaning and continuity. We assume that because we remember one episode, it is representative of many similar episodes that must have taken place. When a new memory of a kindly person is retrieved, the therapist can say that, if one or two kindly actions are remembered, there must have been many more. The therapist also can suggest that every time a bad memory comes to mind, it should be counteracted with the newfound memories of the kindly grandmother, for example, so that the person will carry inside the image of the good grandmother to counteract the image of the cruel parent.

HIERARCHY VERSUS NETWORK

Another new idea that is prevalent has to do with the demystification of hierarchies. For centuries, the pyramid structure was the way we organized ourselves. From the Catholic Church to the army, in General Motors and in the Department of Social Services, power has flowed from the pyramid's top, down to its base; from the Pope, the general, the CEO, down through the lieutenants and managers, to the workers and soldiers at the bottom.

In the 1960s and 1970s, however, the U. S. economy, based on hierarchical structures, fell into disarray. Rising in its place was the new information economy in which greater flexibility was necessary and hierarchies were inappropriate. Humanistic management alternatives were adopted by the Japanese, for example, resulting in impressive productivity gains for Japan.

Our belief in the efficacy of hierarchies began to tumble and the new networking model evolved. Networking is a process that links clusters of people. A powerful tool for social action, it was responsible for the evolution of the women's movement, as well as the many consumer organizations and various other networks, including those for food distribution, environmental protection, education, and information. Networks offer the horizontal link, the egalitar-

ian relationship that those of us crave if we take seriously the ideology of democracy. Hierarchies are about power and control. Networks are about empowering and nurturing.

In preparing for this conference, I thought about my work as a therapist and found that it coincided with these changes in the culture. I had hardly noticed that I had made a transition from hierarchies to networks.

I was always puzzled by how seemingly powerful and competent adults could be such helpless and incompetent parents. And I was even more interested in how little children, apparently helpless, could be powerful helpers in the family. I noticed that although the family appears to be a traditional hierarchical organization, with parents in charge of the children, it rarely is truly organized in this way. How often does a parent side with a child to help the other parent? How many children help their parents' marriage stay together? How many children succeed in separating their parents? These and many similar questions led me to think that perhaps, as a therapist, to organize a family in a hierarchical model was not necessarily the best idea.

I developed new strategies that violate the model of the traditional family hierarchy and that perhaps are part of a new model of the family as a network. The communication style in this new model is lateral, diagonal, and from the bottom up. A network is like a fishnet, where the nodes are all linked together in a three-dimensional structure.

A family can be a complicated organization. There are parents and children, stepparents and stepchildren, grandparents, uncles, aunts, cousins, second cousins, brothers and sisters, stepgrandparents, stepuncles and stepaunts, friends of the family, neighbors, and members of the community. A therapist needs to think in terms of self-help within this network: Who can initiate change and who can help whom? There are the obvious hierarchical possibilities: parents help children; grandparents help parents and children. There are also lateral possibilities: parents help each other; children help each other; members of the older generation help each other; or the younger generation's members help each other. There are also bottom-up choices: children can help the parents; parents can help the grandparents; the younger generation can help the older generation.

The therapist seeks to enter the network through whomever is the best resource for initiating a positive change in the family. In many situations, when parents are drug addicted, abusive, neglectful, or ill, a lateral or bottom-up approach is more conducive to change than a hierarchical one.

Typically, the sequence in therapy is as follows: If a therapist is not making progress with an individual or a family in therapy, the therapist expands the unit. Siblings, grandparents, uncles and aunts, cousins and other relatives, and, ultimately, members of the community are brought in. Eventually, a level is reached at which change takes place, because every time new people are approached, there are new points of view and different resources. Arranging for these new influences enriches everyone's life.

Sometimes when a parent is the problem, the children are the best organizers of the family.

CASE EXAMPLES

Case Four

A father of several teenage children had been addicted to painkillers for many years and repeatedly had been arrested for forging prescriptions. The wife thought he was a bad husband and father, and felt superior to him in every way.

After several failed attempts to improve the marriage and to bring about some good feeling between the spouses, the therapist decided to focus on the children. She invited them to a session, met with them alone, and told them that their father took painkillers because he had a pain in his marriage. Their mother and father had forgotten how to be happy, the therapist said, and she needed the children's help to remind them of what happiness is. In fact, she said that she wanted the children to be in charge of the parents' happiness, telling them what to do so that they would have better times together.

With the therapist's help, the children made various plans. They prepared a candlelight spe-

cial dinner for the parents alone. They arranged for the parents to go out in the evening together. They sent them on a trip to the beach, to the theatre, and to celebrations with friends. The therapy proceeded in this way for six months, during which the father was free of drugs.

The therapy ended when the parents said they now knew how to be happy together. The father was now capable of giving guidance and support to the children and the mother was more tolerant and understanding. The parents, moved by the children's love and concern for them, had responded in kind and had become more kindly and mature. All had the satisfaction of having helped each other. The father continued to be free of painkillers even though, a couple of years later, he had a bout with cancer, from which he was able to recover.

Case Five

Special techniques must be used when a small child presents a problem. As a teacher of psychiatric residents, I was indignant when I heard that the staff of the Department of Child Psychiatry had been trying to hospitalize a five-year-old boy for temper tantrums. Fortunately, the stepfather refused to allow the hospitalization and I was asked to supervise the therapy.

When the mother, son, and younger sister came to the first session, the therapist asked the boy to dramatize his temper tantrums. He puffed up his chest, flexed his arms, made an ugly face, and said, "I'm the Incredible Hulk," as he hit the furniture and screamed. He then showed the therapist how he also could be Frankenstein's monster.

After commenting on how bright and imaginative he was, the therapist asked the boy to pretend to be the Incredible Hulk and Frankenstein's monster again and then the mother to hug and kiss him. Next, the mother was asked to pretend to have a tantrum herself and the boy was to hug and kiss *her*. They were asked to do this at home every day and to end their performance with milk and cookies.

After one session, the boy's tantrums disappeared. The mother and son had helped each other in playful, affectionate ways, without punitive intrusions from outside agents. The tantrums had turned into play in which mother and child could express their love and reassure each other.

Case Six

Another approach is to organize children to take turns in unusual ways. Tommy, a 21-year-old man, was depressed, delinquent, and drug abusing. He said he was the "life ruiner" of the family, and that his brother and sister were perfect.

The therapist suggested that it was not fair that there should be only one "life ruiner" in the family. If the brother and sister were willing to take turns, Tommy only would be the life ruiner one week out of three, so he would have two weeks out of three to do something else—get a job, study, have some fun. The brother and sister agreed, although the parents protested that it would be better not to have a life ruiner at all. When the older brother had his turn at being the life ruiner, he decided it was time to move out of the parents' house. The parents were upset and old conflicts between the father and this son resurfaced. It became clear that Tommy had been drawing the father's anger to himself, distracting the father from his deep resentment toward his intellectual, sensitive older son, who looked down on the father's blue-collar job. As the father and older brother resolved their old conflicts, Tommy did not have to be the life ruiner any more. He found a job and a girlfriend and moved on with his life.

Case Seven

One of the middle children in a family of ten called our institute because she was concerned that her mother might become depressed when the daughter left home to be married. The mother was a widow, a recovering alcoholic who had been overwhelmed by the death of her husband, which had left her with ten children ranging in age from 14 to 30. In the sessions, it was clear that the mother was central to all of their lives, and that no matter how much she gave of herself, it was never enough. The therapist organized the family so that each child was a helper to another child and a helpee of someone else. These helper–helpee relationships between the children were assigned irre-

spective of age, so that, for example, the youngest child ended up being the helper of the oldest. The idea was that the children should take turns at turning to each other for assistance and only ask the mother for help as a last resort. Encouraged by the children's competence and by their love for one another, the mother was able to focus on her own needs, and even developed the courage to introduce the children to a man whom she was considering marrying.

Case Eight

A very different approach can be used to introduce a new person into a family. The parents of a young man were very worried about his abuse of steroids. Even though he was a college student, the young man's main interest was in body building and over several years he had repeatedly abused steroids. Nothing seemed to motivate him to change. He liked to be by himself and said he wasn't very interested in women and didn't mind not having a sex life. The therapist told him that he was focused on himself because he was afraid of rejection, which was his main problem and one that had kept him isolated and unsure of himself.

When the young man admitted that he did have a problem with low self-esteem, the therapist told him that it was clear that what he had to do was to practice being rejected so that he would become immune to it. If he were rejected enough, he would no longer be afraid and it would build his character. The therapist told the young man that in the next two weeks he had to be rejected by at least five different women on five different occasions. He added some advice so that the rejection would occur quickly and not take too much of the young man's time. For example, he could stand at the bottom of an escalator at a fashionable department store and, as a young woman approached, ask her to have a cup of coffee with him. The woman would surely become angry, but, because she was descending on a moving escalator, she wouldn't be able to turn away and would have to answer him with rejection. He could achieve a similar result by standing at the door of a boutique. He should remember that if he approached very attractive, intelligent women, the chances would be greater that they would reject him.

The young man said this was all too difficult to do, but the therapist insisted that he should build his character and not just his body. The therapist knew, however, that because the young man was very handsome and quite charming, it would be highly improbable that he would be rejected by anyone.

In the next session, the young man reported that he had not been able to carry out the assignment because he had become involved with a young woman whom he had met right after the previous session. They had been together for two weeks, and as it was a serious relationship, he could not practice anything with other women. As it turned out, this young woman was strict and demanding and totally disapproved of steroids. The young man had to study and work to make money in order to please her. A new person had been introduced into the young man's life, and she changed things more quickly than a therapist ever could.

THE 18 STEPS

There are so many different kinds of families and so many possible strategies that a therapist can get lost in choosing among them. However, if one considers that the goal is to organize families as self-help networks, then it becomes apparent that certain steps can be followed. In thinking about self-help and about the family network, I developed a program of 18 steps to therapy. These steps are applicable to all kinds of families and taking them will ensure that people will relate to each other in helpful, not harmful, ways.

1. The first step is to listen, showing empathy for and understanding of the position of each family member as one inquires about the problem. This is sometimes difficult to do because people come with conflicting views about the problems that they cannot solve. A therapist needs to evidence understanding of each person's position without antagonizing the others. If one is going to encourage family members to help one another, empathy is essential. One must be able to feel in oneself an echo of what each person in the family experiences. And one must believe that no matter how horrible the deed someone has done, one might have done the same given similar circumstances.

2. The second step is for the therapist to reframe whatever problem is presented, implying hope for change. It is important for a therapist to be optimistic and hopeful. We must believe that all problems are solvable by the family, within the family network. Only death is unsolvable, and even that statement can be debated, depending on one's spiritual orientation. To successfully convey that a problem is solvable depends to a great extent on how the problem is framed. It is important to have small goals that are attainable. For example, a retarded person may never become president of the United States, but can lead a productive, self-sufficient life in harmony with others.

3. The third step is to frame the presenting problem so that each family member must help and each is important to the solution of the problem. In order to become a self-help group, everyone has to be engaged from the beginning as helpers to the therapist.

4. The fourth step is to ask each family member what he or she has done that was a mistake, that was wrong in relation to the others. Sometimes, if one person has committed a crime, it is better not to focus on what mistakes the others have made until later in the therapy and to stay focused on the serious wrongdoings of one person. However, later it is important for everyone to admit to their own mistakes. To function as a self-help network, people need to be responsible for their own actions and to recognize their mistakes so that they won't repeat them.

5. Step 5 is to ask each person to apologize to the others for what he or she has done wrong. Again, one might ask first for the apology of a serious offender, and only later in the therapy, ask for apologies from other family members. Repentance is important as the beginning of change. Depending on the circumstances, people may be encouraged to forgive each other or forgiveness may be postponed to later in the therapy. We know, however, that if people are going to continue as a family, they must forgive each other.

6. Step 6 is to obtain a promise from all family members that they will stay together and no one will be expelled from the family. This step is necessary when there is the possibility of institutionalization, foster care, or expulsion. At this time, it also is necessary to reorganize other professional helpers who may be attempting to hospitalize an adolescent, place a child in foster care, or make a child a ward of the court. When separation is necessary, it is best to place children with relatives within the network of the family and the community rather than with strangers. It is always better to contain a problem and to solve it within the natural tribe than to sever family ties.

7. Step 7 is a pact of nonaggression among family members and toward others outside the family. This includes self-inflicted violence. A goal of all therapy is to prevent violence, and we know that violence is an escalating process that only breeds more violence. A therapist needs to take a clear position in this regard so that if the pact is violated, it will be a betrayal not only of other family members, but also of the therapist.

8. Step 8 requires the therapist to make a statement about the importance of tolerance, love, and compassion. That is what the family is about. The family is the unit in society for these qualities. Many people forget this, and it is necessary for the therapist to repeat it again and again as a reminder of what is really important. Too many people become lost in menial and sordid details of everyday life and behave as though the family were a factory that, at the end of the day, has to produce clean dishes. The family provides refuge from the hardships of society.

9. Step 9 is to assign social control within the family. In almost every therapy, one has to discuss rules and the consequences if the rules are violated. It is necessary to make contracts that specify what is expected between parents and children and husband and wife. If the family members are going to solve their problem so that social-control agents don't have to intervene, there has to be social control within the family.

10. Step 10 is something to look forward to. In every life, there should be some illusion, some hope, some expectation that will keep people alive and interested in living. It may be a trip to California or to Europe, an advancement at work, the possibility of obtaining a professional degree, a visit to distant relatives. This is particularly important with adolescents because so often they are plagued by suicidal thoughts, but it also is needed in everyone's life.

11. Step 11 is protecting the human rights of children, the elderly, the weak, and the sick. We need to accept the fact that it is often only us, the therapists, who are available to organize the family network to defend the human rights of those who cannot speak for themselves and who need to be protected from agents of social control and from the abuses of certain family members and of others outside the family. We have the moral right to act in accordance with the principle that preservation of the individual's human rights is our foremost concern.

12. Step 12 is to help children and adolescents take care of their parents and grandparents in age-appropriate ways. Human beings are the only animals that take care of their parents. The transition from being cared for to taking care of one's own parents is probably the most difficult one in a person's life. Every child dreams of making the parents happy. In every therapy, one can intervene so that this dream becomes feasible within the child's limitations and without harm to the child or to the parents or grandparents. A goal of therapy is to encourage children and adolescents to express love and concern in nondestructive ways and to encourage the older generation graciously to seek out and accept this love and concern. One is not truly a mature adult until one can take care of one's parents.

13. The 13th step is improving the parents' marriage or finding a partner for a single parent. Just as in the movie "Back to the Future," in which the young man has to go back to the past to get his parents to fall in love so he can be born, so a young person is often unable to mature until the relationship between the parents has improved. If a parent is single, the young person needs to help orient the parent in the pursuit of happiness. A therapist has to recognize this need and to collaborate with the youngster in these endeavors.

14. In the 14th step, the therapist discusses sex, drugs, and rock 'n roll. In every therapy, there has to be a discussion about what is sexually safe and appropriate and/or about what is safe and appropriate in relation to drugs. Rock 'n roll refers to issues of having fun—an aspect of life that too often is neglected. It is necessary to remind parents about how to enjoy their children and family members about how to have fun with each other and with other people.

15. Step 15 is heartbreak and disappointment. Everyone at some time experiences pain, disappointment, and heartbreak. We must remember that therapy is about the essential or it is about nothing. The therapist needs to ask, "What is your worst pain, your greatest disappointment? What is your shame? What was the worst, most evil, thing you have ever done? What was the most evil thing done to you?" The only way really to know someone and truly to reach a person is to know about their heartbreak.

16. Step 16 is enhancing relationships. In every therapy, one can remember to do something to enhance the relationship between father and son, child and grandmother, mother and daughter, nephew and uncle, and so on. A brief intervention can have lasting results and improve everyone's life.

17. Step 17 is to promote harmony and balance in people's lives. To love and be loved, to find fulfillment in work, to play and enjoy—all are part of a necessary balance. A balanced life in harmony with others is a desired goal.

18. Step 18 is the "path of the hero." A therapist needs to point people in the direction of a path that may never be completed, but where the search for what may lie ahead gives life a meaning. There are too many people today who are restricted by the banalities of life and who do not have a purpose for their existence. A therapist can orient a person toward a goal in which the search will give trascendence to life and a sense of purposefulness that will help overcome many hardships and tribulations.

SCIENCE VERSUS ART

Today, with people standing in line for hours to see an exhibit of a Renaissance artist, art is becoming a primary leisure activity throughout the world. And with the revival of interest in the arts comes the revival of the question, "Is therapy an art or a science?" Because it is generally accepted that art is accessible to anyone, I think that we, as therapists, should have the courage to accept the fact that therapy is an art that can be taught as such. It can be practiced with the vision and creativity of the artist. In science, we are limited by the real world. In art, there are more complexity and flexibility, communication is metaphorical, and everything is possible.

Of all the arts, therapy is most similar to drama and the strategies of therapy are most similar to the techniques of play construction. Just as a playwright's duty is to keep the audiences awake—to hook, retain, and intensify their interest—so the therapist needs to hold the client's attention or the therapy will fail. In fact, play construction, like therapy, is a body of knowledge gathered from the observation of audience (or client) reaction.

What are some of the characteristics of therapy that are similar to the art of play construction?

For one thing, there has to be a climax, possibly combined with a reversal, perhaps a reframing or a paradox where the action veers around to its opposite. In therapy, as in the theatre, it is not the physical action, but the emotional and mental actions that count. The number of participants is limited to what can be accommodated on the stage or in the therapy room. Censorship and the ethics of the professions do not allow for much physical contact. The action centers on emotional issues.

People come to therapy when they are involved in an opposition of evenly matched forces that strain against each other. There are stress, tension, a struggle until the issue is resolved. It may be a conflict of individual wills, of ideas, of moral choices, of a person's purpose with some obstruction or flaw in his or her own nature. It is best for the therapist to think in terms of the individual striving to achieve a goal (to dominate, to be loved, to give love, to repent) and meeting resistance from an obstacle or succession of obstacles.

In every therapy, there has to be a central character who propels the action forward, an activator, a doer, someone who makes things happen. This may be a hero or a villain, a competent operator or a perpetrator of comic disasters. If the therapy is in danger of running out of steam, one can always expand the unit, bring in more family members, and a new driver can be introduced. The therapist, like the dramatist, needs to show the beginnings of a particular change, trace it through its natural turmoil, and bring the contending forces into a different, though not necessarily a perfect, balance. Things were one way; now they are another.

The art of therapy is the art of preparation. Preparing a family skillfully so that it will grasp, and be moved by, suggestions later in the therapy is a vital ingredient of our work. Atmosphere, tone, and mood are parts of preparation that inspire motivation and make the therapist believable. Preparation suspends disbelief and lays the groundwork for the possibility of major change. For example, a therapist can start a session by asking everyone present if they believe in magic or in miracles. After such a beginning, anything is possible.

Sometimes the therapist makes the family believe the therapy is about one thing, until it is suddenly revealed to be about something else altogether. For example, the anorectic is not trying to destroy herself, but is trying to help her alcoholic father. The boy who steals cars is only trying to draw the father's anger toward himself and so protect the mother.

Every therapist is a detective. Every successful therapy is an investigation brought to the fruitful conclusion.

Preparation is linked with emphasis. Repetition, elaboration, and timing will underline a point, so that it stays in the memory. Repetition is necessary to ensure that important points are clear in the family's mind. Great orators believe in saying a thing three times; therapists need to say it ten times. Therapy has to be redundant.

There has to be dramatic tension. A therapist needs to elicit, suspend, heighten, and resolve a state of tension. One has to know what material to milk for its dramatic potential. Tension cannot be endured without breaks, and the therapist occasionally will discuss trivial matters and then return to the dramatic tension.

Just as the playwright must be interested in his or her characters, we must feel sympathy for the people we work with or we will not care about their suffering and we will not have

enough hope and fear to be motivated to change them.

Most of all, we need to know how to ask questions. The movement of therapy is from question to answer, from problem to solution. Similarly in drama, will Hamlet kill the king before the king kills him?

Each session in therapy ends with a question mark, as does each episode of a television serial. In "Dallas," who shot J.R.? In *A Chorus Line*, who will get the job? Many cunning therapists create questions at a faster rate than they can be answered. They propose pleasing ambiguities, leaving several options open, never being too explicit or giving the game away, and rationing information until the characters in the therapy are sufficiently motivated to follow suggestions.

Expectations, once aroused, normally should be satisfied or the family may feel cheated. If the family has been led to expect, for example, a major confrontation, then that scene becomes virtually obligatory. If a couple, for example, expects an opportunity to express all of each spouse's resentments in the presence of the therapist, then that scene becomes mandatory.

Another important element is suspense. A therapist can create a word-by-word kind of suspense where people are thinking, "What will he say to that?" or, "Is she siding with me?" The better the therapist, the more suspense is possible, because the therapist can surprise the family with his or her choice of words. A therapist speaking slowly and thoughtfully, but with immense verbal precision, is very suspenseful. Milton Erickson was, of course, a master in this area.

Ideally, clients should develop insight without realizing they are doing so; they should follow suggestions without necessarily knowing that they have been given. The family becomes so enthralled in the conflicts of the present that the past can remain shadowy.

The therapist asks questions in such a way that the answers are presented in the form of a conflict. If your father had to choose between his wife and his mother, whom do you think he would choose? It must seem perfectly natural that the facts should come out in the way they do. An expository device, to be really successful, must be invisible.

The therapist asks questions in such a way as to create a conflict that can be resolved and the family becomes convinced that the conflict already existed.

ETHICS AND SPIRITUALITY

Another area of concern today is ethics and spirituality. A new concern with ethics is reflected in every field as we consider the possibility of manipulating life through biotechnology, and as we witness insider trading, bribery, and the common occurrence of fraud. Philosophers are being pursued to advise hospitals, legislatures, computer factories, and prisons. Ethics is being taught in more and more schools and universities.

In the field of therapy, we are being called upon not only to protect the human rights of individuals, but also to organize family members to do what is morally and ethically right. Morality has come back into therapy and the understanding is developing that what is ethically correct is also therapeutic.

Nowhere is an ethical approach as needed as in dealing with the problems of incest and sexual abuse that have reached crisis proportions in our society. No therapist can avoid treating the offenders or victims. Incest and sexual abuse relate not only to ethical issues, but to spiritual ones as well. Sexuality and spirituality are related in human beings, so that a sexual attack is an attack on the spirit of the person. Ethics and spirituality must be addressed in these therapies. I have developed a standard approach that ensures that further harm will not occur, introducing metaphors of spirituality and unity and emphasizing symbols of compassion and higher emotion. Family members are moved step-by-step from abuse to repentance, reparation, and protection of one another.

The field of therapy is moving in the direction of organizing the family as a self-help network, of teaching therapy as an art form, and of incorporating morality and spirituality. Spirituality includes a sense of humor that helps us to take ourselves less seriously and to laugh at our plight in the world. Humor helps us to bring out the best in people and to release them from

the grimness with which they usually come to therapy. I would like to end on a humorous note with one of my favorite therapy stories.

CASE EXAMPLE

Case Nine

A couple came to therapy with a serious problem. The wife was severely diabetic and was drinking herself to death. She drank a half-bottle of vodka a night and was not paying attention to her diet or her medications. The husband was not quite violent, but he was a very tall, large man who had violent temper tantrums. He would take a plate of spaghetti, for instance, and smash it against the wall. The wife was a tall, bloated woman who came to the sessions wearing shorts and with curlers in her hair. They talked endlessly about messes: the attic, the garage, cleaning up after the dog, taking out the garbage.

The therapist was a nice young man. As he struggled with this couple, he seemed to be getting more and more depressed. They were the kind of people who make the most dedicated of therapists ask themselves, "For this I struggled through a Ph.D.?" As the supervisor, I had the challenge of motivating the therapist to become more interested in the couple.

One day, after several sessions, I said to him, "Today I would like you to go in and ask the wife whether she has seen the movie or read *Gone with the Wind*. She is going to ask, 'Why are you asking?' Tell her that she and her husband remind you of Rhett Butler and Scarlett O'Hara. They also had a passionate relationship, and were always fighting. Like Rhett, the husband is always on the verge of violence. Like Scarlett, the wife is always trying to change her husband, but she never succeeds; she never changes him at all."

When the therapist asked the question, the husband immediately looked at himself in the mirror. The only resemblance he had to Clark Gable was his mustache, but he started to stroke it. The wife said, "*Gone with the Wind* is my favorite novel! I've read the whole book five times. I've seen the movie probably eight or nine times. And Scarlett *did* change Rhett."

The therapist said, "No, she didn't. I'll bet you $10 that you won't find a passage in the book that shows that she changed him. I'm surprised that, if you know the novel so well and you are so similar to Scarlett, you continue trying to change your husband instead of just enjoying his unpredictability and the passionate relationship that you have with him." The woman said she would read the book again, but the questions already had set up the context for a different type of interaction. They were identifying with a cultural stereotype of a romantic, passionate couple. The therapist had momentarily raised them to a higher level of being.

Then the therapist proceeded, "I'd like you to describe to me your best memories of your life together. Way back in the past when you first met, what were the best times that you had together?" At first, they could not think of any good memories at all. The therapist insisted: "There must have been some good times. Perhaps your honeymoon or the birth of the first child." Slowly they began to remember. The husband described how they had gone on their honeymoon to a place in Florida where there were dolphins. One day, he went by himself to the dolphin lagoon and learned the signals that the trainer gave to the dolphins for the show. The next morning, he took his wife for a walk to the lagoon, gave the signals, and the dolphins came out of the water and put on a show just for her. In listening to this, the therapist began to become interested in the man. The wife softened as she remembered the episode.

Then the couple remembered some other charming incidents. The therapist told them that in the next two weeks he wanted them to just do one thing—to have one good experience that would be remembered ten years from now. Who did the dishes, who took out the garbage, or who cleaned the attic was not going to be remembered in ten years, but an unusual event, like that with the dolphins, would be remembered always.

That day saw the first snow of the winter. When the couple left the session, the husband built a big snowman right at the door of the institute, which is something *we* always remember. This couple discovered wonderful things to do in Washington. For two months, the only directive was to create good memories. All conversation about the relationship and her diabetes was abandoned, except as it related to the good memories that they were creating. In less than three months, the wife's health improved greatly. She had quit drinking, even though the therapist had never talked about the drinking, and she was taking care of her diet. They thanked the therapist, and the therapy ended.

Creating good memories is one of my favorite strategies for therapy and one that is good to apply to our own lives. I hope that this Evolution Conference will create many good memories for all.

Discussion by Mary McClure Goulding, M.S.W.

◆

I wish to thank Ms. Madanes for a very beautiful paper. As she was speaking, I was thinking that the glory of this conference is that we are all here together, and that we have so many different approaches. I also realized that I had thought of her as intellectual and bright, but as working by kind of fooling people. But as she spoke, it was as if Virginia Satir were here, because Madanes has the love and kindness that I associate with Virginia. I am sure one of the reasons that Madanes' families come back and get well is that she believes in them so intensely and cares about them. That came through beautifully.

I like the list (it's a great list) of the 18 things to remember while seeing a family. I especially liked the observation that the therapist has to demonstrate tolerance, love, and compassion, that that is what family living is all about. I liked the temper-tantrum technique. If we had more time, it would be a fun exercise for people in the audience. In pairs, each could be Frankenstein monsters and then hug. It's similar to the "no–no" dance I do with my grandchildren when they are age two. We do a march yelling, "No. No. No."

I liked the idea of remembering the good person instead of the bad. So many therapists think that they have to spend a lot of time reviewing past horrors. I don't go to the dentist if I can possibly avoid it. When I do, I go to one who works fast. I feel the same way about reliving terrible things. It is a nice technique to orient to the person who was good in one's life. Sometimes people do not think of people who were good. Sometimes there really wasn't anyone good around much; then they can make it up. "What type of a good person had you wanted?" "Will you treat yourself that way?" "You can begin reparenting yourself: Pick an age when you really needed this good person and spend 15 minutes every evening reparenting that child at that age, being all the good things that the child needed." Then the person usually does come up with a good person in the past that he or she is modeling from.

Where Madanes and I differ in our therapeutic approach is that I like to have people know when they have good insight. I think it is important for clients to demonstrate good insight. I am interested in their taking charge and thinking for themselves and being proud of their ability to be their own therapists. I think the really important thrust is believing in families, believing in family members helping each other.

I would like to say also that there are times when a person desperately needs help to leave the family. We primarily see therapists at our institute. I am appalled at the number of therapists who become therapists because there was grave mental illness within the family when they were children. And many still struggle with a family member who is gravely mentally ill. Yet many therapists believe families have to stay together. I think it is important to know when to leave, when to cut loose, when to let the State take charge.

Another point is that if family members are going to stay together, they may need money. A horror that has happened to this country today is that we have the money for the military, but we don't have the money to keep families together. We have to be vocal about this inequity.

I have had a bad year. A lot of people I know have died, and for the first time, I have been working intimately with friends who are dying. The hospice movement in our area is fantastic. The last two people for whom I cared a great deal died at home. My ex-husband is dying now, and he also will die at home. This is possible because of hospice care, because people in the community come in and do the things the family members can't quite do, and they provide relief.

We need something similar for the young and for families. We need something like hospice visitors who will come in to help the single mother, the overworked and underpaid parents, the dysfunctional. I think that would make self-help much more possible for many families. We need the national caring and compassion that Madanes demonstrates toward the families she treats.

QUESTIONS AND ANSWERS

Question: I was very moved by this presentation talk. I would like you to speak a little bit about your use of self-disclosure in therapy.

Madanes: I think that the more experienced you are as a therapist, the more comfortable you can be in disclosing aspects of your own life. If the problem is such that it is difficult for the family members to feel that you can be sympathetic to their situation, self-disclosure can be used to disclose a similar experience so that a bond of intimacy will be established.

Question: I am a teacher, and within the school system, we run groups. Could you see a group of students forming their own family? How could we use some of the 18 steps you suggested in terms of a group of adolescents as a family? Does it really need to be a biological family?

Madanes: Families have a past, a present, and a future together. A group of students in a school can be friends and can help each other in many ways, but it is a different type of organization. Certainly, some steps can be adapted to make the group have more continuity and more collaboration. But you don't want to transform them into a family, because they have their own families.

Question: I have a concern about the family in which the child takes care of the parent. This role can create a great deal of pain for that child. You suggested that a child can be utilized to help parents out of their dilemmas. Are there families where this would not be appropriate? Where we need to help the family to develop a hierarchy and to firm up their boundaries? And is the effectiveness of this maybe perhaps due to the fact that the child has been trying so hard, but has tried in ways that were not effective?

Madanes: This is why I presented the view that in my approach, one can enter the family system either at the higher echelon of the hierarchy and intervene through the parents, or intervene laterally between the parents, or intervene bottom up from the child to the parents. Of course, there are situations where it is more appropriate to appeal to the grandparents, who can give caring and protection to the younger generation. There are other situations in which the most competent members and the most dedicated are the children. However, in our society, many children take care of their parents, and the problem is that they often do it without recognition and without appreciation. They do it in ineffective ways. With the help of the therapist, the children can get the appreciation they deserve and feel satisfied because they are effective and appropriate helpers.

Question: I would like to hear the presenters' thoughts about the use of psychotropic medication in combination with therapy.

Haley: I think medication is the worst problem in the therapy field. It has complicated everyone's work—particularly that of psychiatrists.

They are moving into a pharmacological stance that, I think, is limiting their education, as compared with that of residents trained years ago. I don't think it makes people more accessible to therapy to use psychotropic drugs. I certainly don't like drugs that cause tardive dyskinesia and other side effects. I think that drugs are used wrongly and recklessly. To me, therapy is a drug-free enterprise, and I tend to think of drugs as chemical restraints. I would rather not use them. They should be used for social control. If somebody is out of his or her mind and climbing the walls, you do what you can to make that person behave. But I don't think that is related to therapy.

Question: I have a question for Cloé Madanes. I'm wondering about step 7 on your list, the nonaggression pact among family members. When people are violent in families, it's often something that can't be controlled by simply saying, "I'm not going to do it," because it is out of control and it is behavior that just comes up. How do you make a nonaggression pact?

Madanes: I didn't mean that by making a pact of nonviolence the family is not going to be violent. As a therapist, you have to keep in mind that an important goal of therapy is to prevent violence. You have to make clear to the people you work with that you disapprove of violence as a solution to any problem. It doesn't mean that this alone is going to be effective in the sense that there will no longer be violence, but it puts you in the right frame of mind in relation to the problem.

M. Goulding: I would stop all other work and address only the violence issue until it was solved. I would get a nonviolent contract for a single day, if that is all the person is willing to accept, and I would be sure to call the person the next day. "No suicide," "No homicide," and "No violence against self or others" are contracts that must take precedence over all other work. I might get clients to look at what happened in the past, because most people who are violent were raised violently. I would see if I could get them in touch with what it felt like to be the weak one, to be the recipient of violence. I would use whatever techniques and whatever skills I had. I would not leave that issue unresolved.

Question: Is the issue of violence best addressed in a therapeutic situation with the particular therapist? Are there ever appropriate times where an auxiliary referral is made? For example, do you refer a man to an anger-control group? Some people believe that is an effective technique—a group of people dealing with each other and confronting one another about common problems.

Madanes: I think it is most appropriate to deal with violence in the context of the therapy of the family. There are circumstances, however, when you have to separate people. In those cases, as a way of controlling the violence, it is important to connect each spouse to his or her family of origin so that your unit for therapy is not just the couple, but the spouses with their parents and with their relatives. I prefer not to refer to others. We believe that the therapist has to be skillful and patient enough to solve the problem in therapy.

Question: Are two parents necessary for a happy family?

Moderator: You are wondering if you heard a bias toward the nuclear family as opposed to alternative family structures?

Madanes: No, I don't have any bias toward the nuclear family or the two-parent family. I think that single-parent families can work very well, and sometimes better than two-parent families. There is no bias.

Question: I'd like to ask Cloé whether or not she ever sees members of the family alone, or is it a requisite to see all of them together?

Madanes: We see family members individually, in dyads, in triads, in a variety of combinations. This is not an orthodox setting where you have to see people in a certain way.

Question: When you have a couple, each of whom thinks the other is paranoid or mentally ill, is it appropriate to see other members of the

family, such as a sister, separately to give further background on each of the individuals to get a picture of what is going on? I hear diametrically opposite stories from the husband and the wife.

Madanes: Yes, it is always a good idea to bring as many people in as possible to inform you about what is happening. Each person's different view furthers your understanding. It is very good for the therapy.

Question: I would like you to talk about step 18, the "path of the hero." Could you give an example of how you used that in your therapeutic work?

Madanes: The idea is to help each individual in the family find some meaning in life—something the person would like to pursue, with the emphasis not necessarily on what is accomplished—not on what is at the end of path—but on the importance of following a certain path, going in a certain direction, having some goal. For example, the goal can be an artistic one, like the idea of self-expression through the theatre. It can be in political action. It can be studying Eastern philosophy or simply helping others. This is very important, particularly with people who have been abused or who have suffered trauma. You take them away from the issue of pain that they have suffered. From the injustice that was perpetrated on them, you take them to the idea of helping others and future generations so that others will not go through that suffering.

Question: Cloé, you mentioned hope and optimism as being keys to instilling hope in families. I wonder how you might apply these to families that have experienced the accidental death of a child, for example, a two-year-old who drowns. Mom thought Dad was watching the child, Dad thought the sister was watching the child, and the child died.

Madanes: There are many different things you can do. One that comes to mind is to emphasize that the sadness that they feel is because of the love that they had for the child. They have that love within them and their love hasn't died with that child. The issue is to channel that love into another child, another being, others who can be the object of that love. The love is within the parents; it hasn't been lost with the child.

Question: When Cloé talked about networks and the use of people in a nonhierarchical way, it brought to my mind an organization called the National Association for the Mentally Ill, which proposes to be a network outside the institutional framework. Its members have some interesting views that are divergent from those we are hearing, and I would like to hear comments. For one thing, there is resentment of family therapy. Also, there is a desire to make psychotropic drugs and custodial and institutional care available.

Madanes: The fact that I disagree with the objectives of certain self-help networks doesn't mean that I don't defend their rights to organize their networks. Fortunately, democracy is such that it allows for many different kinds of organizations. That interchange is good for all.

The Construction of Clinical "Realities"

Paul Watzlawick, Ph.D.

Paul Watzlawick, Ph.D.

Paul Watzlawick received his Ph.D. degree from the University of Venice in 1949. He has an Analyst's Diploma from the C.G. Jung Institute for Analytic Psychology in Zurich. Watzlawick has practiced psychotherapy for more than 35 years. Currently, he is Research Associate at the Mental Research Institute and Clinical Professor in the Department of Psychiatry and Behavioral Sciences, Stanford University Medical Center.

Watzlawick received the Distinguished Achievement Award from the American Family Therapy Association and the Lifetime Achievement Award from the Milton H. Erickson Foundation. He is the author, coauthor, or editor of 12 books on the topics of interactional psychotherapy, human communication, and constructivist philosophy.

Paul Watzlawick presents tenets of constructivism, pointing out that psychological normalcy is a convention, not a fact. The criterion of "reality adaptation" as a measure of mental health or pathology is fictitious, since what reality "really" is remains an arbitrary definition that is often reified. These reifications can lead to both positive and negative practical consequences. Implications for therapy are offered.

As clinicians, we are not usually also epistemologists, that is, we have no training in that branch of science that studies the origin and nature of knowledge. The implications and consequences of this are far-reaching and certainly go well beyond my own meager training in philosophy. However, I believe that at least some basic epistemological considerations determine the direction our field is taking, and they thus do enter into the subject matter of this conference.

DEFINING NORMALCY

Let me begin with one such consideration that may be trivially obvious to some and almost scandalous to others: in contrast to the medical sciences, our field does not have a generally accepted, final definition of normalcy. Physicians are in the fortunate position of possessing a fairly clear, objectively verifiable idea of what may be called the normal functioning of the human body. This enables them to identify deviations from the norm and allows them to consider them pathologies. It goes without saying that this knowledge does not also enable them to treat every such deviation. But it definitely means that they presumably can make distinctions between most manifestations of health or of illness.

The question of the emotional or mental health of an individual is a totally different matter. It is not a scientific, but a philosophical, a metaphysical, or even a plainly superstitious assumption. For us to become aware of what or who we "really" are would require us to step outside ourselves and look at ourselves objectively, a feat coming close to what so far only Baron von Münchhausen was able to accomplish when he saved himself and his horse from drowning in a quagmire by pulling himself out by his own pigtail.

Any attempt by the human mind to study itself leads to the problems of recursiveness or self-reference, which have the same structure as certain jokes, such as the question, "What is intelligence?" and the answer, "Intelligence is that mental capacity that is measured by intelligence tests."

Throughout the ages, insanity was considered the deviation from a norm that itself was considered to be the final, ultimate truth. So "final" was that truth, that to question it was itself a symptom of madness or badness. The age of enlightenment was no exception, except that instead of some divine revelation it was now the human mind itself that had divine properties and was referred to as *déesse raison*. According to her pronouncement, the universe was governed by logical principles, the human mind was capable of grasping these principles, and the human will was capable of acting according to them. Let me mention only as an aside that the enthronement of the Goddess Reason led to the killing of about 40,000 people by means of Dr. Guilletin's enlightened invention, and eventually, feeding back upon itself, to the establishment of yet another traditional monarchy.

Over 100 years later, a far more pragmatic and humane definition of normalcy was introduced by Freud, who defined it as "the ability to work and to love." For many people, this definition seemed to serve its purpose and thus found wide acceptance. Unfortunately, however, according to this definition, Hitler would have been sort of normal, because, as we all know, he worked very hard and he loved at least his dog, if not also his mistress, Eva Braun. Freud's definition is found lacking when we are faced with the proverbial eccentricities of particularly outstanding people.

These problems may have contributed to the general acceptance of yet another definition of normalcy, namely, that of *reality adaptation*. According to this criterion, normal people (and especially therapists) see reality as it really is, while people suffering from emotional or mental problems see it in a distorted way. This definition unquestioningly assumes that there is a real reality that is accessible to the human mind, an assumption that has been philosophically untenable for at least 200 years. Hume, Kant, Schopenhauer, and many others have insisted that of the "real" reality we can only have an opinion, a subjective image, an arbitrary interpretation. According to Kant, for instance, every error consists in taking the way *we* determine, divide, or deduce concepts for qualities of the *things* in and of themselves. And Schopenhauer, in *The Will in Nature* (1912) wrote: "This is the meaning of Kant's great doctrine, that teleology [the study of evidences of design and purpose in nature] is brought into nature by the intellect, which thus marvels at a miracle that it has created itself in the first place" (p. 346).

It is quite easy to dismiss such views scornfully as merely "philosophical" and therefore devoid of practical usefulness. But similar statements can be found in the works by representatives of what is generally considered to be natural science at its best: theoretical physics. In 1926, during a conversation with Heisenberg on theory building, Einstein is supposed to have asserted that it is quite wrong to try founding a theory only on objective observation. The very opposite is true: It is the theory that decides what we can observe.

In a similar vein, Schrödinger (1958), in his book *Mind and Matter*, asserts, "Everyman's world picture is and always remains a construct of his mind and cannot be proved to have any other existence" (p. 52).

And Heisenberg (1958) on the same subject:

The reality that we can talk about is never the "a priori" reality, but a known reality shaped by us. If with regard to this latter formulation it is objected that, after all, there is an objective world, independent from us and our thinking, which functions, or can function, without our doing, and which is that which we actually mean when doing research, this objection, so convincing at first blush, must be countered by pointing out that even the expression "there is" originates in human language and cannot, therefore, mean something that is unrelated to our comprehension. For us "there is" only the world in which the expression "there is" has meaning. (p. 236)

The self-referential circularity of the mind subjecting itself to a "scientific study" was well described by the famous biocybernetician Heinz von Foerster (1974):

We are now in the possession of the truism that a description (of the universe) implies one who describes (observes) it. What we need now is the description of the "describer" or, in other words, we need a theory of the observer. Since it is only living organisms which would qualify as being observers, it appears that this task falls to the biologist. But he himself is a living being, which means that in his theory he has not only to account for himself, but also for his writing this theory. This is a new state of affairs in scientific discourse for, in line with the traditional viewpoint which separates the observer from his observations, reference to this discourse was to be carefully avoided. This separation was done by no means because of excentricity or folly, for under certain circumstances inclusion of the observer in his descriptions may lead to paradoxes, to wit the utterance "I am a liar." (p. 401)

And perhaps even more radical (in the original sense of "going to the roots"), the Chilean biologist Francisco Varela (1975) in his *Calculus for Self-Reference*:

The starting point of this calculus [...]is the act of indication. In this primordial act we separate forms which appear to us as the world itself. From this starting point, we thus assert the primacy of the role of the observer who draws distinctions wherever he pleases. Thus the distinctions made which engender our world reveal precisely that: the distinctions we make—and these distinctions pertain more to a revelation of where the observer stands than to an intrinsic constitution of the world which appears, by this very mechanism of separation between observer and observed, always elusive. In finding the world as we do, we forget all we did to find it as such, and when we are reminded of it in retracing our steps back to indication, we find little more than a mirror-to-mirror image of ourselves and the world. In contrast with what is commonly assumed, a description, when carefully inspected, reveals the properties of the observer. We, observers, distinguish ourselves precisely by distinguishing what we apparently are not, the world. (p. 24)

All right, one may say, but what has all of this to do with our profession in which we are up against the stark realities of behavior whose insanity not even a philosopher could deny?

In reply, let me quote (again) that strange incident that took place more than two years ago in the Italian city of Grosseto. A woman from Naples, on a visit to Grosseto, had to be admitted to the local hospital in a state of acute schizophrenic excitement. Since the psychiatric ward was unable to admit her, it was decided to send her back to Naples for proper treatment. When the ambulance attendants arrived and asked where the patient was, they were told in what room she was waiting. Upon entering, they found the patient sitting on a bed, fully dressed and her handbag ready. When they invited her to come downstairs to the waiting ambulance, she again became quite psychotic, physically resisting the attendants, refusing to move, and, above all, depersonalizing. She had to be forcibly tranquilized, and carried down into the ambulance, and off they went to Naples.

On the *autostrada* outside Rome, the ambulance was stopped by a police car and sent back to Grosseto: There had been a mistake; the woman in the ambulance was not the patient, but an inhabitant of Grosseto who had gone to the hospital to pay a visit to a relative who had undergone minor surgery.

Would it be exaggerated to say that the mistake had created (or, as we radical constructivists would say, "constructed") a clinical reality in which precisely the "reality-adapted" behavior of that woman was clear evidence of her "insanity"? She became aggressive, accused the staff of evil intentions, began to depersonalize, and so on.

Whoever is familiar with the work of the psychologist David Rosenhan did not have to wait until the Grosseto incident. Fifteen years earlier Rosenhan published the results of an elegant study, "On Being Sane in Insane Places" 1984, in which he and his team proved that the normals are not detectably sane and that psychiatric hospitals create realities of their own.

An essentially analogous example was reported by the news media about a year ago from the Brazilian city of São Paulo. According to this report, it had been found necessary to raise the (very low) railing of the terrace of the Riding Club, since a number of visitors had fallen backwards over the railing and severely hurt themselves. Since, apparently, not all these accidents could be simply explained away by drunkenness, another explanation was suggested, presumably by an anthropologist: Different cultures have different rules regarding the "correct" distance to assume and maintain while engaged in a face-to-face conversation with another person. In Western European and North American cultures, this distance is the proverbial arm's length; in Mediterranean and Latin-American cultures, it is considerably shorter. Thus if a North American and a Brazilian began a conversation, the North American presumably would establish that distance that to him was the "correct, normal" one. The Brazilian would feel uncomfortably distant from the other and would move closer, in order to establish the distance that to the Brazilian was the "right" one; the North American would move back, the other would move closer, and so on, until the North American would fall backwards over the railing. Thus two different "realities" had created an event for which, in the classical monadic view of human behavior, the diagnosis of accident proneness or even of the manifestation of a "death instinct" would not be too far-fetched and would thus construct a clinical "reality."

The reality-creating power of such cultural rules is the subject of Walter Cannon's (1942) classic paper, "Voodoo Death," a fascinating collection of anthropological case material demonstrating how a person's firm belief in the power of a curse or evil spell may lead to the death of that person in a matter of hours. In one instance, however, the other members of an Australian bush tribe forced the medicine man to withdraw his curse and the victim, who had already sunk into lethargy, recovered in a very short time.

As far as I know, nobody has studied the construction of such clinical "realities" in greater detail than Thomas Szasz. Of his many books, *The Manufacture of Madness—A Comparative Study of the Inquisition and the Mental Health Movement* (1970) is of particular relevance to my subject. Of the many historical sources utilized by him, let me quote from the one with which I am most familiar. It is the book *Cautio Criminalis*, dealing with the witches' trials, written by the Jesuit Friedrich von Spee in 1631 (republished by Ritter, 1977). In his capacity as father confessor of many people accused of witchcraft, he witnessed the most atrocious torture scenes and wrote the book in order to make the court authorities aware of the fact that under their rules of trial procedure, *no* suspect could ever be found innocent. In other words, these rules constructed a reality in which, once again, *any* behavior of the accused was evidence of guilt. Here are some of the "proofs":

- God would protect the innocent from the beginning; "therefore," not being saved by God is in and of itself already proof of guilt.
- A suspect's life is either righteous or not. If not, this is additional proof. If it is, this gives rise to additional suspicion, for it is known that witches are capable of creating righteous impressions.
- Once in jail, the witch will either be fearful or not. If fearful, this is obvious proof of a guilty conscience. If without fear, this confirms the probability of guilt, for it is well known that the most dangerous witches are capable of appearing innocent and calm.
- The suspect either tries to flee or not. Any attempt to flee is obvious and additional proof of guilt, while not attempting to flee means that the devil wants her death.

As we can see again, the *meaning* attributed to a set of circumstances within a given frame of assumptions, ideologies, or beliefs constructs a reality all of its own and reveals that "truth," so to speak. In Gregory Bateson's terms, these are double-bind situations, logical impasses, of which he gave countless clinical examples, in particular, in his book *Perceval's Narrative—A Patient's Account of His Psychosis* (1961).

John Perceval, son of the British prime minister Spencer Perceval, became psychotic in 1830 and remained hospitalized until 1834. In the years following his release, he wrote two biographical accounts, entitled *Narrative*, detailing his experiences as a mental patient. To give just one quotation from Bateson's Introduction, referring to the interaction between the patient and his family:

[The parents] cannot perceive their own perfidy except as justified by the patient's behavior, and the patient will not let them perceive how his behavior is related to his view of what they have done and are now doing. The tyranny of "good intentions" must endlessly be served while the patient achieves an ironic sainthood, sacrificing himself in foolish or self-destructive actions until at least he is justified in quoting the Saviour's prayer: "Father, forgive them, they know not what they do.——Amen" (p. xviii)

However, the ancient wisdom *similia similibus curantur* (likes are cured by likes) also applies to these situations. The most ancient example known to me of the construction of a positive clinical reality is reported by Plutarch in his *Morals* (Goodwin, 1989) and deals with the extraordinary success of the "Mental Health authorities" of the ancient city of Milesia in Asia Minor:

A certain dreadful and monstrous distemper did seize the Milesian maids, arising from some hidden cause. It is most likely the air had acquired some infatuating and venomous quality, that did influence them to this change and alienation of mind; for all on a sudden an earnest longing for death, with furious attempts to hang themselves, did attack them, and many did privily accomplish it. The arguments and tears of parents and the persuasion of friends availed nothing, but they circumvented their keepers in all their contrivances and industry to prevent them, still murdering themselves. And the calamity seemed to be an extraordinary divine stroke and beyond human help, until by the counsel of a wise man a decree of the senate was passed, enacting that those maids who hanged themselves should be carried naked through the market-place. The passage of this law not only inhibited but quashed their desire of slaying themselves. Note what a great argument of good nature and virtue this fear of disgrace is; for they who had no dread upon them of the most terrible things in the world, death and pain, could not abide the imagination of dishonor and exposure to shame even after death. (p. 354)

Maybe that wise man was aware of the equally ancient wisdom of Epictetus, who said that it is not the things that bother us, but the opinions that we have of the things.

But these are exceptions. By and large, our field has never stopped assuming that the existence of a name is proof of the "real" existence of the thing named, Alfred Korzybski (1933) and his warning notwithstanding, namely, that *the name is not the thing, the map is not the territory.* The most monumental example of this kind of reality construction, at least in our days, is the *Diagnostic and Statistical Manual of Mental Disorders* (DSM). Its creators must be credited with what is probably the greatest therapeutic success of all times. Reacting to growing social pressure, they no longer included in the third edition (DSM-III) homosexuality as a psychiatric condition, thereby curing millions of people of their "disease" by the stroke of a pen. But, leaving facetiousness aside, the practical, clinical consequences of the use of diagnostic terms are being studied seriously by Karl Tomm and his team in the Family Therapy Program, Department of Psychiatry, University of Calgary.

What practical, useful conclusions may be drawn from all of this?

If it is accepted that mental normalcy cannot be defined objectively, then, of necessity, the concept of mental illness is just as undefinable. But then, what about therapy?

IMPLICATIONS FOR THERAPY

It is at this point that we should turn our attention to a phenomenon that has been known for a long time, albeit almost exclusively as a negative, undesirable set of circumstances: the self-fulfilling prophecy. The first, detailed study goes back to the research of Russel A. Jones (1974) (and here I quote the subtitle of his book) into the social, psychological, and physiological effects of expectancies.

As is by now generally known, a self-fulfilling prophecy is an assumption or prediction that, precisely because it has been made, causes the expected or predicted event to occur, and thus, recursively, confirms its own "accuracy." The study of interpersonal relations offers numerous examples. For instance, if a man assumes, for whatever reason, that people do not like him, he will, because of this assumption, behave in such a hostile, overly sensitive, suspicious manner as to produce in his human environment that very dislike that he expected, and that "proves" to him how right he was from the beginning.

A self-fulfilling prophecy on a statewide scale occurred in March 1979, when the California mass media reported an imminent, severe gasoline shortage as a result of the Arab oil embargo. As a result, California motorists did what, under the circumstances, was the only reasonable thing: they stormed the gas stations to fill up their tanks and to keep the tanks as full as possible. This filling up of 12 million gas tanks (which up to that point had probably been about 70 percent empty) depleted the enormous fuel reserves and brought about the predicted shortage, literally within a day. Endless lines formed at the gas stations, but about three weeks later, the chaos came to an end when it was officially announced that the allotment of gasoline to the state of California had been reduced only minimally.

Other by now classical studies are the highly interesting investigations of Robert Rosenthal, in particular, his book *Pygmalion in the Classroom* (Rosenthal & Jacobson, 1968), to say nothing of a plethora of investigations into the effects of placebos, those chemically inert substances that the patient assumes are newly developed, powerful medications. Although known since ancient times and used by all sorts of "spiritual" healers, curanderos, and the like, the placebo effect did not receive much scientific attention until about the middle of our century. According to Shapiro (1960), more research reports on this subject were published between 1954 and 1957 alone than during the 50 preceding years.

To what extent mere assumptions or attributions of meaning to perceptions can have a powerful effect on a person's physical state is well borne out by an example, already reported elsewhere (Watzlawick, 1990).

A hypnotist, highly respected for his skills and clinical successes, was invited to give a workshop for a group of doctors in the home of one of them. Upon entering the house, he noticed that, as he put it, "every horizontal surface was filled with flower bouquets." Being afflicted with a strong allergy to freshly cut flowers, almost immediately the well-known burning sensations made themselves felt in his eyes and nose. He turned to the host, and mentioned his problem and his fear that under these circumstances he would be unable to give his talk. The host expressed surprise and asked him to examine the flowers, which turned out to be artificial. Upon making this discovery, his allergic reaction subsided almost as quickly as it had come on.

This example seems to provide clear evidence that the criterion of reality adaptation is, after all, fully valid. The man *thought* that the flowers were real, but as soon as he discovered that they were only nylon and plastic, this confrontation with reality resolved his problem and he returned to normalcy.

FIRST- AND SECOND-ORDER REALITIES

At this point, it becomes necessary to draw a distinction between two levels of reality perceptions that are usually thrown into one pot. We need to distinguish between the image of reality that we receive through our senses and the meaning we attribute to these perceptions. For instance, a neurologically healthy person can see, touch, and smell a bunch of flowers. (For simplicity's sake, we shall disregard the fact that these perceptions also are the result of fantastically complex constructions carried out by our central nervous system. Let us further disregard the fact that the phrase "bunch of flowers" has meaning only for English-speaking people. It is meaningless noise or a series of letter symbols for anybody else.) Let us call this the *reality of the first order*.

However, matters rarely rest at this point. Almost invariably, we attribute a sense, meaning, and/or value to the objects of our perception. And it is at this level, the level of the *second-order reality*, that problems arise. The crucial difference between these two levels of reality perception is well illustrated by the old joke

"What is the difference between an optimist and a pessimist?" The answer: "An optimist says of a bottle of wine that it is half full; a pessimist says that it is half empty." The first-order reality is the same for both of them (a bottle with some wine in it); their second-order realities are different, and it would be totally useless to try to establish who is right and who is wrong.

In the case of the allergic hypnotist, then, his allergy can be considered a phenomenon that usually takes place on the level of his first-order reality, that is, his system reacts in typical, objectively verifiable ways to the presence of pollen in the air. But, as the example demonstrates, the mere assumption of the presence of flowers (in other words, the construction of a second-order reality) produced the same result.

As already mentioned at the beginning, the medical sciences do have a reasonably reliable definition of such first-order-reality events and processes. In the realm of psychotherapy, on the other hand, we are in a universe of mere assumptions, convictions, and beliefs that are part of our second-order reality and, therefore, are constructions of our minds. The processes whereby we construct our personal, social, scientific and ideological realities, and then consider them "objectively real," are the subject matter of that modern epistemological discipline called *radical constructivism.*

REALITY AND PSYCHOTHERAPY

Probably one of the most shocking tenets of this school of thought is that of the "real" reality, we can at best know what it is *not.* In other words, only when our reality construction breaks down do we realize that reality is not the way we thought it was. In his *Introduction to Radical Constructivism*, Ernst von Glasersfeld (1984) defines knowledge as

something the organism builds up in the attempt to order the as such amorphous flow of experience by establishing repeatable experiences and relatively reliable relations between them. The possibilities of constructing such an order are determined and perpetually constrained by the preceding steps in the construction. This means that the "real" world manifests itself exclusively there where our constructions

break down. But since we can describe and explain these breakdowns only in the very concepts that we have used to build the failing structures, this process can never yield a picture of a world which we could hold responsible for their failure. (p. 39)

But it is these failures, these breakdowns that we are faced with in our work, those states of anxiety, despair, and madness that befall us when we find ourselves in a world that gradually or suddenly has become meaningless. And, if we can accept the possibility that of the real world we can only know for certain what it is not, then psychotherapy becomes the art of replacing a reality construction that no longer "fits" with another, better-fitting one. This new construction is just as fictitious as the former, except that it permits us the comfortable illusion, called "mental health," that we now see things the way they "really" are and that we are thus in tune with the meaning of life.

Seen in this perspective, psychotherapy is concerned with *reframing* the clients world view, of constructing another clinical reality, of bringing about deliberately those chance events that Franz Alexander (1956) called corrective emotional experiences. Constructivist psychotherapy is under no illusion of making the client see the world as it really is. Rather, constructivism is fully aware that the new world view is, and can only be, another construction, another fiction—but a useful, less painful one.

At the end of a brief therapy (of nine sessions), the client, a young woman, had this to say, "The way I saw the situation, it was a problem. Now I see it differently, and it is no problem any more."

To me, these words are the quintessence of successful therapy: the reality of the first order has, of necessity, remained unchanged, but the client's second-order reality now is different and bearable.

And these words bring us back to Epictetus: It is not the things that bother us, but the opinions that we have about these things.

REFERENCES

Alexander, F. (1956). *Psychoanalysis and psychotherapy.* New York: Norton.

Bateson, G. (1961). *Perceval's narrative*. Stanford, CA: Stanford Univ. Press.

Foerster, H. von (1974). Notes pour une éspistemologie des objets vivants. In E. Morin and M. Piatelli-Palmarini (Eds.), *L'unité de l'homme*. Paris: Le Seuil.

Glasersfeld, E. von (1984). An introduction to radical constructivism. In P. Watzlawick (Ed.), *The invented reality*. New York: Norton.

Goodwin, W.W. (Ed.). (1889). *Plutarch's miscellanies and essays in 5 volumes* (vol. 1). Boston: Little, Brown & Co.

Heisenberg, W. (1958). *Physics and philosophy*. New York: Harper.

Jones, R. A. (1974). *Self-fulfilling prophecies*. New York: Halsted.

Korzybski, A. (1933). *Science and sanity*. New York: International Non-Aristotelian Library.

Ritter, J. F. (1977). *Friedrich von Spee*. Trier: Spee-Verlag.

Rosenhan, D. L. (1984). On being sane in insane places. In P. Watzlawick (Ed.), *The invented reality*. New York: Norton.

Rosenthal, R., & Jacobson, L. (1968). *Pygmalion in the classroom*. New York: Holt, Rinehart & Winston.

Schopenhauer, A. (1912). *Uber den Willen in der Natur*. Munich: Piper.

Schrödinger, E. (1958). *Mind and matter* Cambridge, England: Cambridge Univ. Press.

Shapiro, A. K. (1960). A contribution to the history of the placebo effects. *Behavioral Science, 5* (109–135).

Szasz, T. (1970) *The manufacture of madness*. New York: Dell.

Varela, F.J. (1975). A calculus for self-reference. *International Journal of General Systems, 2*, (5–24).

Watzlawick, P. (1990). Therapy is what you say it is. In J.K. Zeig and S.G. Gilligan (Eds.), *Brief therapy: Myths, methods, and metaphors* (pp. 55–61). New York: Brunner/Mazel.

Discussion by Cloé Madanes

◆

I want to say first of all that it is a great pleasure for me to comment on Dr. Watzlawick's paper because I considered him my teacher in the 1960s in California. He gave me my first job in the United States as his research assistant. I must say, though, that it was a volunteer job. But I published two papers out of that project at the Mental Research Institute, and I will always remember Dr. Watzlawick's encouragement and confidence in my intelligence. Looking back now, I realize that I was 26 years old then and incredibly naive and presumptuous. I thought I knew everything and Paul, in his unique restrained kindness, not only never told me that I didn't know anything, but he helped me to believe that I actually had something to say and that I could make a contribution.

I think that my experience in working many years ago with Paul reflects what I consider the two most important aspects of his work as a therapist and teacher of therapy. These two essential characteristics are respect and hope.

His interest in the mind, in second-order realities, in how a person views the world, reflects a great respect for every human being as a thinking person. His emphasis on the meaning of life in every therapy speaks of his deep respect for the individual.

Equally important are the optimism and hope that he brings to therapy. As he told us, "We are faced in our work with breakdowns, those states of anxiety, despair, and madness that befall us when we find ourselves in a world that gradually or suddenly has become meaningless. Psychotherapy becomes the art of constructing a reality that permits us the illusion that we are in tune with the meaning of life."

I agree completely. Psychotherapy is the art of finding the angel of hope in the midst of the terror of despair and madness. I would like to tell a story from Greek mythology that I think explains why God created therapists. It is the story of Pandora as told by Virginia Hamilton (1988).

Pandora was a woman made in heaven. Zeus, the Creator, wrapped her in a robe of innocence and gave her a box with a surprise inside. Before she left heaven, Apollo said to her, "Pandora, don't ever open the box!"

But Pandora had one defect. She was curious about everything. She had to look into all she saw.

Pandora was sent to Epimetheus, and as soon as she entered his house, he fell in love with her beauty. When she told him that she had been sent by Zeus, he said, "There must be a trick somewhere! What do you carry in that box?" Pandora said she didn't know and Epimetheus put it on the highest shelf, saying that it must be an awful surprise.

When his brother, Prometheus, came home, he warned Epimetheus that Pandora herself was dangerous, not just the box. But Pandora was good. The only problem was that she had to know what was in that box.

One day, when she was alone, she decided that she would just take it down and shake it and listen to it without opening it. She put a small chest on a stool, climbed up and stretching as high as she could, slid the box toward herself. As she tried to lift it, it flew out of her hands. There was a great jumble of noise—roars and screams, howls and cries. For a moment, the room was dark.

Out of the box came awful things—winged things and crawling things, slithering things and creeping things—bringing with them a slime of dark and gray despair. There were plagues of sorrow and pain. There was misery, holding its dripping head. Envy took hold of Pandora and tried to tear her hair out. Poverty slid hungrily across the floor.

Pandora tried to cover the box, but it was too late. All of the awful things were clamoring through the house and on out into the street, the town, the whole world.

There was one little thing left quivering on the floor. It must have been on the very bottom of the box. As Pandora held it, she could see its great heart swell and sink in its chest. "I must go," it said, rising weakly to its crooked feet. "But who are you?" Pandora asked.

The thing smiled a wan smile, unfolding its brightly colored wings. "I am Hope," it said. "If I do not hurry, humans will have so little reason to live." With one great leap, Hope sprang from the room, from the house, and into the world.

Pandora saw Hope catch up to the ugly things of the world. When Hope was among them, the creatures seemed less sure of themselves.

So it was that hunger and poverty, despair and ugliness, came into the world of humans. Epimetheus would have to live forever with Pandora, who had let one disaster after another out to torment life.

"Well, it's not all bad," Pandora thought, "There is always Hope." Hope stays in the world. It is the one good thing out of Pandora's gift box from the jealous god.

I think that God created therapists to be like Hope, destined to follow all the horrors of the world of humans. We need always to remember that our task is to make the monsters less sure of themselves or, as Paul would say, to create a reality that makes the world a brighter place.

REFERENCE

Hamilton, V. (1988). *In the Beginning—Creation Stories From Around the World*. New York: Harcourt Brace Jovanovich.

QUESTIONS AND ANSWERS

Meichenbaum: Although I am scheduled to be the discussant of the next Invited Address, I would like to share an observation concerning this thoughtful paper. While I do not wish to be viewed as a defender of psychiatry and DSM-III-R, I would like to comment on the David Rosenhan study that you highlighted in your presentation. Several years ago, in a paper published, I believe, in the journal of *Professional Psychology*, one of the confederate "pseudo-patients" in Rosenhan's original study reported on his hospitalization experience. In contrast to Rosenhan's general findings of the pseudopatient's negative experience, this patient/confederate reported on positive staff treatment consisting of compassionate and humane care. Furthermore, this author claimed that his experience was not included along with those of the other eight pseudopatients whom Rosenhan cited. This account does not detract from Rosenhan's innovative research, but it should give pause in considering whether Rosenhan has also "constructed reality."

I believe that there is a real danger in using

anecdotes to illustrate points about "constructive realities."

Watzlawick: The Rosenhan paper created a great deal of outcry, it has been replicated many times. The controversies surrounding this work are by no means resolved.

Question: How effective is it going to be once the lay public becomes aware that one of psychology's main tenets is replacing an old constructed reality with a new one. Will the old intervention be as effective?

Watzlawick: I agree with you. Popularization can be a rather negative factor. But in my own work, I have found a way around it. People may come for help and say, "I have a problem. But I have read most of your books and I know most of your tricks. Can you still help me?" I then try to reframe the situation by saying, "If you have read it all, then this is a great advantage. We don't have to talk about it in detail. We can simply engage in a new kind of behavior to see what practical consequences come from it."

Another problem is that once a particular approach is popularized, there can be strong public reactions. For instance, we constructivists are accused of being nothing but the representatives of a warmed-over version of nihilism; we are destructive because we deny all values. Well, that is a misunderstanding. People also misunderstand paradoxical therapy because they see paradox only in the colloquial sense of something strange, unexpected. That is not what Gregory Bateson meant.

I had a discussion with an eminent colleague who claimed that systemic therapy was useless. I found out only gradually that for him "system" meant those in government. Of course, when you take it in this colloquial sense, that is not exactly what "systemic therapy" means.

Question: Ms. Madanes responded earlier about the witch trials. A recent study on television revealed the thinking of the witch hunters, who genuinely believed that freeing the souls of witches from their earthly torment was more critical than the lives of the women themselves. The witch hunters thought they were freeing these poor women's souls from agony and tor-

ment by burning them and that their method was the only way to free them. Today, we can't even imagine thinking like that, although we can see something similar in the horrors of World War II. I think the Nazis truly believed they were improving the world. So I think we have to be careful. We can't assume that our new construction will be more morally pure.

Watzlawick: I am in full agreement with you. But this is the essence of all similar assumptions based on an ultimate "truth" and a Messianic obligation to change the world so that this truth is accepted. As I mentioned in my presentation, this goes back to Plato and his books on the state and the law. He proposed institutions very similar to Nazi concentration camps for those people who either were incapable of grasping the truths that the philosopher king offered or were unwilling to accept the truth. So I am extremely apprehensive of any ultimate explanation of "reality" that does not consider the fact that it is only another constructed fiction. And I am in favor of realizing that the task of science, and also the task of psychotherapy, cannot be the discovery of truth, but only the elaboration of techniques that are useful for a given purpose. For me, the given purpose of therapy is exclusively the lessening of pain, there are no great fantastic ideals that need to be achieved.

Question: Please address, if you would, the implications of constructivist thinking for family violence.

Watzlawick: Families construct their own realities, and there are cultural realities and there are the personal experiences of family members. In the systemic approach, we try to understand as quickly as possible the functioning of this system: What kind of reality has this particular system constructed for itself? Incidentally, this rules out categorizations because one of the basic principles of systems theory is that "every system is its own best explanation." And so, as a systemic therapist, in early sessions I try to find out how the system works. I try to discover the function of the symptom within the functioning of this system, and, needless to say, the reality of that system is a constructed reality.

Question: Can I follow up on that? More specifically, how would you intervene if there were a physical reality of physical violence in the family?

Watzlawick: It is very difficult to talk about a hypothetical case. I would need to know a great deal about the function of the physical violence. I cannot just say that physical violence is a particular mental deviation and that is it. That is not good enough. I need to know how it fits into this family's reality.

Question: There is a basic debate at this conference between individual and family therapy. You present the idea that we construct reality on the basis of individual perception that is totally self-contained within us. Yet, at the same time, reality is also collectively determined. My problem with systems therapists is they focus on the collective determination of reality and they ignore the fact that individuals also contribute.

Watzlawick: I think it is a vicious circle. The system imposes a certain world view, for example, on the child. But the child, being a person in his or her own right, reacts in a certain way. So you cannot just look at pieces of the system. It is wrong to believe that systems theory denies the dignity of the individual and the depth of his or her soul. Rather, mutual influences need to be taken into account: The way one behaves influences the system; the reactions of the system influence the person. That in no way denies one's dignity as an individual, although this accusation frequently is made.

Question: First of all, Dr. Watzlawick, it is great to hear you because for the past 15 years I have been listening to you, and I get excited and then I don't understand it, and I tend to try to figure this out. My question concerns time. This is one of the things I have been writing about myself—that is, in my constructivism of how I view the world, there are three time zones in which we live past, present, and future, and usually in our language, as we describe things, we describe primarily from the past. In your presentation, you described many things from the past that we can analyze and look at in terms of what went wrong, and then think about the present in a certain way. Constructivism is like describing how we have to build a shelter for ourselves, like a house. Can one talk about the future, which is something that doesn't exist, until it exists, and then it becomes present and past? Is there a way to frame to something beyond constructivism or beyond saying, yes, we construct things and, therefore, we think about it after it occurs, which is a feedback loop? Can you talk more about feed-forward loops?

Watzlawick: I can refer to the phenomenon of the self-fulfilling prophesy. I have an assumption about how things will go in the future. This assumption in the here-and-now, which may have roots in the past, determines the events. The prophecy of the event leads to the event of the prophecy. So getting people to behave differently in the here-and-now from the ways they have tried to solve their problems can create new futures for them.

Question: So in essence you have to go backwards, not forward?

Watzlawick: No, you have to work in the here-and-now in order to go forward. I am not interested in how this problem arose. I am not interested in the "why" of the behavior that needs to be changed. I am interested in what can I do here-and-now to lessen this person's pain. There is no doubt that the problem has its roots in the past; however, in order to change something, the knowledge of the past is irrelevant. And I say that even though I was trained as a Jungian analyst.

Identifying the Various Recurring Processes in the Family That Lead to Schizophrenia in an Offspring

Mara Selvini Palazzoli, M.D.

Mara Selvini Palazzoli, M.D.

Mara Selvini Palazzoli received her M.D. degree from the University of Milan in 1941. Currently, she is Director of the New Center for Family Therapy in Milan, and also serves on a number of editorial boards. The recipient of the Distinguished Contribution to Research in Family Therapy Award from the American Association for Marriage and Family Therapy, she is the author or coauthor of five books, primarily on her approach to understanding and treating families.

Mara Selvini Palazzoli describes the research of her group into some of the family processes that lead to psychosis in an adolescent member. As a direct consequence of strife between the spouses, one of the parents places the child in a position of pseudoprivilege above the spouse and shapes the child's upbringing to make the child the opposite of the spouse in every possible way. Deception about feelings increases the possibility of a psychotic breakdown when the child reaches adolescence.

Our recent work (Selvini Palazzoli, Cirillo, Selvini, & Sorrentino, 1988) focuses on the relational roots of serious mental disorders in adolescents. More recently we have singled out and characterized subgroups of the syndrome we customarily call "schizophrenia" and constructed precise models of the recurring interactive family processes leading to symptoms of the syndrome. However, before I present the specific subgroup of schizophrenic adolescents that I have chosen as my subject, I will return to "the roots," that is, to the first presentation I made, in New York in 1985, describing our general model of the psychotic process in the family. On that occasion, I tried to synthesize theoretical concepts about psychosis we had gathered during our many years of qualitative clinical research. This research used a series of invariant prescriptions, which we assigned routinely at our center to all families that featured a child afflicted with a serious mental disorder.

The use of invariant prescriptions allowed us to take a significant step forward, because the invariant nature of the assignments we gave to families allowed us to make a comparative study both of how different families reacted to them and of the reactions of the different members within the same family.

This research design is a basic instrument for garnering new knowledge. And during the eight years we carried out this experiment, we began to recognize certain recurring phenomena, which in time we were able to predict, group, and label. What began to emerge was a number of recognizable phenomena that gradually allowed us to find our way through the confusing and indistinguishable background "noise" that is part of the interactive processes in such families.

OUR MODEL OF A RELATIONAL PROCESS

The synthesis I presented in New York was a model of a six-stage relational process that elicits serious mental disorders in a child. From a theoretical point of view, in order to construct this model, it was essential for us to abandon some of the rigidity of systemic thinking and adopt a game metaphor as a fundamental aid to developing the complex way of thinking necessary to understand these families. The game metaphor provides a language of human relationships allowing for the integration of *individual* and *relational* variables through the dimension of a historical process (time).

Next I will briefly examine the six stages of our model as they were formulated in 1985 (Selvini Palazzoli, 1986).

THE SIX STAGES

First Stage: Couple Stalemate

The term "stalemate," borrowed from the game of chess, refers to a specific pattern in couples that consists of an endless game of covert reciprocal provocations, which, since they never receive an adequate outcome (or response), do not produce significant escalation, crises, or definite breaks in rapport. For example, if a husband is gallant with a lady, his wife will never react with jealousy, she will remain impossible! So, the situation remains stable over time.

Second Stage: The Child Enters the Parents' Game

The future identified patient eventually becomes more interested in the parents' problems. He or she becomes emotionally involved with the parent he or she considers the weaker one and is deluded into thinking that he or she enjoys with this parent a privileged relationship (imbroglio of the affections). The child is also covertly induced by this parent to secretly ally with him or her.

Third Stage: The Child's Unusual Behavior

Instances of unusual but not yet symptomatic behavior subsequently are directed at both parents, for the purpose of challenging the power of the ostensible "winner" and showing the "loser" (the trusted ally) how to cope with the other parent.

Fourth Stage: The About-Face of the Trusted Ally

The parent who is incorrectly seen by the child as the weaker does not join the child's attempted rebellion. Instead he or she becomes hostile towards the child and sides with the spouse. The privileged relationship is revealed to have been a delusion.

Fifth Stage: The Symptom Erupts

One can well imagine that the child's emotional response to "traitorous" behavior on the part of a presumed ally must be highly passionate, including feelings of betrayal, humiliation, indignant anger, and confusion. And yet the adolescent is unable to voice these sentiments, since invariably they will be disavowed by the presumed ally, who is in no way willing to jeopardize the relationship with the spouse. By his or her incomprehensible behavior, the patient both signals and conceals that his or her position is untenable.

Sixth Stage: Symptom-Based Strategies

Once symptoms occur, every member of the family unconsciously stands to gain by them, either by feeling reassured about some personal anxiety or by obtaining some kind of indirect advantage. These indirect advantages tend to reinforce the persistence of symptoms.

Our original model required great effort on our part owing to the extreme complexity of the phenomena we were studying; it was difficult to reduce our findings to simple terms. The model took into account only the parent–child triad and entirely neglected both the parents' rapport with their families of origin and the role played in the family game by any siblings. This latter information, however, is of vital importance for reconstructing and understanding the process.

THE GAME REVISITED

Having chosen not to examine any unsettled problems the parents might have had with their respective families allowed us to devise a simple descriptive schema of the nature of the couple's stalemate. However, it prevented us from inquiring into the bitter origins of this stalemate and understanding what is was that led each to choose this particular spouse and had caused the choice to turn sour—a failure all the more tragic since it cannot be admitted because the spouse would never understand the reasons for it and since couples often are strongly obligated to keep personal information strictly under cover. In the ensuing bitter loneliness and resentment, one can understand how a parent might see in a child (or in children), someone to cling to, to make up for his or her own injured affections, or else someone to use to covertly inflict some kind of punishment on a spouse. The trouble is that, in so doing, the parent fails to realize the possible serious consequences of such an attitude or the fact that such a process, once started, cannot be stopped and ends by someone getting out of control.

Today, we define this game even more precisely as a situation of great (and concealed) suffering for both parents. Both parents, however, often are incapable of admitting and recognizing this personal suffering in all its magnitude. The malaise is negated or, in certain cases, expressed through some sort of camouflaged conflict, that is, through a shifting away of this suffering from its real matrix toward irrelevant matters.

I will retrace why each partner cannot trust the other and feels it necessary to be vigilant and incessantly devise new moves to neutralize those enacted by the partner. In this context, the term "power" as we use it to describe the couple stalemate is not power in a conventional sense, that is, the capacity too force another to do what one wants. Power, in the couple stalemate, has a purely defensive goal: to frustrate expectations of the partner in order to maintain a personal sense of integrity and save one's own dignity.

There are, of course, many different types of couples stalemates, and they give rise to different family games. Here I describe only one of the games that frequently occur in our clinical work with schizophrenic patients. In all subspecies of games, significant warping takes place within the realm of affections.

In the particular subspecies we are examining, the imbroglio consists of literally, although unwittingly, "using" a child as a tool with which to frustrate the spouse. This child will be treated as though he or she enjoys a privileged rapport with one of the parents. Unfortunately, the child will become persuaded that this is true. The symptom will erupt when an emotional betrayal on the part of this parent leads him or her to suspect that this privilege was never genuine.

In our research, we also are working on models of another subspecies of game that gives rise to serious mental disorders. A typical situation is one in which the parents, competing with each other, simultaneously or alternately act out the *instrumental* seduction of one of their children, for whom, in actual fact, neither of the dyad feels much empathy or esteem. Another subspecies of game is played when the child is denied his or her proper place in the family and is not given sufficient attention. Here, deprivation and neglect are covert and denied, and the parents seem perfect on both accounts.

With regard to the patient's siblings, we now feel quite sure that with such a covert, potentially pathogenic process under way in a family, all of them will be harmed to some degree. The extent of the damage, however, differs greatly according to the specific role each child plays in the game. One often finds in families with a schizophrenic child that a so-called "sane" sibling will be singled out by one of the parents as a sort of "stand-in" for affective attachment; that child will be appointed a substitute for a spouse's starved affections. However, in such a case, the parent's feelings are genuine, and do not cause the irreparable damage brought on by an instrumental imbroglio. I do not intend to go into this any further here, and I only mention it to orient the reader to the new horizons our team is exploring.

Next, I will present the core of my chapter: *when a child is designated to become the exact opposite of the spouse.*

As I mentioned previously, I will present only one subgroup our team identified and characterized from within the population we have treated of families with schizophrenic children, adolescents, or young adults.

I have done this for several reasons. With the help of our model, our team was able, for this subgroup, to (1) retrace the course of the interactive process, or game, starting from the couple's stalemate; and (2) present it in a manner easy to convey and render understandable.

I will begin with a brief description of the way in which this subgroup is characterized by the following intrafamilial process. One of the parents, who conceals the suffering and resentment he or she experiences in marital rapport, gets a son or daughter enmeshed in an ostentatiously privileged rapport. The parent will appear to discover and enthusiastically praise in this child precisely those qualities that the spouse lacks, and will try to inhibit, without seeming to do so, any qualities or personal traits the spouse possesses. A detailed reconstruction of this process shows in a convincing manner how a certain type of interactional game involving the child for years has catastrophic effects on his or her identity formation and psychological evolution, and, later, on his or her psychoaffective survival.

It is interesting to consider the process by focusing on the future patient. He or she labors under the delusion, during the entire presymptomatic phase, that he or she is very important for one of the parents. The child has a distant relationship with the other. This latter parent, in turn, will treat the future patient coldly, barely hiding contempt. Such an attitude of thinly disguised hostility on the part of the "distant" parent will inevitably reinforce the bond of dependency that ties the patient to the enmeshing parent.

One can imagine how such a situation may, over time, have a catastrophic effect on the child's identity structure. It if easier to consider the effect if we posit a family in which the future patient is a boy and the only child, the enmeshing parent is the mother, and the distant parent is the father. The mother, according to the rules that require concealment of real sentiments about the couple's rapport, will not tell her husband anything about what it is that really frustrates her (although she may have tried to do so once and found him unresponsive). Neither will she divulge to her son what it is about her husband's behavior that hurts, offends, and exasperates her. Therefore, under the constant pressure of the frustrations her husband inflicts upon her day after day—not to mention the stress of her own furious reactions to his behavior and her desire to get even—the mother will find no other way out of her predicament. Subsequently she will cling morbidly to her son, thereby thrusting back on her husband, without fully realizing what she is doing, a very powerful frustration—that of having a son who is a rival.

Note that, in our case histories involving this subgroup, the husband often will have a history of "affective deprivation" and be greatly in need of a mother. Therefore, the fact that the son has become a rival wounds him even more deeply. And that is not all. The instrumental attachment the mother forms with her son, almost in antithesis to her husband, leads her to behave in a manner consistent with this attachment, a behavior that can range from the most superficial and obvious to the most deeply concealed. More obvious behavior of this kind consists of unconditional approval of certain qualities the son is supposed to have and the father lacks: The boy is a brilliant athlete, with a promising career in sports; he is exceptionally gifted intellectually, and even at this tender age, has already shown his worth; his drawings show he is a real artist, and so on.

If the father tries to object and reduce his

son's achievements to normal size, his wife immediately will exclaim, in a pained tone of voice, "You have no faith in Robert." These exaggerated expectations on the part of the mother, together with the father's reservations, rectifications, and growing aloofness toward his son, begin to weigh increasingly on the shoulders of the boy, who fears that he may not be able to live up to his mother's expectations. If he cannot achieve his mother's expectations, it poses an even greater problem, because in that case the father's opinion would be right. Indeed, in many cases, although not in all, the father is very critical of the way his wife has reared their son.

On the most deeply hidden level of the mother–son interaction, however, the damage is far greater, since it is mainly the mother who brings up and educates her child. One easily can imagine, then, that she will strongly wish her son to exhibit talents and skills that her husband lacks, and also not develop certain tendencies, qualities, or tastes that her husband possesses in full measure and that shape his personality. But, according to the dictates imposed by concealment, she must keep her motives to herself, without ever mentioning them to her son.

Her educational efforts will consist of analogical moves. Whenever the boy exhibits behavior that in some way reminds his mother of her husband, she will respond by darkly signaling that she is feeling sad; she will grow distant or lapse into silence. The boy will not be able to see any clear reason for these signals, but they will make him feel ill at east and anxious. He gradually learns to identify what behavior brings on these special signals, and he learns to avoid those actions and repress them, even though he does not understand why this should be. Any explanation will seem too confusing or arbitrary.

The type of boy who develops because of being treated this way will be someone who in many ways (and also superficially) will be the exact opposite of his father. For instance, should the father be a great sports fan, the son will be fond only of classical music; if the father is a bit coarse, the son will behave like a true aristocrat. Another important consideration is that such a permanent dependency on the mother is a powerful obstacle to socializing, both within the family (not only with the father but also with the siblings, if any, with whom the boy could ally in order to make friends) and in the outer world.

An illustration may provide clarification. Take the case of the elder brother during his childhood, "When I was little, it would get on my nerves to see this smug little genius pampered and admired by our mother. This baby genius, who at the age of five would refuse to play with me and spent all his time reading important books. I even went so far at times as to hit him hard, but I stopped that, because my mother would get terribly mad at me. Then, when I became a teenager, I'd smoke a bit of pot now and then, just to divert Mom's attention away from him a little. It worked. She got real worried. Then, after he failed several times at school, he started acting disturbed, and I took over to some extent as his male nurse. I'd keep him company, and take him out for walks . . . But the therapy sessions have shown me now that maybe I was just doing this to win back my mother. When he got worse and tried to kill himself, and started being a chronic case, well, I started hating him. I'd go around saying, for all I cared, he was dead. It would make me so furious to see Mom worrying about him and pampering him in every way. I'd wanted her to kick him out of the house."

It seems obvious that this type of interactive process between mother and son leads to serious deprivation and warping of the son's identity structure, his sense of personal identity, and his social skills. The boy will feel increasingly ill at ease, especially in extrafamilial contexts and in regard to the demands and trials that adolescence inevitably place on him. The erosion of the pseudoprivileged rapport with the mother usually comes about gradually, in the shape of a growing series of minor fiascos, until some more conspicuous failure in school, sports, or social achievement lets the patient perceive that the excollusive parent is disappointed in him and despises him.

At this point, the adolescent sinks into a dramatic state of abandonment. He feels let down by the enmeshing parent. Rapprochement with the other is extremely difficult. There has been no preexisting template for such closeness, because the distant parent secretly has felt this child to be a rival. The siblings, previously envious of the patient's pseudoprivileged rapport with one parent, provide no empathy, no relief for the patient's isolation, "What could be expected of Mom's pet!" For her part, the inveigling parent discovers that the child she has reared and molded as the exact antithesis of the spouse is a failure, and angrily realizes that the child is a "waste product" whose inferior quality increasingly justifies the spouse's insistent criticisms. This creature has become a sort of boomerang. The ex-enmeshing, enamored parent now will turn to someone else, perhaps one of the other children, the spouse, or even a third party. The explosion of psychotic behavior in the child results from the backfiring of all the beliefs and certainties of which he had built his narrow affective and cognitive universe.

The tragedy in the child is triggered by the feeling, at once violent and obscure, of having been the victim of an affective *imbroglio*, having served the mother's purpose, but one that did not entail real love. Actually, it is not the emotional deprivation per se that brings on psychosis, but the concealment: The child continues to believe his parents are perfect, and if they are criticized at all, it will happen in a totally distorted fashion and for the wrong reasons: They will be seen as being "too bourgeois," "overprotective," or the like.

SUMMARY OF THE MODEL

We have now constructed a summary of the model that is specific for a subgroup of adolescent schizophrenic psychotics. It can be outlined as follows:

1. The couple's stalemate.
2. A pseudoprivileged relationship of a child with one of the parents, while the other withdraws from the child. The future patient construes himself or herself, and is constructed, as the opposite of the distant parent.
3. Initial failures and difficulties in the preadolescent who is emotionally handicapped by a pseudoprivileged dependence on one of the parents. There follows increased distancing by the other parent, serious distortions

in the child's identity formation and commitment, and a failure to acquire social skills.
4. A breakdown of the pseudoprivileged relationship when a critical event (or series of events) shows the patient the real disappointment and contempt that the inveigling parent feels for him or her. In a vague and confused way, the patient begins to perceive that he or she has been "used" by the parent and is not really important. He or she also feels let down by the other parent and by the siblings. Subsequently, symptomatic behavior erupts.
5. A subsequent evolution consisting of diverse possibilities: The inveigling parent and the child can remain prisoners of their bond. The child can be episodically aggressive and the inveigling parent exasperated. The relation may deteriorate and become charged with suffering, but it can continue endlessly, even assuming grotesque characteristics, while the other parent remains distant.

A REVEALING EVOLUTION THAT COMES TO LIGHT AT A LATER TIME

At this point, I would like to emphasize strongly that frequently there is a different evolution in these cases, one that we have observed in this special subgroup of young psychotics when they come to us in a state that has deteriorated into chronicity. The phenomena we observe are the exact opposite of those I described in the foregoing. That is, there is an inversion, a shifting of roles between the two parents. The formerly "enamored" parent appears intolerant of the patient and wants back his or her peace of mind. The erstwhile "distant" parent now takes his or her turn in being enamored with the patient, becomes increasingly anxious about the child, and finds time to help the child that he or she never found for the spouse. The parent assumes the role of the child's saviour. However, the overprotective relationship he or she sets up with the child is unwittingly as false and manipulative as the one the other spouse had formerly devised. It is as though the erstwhile distant parent is now jumping at the chance to adopt an identical strategy and to retaliate against the spouse by subjecting him or her to the same painful feelings of exclusion, jealousy, and rage of which he or she previously had been the victim.

In this way, the patient becomes involved a second time in a pseudoprivileged rapport (imbroglio of the affections), whose real goal is to square accounts in the couple's stalemate. As was the case in the first of these positions, this second pseudoprivileged relationship will not be of help to the patient, who does not receive any message of hope or a real incentive to disentangle, to become autonomous and assume responsibility: What reaches the patient will be a message of anxiety and overprotectiveness.

Such a shift of roles between the two parents in their rapport with their child–patient is, therefore, a shift that leaves things unchanged. What I particularly want to stress here, however, is the way in which this exchange of roles, once it has come about, confronts the therapist with conflicting requests. The erstwhile distant parent, who has now changed into a loving saviour, will come to the therapist with an open emotional and pressing request, "Help me save my child. I have no object in life other than to save him."

The erstwhile inveigling parent, on the other hand, will act glum and tense. In a covert and confused manner, this parent will admit that he or she has given up all hope or confess to an uncontrollable fear of the patient's possible violent behavior or to the fact that too close an association with the patient could have dangerous personal consequences for the patient. He or she may even go so far as to voice the fear that the heavy burden of caring for the child, a burden from which he or she now considers himself or herself exempt since it can harm the child, may actually harm the spouse. Statements of this kind, which at first used to puzzle our team, are now interpreted to mean: "I've really had enough of this child. I want my spouse back, who currently does nothing but worry and care about the patient..."

The fact that we were able to detect this phenomenon featuring two incompatible requests addressed to the therapist (and saw it surface repeatedly when dealing with the families of chronic schizophrenics apparently different from one another) was a big step forward for our team. We thought we might have found a recapitulation here, a phenomenon of which we had former knowledge and that could help serve as a guide in exploring the unknown, as we attempted to trace back during the particular course of a familial process, the schema of which, however, was previously known to us. In such an unhappy parental couple, the parent presenting as exhausted, and who longed to have the spouse back, would be the one who had previously unwittingly "used" the child in order to shape the child into "the rival in the family affections" (without realizing that this could have disastrous effects). The parent who now came on as the "saviour," ready to sacrifice anything in order to save the child, was, in fact, the parent who had formerly been "distant." This parent would now strongly disapprove of the other spouse's coolness toward this poor, sick child, and would be quite unaware of the fact that he or she was thereby simply getting back at the spouse by inflicting the same pain he or she had previously suffered at the other's hands.

This fact, which we have since tested on 14 families we treated that presented with these "signs," enabled us to shorten considerably the length of time required to understand the process that led to the adolescent's serious mental disturbance. To be sure, understanding is not equivalent to curing, but, in our opinion, for these extremely serious cases, it is a *sine qua non* point of departure. This is all the more true in view of the fact that, due to the peremptory rule that imposes concealment, what most of all harms the patient's chance of improving through treatment is precisely this permanent state of confusion—of not being able to understand the incredibly intricate web into which all members of the family, and the patient most of all, have become entangled.

A NECESSARY CLARIFICATION

Before concluding, it is important to clarify one other important matter. I fear that descriptions of the parents' moves and countermoves in the interactive family process that I have presented as typical for cases involving a certain subgroup of adolescent schizophrenics will induce in the reader the shocking feeling that parents of schizophrenic children are some sort of ogres. As far as I am concerned, I must confess that I had to reach my present age before I could break free from my naive moralism and, for example, lose my certainty that in their place I would have fared much better!

Moreover, semantics itself betrays us. We often are unable, when we observe a new phenomenon or grasp a new idea, to invent a language or a term that does not lead to misinterpretation. How could our team reinvent a term such as "instigation," which in common parlance means "set a person against another," and deprive this word of its implicit connotation of conscious bad intention? How could we do the same with our term "imbroglio of the affections," which implicitly conveys the idea of a trick plotted in cold blood? And how often have we had proof that a father voicing his attachment to a chronic schizophrenic child was acting in good faith? (Still, at the root of this attachment there was always a certain resentment toward his wife.)

This is why our therapeutic work with the family of a psychotic or schizophrenic adolescent will aim, first of all, at understanding the nature of the parents' plight—not the plight that is apparent (namely, the tragedy of having a sick child), but that which is hidden and has been with them silently for so long. Our attitude is one of openness, devoid of any reticence, manipulation, or cunning. Our working hypothesis is that the roots of a child's or an adolescent's serious mental disorder are to be found in the parents' covert suffering. We will explain our theory to the family members quite openly, right at the start, so that they will have time to accept or deny it. There is not the slightest aura of moral indignation during any of the sessions.

But here I must stop. The subject of how to handle this subgroup therapeutically is highly complex and will be set forth in detail in a paper we are now preparing. I only want to add here that parents such as these can be led to understand and accept their responsibility for their child's serious disorder *only* if they feel they themselves have met with understanding and have been helped to face the frustrations and pain they suffered in the past, whether individually or as a family. This *certainly* cannot be achieved if the couple is indicted by, and then excluded from, the therapeutic process.

REFERENCES

Selvini Palazzoli, M. (1986). Toward a general model of psychotic family games. *Journal of Marital and Family Therapy, 12*(4), 339–349.

Selvini Palazzoli, M., Cirillo, S., Selvini, M., & Sorrentino, A.M. (1988). *Family games: General models of psychotic processes in the family.* New York: Norton.

Discussion by Donald Meichenbaum, Ph.D.

◆

It is not an accident that in my own area of cognitive behavior modification most research has focused on children and adults, and researchers have wisely skipped adolescents. This is especially true when the adolescent is suffering from serious forms of psychopathology such as schizophrenia. It takes a brave and perceptive clinician to explore the complexity of adolescent schizophrenia and its impact, especially as evident on the family. Moreover, to argue that the "recurring family process leads to the adolescent's serious disturbance," as Palazzoli does, takes a particularly brave theoretician. One may, however, raise several questions about the clinical descriptive account offered by Dr. Palazzoli.

First, much research on developmental psychopathology has highlighted *bidirectional influences*. Not only do parents affect children and adolescents, but children and adolescents significantly influence parents. Whether one looks at the writings of Richard Bell, Gerald Patterson, or Donald Kiesler, their concepts of "coercion," "reciprocity," and "complementarity of interactive sequences," underscore the need to be cautious when making directional causative claims. Thus one might question Palazzoli's proposal that "the roots of a child's or an adolescent's serious mental disorder are to be sought for in the parents' covert suffering." Such propositions place a major onus on parents and underemphasize (if not overlook) the interactive influences of the adolescent in cocreating and engendering parental reactions. There is a danger of replacing the misguided concept of "schizophrenogenic mother" with the concept of a "schizophrenogenic family." One needs to keep in mind the biological underpinnings of the schizophrenic disorder and their impact on social interactions. A biopsychosocial model provides a heuristically useful perspective from which to understand and treat the adolescent schizophrenic disorder.

Second, a family-systems perspective that embraces game theory yields rich metaphorical terms such as couple stalemates, camouflage conflict, instrumental seduction, enactments, and imbroglio of affect. These concepts also pose a danger. The paradigms we adopt, such as "games," influence the concepts we employ, color the way we see things, and determine the data we attend to and how they are collected and analyzed. The language of game theory implies "winners" and "losers," implicit and explicit rules, goals and strategies, and the like. These constructs convey a level of intentionality and mindfulness that does not fit the often "scripted automatic nature" of social interactions.

Third, a related concern is the absence of evidence for stage theories of social interactions and emotional adjustments, thus raising additional concerns about the Palazzoli model. In addition, given the difficulty in finding data to support the more simplistic double-bind communication model, it is difficult to envisage the research paradigms or naturalistic observational coding schemes that could be used to document the complex interpersonal patterns described by Palazzoli. How shall we measure such constructs as identity structuring, sense of personal identity, imbroglio of affection, and the like?

Fourth, one must be cautious in drawing causative conclusions from retrospective clinical accounts. No matter how perceptive and astute the clinician, without prospective studies with appropriate clinically matched control groups, there is a danger in drawing causal inferences based on clinical observations.

Finally, Palazzoli's chapter represents the work of a sensitive and astute clinician at work tracing complex interactional patterns. But why do such familial patterns give rise to schizophrenic disorders and not to other forms of psychopathology? Moreover, why is one sibling more vulnerable to adolescent schizophrenia than others? How do Palazzoli's descriptive accounts relate to the work on high expressed emotion with its emphasis on social criticism, negative familial interactions, and the like? Answers to such questions will help translate challenging clinical observations into testable propositions.

QUESTIONS AND ANSWERS

Question: Have you found any similarities between psychotic adolescents and anorexics? A second question concerns the parents of the marital dyad. What research have you done on generational forces?

Palazzoli: I have looked into the difference between the families of anorexics and families of schizophrenics, and we have presented two distinct models in our latest book entitled *Family Games.* In short, we do not find in the anorexic family the tremendous concealment of relational problems that is always present in the schizophrenic family. In our book, we present a simplified model because, owing to the enormous complexity of these problems, we have excluded from our research the relationship of the parents with the respective extended families. We could only describe in our recent work what we could see of this particular game of the couple. We had not yet started to discover for what reason the man had married that specific woman, or the woman that specific man. After the publication of the book, we started to study the spouses' relationships with members of their families of origin—because it is in the relational root of the family of origin, where they have suffered very much, that we can find the reason for the marriage. Also, we can find there the reasons they have for concealment. Time is needed before we can explain these things satisfactorily.

Question: I was actually wondering, with regard to the cases that you have seen, whether you have had a case in which one of the spouses has died. What happens to the game in this case?

I know of a case in which, after the father died of natural causes, the son, who was the identified patient, assumed a lot of the unwanted characteristics of the father.

Palazzoli: We have had no cases in which one of the parents died during the treatment.

Matteo Selvini: But we have seen single-parent families. In some cases, we hypothesized that perhaps the couple's stalemate was not between the two spouses, but between the mother and her own mother. It also can be seen between a mother and her sister, for example.

Palazzoli: We are convinced that there are no single-parent families because there is always some other involved person in a triadic position with the identified patient. Grandmothers are very often the third person.

Question: I wonder if you have any hypothesis about which child becomes the identified patient. How does the identified patient evolve in the system?

Palazzoli: This problem is very interesting, and for the time being, in my opinion, there is no answer. In the complexity of the developmental process of the family, there are so many events we cannot know. Factors include the physical aspects of the child, such as gender, sex, and physical resemblance to either parent. There are so many possibilities that currently it is impossible to decide on how someone becomes the identified patient.

Jay Haley maintains that each child in the family occupies a different position. Only one usually is in the position to be involved in the parents' problem, and for that reason, only one of the brothers or sisters, or seldom two, becomes psychotic or schizophrenic. But not all the other brothers or sisters do.

Matteo Selvini: We have collected some data about the subgroup of game that we discussed. In our initial data, it is more common to find this kind of pseudorelationship between a mother and son. Frequently, we find it in a mother and daughter. In rare cases, we find the same factor between the father and the daughter, but in these cases, the situations are very much worse. I want to add another thing to this problem of who becomes the identified patient. The couple's stalemate is not stable over time. For example, the first child could be born in a situation where the balance in the couple was good. But when the second boy was born, the couple had a period of serious crises and the mother was incapable of expressing anger directly to the husband. She chose a contorted way of provocation, and started to exalt the second son's qualities, precisely because she wasn't capable of reacting directly with her disappointment toward her husband. Perhaps certain physical characteristics of the son also favored this situation. The factors are very complex.

I want to add also that I agree with Dr. Meichenbaum's observation that in building this model, we also have to be cognizant of the part the adolescent takes in this process. This is something we want to develop further. We have some preliminary information, but we do not have time to develop it in this presentation. However, I believe that often the son or the daughter in this sort of privileged relationship has mixed feelings because he or she is in some way aware of being involved in something that is not fair. This child actively tries to ally one of the parents with him or her. And so there is a certain feeling of guilt about being in this position. Or, better, there is a mixed feeling of guilt and privilege.

Palazzoli: In studying different processes of families with a psychotic child, we find that two phenomena are fundamental—transgenerationality and concealment. Transgenerationality is very important because it cannot be openly admitted and discussed: Nobody can declare that his or her father or mother enticed and betrayed him or her. To pretend special feelings, to make an allusive promise, to break it—all this runs on the analogic level. It can never be said.

SECTION II

◆

Cognitive-Behavioral Approaches

The Revised ABCs of Rational-Emotive Therapy (RET)

◆

Albert Ellis, Ph.D.

Albert Ellis, Ph.D.
Albert Ellis is the President of the Institute for Rational-Emotive Therapy in New York. He has practiced psychotherapy, marriage and family counseling, and sex therapy for more than 45 years. Ellis has received the Humanist of the Year Award from the American Humanist Association, the Distinguished Professional Contribution to Knowledge Award from the American Psychological Association, and the Personal Development Award from the American Association for Counseling and Development, and has written or edited more than 50 books and monographs. A Fellow of six professional organizations and a Diplomate of three professional boards, he received his Ph.D. degree in Clinical Psychology from Columbia University in 1947.

Albert Ellis describes the evolution of his Rational-Emotive Therapy and presents a revision of the original ABCs of RET. He shows that people's Belief Systems about the Activating Events of their lives largely contribute to their emotional and behavioral Consequences, and that each of these three elements influences and includes the others. Moreover, all three include interacting cognitive, emotive, and behavioral elements. Ellis also addresses the use of these concepts in psychotherapy.

When I first formulated the ABCs of rational-emotive therapy (RET) and of cognitive-behavior therapy (CBT), I fully realized how complex cognitions, emotions, and behaviors are and how they inevitably include and interact with one another. Thus in my first paper on RET, presented at the American Psychological Convention in Chicago in August 1956, I said:

Thinking . . . is, and to some extent has to be, sensory, motor, and emotional behavior. . . . Emotion, like thinking and the sensory-motor processes, we may define as an exceptionally complex state of human reaction which is integrally related to all the other

perception and response processes. It is not one thing, but a combination and holistic integration of several seemingly diverse, yet actually closely related, phenomena. (Ellis, 1958, p. 35)

In this first presentation on RET, I also cited my 1953 paper, given at the University of Minnesota conference, on the foundations of science and the concepts of psychology and psychoanalysis (Ellis, 1956). Adapting some ideas from this paper, I stated:

A large part of what we call emotion, in other words, is nothing more than a certain kind—a biased, prejudiced, or strongly evaluative kind—of thinking. . . . thinking and emoting are so closely interrelated that they usually accompany each other, act in a circular cause and effect relationship, and in certain (though hardly all) respects are essentially the same thing, so that one's thinking becomes one's emotion and emotion becomes one's thought. (Ellis, 1958, p. 36)

As can be seen from these quotations, RET always has had a complex, interactional, and holistic view of the ABCs of human personality and disturbance. Simply stated, the ABC theory of RET, following the views of several ancient philosophers—especially Epictetus and Marcus Aurelius—and of Robert Woodworth's stimulus–organism–response (SOR) theory, holds that Activating Events (As) in people's lives contribute to their emotional and behavioral disturbances or Consequences (Cs), largely because they are intermingled with or acted upon by people's Beliefs (Bs) about these Activating Events (As). When I formulated this theory early in 1955 I, was not aware that George Kelly (1955) had a little earlier created a similar theory of personal constructs. Following the publication of Kelly's and my writings, and influenced largely by my active-directive cognitive-emotive-behavioral methods of helping people to change their Belief System (B) and concomitantly improve their neurotic Consequences (Cs), a number of other therapists began to develop systems of CBT that subscribed to the ABC theory of emotional disturbance, including Beck (1967), Glasser (1965), Goldfried & Davison (1976), Lazarus (1971), Mahoney (1977), Maultsby (1984), Meichenbaum (1977), Raimy (1975), Seligman (1991), and Wessler & Hankin-Wessler (1986).

Using the ABC theory, cognitive-behavioral therapy has made enormous progress since the 1970s and is now one of the most popular forms of psychological treatment. Literally hundreds of controlled research studies show that RET and CBT significantly helped clients to become less disturbed than have other methods of psychotherapy with similar clients and are more effective than having clients remain on a waiting list (Beck & Emery, 1985; Beck, Rush, Shaw, & Emery, 1979; DiGiuseppe, Miller, & Trexler, 1979; Engels & Diekstra, 1986; Haaga & Davison, 1989; Jorm, 1987; Lyons & Woods, 1991; McGovern &

Silverman, 1984; Miller & Berman, 1983). Several hundred other studies also have shown that irrational belief and dysfunctional attitude tests, based on the ABC theory, significantly distinguish between groups of disturbed and less disturbed individuals (Baisden, 1980; DiGiuseppe, Miller, & Trexler, 1959; Ellis, 1979a; Hollon & Bemis, 1981; Schwartz, 1982; Smith & Allred, 1986; Woods, 1987; Woods & Lyons, 1990; Woods, Silverman, Gentile, & Cunningham, 1990).

My hypothesis, then, that people's positive and negative thoughts contribute significantly to their emotional and behavioral disturbance, and that helping them to change their thinking also will help them become significantly less disturbed, has led to hundreds of research and clinical studies that tend to support these theories and to contribute to our knowledge of healthy and unhealthy personalities. Many attacks, however, have been made on the ABC theory, especially by radical behaviorists (Ledwidge, 1978; Rachlin, 1977; Skinner, 1971), and some of the attackers' points are well taken.

A number of rational-emotive and cognitive-behavior therapists who subscribe to and use the ABC theory of personality and personality disturbance also have suggested additions to and modifications of my original ABC model, including Beck (1976); Brown and Beck (1989); DeSilvestri (1989); DiGiuseppe (1986); Dryden (1984); Greenberg and Safran (1987); Grieger (1985); Guidano (1988); Guidano and Liotti (1983); Lazarus (1989); Mahoney (1988); Maultsby (1984); Muran (1991); Rorer (1989a, 1989b); Schwartz (1982); Wessler (1984); and Wessler and Wessler (1980).

Spurred by the criticism of my original ABC theory, as well as by my own clinical and research findings, I began to revise and add to this model in the 1950s and continue to do so today (Bernard & DiGiuseppe, 1989). For example, I developed a self and a self-acceptance theory of RET (Ellis, 1962, 1969a, 1969b, 1971, 1973, 1985). I stressed the humanistic and existential elements of RET (Ellis, 1962, 1972, 1973, 1976). I Emphasized the emotive and behavorial aspects of dysfunctional thinking. (Ellis, 1962, 1972, 1973, 1976). I emphasized the emotive and behavioral aspects of dysfunctional thinking (Ellis, 1962, 1968, 1972, 1973). I spotlighted the rigidity and "musturbatory" quality of my original 12 irrational beliefs and distinguished between dysfunctional inferences and attributions and the core dogmatic "musts" from which they are usually derived (Ellis, 1977a, 1984, 1985a, 1985b, 1987a, 1987b; Ellis & Dryden, 1987, 1990b, 1991; Ellis & Harper, 1975). I changed my adherence to logical positivism to a more flexible adaptation of Popper's (1985) critical realism (Ellis, 1985a, 1985b, 1987a, 1987b; Ellis & Dryden, 1987, 1990, 1991).

I also showed how secondary disturbance symptoms occur: how people make their Cs into new As, to create emotional problems about emotional problems. I originated the concept of discomfort anxiety, as well as ego anxiety. And I applied the ABCs of RET to couples, to families, to organizations, and to other complex systems (Ellis, 1985b; Ellis, Sichel, Yeager, DiMattia, & DiMattia, 1989).

I specifically expanded the ABCs of RET (Ellis, 1985a) and showed how RET is unusually constructivist, contrary to the views of Guidano (1988) and Mahoney (1988), who wrongly put it in the associationist and rationalist camp (Ellis, 1989, 1990a). In my paper "Expanding the ABCs of RET," I noted that this model is "oversimplified and omits salient information about human disturbance and its treatment" (Ellis, 1985a, p. 313). I still agree with this statement, and I may well write a book one of these days further expanding the ABCs and rendering them more complete. In the rest of this chapter, I shall present something of an outline for this future book.

BASIC HUMAN GOALS AND VALUES

To start on this outline, let me mention the letter G, which stands for the Goals, values, and desires that people bring to their ABCs of human health and disturbance. Humans, biologically and by social learning, are goal-seeking animals and their Fundamental Goals (FG), normally, are to survive, to be relatively free from pain and to be reasonably satisfied or content. As subgoals or Primary Goals (PG), they want to be happy (1) when by themselves; (2) gregariously, with other humans; (3) intimately, with a few selected others; (4) informationally and educationally; (5) vocationally and economically; and (6)

recreationally. I agree with Epstein (1990) that the chief goals or motives of people who are likely to survive are (1) the desire to achieve pleasure and avoid pain; (2) the desire to understand and assimilate the data of experience and, therefore, to maintain the stability and integrity of the information-gathering and assimilating system; (3) the desire to relate to other people; and (4) the desire to have an integrated self-system and to rate one's traits and oneself as competent, achieving, and lovable.

I would add these basic goals to Epstein's list: (5) the desire to use reason, logic, and some aspects of the scientific method; (6) the desire to solve and master life problems and to succeed at tasks that aid survival, pleasure, removal of pain, and feelings of mastery; (7) the desire to have new experiences, especially those perceived as novel and stimulating; and (8) the desire to achieve some stability and security in one's work and social life. As Grieger (1986) notes, these goals (which are also basic stances or Beliefs and emotions) provide a context that affects how people *perceive* their Activating Events *and* how they *evaluate* their world.

Otherwise stated, almost all humans seem to be born and reared with strong tendencies to see their world and their lives as benign rather than malevolent; to see their environment and other people as meaningful (including predictable, controllable, and just); to view others as a source of support and happiness rather than as a source of insecurity and unhappiness; and to see themselves and their traits as capable, good, and lovable rather than as incapable, bad, and unlovable (Epstein, 1990). When reality impinges on them and demonstrates that they, others, and life are not this benign, they feel appropriately frustrated and sad, but also they often choose to feel inappropriately panicked, depressed, and enraged and thereby neuroticize themselves.

My ABC theory of personality holds that when humans experience—or even think about experiencing—stimuli or Activating Events (As) that they interpret as aiding or confirming their goals (Gs), they normally explicitly and/or tacitly (unconsciously) react with their Belief System (B) and their Consequences (Cs) in a pleasurable, approaching manner. Thus they preferentially (rather than demandingly) think, at point B, "This is good! I like this Activating

Event," and they experience the emotional Consequence (C) of pleasure or happiness and the behavioral Consequence (C) of approaching and trying to repeat this Activating Event. When these same people experience As that they perceive as blocking or sabotaging their Goals (Gs), they normally explicitly or tacitly react at points B and C in an unpleasurable, avoiding manner. Thus they preferentially think, at point B, "This is bad! I dislike the Activating Event," and they experience the emotional Consequence (C) of frustration or unhappiness and the behavioral Consequence (C) of avoiding or trying to eliminate this Activating Event.

This ABC theory of personality seems fairly simple and clear and was more or less endorsed by Freud (1920/59), who called it the pleasure principle, and by most psychologists. It is also favored by existential and humanistic theorists, who abjure the stimulus–response conditioning models of the radical behaviorists, and who like the stimulus–organism–response model because it includes B, people's Belief System, and thus leaves more room for individual difference and choice (Heidegger, 1962).

THE ABCs OF EMOTIONAL DISTURBANCE

The ABC model of RET becomes more complex and controversial when applied to neurotic disturbance. Because it hypothesizes that when people's Goals (Gs) are thwarted or blocked by Activating Events (As) inimical to these Goals, they have a (conscious or unconscious) choice of responding with disturbed (inappropriate) or undisturbed (appropriate) negative Consequences (Cs). If their Belief System (B) is rational or self-helping, it will include attitudes or philosophies that help them to achieve their Goals and these rational Beliefs (rBs) will mainly create healthy emotional Consequences (Cs)—such as appropriate feelings of disappointment, sorrow, regret, and frustration—and also encourage healthy behavioral Consequences—such as appropriate actions, like trying to change, improve, or stay away from Activating Events that sabotage their Goals.

This ABC model of emotional/behavioral disturbance is still fairly simple and, as noted

above, is followed by most RET and CBT practitioners and theorists. It becomes more controversial when it hypothesizes that the irrational Beliefs (iBs) or Dysfunctional Attitudes (DAs) that constitute people's self-disturbing philosophies have two main qualities: (1) They have at their core explicit and/or (usually) implicit rigid, dogmatic, powerful demands and commands, usually expressed as *musts*, *shoulds*, *ought to's*, *have to's*, and *got to's* such as, "I absolutely must have my important Goals unblocked and fulfilled!" (2) They have, usually as derivatives of these demands, highly unrealistic, overgeneralized inferences and attributions—such as, "If I don't have my important Goals unblocked and fulfilled, as I must," (a) "It's awful" (that is, totally bad or more than bad!); (b) "I can't bear it" (that is, survive or be happy at all!); (c) "I'm a worthless person" (that is, completely bad and undeserving!); and (d) "I'll always fail to get what I want and only get what I don't want (now and in the future!)."

This specific ABC model of human disturbance is followed, in RET, by D—the Disputing of people's irrational Beliefs (iBs)—when they feel and act in a self-defeating way, until they arrive at E, an Effective New Philosophy, or sound set of preferential Beliefs, for example, "I'd prefer to succeed and be lovable, but I never have to do so!" or "I'd very much like others to treat me fairly and considerately, but there is no reason why they must do so," or "I greatly desire my life conditions to be comfortable and pleasant, but I never need them to be that way."

RET Disputing (D) is done, first, cognitively by using scientific questioning and challenging to uproot people's musts and demands. For example, "Why must I perform well, even though it's desirable that I do so?" "Where is the evidence that you have to treat me considerately, however much I'd like you to do so?" Disputing is also done emotively. For example, using rational-emotive imagery (Maultsby & Ellis, 1974), disturbed people imagine one of the worst failures to achieve their goals, let themselves feel, say, very depressed, and forcefully work to change their inappropriate feeling of depression to the appropriate one of keen disappointment or regret. Disputing is also done behaviorally. For example, people who avoid socializing will force themselves to socialize, while simultaneously convincing themselves that it is not awful, but only inconvenient, to get rejected.

This more specific clinical application of the ABCs of RET has been successful in thousands of reported cases and, as noted above, in scores of studies. Most of these studies have mainly used RET cognitive Disputing and have failed to add its emotive and behavioral active Disputing methods. Therefore, I predict that when RET is properly tested, it will do even better against control groups than it has up to now.

If the ABCs of RET work so well, why should I bother to revise them and perhaps overcomplicate them? The answer is that I want to do so mainly because they omit a good deal of information about human thoughts, feelings, and behavior that would provide a more detailed and accurate picture of how humans relate to themselves and to each other. If this picture is better drawn, it also may provide better knowledge of human disturbance and what can be done to ameliorate it.

So let me, in this chapter, try to fill in some more—though hardly all—the salient details that I have not previously outlined. The main thing that I want to emphasize is that not only, as I have previously theorized, are cognitions, emotions, and behaviors interactional, and not only are they practically never entirely disparate and pure, but the same thing seems to be true of the ABCs of RET: G, A, B, and C continually interact with one another, and they all seem to be part of an interactive collaboration.

INTERACTIONS OF As, Bs, AND Cs

Let us take, first, G, a person's Goals. These consist of purposes, values, standards, and hopes that are often biological propensities (e.g., the urge to eat), are learned (e.g., the desire for cookies), and are also practiced and made habitual (e.g., compulsive overeating). Most strong and persistent Goals include pronounced cognitive, emotive, behavioral, and physiological elements. Thus the urge to eat is cognitive (e.g., "Food is good and nourishing, so I'd better obtain it"); is emotive (includes the pleasure of eating "good" and the displeasure

of eating "bad" food); is behavioral (includes purchasing, cooking, and chewing "proper" food); and is physical (includes sensations of touch, taste, smell, and sight).

Goals also are a part of the ABCs of human behavior. Thus one's Goal of surviving involves one's healthfully Believing (B) that food is desirable, feeling good (C) when it is available, going out of one's way to find and prepare it (C), and seeing it (B) as a (good or bad) Activating Event (A) when it is plentiful or scarce. Having the real (conscious or even unconscious) Goal (G) of surviving, and the specific Goal of eating in order to survive, normally includes and involves some As, Bs, and Cs. Similarly, having the Goal (G) of not surviving, and specifically of starving oneself to death, also involves several As, Bs, and Cs—particularly the Belief (B) that one had better not eat anything, the feeling (C) of loathing food, and the behavior (C) of avoiding all food.

Goals (Gs) also normally interact with and create various kinds of As, Bs, and Cs. Thus the Goal of surviving and of eating to survive will frequently greatly affect one's Activating Events (As) (the presence or absence of food), influence one's Beliefs (Bs) and these As, and help to create strong feelings and behaviors about these As. Would-be survivors who are starving (A) will see even bark or skin as food (A), will believe (B) that even this poor kind of food is nutritious, will strongly desire it (C) and will actively look for it and eat it (C). Goals (Gs), then, include and influence cognitions, emotions, and behaviors, and, of course, thoughts, feelings, and actions often include and influence Goals.

Let us now look at Activating Events (As), particularly those that block or sabotage people's Goals (Gs) and encourage or contribute to disturbances (Cs). Let's take the loss of approval or of love (A): Assuming that one values or has the goal of gaining approval, even a slight lack of it (A) often includes several Bs: (1) nonevaluative perception or observation (e.g., "This person is frowning"); (2) nonevaluative inferences or attributions (e.g., "This person is frowning at me and probably dislikes what I am doing and may dislike me"); (3) negative preferential evaluations (e.g., "Because this person doesn't like my behavior and doesn't seem to like me, as I prefer her to do, I find that unfortunate, but I can still accept myself and be reasonably happy"); (4) negative musturbatory evaluations (e.g., "Because this person doesn't like my behavior and dislikes me, as she must not do, this is awful, I can't bear it, and I am an incompetent, worthless individual!").

The relationships between Activating Events (As) and Beliefs (Bs) about these As are interactional and reciprocal. The As often significantly influence Bs, and Bs also often significantly influence As. Thus if A is perceived as loss of approval, the Belief "I prefer to be approved but I don't have to be" can influence a person to perceive A as a slight affront, while the Belief "I must be approved and I'm worthless if I am not!" can influence a person to perceive A as a cruelly intended, persistent, enormous assault.

Similarly, the frequency, kind, and degree of the Activating Events (As) one experiences may easily influence or contribute to one's Beliefs. Thus if one's behavior is occasionally criticized by another person, one may Believe, "I'd like this other to approve of me, but if he doesn't, it's slightly bad and I can easily stand it." If, however, one's same behavior is continually heavily excoriated and one is strongly attacked (A) for it, one may construct the Belief, "This criticism (A) is unfair and must not exist! I can't stand it! My attacker is a rotten person for treating me this way!"

Just as Activating Events (As) encourage or contribute to Beliefs (Bs), so do they also include Cs. Thus assuming again that one strongly has the Goal (G) of getting others' approval and is actually disapproved (or perceives disapproval), one will almost always feel the emotional Consequence (C) of appropriate feelings of disappointment, sorrow, regret, and frustration, and also take functional actions (Cs), such as discussing and possibly changing one's disapproved behaviors. These Consequences—or some other feelings and actions—are almost inevitable concomitants of As that seriously block one's Goals.

Practically all humans have powerful innate tendencies to take their strong preferences and change them to dogmatic, absolute musts and demands. Once they experience what they consider to be serious negative Activating Events, they frequently musturbate about them (at B) and thereby quickly bring on inappropriate Consequences (Cs) of disturbed feelings—like

panic, depression, and rage—and dysfunctional behaviors—like withdrawal, procrastination, drinking, and violence—when they are disapproved of by others. So negative Activating Events—or what Seligman (1991) calls Adversities—almost always include and involve appropriate emotions and actions, and frequently they also have concomitants of self-defeating feelings and behaviors.

Consequences (Cs) also significantly influence or even create As. Thus if a woman feels horrified and self-hating because her lover has "rejected" her, she may fairly easily see (interpret) him as "rejecting" (A), when he actually only may be focused on something else. She can even feel so horrified (C) about his rejection (A) that she falsely and defensively sees (interprets) him, at point A as accepting her when he is really being indifferent or rejecting.

Activating Events (As), as well as Bs and Cs, almost always—and perhaps always—have cognitive, emotive, and behavioral aspects. They may seem to be factual, objective, or impersonal—as when you desire good health (G) and you meet with an accident (a car hits you) and you end up with a broken leg and with pain (As). Actually, however if A (the accident) is to lead to B (your Beliefs about it) and C (your emotional and behavioral consequences), you somehow have to perceive (cognize) what "objectively" happens at A. You will view (cognize) it in several ways. You will experience (emote) about it; and do something (act) in connection with it. It, this event or happening, may possibly just happen in the world. But as long as it happens to you, a thinking, emoting, and behaving person, it seems to involve some of your thoughts, feelings, and reactions. Even if you go into a coma as a result of the event (the car's hitting you), as soon as you come out of the coma and know about it, you immediately react to it cognitively, emotionally, and behaviorally. Only if you should die (at the time or immediately after A occurs), do you not react to it at all. Nor, in all probability, will you ever! A, then, is an Activating Event that happens to a person, and people usually add cognitive, emotive, and behavioral elements to A. They are intrinsically phenomenalists and constructivists, which seems to characterize their essential nature as living, and usually conscious, humans.

As already noted, Beliefs (Bs) often strongly interact with and reciprocally influence As. They also—as the original ABC theory of RET and of the other cognitive-behavioral therapies hold—powerfully interact with and reciprocally influence Cs. Thus preferential Bs—for example, "I would like very much to be loved by So-and-So, but I never have to be"—normally lead one to feel appropriately sad and frustrated when one thinks one is rejected by that person, and musturbatory Bs—for example, "I absolutely must be loved by So-and-So or else I am worthless"—usually lead one to feel inappropriately panicked and depressed.

At the same time, Consequences (Cs) often significantly interact with and reciprocally influence Bs. Thus if one feels depressed (at C) after being rejected (at A) and avoids approaching potential rejectors (C), one will frequently invent Bs, such as "So-and-So is stupid and is not worth approaching"; or "I can easily find better people than So-and-So to approach"; or "So-and-So dislikes me because she is envious of my ability."

Somewhat like G and A, B (one's Belief system) is cognitive, emotive, and behavioral, although it may seem, at first blush, to be heavily cognitive or philosophical. Thus when a car hits you, and breaks your leg and you are in physical pain (As), you often will have both preferential Beliefs ("I don't like this!") and musturbatory Beliefs ("This absolutely should not have occurred and it's horrible that it did!"). Both of these Beliefs are strongly affected by your feelings of pain; and when these Beliefs lead to feelings of frustration and horror, these feelings, by a feedback loop, seem to "confirm" the Beliefs. They also have strong behavioral concomitants or components: "I don't like this!" implies that you will quickly do something about your leg and your pain; and "This should not have happened and it's horrible that it did!" implies that you will frantically try to do something about your accident—complain, sue, go to a hospital, and so on. As noted above, it is you, a person, who has preferential and musturbatory thoughts about Activating Events. But persons almost simultaneously have feelings and behaviors along with their evaluative thoughts, though actually thoughts may precede feelings and behaviors and then, milliseconds later, the latter, by a feedback loop, may affect evaluating thoughts. Therefore, it is almost impossible for one to think evaluatively about any Activating Event in life without also having feelings and actions (or inactions) involving it.

Paul Woods (1987, 1990) suggests a more neurological interpretation of how As, Bs, and Cs almost inevitably interact. Thus Activating Events (As) include:

- External happenings.
- Stimulus energy transmitted by these external happenings.
- Activity in the sensory area of the brain (stimulus experienced).
- Activity in sensory association area of brain (sensation interpreted).

Belief systems (Bs) take place largely in the cortical area of the brain, where experience is tied in with Belief systems and is evaluated. Consequences (Cs) consist of emotional and behavioral reactions to As and Bs.

Neurologically, then, the sensations we interpret at A influence our emotional and behavioral reactions at C; but the reverse is also true, so that the interpretation of our sensations at A also influences our emotional and behavioral reactions at C. Again, the sensations we interpret at A influence our cortical area (experience tied in with Belief systems and evaluated), and also our cortical area experiences and evaluations influence and interact with our interpretation of our sensations at A.

Finally, our cortical-area experiences and evaluations at B influence our emotional and behavioral reactions at C, and our C reactions influence our cortical area experiences and reactions at C.

THE ABCs OF INTERPERSONAL RELATIONSHIPS

As can be seen by the above examples, interactions and mutual influences among the ABCs of healthy and unhealthy functioning are multiple and almost endless—as is also true of interactions among the ABCs of two or more people in an intimate relationship. As I and my coauthors showed in *Rational-Emotive Couples Therapy* (Ellis, Sichel, Yeager, DiMattia, and DiGiuseppe, 1989), two people's Cs often powerfully influence each other's As. Thus if a husband criticizes his wife (A), she may tell herself, "He must not be so critical! What a louse he is!" and she may react with rage at C. Then he may view her rage as a negative Activating Event (A) and may react at C with depression. Then she can view his depression as a negative Activating Event (A) and react at C with guilt and self-pity. Etcetera!

In the case of intimate interpersonal relations, a couple's As may also strongly influence their Bs—and their Bs can significantly influence their As. Thus in the frequent illustration, the husband's constant criticism of some of his wife's *actions* may lead her falsely to interpret this as criticism of *her* and then to Believe, "He completely hates me!" And her comment, "You hate me, you bastard!" (her C), may encourage him to criticize her severely further and to hit her (his C2 and her A2). Noting his As, the wife may then conclude, "See! Now I'm sure that he completely hates me!" (her B2), and file for divorce (her C2).

The interactions among the ABCs of two people, then, may be immense and profound; and in a family system, where there are three or more members, they may be almost infinitely complex. This does not mean that in therapy all of these interactions create disturbances, or that they all must be completely revealed and understood by the therapist and the clients. The ones that are crucial to disturbance usually still involve thoughts, feelings, and actions that overtly or tacitly involve musts and demands.

Suppose, for example, that a married woman is criticized badly by her husband (A1). She can rationally tell herself, "I don't like his treating me this way; I think I'll have little to do with him" (B1), and feel appropriately disappointed and withdraw from him sexually (C1). But she can also rationally believe, "I don't think it's right to withdraw sexually from my husband" (B2) and can thereby make herself feel appropriately sorry and regretful (B2) about his bad treatment (A1), about her thought, "I think I'll have little to do with him" (B1), and about her

sexual withdrawal (C1). If so, she is not, in RET terms, thinking, feeling, or behaving neurotically.

She can, however, easily take her husband's critical treatment of her (A1), add irrational *musts* to her sensible *preferences*, and tell herself, "He *must* not criticize me this way and he is a complete *bastard* for doing so!" (B1), and then feel inappropriately enraged and homicidal and may actually assault her husband (C1). Her musturbatory *demand*, instead of her strong *preference* that A not occur, now neuroticizes her and creates dramatically different feelings and behaviors (C1).

As she is disturbing herself, this woman may secondarily disturb herself with musts about her A1, B2, and C1. Thus she may powerfully insist that: (1) "I *must* not let my husband criticize me!" (A1); (2) "I *must* not view my husband as a bastard!" (B1); and (3)"I *must* not feel homicidal and act assaultively!" (C1). With these demands about her original A, B, and C, this woman can easily make herself anxious and depressed about her anxiety, and her depression and her secondary disturbances can easily outweigh her primary ones!

At the same time, her husband can negatively view her A, B, and C and rationally can strongly *wish* or *prefer* her not to see him as critical (her A), not to believe that he is a bastard (her B), and not to be enraged and assaultive (her C). Or he can irrationally *demand* that she absolutely *must* not experience her A, B, and C and may thereby make himself anxious, depressed, and enraged about her experiences.

In other words, if this husband and wife fully understand the ABCs of their own and the other's life, they will have a much better view of what is happening—and what they are making happen—in their relationship. And so will their therapist. But, as the theory and practice of RET originally proposed, and still does, to understand the process of their disturbances about these ABCs, they had better clearly see their preferences and their demands concerning their own and the other's cognitive-emotive ABCs. If their own cognitive-emotive Bs are preferential, they will most probably not be disturbed; if they are distinctly musturbatory, they probably will be.

By stating this, it may seem as though I am

espousing the old RET, which made Beliefs (Bs) crucial in the creation of disturbed Consequences (Cs). This is partly true. But I am also going back to the original RET that saw thoughts and feelings as conjoint and allied rather than as disparate (Ellis, 1962). Although I have usually refered to Bs as Beliefs, which they are, when they have emotional and behavioral Consequences, they strongly interact with each other and are cognitive-emotive.

Thus as Abelson (1962) has shown, cognitions can be "cold" and "hot" and, as I have added (Ellis, 1985a, 1985b), they can also be "warm." The husband mentioned above thus has his choice of all three kinds of cognitions if his wife is violently angry: (1) "I see that my wife is violent" (cool cognition): (2) "I don't like her violence, I wish she didn't act that way. How annoying that she does" (warm cognitions-feelings): (3) "I utterly loathe her attacks! She *must* not assault me! She's no damned good for acting that way! I'll kill her!" (hot cognitions-feelings). Cold cognitions may include little or no feelings. Warm cognitions include evaluations of cold cognitions, ranging from weak to strong evaluations; and evaluations include weak to strong feelings. Hot cognitions include distinct feelings, usually ranging from strong to very strong.

Like their Gs, As, and Bs, people's Cs also include powerful emotive and behavioral elements mutually interacting with powerful cognitive elements. Thus when you are hit by a car, have a broken leg, and are in pain (As) and you tell yourself, "This shouldn't have happened! This is terrible!," you will not only act at point C (e.g., complain and go to the hospital), but also you often will feel displeased and enraged and ruminate and obsess about what happened and its unfortunate results. You also may have self-pitying, paranoid, or suicidal thoughts, and you may have feelings of depression, despair, vindictiveness, and so on. As usual, you are a *person* who reacts to Activating Events.

If what I have said thus far is valid, then what we call personality normally applies to persons—to humans. It is the way humans are, or how they fairly consistently, and often inconsistently, behave. To understand them, we have to understand our environment or Activating Events, because we only and always exist in an environment, and we are not, as far as we can tell, entirely in, of, by, and for ourselves. We react, moreover, to this environment, as well as to ourselves, and we react to it, physically and emotionally, biologically and psychologically. Our "emotional" and "psychological" reactions are cognitive, emotional, and behavioral. That is our "nature." We can define our thoughts, feelings, and behaviors as if they are disparate or separate kinds of processes; but rarely, if ever, is this true. In one sense or another, as I first said in 1956, "Thinking and emoting ... in certain (though hardly all) respects are essentially the same thing so that one's thinking becomes one's emotion and emotion becomes one's thought" (Ellis, 1962, p. 36). It is good to know that many other cognitive-behaviorists have endorsed this same view (Epstein, 1990; Greenberg & Safran, 1987; Guidano, 1988; Mahoney, 1988; Meichenbaum, 1990; Muran, 1991).

USING THE ABCs IN PSYCHOTHERAPY

To understand our thoughts, feelings, and behaviors, and to see how they are integrally and holistically related, does not necessarily help us to devise efficient and effective theories of psychotherapy (Bernard, 1986; Ellis, 1985b; Ellis & Dryden, 1990, 1991; Ellis & Grieger, 1977, 1986; Yankura & Dryden, 1990). The question still arises: Which, if any, of these processes—assuming that we can partially distinguish them—contributes more to human disturbance and which can be more efficiently changed in order to achieve greater, more comprehensive, and more lasting personal change, or to achieve what we call good personality functioning or mental health?

As the clinical and research literature of the past 100 years has shown, therapists can help their clients change their thoughts, feelings, and actions, and to really focus on one, two, or all three of these processes, and in many instances contribute to both ephemeral and lasting personality change. None of the hundreds of techniques that have been used have yet been conclusively shown to be superior to the other methods. Rational-emotive theory (along with CBT) has taken an integrative stand and stresses the active-directive use of a number of cognitive, emotive, and behavioral methods with almost all clients (Ellis, 1957, 1962, 1988; Ellis & Dryden, 1987, 1990, 1991). However, RET uses different emphases and proportions of direct and indirect, collaborative and forceful, persuasive and homework, cognitive and emotive methods with different, and particularly with resistant, clients—because all people are individuals and have similarities with and differences from others (Ellis, 1985b; Ellis & Dryden, 1987, 1991; Ellis & Watzlawick, 1988; Ellis & Zeig, 1988).

Let me conclude this chapter on a more controversial, and even somewhat contradictory, note. Because humans are human, because they are more cognitive than other creatures, I hypothesize that certain cognitive methods of therapy will particularly and more elegantly help many (not all!) clients to make faster, greater, more pervasive, more lasting personality changes than will some other less cognitive techniques—and that this will be particularly true of more neurotic (rather than borderline and psychotic) clients. Moreover, our cognitive modality, as Russell Grieger (personal communication) has rightly reminded me, is (1) most uniquely human and (2) the most interpersonally influential of all human modalities.

Yes, I realize the trouble I am getting myself into with these hypotheses. According to what I have said in this chapter, what we call cognitive is by no means only intellectual, but often includes profound emotional and motor processes. Moreover, the special cognitive methods I shall describe all include the emotive and behavioral elements, and are not purely intellectual or philosophic. So the points I am about to make include confounded, imprecise terms that may water down some of my arguments. Nonetheless, where angels fear to tread, let me venture on!

First, let me add an important aspect of my ABCs of RET that often gets lost and that one of my perspicacious clients clearly saw. People, as I stressed with this client after he had previously failed to surrender his severe and chronic anger with five years of psychoanalysis, largely construct their own irrational Beliefs (iBs), rather than accept them from their parents. They take the Activating Events of their lives (in his case, constant criticism and abuse), and cre-

ate about them rational Beliefs (rBs) (e.g., "I am acting badly and will gain disapproval, and that is unfortunate") and also create irrational Beliefs (iBs) (e.g., "I must not act badly and have to please my parents and significant others, else I am a bad person!").

People's iBs—as I note in this chapter—while cognitive, also regularly interact with emotive and behavioral components, so that they all mutually affect each other. But because humans are language-creating, symbol-making, self-talking creatures, they are largely, in a form of symbolic shorthand, encoded in conscious and unconscious hot cognitions, such as (in the case of this client), "I am no good! I can't stand significant people's disapproval! I must make a lot of money to prove that my parents were wrong and that I deserve happiness!"

These iBs are largely reactions to the unfortunate Activating Events (As) of clients' early and later lives. But once they construct them many times and they practice and practice them as self-statements, they are made into Basic Philosophies that seem, and feel, absolutely right and true, even though they may be dogmatic, false assumptions. As my client nicely put it, "B starts off by following A, but then it becomes before A and is brought to new As."

I immediately agreed. "Yes. B is first created or constructed—especially the self-defeating musts in B—about A. But then it becomes, by repetition and by acting as if it were true, basic—a Basic Philosophy that we thereafter tend to bring to A. In so doing, we often distort and change A—for example, we see ourselves as rejected totally when someone only makes a slightly negative remark about what we are doing."

As this client and I went on to discuss, at length, the hot irrational cognitions that we encode in B often become Basic Philosophic Assumptions—what Kelly (1955) called dysfunctional personal constructs—that we use as virtual cornerstones of our lives. They significantly affect our Goals (Gs), Activating Events (As), and Consequences (Cs). They even, RET holds, importantly influence our derivative Bs. Thus my client's main musturbatory iBs—"I must not act badly and must please my parents and significant others!"—led him steadily to conclude, "Because I often do not act well and do displease my parents and significant others, I am no good! I don't deserve happiness! I must succeed more than others. I can't stand failing! I'll never do well enough!" Etcetera.

Why are musts and shoulds that people accept, create, and disturb themselves with often so difficult for them to surrender? The answer is that they tend to have a special, inter-related kind of cognitive, emotive, and behavioral nature.

Cognitively, they are absolutist and necessitous: for example, "At all times and under all conditions, I must perform adequately!" "I must *completely* and *perfectly* perform well!" "Unless I perform well, as I of course must, I shall suffer utter disaster, may well die, and if I continue to live, I cannot be happy *at all*!"

Emotively, the musts with which people disturb themselves are held strongly and powerfully and consist of what Abelson (1962) calls "hot cognitions." For example, "I *really* have to perform *very* well!" "Because this is the *most* important relationship in my life, I *truly* must succeed in it!" "Because my desire for food is *so* great, I must keep eating and eating to satisfy it!" "Because I *feel* so anxious when I fail, my feeling proves that I *have* to succeed!"

Behaviorally, musts that lead to disturbance are *rigidly* held and clung to, and the behaviors that they lead to are constantly practiced and reinforced. Examples: "Because I so greatly *need* your affection, I cannot *ever* leave you, I *have to* keep begging you to love me, and I *can't stop* following you around. My following you and obsessing about you *proves* that I really love you and that I *must* have you!" "Every time I get a raise, I jump with joy, so I *must* keep getting raises."

Dogmatic musts often include compound Beliefs that simultaneously have strong cognitive, emotive, and behavioral elements. Thus: "I *have* to be completely successful and thereby win your approval, or else I am a total clod, my life will be *awful* and *terrible*. I'll *never* be able to succeed or be approved, and I might as well kill myself! Moreover, if I fail and you don't approve of me, that will make me feel horribly anxious and depressed, and I *can't stand* having those feelings and am a worthless nincompoop for having them!" (Muran, 1991).

Imperative musts usually have powerful emotive and behavioral components that help create and intensify them and that lead to miserable cognitive, emotive, and behavioral results that require attention in their own right, that consume considerable time and energy, that sidetrack people from actively Disputing these musts, and that encourage them to create more disturbing (cognitive-emotive) musts about them. For example: "I must not think irrationally and must not feel anxious and depressed when I do think that way! I *can't bear* having these musts and getting horrible results from having them! It's *too* hard to keep fighting them and giving them up—in fact, it's so hard that I *can't* give them up! And I'm *no damned good* for creating these terrible thoughts and feelings and for not stopping them!"

People's imperative, unconditional musts, then, seem to be inevitably cognitive, emotive, and behavioral, and in turn lead to poor thinking, feeling, and motoric results that they then have disturbing thoughts, emotions, and actions about and that serve to impede their clearly seeing and forcefully Disputing and alleviating these musts. No wonder that so-called intellectual insight and Disputing usually will not help people very much to surrender and keep giving up their profound musts! That is why RET actively encourages clients and other people with disturbances to keep using a number of strong, vigorous cognitive, emotive, and behavioral methods to include in the Disputing of self-defeating musts and commands.

All told, then, RET still holds that profound, dogmatic, absolutist, imperative musts are probably the most important aspect of neurotic disturbance. But the revised RET theory contends that these musts are not merely intellectual, cognitive, or philosophic, but that they also are highly emotive and behavioral and that they are an integral part of people's Goals, Activating Events, Beliefs, and disturbed Consequences when they become—or *make themselves*—neurotic.

If irrational Beliefs (iBs) are held both consciously and unconsciously, and often held vigorously, as RET hypothesizes, they had better be clearly revealed, shown to be destructive, and be strongly and persistently attacked by both therapists and their clients. Because these Beliefs (Bs) and their Consequences (Cs) are cognitive, emotive, and behavioral, RET uses many thinking, emotional, and activity techniques to change them. But it uses these methods largely to help clients make—or, rather, give themselves—a profound philosophic change, and especially to change their rigid musturbatory to alternative-seeking preferential thinking.

We can encourage our clients to think creatively and inventively for themselves, rather than only following their therapist's ideas and assignments, so that they ideally become more open-minded and less dogmatic in their thinking and tend to create fewer and fewer bigotries and rigidities in the future. As they acquire and keep using an and/also, both/and, open-to-change general view, they will keep constructing specific philosophies and tentative solutions to life problems that will help them avoid self-defeating and socially destructive behaviors and open the road to maximum self-and other-fulfillment (Ellis, 1990b).

For all its old and newer emphasis on the holistic understanding of how cognitions, emotions, and behaviors include each other and how Activating Events (As), Beliefs (Bs), and emotional and behavioral Consequences (Cs) intricately and strongly interact when people live healthfully and when they make themselves disturbed, RET, then, still stresses the advantages of people's making and continuing to make a profound basic philosophic change. I now see, more than I ever did before, that this profound philosophic change is extremely cognitive, emotive, and behavioral. It means that those who make it will, first, truly, and much of the time, choose to keep thinking in a flexible, preferential rather than rigid, musturbatory way. It means, second, that they will strongly, vigorously, and quite emotionally involve themselves with scientific, and against bigoted, ways of viewing and relating to themselves, to others, and to the world. It means that they will steadily and determinedly keep fighting and acting against cognitive-emotional rigidity and for open-mindedness.

REFERENCES

Beck, A. T., & Emery, G. (1985). *Anxiety disorders and phobias*. New York: Basic Books.

Beck, A. T., Rush, A.J., Shaw, B.F., & Emery, G. (1979). *Cognitive therapy of depression*. New York: Guilford Press.

Bernard, M. E. (1986). *Staying alive in an irrational world: Albert Ellis and rational-emotive therapy*. South Melbourne, Australia: Carlson/Macmillan.

Bernard, M. E., & DiGiuseppe, R. (1989). *Inside rational-emotive therapy*. San Diego, CA: Academic Ps.

Brown, G., & Beck, A. T. (1989). The role of imperatives a psychopathology: A reply to Ellis. *Cognitive Therapy and Research, 13*, 315–321.

Crawford, T. (1990, May 7, May 11, May 26). Letters to Albert Ellis.

DeSilvestri, C. (1989). Clinical models in RET: An advanced model of the organization of emotional and behavioral disorders. *Journal of Rational-Emotive and Cognitive Behavior Therapy, 7*, 51–58.

DiGiuseppe, R. (1986). The implication of the philosophy of science for rational-emotive theory and therapy. *Psychotherapy, 23*, 634–639.

DiGiuseppe, R. A., Miller, N. J., & Trexler, L.D. (1979). A review of rational-emotive psychotherapy outcome studies. In A. Ellis & J.M. Whiteley (Eds.), *Theoretical and empirical foundations of rational-emotive therapy* (pp. 218–235). Monterey, CA: Brooks/Cole.

Dryden, W. (1984). Rational-emotive therapy. In W. Dryden (Ed.), *Individual therapy in Britain* (pp. 235–263). London: Harper & Row.

Ellis, A. (1956). An operational reformulation of some of the basic principles of psychoanalysis. In H. Feigl & M. Scriven (Eds.), *The foundations of science and the concepts of psychology and psychoanalysis* (pp. 131–154). Minneapolis: University of Minnesota Press. (Also: *Psychoanalytic Review, 43* 163–180.)

Ellis, A. (1957). *How to live with a neurotic: At home and at work*. New York: Crown. Rev. ed.: North Hollywood, CA: Wilshire Books, 1975.

Ellis, A. (1958). Rational psychotherapy. *Journal of General Psychology, 59* 35–49. Reprinted: New York: Institute for Rational-Emotive Therapy.

Ellis, A. (1962). *Reason and emotion in psychotherapy*. Secaucus, NJ: Citadel.

Ellis, A. (1968). *Homework report*. New York: Institute for Rational-Emotive Therapy.

Ellis, A. (1969a). A cognitive approach to behavior therapy. *International Journal of Psychiatry, 8*, 896–900.

Ellis, A. (1969b). A weekend of rational encounter. *Rational Living, 4*(2), 1–8. Reprinted in A. Ellis & W. Dryden, *The practice of rational-emotive therapy*. New York: Springer, 1987.

Ellis, A. (1971). *Growth through reason*. North Hollywood, CA: Wilshire Books.

Ellis, A. (1972). *Psychotherapy and the value of a human being*. New York: Institute for Rational-Emotive Therapy. Reprinted in A. Ellis & W. Dryden, *The Essential Albert Ellis*. New York: Springer, 1990.

Ellis, A. (1973). *Humanistic psychotherapy: The rational-emotive approach*. New York: McGraw-Hill.

Ellis, A. (1976). RET abolishes most of the human ego. *Psychotherapy, 13*, 343–348. Reprinted: New York: Institute for Rational-Emotive Therapy.

Ellis, A. (1977). *Anger—how to live with and without it*. Secaucus, NJ: Citadel Press.

Ellis, A. (1979a). Rational-emotive therapy: Research data that support the clinical and personality hypotheses of RET and other modes of cognitive-behavior therapy. In A. Ellis & J.M. Whiteley (Eds.), *Theoretical and empirical foundations of rational-emotive therapy* (pp. 101–173). Monterey, CA: Brooks/Cole.

Ellis, A. (1979b). Rejoinder: Elegant and inelegant RET. In A. Ellis & J.M. Whiteley (Eds.), *Theoretical and empirical foundations of rational-emotive therapy* (pp. 240–271). Monterey, CA: Brooks/Cole.

Ellis, A. (1983). *The case against religiosity*. New York: Institute for Rational-Emotive Therapy.

Ellis, A. (1984). The essence of RET—1984. *Journal of Rational-Emotive Therapy, 2*(1), 19–25.

Ellis, A. (1985a). Expanding the ABC's of rational-emotive therapy. In M. Mahoney & A. Freeman (Eds.), *Cognition and psychotherapy* (pp. 313–323). New York: Plenum.

Ellis, A. (1985b). *Overcoming resistance: Rational-emotive therapy with difficult clients*. New York: Springer.

Ellis, A. (1987a). The impossibility of achieving consistently good mental health. *American Psychologist, 42*, 364–375.

Ellis, A. (1987b). A sadly neglected cognitive element in depression. *Cognitive Therapy and Research, 11*, 121–146.

Ellis, A. (1988) *How to stubbornly refuse to make yourself miserable about anything—yes, anything!* Secaucus, N.J.: Lyle Stuart.

Ellis, A. (1989). A rational-emotive constructivist approach to couples and family therapy. In A. Ellis, J. Sichel, R. Yeager, D. DiMattia, & R. DiGiuseppe, *Rational-emotive couples therapy* (pp. 106–115). New York: Pergamon.

Ellis, A. (1990a). Is rational-emotive therapy (RET) "rationalist" or "constructivist"? In A. Ellis & W. Dryden, *The essential Albert Ellis* (pp. 114–141). New York: Springer.

Ellis, A. (1990b). Rational and irrational beliefs in counseling psychology. *Journal of Rational-Emotive and Cognitive-Behavior Therapy, 8*, 221–233.

Ellis, A. (1990c). A rational-emotive approach to peace. Paper presented at the 98th Annual Convention of the American Psychological Association, Boston, August 10.

Ellis, A. (1991). The philosophical basis of rational-emotive therapy. *Psychotherapy in Private Practice, 8*(4), 99–106.

Ellis, A., & Dryden, W. (1987). *The practice of rational-emotive therapy*. New York: Springer.

Ellis, A., & Dryden, W. (1990). *The essential Albert Ellis*. New York: Springer.

Ellis, A., & Dryden, W. (1991). *A dialogue with Albert Ellis: Against dogma*. Stony Stratford, England: Open University Press.

Ellis, A., & Grieger, R. (Eds.). (1977). *Handbook of rational-emotive therapy. Vol. 1*. New York: Springer.

Ellis, A., & Grieger, R. (Eds.). (1986). *Handbook of rational-emotive therapy. Vol. 2*. New York: Springer.

Ellis, A., & Harper, R. A. (1975). *A new guide to rational living*. North Hollywood, CA: Wilshire Books.

Ellis, A., Sichel, J., Yeager, R., DiMattia, D., & DiGiuseppe, R. (1989). *Rational-emotive couples therapy*. New York: Pergamon.

Ellis, A., & Watzlawick, P. (Speakers). (1986). *Debate: Direct vs. indirect psychotherapy*. Cassette recording. Garden Grove, CA: InfoMedix and Milton H. Erickson Foundation.

Ellis, A., & Zeig, J. (Speakers). (1988). *Dialogue*. Cassette recording. Garden Grove, CA: InfoMedix and Milton H. Erickson Foundation.

Engels, G. I., & Diekstra, R.F.W. (1986). Meta-analysis of rational emotive therapy outcome studies. In P. Eelen & O. Fontaine (Eds.), *Behavior therapy: Beyond the conditioning framework* (pp. 121–140). Hillsdale, NJ: Erlbaum.

Epstein, S. (1990). Cognitive experiential self-theory. In L. Pervin (Ed.), *Handbook of personality and research*. New York: Guilford Press.

Freud, S. (1920/1959). *Beyond the pleasure principle*. New York: Basic Books.

Grieger, R. M. (1986). *Rational-emotive couple counseling: A special issue of journal of rational emotive therapy*. New York: Human Sciences Press.

Glasser, W. (1965). *Reality therapy*. New York: Harper & Row.

Goldfried, M.R., & Davison, G.C. (1976). *Clinical behavior therapy*. New York: Holt, Rinehart & Winston.

Greenberg, L.S., & Safran, J.D. (1984). Integrating affect and cognition: A perspective on the process of therapeutic change. *Cognitive Therapy and Research, 8*, 591–598.

Grieger, R. (1985). From a linear to a contextual model of the ABCs of RET. *Journal of Rational-Emotive Therapy, 3*(2), 75–99.

Guidano, V. F. (1988). A systems, process oriented approach to cognitive therapy. In K.S. Dobson (Ed.), *Handbook of cognitive behavior therapies* (pp. 307–356). New York: Guilford Press.

Guidano, V. F., & Liotti, G. (1983). *Cognitive processes and emotional disorders*. New York: Guilford Press.

Haaga, D.A., & Davison, G.C. (1989). Outcome studies of rational-emotive therapy. In M. E. Bernard & R. DiGiuseppe, Eds., *Inside rational-emotive therapy* (pp. 155–197). San Diego, CA: Academic.

Heidegger, M. (1962). *Being and time*. New York: Harper & Row.

Hollon, S.D., & Bemis, K.M. (1981). Self-report and the assessment of cognitive functions. In M. Hersen & A.S. Bellack (Eds.), *Behavioral assessment* (pp. 125–174). New York: Pergamon.

Kelly, G. (1955). *The psychology of personal constructs*. 2 vols. New York: Norton.

Lazarus, A.A. (1971). *Behavior therapy and beyond*. New York: McGraw-Hill.

Ledwidge, B. (1978). Cognitive behavior modifications: A step in the wrong direction. *Psychological Bulletin, 85*, 353–375.

Lyons, L.C., & Woods, P. (1991). The efficacy of rational emotive therapy: A quantitative review of the outcome research. *Clinical Psychology Review, 11*, 357–369.

Mahoney, M. J. (1977). Personal Science: A cognitive learning theory. In A. Ellis & R. Grieger (Eds.), *Handbook of rational-emotive therapy* (pp. 352–366). New York: Springer.

Mahoney, M. J. (1988). The cognitive sciences and psychotherapy: Patterns in a developing relationship. In K.S. Dobson (Ed.), *Handbook of the cognitive-behavioral therapies* (pp. 357–386). New York: Guilford Press.

Maultsby, M.C., Jr. (1984). *Rational behavior therapy*. Englewood Cliffs, NJ: Prentice-Hall.

Maultsby, M.C., Jr., & Ellis, A. (1974). *Technique for using rational emotive imagery*. New York: Institute for Rational-Emotive Therapy.

McGovern, T. E., & Silverman, M.S. (1984). A review of outcome studies of rational-emotive therapy from 1977–1982. *Journal of Rational-Emotive Therapy, 2*(1), 7–18.

Meichenbaum, D. (1977). *Cognitive-behavior modification.* New York: Plenum.

Meichenbaum, D. (1990). Cognitive-behavior modification. Invited address to Evolution of Psychotherapy Conference, Anaheim, CA, December 13.

Muran, J. C. (1991). A reformulation of the ABC model in cognitive psychotherapies: Implications for assessment and treatment. *Clinical Psychology Review, 11,* 399–418.

Popper, K. R. (1985). In D. Miller (Ed.), *Popper selections.* Princeton, NJ: Princeton University Press.

Rachlin, H. (1977). Reinforcing and punishing thoughts. *Behavior Therapy, 8,* 659–665.

Raimy, V. (1975). *Misunderstandings of the self.* San Francisco: Jossey-Bass.

Rorer, L. G. (1989). Rational-emotive theory: An integrated psychological and philosophical basis. *Cognitive Therapy and Research, 13,* 475–493; *13,* 531–548.

Schwartz, R. M. (1982). Cognitive-behavior modification: A conceptual review. *Clinical Psychology Review, 2,* 267–293.

Seligman, M. E. P. (1991). *Learned optimism.* New York: Knopf.

Skinner, B. F. (1971). *Beyond freedom and dignity.* New York: Knopf.

Smith, T. W., & Allred, K.D. (1986). Rationality revisited: A reassessment of the empirical support for the rational-emotive model. In P.C. Kendall (Ed.), *Advances in cognitive-behavioral research and therapy* (Vol. 5)(pp. 63–87). New York: Academic.

Wessler, R. L. (1984). Alternative conceptions of rational-emotive therapy: Toward a philosophically neutral psychotherapy. In M.A. Reda & M. L. Mahoney (Eds.), *Cognitive psychotherapies: Recent developments in theory, research and practice* (pp. 65–79). Cambridge, MA: Ballinger.

Wessler, R. L., & Hankin-Wessler, S.W.R. (1986). Cognitive appraisal therapy. In W. Dryden & W. Golden (Eds.), *Cognitive-behavioral approaches to psychotherapy* (pp. 196–223). London: Harper & Row.

Wessler, R. A., & Wessler, R.L. (1980). *The principles and practice of rational-emotive therapy.* San Francisco, CA: Jossey-Bass.

Wolfe, J. L., & Naimark, H. (1991). Psychological messages and social context: Strategies for increasing RET's effectiveness with women. In M. Bernard (Ed.), *Using rational-emotive therapy effectively.* New York: Plenum.

Woods, P. J. (1987). Reduction in type A behavior, anxiety, anger, and physical illness as related to changes in irrational beliefs. *Journal of Rational-Emotive and Cognitive-Behavior Therapy, 5* 213–237.

Woods, P. J. (1990, October 23). Personal communication.

Woods, P. J., & Lyons, L.C. (1990). Irrational beliefs and psychosomatic disorders. *Journal of Rational-Emotive and Cognitive-Behavior Therapy, 8,* 3–20.

Woods, P. J., Silverman, E.S., Gentilini, J.M., & Cunningham, D.K. (1990, June). Cognitive variables related to suicidal contemplation in adolescents with implications for long-range prevention. Paper presented at the World Congress on Mental Health Counseling, Keystone, CO.

Yankura, J., & Dryden, W. (1990). *Doing RET: Albert Ellis in action.* New York: Springer.

Discussion by Salvador Minuchin, M.D.

◆

Jeff Zeig's hope to develop a dialogue between people who have different perspectives on the process of psychotherapy is a hope I do not think it is really possible to realize. As I was listening to Dr. Ellis, I was thinking that he was describing changes in his theory. He is a man who has worked for a lifetime on a particular therapy. I am supposed to be a discussant of his paper. But I am a person who has spent a lifetime in a completely different way of thinking. And as much as I try to be respectful of his ideas and to understand what he is saying, the truth is that we are speaking completely different languages. I do not recognize people outside of context. I do not recognize the people whom Albert Ellis describes. To me, the concepts of circularity and feedback are concepts between people, not within people. Patients are part of the same system, and I do not see the therapist and the mutual influence of therapists and patients in the way that Dr. Ellis does.

I told Jeff Zeig that I would not be a good discussant of this paper, and that I did not want to discuss it. I explained to him that I am not an expert in the works of Dr. Ellis. I left individual psychotherapy 25 years ago because it seemed too narrow, and my knowledge of the cognitive therapy field, I said, is limited to two books Aaron Beck sent to me when we were colleagues at the University of Pennsylvania, and having played poker with Martin Seligman for a year. Out of a recognition of my ignorance and limitations, I told Zeig that I preferred not to review this paper.

He insisted that I do it. Recognizing a musturbatory must in Zeig, I countered that I should not do it, that I could not do it. I said, "I will appear ridiculous in front of hundreds of people, maybe thousands." And since I thought this would be videotaped, I said, "It will become a document of my incompetence for posterity." On the telephone, my voice trembled; I was sweating.

In response, Zeig's voice was firm. Happiness, he said, comes from avoiding unnecessary overcaution and anxiety. He said that I needed to dispute my belief system—that I needed to shine in front of an audience. I do not need to be loved, he told me firmly, I merely prefer to be loved. I hesitated. I thought and felt reassured that I probably would not make myself a complete ass, and though I prefer to shine and be loved, I could probably survive embarrassment.

But as I was talking—

My eyelids felt heavy. My left hand began to levitate. My unconscious knew that Zeig had uncoded indirection in his directive message. I fell into a trance. I was running with two foxes that were faster than me, and I tried to catch them. I stopped under a tree and looked at its leaves. I woke up. I thought of my time as a psychoanalyst, and I thought that the two foxes were obviously Zeig multiplied by two. The F in foxes is the F of fathers—Zeig's father. Obviously, the tree stood for Milton Erickson. I felt strangely relaxed.

I talked with my wife, with whom I share belief systems, and at this point, a combined memory. I asked her for advice. "What can I do with the author's oversimplification, absolute clarity and shameful certainty?"

Her answer was firm. "You should answer as a family therapist," she said. "You can challenge his simplification with overcomplexity, his clarity with confusion, his certainty with obscure and multiple meanings."

As a family therapist, I agree with her. I was up to the task.

I do feel comfortable with some of the theoretical constructions of Dr. Ellis: the mutual influence of the cognitive, the emotional and the behavioral, and the way in which belief systems participate in the creation of meaning. I see the circular interconnection of goals, beliefs, and consequences, and the power of irrational beliefs in the construction of rigidly held musts and shoulds. I think that, at the core, all therapists are constructivist therapists. But I find it difficult to envision a world populated by people who have clearly defined activating events leading to differentiated beliefs about them that activate nonambivalent consequences.

My world as an individual and as a family therapist is a world of multiple contexts populated by significant people who frequently impinge on me with simultaneous activating events that are frequently in conflict with each other. My belief systems and my responses vary in different social contexts.

As I think of my practice as a family therapist, I recognize that here I am countering Ellis' rigidity with my rigidity, his way of thinking and seeing with my way of thinking and seeing. We are really in two parallel worlds. I don't think there is a dialogue. I think that at the most there can be a mutual recognition that we are competent in what we are doing and that we are helpful to *some* people.

I attended a workshop given by Dr. Ellis and I was impressed by his sense of humor, by his level of energy. I was also impressed by his hands. There is a way in which Dr. Ellis moves his hands that is like a conductor of an orchestra. There is a staccato movement, a punctuation that he does, that is very powerful. At the same time, I observed the way he interviewed a colleague who volunteered for an interview. I saw that he can join. His pushing at people can become benign. At times, he can be convincing and pushing. At times, he can be benign Uncle Albert. So I recognize something that I did not see in his paper: Dr. Ellis as a therapist. I felt the lack of the therapist and the therapist's influence on the patient in the paper when it was so evident in this interview.

Now, as a family therapist, I am usually directive. I think Zeig thought I could be a discussant because I can be as confrontative in my practice as Dr. Ellis is in his. And I also can be as seductive and convincing as he is. But at other times, I am very undirective. I may challenge a phobic system in a patient by working with the total family and dealing with issues of proximity and control in the family and not with the meaning of the phobia. Or I may attribute multiple meanings to the symptom, thus creating confusion. I can say to people who have a phobia, "You don't own the phobia; your parents own it." I change the control of the symptom and give it to other family members. Or I may shift the locus of control from the patient to other family members, and so on. I am never certain that I have all the answers or that my interventions are always appropriate. I am always in doubt, and, therefore, I am continuously overkilling. I introduce many, many different ways of challenging a symptom. I see therapy as a dialogue in which I look from different perspectives at complex human systems in which the same activating events impinge differently on family members with different needs, activating similar or different or conflicting responses. After 39 years as a therapist, probably the same length of time as Dr. Ellis, I have become less certain that we have a magic bullet. In attending workshops over the last three days, I have been more and more impressed by the certainty with which we describe our deepest beliefs. The truth is that the longer I am in this field, the less certain I am. Therefore, I envy, but I question, Dr. Ellis' certainty.*

RESPONSE BY DR. ELLIS

I am going to respond very briefly because I had really bad luck this morning; the gremlins are after me. First, my watch battery broke down; then my hearing-aid battery broke down, so I did not hear clearly what Dr. Minuchin said. But let me respond to what I think some of the points were that he made. His first comment, I think, was that I am too definite and absolutistic

---

* *Editor's Note:* As Conference organizer, the editor is extremely grateful to Dr. Minuchin for serving as discussant for Dr. Ellis' address. As a practitioner of Ericksonian therapy, the editor is extremely grateful to Dr. Minuchin for this object lesson in the elegant use of indirect methods of influence and communication, and hopes that Dr. Minuchin will enjoy finding more foxes beckoning to him in future dreams....

in what I say and in my theory, but in my practice and in my workshop I am quite emotive, I benignly push people, and I have a great energy and a good sense of humor. I think he was surprised by my emotionality in the demonstrations that he witnessed.

Actually, there is no contradiction here because most people wrongly think that rational means unemotional. However, rational, as I define it in RET, means *appropriately emotional*—so that you feel appropriately sad, sorry, and regretful when anything goes wrong in your life, but you feel appropriately happy and pleased when something goes right. And if you use RET, you do not feel inappropriately horrified when something goes wrong. I still say, and have some supporting evidence for this, that when people give themselves absolutist commands and demands, they experience radically different feelings and behaviors than they do when they give themselves preferences and differences.

Rational-emotive therapy has often been misunderstood because I, perhaps unfortunately, used the word rational to describe it. Years ago, I thought of calling it reality therapy. But then I told myself, "Practically all therapies try to help people to get in touch with reality. So I would have chutzpah to call RET reality therapy." And so I stayed with calling it rational-emotive therapy. But *rational* has a lot of connotations in people's minds that it does not have in my own mind. In RET, it largely means self-helping and socially constructive. Consequently, RET is not only rational, logical, and consistent in showing people how scientifically to rip up their dogmatic musts, but it is also a very emotive, dramatic, and evocative set of procedures. Probably, RET is the most emotive of all the cognitive-behavioral therapies. It is deliberately very emotive because it theorizes and observes that people very *hotly* hold onto their prejudices, just as is evident during this conference. The various presenters hotly hold onto their own prejudices and are loath to change them. Therefore, if clients are to be helped, and let us assume that they usually come for help, their therapist had better not just be cool, calm, and nice. Such therapeutic behavior often pleases clients and will help them to *feel* better. But they are not likely to *get* better unless the therapist also shows them how to rigorously and emotively change their Jehovian musts and demands—because they usually very strongly hold onto their *must*urbation and keep "confirming" it. It is the *power* of their dysfunctional beliefs, not merely their illogicality, that gets them and keeps them disturbed.

Dr. Minuchin mentioned my pushing clients during my demonstrations—and, of course, that is what I do. In following, to some degree, Alfred Adler, who was a brilliant cognitive therapist, but who also encouraged and pushed people. I also actively do the same. I push people because my notion is (and it may be an odd notion) that therapy is largely teaching. It consists of strongly interacting with clients in order to teach them how to help themselves. Alas, people often strongly stick to their nutty convictions. So unless you push them, encourage them, and keep after them, they will feel good, but will not greatly work to change themselves.

To help people change, you often have to push, and push, and push; and to use all possible modalities, including—and here I think I agree with Dr. Minuchin—the personality, the drive of the therapist. If the therapist is namby-pamby, is Boy Scout-ish or Girl Scout-ish, as lots of therapists are, I doubt whether the therapist will be too helpful. Unless you use your own personality traits and have a good deal of push and drive to help your many unpushing clients, you will not greatly help those who are pushing very hotly in the wrong direction. As a therapist, you won't get very far unless you use every cognitive, emotive, and behavioral technique that you can possibly dream up, and then invent some more!

QUESTIONS AND ANSWERS

Question: Dr. Ellis, in the context of RET, I find it interesting you use the word "unconscious." I wonder how you define unconscious. And second, in the context of RET, to what extent is it necessary to make the unconscious conscious before you can use it to bring about change?

Ellis: That is a very good question. Freud didn't originate the concept of the unconscious. People forget that there was a lengthy book by a professor of psychology, I think his name was William Hartman, in about 1870 called the *Psychology of the Unconscious*. Also, many dramatists and novelists talked about unconscious things back in the 18th century. But Freud did, unfortunately, originate the idea of a deep, repressed unconscious. I would say that he led the field vastly astray. There are a few things that people really repress, but as recent research has shown, there are thousands of things just below the level of consciousness of which one is unaware. You really think, believe, feel in an unaware manner, but you don't have to dig deeply to get at important unconscious attitudes—like people's underlying shoulds and musts that disturb them.

You can easily disclose what Freud called our preconscious thoughts and feelings. Preconscious was a good term, one of the best that Freud originated. But he unfortunately abandoned it, which just shows how, as I keep saying, Freud had a gene for inefficiency, while some other therapists have a gene for efficiency.

So when you have a philosophy behind what you are doing, and you are doing something dysfunctional, but don't know what your dysfunctional philosophy is, the answer is, "Seek and ye shall find." Assume on theoretical grounds, such as the theory of RET, that you are searching for some preconscious "tyranny of the shoulds," as Karen Horney called it. Assume that disturbed clients have these absolutist shoulds and musts, and then test it out with each individual client. Test it out and, I won't say invariably, but most of the time, you will find that clients easily accept these preconscious musts. When clients say, "I am terribly afraid of public speaking," I ask, "What are you telling yourself to make yourself afraid?" They say, "I don't like to fail." I ask, "Is that all you are thinking?" Either they quickly reply, "I'm telling myself, I must not fail!" or I ask, "Aren't you saying, 'I don't like to fail and I shouldn't!'" They immediately say, "Yes, that's exactly it! I must not fail!"

Thus most of what we call the unconscious, especially our disturbed unconscious, is just below the level of consciousness, and it can easily be brought up by questioning clients about it. Most of the time, they will admit to clear-cut unconscious thoughts. Don't think you need some mysterious Ericksonian way of indirectly getting at it; you don't need that. Direct questioning will help them acknowledge unconscious or preconscious shoulds and musts, usually in about three minutes. Occasionally, unconscious material is deeply repressed, and then you can figure it out through other data, including behavioral data and emotive data. If you suspect its presence, you can keep probing for it and usually find it. In the vast majority of cases, however, what we call "the unconscious" consists of tacit, implicit, or preconscious ideas. It's rarely deeply hidden or repressed.

Question: First a comment: I would agree with Dr. Minuchin that what is going on here is not a dialogue. To me, it more approximates parallel play. At the risk of sounding like there is nothing new "under the sun," and maybe attacking a "must" that you be given credit for what you are saying. I am hearing a lot of what you are saying as similar to Adlerian theory. What is the contrast between what you describe and the Adlerian idea of the early structure of perceptions that are then played out in later life based on making events occur the way one expects them to by the people one selects to have in one's life and the way one operates with those people, thus creating a self-fulfilling prophesy?

Ellis: If I understand your question, you are right that RET overlaps significantly with Adlerian approaches. I have said this in several papers. Alfred Adler was a brilliant cognitivist. I have been a member of the North American Society for Adlerian Psychology for about 20 years, and I think that Adler was an unusually creative theorist and therapist. Unfortunately, he digressed into some Freudian theory, such as the enormous importance of first memories and early childhood. And he may have overdone the concept of a style of life. In RET, we overlap to some degree with Adler—to a considerable degree on the cognitive side. Adler had relatively few behavioral or even emotive interventions except the one, which I mentioned before, of encouragement and hope. He was very good on that. He was very sensible. He wrote in plain language, not jargon, and he wrote largely for the public. To our misfortune, he has been one of the most neglected psychotherapists of all time. He was much saner than Freud and Jung, who were often vague and untherapeutic. I think we should pay much more homage to Alfred Adler than is usually paid.

Question: We develop defenses over the years from powerful influences in our relationships with our parents. It seems that changing people's beliefs doesn't address the powerful defenses that develop when we are very vulnerable. Do you agree?

Ellis: What are called "defenses" is one of the few good parts of the Freudian system. And again, Freud didn't originate that idea, but he went further with it—he and his daughter, Anna. Defenses mean that when one feels ashamed of something, such as hating one's mother or wanting to have sex with her, one is horrified at one's own thoughts and behavior. Therefore, Freud said, people construct a series of defenses to avoid facing that "shameful" fact.

The Freudians often show clients their defenses. But insight into them won't change the irrational beliefs that lead you to construct your defenses. Thus when you are defensive, you may well have the core philosophy, "I *must* not hate my mother!" or, "I *must* not think of sex with my mother," or some other absolutist demand. With such a self-command, you make yourself guilty and depressed, and then you refuse to face your actually hating or lusting after your mother. The RET therapists agree with the Freudians that you are defensive, but then they ask you, "What are you telling yourself to create your guilt and depression?" Dysfunctional feelings of shame, guilt, and depression are intrinsic to defensiveness. And so, in RET, we find your musturbatory ideas that lead to your shame, self-downing, or shithood, we help you to change them and the disturbed feelings they create and thereby uncreate the basic reasons for your defensiveness. Freud wrongly thought that if you show people that they have defenses, they will give them up. But that's not true. You had better, in addition, get to the basic core of philosophy that creates the defenses. That is where Freud failed and Adler succeeded. By showing people that they have a reason for creating their defenses and that the reason is almost always some kind of self-condemning philosophy, RET, like the Adlerians, helps you to reveal this philosophy and effectively change it.

Question: My question pertains more to the process of therapy than to the theory. You said that irrational belief systems are an innate tendency and that most of the therapists who attend this conference will go home with the prejudices that they had when they came. I'm concerned with the process of the therapist who starts to dispute irrational beliefs. Is there an assumption that therapists are rational persons who believe they are disputing the process or beliefs they ought to dispute? It would seem to me that I have my own bias about what is rational and what is not rational. With regard to some obvious things, there may not be a problem, but I'm concerned about the subtle differences a client may bring in.

Ellis: You are assuming, which is what RET assumes, that "rational" means illogical and that there is some realistic or rational answer that therapists know somehow and that clients don't know, and that the therapist gives the client this "rational" answer. "Irrationality" in RET means any thought, feeling, or behavior against the basic interest of the client and his or her social group. If the therapist is not able to see that the client is defeating himself or herself—is not able to figure out that this self-defeating is being constructed and cannot figure out what the person is irrationally thinking, inappropriately feeling, or dysfunctionally doing to needlessly disturb himself or herself—then the therapist had better become a ditch digger and give up therapy!

It is *not* that the therapist has a correct view of rationality, is an intellectually rational person, and the client is not. The client may be more rational than the therapist about many things. Incidentally, some of my clients are professors of logic, and they are better at logic than I am. But they still believe that if they give a lousy lecture, as they absolutely *must* not, that they are real *shits*. I'm not going to argue logic with them; they know it better than I. I just say to them, "When you give a lousy performance,

you don't have to prove that it is sad and unfortunate, because you desire to succeed and by this value, you *make* failure 'unfortunate' or 'bad.' What I want you to prove—or falsify—is the proposition that you completely *must* succeed and are a *total turd* if you don't." So far none of them has shown me any evidence for absolute musts or for turdhood!

In RET, we only dispute unrealistic or irrational Beliefs that are against the client's own interest. But we are not just logicians. We also employ many other cognitive, emotive, and behavioral techniques of disputation. My contention still is when people are neurotic and not when they are borderline or psychotic, they just about invariably seem to have the "tyranny of the shoulds," which Horney nicely pointed out in 1950. I took the idea from her. But I don't think she had a good method of helping people to give up their Jehovian "shoulds." Not only does RET show people that they have grandiose commands ("I must do well!" "You have to treat me beautifully!" "The world must give me exactly what I want!"), but it also shows people how to change these unconditional demands. If they don't want to do that, it gives them full leeway to be just as nutty as they now are!

Minuchin: I think that Dr. Ellis didn't answer that question. The question was about the way in which the therapist's point of view is significant in convincing the patient that the patient's belief is not rational. There is a dialogue between two points of view. The therapist is an expert and is in the position of the one who is the convincer. But it is the therapist's point of view and the point of view of the patient that enter into dialogue. I think Dr. Ellis is an excellent convincer, and it is difficult to argue with him. But at this point he did not answer the question, which was the significance of his point of view and its interaction on the particular way in which he influences the point of view of the patient.

Ellis: I didn't hear it that well. My hearing aid, again, is not working right now.

Minuchin: I think this is wonderful because I don't hear Dr. Ellis's point of view and he doesn't hear what I say very well, so I think we are involved in a most magnificent parallel play.

Ellis: Let me say what I think I heard you say, but I'm not sure. I think you said something to the effect that I have a certain point of view and a certain way of putting it over, and then I can convince the client that he has that point of view, and, therefore, I am effective in getting the client to see my "rational" viewpoint.

Minuchin: I also think there is nothing wrong with that.

Ellis: Right. But the answer to that question is that we now have over 500 experimental studies of RET and cognitive behavior therapy (Lyons & Woods, 1991). (Only one was done by me—a pioneering study years ago; the rest were done by other people.) In these studies, the therapists, trained by us or by Aaron Beck or Don Meichenbaum, help people to challenge and dispute and give up their irrational ideas, and almost all of these studies tend to prove that when people take their irrational ideas—or what Tim Beck calls "dysfunctional attitudes," which is just another name for irrational ideas and attitudes—and change them, the people become significantly improved. We have considerable empirical data of this sort. So it isn't the way I present it or the way I personally convince the client or anything like that.

The studies I just mentioned are not case histories, but controlled research studies. The only kind of therapy that has been more researched than rational-emotive and cognitive-behavior therapy is pure behavior therapy. There are few studies over the years of the effectiveness of psychoanalysis and most other forms of therapy, including family therapy, but there are 500 on the effectiveness of RET and CBT. Thus which of the client's beliefs the therapist *personally* considers "rational" or "irrational" does not seem to be relevant in RET and CBT.

Question: This is a question for Dr. Minuchin. Would you comment on parallels between rational-emotive therapy and Murray Bowen's concept of differentiation of intellectual and emotional systems?

Minuchin: I don't think I can do that.

Ellis: Well, I'll give it a try. I don't remember Bowen's complete theory, but it does overlap with RET in many respects, because Murray Bowen, as I understand him, was a systems therapist. However, he was a different kind of systems therapist. He said that human beings in families often get taken in by the family system, and thus he helped them become individuated. Individuation was a good concept that Carl Jung originally proposed. A lot of what Bowen did was to get people untied from the family system and that overlaps with RET, which tries to get people untied from any system. It tries to enable them to be *in* the system effectively, to get along with family members and with other humans within the system, but not to think they have a dire need for the approval and love of the other members of the system and so become too subservient to and too fused with those system members. I think that, in that respect, we would overlap significantly with Murray Bowen.

Minuchin: I don't think so. This concept of the differentiation is a concept common to all kinds of therapies: it is a universal concept in therapy. Therapists who are system therapists, behavior therapists, or even analysts agree on some level. But differences between RET and Bowen theories are differences that can be expounded on in many volumes. That is why I didn't want to try to answer the question. The way in which Murray Bowen dealt with the process of differentiation is completely different. It involves ways of intervention that are so different that it is beyond the possibility of dialogue here.

One of the things, Dr. Ellis, that I realize here is that I am also hard of hearing, and you are hard of hearing, and I think that this is symbolic of our two worlds. I think we are hard of hearing because we use different languages.

Question: Dr. Ellis, would you comment on the use of RET with children and/or teenagers?

Ellis: Originally, RET was to be used with adults, but it was also available for use by parents, and so many adults I saw started using it with their children. They told me that they could teach bright children, as young as 4 years of age not to be arrant demanders and commanders, and that the children did much better emotionally and behaviorally.

In 1966, I wrote a book on the use of RET with families and children in 1966, *How to Raise an Emotionally Healthy, Happy Child*. From 1971 to 1975, the Institute for Rational-Emotive Therapy in New York ran a school for children where we actually taught RET in the classroom. Therapists taught the teachers and the teachers taught the children how to use RET. For five years, we found it pretty effective, although we didn't have a control group, because we only had two small classes in our school and they both used RET. But, since that time, almost 20 empirical studies have been done showing that when RET is taught to children in a classroom situation, or by their parents, or by a therapist, the children become significantly less disturbed. If you want further material on this, there is a book edited by myself and Michael Bernard (Ellis & Bernard, 1983), *Rational-Emotive Approached to the Problems of Childhood*. Michael Bernard and Maria Joyce (1984) have also published *Rational-Emotive Therapy with Children and Adolescents*, and Dr. Ann Vernon (1989) has a book, *Thinking, Feeling and Behaving*, which has exercises for teachers and parents to use to help children use RET.

I thought at first we could get children of 6 or 7 years of age in our classroom to learn RET. We found that they learned it, but they didn't use it. Piaget was more correct than I was because he said that children don't reach the age of formal operations until 8. We found that from the age 8 onward children not only could learn RET, but could use it and give up some of their low frustration tolerance and their self-downing. If you look at our catalog, available from the Institute for Rational Emotive Therapy (45 East 65th Street, New York NY, 10021), you will see considerable RET material for and about children. We find that although the disputing of irrational Beliefs doesn't work as effectively with young children as with older ones, they do quite well with coping self-statements. From the age of 12 to 14 upward, adolescents do pretty well with regular cognitive, emotive, and behavioral RET.

Minuchin: All my life, I have worked with children. I was a child psychiatrist, and then I became a child analyst. I left all of that because I began to think that one could not work with children without including their families. The idea of working in any kind of therapy with young children that does not include the influence of the family and working with the family is one of the scotomas that therapists have. Child therapy is family therapy. Sometimes one can intervene in particular ways—RET, or psychoanalysis, or whatever—but it is, in effect, an intervention that needs to take place in the midst of the family. I really don't see how one can work with children without including parents.

Ellis: I agree that working with both parents and their children is highly preferable, but we also have many instances where RET has helped children when used with them mainly by therapists and teachers.

REFERENCES

Bernard, M. E., & Joyce, M. R. (1984). *Rational-emotive therapy with children and adolescents*. New York: Wiley.

Ellis, A., & Bernard, M. E. (Eds.). (1983) *Rational-emotive approaches to the problems of childhood*. New York: Plenum.

Ellis, A., Wolfe, J. L., & Moseley, S. (1966). *How to raise an emotionally healthy, happy child*. North Hollywood, CA: Wilshire Books.

Lyons, L. C., & Woods, P. J. (1991). The efficacy of rational-emotive therapy: A quantitative review of the outcome research. *Clinical Psychology Review, 11*, 357–369.

Vernon, A. (1989). *Thinking, feeling, behaving: An emotional education curriculum for children*. Champaign, IL: Research Press.

Clinical/Therapeutic Effectiveness: Banning the Procrustean* Bed and Challenging 10 Prevalent Myths

Arnold A. Lazarus, Ph.D.

Arnold A. Lazarus, Ph.D.

Arnold Lazarus is Distinguished Professor at the Graduate School of Applied and Professional Psychology at Rutgers University. Lazarus serves on the editorial board of nine professional journals. He also has served as president of the Association for Advancement of Behavior Therapy, and he is a recipient of the Distinguished Service to the Profession of Psychology Award from the American Board of Professional Psychology. He received the Ph.D. degree in 1960 from the University of the Witwatersrand, Johannesburg, South Africa. He has written, been the coauthor, editor, or coeditor of 14 books, and has written and been the coauthor of more than 200 professional papers and chapters.

Arnold Lazarus outlines ten myths about psychotherapy and then presents a detailed exposition and rebuttal. The treatment of a young man with panic disorder is discussed as an exemplar of the need to apply data-based treatments of choice within the context of clinical artistry. Technical eclecticism is defined and is offered as a possible solution to many common misconceptions.

The extraordinary growth of psychotherapy has spawned a profusion of theories, methods, and techniques, plus a host of ill-defined terms and a slew of misconceptions. The resultant chaos appears to be perpetuated mainly by several widespread myths, some contradictory to others, some interconnected:

Myth 1.   The in-depth training provided by a specific system or school of psychotherapy is the best way to advance knowledge and help clients.

Myth 2.   Integration or theoretical eclecticism augments the psychotherapeutic database and has synergistic effects.

Myth 3.   A sound therapeutic relationship is usually both necessary and sufficient to produce significant change.

Myth 4.   Common factors account for most of the outcome variance, and all approaches achieve essentially equal results.

Myth 5.   There are no well-documented treat-

---

*In Greek mythology, Procrustes was a villainous son of Poseidon who forced travelers to fit into his bed by stretching their bodies or cutting off their legs.

ments of choice for particular problems or specific strategies for specific syndromes.

Myth 6. Cognitive therapy and behavior therapy are, at best, superficial; genuine change calls for attention to dreams, unconscious motivation, and intense feelings.

Myth 7. The therapist should have all members of the social network present at the initial interview, and unless all members of that network are treated, outcomes will be unbalanced or otherwise unsatisfactory.

Myth 8. What transpires in the patient–therapist relationship is a microcosm of all significant interactions in the patient's environment.

Myth 9. Changes that accrue in the office, in the consulting room, or in a therapeutic group automatically generalize to the extratherapeutic environment.

Myth 10. Terms without concrete referents contribute to the understanding of problem generation or resolution (e.g., archetypes, borderline personality, transference).

Some of these beliefs represent occasional or half-truths. For example, there are instances where common factors do play a more significant role than specific techniques, and with certain clients, it is essential to involve the entire social network. Nevertheless, as I hope to show, most of these beliefs are blatantly untrue. They stem from the psychotherapeutic literature; from workshops, panels, seminars, lectures, and other professional meetings; and from discussions with colleagues who do not necessarily share my opinions. A systematic rebuttal of each one will occupy more space than I have been allotted, but by the end of the chapter, all ten will have been covered.

What have we learned from the 1985 Evolution of Psychotherapy Conference in Phoenix, Ariz.? I was amazed to discover that many attendees avoided all addresses, workshops, debates, and panels that did not feature their particular hero. Likewise, most faculty members did not avail themselves of the opportunity to learn something from one or more of the other world authorities in attendance. The *Proceedings* of this landmark conference (Zeig, 1987) reveals remarkably little interdigitation; it would seem that each personage is lost in his or her own ivory tower and is concerned only with the intellectual icons contained therein.

Now, five years later, will this conference be different? Borrowing the punch line of an old joke, I submit that it will be exactly the same— only worse! What Larson (1980) described as a "dogma eat dogma" environment now also seems to suffer from what has been referred to as a "hardening of the categories" (see O'Hanlon, 1990). One who pays close attention to the views expressed by many of the authorities at this conference will discover considerable dogmatism, scorn for nonbelievers, a sense of mission, unwarranted faith in the efficacy of notions and methods that have little or no experimental backing, and ardent support for one or more of the ten fallacious beliefs that I will address.

CULTISM

We all know more or less why cultism holds such mass appeal. Committed cult members find that ingatherings satisfy their need for belonging, while providing a sense of identity, purpose, meaning, affiliation, and cohesion. The in-group spirit of solidarity usually offers a context wherein truth and virtue become the sole province of the members of that particular clan, tribe, order, gang, brotherhood, sisterhood, political party, or school of psychological thought. The widespread need for leaders, gurus, and padrones seems so compelling that virtually anyone with a tinge of charisma and a credible party line can attract overzealous adherents who soon assume the cloaks of disciples and eagerly recite lists of grievous consequences to all dissenters. In this atmosphere, the perpetuation of self-proclaimed truths becomes assured, and disconfirming facts are not only dismissed, but strongly censured and censored.

The history of the psychotherapeutic movement is replete with instances of the foregoing dynamics. Doctrinaire and dogmatic leaders and followers waged bloody battles against rival theorists long before and after Freud, Jung, and Adler parted company. The high priests of psychological health engaged in competitive strife and internecine battles and displayed blind hostility to alternative concepts and techniques. Thus today we have literally hundreds of schools of psychotherapy that have produced "a deafening cacophony of rival claims" (Norcross & Grencavage, 1990, p. 4).

Many are of the opinion that bloody professional warfare is a relic of earlier decades of psychotherapy. They claim that reapprochement, convergence, and integration have replaced the territoriality and petty rivalries of bygone years. I think they are mistaken. For example, a book by Saltzman and Norcross (1990) with the ironic and provocative title *Therapy Wars* supposedly emphasizes the virtues of transtheoretical dialogue, but I assert that the discerning reader will find more contention than convergence and no shortage of divarication. There is still a powerful propensity to promote preconceived agendas instead of embracing the pragmatic dictum of using what works. It is unfortunate that reputations seem to profit more from emphasizing putative differences than from stressing real similarities.

Recently, at a conference where most of the presenters and attendees were members of a particular psychotherapeutic school, I managed to gain further insights into the workings of cults. In addition to the sense of belonging and identity that the faculty and their followers enjoyed, another powerful reinforcer was evident. Within that orbit, prestige and status could be dispensed. Thus I witnessed the crowning of a new Director of Clinical Training. Outside the orbit of this particular school of thought, he was by no means a ranked player, let alone a top seed (to use a tennis analogy). But within the confines of that peer group, he was now Number 3, an acknowledged leader—only the system innovator and his chief-of-staff were higher on the totem pole. Where else could he have achieved such recognition? Is it not easier to learn to ride one particular horse than to become an all-round equestrian?

Many continue to inquire why I refuse to launch a *Journal of Multimodal Therapy* or to distribute a *Multimodal Therapy Newsletter*. The reason is simple. To do so would be to foster the very thing to which I am ideologically opposed—an in-group mentality and the formation of yet another school or system to add to the hundreds in existence. Instead, the multimodal orientation (Lazarus, 1989) espouses a *technical eclecticism* that remains open to effective methods and tactics from any discipline and rests mainly on a broad cognitive-social learning theory (Bandura, 1986). There is little doubt that had I assembled a coterie of multimodal adherents and offered training workshops leading to certificates of competence (and perhaps thrown in a multimodal picnic here and there), a lively and perhaps profitable band of zealots could have been created. However, these maneuvers do not promote knowledge; they only encourage reiteration of findings that fit the needs and perceptions of the protagonists and their followers.

While several surveys suggest that between one third and one half of American psychotherapists identify themselves as eclectics (see Dryden & Norcross, 1990), in many quarters, it is still *in*, or highly fashionable, to belong to a particular school of thought. "I'm a person-centered therapist." "I'm a cognitive therapist." "I'm a psychoanalyst." What happens when a client who needs a cognitive therapist consults a person-centered therapist and vice versa? A survey led me to conclude that consumers usually get not necessarily what they need, but what the therapist happens to practice (Lazarus, 1989). "You are my client. This is what I do." Never mind what the client requires. Imagine a patient in need of a tonsillectomy who undergoes a prostatectomy because the surgeon whom the patient consulted just happens to practice urology!

What may we infer when someone identifies himself or herself as a Jungian, a Freudian, a neo-Freudian, an Adlerian, a Rogerian, a behaviorist, a cognitive therapist, a Transactional Analyst, a Gestalt therapist, and so forth? I submit that a careful history will reveal motivations that have little or nothing to do with the objective merits of the orientation they embrace. System innovators and their followers tend to believe what they believe, and do what they do, not on the basis of objective data, but as the direct consequence of personal appeal. Obviously, our experiences shape our beliefs and perceptions, but might not our clients derive more benefit if our theories and methods were selected not on the basis of subjective meaning and attraction, but on the grounds of scientific evidence and relevance to their particular problems? (So much for myth 1, that committed school adherents are most likely to advance knowledge and promote clinical results.)

Perhaps a case history might consolidate and clarify several points that have been raised and underscore a number of additional facts and fallacies.

TREATING A YOUNG MAN WITH PANIC DISORDER

A 33-year-old accountant experienced a panic attack while driving to work. He thought that something had gone wrong with his heart and that he was dying. He drove to the side of the road, stopped his car, opened the door, and "collapsed in the street." The young man ended up in the emergency room of a local hospital and was discharged a few hours later. "The doctor said I had an anxiety reaction." The next morning, as he started up his car, he experienced the same sensations (fear, tachycardia, dizziness, dyspnea, trembling, sweating, chest pains, nausea, and chills). His wife drove him to his family doctor, who examined him and then prescribed Ativan. "Every day became a struggle," he said. Within a month, he had accumulated a wide range of avoidant behaviors. "These attacks starting coming on anywhere and everywhere, not only while driving, but also at movies, in restaurants, in crowded places, and even when just relaxing and visiting friends.... So I tried to keep away from all those people and places, and this ended up putting a huge strain on my marriage."

On the advice of a relative, he consulted a social worker, who saw him approximately four times a week for two months. "I wasn't getting anywhere so I quit and called a psychologist whose name I picked out of the Yellow Pages. ... He wanted me to come in with my wife and my brother. If my parents weren't in Florida, he'd have wanted them to come in too."

"I guess he practices family therapy," I said. "So how long did you see him?"

"Are you kidding?" he replied. "I wouldn't go near the guy. It serves me right for trying to do a thing like that through the Yellow Pages. ... I'm not a kid or a basket case. Besides, I'd sooner ask my worst enemy for help than turn to my brother."

"Why is that?" I inquired.

"Because my brother is envious of me ... and would gloat and put me down. ... He was an only child for 10 years before I came along."

A brief discussion about his family interactions pointed to the destructive role that somewhat distant but overly critical parents seemed to have played. As will be seen, a specific treatment plan was formulated to meet the client's personal needs, while administering research-based treatments of choice. (This touches on myth 7, the need for all significant others to be present.)

I obtained a report from the social worker, which was, in my estimation, an astonishing document. It started out with relatively benign speculations concerning the client's supposed ambivalence, dependency, resistance, regressive tendencies, passive-aggressive penchant, and some lingering, unresolved oedipal issues. But then it referred to cannibalistic images that were somehow tied to his poor object relations and sibling rivalry, and involved another employee at his place of work towards whom the client allegedly harbored homosexual and homicidal impulses. Prognosis was "poor" for this "narcissistic, borderline personality disorder." The treatment of choice, of course, was intensive psychoanalysis, but the catch-22 was that his entrenched resistance would probably undermine the therapy.

For many years (Lazarus, 1971, 1989), I have advocated a flexible, personal therapeutic stance that tries to calibrate the goodness-of-fit of the treatment to the client's basic style. Many therapists agree with this in principle, but fail to carry it out in practice. There is a quote from Milton Erickson in the front of Zeig and Gilligan's (1990) edited book on *Brief Therapy*: "Each person is a unique individual. Hence psychotherapy should be formulated to meet the uniqueness of the individual's needs, rather than to tailor the person to fit the procrustean bed of a hypothetical theory of human behavior."* I submitted the title of this invited address before the Zeig–Gilligan volume appeared, and was pleased to learn that Erickson, who seemed to practice what he preached, would have applauded the title (if not the content) of my presentation. But Jay Haley will doubtless speak to that with great authority.

When it comes to the treatment of panic disorders, are there data attesting to prescribed treatments of choice? Indeed there are. "At the heart of the psychological treatment of panic are reproduction of and exposure to the somatic symptoms of panic. . . . All psychological treatments for panic with any demonstrable success have this process as a core ingredient" (Barlow, 1988, p. 447). Moreover, after reviewing the wide-ranging drug studies, Barlow concluded that tricyclics seem preferable to benzodiazepines and noted that the addition of imipramine to exposure-based treatment may enhance the clinical effects.

By contrast, what are the chances of overcoming most panic disorders if we provide a therapeutic relationship based on congruence, unconditional positive regard, and empathic understanding, which Rogers (1957) considered necessary and sufficient conditions for constructive personality change and problem resolution—an opinion that his followers still echo to this day (Bozarth, 1990)? While there are instances where the therapeutic relationship is itself the vehicle for therapeutic change, in which case it may be sufficient and even necessary, most people with panic disorder will find the context of patient–therapist rapport the soil that enables the techniques to take root (Lazarus & Fay, 1984a). Thus scientific studies tell us what needs to be done, but ultimately, it is the therapist's *artistic talents* that determine how proven methods are best implemented.

Ed. Note: The history of the quote is as follows: When I organized the 1980 International Congress on Ericksonian Approaches to Hypnosis and Psychotherapy, I asked Erickson for a quote to be printed in the Congress promotional brochure that was first distributed in 1979. The quote was published in the printed proceedings of that Congress and appears in the front of the proceedings of the three subsequent International Erickson Congresses.

Artistic competence, however, is seldom sufficient. If someone with a severe panic disorder is treated by the most gifted artists within Freudian, Jungian, Adlerian, Gestalt, Transactional, or existential camps, whatever gains may accrue, rapid and durable elimination of the panic per se is not likely to be one of them. Too many clinicians are apt to adhere to their favorite ideological structure, even when clinical facts do not support it. Poseidon's villainous son Procrustes lives on in many guises. But let me stop digressing (or regressing) and return to the 33-year-old man and his severe panic disorder who was left dangling several paragraphs ago.

It was soon clear that the young man had an inquiring mind. He was delighted when I pulled books off my shelf and shared conclusions from data-based studies with him. A therapist's credibility is often buttressed by demonstrating that the recommended procedures have been endorsed by respected researchers. The position I endeavored to assume was that of an inspiring teacher, a role that the client found especially congenial. As he put it: "I like how you explain what you do and why you do it." Initially, my stance was one of high direction and high support (Howard, Nance, & Myers, 1987), but as therapy progressed, I became somewhat less directive. When it became clear, early in treatment, that the client secretly attributed his problems to cardiac insufficiency, I urged him to have a complete physical examination, including an electrocardiogram. This provided him with a clean bill of health. He also drew considerable comfort from perusing the diagnostic criteria in the revised third edition of the *Diagnostic and Statistical Manual of Mental Disorders* for panic disorder with and without agoraphobia (300.21 and 300.01). "That's amazing!" he exclaimed. "It describes me to a tee!"

When he wondered how the panic attacks came about, I explained that they could be precipitated by cognitions, images, or sensations, and asked him to hyperventilate for two minutes. He experienced a full-blown panic attack before reaching the 90-second mark. Immediately, he was shown how to gain control of his unpleasant sensations and their accompanying terrors via deep muscle relaxation, rhythmic diaphragmatic breathing, calming self-statements, and mental imagery. The fact that a panic attack had been deliberately evoked and extinguished seemed to inspire confidence in his capacity to overcome his problem. We then focused on the *preventive* aspects of slow abdominal breathing, relaxation, meditation, mental imagery, and similar stress-reducing methods (Lazarus, 1984; Zilbergeld & Lazarus, 1988).

His physician had no objection to prescribing imipramine instead of Ativan, although he recommended that the client take both medications for the first three weeks while gradually tapering off the Ativan. The next step consisted of urging the client to enter into all situations that he had been avoiding. Armed with a brown paper bag into which he could breathe to offset possible undercurrents of hyperventilation, together with the knowledge that he was on "antipanic medication" and had acquired an arsenal of panic-control techniques, he carried out his homework with increasing confidence, despite initial trepidation.

Cognitive restructuring and assertiveness training were then implemented. He was disabused of several common mistaken beliefs (Lazarus & Fay, 1975) and related issues, such as perfectionism, dichotomous reasoning, excessive shoulds and musts, and needless self-blame (Ellis & Harper, 1975). Particular emphasis was placed on disputing catastrophic thoughts linking unpleasant physical sensations to imminent death.

Session frequency was reduced from twice weekly to once a week, then to once a fortnight, and finally to once a month. His family dynamics (e.g., mutual antagonism vis-à-vis his brother and reactions to his hypercritical parents) and other interpersonal issues (e.g., coping with difficult co-workers) became the main focus of our attention. Role-playing methods, the empty-chair technique, and some training in paradoxical communications seemed to take the sting out of these negative encounters and enabled him to put his assertiveness training to good use. He took comfort in my observation that whereas it is preferable to have loving closeness between siblings, this is not always achievable and is certainly not mandatory. With a wry smile, he remarked: "I'll take that as per-mission from an objective authority not to give myself a hard time for hating my brother's guts!"

My plan was to have him weaned from the imipramine while augmenting in vivo exposure, but after a month's hiatus, he announced that he had summarily stopped the medication without ill effects. "In fact, I feel better all around," he remarked, "and it certainly feels great not having a dry mouth all the time" (a common side effect of the medication). A couple of booster sessions three months apart put the cap on his therapy.

This was not a case of short-term, time-limited, or brief therapy. Most of the work was carried out during 44 sessions extending over 10 months. A follow-up indicated that he has had no panic attacks for well over a year, although he suffers occasionally from anticipatory anxiety. Nevertheless, he claims that these attacks are short-lived and readily aborted. As a relevant aside, the client attributed most of his gains to his new-found assertiveness and communication skills. He mentioned in passing that his marriage had improved considerably.

Might I add that in the many hours I spent with this man, I found nothing to support the homicidal, homosexual, narcissistic, or borderline features that his previous therapist had underscored. Nevertheless, drawing on the equivalency of outcome hypothesis, (i.e., that all approaches to therapy yield identical outcomes and that there are no well-documented treatments of choice), some may contend that the client would have fared no better, and no worse, had he received psychoanalysis, family therapy, or any other approach, provided that he and the therapist "hit it off." Let us examine this unfortunate but persistent belief. (Some attention has now been given to rebutting myths 3, 5, and 6—that a sound therapeutic alliance is usually necessary and sufficient, that no well-documented techniques exist for specific conditions, and that cognitive therapy is superficial.)

THE COMMON-FACTORS MYTH

I now wish to challenge the widely held view that factors common to all therapies are the true agents of change, that specific differences in method and technique are largely irrelevant, and that all approaches to therapy achieve equivalent outcomes (Myth 4).

As Giles (1983a, 1983b, 1990) has shown, these unwarranted conclusions derive mainly from flawed studies, such as that by Luborsky, Singer, and Luborsky (1975), and from erroneous meta-analyses, such as the work of Smith, Glass, and Miller (1980). They are confounded by the fact that a large number of conditions tend to remit spontaneously, may be helped by fortuitous life circumstances, or are positively influenced by expectancy or placebo effects (Lambert, 1986). Thus even a rather inept clinician may achieve a pretty consistent 50 percent remission rate, unless he or she happens to be truly noxious or specializes in the treatment of clients with heavy substance-abuse problems, severe character disorders, extreme impulse-control disorders, or other especially difficult disturbances.

Nevertheless, treatments of choice or prescriptive therapies have been well documented for a variety of conditions, including bulimia nervosa, compulsive rituals, social-skill deficits, bipolar depression, schizophrenia, focal phobias, tics and habit disorders, asthma related to large-airway obstruction, pain management, hyperventilation, panic disorders, autism, enuresis, vaginismus and other sexual dysfunctions, and a variety of stress-related disorders (e.g., Bandura, 1986; Barlow, 1988; Clark, Salkovskis, & Chalkley, 1985; Fairburn, 1988; Foa, Steketee, Grayson, & Doppelt, 1983; Franks, Wilson, Kendall, & Foreyt, 1990; Grayson, Foa, & Steketee, 1985; Hersen & Bellack, 1985; Lehrer, Hochron, McCann, Swartzman, & Reba, 1986; Mueser & Berenbaum, 1990; Murphy, Lehrer, & Jurish, 1990; Leiblum & Rosen, 1989; O'Leary & Wilson, 1987; Öst & Sterner, 1987; Rachman & Wilson, 1980; Salkovskis & Westbrook, 1989; Wilson & Smith, 1987; Woolfolk & Lehrer, 1984). It is significant that virtually all the aforementioned sources are drawn from the field of cognitive-behavior therapy. Whether it is necessarily the preferred or optimal form of psychological treatment for the above-mentioned disorders is open to debate. But as Wilson (1990) has stressed: "What is undeniable is that the approach has been shown to work; no evidence

suggests that it might be less effective than alternative methods" (p. 282).

To offset a possible misunderstanding, let us inquire whether I am guilty of the same dogmatism and procrustean maneuvers of which I am so critical. Do I carry a torch for cognitive-behavior therapy? Not at all. I am not a "cognitive behavior therapist," but a *clinical psychologist* who adopts a flexible technically eclectic position. I draw heavily from social and cognitive learning theory because its tenets are grounded in research and are open to verification or disproof, but I am aware of its limitations (e.g., it cannot, in my estimation, adequately account for dissociative phenomena). But I respect empirical research, and those with a cognitive-behavioral bent are the ones who conduct most of the nonbiologically based studies. As a therapist, I do not slavishly adhere to any orientation. Instead, while attempting to offer what each client appears to require, I span the gamut of styles, ranging from quiet, pensive, existential reflection to active, directive coaching, teaching, modeling, and instructing. My focus swings back and forth between the individual and his or her agenda, to the client's social milieu and its contextual relevance.

Legal definitions concerning standards of patient care and the criteria for malpractice and negligence are changing. Patients have a right to the proper treatment, and therapists have a responsibility to administer effective treatment. As Klerman (1990) underscored, "Practitioners and institutions who continue to rely on forms of treatment with limited efficacy will be on the defensive and at possible jeopardy for legal action" (p. 417). With so-called common or garden-variety neurotics, good listening skills, a touch of empathy, and a shoulder to cry on can go a long way. Results will probably be quite similar whether these clients lie on a couch, jump up and down, punch pillows, scream, relax, think, meditate, examine their dreams, delve into their past, undo their family triangulations and collusions, or contemplate their navel. But let us hope that therapists of all persuasions will soon know when to give up their favorite playthings and provide the highly focused, specific, and systematic forms of treatment that are demonstrably effective and often required. The literature often has made reference to patients' right to treatment and their right to refuse treatment. Now we will be hearing more about patients' rights to safe and *effective* treatment (Wilson, 1990).

INTEGRATION—A PSEUDOSOLUTION

Most would agree on the virtues of a unified, integrated approach to psychological treatment based on effective therapeutic strategies drawn from diverse theories and approaches. On paper, this appears to be distinctly antiprocrustean. Unfortunately, in practice, this ideal has resulted in the indiscriminate use of ill-defined concepts and dubious methods drawn from incompatible notions, often including fads that have no adequate theoretical rationale or any empirical support (Norcross, 1986). Psychodynamic and behavioral orientations figure most prominently in the literature on integration. The rationale is that psychodynamic and behavioral approaches each have particular strengths that can complement the weaknesses of the other. The major strength of a psychodynamic orientation is said to be its focus on underlying processes, whereas the strength of behavior therapy is the manner in which emphasis is placed on target behaviors and interventions that enable patients to act in ways that can facilitate corrective experiences.

On the face of it, this rapprochement sounds sensible, but logic and reason fall by the wayside when we look for guidelines concerning which of the putative "underlying processes" to accept, which ones to discard, and upon what grounds to arrive at these conclusions. The psychodynamic orientation is distinguished by the failure of its proponents to arrive at any consensus regarding "underlying processes." Apart from the well-known rift among Freud, Jung, Adler, and the large number of splinter groups that developed, one finds more contemporary psychodynamic thinkers—Kohut, Winnicott, Hartmann, Mahler—at odds both with their progenitors and with one another. All too typical of psychodynamic thinking are the comments of Jacob Arlow (1989), a prominent spokesperson within psychoanalytic and psychodynamic circles: "Unfortunately, there exists no adequate study evaluating the results of psychoanalytic

therapy. In a general way, this is true of almost all forms of psychotherapy. There are just too many variables to be taken into account to make it possible to establish a controlled, statistically valid study of the outcome of the therapy" (p. 42). One paragraph later he states: "Nonetheless, the fact remains that when properly applied to the appropriate condition, psychoanalysis remains the most effective mode of therapy yet devised" (p. 43). What an immaculate leap of faith!

Agras (1987) has suggested that if and when outcome studies establish the effectiveness of psychodynamic psychotherapies, one might begin to consider the potential value of a behavioral–psychodynamic integration. Nevertheless, it remains unclear how one would ever integrate psychoanalysis and behavior therapy since behavioral constructs are grounded in operational definitions, whereas most psychoanalytic tenets are not experimentally verifiable.

Technique effectiveness is not proof of the theory that spawned it. Methods may prove effective for reasons other than those that initially gave birth to it. You need not subscribe to Gestalt theory in order to employ a Gestalt technique. Often, when trying to combine different theories, one ends up inadvertently embracing incompatible notions. While some theories, such as social learning theory and general systems theory, lend themselves to integration (Kwee & Lazarus, 1986), practitioners are well advised to avoid selecting bits and pieces from divergent theories, and to search instead for testable, replicative, and effective methods of therapeutic change, unsullied by any notions culled from hearsay.

If practitioners paid heed to more data-based findings, myths 8 and 9 could hardly be endorsed (i.e., that patients' responses within the therapeutic relationship are a veridical microcosm of significant life encounters, and that changes inside therapy are necessarily reflected in corresponding gains outside of the treatment setting). At times, a client's predominant reaction to a therapist may stem from past encounters with a person or people who had had a particular impact, but situation and person specificity should not be ruled out. There is little cross-situational consistency of personality traits (Mischel & Peake, 1982), which makes it essential to promote corrective emotional experiences in the appropriate situational context, rather than exclusively within the confines of the therapist's office. The relationship to a therapist in an artificial setting is secondary to the specific significant interpersonal relationships in daily life. A major goal in all treatments is to ensure that changes extend to the world outside the therapist's office. Generalization of treatment-induced change calls for homework and other bridging maneuvers (Lazarus & Fay, 1984b).

Perhaps a good deal of confusion derives from the tendency to assume that when exploring conflicts and getting clients in touch with their emotions, one is necessarily practicing "psychodynamic psychotherapy." A well-rounded clinician may address defensive reactions (not "defense mechanisms") and examine unconscious processes or nonconscious reactions (not the reified "unconscious mind") without subscribing to the surplus constructs and putative complexes that so many "psychodynamic" practitioners espouse (see Lazarus, 1989).

JARGON

I have touched on each of the fallacious beliefs outlined at the beginning of this chapter except for the last—the use of ill-defined terms. Jargon appears to be used for three main reasons. First, it covers up the speaker's ignorance and presents a front of erudition to the uninitiated. Second, it provides a vehicle for group identification. And third, it lends an air of mystification that has an allure for all too many. I have friends and colleagues who enjoy joking around with Orwellian double-talk coupled with psychobabble and pure gibberish: "The transferential preparadigmatic, pseudoepistemological, dialectical, hermeneutic ontological apperceptions have metaphysical and positivistic lacunae that attenuate constructionistic metatheoretical and fundamental phenomenological contextualized and deterministic intentionality."

In the interest of space limitations, let us focus only on the terms "transference" and "countertransference," since they are bandied about with great regularity.

We hear about positive transference, nega-

tive transference, transference neurosis, analysis of transference, and transference cure. Many will say, "I have a negative countertransference," implying simply that they dislike a particular client. Of course, the term stands for much more; at the very least, that the therapist's repressed feelings are coming into play through identification or through responding subjectively to the patient's expression of hostility.

Who would question the observation that human beings are capable of behaving toward people in the present as they once behaved toward significant others in the past? And who would disagree that people tend to repeat past relationships that are sometimes inappropriate to the present? When using the term transference, many are referring to these processes. But transference is not simply a matter of attributing to new relationships various characteristics belonging to old or former ones. Were this the case, transference would be a synonym for stimulus and response generalization. However, transference is far more complex. The term refers to reliving or reestablishing, with whomsoever will permit it, an infantile situation that is deeply desired because it previously had been either greatly enjoyed or greatly missed. It involves forgotten but significant conflict-laden childhood memories and repressed unconscious fantasies, and much more (Arlow, 1989).

The point I am stressing here is that we often use ill-defined terms, or employ well-defined terms idiosyncratically, thereby obfuscating meaningful dialogue. Our discipline spawns more confusion than any of us can handle. We certainly do not need to add unnecessary linguistic hurdles to boot. My plea is that we replace jargon with everyday language whenever possible.

It seems to me that the evolution of psychotherapy has arrived at the point where the prescriptive selection of psychosocial interventions can respond to the question "What, when, and for whom?" As Beutler and Clarkin (1990) have shown, we now know enough to include sequential assessments of patient dimensions, environments, settings, therapists, and therapies. If we genuinely desire to become efficient and effective clinicians, it seems to me that inquiring and flexible attitudes and a systematic, technically eclectic viewpoint are essential.

REFERENCES

Agras, W. S. (1987). So where do we go from here? *Behavior Therapy, 18,* 203–217.

Arlow, J. A. (1989). Psychoanalysis. In R. J. Corsini & D. Wedding (Eds.), *Current psychotherapies* (4th ed.) (pp. 19–62). Itasca, IL: Peacock.

Bandura, A. (1986). *Social foundations of thought and action: A social cognitive theory.* Englewood Cliffs, NJ: Prentice-Hall.

Barlow, D. H. (1988). *Anxiety and its disorders.* New York: Guilford Press.

Beutler, L. E., & Clarkin, J. F. (1990). *Systematic treatment selection: Toward targeted therapeutic interventions.* New York: Brunner/Mazel.

Bozarth, J. D. (1990). The essence of client-centered/person-centered therapy. In G. Lietaer, J. Rombauts, & R. Van Balen (Eds.), *Client-centered and experiential psychotherapy: Toward the nineties* (pp. 44–51). Leuven: Katholieke Universiteit te Leuven.

Clark, D. M., Salkovskis, P. M., & Chalkley, A. J. (1985). Respiratory control as a treatment for panic attacks. *Journal of Behavior Therapy and Experimental Psychiatry, 16,* 23–30.

Dryden, W., & Norcross, J. C. (Eds.). (1990). *Eclecticism and integration in counseling and psychotherapy.* Essex, England: Gale Centre Publications.

Ellis, A., & Harper, R. A. (1975). *A new guide to rational living.* North Hollywood, CA: Wilshire.

Fairburn, C. G. (1988). The current status of the psychological treatments for bulimia nervosa. *Journal of Psychosomatic Research, 32,* 635–645.

Foa, E. B., Steketee, G., Grayson, J. B., & Doppelt, H. G. (1983). Treatment of obsessive-compulsives: When do we fail? In E. B. Foa & P. M. G. Emmelkamp (Eds.), *Failures in behavior therapy* (pp. 10–34). New York: Wiley.

Franks, C. M., Wilson, G. T., Kendall, P. C., & Foreyt, J. P. (1990). *Review of behavior therapy: Theory and practice.* Vol. 12. New York: Guilford Press.

Giles, T. R. (1983a). Probable superiority of behavioral interventions—I: Traditional comparative outcome. *Journal of Behavior Therapy & Experimental Psychiatry, 14,* 29–32.

Giles, T. R. (1983b). Probable superiority of behavioral interventions—II: Some implications for the ethical practice of psychological therapy. *Journal of Behavior Therapy & Experimental Psychiatry, 14,* 189–196.

Giles, T. R. (1990). Bias against behavior therapy in outcome reviews: Who speaks for the patient? *The Behavior Therapist, 13,* 86–90.

Grayson, J. B., Foa, E. B., & Steketee, G. (1985). Obsessive-compulsive disorder. In M. Hersen & A. S. Bellack (Eds.), *Handbook of clinical behavior therapy with adults* (pp. 133–165). New York: Plenum.

Hersen, M., & Bellack, A. S. (1985) (Eds.). *Handbook of clinical behavior therapy with adults.* New York: Plenum.

Howard, G. S., Nance, D. W., & Myers, P. (1987). *Adaptive counseling and therapy: A systematic approach to selecting effective treatments.* San Francisco: Jossey-Bass.

Klerman, G. L. (1990). The psychiatric patient's right to effective treatment: Implications of *Osheroff v. Chestnut Lodge. American Journal of Psychiatry, 147,* 409–418.

Kwee, M. G. T., & Lazarus, A. A. (1986). Multimodal therapy:

The cognitive-behavioural tradition and beyond. In W. Dryden & W. Golden (Eds.), *Cognitive-behavioural approaches to psychotherapy* (pp. 320–355). London: Harper & Row.

Lambert, M. J. (1986). Implications of psychotherapy outcome research for eclectic psychotherapy. In J. C. Norcross (Ed.), *Handbook of eclectic psychotherapy* (pp. 436–462). New York: Brunner/Mazel.

Larson, D. (1980). Therapeutic schools, styles and schoolism: A national survey. *Journal of Humanistic Psychology, 20,* 3–20.

Lazarus, A. A. (1971). *Behavior therapy and beyond.* New York: McGraw-Hill.

Lazarus, A. A. (1984). *In the mind's eye: The power of imagery for personal enrichment.* New York: Guilford Press.

Lazarus, A. A. (1989). *The practice of multimodal therapy: Systematic, comprehensive and effective psychotherapy.* Baltimore: Johns Hopkins University Press.

Lazarus, A. A., & Fay, A. (1975). *I can if I want to.* New York: Warner Books.

Lazarus, A. A., & Fay, A. (1984a). Behavior therapy. In T. B. Karasu (Ed.), *The psychiatric therapies* (pp. 485–538). Washington, DC: American Psychiatric Association.

Lazarus, A. A., & Fay, A. (1984b). Some strategies for promoting generalization and maintenance. *The Cognitive Behaviorist, 6,* 7–9.

Lehrer, P. M., Hochron, S. M., McCann, B., Swartzman, L., & Reba, P. (1986). Relaxation decreases large-airway but not small air-way asthma. *Journal of Psychosomatic Research, 30,* 13–25.

Leiblum, S. R., & Rosen, R. C. (Eds.). (1989) *Principles and practice of sex therapy* (2nd ed.) New York: Guilford Press.

Luborsky, L., Singer, B., & Luborsky, L. (1975). Comparative studies of psychotherapies: Is it true that everyone has won and all must have prizes? *Archives of General Psychiatry, 32,* 995–1008.

Mischel, W., & Peake, P. (1982). Beyond deja vu in the search for cross-situational consistency. *Psychological Review, 89,* 730–755.

Mueser, K. T., & Berenbaum, H. (1990). Psychodynamic treatment for schizophrenia: Is there a future? *Psychological Medicine, 20,* 253–262.

Murphy, A. I., Lehrer, P. M., & Jurish, S. (1990). Cognitive coping skills training and relaxation training as treatments for tension headaches. *Behavior Therapy, 21,* 89–98.

Norcross, J. C. (Ed.). (1986) *Handbook of eclectic psychotherapy.* New York: Brunner/Mazel.

Norcross, J. C., & Grencavage, L. M. (1990). Eclecticism and integration in counseling and psychotherapy: Major themes and obstacles. In W. Dryden & J. C. Norcross (Eds.), *Eclecticism and integration in counseling and psychotherapy.* Essex, England: Gale Centre Publications.

O'Hanlon, W. H. (1990). A grand unified theory for brief therapy: Putting problems in context. In J. K. Zeig & S. G. Gilligan (Eds.), *Brief therapy: Myths, methods and metaphors* (pp. 78–89). New York: Brunner/Mazel.

O'Leary, K. D., & Wilson, G. T. (1987). *Behavior therapy: Application and outcome* (2nd ed.). Englewood Cliffs, NJ: Prentice-Hall.

Öst, L. G., & Sterner, U. (1987). Applied tension: A specific behavioral method for treating blood phobia. *Behaviour Research and Therapy, 25,* 25–30.

Rachman, S., & Wilson, G. T. (1980). *The effects of psychological therapy*. London: Pergamon.

Rogers, C. R. (1957). The necessary and sufficient conditions of therapeutic personality change. *Journal of Consulting Psychology, 21,* 95–103.

Salkovskis, P. M., & Westbrook, S. (1989). Behaviour therapy and obsessional ruminations: Can failure be turned into success? *Behaviour Research & Therapy, 27,* 149–160.

Saltzman, N., & Norcross, J. C. (1990). *Therapy wars: Contention and convergence in differing clinical approaches.* San Francisco: Jossey-Bass.

Smith, M. L., Glass, G., & Miller, T. (1980). *The benefits of psychotherapy.* Baltimore: Johns Hopkins University Press.

Wilson, G. T. (1990). Clinical issues and strategies in the practice of behavior therapy. In C. M. Franks, G. T.

Wilson, P. C. Kendall, & J. P. Foreyt (Eds.), *Review of behavior therapy*, Vol. 12 (pp. 271–301). New York: Guilford Press.

Wilson, G. T., & Smith, D. (1987). Cognitive-behavioral treatment of bulimia nervosa. *Annals of Behavioral Medicine, 9,* 12–17.

Woolfolk, R. L., & Lehrer, P. M. (Eds.). (1984). *Principles and practice of stress management.* New York: Guilford Press.

Zeig, J. K. (Ed.). (1987). *The evolution of psychotherapy.* New York: Brunner/Mazel.

Zeig, J. K., & Gilligan, S. G. (Eds.). (1990). *Brief therapy: Myths, methods and metaphors.* New York: Brunner/Mazel.

Zilbergeld, B., & Lazarus, A. A. (1988). *Mind power: Getting what you want through mental training.* New York: Ivy Books.

Discussion by Jay Haley, M.A.

◆

It is a pleasure to be asked to comment on the presentation by Dr. Lazarus. I think it is a good one and it is stimulating. It raises many issues related to the evolution of therapy.

A problem for me is that it is so rich and offers such a variety of ideas that it is difficult to make a comprehensive comment. Instead, I will choose aspects of it that interest me and make a few points. One point is that I agree with his myths; I do not see how one could object to them.

I think Dr. Lazarus is approaching therapy as if it ought to be a rational endeavor based on scientific data. Myths should be eliminated and facts should be emphasized. I don't think that is the map that has been, or is being, used for the territory of therapy. It is not that there are scientific truths and there are myths, but rather that, in the therapy field one person's myths are another person's truths.

Suppose, for instance, that therapy had been born as a scientific endeavor with a group of intelligent men and women focused on how to change people with psychological problems who wanted to be changed. They would describe problems in such a way that certain therapy operations would follow and these would lead to the desired changes. Techniques would have been devised, outcome measured, improvements in interventions made, and today there would be a consensus based on scientific data about how to change people. If a man were in a panic about his heart when nothing was wrong with it, certain therapy procedures would logically follow and there would be a consensus on what should be done. Such a rational approach would be preferred by Dr. Lazarus, as I understand his presentation.

However, a scientific consensus has not been achieved among therapists who set out to change people. There is not even an agreement in the field that it is the therapist's task to change people. If one were to ask many people with a psychoanalytic orientation if it is their job to change a client, it is likely that they would say that it is not. Their job is to help people understand themselves, and whether the people change or not is up to them. There is also no agreement about how a therapist should define a problem that is to be changed. Without agreement on the problem, it is difficult to agree on appropriate therapy techniques. To one therapist, an unreasonable fear of dying of a heart attack is a problem of an individual's irrational belief system. To another person, such a fear is a way of defining a relationship with a wife and requiring certain behavior on her part. Many therapists would consider a severe symptom to be best approached through the marriage and would expect improvement in the symptom to correlate with changes in the marriage.

Once I did an outcome study with a few hundred families; I wanted to see if the therapy outcome was better if the client and therapist agreed on what was the problem. This simple task turned out to be quite complex. A mother, for example, would say that the problem was that her child never did what she asked. The therapist reported that the child lacked ego differentiation. Was this the same problem? Often client and therapist do not agree on the problem and speak different languages until the client is taught a clinical view by the therapist.

If we cannot agree on whether or not the task is to change people, and we do not agree on the problem, how can we agree on the cause of the problem? We cannot even agree that the cause is relevant to changing the problem. For example, there once was a theory that a past trauma caused a current phobia. Today some therapists would not agree with that cause. Other therapists would not consider that theory relevant to changing the problem. They argue that theories of how someone got the way he or she is are inappropriate as theories of how to induce change.

It seems to me that it is asking too much to expect a consensus in the therapy field about whether or not to change people, what to change, and how to change them as determined by scientific facts. It is important that we have people like Dr. Lazarus attempting to derive such a consensus, but it can be frustrating.

If one likes history, it might be noted that a century ago there was a serious attempt by intelligent people to define the therapy problem and the psychological field (Ellenberger, 1970). In the 1880s, various investigators attempted to explain a particular phenomenon. They observed that a person would do something and say that he or she could not help it. The person would even do something and then be amnesiac about having done it. Or a person would do something and say he or she could not stop doing it and did not know why. That is, the peo-

ple were trying to explain the involuntary behavior that is characteristic of psychological symptoms. If a person said he or she could not help himself or herself, a rational discussion to persuade the person that such thinking was not rational did not seem helpful. Yet why would the person behave that way?

There were three explanations of such behavior that emerged in the 1880s. One was the idea that the person was driven by ideas outside of awareness. This was the birth, or the creation, of the unconscious as an explanation. If a person did something, did not know why he or she did it, and even had amnesia about doing it, there must be some part of the mind functioning outside of consciousness. Because of the legacy of Mesmer, hypnosis was used to demonstrate that a subject could have amnesia for suggestions, and this supported the hypothesis of an unconscious.

A second explanation that became popular was that the person was possessed by another entity, a spirit, that caused him or her to do what he or she did, and this explained the involuntary behavior. We might note that throughout the world this probably becomes the most popular explanation of involuntary behavior, and whole systems of healing are based on it. That is their science. (Curiously, that work does not seem to be considered as relevant to the evolution of therapy at this conference.)

A third explanation was that the person behaved in this involuntary way because another personality had taken over. It was a popular view that different personalities appeared at different times and amnesia occurred. On this 100th anniversary of these explorations, multiple personality is back in vogue as an explanation. Cases are multiplying. It is reported that in 1980 only about 200 cases of multiple personality disorder were reported in the world literature. In the next decade an estimated minimum of 6,000 cases have been diagnosed in North America alone (Ross & Wozney, 1989).

When it came to the problem of changing involuntary behavior, the most practical technique to use seemed to be hypnosis since it could influence ideas in the unconscious that were causing a person's behavior. That approach proved to be the most popular in the western world and was the nucleus of psycho-dynamic theory, even though hypnosis was later abandoned by that group. It might be noted that the main healing technique in spirit possession is ritual trance, and hypnosis is commonly used with multiple personalities.

In this century, the different techniques of therapy that developed began as deviations from the psychodynamic view. For example, different brief therapies had to defend them-selves as deviations from that orientation, and therapists who wished to use the new approaches had to recover from their training in the psychodynamic view.

As Dr. Lazarus points out, there are now hun-dreds of different therapies and no consensus. We still tend to define a problem as an involun-tary behavior, but many different ways have developed to make a change. Which approach a therapist chooses might be based on, as Dr. Lazarus suggests, a leader of a group, if not a cult leader, rather than on scientific research. I have found it a mystery why one approach in therapy is followed rather than another. The choice of a therapy approach does not seem based on scientific studies of outcome, or even on outcome at all. It seems to be a political mat-ter related to factions in the field. I know of a number of therapeutic approaches to particular problems that prove successful in outcome and yet are overlooked. As an example, an active family therapy with serious drug abusers has been quite successful. Outcome has been stud-ied and written up. Yet addicts are still routinely put in artificial groups and their families are ignored.

The case Dr. Lazarus offers is a classic one in the field. The presenting problem is a man who is in a panic state for fear of dying of a heart attack when there is nothing wrong with his heart. Such a man will say he cannot help himself; it is an involuntary fear. Therefore, reassurances that there is nothing wrong with his heart do not solve the problem. No matter how many doctors have examined him and reassured him, he continues to be in a panic about his heart.

If we approached this case in terms of the myths about therapy outlined by Dr. Lazarus, they are all possible. One way to put them is in terms of opposite dimensions:

1. One can think of therapy as determined by the personality of the therapist or as one that requires training in therapeutic skills. As Dr. Lazarus put it, there is a myth that a sound ther-apeutic relationship is all that is necessary for change. The opposite view is that a therapist needs to know what to do and how to do it to solve such a heart problem.

2. One can think of the problem as a medical problem or as a human dilemma. Even though there is nothing physically wrong with the cli-ent, one might consider it to be in the medical domain. If so, one might use medication. In con-trast, if it is defined not as a medical problem, but as a psychological problem deserving ther-apy, one would examine the person and his social situation in the search for a way to pro-duce a change. Of course, some people would try to define it as both. In such a case, the result can be a social worker's trying to deal with a medical problem without having gone to med-ical school. Or the medical diagnosis can mean trying to collaborate with a physician who is in conflict with the therapy approach, thus con-founding the problem.

3. One can think of the problem as caused by the past or one can think of it as having a func-tion in the present. A past explanation leads to examining the past and assuming that the per-son has interiorized a program from previous experience. If one is focused on the present, the social situation of the person must be examined to find a function of the symptom.

4. One can believe that change requires the client to become aware of what is behind the problem and to understand it according to the therapist's theory. Or, the change can be based on an intervention of a therapist that is not educative of the client; in fact, it can be done outside of awareness. To put it another way, some therapists believe that the machinery of the therapy, and all the techniques used, should be shared by the therapist with the cli-ent. Others believe that the design of the ther-apy should be confined to the therapist.

There are other dimensions, of course, and they come to mind because of the variety of ideas presented by Dr. Lazarus. His case of the fear of heart failure illustrates an important issue that all therapists must consider. The question is whether one should learn a method and apply it to all clients or should design a therapy for each case. Learning a method is easier than learning to innovate a therapy for each client. Yet obviously, with the great variety of problems therapists are expected to solve today, no single method is going to be appropriate for all of them. Once one has learned a variety of interventions, one then faces the question of whether to use a variety of approaches in a single case or to economize and make a single intervention, if that is effective.

Dr. Lazarus dealt with this heart panic by choosing to use a variety of interventions. Over the 44 sessions, he used multiple techniques. The one approach he did not use was to involve the wife or the family in the therapy, except as an empty chair. The client later reported an improvement in the marriage that coincided with the improvement in the symptom, which would be a correlation expected by a family therapist.

If we think of a single intervention or multiple interventions, the heart-panic case chosen by Dr. Lazarus happens to be one where two classic single interventions were reported as successful. One of the earliest published cases involving the use of paradox concerned a client with such a problem. Victor Frankl reported a paradoxical way of dealing with a person who feared a heart attack although nothing was wrong with the person's heart. As I understand it, Dr. Frankl would say to the person who came in with an irrational fear of dying of a heart attack. "Why don't you drop dead of a heart attack right now, here in my office." As he insisted the person drop dead, the person would become angry and not anxious, and at some point would laugh which was what Dr. Frankl wanted the person to do. The panic would subside after that.

A somewhat different approach was used by Milton H. Erickson when dealing with a similar heart panic. He chose to use a family therapy approach. Since such a fear typically involves controlling everyone around by constantly complaining about the heart, the family is usually exasperated by such a person, while also concerned. In one such case, Dr. Erickson interviewed the patient's wife alone and asked her to go to the various funeral parlors in town and collect their literature. When her husband complained of his panic about his heart, she was to quietly distribute the mortuary literature in various places around the house. As she repeated this behavior, the husband recovered from his panic. I have replicated this approach and it is effective. However, it requires some skill in marital therapy, as marital issues come out with the abandonment of the symptom. The family view has now been added to the hypothesis of the unconscious, or spirit possession, or multiple personalities when explaining the involuntary symptom.

I think we can all benefit from differences in our theories and our myths. The approach of Dr. Lazarus in this case is based on a set of assumptions appropriate to the interventions he made. As he points out, if we are to be effective with the variety of problems in therapy, we need flexible attitudes and different technical viewpoints.

REFERENCES

Ellenberger, H. F. (1970). *The discovery of the unconscious.* New York: Basic Books.

Ross, G. R., & Wozney, B. A. (1989). Multiple personality disorder: An analysis of 236 cases. *Canadian Journal of Psychiatry, 314.*

Evolution of Cognitive Behavior Therapy: Origins, Tenets, and Clinical Examples

Donald Meichenbaum, Ph.D.

Donald Meichenbaum, Ph.D.

Donald Meichenbaum (Ph.D., University of Illinois, 1966) is a Professor of Psychology at the University of Waterloo, Canada. He is the associate editor of Cognitive Therapy and Research *and the editor of the* Plenum Series on Stress and Coping. *Meichenbaum serves on the editorial board of a dozen journals. He is a recipient of the Izaak Killam Fellowship Award from the Canada Council. He has published six books and numerous articles, mostly on cognitive behavior modification and coping with stress.*

Donald Meichenbaum surveys the history of cognitive behavior therapy, describes some of the theoretical understructure, and indicates possible applications. Cognitive behavior modification attempts to integrate the clinical concerns of psychodynamic and systemic approaches with the technology of behavior therapy.

Since its inception in the early 1970s, cognitive behavior therapy (CBT) or cognitive behavior modification (CBM) has attempted to integrate the clinical concerns of psychodynamic and systems-oriented psychotherapists with the technology of behavior therapy. It has contributed to the current integrative efforts in the field of psychotherapy. In this chapter, I will briefly describe the origins of CBT and discuss some of the major tenets and theoretical constructs underlying CBT. A comprehensive empirical review of CBT is beyond the scope of this chapter, but a bibliography of such review articles is listed in the references. Finally, the potential integrative focus of CBT in the field of psychotherapy is highlighted.

ORIGINS OF COGNITIVE BEHAVIOR THERAPY

It is difficult to pinpoint a specific person or date to which to attribute the origins of any psychotherapeutic approach. As in most forms of psychotherapy, CBT was the result of an evolutionary process and was part of a zeitgeist. These cross-currents included:

1. A growing dissatisfaction with both the empirical and theoretical basis of a strictly behavioral therapeutic approach (e.g., see Breger & McGaugh, 1965; Brewer, 1974; McKeachie, 1974). Each of these authors questioned the adequacy of learning theory explanations of both psychopathol-

ogy and behavioral change. A related concern was the *limited* generalized improvement that followed from behavioral interventions (see Meichenbaum, 1977).

2. The work on social learning theory, as evident in the writings of Rotter (1966), Bandura (1974), Mischel (1975), and Kanfer and Phillips (1970), highlighted the role of mediated self-regulatory processes. In short, the client's thoughts and feelings were given a primary role in the behavioral change process. Individuals not only reacted to environments, but also helped to create environments. This point was underscored by Richard Lazarus (1966) in his transactional model of stress when he emphasized the role of primary and secondary appraisal processes influencing an individual's coping efforts.

3. As documented by Victor Raimy (1975), a long tradition of semantic therapists from Dubois to George Kelly laid the foundation for CBT. In particular, the work of Albert Ellis, Arnold Lazarus, and Aaron Beck and their colleagues provided a theoretical framework for the development of CBT. As we shall consider below, more recent theoretical and clinical developments in CBT have raised questions about the adequacy of their directive, disputational, rationalist psychotherapeutic approaches. Historically, however, they have contributed significantly to the development of CBT.

4. Finally, CBT developed in the midst of a "cognitive revolution," as Dember (1974) characterized it. Perhaps, a more apt description would be that CBT was part of a "cognitive evolution." The work of such cognitive psychologists as Kruglanski (1980, 1990), Mandler (1975), Nisbett and Ross (1980), Simon (1957), and Tversky and Kahneman (1974) provided a theoretical framework for the further development of CBT. Another somewhat related influence, especially in the development of CBT with children, was the work of the Soviet psychologists Lev Vygotsky (1978) and his student A. R. Luria (1976). They proposed that children become socialized by internalizing interpersonal communication into private (intrapersonal) speech. Their socialization and internalization

models provided a theoretical framework for the development of cognitive behavior modification with children.

These historical cross-current trends are discussed further in the works of Mahoney (1974) and Meichenbaum (1977).

REACTIONS TO COGNITIVE BEHAVIOR THERAPY

What was offered as a clinically sensitive integrative approach was often unwelcome, especially to behaviorally oriented psychotherapists. "Cognitive-types," as they were pejoratively described, were labeled as "malcontents." Pressure was exerted by behaviorists to have cognitive behavioral researchers excluded from the Association for the Advancement of Behavior Therapy (AABT) conferences, editorial boards, and even the organization.

Surely, these sparks of controversy were not as exciting as those in Vienna when Freud and Jung exchanged jibes, but in its own fashion, the present controversy illustrated the commitment with which theoretical positions were held. Like our clients, the scientist's passions (not reason or data) ruled the day.

One of the results of the resistance to CBT was the creation of a new journal, *Cognitive Therapy and Research*, in March 1977, with Michael Mahoney as editor and Aaron Beck, Marvin Goldfried, and Meichenbaum, as associate editors. The "malcontents" had created an outlet in which critically to discuss and evaluate CBT.

Since its inception in the early 1970s, CBT has emerged into one of the most widely adopted forms of psychotherapeutic intervention. Next, a model of CBT will be offered.

THE EVOLVING MODEL

Subsumed under the heading of CBT are a variety of diverse psychotherapeutic techniques, including cognitive restructuring, problem solving, stress-inoculation training, anxiety management training, and self-instructional training (see Mahoney & Arnkoff, 1978). Each particular psychotherapeutic approach and each proponent of CBT has a particular theoretical slant. A partial list of the innovators and advocates of CBT follows: Arnkoff, Baucom, Beck, Chambless, Craighead, Deffenbacher, Dryden, D'Zurilla, Ellis, Emery, Epstein, Foa, Foster, Freeman, Glass, Goldfried, Goldstein, Guidano, Hawton, Hollon, Jacobson, Kendall, Linehan, Liotti, Mahoney, Marlatt, Meichenbaum, Novaco, Padeskey, Persons, Robin, Rush, Safran, Shaw, Segal, Suinn, Turk, and Wilson. Any attempt to capture the commonalities and differences across these important contributors to CBT is not feasible within the present space. Instead, I will consider the major theoretical tenets of CBT, or of cognitive behavior modification, as I view them.

BASIC TENETS

1. Behavior is reciprocally influenced by the client's thoughts, feelings, physiological processes, and resultant consequences. As Bandura (1978) highlighted, behavior is "reciprocally determined."

According to CBT, cognitions are *not* viewed as being primary or as being causative of maladaptive behavior. Clients' thoughts are as much influenced by their feelings, as their feelings are influenced by their thoughts. Cognition and emotion are viewed as being two sides of the same coin. Cognition, in all of its complexity, is only one part of a causative chain, and often is not the more critical. For example, when trying to predict relapse in clients suffering from unipolar depression, the amount of criticism from the client's spouse proves to be a better predictor than any specific cognitive measure (Hooley et al., 1986).

2. Cognitions are complex in nature and can be viewed in terms of cognitive events, cognitive processes, and cognitive structures. *Cognitive events* refer to individuals' automatic thoughts, internal dialogue, and images. It should be noted, however, that this does not mean that individuals constantly go around talking to themselves. Rather, most of the time an individual's behavior is mindless, automated, or "scripted," as described by Abelson (1976), Langer (1978), and Thorngate (1976). Still, there

are occasions when the automaticity of an individual's behavior is interrupted or when an individual has to make decisions under conditions of uncertainty, and as a result, mindful private speech occurs. Cognitive behavior therapy proposes that the content and nature of such thoughts can influence how individuals feel and how they behave. But, as already noted, how individuals' feel, behave, and elicit reactions from others can significantly influence their thoughts.

Cognitive behavior therapy does not believe that cognitions (so-called "irrational" beliefs, or cognitive errors, or specific thoughts) cause emotional disturbance and maladaptive behavior. Rather, CBT holds that such a position is simplistic and does not fit the data. Cognitions are only one part of a complex reciprocally interactive process.

Cognitive events are only one way to view cognitions. Another important way to view cognition is *cognitive processes*. Social, cognitive, and developmental psychology have been particularly helpful in describing and explicating several cognitive processes, including confirmatory biases, mental heuristics, and metacognition. (See Meichenbaum and Gilmore [1984], Hollon and Kriss [1984], and Taylor and Crocker [1981] for a fuller discussion of these cognitive processes.)

Briefly, *confirmatory bias* refers to the fact that individuals hold certain views of themselves and the world and they rarely look for anomalous or disconfirming evidence. *Mental heuristics* refers to the "mental habits" that individuals employ when they have to make judgments under conditions of uncertainty (e.g., availability and representation heuristics, as described by Tversky and Kahneman [1977]). Moreover, one's emotional state (i.e., being depressed, anxious, etc.) can influence and color what specific heuristic examples from the past are called upon. Individuals do not merely respond to events, but they call forth in a mood-congruent fashion salient, ready at hand, examples. Thus the client's emotions influence what information is attended to, what inferences are drawn, and what attributions are offered.

Metacognition refers to the executive self-regulatory processes one engages in and how one reflects upon them. The CB therapist helps clients develop the ability to "notice," "catch," "interrupt," "monitor," and "evaluate," their thoughts, feelings, and behaviors. Such metacognitive transitive verbs constitute a central feature of the social discourse of CBT. These therapists identify, reflect, model, and reinforce the client for engaging in such metacognitive self-regulatory activities. Moreover, CB therapists ensure that clients take credit or make self-attributions about the behavioral changes they implement.

Finally, CBT highlights the critical role of *cognitive structures* or *personal schemas*. It has moved from a more simplistic emphasis on cognitive events and self-statements to highlight the importance of schemas, a concept borrowed from the information-processing paradigm as initially emphasized by Bartlett (1932). Schemas refer to the cognitive representation of past experience that assists and influences the construction of current experience and that guides the organization of new information (Goldfried, 1988; Neimeyer & Feixas, 1990). In the same spirit, Safran and Segal (1990) highlight that schemas act like tacit rules that organize and guide self-related information. Such schemas influence how individuals appraise events and their coping efforts (Meichenbaum, 1977).

3. Given the emphasis placed on schemas, a central task for the CB therapist is to help clients come to understand how they construct and construe reality. In this sense, CBT operates in a constructivist mode.

The CB therapist also helps clients appreciate how they inadvertently and unwittingly create the data that confirm their views of themselves and of their world. Cognitive behavior therapy embraces an interactional perspective of behavior, as espoused by Coyne and Gotlib (1983), Kiesler (1982), and Wachtel (1982). For instance, chronically depressed clients often turn others off, thus eliciting the reactions that confirm their concerns about rejection and fears of abandonment. Thus when depressed clients contend that "no one likes them," this may be more of a veridical description than a cognitive distortion. What they fail to appreciate, however, is how they may unknowingly contribute to this interactional pattern. In a collaborative fashion, the CB therapist helps clients discover and alter this self-defeating pattern.

An important corollary of the constructivist position is that CBT does not hold that there is "one reality," or that the task for the therapist is to educate or correct clients' misconceptions (errors in thinking, irrational thoughts). Rather, in the tradition of the Kurosawa movie *Rashomon*, CBT holds true that there are "multiple realities." The collaborative task for clients and CB therapists is to help clients appreciate how they create such realities and what "price" they must pay for such constructions. Moreover, is this the emotional and interpersonal "price" clients wish to pay? What is the "impact," the "toll," for holding such views of oneself and of the world? This question is not answered in the abstract, but experientially and emotionally examined in CB therapy sessions and in vivo, contributing to what Alexander and French (1946) called "corrective emotional experiences."

Cognitive behavior therapy also explores in a collaborative problem-solving fashion what else clients can do to change their personal constructions and behaviors. Moreover, the CB therapist and client explore what barriers will get in the way of implementing such behavioral changes.

4. The present version of CBT takes issue with those psychotherapeutic approaches that adopt a rationalist or objectivist position. As Neimeyer (1985) and Mahoney (1988) observe, rationalist therapeutic approaches attempt to have clients monitor and correct "disturbed" or "irrational" beliefs, and they attempt to help clients develop more accurate or objective views of reality by such means as logical disputation, instruction, and the collection of empirical evidence in order to test one's beliefs against external reality.

In contrast, CBT, which is phenomenologically oriented, attempts to explore by means of nondirective reflective procedures the client's world view. There is an intent to see the world through the client's eyes, rather than to challenge, confront, or interpret the client's thoughts. A major mode of achieving this objective is for the CB therapist to "pluck" (pick out) key words and phrases that clients offer, and then to reflect them in an interrogative tone, but with the same affect (mirroring) in which they were expressed. The CB therapist also may use the client's developmental accounts, as well as in-session client behavior, to help the client get in touch with his or her feelings.

5. A critical feature of CBT is the emphasis on *collaboration* and on *discovery* processes. The CB therapist will be at his or her best when the client is one step ahead of the therapist, offering the suggestion that the therapist would otherwise offer. The CB therapist works carefully and operates strategically to help clients collect data (for example, about the situational variability of their presenting problems); and then raises Socratic questions with clients about what they could do differently. If the client answers, "I don't know," the CB therapist answers, "I don't know, either. How can we go about finding out?" Thus a collaborative "we" team approach is nurtured in an attempt to share responsibility and to empower clients. The goal of CBT is to help the client become his or her own therapist. In order to achieve this objective, the CB therapist is not didactic, but acts more like Peter Falk playing the television detective Columbo. In this way, CB therapists help clients recognize the circular self-perpetuating nature of their behaviors and they enlist, cajole, and challenge clients to perform personal experiments whereby they can test out their social constructions, beliefs, and tacit assumptions, and experiment with new outlooks. Some patients require explicit behavioral training (e.g., modeling, behavioral rehearsal, role playing) in acquiring and consolidating the skills to perform such personal experiments.

6. A central feature of CBT is the importance of the concept of *relapse prevention*. While this concept was initially emphasized by such CB therapists as Marlatt and Gordon (1985) in work with clients who had problems with addiction, the concept of relapse prevention is relevant to all forms of CB interventions. Relapse prevention refers to the need for CB therapists and clients to explore the high-risk situations that are likely to contribute to relapse, and also to consider the nature of clients' thoughts and feelings that may contribute to lapses and that escalate lapses into relapses (going back to baseline). Cognitive behavior therapists anticipate and subsume such emotional reactions into ther

apy (e.g., see Meichenbaum, 1985). In fact, the CB therapist will highlight the fact that clients, like scientists, often learn most from failures and frustrations. Without such failures, clients would not be making progress.

In short, CB therapists help clients cognitively reframe failures and disappointments as learning trials rather than as occasions to "catastrophize." The CB therapist acts as a purveyor of hope, combating the sense of demoralization and of hopelessness, helplessness, and victimization that often characterize clients' internal dialogue when they enter treatment (Frank, 1974). The CB therapist may even compliment clients on their initial symptoms and distress, conveying that this distress indicates that they are "in touch" with their feelings. "Given what you [the client] have gone through, if you were not depressed [anxious, angry], I [the therapist] would be really concerned." In other words, CBT holds that it is not that clients become depressed, anxious, angry, and so on—each of which reflects normal emotional reactions to the vagaries of life—but what clients say to themselves about such emotional reactions that is critical to the behavior change process. Cognitive behavior therapists use the full array of cognitive restructuring procedures, such as social comparison, paradoxical techniques, reframing, and the like, to foster hope and to nurture change.

7. These techniques will only work within the context of a therapeutic collaborative relationship. Cognitive behavior therapy holds that the relationship that develops between the client and the therapist is critical to the change process. Safran and Segal (1990) recently reviewed the literature on the various variables that influence therapeutic outcome and convincingly documented that relationship and therapist variables are significantly more important than specific technical factors in influencing treatment outcome (namely, some 45 percent versus 15 percent of the variance of treatment outcome was accounted for, respectively, by therapist-relationship variables versus technical factors). Consistent with these findings, CB therapists expend a great deal of effort in establishing and nurturing a therapeutic alliance. Such features as collaboration, warmth, empathy, emotional attunement, acceptance,

hope, inspiring confidence, and being a coping model are emphasized by CB therapists. Out of the strength of the relationship with the CB therapist, clients muster the courage to undertake the demanding tasks of changing. Moreover, as Meichenbaum and Turk (1987) reported in their book on facilitating treatment adherence, such relationship factors are critical in overcoming client resistance and client noncompliance. This is essential when we learn that approximately 70 percent of patients drop out of psychotherapy by the fourth session (Phillips, 1986). As Safran and Segal (1990) observe, CBT recognizes the "inseparability of therapy techniques, personal qualities of the therapist and the therapeutic relationship" (p. 35).

All too often, psychotherapy becomes too didactic, sounding too much like Logic 101, rather than helping clients collaboratively discover, explore, experiment with how they view things (construe and construct reality), and then consider what the impact is of such constructions. Out of the therapeutic alliance, clients evidence the courage to undertake "personal experiments" to view things differently and to behave differently. Often such changed views of oneself follow from changed behaviors and their resultant consequences.

8. This learning process is highly emotional. Emotions play a critical role in CBT. As Greenberg and Safran (1986) have observed, emotion all too often has been overlooked and undervalued in psychotherapy. However, CBT views emotions as critical in understanding clients' cognitive structures or schemas. In the same way that dreams were the "royal road to the unconscious" for Freud, emotions are viewed as the "royal road" to clients' personal schemas.

There are many ways to tap clients' emotions, but one way that will be highlighted here is the use of in-session "transference behaviors." Clients often bring into therapy the nature of the emotional experiences they have had with significant others. The CB therapist "goes public with the data" as he or she observes them (acting as a participant/observer), and then reflects on these observations with the client. In this instance, the "unit of analysis" may not be a specific set of automatic thoughts or the pattern of thinking, but the manner in which

the patient is interacting with the therapist. In an invitational and exploratory manner, rather than in a directive and disputational fashion, the CB therapist explores with clients both their immediate emotional experiences, and the developmental and historical factors that contributed to their present emotionally charged interactions. In short, CBT is not ahistorical, but it attempts to help clients make sense out of or fabricate a meaning for the ways in which they behave. Formulating such meaning nurtures hope and helps to convince clients that they are not "going crazy," and that their beliefs are not "pathogenic," as control mastery theorists propose (Weiss & Sampson, 1986). Rather, the clients' beliefs and social constructions make sense given their life experiences, but now such beliefs, such social constructions, have negatively transferred and have been overextended, reflecting "burdensome baggage" that is getting in the way of their personal goals. As systems-oriented therapists suggest, the clients' solutions often represent part of the problem.

It is important to note that from a CBT perspective, the importance of this historical fabrication of meaning is not in its veridicality, but in its *viability*. As Neimeyer and Feixas (1990) have observed, the constructionist approach is more concerned about the viability, than the validity of one's meaning system. In fact, Taylor and Brown (1988) have observed that motivated reasoning (holding false illusions, using denial instead of engaging in problem solving, holding positive views of oneself and the world) often is adaptive. This seems true for illusory beliefs that do not serve as the basis for important action. Where not doing something is not important, motivated reasoning may be adaptive (Kunda, 1990).

Cognitive behavior therapy recognizes that one should neither confront nor challenge clients' beliefs head-on, as doing so is likely to "freeze" such beliefs (Kruglanski, 1990). If the therapist wishes to help change clients' beliefs, then he or she should "go through the back door." By enlisting the client as a collaborator, reducing defensiveness, or by "blowing the client's belief up" to an extreme and then having clients react (moving more to the center), such emotionally charged beliefs are more open to change. This change process is filled with what

Zajonc and Markus (1984) called "hot cognitions." Cold cognitions—giving information, disputation, and logic—rarely change strongly held beliefs and accompanying behaviors (see Meichenbaum & Turk, 1987).

9. While an examination of in-session behavior with the therapist is viewed as critical to the change process, CB therapists are now recognizing the benefits of conducting CBT with couples and families. Work by Baucom and Epstein (1990), Jacobson (1987), and Robin and Foster (1989), among others, illustrates the influence of system-oriented therapists on CBT. The unit of analysis, the data that the CB therapist reflects and focuses on, is the interlocking interactional familial patterns and the shared construct systems. Moreover, CBT also has become interested in how particular societal and cultural groups exert their influence on the clients' belief systems and behaviors. For instance, stress inoculation training has been extended to entire groups, organizations, and community groups (see Meichenbaum, 1985).

10. Finally, CBT provides a useful means to extend interventions well beyond the clinic setting, on both a treatment and a preventative basis. Meichenbaum and Jaremko (1983) describe how CBT has been extended to such groups as probation officers, hospital nurses, military officers, school teachers and principals, and other psychiatric, medical, and community groups. One of the more exciting efforts "to give CBT away" involves Barbara Wasik and her colleagues' (1990) program at the University of North Carolina where she trained home visitors to do CBT with urban and rural single mothers of premature infants. My own present efforts involve the training of front-line staff, school teachers, as well as clinicians, to conduct CBT on an inpatient individual and group basis with distressed children and adolescents (6 to 16 years of age) and their families.

polar depression (Hollon & Najavits, 1988), anxiety disorders (Barlow & Cerny, 1988), and anger problems (Novaco, 1975), as well as for distressed couples (Baucom & Epstein, 1990), pain patients (Turk et al., 1983), patients with addictions (Marlatt & Gordon, 1985), and other clinical groups. More recently, CBT has turned its attention to Axis II personality disorder patients (Beck et al., 1990). Clearly, this last group of borderline, narcissistic, and antisocial personality disorder patients will require more extensive long-term CBT interventions than the Axis I psychiatric patients. It is likely that the clinical efforts of CB therapists with Axis II clients will further heighten integrative influences in the field of psychotherapy.

As discussed in this chapter, CBT emphasizes:

1. Both constructivist and interactive perspectives.
2. The important role of schema.
3. The critical role of emotion.
4. The significance of the therapeutic relationship, especially the therapeutic alliance.
5. The role of historical, developmental, familial, and sociocultural influences.
6. The need to consider transference (and one might also add countertransference relationship factors).
7. The importance of behavioral and relapse prevention skills training.
8. The desire to employ a consultative CBT training model with "paraprofessionals."

Following these guidelines will hasten the integrative forces of psychotherapy. Perhaps a set of guiding principles is emerging that can bring order to the Babel surrounding the field of psychotherapy. It is proposed that CBT can contribute significantly to this integrative process.

SUMMARY

In summary, since its inception, CBT has emerged into an influential psychotherapeutic model, in terms of both practice and theory. The clinical practice of CBT has provided encouraging data for the treatment of patients with uni-

REFERENCES

Abelson, R. P. (1976). Script processing in attitude information and decision making. In J. Carroll and J. Payne (Eds.), *Cognition and social behavior*. Hillsdale, NJ: Erlbaum.

Alexander, F., & French, T. (1946). *Psychoanalytic therapy: Principles and applications*. New York: Ronald Press.

Bandura, A. (1978). The self-system in reciprocal determinism. *American Psychologist, 33,* 344–358.

Barlow, D., & Cerny, J. (1988). *Psychological treatment of panic.* New York: Guilford Press.

Bartlett, F. (1932). *Remembering.* Cambridge, England: Cambridge University Press.

Baucom, D., & Epstein, N. (1990). *Cognitive-behavioral marital therapy.* New York: Brunner/Mazel.

Beck, A. T., Freeman, A., et al. (1990). *Cognitive therapy of personality disorders.* New York: Guilford Press.

Breger, L., & McGaugh, J. (1965). Critique and reformulation of "learning theory": Approaches to psychotherapy and neurosis. *Psychological Bulletin, 63,* 338–358.

Brewer, W. (1974). There is no convincing evidence for operant and classical conditioning in adult humans. In W. Weimar & D. Palermo (Eds.), *Cognition and the symbolic processes.* New York: Halsted Press.

Coyne, J. C., & Gotlib, I. H. (1983). The role of cognition in depression: A critical appraisal. *Psychological Bulletin, 94,* 472–505.

Dember, W. (1974). Motivation and the cognitive revolution. *American Psychologist, 29,* 161–168.

Frank, J. (1974). *Persuasion and healing.* New York: Schocken.

Goldfried, M. (1988). Personal construct therapy and other theoretical orientations. *International Journal of Personal Construct Therapy, 1,* 317–327.

Greenberg, L., & Safran, J. (1986). *Emotion in psychotherapy.* New York: Guilford Press.

Guidano, V. F., & Liotti, G. (1983). *Cognitive processes and emotional disorders.* New York: Guilford Press.

Hollon, S., & Kriss, M. (1984). Cognitive factors in clinical research and practice. *Clinical Psychology Review, 4,* 35–76.

Hollon, S., & Najavits, L. (1988). Review of empirical studies on cognitive therapy. In A. J. Frances & R. Hales (Eds.), *Review of Psychiatry, 7,* 643–647.

Hooley, J., Orley, J., & Teasdale, J. (1986). Levels of expressed emotion and relapse in depressed patients. *British Journal of Psychiatry, 148,* 642–647.

Jacobson, N. S. (1987). *Cognitive and behavior therapist in clinical practice.* New York: Guilford Press.

Kanfer, F., & Phillips, J. (1970). *Learning foundations of behavior therapy.* New York: Wiley.

Kiesler, D. J. (1982). Interpersonal theory for personality and psychotherapy. In J. C. Anchin & D. J. Kiesler (Eds.), *Handbook of interpersonal psychotherapy.* Elmsford, NY: Pergamon.

Kruglanski, A. W. (1980). Lay epistemiology process and contents. *Psychological Review, 87,* 70–87.

Kruglanski, A. (1990). Lay epistemic theory in social-cognitive psychology. *Psychological Inquiry, 1,* 181–197.

Kunda, Z. (1990). The case for motivated reasoning. *Psychological Bulletin, 108,* 480–498.

Langer, E. (1978). Rethinking the role of thought in social interaction. In J. Harvey, W. Ickes, & R. Kield (Eds.), *New directions in attribution research,* Vol. 2. Hillsdale, NJ: Erlbaum.

Lazarus, R. (1981). The stress and coping paradigm. In C. Eisdarfer (Ed.), *Models for clinical psychopathology.* New York: Spectrum.

Luria, A. R. (1976). *Cognitive development: Its cultural and social foundations.* Cambridge, MA: Harvard University Press.

Mahoney, M. (1974). *Cognition and behavior modification.* Cambridge, MA: Ballinger.

Mahoney, M. (1988). Constructive metatheory: Implications for psychotherapy. *International Journal of Personal Construct Psychology, 1,* 299–315.

Mahoney, M., & Arnkoff, D. (1978). Cognitive and self-control therapies. In S. Garfield & A. Bergin (Eds.), *Handbook of psychotherapy and behavior change.* New York: Wiley.

Mandler, G. (1975). *Mind and emotion.* New York: Wiley.

Marlatt, A., & Gordon, J. (1985). *Relapse prevention: Maintenance strategies in the treatment of addictive behaviors.* New York: Guilford Press.

McKeachie, W. (1974). The decline and fall of the laws of learning. *Educational Researcher, 3,* 7–11.

Meichenbaum, D. (1977). *Cognitive behavior modification: An integrative approach.* New York: Plenum.

Meichenbaum, D. (1985). *Stress inoculation training.* New York: Plenum.

Meichenbaum, D., & Gilmore, J. (1984). The nature of unconscious processes: A cognitive behavioral perspective. In K. Bowers & D. Meichenbaum (Eds.), *The unconscious reconsidered.* New York: Wiley.

Meichenbaum, D., & Jaremko, M. (1983). *Stress reduction and prevention.* New York: Plenum.

Meichenbaum, D., & Turk, D. (1987). *Facilitating treatment adherence: A practitioner's guidebook.* New York: Plenum.

Mischel, W. (1975). The self as the person: A cognitive social learning view. In A. Wandersman (Ed.), *Behavioristic and humanistic approaches to personality change.* New York: Pergamon.

Neimeyer, R. A. (1985). Personal constructs in clinical practice. In P. Kendall (Ed.), *Advances in cognitive behavioral research and therapy.* New York: Academic.

Neimeyer, R., & Feixas, G. (1990). Constructivist contributions to psychotherapy integration. *Journal of Integrative and Eclectic Psychotherapy, 9,* 4–20.

Nisbett, R., & Ross, L. (1980). *Human inference: Strategies and shortcomings of social judgment.* Englewood Cliffs, NJ: Prentice-Hall.

Novaco, R. (1975). *Anger control.* Lexington, MA: D.C. Heath.

Phillips, E. L. (1986). Are theories of psychotherapy possible? Paper presented at the Fifth Cognitive Behavior Therapy Conference, Clearwater Beach, FL.

Raimy, V. (1975). *Misunderstanding of the self: Cognitive psychotherapy and the misconception hypothesis.* San Francisco: Jossey-Bass.

Robin, A., & Foster, S. (1989). *Negotiating parent-adolescent conflict.* New York: Guilford Press.

Rotter, J. (1966). Generalized expectancies for internal versus external control of reinforcement. *Psychological Monographs, 80.*

Safran, J., & Segal, Z. (1990). *Interpersonal processes in cognitive therapy.* New York: Basic Books.

Simon, H. (1957). *Models of man: Social and rational.* New York: Wiley.

Taylor, S. E., & Brown, J. (1988). Illusion and well-being: A social psychological perspective on mental health. *Psychological Bulletin, 103,* 193–210.

Taylor, S. E., & Crocker, J. (1981). Schematic basics of social information processing. In E. Higgins, C. Herman, & M. Zanna (Eds.), *Social cognition: The Ontario Symposium.* Hillsdale, NJ: Erlbaum.

Thorngate, W. (1976). Must we always think before we act? *Personality and Social Psychology Bulletin, 2,* 31–35.

Turk, D., Meichenbaum, D., & Genest, M. (1983). *Pain and behavioral medicine*. New York: Guilford Press.

Turk, D., & Salovey, P. (1985). Cognitive structures, cognitive processes and cognitive behavior modification. *Cognitive Therapy and Research, 9*, 1–35.

Tversky, A., & Kahneman, D. (1974). Judgment under uncertainty: Heuristics and biases. *Science, 185*, 1124–1131.

Vygotsky, L. S. (1978). *Mind in society: The development of higher psychological processes*. Cambridge, MA: Harvard University Press.

Wachtel, P. (1982). What can dynamic therapies contribute to behavior therapy? *Behavior Therapy, 13*, 594–609.

Wasik, B. H., Bryant, D. M., & Lyons, C. M. (1990). *Home visiting: Procedures for helping families*. New York: Sage.

Weiss, J., Sampson, H., & the Mount Zion Psychotherapy Research Group. (1986). *The psychoanalytic process*. New York: Guilford Press.

Zajonc, R., & Markus, H. (1984). Affect and cognition: The hard interface. In C. Izard, J. Kagan, & R. Zajonc (Eds.), *Emotions, cognition and behavior*. Cambridge, England: Cambridge University Press.

Discussion by Albert Ellis, Ph.D.

◆

In general, I agree with almost everything Meichenbaum said. I'll have some disagreements later, but I agree with most of his presentation. However, he unfortunately follows Michael Mahoney, who has a crusade against the so-called "rationalist" cognitive behavior therapies, such as Don's original theories and those of Tim Beck (1976), Arnold Lazarus (1989), David Burns (1980), and Maxie Maultsby (1984). But if they all replied to Mahoney and now to Don, they would probably all say that they are not rationalists.

Mahoney has some very good points in his constructivist position, and Don repeated some of them. But let me go through the constructivist position and show that it is not opposed to RET, because RET, as I said in my recent book *The Essential Albert Ellis* (Ellis & Dryden, 1990), is probably the most constructivist of all the cognitive behavior therapies, and yet Mahoney and Meichenbaum peculiarly insist that it is "rationalist."

Let me show why RET is constructivist by going through the main points that Don made. First of all, constructivism means, as Don and Mike Mahoney say, that people are not just associationistic, empirical, and logical, but that they actually *construct* (or at least *partly* construct) their own disturbances. Now Don and Mike have not said exactly why this is true. They don't seem to say as clearly as I have said

for many years that humans largely construct their disturbed thoughts, feelings, and actions because they are born constructivists. They have innate biological tendencies to think, feel, and act that way. And they are also born learners. Being born teachable or gullible, they learn standards from their parents and their culture. But I theorize, and I may be wrong about this, that people's goals and standards practically never make them emotionally disturbed. Mainly, they are emotionally disturbed because they take theirs parents' goals and standards, and they either follow them or don't follow them, neither of which path will usually get them into too much trouble. Even when they rebel against these parental and cultural standards, and they are therefore criticized, they can tell themselves, "It's too bad that I went against this sex, monetary, or other standard and thereby fell on my face. But I'm a fallible human. That's the way I am. Too bad! Maybe I'd better follow this standard in the future or live with poor consequences." So it isn't the standard that upsets people. They largely learn goals and rules from their parents and their culture, but they *create*, they often *construct*—just because they are human—rigid musts, shoulds, and oughts *about* these standards. Thus people often think, "Because it is good in my culture to have sex, to marry, and to raise a family, and because I am not doing that good thing as well as I *must*, I am incompetent and worthless!" By accepting *and* creating *must*urbatory expectations about their (largely learned) standards, they largely create most of their emotional disturbances. Yes, they easily tend to *construct*, not *merely* learn them. But they also have another constructive tendency, and that is to think about what they do, to observe, to think about their thinking, and to *change* themselves.

Humans have *two* main constructivist's propensities: One is a self-defeating tendency—to take their standards and goals and insist that they *have* to do well, they *have* to be loved, and *have* to be comfortable and safe. Their second biological (and sociological) tendency is to question and challenge that which they often dysfunctionally think, feel, and do. However, they often use their self-constructive tendencies sloppily and poorly, and I think that good cognitive behavior therapy, notably RET, shows them how to utilize their self-constructive propensities and to minimize their self-destructive and socially sabotaging absolutist shoulds, oughts, commands, and demands.

Thus RET acknowledges people's developmental history and its influences on their desires, goals, and values. But it also stresses that it isn't their preferences that upset them; it's their demands, commands, Jehovian musts that these preferences *must* be achieved. I usually give the illustration that in the United States boys learn to cherish baseball. In England, boys learn to want to excel at cricket, and in South America they learn to prefer soccer. But in all three places, they foolishly tend to *demand*, "I *must* be good at baseball!" or, "I *have to* be good at cricket, or soccer!" It isn't their learned "I'd like to be!" but their constructed insistence "I *have* to be!" that disturbs them. So RET is very phenomenological. It always has said, "You largely *create* your disturbances. You usually *don't* get them from your parents. You get the standards and goals, but you both accept *and* create musts about accepted standards. Along with Mahoney and Meichenbaum, RET is strongly phenomenological and constructivist (Ellis, 1958, 1962, 1973, 1988, 1989, 1990; Ellis & Dryden, 1987, 1990, 1991).

As far as interaction is concerned, the CB therapies finally recently got around to the fact that cognitions, emotions, and behaviors all interact in an important manner. People rarely, if ever, have any pure thoughts, pure feelings, or pure behaviors, as I said about 35 years ago. Let me repeat what I wrote in *Reason and Emotion in Psychotherapy*, and what I originally said in 1956 at the American Psychological Association Convention in Chicago:

Thinking is, and to some extent has to be, sensory, motor, and emotional behavior. Emotion, like thinking and the sensory motor processes we may define as an exceptionally complex state of human reaction which is integrally related to all the other preception and response prostheses. It is not one thing but a combination and wholistic integration of several seemingly diverse, yet actually closely related phenomena. (Ellis, 1988, p. 35)

I said this in 1956, and it's nice that the other cognitive behavioral therapists, like Don Meichenbaum and Greenberg and Safran (1986), are finally coming around to saying this again—but are completely ignoring the fact that I said it many years ago! Let me repeat what I said in 1953, which was even before I started RET. Adapting ideas from a 1953 address, I wrote:

A large part of what we call emotion, in other words, is nothing more than a certain kind—a biased prejudiced or strongly evaluative kind of thinking. Thinking and emoting are so closely interrelated that they usually accompany each other, act is a circular cause and effect relationship, and in certain, though hardly all, respects are essentially the same things, so that one's thinking becomes one's emotion and emotion becomes one's thought. (Ellis, 1958, p. 36)

My 1953 paper was given at the University of Minnesota, was published in 1956 (Ellis, 1956), and that is what I said in it. So RET is exceptionally emotive, evocative, and interactional (Huber & Baruth, 1989). Now it is nice that the others are finally getting to this view—while falsely accusing RET of being "rationalist" and of only emphasizing empiricism and logic, which again is false.

Let me briefly go through some of the other main points of Don's paper. Like Don, RET stresses the important role of people's schemata and core philosophies. It holds that humans have basic philosophies and biosocial tendencies to construct and reconstruct new schemata and philosophies. They tend to bring these philosophies of life to any stimuli, including their parental-given stimuli, and, therefore, perceive and deal with "external" stimuli in a biased manner. They derive their core beliefs from their experiences with their environment and *from* themselves. They are self-creating organisms who take over (accept) desires, goals, and preferences from others, because that is the kind of an animal they are. But they often accept parental and cultural standards because of their innate suggestibility. They then frequently change and transmute these standards by making a "magical jump" from a preference to a dire need. Almost all people do this, in all parts of the world. They adopt different goals and preferences remedially and culturally, but then they seem to have the tendency not only to create schemata, but also to transmute them into Jehovian musts. Their nondisturbed schemata are important aspects of their personality, but in psychotherapy we want to know not only about the personality of humans, but also how and why they upset themselves about their desires and standards. Rational-emotive therapists have always said, and still do, that humans frequently schematicize by constructing rigid musts and that they bring their musturbation, along with their preferences, to situations that they experience.

The critical role of emotion in creating and treating disturbance has always been stressed in RET, because people start with goals and *desires*, especially the strong desires to stay alive and be happy and nonmiserable. Virtually all humans are that way. Then they meet what RET calls Activating Events (A) or what Marty Seligman (1991) calls Adversities, or situations they dislike. Then, at point B, their Belief System, they have the rational, self-helping Belief, "I *would* like to do well and change the Adversity"—which encourages them to feel appropriately sorry and regretful when A still exists. But at B, they frequently *also* have the irrational, self-defeating Belief, "Because I would *prefer* to change the Adversity, I absolutely *must* do so. I *have to* be successful, loved, and comfortable!" They then *in*appropriately feel panicked and

depressed when Adversity still exists. Put differently, they take warm cognitions—for example, "I like this table and hope you don't harm it, but if you do, I can still have a good life"—and they make them into hot cognitions—for example, "Because I like this table so much, you absolutely *must not* harm it, and if you do, I *can't stand* it. It's *awful*, and you are a *rotten person* who deserves to be drawn and quartered!"

When people hold dysfunctional Beliefs and accompany them with inappropriate feelings and behaviors, they not only command that the universe be *their* way, but often also make these commands heartily, strongly, emotively, rigidly and persistently. That is why, in 1961, Bob Harper and I changed the term rational therapy, which I first called it, to rational-emotive therapy, to emphasize the cognitive-*emotional* aspect of neurosis and the strength, the power, and the hotness with which disturbance-creating ideas are created and maintained. Consequently, RET does not merely stick to the empirical techniques of disputing irrational Beliefs (iBs) that are largely used by Beck (1976), Burns (1980), Maultsby (1984), and the early Don Meichenbaum (1977). They mildly, realistically, and "rationally" talk clients out of their dysfunctional ideas. But, as Don now is beginning (somewhat belatedly) to see, much of the time that won't work.

Sometimes, however, this "rationalist" method does work; and those self-help books that Don parodies have possibly helped more people than all modern therapists combined have helped. More neurotic people may improve by reading self-help books, including the questionable Bible, than they do in psychotherapy. So it is silly to say that just because people read or listen to therapeutic talks, they cannot significantly help themselves, and that they can *only* do so in a relationship with a therapist (Ellis, 1959; Rogers, 1957).

People are never purely cognitive, or purely emotional, or purely behavioral. As I noted in 1953 and 1956, and as I note in my invited address to this Evolution of Psychotherapy Conference (see pp. 79–90), thinking, feeling, and behaving are interactional and had better *all* be explored and changed in effective psychotherapy (Ellis, 1956, 1958, 1991). It is nice that Mahoney and Meichenbaum have finally acknowledged this, but for them to say that RET, a pioneer in this area, "rationalistically" ignores emotion is truly incredible!

Let me briefly consider Don's main points against "rationalism" and show how they don't apply at all to RET. And if Aaron Beck were with us, he would probably say that they don't apply to him. Incidentally, Mahoney originally accused me and Beck and Meichenbaum together, and now Don is becoming a purer "constructivist" by accusing Beck and me!

Rational-emotive therapy gives emotion a critical role in therapy because, it holds, humans start to disturb themselves by experiencing goals, purposes, and desires, all of which are highly emotive and motivational. They then *strongly* and *vigorously*—that is, *emotionally*—feel them and, often, change them to *powerful demands*. Rational-emotive therapy helps clients to keep (and sometimes increase) their desires and feelings, while, at the same time, it uses *several* cognitive-emotive methods to minimize their grandiose demands. It partly does this by logically and empirically disputing their dysfunctional Beliefs. But, more important, it helps clients to think for themselves, and not by "rational" rote, and it strives for clients' achieving a *profound philosophical change*, a new *method* of open-ended, open-minded thinking, feeling, and behaving.

Like most other therapies, RET encourages a therapeutic alliance between therapist and client, but holds that a good alliance includes collaborative *teaching*. That is what Don has significantly omitted in his chapter—that in order to help people change, you ally with them and you achieve their trust, but you *also* teach them how they are needlessly upsetting themselves and how to look at their own malfunctioning and change it and the core philosophies that create and maintain it. Carl Rogers' (1961) therapeutic alliance, for example, helped people by modeling self-acceptance through therapist acceptance. But this modeling mainly provides *conditional* and not *un*conditional acceptance, because, as Rogers admitted, clients tend to accept themselves *because* the therapist accepts them. In *unconditional* self-acceptance, which RET models *and* teaches, clients are shown how to accept themselves *whether or not* the therapist (or anyone else) accepts them

(Bernard, 1986; Ellis, 1973, 1988; Walen, DiGiuseppe, & Wessler, 1980).

In RET sessions, we teach people to have a therapeutic alliance with themselves, not just with the therapist. So they feel that a therapist loves them. That's nice! But they had better have a therapeutic alliance with themselves, so that they fully and unconditionally accept themselves whether or not they do well and whether or not anybody else, including the therapist, loves them. Practically all the existing studies of the outcome of therapy have been weak because they only test how people *feel* better, but not how they *get* better, which I said in 1972 (Ellis, 1972). When clients feel better because the therapist approves of them, they are still usually quite neurotic. They still strongly believe, "I *must* be approved and now that Carl Rogers or Al Ellis likes me, I'm okay." But because they quickly discover that the rest of the world doesn't give a shit for them, back to wormhood they go (Ellis & Dryden, 1991; Yankura & Dryden, 1990).

The therapeutic alliance is fine, as used by Carl, Don, and me, but RET also tries to show people that they don't need even a therapist's approval. Good therapy, which can also be done through books and lectures, actually *can* teach this. I would like to see an experiment with one group of clients receiving personal Rogerian therapy and another group only reading Carl Rogers' books that include the *philosophy* of unconditional positive regard. My hypothesis is that the second group would acquire significantly more *un*conditional self-acceptance than the first. And if a third group read and listened to only RET materials, it, I hypothesize, would gain more self-acceptance than the other two groups.

Don Meichenbaum talks about the role of historical development, mental, familial, and social cultural differences. These are, of course, important. But how did clients first construct their irrational beliefs? They didn't do it through their culture, but largely did it, RET holds, through *themselves*. They are *both* talented screwballs and talented self-actualizers. Both are constructive biological tendencies. Again, they are *influenced* by social goals, standards, and values, but they *add* unhealthy Jehovian commands over and above such pressures.

What about the need to consider transference and countertransference factors? Transference means several things. First, clients transfer, overgeneralize from the past and from their experience with their transactions with their therapist. This is often part of their disturbance and had better be therapeutically addressed. Transference also means that the clients have strong needs to relate to significant people and that because the therapist is significant to them, they bring their needs to win the therapist's approval and do everything possible to gain his or her support. The therapist may use that need to attach the client healthfully or unhealthfully to himself or herself, thus helping or harming the client—and especially sabotaging the client when and if the client's overgeneralizing and dire need for love tendencies are reinforced. In RET, we reveal and analyze transference relationships—as they occur in therapy and in clients' outside lives—and show them how to undo unhealthy transference, how to stop *over*generalizing, and how to stop direly *needing* their therapist's approval (Ellis, 1962, 1973; Ellis & Dryden, 1991).

Don agrees with Neimeyer and Feixas (1990) that "the constructionist approach is more concerned about the *viability* rather than the validity of one's meaning system." Quite right! As I have tried to make clear for many years (Ellis, 1962, 1973, 1988, 1990, 1991, 1992; Ellis & Dryden, 1987, 1990, 1991; Ellis & Harper, 1975; Ellis & Whiteley, 1979), "rational" in RET does not merely mean realistic, logical, or consistent; it mainly means self-helpful *and* socially viable. It hypothesizes that people *usually* help themselves and others when they realistically and logically stay with strong preferences rather than absolutist musts and demands. However, it has acknowledged for years that "irrational" and Pollyannaish philosophies may *sometimes* help people survive and be happy and, therefore, that RET *at times* includes *ir*rational and *un*realistic methods (Ellis, 1989; Young, 1977).

Don emphasizes the importance of behavioral and relapse-prevention skills training. That is what RET always has done. It always assumed that people largely construct their disturbances and that they easily reconstruct them and fall back. Therefore, they rarely get completely over a disturbance, but only minimize it.

When they fall back or construct new dysfunctional thoughts, feelings, and behaviors, RET tries to help people prevent and overcome them. It tries to help them achieve an *elegant* solution: that is, to see over and over again that they do not *need* what they *want*, and that there is no reason why hassles, failures, and disapprovals *absolutely must not exist*. Ideally, RET shows clients how to make themselves less disturbed and less disturb*able* (Ellis, 1973, 1988; Ellis & Dryden 1987, 1990, 1991; Ellis & Whiteley, 1979). It often teaches skills training, practical solutions, and problem solving, but basically RET tries to help clients make a "basic philosophic change" that abets relapse prevention and *re*construction of dysfunctional behavior.

With regard to Don Meichenbaum's goal of extending CBT well beyond the clinic setting, including family therapy and paraprofessional training, RET has pioneered in this respect since I first published *How to Live with a Neurotic* (Ellis, 1957). The Institute for Rational-Emotive Therapy in New York has given paraprofessional training certificates for many years; it has run an experimental school for children; it includes a corporate services division that trains businesspeople and trainers; it is allied with Rational Recovery Systems, a large organization of self-help groups; since 1965, it has conducted over 2,000 courses and workshops for the public; and it has sponsored many other nonclinical applications of RET (Institute, 1991).

To summarize: Don Meichenbaum has nicely extended his original formulations of cognitive behavior therapy in his chapter and I heartily agree with almost all of his reformulations. As I unmodestly note above, RET has even pioneered in adopting many of the points he makes. But his view of RET as "rationalist" rather than "constructivist" is mistaken. I am sure that Arnold Lazarus would agree that this kind of CBT is not "rationalist" either; and I am not sure whether any major form of CBT is. Mike Mahoney (1991) and Don Meichenbaum have partly set up a strawperson that supposedly makes them radically different from RETers and other cognitive behavior therapists. Fortunately, RET has predated them by a number of years.

REFERENCES

Beck, A. T. (1976). *Cognitive therapy and the emotional disorders*. New York: International Universities Press.

Bernard, M. (1986). *Staying alive in an irrational world*. Melbourne: Macmillan.

Burns, D. (1980). *Feeling good*. New York: Morrow.

Ellis, A. (1956). An operational reformulation of some of the basic principles of psychology and psychoanalysis. *Psychoanalytic Review, 43*, 163–180.

Ellis, A. (1957). *How to live with a neurotic: At home and at work*. New York: Crown. Rev. ed., North Hollywood, CA: Wilshire Books, 1975.

Ellis, A. (1958). Rational psychotherapy. *Journal of General Psychology, 59*, 35–49. Reprinted: New York: Institute for Rational-Emotive Therapy.

Ellis, A. (1959). Requisite conditions for basic personality change. *Journal of Consulting Psychology, 23*, 538–540.

Ellis, A. (1962). *Reason and emotion in psychotherapy*. Secaucus, NJ: Citadel.

Ellis, A. (1972). Helping people get better rather than merely feeling better. *Rational Living, I*(2), 2–9.

Ellis, A. (1973). *Humanistic psychotherapy: The rational-emotive approach*. New York: McGraw-Hill.

Ellis, A. (1985). *Overcoming resistance: Rational-emotive therapy with difficult clients*. New York: Springer.

Ellis, A. (1988). *How to stubbornly refuse to make yourself miserable about anything—yes, anything!* Secaucus, NJ: Lyle Stuart.

Ellis, A. (1989). A rational-constructivist approach to couples and family therapy. In A. Ellis, J. L. Sichel, R. J. Yeager, D. J. DiMattia, & R. DiGiuseppe, *Rational-emotive couples therapy* (pp. 106–119). New York: Pergamon.

Ellis, A. (1990). Is rational-emotive therapy (RET) "rationalist" or "constructivist." In A. Ellis, & W. Dryden, *The essential Albert Ellis* (pp. 114–141). New York: Springer.

Ellis, A. (1991). Achieving self-actualization. In A. Jones & R. Crandall (Eds.), *Handbook of self-actualization*. Corte Madera, CA: Select Press.

Ellis, A., & Dryden, W. (1987). *The practice of rational-emotive therapy*. New York: Springer.

Ellis, A., & Dryden, W. (1990). *The essential Albert Ellis*. New York: Springer.

Ellis, A., & Dryden, W. (1991). *A dialogue with Albert Ellis*. Stony Stratford, England: Open University Press.

Ellis, A., & Harper, R. A. (1975). *A new guide to rational living*. North Hollywood, CA: Wilshire Books.

Ellis, A., & Schoenfeld, E. (1990). Divine intervention and the treatment of chemical dependency. *Journal of Substance Abuse, 2*, 459–468.

Ellis, A., Sichel, J., Yeager, R., DiMattia, D., & DiGiuseppe, R., (1989). *Rational-emotive couples therapy*. New York: Pergamon.

Ellis, A., & Whiteley, J. (1979). *Theoretical and empirical foundations of rational emotive therapy*. Monterey, CA: Brooks/Cole.

Huber, C. H., & Baruth, L. G. (1989). *Rational-emotive and systems family therapy*. New York: Springer.

Institute for Rational-Emotive Therapy (1991). *Catalogue*. New York: Author.

Lazarus, A. A. (1980). *Multimodal therapy*. Baltimore: Johns Hopkins University Press.

Lazarus, A. A. (1989). *The practice of multimodal therapy: Systematic, comprehensive, and effective psychotherapy*. Baltimore: Johns Hopkins University Press.

Mahoney, M. J. (1991). *Human change processes*. New York: Basic Books.

Maslow, A. H. (1973). *The farther reaches of human nature*. Harmondsworth, England: Penguin.

Maultsby, M.C., Jr. (1984). *Rational behavior therapy*. Englewood Cliffs, NJ: Prentice-Hall.

Meichenbaum, D. (1977). *Cognitive-behavior modification*. New York: Plenum.

Neimeyer, R., & Feixas, G. (1990). Constructivist contributions to psychotherapy integration. *Journal of Integrative and Eclectic Psychotherapy, 9*, 4–20.

Rogers, C. R. (1957). The necessary and sufficient conditions of therapeutic personality change. *Journal of Consulting Psychology, 21*, 95–103.

Rogers, C. R. (1961). *Becoming a person*. Boston: Houghton Mifflin.

Seligman, M. (1991). *Learned optimism*. New York: Knopf.

Walen, S. R., DiGiuseppe, R., & Wessler, R. L. (1980). *A practitioner's guide to rational-emotive therapy*. New York: Oxford.

Yankura, J., & Dryden, W. (1990). *Doing RET: Albert Ellis in action*. New York: Springer.

Young, H. S. (1977). Counseling strategies with working class adolescents. In J. L. Wolfe & E. Brand (Eds.), *Twenty years of rational therapy* (pp. 187–202). New York: Institute for Rational-Emotive Therapy.

RESPONSE BY DR. MEICHENBAUM

My association with Albert Ellis goes back to my beginning days as a graduate student in clinical psychology. I have described my initial provocative encounter with Al in my 1977 book, *Cognitive Behavior Modification*. Even in that first meeting Al was continually correcting me. It is impressive that not much has changed in the interim 25 years.

Another indicator of consistency is the religious fervor with which Al espouses RET doctrine. Indeed, there is a Biblical flavor to his response. The "Biblical" aspect derives from his assessment that any criticism of RET is misguided and that any new idea has been subsumed in his prior RET writings. While I concur that Al Ellis deserves credit for being a strident voice for the position that cognitions play a role in maladaptive behavior, I also have misgivings about the degree to which he has highlighted cognition, in the form of so-called "irrational beliefs," in his formulations of emotional disturbance and maladaptive behavior.

As Mahoney (1991) and I have noted, it is both presumptuous and pejorative to characterize someone's beliefs as "irrational," as if one holds the axiomatic system of rationality. At times, I must confess, I feel Albert Ellis believes that he has been "chosen" to educate us all about what constitute "rational beliefs."

In addition, Ellis' emphasis on the logical disputation of his clients' beliefs belie his pronouncements of being a "constructivist." I argue that there is not one reality, or one set of beliefs, that is to be evaluated on the dimensions of rationality and validity. Rather, individuals are continually selecting and helping to orchestrate their own realities. The task for the therapist is to collaborate with clients in having them appreciate how they narratively script, architecturally sculpt, and behaviorally enact their own realities. Moreover, the therapist considers with clients the impact their metaphorical constructions have on them and on others. What is the price they pay, what is the toll such views take? Is this the price they wish to pay? If not, what could be done to change things? The therapist acts as a collaborator in helping clients to achieve their personal goals. It is the viability and adaptiveness of personal constructions, not their "rationality," that is central to a constructivist perspective. I suspect that Al must have said this somewhere.

Moreover, clinicians should be concerned that confronting clients in the form of logical disputation and challenging their beliefs are likely to "freeze" these beliefs rather than encourage clients to perform personal experiments that will allow them to collect disconfirmatory data. The therapist helps clients to take such data as evidence to "unfreeze" their views of themselves, the future, and the world.

Speaking of evidence, I would encourage Al to qualify his enthusiasm for bibliotherapeutic procedures. Both Rosen, in his many reviews of the questionable benefits of self-help manuals, and our review on patient education (see Meichenbaum & Turk, 1987) underscore the limited therapeutic effectiveness of patients' reading clinical material. For instance, what would it take for Al Ellis to reconsider his commitment to RET doctrine? Clearly, not anything Mahoney or I have written. Like our patients, Al has the ability to reframe any criticism as a reaffirmation of his original RET position. My hope is that he will remain well for many years so we can continue to have this dialogue. There are few things I can truly count on in this changing world. Al's consistency is reassuring!

REFERENCES

Mahoney, M. J. (1991). *Human change processes*. New York: Basic Books.

Meichenbaum, D. (1977). *Cognitive behavior modification*. New York: Plenum.

Meichenbaum, D., & Turk, D. (1987). *Facilitating treatment adherence: A practitioner's guidebook*. New York: Plenum.

Toward Better Results in the Treatment of Depression: The Analysis of Individual Dynamics

◆────────◆────────◆

Joseph Wolpe, M.D.

Joseph Wolpe, M.D.

Joseph Wolpe, M.D., D.Sc., received his M.D. degree in 1948 from the University of Whitwatersrand in Johannesburg, South Africa. He is Professor of Psychology and Psychiatry at Pepperdine University and at the University of California, Los Angeles. A recipient of the Distinguished Scientific Award for Applications of Psychology from the American Psychological Association and the Lifetime Achievement Award from the Phobia Society, he is one of the leading practitioners of behavior therapy. Wolpe has written seven books and coedited two, has more than 500 professional publications to his credit, and is the cofounder of the Journal of Behavior Therapy and Experimental Psychiatry.

Joseph Wolpe alerts us to the fact that accepted thinking about nonbipolar, nonpsychotic depression is marred by inattention to research, showing that some cases are masked endogenous depressions, while others are anxiety-based in several possible ways. Therefore, individual cases must be investigated to decide appropriate treatment. This would make it possible to surpass the mediocre results typified in the "Collaborative Study."

Despite an outward appearance of sophistication and scientific respectability, serious confusion marks the currently accepted approach to the treatment of nonbipolar, nonpsychotic depression. Several methods of treatment of depression exist, all of which are erroneously regarded as applicable "across the board." Responsible for this error is the assumption that depression is a uniform "entity" wherein cases differ from each other only in severity.

What I intend to show in this chapter is that depression is the result of several different kinds of circumstances, and it is necessary to determine what lies behind the individual case in order to decide what treatment is likely to succeed.

HISTORICAL BACKGROUND

Over the ages, depression was called melancholia, supposedly a specific illness caused by "humors" or other processes within the person. About a century ago, an association between depressive and manic states was noted (Klerman, 1989), and they were seen as different manifestations of the same disorder. Later, Kraepelin (1904) noted that certain cases of depression displayed unusual emotional reactivity, and he proposed that these were a separate type, psychologically caused. His dichotomy came to be generally recognized and was given various labels, of which endogenous-neurotic (Kendall & Gourlay, 1970) was in recent years the most widely used. The 1987 revised third edition of the *Diagnostic and Statistical Manual of Mental Disorders* (DSM-III-R) renders the dichotomy as major depression, on the one hand, and dysthymic disorder, on the other.

Clinicians, however, often found it difficult to decide on which side of the dichotomy to assign a particular case. They could positively diagnose endogenous depression on the basis of such features as psychomotor retardation, agitation, delusions, hallucinations, and negativism, but the diagnosis of psychogenic depression was mainly based on exclusion, being made when cases lacked the features pathognomonic of endogenous depression (Foulds, 1975; Kiloh, Andrews, Neilson, & Bianchi, 1972; Mendels & Cochrane, 1968).

A study by Akiskal et al. (1979) conducted on patients with "neurotic depression" showed that they are not a homogeneous population. A depressed patient was eligible for inclusion in the study if reality testing was preserved, if there was insight into the psychological nature of the illness, and if hallucinations and delusions were absent. Out of a substantial population of depressed subjects, Akiskal and his colleagues identified 100 as having "neurotic depression." These patients were followed up three to four years later, at which time much evidence of other psychiatric diagnoses emerged. Thirty-six patients had melancholic episodes, and half of these (18% of the total) also had changes of polarity, 10 cases were attributable to medical-surgical illness, and three were schizophrenic or schizo-affective. Most of the remainder were labeled "chronic secondary dysphorias," which Akiskal (1983) later saw as including neurotic sources of depression. He was not aware that at that time there already were both physiological and clinical grounds for the existence of anxiety-based depressions. However, most germane to our immediate concern is the finding of the Akiskal study that cases diagnosed as "neurotic depres-

sion" (which could just as readily be labeled "nonpsychotic depression") are not a homogeneous group, but a mixed bag.

NEUROTIC ANXIETY AS A CAUSE OF DEPRESSION

Anxiety is often the sole manifestation of a neurosis, but it is also the basis of such disorders as psychosomatic states, stuttering, sexual inadequacy, and obsessions and compulsions. In these, the causal role of anxiety usually becomes clear upon close scrutiny. Its role is less obvious when neurotic anxiety is the antecedent of depression. Occasionally, during this century, there were psychiatrists who observed clinically a connection between anxiety and certain cases of depression. Rogerson (1940) was one of the first to show awareness of this when he suggested that the term "affective psychosis" be used for biological depressions and "affective neurosis" for anxiety states (which he subcategorized into depressive neuroses and anxiety neuroses).

PHYSIOLOGICAL EVIDENCE FOR AN ANXIETY-LINKED SUBCLASS OF DEPRESSIONS

Three decades ago, Shagass, Naiman, and Mihalik (1956), using the sedation threshold (Shagass, 1954) as a measure of anxiety, demonstrated that whereas its levels are low in endogenous depression, they are high in neurotic depressions. The sedation threshold is the amount of sodium amobarbital (Amytal) injected at a steady rate that is needed to produce certain electroencephalographic effects, together with such behavioral effects as cessation of conversational responding. They found, in general, that there was a direct relationship between the level of ongoing anxiety and the amount of Amytal required to combat it. Endogenous depressions were diagnosed according to the usual criteria of psychomotor retardation, agitation, delusions, hallucinations, mutism, and negativism. In the neurotic group, there were none of these features, but, instead, a depression would be combined with neurotic symptoms, among which anxiety was prominent. In a comparison of 25 matched pairs, 23 of the endogenous cases and only one of the neurotic patients had a sedation threshold of less than 4 mg/kg. Significantly, the mean sedation threshold in the neurotic depressions (mean 5.05) was only slightly lower than that in a separate group of subjects diagnosed as having anxiety states (mean 5.32).

Other workers (e.g., Gilberti & Rossi, 1962; Nymgaard, 1959; Perez-Reyes, 1972a, 1972b) corroborated these observations in a variety of ways. Perez-Reyes observed that the thresholds of neurotic depressives were significantly higher, and those of psychotic depressives significantly lower, than those of normal controls. He persuasively argued that endogenous depression and neurotic depression must be separate syndromes if their sedation thresholds are on opposite sides of normal.

Gilberti and Rossi found that endogenous and neurotic depression could also be differentiated on their responses to stimulant drugs, which Shagass (1981) called "a kind of a reverse direction sedation threshold." They injected methamphetamine or methylphenidate at a steady rate and measured blood pressures and pulse changes. They predicted and found high stimulation thresholds in endogenous depressives (mean–17 mg/kg of methamphetamine) and low thresholds in neurotic depressives (mean = 7.1 mg/kg).

Impressive though the above observations are, they made little impact on psychiatrists. Typically, Roth et al. (1972), in a paper dealing specifically with the relationship between anxiety states and depression, did not mention the work of Shagass. This is important because if psychiatrists had realized that there are cases where high measures of anxiety are associated with depression, they might have considered the possibility that overcoming the anxiety might also overcome the depression. As will be seen, there are clinical data showing this to be the case.

THE VARIABLE DYNAMICS OF NEUROTIC DEPRESSION

Independently of the foregoing physiological research, I had observed, in the early 1950s, cases in which depression appeared to be related to neurotic anxiety. Most frequently, the patient would have presented as a neurotic case, and clinical assessment would have revealed depression as a feature of the symptomatology. Further study would have shown the depression to be secondary to anxiety. The causal role of the anxiety was regarded as confirmed if depression was resolved as a sequel to the deconditioning of anxiety.

About a decade ago, I represented the findings of a long experience in a randomly sampled group of 25 patients (Wolpe, 1979). The basic data are presented in Table 1. Clinical data from these patients indicated that the depression could be dynamically related to anxiety in four different ways.

Before detailing this, it is necessary to make

Table 1. SUMMARY OF DATA

PREDOMINANT BASIS OF CAUSATIVE ANXIETY	NUMBER OF CASES	MEAN TIME SINCE ONSET OF DEPRESSIVE SYMPTOMS	MEAN NUMBER OF TREATMENT SESSIONS	NUMBER RECOVERED OR MUCH IMPROVED
Classically conditioned	11	9.6 years	35.2	11
Cognitively based	6	7.3 years	24.5	5
Interpersonal inadequacy	8	4.9 years	27.5	6
Bereavement	—	—	—	—
TOTAL	25	7.4 years	30.2	22

Number of cases followed up 6 months or more: 19
Mean follow-up: 5.2 years

Source: Wolpe, 1979

some general remarks about the behavioral approach to neuroses, because it is widely misunderstood. The popular assumption is that behavioral treatment is rigidly determined by the simple description of the case. For example, a phobia is treated by desensitization and a social fear by assertiveness training. This simplistic picture only can be held by a person who has no knowledge of the behavioral conception of neuroses as learned maladaptive anxiety response habits (Wolpe, 1958, 1990). A therapeutic strategy directed against such habits must vary from case to case, since it must be formulated on an accurate analysis of the dynamics of the anxiety. The anxiety must be comprehensible in terms of the conditionings and motivations operative in the individual case. Hence one does not diagnose neurotic depression and then apply a "textbook" treatment, such as cognitive therapy. Instead, one individualizes the treatment in accordance with the identified dynamic structure of the case. How the analysis is conducted is described in the section that follows.

DIAGNOSIS AND SUBDIAGNOSIS OF NEUROTIC DEPRESSION

Details of individual cases determine the conduct of treatment. As Table 1 indicates, a high measure of success attends programs tailored to individual dynamics. The possibility of a basis in anxiety should be considered in any depression in which the criteria for major depression are absent. As demonstrated by Akiskal et al. (1979), a large number of those failing to meet these criteria are found in time to be endogenous, another subgroup to be neurotic, and there are probably depressions with other etiologies, as suggested by Akiskal (1983) and Winokur (1985). Only the identification of the neurotic cases will be considered here.

For a depression to be eligible for consideration as neurotic, there must be evidence of maladaptive anxiety. Anxiety is maladaptive when it is elicited in circumstances in which there is no objective threat. The first source of information about maladaptive anxieties is the patient's history. Events, persons, and thoughts that were present at a time of high anxiety

arousal may have become persistent triggers to anxiety. Sometimes, later events will modify the character of the anxiety or give new stimuli the ability to arouse it (second-order conditioning). The central aim of history-taking is to define the stimulus areas that currently elicit maladaptive anxiety. These areas will later be the focus of therapy. The dynamics of each stimulus must be analyzed. It is, for example, not enough to know that a patient is anxious in social situations; one needs to define the situations that are distressing and the factors within these that control the magnitude of the distress. If a man is made anxious by being the center of attention, factors that may influence the magnitude of the anxiety include the number, age, or status of the people looking at him; the requirements to perform (e.g., speak); and disapproval that he may infer (whose content must be elucidated). All relevant factors will be taken into account in the treatment program.

Complexity of antecedents of neurotic anxiety is the rule. This is often true even of phobias labeled "simple." Agoraphobia well illustrates complexity. Only a minority of these cases are nothing but fear of separation from a "safe" place or person; some are primarily fears of physical or emotional crises, which include panic attacks of heterogeneous etiology (Wolpe & Rowan, 1988). Others are fears of what may be encountered in the outside world (as is found in one variety of school phobia). Yet another group are the agoraphobias of unhappily married women, who are low in self-sufficiency, whose dynamics are fascinatingly varied, and whose treatment involves the acquisition of social control (Wolpe, 1990).

The clinical history concludes with surveys of early relationships, educational experiences, and love life. Additional data are obtained from questionnaires that are routinely administered: the Willoughby Neuroticism Schedule, the Fear Survey Schedule, and the Bernreuter Self-Sufficiency Inventory. These questionnaires, in different ways, provide a conspectus of social anxiety and emotional lability.

The therapist plans treatment to meet the dynamic structure of each area of maladaptive anxiety (Wolpe, 1990). Two thirds of anxiety cases (Ost & Hugdahl, 1981; Wolpe, 1981;

Wolpe, Lande, McNally, & Schotte, 1985) require treatment by deconditioning, using such methods as desensitization, assertiveness training, or emotional flooding, according to the features of the case. In the other one third of cases, cognitive correction is indicated. A few cases require both cognitive and conditioning modalities. Confidence in the diagnosis of neurotic depression is, naturally, enhanced if the magnitudes of anxiety and depression vary concurrently. But even if this is not clearly demonstrable, it is appropriate to embark on deconditioning of maladaptive anxiety, both because this is desirable in its own right and because experience has shown that alleviation of the depression is usually a consequence. Of course, this will not always happen—notably in the occasional case in which the depression is actually endogenous and exists side by side with neurotic anxiety. I have had some cases in which deconditioning of anxiety has been facilitated after a concomitant endogenous depression has been recognized and effectively controlled by lithium.

Incidental features of some diagnostic value in neurotic depression are the absence of early-morning waking and a long continuation of the depression, which is in keeping with the long duration of untreated neuroses. It should be noted that, contrary to what was once believed, precipitation by stress is not a feature of neurotic depression, but is much more suggestive of those that are endogenous (Hirschfeld et al., 1985; Leff, Roatch, & Bunney, 1970; Paykel et al., 1969; Thompson & Hendrie, 1972).

ANXIETY CONTEXTS OF NEUROTIC DEPRESSION

The ways in which anxiety can lead to depression are listed in four contexts. It should be noted that two or more of these may be operative in the same case.

Context 1. Neurotic depression as a consequence of classically conditioned anxiety.

Patients with neurotic anxiety also may report depression, whose fluctuations often are correlated with the intensity of the anxiety. In some cases, depression becomes the dominant emotional tone. Where there has been free-floating anxiety (Wolpe, 1958, 1990), continuous depression may take its place. It is clear from Shagass's studies (see above) that in these cases the autonomic pattern reflects anxiety, even when the subjective report is of depression. The latter diminishes in concert with the deconditioning of anxiety, often ceasing long before the anxiety has been fully overcome. Eleven of the cases of depression in Table 1 were predominantly in this anxiety context.

Context 2. Neurotic depression as a consequence of anxiety based on erroneous cognitions.

This context of neurotic depression differs from the previous one in that the anxiety is not classically conditioned, but is based on self-devaluative misconceptions. Table 1 reflects six cases of this kind, which were appropriately treated by cognitive correction. According to Beck (1967), all cases of depression are due to misconceptions. Our analysis does not support this claim, which is contested in detail in the final section of this chapter. In the majority of our cases, recovery was not associated with any program of cognitive correction.

Context 3. Neurotic depression due to anxiety-based interpersonal inadequacy.

High levels of anxiety may be elicited by a wide range of interpersonal situations, such as the need for self-assertion or the possibility of incurring disapproval. Such anxiety may lead to inadequate handling of other people and the awareness of failure that follows may generate depression. The inhibition of self-expression may itself produce a feeling of ineffectuality that shades into depression. Assertiveness training has a central role in the treatment of such cases. Assertive behavior inhibits, and with repetition weakens, the maladaptive habit of anxiety in relevant interpersonal situations. Individual acts of assertion express anger or whatever other emotion is appropriate to the situation. Occasional patients are unable to begin to be assertive because of fear of a hostile comeback; others are inhibited by guilt. These emotional obstacles are, as a rule, easily overcome by a preliminary program of systematic desensitization.

Context 4. Neurotic depression based on overreaction to bereavement.

When the distress occasioned by bereavement is unusually severe or prolonged, one must always entertain the possibility that a major depression has been precipitated (e.g., Hirschfeld et al., 1985; Thompson & Hendrie, 1972). But in some cases it is previous conditioning of high levels of anxiety to loss that lies behind the persistence of the grief. The anxiety may prevent the reliving of distressing images that would enable the grief to be extinguished (absorbed). Ramsay (1977) obtained striking results in intractable mourning by flooding treatment that made the patient insistently focus on the reality of the death and on precious images from the dead person's life. (See also Lieberman [1978], Phillips [1978], and Wanderer and Cabot [1978] for the parallel treatment of depression resulting from unrequited love.) There were no cases in our series in which bereavement was the primary source of depression, but it was contributory in one case.

THE RESULTS OF TREATMENT

The treatment of depression in the 25 cases presented in Table 1 consisted of overcoming the maladaptive anxiety response habits that were revealed in the assessment of the case. Although the main anxiety context is indicated by the predominant basis, other contexts usually contributed. As Table 1 indicates, the neurotic depression was overcome or markedly improved in 22 of the 25 cases, two cases were unimproved, and one case had repeated recurrences of depression, though at a lower level than before. These three cases were also variously failures in overcoming neurotic anxiety. It is common for depression to cease long before the complete resolution of the underlying anxiety-response habits. Of the 22 successful cases, 19 were followed up six months or more after treatment. None had relapsed.

The study discussed above obviously calls for formal replication, but it does provide prima facie support for the proposition that some depressions are a function of anxiety, and their treatment is the deconditioning of neurotic anxiety. It is relevant that the literature contains frequent intimations of depressions that respond to psychotherapy (e.g., Copeland, 1983; Kiloh & Garside, 1963).

THE FUTILITY OF CURRENT OUTCOME RESEARCH IN DEPRESSION

Endogenous depression is generally treated by biological methods, mainly antidepressant drugs. It has been claimed that "nonpsychotic depression" is more effectively treated by various modes of psychotherapy: interpersonal therapy (Klerman et al., 1974; Weissman et al., 1981), cognitive therapy (Beck et al., 1985; Rush & Watkins, 1981; Shaw, 1977), social skills training (Bellack, Hersen & Himmelhoch, 1983; Hersen, Bellack, & Himmelhoch, 1980, 1984), and reinforcement therapy (Azrin & Besalel, 1981; Lewinsohn et al., 1981). These reports were the impetus for the multimillion-dollar Collaborative Research Program sponsored by the National Institute for Mental Health (Elkins et al., 1989), which compared interpersonal psychotherapy and cognitive-behavior therapy with treatment by imipramine and with controls who received a placebo and 30 minutes of supportive discussion (not psychotherapy). The imipramine was more successful than the psychotherapies, which were not particularly impressive. However, both the Collaborative Program and its predecessors assumed that their case material was uniform, totally ignoring Akiskal's trailblazing demonstration (Akiskal et al., 1979) of the heterogeneity of nonpsychotic depression, to say nothing of the heterogeneous subclasses of neurotic depression described above. To investigate the effects of different agents on psychopathologically mixed groups of depression is as futile as to compare the curative effects of medications on cases of pneumonia without subdividing the cases on the basis of causal organisms.

WHY PSYCHOTHERAPIES HAVE SUCCEEDED WITH MIXED POPULATIONS OF NONPSYCHOTIC DEPRESSIVES

It remains necessary to explain why each of the various psychotherapies alleviated many cases of depression. We must first observe that none of the authors considered the matter of diagnostic differentiation and, therefore, the actual distribution of subdiagnoses in their studies is unknown. For the purpose of exposition, we will postulate that in each of the studies there were 100 cases with the same diagnostic distribution as the 100 followed-up patients of Akiskal et al. (1979). Subtracting the 36 cases that they found to be endogenous, the 10 whose depressions were secondary to physical illness, and the two who turned out to be schizophrenic, we are left with 52 patients with what Akiskal (1983) called "chronic secondary dysphorias," which he divided into those in which anxiety dominated (and so the subjects, therefore, presumably were neurotic) and characterological depressions. (Examination of the case descriptions that Akiskal provided to illustrate the latter suggests that many of them were probably also neurotic depressions.) Therefore, without denying the possibility of characterological depressions, we will, for the sake of simplicity, assume that the 52 residual subjects had neurotic depressions. Since about half of Akiskal and colleagues' cases were inpatients, who are, on the whole, less likely to be neurotic, it seems reasonable to suggest that 60 of 100 outpatient nonpsychotic depressions are neurotic. Actually, a somewhat higher proportion of neurotic cases was found by Kiloh and Garside (1963).

Among 60 cases of neurotic depression, psychotherapeutic intervention *of any kind* may be expected to benefit about 30, because up to 50% of neurotic patients improve markedly on the basis of any sympathetic interpersonal interaction (e.g., Coleman, Greenblatt, & Solomon, 1956; Kellner & Sheffeld, 1971; Wilder, 1945). This, of course, is what psychoanalysts call "transference" and behavior therapists call "nonspecific interpersonal effects." Then, of the balance of 40 cases, which we posited as endog-

enous, 11 (27%) may be expected spontaneously to improve substantially in the course of a few weeks on the basis of the Klerman and Cole (1965) observations. Adding to these the 30 recovered neurotic patients provides a baseline recovery rate of 41% to be expected when a heterogeneous group of patients with nonpsychotic depressions have had psychotherapy *of any kind.*

Out of the four types of psychotherapeutic intervention noted above, we will select cognitive therapy to illustrate the misleading character of the outcome studies that have been published. We may assume, on the basis of the findings of Ost and Hugdahl (1981) and Wolpe (1981), that 20 (one third) of Beck's neurotic cases were predominantly cognitive. If the cognitive methods were found to benefit all of these, his projected success rate would rise from the baseline 41% to 61%.

This projection is fairly similar to the actual results obtained. In a report by Beck et al. (1985) of 37 cases treated by cognitive therapy, 25 (67%) were rated as "recovered" or "much improved." The success of the entire 67% is credited to cognitive therapy, in contrast to the actual 20% calculated above. Even though the calculation is based on a hypothetical projection, it suffices to show how the proponents of particular psychotherapeutic methods may have been misled into believing that their methods have specific efficacy for nonpsychotic depression.

SUGGESTIONS FOR THE FUTURE CONDUCT OF OUTCOME RESEARCH ON NONPSYCHOTIC DEPRESSION

Outcome studies on mixed pathologies have little value, except when the explicit object is symptom control, in the way that an analgesic may control pain no matter how it is caused. In populations with nonpsychotic depression, it is possible to distinguish neurotic cases with considerable assurance, as well as those that are endogenous. In due time it no doubt will become possible to diagnose others differently caused. Outcome studies should be confined to particular causal categories. With respect to neurotic cases, in addition to the categorical diagnosis, it is also necessary for comparisons of outcome to take into account the different ways in which anxiety is related to depression. Of course, the results of a total behaviorally based treatment package targeted on the basis of subcategorization could appropriately be compared with those of other packages. When other etiological categories of cases within the rubric of nonpsychotic depression are identifiable (e.g., Akiskal, 1983; Winokur, 1985), these, too, will be appropriate subject matter for comparative outcome studies.

REFERENCES

Akiskal, H. S. (1983). Dysthmic disorder: Psychopathology of proposed chronic depressive subtypes. *Am J Psy, 140,* 11–20.

Akiskal, H. S., Rosenthal, R. H., Rosenthal, T. L., et al. (1979). Differentiation of primary affective illness from situational, symptomatic and secondary depression. *Arch Gen Psy, 36,* 635–643.

Ascher, E. (1962). A criticism of the concept of neurotic depression. *Am J Psy, 108,* 901–908.

Azrin, N. H., & Besalel, V. A. (1981). An operant reinforcement method of treating depression. *J Behav Ther Exp Psy, 12,* 145–151.

Beck, A. T. (1967). *Depression.* New York: Harper & Row.

Beck, A. T., Hollon, S. D., Young, J. E., et al. (1985). Treatment of depression with cognitive therapy and amitriptyline. *Arch Gen Psy, 42,* 142–148.

Bellack, A. S., Hersen, M., & Himmelhoch, J. (1983). A comparison of social skills training, pharmacotherapy, and psychotherapy for depression. *Behav Res Ther, 21,* 101–107.

Brown, G. W., Davidson, S., Harrison, U., et al. (1977). Psychiatric disorder in London and North Uist. *Soc Sci & Med, 11,* 367–377.

Coleman, J. V., Greenblatt, M., & Solomon, H. S. (1956). Physiological evidence of rapport during psychotherapeutic interview. *Dis Nerv Syst, 17,* 71–77.

Copeland, J. R. M. (1983). Psychotic and neurotic depression: Discriminant function analysis and five-year outcome. *Psychol Med, 13,* 373–383.

Elkins, I., Shen, T., et al. (1989). NIMH treatment of depression collaborative program. *Arch Gen Psy, 46,* 971–982.

Foulds, G. A. (1975). The relationship between the depressive illnesses. *Br J Psy, 123,* 531–532.

Gilbert, R., & Rossi, R. (1926). Proposal of a psychopharmacological test ("stimulation threshold") for differentiating neurotic from psychotic depression. *Psychopharmacologia, 3,* 128–131.

Hersen, M., Bellack, A. S., Himmelhoch, J. M. (1980). Treatment of unipolar depression with social skills training. *Behav Mod, 4,* 547–556.

Hersen, M., Bellack, A. S., Himmelhoch, J. M., et al. (1984). Effects of social skills training, amitriptyline, and psychotherapy in unipolar depressed women. *Behav Ther, 15,* 21–40.

Hirschfeld, R. M. A., Klerman, G. L., Andreasen, N. C., et al. (1985). Situational major depression disorder. *Arch Gen Psy, 42,* 1109–1114.

Kay, D. W. K., Garside, R. D., Roy, J. R., et al. (1969). "Endogenous" and "neurotic" symptoms of depression: A 5- to 7-year follow-up of 104 cases. *Br J Psy, 115,* 389–399.

Kellner, R., & Sheffield, B. F. (1971). The relief of distress following attendance at a clinic. *Br J Psy, 118,* 195–198.

Kendell, R. E., & Gourlay, J. (1970). The clinical distinction between psychotic and neurotic depressions. *Br J Psy, 117,* 257–266.

Kiloh, L. G., Andrew, G., Neilson, M., & Bianchi, G. N. (1972). The relationships of the syndromes called endogenous and neurotic depression. *Br J Psy, 121,* 183–196.

Kiloh, L. G., & Garside, R. F. (1963). The independence of neurotic depression and endogenous depression. *Br J Psy, 109,* 451–463.

Klerman, G. L. (1989). Mood disorders. In *Treatments of psychiatric disorders.* Washington, D.C.: American Psychiatric Association.

Klerman, G. L., & Cole, J. O. (1965). Clinical pharmacology of imipramine and related antidepressant compounds. *Pharmacol Rev, 17,* 101–141.

Klerman, G. L., DiMascio, A., Weissman, M. M., et al. (1974). Treatment of depression by drugs and psychotherapy. *Am J Psy, 131,* 186–191.

Kraepelin, D. (1913). *Lehrbuch der Psychiatrie* (ed 8). Leipzig: Barth.

Leff, M. J., Roatch, J. F., & Bunney, W. E. (1970). Environmental factors preceding the onset of severe depressions. *Psychiatry, 33,* 293–311.

Lewinsohn, P. M., Steinmetz, J. L., Larson, D. W., et al. (1981). Depression related cognitions: Antecedent or consequence? *J Abnorm Psychol, 90,* 213–219.

Lewis, A. J. (1938). States of depression: Their clinical and aetiological differentiation. *Br Med J,* 4060.

Lieberman, S. (1978). Nineteen cases of morbid grief. *Br J Psy, 132,* 159–161.

Masserman, J. H. (1946). *Principles of dynamic psychiatry.* Philadelphia: Sanders.

Mendels, J., & Cochrane, C. (1968). The nosology of depression: The endogenous-reactive concept. *Am J Psy, 124* (Suppl.), 1–11.

Nymgaard, K. (1959). Studies on the sedation threshold. *Arch Gen Psy, 1,* 530–536.

Ost, L., & Hugdahl, K. (1981). Acquisition of phobias and anxiety response patterns in clinical patients. *Behav Res Ther, 19,* 439–477.

Pavlov, I. P. (1941). *Conditioned reflexes and psychiatry.* Translated by W. H. Gantt. New York: International.

Paykel, E. S., Myers, J. K., Diehelt, M. N., et al. (1969). Life events and depression. *Arch Gen Psy, 21,* 753–760.

Perez-Reyes, M. (1972a). Difference in sedative susceptibility between types of depression: Clinical and neurophysiological significance. In T. A. Williams, M. M. Katz, & J. A. Shields, Jr. (Eds.), *Recent advances in the psychobiology of the depressive illnesses* (pp. 119–130). Washington, DC: U.S. Government Printing Office.

Perez-Reyes, M. (1972b). Differences in the capacity of the sympathetic and endocrine systems of depressed patients to react to a physiological stress. In T. A. Williams, M. M. Katz, & J. A. Shields, Jr. (Eds.), *Recent advances in the psychobiology of the depressive illnesses* (pp. 131–135). Washington, DC: U.S. Government Printing Office.

Ramsay, R. W. (1977). Behavioural approaches to bereavement. *Behav Res & Ther*, *15*, 131–135.

Rogerson, C. H. (1940). The differentiation of neurosis and psychosis with special reference to states of depression and anxiety. *J Ment Sci*, *86*, 632.

Roth, M., Gurney, C., Garside, R. F., et al. (1972). Studies in the classification of affective disorders. The relationship between anxiety states and depressive illness—1. *Br J Psy*, *121*, 147–161.

Rush, A. J., & Watkins, J. T. (1981). Group versus individual cognitive therapy: A pilot study. *Cog Ther Res*, *5*, 95–103.

Shagass, C. (1954). The sedation threshold: A method for estimating tension in psychiatric patients. *Electroenciphalogr Clin Neurophysiol*, *6*, 221–228.

Shagass, C. (1981). Neurophysiological evidence for different types of depression. *J Behav Ther Exp Psy*, *12*, 99–111.

Shagass, C., Naiman, J., & Mihalik, J. (1956). An objective test which differentiates between neurotic and psychotic depression. *Arch Neurol Psy*, *75*, 461–471.

Shaw, B. F. (1977). Comparison of cognitive therapy and behavior therapy in the treatment of depression. *J Consult Clin Psychol*, *45*, 543–551.

Thompson, K. C., & Hendrie, H. C. (1972). Environmental stress in primary depressive illness. *Arch Gen Psy*, *26*, 130–132.

Weissman, M. M., Klerman, G. L., Prusoff, B. A., et al. (1981). Depressed outpatients: Results one year after treat

ment with drugs and/or interpersonal psychotherapy. *Arch Gen Psy*, *38*, 51–55.

West, E. M., & Dally, P. G. (1959). Effects of iproniazid in depressive syndromes. *Br Med J*, *1*, 1491–1494.

Wilder, J. (1945). Facts and figures on psychotherapy. *J Clin Psychopath*, *7*, 311.

Winokur, G. (1985). The validity of neurotic-reactive depression: New data and appraisal. *Arch Gen Psy*, *42*, 1116–1122.

Wolpe, J. (1958). *Psychotherapy by reciprocal inhibition*. Stanford, CA: Stanford University Press.

Wolpe, J. (1979). The experimental model and treatment of neurotic depression. *Behav Res Ther*, *17*, 555–565.

Wolpe, J. (1981). The dichotomy between directly conditioned and cognitively learned anxiety. *J Behav Ther Exp Psy*, *12*, 35–42.

Wolpe, J. (1985). Panic attacks are not homogenous. *Proceedings*, Fourth World Congress of Biological Psychiatry, Philadelphia.

Wolpe, J. (1986). The positive diagnosis of neurotic depression as an etiological category. *Comp Psy*, *27*, 449–460.

Wolpe, J. (1990). *The practice of behavior therapy* (4th ed.). New York: Pergamon.

Wolpe, J., Lande, S. D., McNally, R. J., & Schotte, D. (1985). Differentiation between classically conditioned and cognitively based fears: Two pilot studies. *J Behav Ther Exp Psy*, *16*, 287–293.

Wolpe, J., & Rowan, V. C. (1988). Panic disorder: A product of classical conditioning. *Behav Res Ther*.

Discussion by Thomas Szasz, M.D.

Dr. Wolpe's chapter exemplifies what makes much of the modern literature on psychotherapy, to me at least, unsatisfactory and uninspiring. Everything he says is couched in jargon. Prominently disfiguring the text are such terms as "endogenous-neurotic," "dysthymic disorder," "secondary dysphorias," "mixed pathologies," "nonbipolar," and, of course, "patient" and "treatment." Like the woman in the famous Wendy's ad who asked "Where is the beef?", I cannot help but ask "Where is the illness? Where is the treatment?" They are nowhere in sight. All that is in sight is Dr. Wolpe's claim of his success in "treating" 22 out of 25 persons who came to see him, I assume, voluntarily. Dr. Wolpe doesn't even tell us that.

Anyone who embraces the medical model as

fervently as does Dr. Wolpe may be judged fairly in terms of that model. Physicians who treat patients suffering from AIDS, lymphoma, or multiple sclerosis present not only objective evidence for what ails their patients, but also treatment failures. But would Dr. Wolpe have presented the results of his "therapy" if 22 out of his 25 "patients" had failed to improve or got worse? To my knowledge, Dr. Wolpe has never presented a series of cases where his treatment failed. Moreover, although he and I seem to agree that what other people call (mental) diseases are simply, but upsettingly to self or others, behaviors, he attaches names that sound like medical diseases to certain (undesirable) behaviors and treats them *as if* they were diseases rather than, as he himself acknowledges, behaviors. For example, Dr. Wolpe speaks of a "therapeutic strategy directed against such habits . . ." But bad habits are not diseases. The matter before us is much richer than Dr. Wolpe's approach admits. After all, changing people's habits is an occupation that psychotherapists share with advertisers, politicians, teachers, televangelists, and, of course, parents, spouses, and virtually everyone else in the world. Thus, like Dr. Wolpe, I too have been interested in people's habits, as my following research into marital relations illustrates:

Women marry hoping their husbands will change; men, hoping their wives won't. Both will be disappointed. Bad enough, but couples can make it worse by going to a psychiatrist to fix the problem. (Adapted from Szasz, 1990)

In effect, then, Dr. Wolpe claims to have a key for a nonlock. (He is not alone. Many psychotherapists indulge in this inconsistency.) I, for one, refuse to abide by the illogic of a person's asserting that "X is not a lock" (mental illness is *not disease* [it is behavior]), and then claiming that he, and he alone, has the key to unlock it (behavior *therapy*).

I should like to say that I find Dr. Wolpe's style of describing persons, and what he calls "diagnosis" and "therapy," so unappealing that I feel impelled to satirize it. I submit that a line such as "neurotic depression as a consequence of anxiety based on erroneous cognition" is positively funny. In case the humor escapes you, let me demonstrate it. Now, "erroneous cognition" is something real, something we can really sink our teeth into and almost taste. I can assure you, it's delicious, provided it is the other person's "erroneous cognition." If it's your own, it is bitter as bile. I don't recommend it all. Instead, stick to Mark Twain's recipe: "Nothing so needs reforming as other people's habits (Twain, 1884/1964).

REFERENCES

Szasz, T. S. (1990). *The untamed tongue: A dissenting dictionary* (p. 94). LaSalle, IL: Open Court.

Twain, M. (1884/1964). *Pudd'nhead Wilson* (p. 113). New York: Signet.

RESPONSE BY DR. WOLPE

I would like to answer some of the arguments Dr. Szasz raised. First, the cases he has accused me of selecting were chosen in a passive way. The 25 cases came from my file on depression, randomly selected by an assistant who knew nothing about psychotherapy or the contents of the file. Second, every single case came voluntarily. I've never treated a person who didn't come voluntarily for treatment. Dr. Szasz has been critical of cases whose treatment is involuntarily imposed. Third, I call people I see "patients" because they suffer, and that is the meaning of the word "patient." This is merely a matter of dictionary meaning.

Dr. Szasz does notice one very important thing, the fact that what I'm concerned with is habits. All behavior therapy is the treatment of maladaptive habits. In the area of emotional problems, it consists of the removal—the psychological overcoming—of habits of anxiety in response to situations that are not threatening. To have anxiety in response to harmless situations is to have pain that is unnecessary. For example, one person is anxious when the center of attention; another is made anxious by criticism from unimportant people. If patients are upset by these things, procedures such as systematic desensitization enable us to overcome their sensitivities. Perhaps Dr. Szasz does not realize that emotional habits are just as much habits as is the habit of taking off your hat when you go into a house. But where there is a *maladaptive* anxiety, we exercise our ability to remove the habit.

Since Dr. Szasz approves of the term "erroneous cognitions," I'll briefly describe a severe case of depression that was based on erroneous cognitions. This woman had been very depressed and anxious for 10 years, during which time she had undergone psychoanalysis with two different analysts. During my first three sessions with her, I went into her background and current circumstances very carefully to find associations of the depression. It turned out that her depression had been set off after she married by the fact that she had been unable to have coital orgasms. There was a consensus between her husband and the two psychiatrists that this inability indicated that something was wrong with her "deep down." She came to regard herself as a very inferior human being. For example, if at a party she were to see her husband engaged in a more or less animated conversation with another woman, she would become filled with envy because even if the other woman were quite unattractive, she would think, "At least she doesn't have my terrible affliction."

In the course of those first three sessions, the fact emerged that the reason why she didn't have coital orgasms had nothing to do with anything "deep down," but was a consequence of certain behavior by her father that had led to her distrusting people. He often did things behind her back. For example, when she was 13, she had a dog she loved, but her father took a dislike to it and had it destroyed while she was at school. By generalization, she became fearful of trusting anybody who was close to her: It emerged that she was unable to have orgasm with her husband because it implied, in her mind, total abandonment to him.

In the sexual situation, there is obviously a major commitment, a kind of letting go during an orgasm, and she couldn't bear to have her husband witness it. She could, by contrast, have orgasms quite easily by masturbation. Once she realized the cause of her failure to have orgasms, there was an enormous rise in self-esteem and an end to her depressions. After our first three sessions, her depressions stopped and have not recurred in 13 years. I went on to decondition her fear of trusting so she could have orgasms in the presence of her husband. First, she would reach them through masturbation, and when she was desensitized to that, she could go on to coital ones. Then after removing the wrong belief that caused the depression, we moved on to deconditioning the fear of trusting that was at the bottom of everything.

QUESTIONS AND ANSWERS

Question: Dr. Wolpe, I have two questions for you about the study you presented. First, what were the criteria measures for improvement?

Wolpe: After these treatments, the patient stopped being depressed. He stopped applying the word "depressed" to himself.

Question: So they improved according to self-report?

Wolpe: Yes, that is what is usually done in the treatment of neurotic patients. They come to you and say, "I'm afraid of criticism." They'll tell you what they are afraid of and then you treat them. At the end of treatment, they say, "Those absurd criticisms that used to distress me no longer do." Clinically, the situation is that the patient suffers. The patient comes to you telling you he or she is suffering, and at the end, if you have success, the patient tells you he or she is no longer suffering, but feels fine.

Question: So these patients were no longer depressed and never again became depressed?

Wolpe: That is correct. This is not to say that if one lost money in the stock market, he or she did not temporarily feel depressed.

Question: My second question is, was there a control group that was given some kind of supportive conversation but no therapy?

Wolpe: There was no control group. Obviously, in order to vindicate a treatment, you need control groups. But first you have to think that a good case exists for the efficacy of the treatment.

SECTION III

Humanistic Approaches

The Self in Action: A Gestalt Outlook

◆

Erving Polster, Ph.D.

Erving Polster, Ph.D.

Erving Polster (Ph.D., Western Reserve University, 1950) is codirector of the Gestalt Training Center, San Diego, and is also on the Clinical Faculty at the University of California, San Diego Medical School. Polster is the coauthor, with his wife, Miriam, of the landmark text, Gestalt Therapy Integrated. *He also published a book on his approach titled* Every Person's Life is Worth a Novel.

The concept of the self has come to imply a consistent cluster of characteristics that are often given fixed and universal attributes, such as the narcissistic self, top dog and underdog, and false and true self. In this chapter, Erving Polster expands the concept of self to include the versatility and unique aliveness of the individual's many selves and shows how these selves help people make sense of their lives. Special attention is directed to broadening the concepts of introjections, transference, and gestalt formation, showing how these may be instrumental in harmonizing alienated selves.

In this chapter, I will discuss four points related to Gestalt therapy's concept of the self. The first concerns the special significance of a sense of self for people in search of their identity. With regard to my second point, I will discuss a unified sense of self and its relation to constituent selves. Next, I will introduce a revised perspective of introjection, one that makes clear how vital introjection is to the early formation of selves, as well as to the reconstruction of selves. Finally, I will specify three therapeutic procedures that will tap into the infusion potential of the introjection process.

BACKGROUND

A concept of the self was one of Gestalt therapy's most important early contributions. However, the concept became a casualty—wounded, but not dead—in a post–World War II theoretical struggle. Many readers of this chapter were not yet born then, so it may be hard to realize the extremes to which therapists had gone in classifying people, often disregarding the person's individual experiences. In those days, we were replete with possibilities for understanding people, especially those of us who were psychoanalytically oriented, and we often would assume this understanding prematurely, giving only superficial attention to what people actually wanted, what they actually felt, and what they actually did, using these concerns merely as intellectual stepping-stones.

I look back with nostalgia at those exhilarating days in the late 1940s when I was a graduate student. As young zealots, we exaggerated what we learned, for example by identifying someone as an oral personality, often obscuring—not even caring about—the person's unique individuality. To our credit, we were incredibly agile in divining each other's psyches from the barest information and only the most stubborn among us would scoff at these designations. As a coffee-break calisthenic, it was a great exercise for our galloping minds, but a parlor game does not a person make.

A corrective to this system of stagnant classification had to come and it was most forcefully evident in existentialist circles, one of which was Gestalt therapy. In 1951, Perls, Hefferline, and Goodman, in their seminal book *Gestalt Therapy*, reacted against classifications and put the self into action, making it a centerpiece of their theory. Their view, in a nutshell, was that the self was a system of continuing contacts, a process rather than a structure, and they emphasized its engagements and its fluidity. They said, "The self is not . . . a fixed institution; it exists wherever and whenever there is . . . interaction. To paraphrase Aristotle, when the thumb is pinched, the self exists in the painful thumb" (p. 373). This was a key perspective because of the emphasis on flux rather than on an enduring class of characteristics; even though they said the *self* exists in the painful thumb, they made clear that the infinity of all of our experiences was of greater interest than the abstract self.

In a later work written with my wife, Miriam (Polster & Polster, 1973), we were more hospitable to classifications of the self and presented the concept of the I-boundary. Without going into details here, we named classes of self that were pivotal in regulating contact. But our interest in examining the activities and awarenesses of the person predominated and we focused the rest of our book on those processes. The self once again receded into the background.

Misgivings about abstractions and a yearning for a greater appreciation of actual experience went beyond psychology. One of the voices warning against the petrifaction that occurs in classifying experience was that of the novelist Joyce Cary (1961), who said that if you tell a child the name of a bird, the child loses the bird. That fear was and remains, real. Yet it also seems timely now to recognize that, although the danger of losing Cary's bird is substantial, there is an equal but opposite truth—if you know the name of the bird, its history, and its habits, you may know the bird better. Given these opposite truths, losing the bird and enhancing the bird, it is evident that the principles that win out in any method—the ones that come to be a method's melody, so to speak—always are accompanied by counterpoints. These counterpoints could enrich the melody, like the harmonic undercurrents that deepen primary musical themes. In music, however, the different voices resonate spontaneously in the listener's ear, but in therapeutic theories, the mind easily narrows in on the main theme, shifting away from contrapuntal intricacy.

I do not think this has to happen. Let us revisit the self as harmonic counterpoint to our focus on raw experience. After 40 years of growth in experiential know-how, we see again—perhaps more than ever—a yearning to know who we are, to know the self that evolves from an infinity of ephemeral experiences, unnamed wisps, each by itself having no form and going nowhere. Perhaps now, less defensive about being classified, we can respond to this craving for a personal synopsis by searching out raw experience and, at the same time, as musicians do with their counterpoints, using the concept of self to add depth and identity to these experiences.

WHAT IS THE SELF?

The concept of the self calls for the person to transform the pronoun I from a grammatical stand-in—without further meaning—into a recognition of essential qualities with which the person may be identified. Real self, narcissistic self, nuclear self, and false self all refer to essential qualities of the person. But the self is more than essential qualities. It is also a representative of the person. This inner being is formed through those patterning powers of the mind that unite elemental experiences into wholes. Long ago, Gestalt learning theorists pointed out the innate capacity for gestalt formation, a magnificent capacity that enables us to see unified faces rather than disconnected eyes, ears, nose, and lips. Beyond this simple perceptual feat, it is only a short step to believing that the same patterning process also organizes personal characteristics into coherent clusters, from which we form our sense of self.

Where such formations of self are concerned, patterns are much more freely created than in simple perceptions. At a high level of generalization, we may see that the self integrates the events of a lifetime, of which an epitaph is one example. The 19th-century novelist Machado de Assis (1990) wrote, "Among civilized people (epitaphs) are an expression of a secret . . . egoism that leads men . . . to rescue from death at least a shred of the soul that has passed on . . ." (p. 202).

This rescue of a shred of our souls does not wait for death, however. Many of us spend our lives reaching for measures of our true proportions in a potentially shapeless existence. The search for a single guiding image of our enduring nature is a temptation at least as old as the Greek adage, "Know thyself."

Let me give you an example of a blessed unity of self. One chronically angry patient of mine realized one day, as though hit between the eyes, how hard his life had been. In great self empathy, instead of getting angry, he cried convulsively. After he emerged, released from his anger and tension, he said, "This is the real me, peaceful and soft." He loved this self, the self that was free to cry when overwhelmed and to enjoy the breath of fresh air inside. But was it real? No, it was no more real than his angry rigidity had been.

The appearance of my patient's "real me"—peaceful and soft—gave him a unified sense of self that we all seek; he was all of a piece, à la Kierkegaard (1948), who wrote a book titled, *Purity of Heart Is to Will One Thing*. The marvelous wholeness my patient felt in this self was devoutly sought as he was happy to identify with it and to pray that it would become more easily accessible. However, this was only one elusive aspect of his self. At other times, there would be other states of mind—religious, scholarly, sexual—that also could cause him to experience himself as whole, and even "real."

Whatever this unified self may be, no matter how pivotal in restoring personal cohesion, the one self that represents his "all" also is accompanied by constituent selves. These constituent selves may coordinate well with each other and with the unified self or they may compete or be alienated. They may live in war or peace. They may be cunning or resigned. They may each go through periods of being favored or neglected. And they face stimulation, accepting it or fending it off.

In the consequent fluctuations, selves may be formed with great versatility. Let us examine a man who has the following four characteristics: he is careful in his choice of words, noticeably obstructionistic about things he is told to do, passive in conversation, insufficiently interested in his work. Given this cluster of characteristics, we may name the cluster a "procrastinating self." Or this formulation may change according to the chemistry created by combining these characteristics with others. For example, if this procrastinating person were to show nonchalance, we might name this self his "who cares self." If he seems quite confident, we may call it his "biding-my-time self." If he is clumsy, we may call it his "nerd self." How we resonate with our patients in identifying relevant selves from a multitude of possible configurations will be influential in treatment. Moreover, the sense of selves changes as new experiences call for change.

Before we move to therapeutic applications, there is one other consideration to take into account in formulating the concept of self. Ordinarily, we see people as having *characteristics*, not selves. At what point do the discrete characteristics—carefulness, obstructionism, passivity, and disinterest—coalesce into a procrastinating *self*. To use another example, when a person pretends to trip over your feet, tells funny stories, turns serious conversation upside down, one may laugh with that person or ridicule the person or stiffen against him or her as a matter of simple reactivity. At a certain point, however, these events and the person's evolving characteristics may be so enduringly interwoven and so clearly recognizable as a class of experiences that they may warrant designation as a self; in this case, let us say, a clownish self. This clustering, named or unnamed, will incline the person to clown, sometimes irrespective of current needs. In a sense, therefore, the self has a life of its own, a configuration extending its guidance, often without awareness.

The therapist often will recognize these influential clusters of experience before the patient does. He or she may then make an integrative leap, identifying these clusters as the entity we call the self. By naming the self, then by evoking the self's story with its struggles, climax, and, it is hoped, resolution, the therapist breathes life into these clusters of characteristics.

In other words (and this point is crucial) *the formation of self is a small work of fiction.* Characters are created and put into action in the context of the patient's life circumstances. Let me give you an example of how this creation of characters and their thematic development works. I have a patient whose antiestablishment self was so firmly embedded that it was damaging his life. We identified this self through his stories of many geographical moves, a largely absent but authoritarian father, the many exclusions that kept him from feeling part of the new communities into which he moved, and the frustrated, defeated attitude he expressed toward his current employers.

Paradoxically, in spite of this antiestablishment self, my patient is an executive with a large corporation. With his humane attitude, he tried to merge corporation and community needs, but his purposes were at odds with what the corporation saw as its bottom-line requirements. Because of this incompatibility, as well as his life history, he would speak of himself as an outsider, more like a token of corporate humanity than a serious contributor.

However, not surprisingly, he also had an ambitious self, bordering on the grandiose and requiring him to succeed regardless of the clash of values. But the ambitious self as a servant to the antiestablishment self kept him tilting at windmills, dreaming the impossible. When he began to see his ambitious self more broadly, not as a servant of the antiestablishment self, but as a part of his own overall good sense, he found doable tasks to serve his humanitarian purposes. One of the things he did was to create a successful film on the use of company nurseries; he also set up a system to help needy workers. Subsequently, he developed respectful relations among his peers, and then his ideas were welcomed into the corporate decision-making process. Furthermore, cracking through

his seriousness, he let himself enjoy his success, a pleasure previously strictly forbidden by the imperious antiestablishment self.

These new experiences called for revision of his antiestablishment self, and one day I told him that I now saw him as a corporation man. He seemed insulted for a moment, but then laughed at the truth of my observation. Nevertheless, corporation man or not, he is clearly his own man—bright, diligent, kind, and cooperative. And all of these characteristics became real to him. He had previously subsumed these characteristics within his antiestablishment self and now they were released to be reapplied in his corporation self, a composite self accepting membership in the workplace he had chosen.

In spite of what I have said, to talk about selves seems a strange way to talk about a person, as though these selves were the person's tenants or employees or internal sprites. Why not just say that my patient was a person who hated the establishment, but also was ambitious, and that he had overestimated how much he would have to sacrifice his values in order to do his job? Isn't that enough? Often it is. But, what is added by addressing selves is that they become agents of the person: brightly organized, spotlights on otherwise ephemeral existences, banners, so to speak, around which the person rallies his or her psychological energies. Just as the novel creates human images that echo in the minds of its readers, the image of selves also comes alive, giving membership and coherence to otherwise disconnected parts of the person. The therapist uses the device of the self to give life to the patient's experiences, registering them so vividly that the abandoned aspects may be more fully reexperienced and the fragmented person made whole.

HOW DOES THE SELF FORM?

This brings us to another crucial point. Especially important in the formation of self is the role of introjection, a much maligned function. Perls (1947) said that introjection "means preserving the structure of things taken in, whilst the organism requires their destruction.... Any introjection must go through the mill of the molars if it is not to become ... a foreign body—a disturbing isolated factor in our existence" (p. 129). This point of view, that metaphorical chewing is crucial, often has been taken to mean that the introjecting person is a passive vessel who ingests what the environment serves. If parents do not listen, for example, when a young girl talks, she assumes she is not worth listening to; if people laugh derisively at her, she believes she is a shameful person; if people play with her happily, she infers that she has a right to whatever she wants.

According to this, limited and limiting interpretation, introjection, through its indiscriminate inclusiveness and its enduring effects, is seen as a major source of mistaken beliefs about one's self, which it often is. But that is only half of the story. To incorporate the other half, I would like to redefine introjection as *spontaneous receptivity, unimpeded by the deliberative faculties of the mind*. Introjection, in this sense, is to receptivity what Freudian free association is to verbal expression. That is not to say that deliberateness has no place; it is a partner. From this position, we may better appreciate two of introjection's major attributes, which were overlooked by Perls and which contribute enormously to the powers of therapy.

The first attribute of introjection is that it is a wondrous source of learning, extending hospitality to the abundance of the world's offerings. Though introjection is receptivity, it can be an appetitive receptivity. We see the effects of its vibrancy all the way forward from the infant who spontaneously picks up English as a spoken language to a concertgoer enthralled by the music. This same fascination is available in psychotherapy, where the patient may be introjectively infused with the messages implicit in psychotherapeutic exchange.

The second attribute of introjection is that it does not stand alone. In and of itself, introjection has no implications for psychological well-being, no more so than blood circulation does for blood pressure levels. The key to well-being is not whether we introject, but how well the introjected experiences are integrated into the person. This integration is facilitated by three operations that together compose the process of introjection: contact,

configuration, and tailoring. Each operation will be examined in turn.

THE CONTACT FUNCTION

Though the Gestalt principles of contact are extensive, perhaps it is enough to say that contact is the instrument of connection between the individual and the world. Only through contact does the individual meet the world and discover anything to introject. One *hears* one's mother's cooing or scolding voice. One *sees* a smile or a scowl. One is *touched* gently or harshly. When *drinking* milk, the infant *feels* the touch of the mother and *tastes* the milk and *senses* its fluidity and texture. Such contacts, multiplied in power and complexity, are the raw material for introjection.

Whereas it is often believed that a person in good contact is not introjecting, contact and introjection are actually interwoven. So close in touch is the contacting person, as a matter of fact, that he or she merges momentarily with the other person while paradoxically maintaining an individual identity. This closeness enables the contacting person to tune in sensitively, providing a head start on integrating the introjection. In this sense, good contact is a lubricant for the introjective process. Take, for example, a person who always has felt isolated and lives life according to the expectations of this isolated self. If, in good contact with a therapist or others, the person were to feel understood and valued, this new contact might cause a relaxation of his or her isolated self, while newly introjecting a sense of belonging.

CONFIGURATION

The individual seeks a rightful place within the self for new experience and to give relevance and coherence to as much experience as possible. This configurational reflex is a crucial determinant of the future of the introjection, particularly as to whether or not it turns out to be "healthy."

At first, in the earliest days, the child, with only scant experience, has little that is already established to which he or she must connect any new experience; the child's skill in determining what fits is minimal. Certain early difficulties, such as terrible milk and brutal treatment, would be manifestly alien to the already formed biological needs. But most of what enters comes in on the ground floor of the organism, and the child's freedom to introject is great because it is easy to fit his or her experiences into the relatively few requirements. Much of what happens just fits, and it is only natural to feel that life is just as it uncomplicatedly is.

The fewer the contradictions between what already exists in the child and what he or she is newly receiving, the easier the configurational process becomes. But as this world of connections achieves greater definition—as in learning a particular language, developing individual bodily posture, living by certain moral rules, or recognizing dangers—the requirements for acceptable fit become more challenging. For example, it makes less difference who is tending the baby at 2 months of age than at 7 months, as the connections with the mother have been strongly formed by then and the baby will find it difficult to accept a substitute.

Other examples of differing experiences that would be hard to integrate would be experiences of hunger and the contradictory delay of food, aggressive impulses and the contradictory behavioral suppression, or sensuality and the contradictory requirement for distance. Or a generous little boy may have to reconcile his own actual generosity with his father's scolding him for being stingy. Or a girl trained to crave success may be thrown by being told she is stupid. Clearly, it is no small matter to navigate through the sea of contradictions we all face, especially because the formation of our selves is always on the line.

TAILORING

This is a process similar to the Perlsian concept of the mill of the grinding molars, which calls for the destructuring of gestalt patterns. As the child grows and as failures in connection accumulate, causing psychological pain, the individual must, first, assess the prospects for

successfully interconnecting new stimulations with those already in place, rejecting those that would not fit. Then he or she also remodels experiences that would not fit in their present state, but would if they were altered. The remodeling comes through a number of activities, such as criticizing, objecting, revising, educating, digesting, suggesting, commanding, and all the range of things people do to try to make the world of ideas, things, and other people harmonious with themselves. These tailoring functions are all devoted to maximizing the success of the configurational reflex in interconnecting all that is taken in.

Nevertheless, in spite of our skills in contact, configuration, and tailoring, we are all more or less in trouble because, in trying to get a coherent sense of self, we often will have to isolate those parts of our experiences that do not fit. In the service of coherence, alienation among seemingly incompatible characteristics or selves leaves the person with a narrow or fragmented self-image. Such alienation—dissociation, when it is extreme—is a major source of self-distortion because certain parts of the person begin to count more than the whole person. Thus it is not the introjection itself that causes trouble, as is commonly believed, but *alienated* introjections—and their dissociative influence.

THERAPEUTIC PROCEDURES

Because of the pivotal disconnections represented in these alienations, therapy becomes an exercise in reconnection. Three primary means for creating connections are (1) the extraordinary engagement between therapist and patient, (2) the restoration of engagement among alienated selves, and (3) the uncovering of a unifying story line that interconnects a sequence of events. Each will be addressed in order.

EXTRAORDINARY ENGAGEMENT
BETWEEN THERAPIST AND PATIENT

The extraordinariness to which I refer is common psychotherapeutic fare. For most people, just walking into a therapist's office makes them feel as though they are putting their very selfhood on the line. It takes no special tricks or charisma on the part of the therapist to turn this event into a great psychological adventure. It is enough for the therapist in this extraordinary context to exercise ordinary kindness, simplicity, clear-mindedness, good language, recognition of implication, and an enduring fascination with the life of the patient. I would especially emphasize an enduring fascination. With an optimal exercise of these qualities by the therapist, the patient's connection with the therapist develops considerable magnitude. The relationship is then in a position to compete for influence with the patient's lifelong adherence to anachronistic selves.

One of the special instruments of this paradoxical interplay between the extraordinary and the therapeutically simple is the concept of sequential fit. Here is what I mean: Each moment of experience gives off its hints for what would seem like a naturally occurring subsequent statement, feeling, or act. Without the therapist's help, the patient cannot move into these moments because he or she is preoccupied or is otherwise geared to disconnect whatever he or she is doing from its immediately following probability. The patient blocks—by repetitions, deletions, changing the subject, abstractions that do not get fleshed out, confusion, circumstantiality, and so on.

If the therapist helps the person out of this choppy existence and into the ensuing experiences, one following the other, the patient soon will enter into the stream of what seems like *inevitably* "next" moments, accompanied by profound absorption and open-mindedness. When the therapist sensitively develops this sequential fluidity, the patient's embeddedness in the process reduces internal deliberations. The patient thus slips into a mental groove where he or she becomes hospitable to thoughts and feelings that previously would have been unacceptable.

This confidence in the power of sequentially faithful experiences has long been evident in the way that Gestalt therapists focus on the awareness continuum. We believe attention to people's own continuing experience stimulates a directionalism that will help lead them to where they need to go. Carl Rogers developed a comparable momentum through his continu-

ing clarifications of his patients' statements, always offering improved language that would better move them forward into the naturally occurring next statement. Milton Erickson's stories, as well, would incline the rapt listener toward moves that he or she would unconsciously pursue.

Upon developing a sense of the rightness of conversational direction, the patient is released from some of the control of the tailoring phase of the introjection process. With a lowered need for tailoring, the chances are greater that one will say whatever one wants to say and will accept new ideas, much as in the early days of guileless receptivity. Here is an example: A patient made a snide reference to his mother's effervescent way of speaking, although it was evident that he, with his heavy vocal tones, could benefit from her style. In discussing her effervescence, as one thing led to the next, I asked him to imitate her voice. At this point, it seemed the natural thing to do, and when he did, the lighthearted self inside him appeared.

The appearance of his lighthearted self led him into further spontaneity and soon he told me what he would not have told me before. At the age of 5, he had had sexual feelings for his mother. It would have been difficult for him to admit these feelings before he imitated her voice, but he welcomed them after doing so. He then went on to tell me that he had been able to smell her and feel himself against her clothes and he adored her. But he was called a "mama's boy," which he accepted as though it were God's own truth. Since the stigma scared him, he stiffened against the mama's-boy image, never at ease in closeness to his mother, believing his sexual feelings might betray a "mama's boy self." When I jokingly added that he had really been "mama's little fucker," he reddened and laughed lyrically.

Through these simple sequences, my patient had swung into a mood in which each next statement or feeling was spontaneously valid, untailored. These pieces just fit together and he absorbed the validity of his sexual self, undeliberately softening the old mama's-boy introjection.

So far I have been discussing the actual relationship between therapist and patient: telling, responding, suggesting, laughing, experimenting, all that is actually going on. Adding, however, to the power of the actual engagement is the symbolic component represented in the transference phenomenon. Historically, transference has been a prime tool of reconnection, but it has had double-edged implications. Transference has been used to take the therapist *out* of the relationship with the patient by assigning implications that deflected from the actual contact, thereby, unfortunately, diminishing connectedness. I think we are all familiar with therapists' denying the direct validity of what patients say about them.

There is another implication, however, that is more empowering. The transference recognition makes the therapist a *party* to the entire life history of the patient, *intertwined* as the interpretations insinuate the therapist into the most intimate fabric of the individual's history. Through the transference, the therapist is no longer just another person, but has elements of everybody who matters in the patient's life. Such consequences are extremely absorbing. This absorption and the accompanying trust often lead to lessened deliberation by the patient, who becomes more open to both the benefits and the dangers of new introjections.

This powerful leverage is often squandered by the therapist's limitations: our pretended knowledge, our undiscerning goals, our ambitions and shame regarding failure and success, our homage to stereotypical procedure, and our insensitivities to the actual process of the patient. It also can be used abusively or exploitatively by therapists who are willing to play God. None of us is safe from such professional hazards and we can only note them here. Yet, in concert with all the necessary cautionary factors, the therapist may make use of the introjective opportunities provided by his or her special centrality to catch up with the advantage already gained by the early infusion of alienating influences. The therapist as a newly unforgettable, merging force is an antidote to the embeddedness of those outdated impressions that are unaffected by *ordinary* new experience. The new experience, therefore, must be so absorbing that the patient will be influenced as though young again.

THE RESTORATION OF ENGAGEMENT AMONG ALIENATED SELVES OF THE PERSON

The therapist promotes reconnection by restoring dialogue among these constituent selves. Befitting the experiential spirit, Gestalt therapy long ago developed a two-part concept of the self in action. First came the concept of neurotic splitting, which also found a place later in object-relations theory. Perls, Hefferline, and Goodman (1953) said, "In a neurotic splitting, one part is kept unconscious, or it is . . . alienated from concern, or both parts are carefully isolated from each other . . ." (p. 240). Second came the technique of personifying the split parts and creating a dialogue among these parts.

As I have previously written (1987), "With all these characters living inside the person, the therapist working with any individual is actually doing group therapy" (p. 115). Let me illustrate this kind of "group" therapy. One patient, a contractor, felt he had made a terrible mistake in taking a certain difficult and unusually lengthy job. He was angry with several people who had advised him to take the job and especially with the other party to the contract, who had lied to him. But he still blamed himself heavily even though he should have been relieved to be almost finished with the project.

I asked him to play out a conversation between his conflicted selves, which he saw as his naive self, referring to the time when he made the decision, and his bitter self, referring to the way he was currently behaving. The two sides spoke carefully to each other, the bitter self with cool anger and the naive self with cool apology. After a few more exchanges, the bitter self got more angry and the naive self became afraid.

At my suggestion, the naive self started to tell the bitter self how afraid he was getting. As he was talking, he remembered a time long ago when he had become furious at a boy in his neighborhood who had plagued him with insults, until he could no longer take them. The naive self said that he had "lost it" one day and finally beat the other kid up so badly that he believed he would have murdered him if the fight had not been stopped. He had blacked out and now "knew" he would have continued mindlessly to bang the boy's head on the cement. He went on to tell of other memories of his many rages and temper tantrums. The naive self, afraid of his murderous self, overlooked the spunkiness that was distorted into the specter of a mad murderer. The bitter self also got into the act, telling me he was afraid his bitterness might be escalated by the dissociated murderer. If not careful, he might throw his chair at my computer, break my statues, turn over my desk, tear my room apart.

Not surprisingly, my patient was greatly relieved just to be able to say these things. More important, though, he was able to reconnect his alienated selves. First, the naive and bitter selves were reconnected in their dialogue. Next, they unearthed another member of the "group," the even more seriously alienated self, the mad murderer, whom my patient was also able to accommodate. Then, his discovering the spunky self under the shadow of his murderous self added one more member to the group, a key participant whose voice merited attention. With all these characters operating safely together, my patient was able to talk to me without the earlier self-recrimination.

UNIFYING STORY LINE

A unifying story line is a vehicle for connection. Stories are the gathering of experiences; through their thematic development, they transform otherwise unconnected events into a meaningful unity. When a patient told me, first, that his mother had died when he was 7 years old, and, second, that from then on his father periodically would mope, and, third, that he would repeat the words, "It can't work," he was connecting these experiences. Then, when he also said that he had made up his mind right then, at age 7, never to feel like a failure, he put down a marker acknowledging the continuity through his life. Normally, stories are so readily heard as a whole unit that their role in connecting discrete experiences is overlooked.

Stories all contain elements of the teller's self, reflected in the characters and their behavior. My earlier patient's murderous self was revealed in his blacked-out battering of the neighborhood boy. When he told the story, he made vivid a vicious fight that had lived in his mind only as a pale abstraction, an immaterial dread of the wanton—felt not even as fear, but as resignation. A patient who tells such stories offers a peephole into his or her self, a hint about the breadth of the patient's life. When this hint is recognized and elaborated through the story line, we have gone beyond stagnant "titles" that, by themselves, keep self designations fixed in position. These designations come to life as they receive clarification from the action, continuity, and thematic developments that evolve.

CONCLUSION

I have tried to show the self as a harmonic interplay between classification and action. The formation of the self and its constituent selves is highly influenced by introjection, a process that creates strong embeddedness. To counteract this embeddedness, it is important to take into account the process of introjection, redefined to embrace its renewal powers. I have described three procedures for creating such renewal, each developing high absorption and each tapping into nondeliberative, introjective learning energy. The first was the immersion in the therapeutic relationship through an inclusive transference and through sequential fit; second was the restoration of connections among alienated selves; and third was the evocation of a story line that reveals the drama in the patient's life and reconnects many experiences. A patient who is enabled to harmonize these contributors to a sense of self will enrich the identity by which he or she measures existence.

REFERENCES

Assis, M. de (1990). *Epitaph of a small winner*. New York: Noonday Press.

Cary, J. (1961). *Art and reality*. New York: Doubleday.

Kierkegaard, S. (1948). *Purity of heart is to will one thing*. New York: Harper.

Perls, F. (1947). *Ego, hunger and aggression*. London: Allen & Unwin.

Perls, F., Hefferline, R., & Goodman, P. (1953). *Gestalt therapy*. New York: Julian Press.

Polster, E. (1987). *Every person's life is worth a novel*. New York: Norton.

Polster, E., & Polster, M. (1973). *Gestalt therapy integrated*. New York: Brunner/Mazel.

Discussion by Ernest L. Rossi, Ph.D.

---◆---

Who could do justice to this extraordinary chapter? I will confine myself to just two points: I will make a scientific point on the new evidence for the scientific foundation for Gestalt psychology. Then I will relate a few personal anecdotes about my encounters with Fritz Perls in order to illustrate what Dr. Polster calls the "extraordinary engagement" between therapist and patient that is one of our most potent vehicles for therapeutic change.

RECENT SCIENTIFIC SUPPORT FOR GESTALT THEORY

In the 1950s and 1960s, neurological research showed that brain fields really did not exist in the way that early Gestalt researchers such as Wolfgang Kohler postulated. There isn't one brain field on which the Gestalt image of the world can be projected in the brain. That seemed to be a scientific death blow to the Gestalt world.

In an extraordinary recent article (Barinaga, 1990), research of Wolfe Singer at the Max Planck Institute in Germany is reported that may become a new foundation for Gestalt psychology. When a brain encodes what we take to be an integrated perception—playing with your pet dog, for example—different parts of the brain pick up the sound (barking), the visual aspects (picturing your dog), the kinesthetic aspects (petting). How do they get integrated into the single experience of playing with your dog? We now find that they are integrated by electrical-wave frequency, by harmonics between the different cells of your brain that encode the experience. There is a 40-hertz wave that integrates all the separate parts of our perception and integrates them into the whole experience—the gestalt.

Is this the way our phenomenological consciousness is put together? The authors do not actually use the word "gestalt" in the article, but certainly this is the new scientific foundation for many phrases in Dr. Polster's presentation, such as the "self as a harmonic counterpoint." This is a new scientific conception of how the mind organizes separate experiences into a whole—a gestalt.

THE SENSITIVITY OF FRITZ PERLS

A personal encounter I had with Fritz Perls many years ago illustrates Dr. Polster's description of the extraordinary engagement between therapist and patient. He says, "It is enough for the therapist in this extraordinary context to exercise ordinary kindness, simplicity, clear-mindedness, good language, recognition of implication, and an enduring fascination with the life of the patient."

In this single sentence, he sums up an optimal therapeutic attitude that I can illustrate by something that happened during my early work with Perls. In the late 1960s, after receiving my Ph.D. degree, I attended one of those extraordinary weeklong workshops at Esalen Institute in Big Sur, Calif., that Perls gave from time to time. At the time, the therapeutic vehicle was called "the hot seat." Each participant would take his or her turn sitting in a chair in the middle of a circle of colleagues, with Perls presiding. This particular evening, I was in the hot seat and reported a dream that mystified me. In the dream, I was simply climbing a vine, like Tarzan, but my feet were stuck in a swamp, from my ankles down. I had no idea what this dream meant.

Fritz encouraged me by saying, "Go ahead, do it." So I stood on the chair and acted out climbing. I climbed and climbed, and suddenly it occurred to me, "Jeez, I'm climbing out of the shit. I'm climbing out of the shitty background of my family." I was battered as a child. I was the victim of incest by my father, who also battered me. Suddenly all that came clear! In my dream, I was climbing out of that. At that moment of insight, I glanced down at Fritz, and what did I see? I saw him staring at me, transfixed by the wonder of this moment of therapeutic insight.

I believe this is the sort of therapeutic encounter that Dr. Polster calls "fascinating interest." Whenever anyone was having a good therapeutic experience, Fritz was in a state of complete "fascinated interest." Of course, if it was poor work, he could be irascible, disinterested, irritable, and so forth.

The next day of that workshop, Fritz took me aside and mentioned that he was starting a new training institute and would welcome my joining to be trained as a Gestalt therapist. Immediately, I was thrown into confusion and consternation because I already had been approved for training as a Jungian analyst. I said, "Look, let me sleep on it tonight and I will tell you in the morning."

Early the next morning on my way to breakfast, I experienced an extraordinary archetypal encounter with Fritz. I was on a long pathway and suddenly Fritz appeared, walking toward me. We were about to meet face to face. Immediately, my whole mind–body galvanized. "Jeez, I'm going to have to tell this great man, 'No, I've decided to go into Jungian training.' And, oh my God, how am I going to tell him?"

When we were within about 100 feet of each other, our eyes met, and, of course, my face must have shown my discomfort. How was I to summon up my courage to tell him? But this extraordinary man immediately sensed what I had to say. As we came closer, he raised his hand, as if to say, "I've got it. I know what your decision is." As we came within a few yards of each other, he brought his hand to his lips, as if to say, "You don't have to talk about it. It's okay." He never used a word, just a significant look of understanding and a few kind gestures. As he came abreast of me, he lightly touched me on the shoulder to reassure me and we walked silently to breakfast together. That's the kind of "extraordinary encounter" I believe Dr. Polster is asking us to access in our daily therapeutic work.

REFERENCE

Barinaga, M. (1990). The mind revealed? *Science, 249,* 856–858.

QUESTIONS AND ANSWERS

Question: You mentioned eliciting the sense of awe in your patient. Could you elaborate a little bit on that? You mentioned how religion does that.

Polster: Religion does induce awe. For example, I went to two very beautiful weddings recently. One was an encounter group type of wedding. There was a gathering of folks in a beautiful large yard. It was warm and friendly and the things people said to each other were truly touching. I was very happy to be there. But I was not awed.

I also went to a Catholic wedding. It was highly institutionalized and little of the ceremony was specific to the actual people getting married, but I was awed. There was a church with architectural splendor and magnificent music. Everything the priest said to the couple went beyond them into the community, the world of people, life itself. Yet though the universal was emphasized, I was also moved for the people who were getting married, I felt so much a part of that particular wedding.

Now the difference was, and I think we lose this awareness in therapy circles, that we tend to be oriented toward ourselves, rather than to the universe. What is often missing is a sense that we are among all of us. It is an incredible thing that we exist at all, that each of us exists with somebody else, that we can come together and get married, that we can get married in front of our beloved friends, and that this event matters in history, a vision that is represented in the church's liturgy, the music, the architecture, the tradition. We psychotherapists have been heavily impressed with how rotten these institutions have become and we have tended to abandon them, thus losing a sense of our proportion in relation to everything else that exists.

Religion does indeed respond to that need and the accompanying awe. In psychotherapy, we don't have the forms yet for doing it communally, though we someday may have them. We have not yet formed a way of breaking through our appreciation of selves, if you will, into the union with all that exists.

In relation to the awe in therapy, we develop

it individually; there already is considerable awe as the patient walks in for the first time. It's always a personal awe. It's the awe of having the freedom of feeling, the freedom of expression, and the freedom of one person knowing you, especially of being known, all of you. Imagine the sense of union.

When I was in therapy with Isadore From, he once saw something in me that I didn't know anybody could see; I was awed by his having seen that quality in me. Being also very cynical, I asked him, "Have you ever said that to anybody else?" He replied, "A few people." I realized his saying something similar to a few people didn't mean that this was a standard spiel. It meant that he really saw this in me and in some others.

That sense of awe at being known, when joined with the feeling of being with another, happens quite frequently in therapy. We don't institutionalize it. Sometimes we even quell the awe by transference disclaimers, rather than accept it as a function of deep interpersonal engagement. I think the private interpersonal experience can be great, but it all too often lacks the continuing force of communally induced awe.

Question: Dr. Polster, how active a role can therapists take in establishing the story line and making the connection for the client?

Polster: Well, the therapist can take a variably active role. There are times when people will say a particular line and you know there is a story in there. Yet they won't say anything further about it. Then you might ask about it or tell a story of your own that could be similar. Alternatively, you could ask what the person felt about what he or she said and that might draw out the story. But one of my fundamental guidelines in therapy is to try as frequently as seems timely to transform abstractions into details. I think of abstractions as the "housing" for the contents of the mind. With abstractions, you have a house but no rooms, no furniture, no photographs, no history. The abstraction provides either an orientation or a summary. If it's orientation, you want to know what patients are orienting you to. If it's summary, you want them to flesh out the summary. Whether I am active or not depends on the particular patient. With some I might just want to listen for the evolving story. The story may come out without my saying anything.

The Betrayal of the Human: Psychotherapy's Mission to Reclaim Our Lost Identity

◆

James F. T. Bugental, Ph.D.

James F. T. Bugental, Ph.D.

James Bugental is semiretired and devotes himself to teaching and writing; he is also an Emeritus Professor, Saybrook Institute, and an Emeritus Clinical Lecturer (formerly Associate Clinical Professor), Department of Psychiatry, Stanford University Medical School. He received his Ph.D. degree (1948) from Ohio State University. In 1987, he was the recipient of the first annual Rollo May Award of the Mentor Society "for contributions to the literary pursuit," and in 1986, he received a certificate "in recognition of the distinguished contribution to the discipline of Clinical Psychology" from the Division of Clinical Psychology, American Psychological Association. He is a past president of the Association for Humanistic Psychology and serves or has served on the editorial boards of eight professional journals. Bugental has written six books and edited another and is the author of approximately 150 articles, reviews, comments, and chapters in books edited by others.

From the rich humanistic tradition, James Bugental presents a manifesto of the subjective. He celebrates the importance of personal mystery, both in life and in therapy, and reminds us to bring subjective life to the forefront. Human experience and actions are centered in subjectivity. Preoccupation with objectivity displaces identity from inner living to the external. Life-changing psychotherapy requires centered awareness and self-direction.

INTRODUCTION

When a person comes to see me for the first time, I am confronted with mystery—immense mystery. Moreover, I know that three years and 300 hours later, when that person bids me a final good-bye, there will still be much that remains a mystery.

The fact is that each person is in many ways a mystery to every other person—whether therapist, spouse, lover, parent, child, friend, or colleague. We are mysteries because each of us quite literally dwells in a separate world. Each lives most truly and fully in his or her inner and irrevocably private world. While our separate worlds have much in common, they also are unique in important ways.

The mystery that is each person adds interest to a relationship, humbles therapists, and may be crucially important when we encounter it in another person. It was just such a mystery that killed my friend, a psychiatrist. He was called to his office door one day by a patient; when he started to greet the patient, the man shot my friend dead.

Our professional skills cannot penetrate all mystery and thus we cannot count on them to save us from disasters that may issue from that mystery.

I am not using fanciful language when I speak of "mystery." I am talking about the deeper nature of each person, which is ultimately ineffable, which each of us can intuit within himself or herself and sense in those with whom we are in genuine relation. This is the mystery that objectivist psychologists deny as superficial, the mystery that manipulative psychotherapists reject as irrelevant. Yet it is the same mystery that I come to know in each person who consults me and that each knows in me.

For many years, the human sciences* dodged the issue of mystery, pretended that it did not exist, contented themselves with cautious answers to timid questions. Gradually, this is changing. Meantime, the arts, literature, religion, and some parts of philosophy have been more courageous. Here we are concerned with psychology's evasion, a resistance arising from phobic reaction to the adjective *subjective*.

CONFRONTING MYSTERY: THE SUBJECTIVE REALM

I recognize that changes are occurring in psychology as the stranglehold of the positivists is lessening (Youniss, 1991), but for therapists, this evolution is overdue. We need to give up this self-defeating avoidance and recognize the subjective for what it truly is: the central fact of human life. By acknowledging it, we can begin to explore it and to learn how to live out its potentials more fully and effectively. Until we do so, our psychologies and our psychotherapies are going to remain partial and limited in their application to living humans.

Appreciating the significance and characteristics of the subjective will help us in our work as therapists. Psychotherapists are relentlessly

*For simplicity of expression, I will subsume our human sciences—psychology, psychiatry, sociology, social work, counseling—under the name "psychology."

confronted with one basic question—a question that frames every encounter with a client, a question that demands provisional (often implicit) answers whenever an intervention is made, a question that (if we are candid) brings us to the limits of our knowledge and training: *What makes a difference in the therapeutic hour?*

At root, the way each of us implicitly or explicitly answers this question reveals our beliefs about what matters to a client's emotions, attitudes, and behavior, and this, in turn, reveals our stand on what matters in human life.

Our journals are full of proposed answers to this basic question: catharsis and working through blocked affect, insight into historical sources of present difficulties, corrective emotional experience, increased choicefulness and decreased compulsion, self-defeating inner sentences changed to self-affirming ones, developed interpersonal skills, and so on and on. Here is the crux of the matter: *Each of these proposed healing, corrective, or growth-evoking influences is an event or an experience in the client's subjectivity.*

EXPERIENCING ONE'S OWN SUBJECTIVITY

Fundamentally, the true psychological realm *is* the subjective. It is the rich, multidimensional, constantly evolving, and fertile inner world that is private to each of us, but that is also the basis of whatever we share deeply among ourselves.

In my oral presentation, at this point the audience was invited to participate in an exercise to demonstrate the pervasive presence of subjectivity. The reader can gain a similar appreciation, if he or she will pause and reflect on what may be going on in her or his awareness in back of the focal attention to the words on this page.

Pause now and see what you can find.

Take note of the words in your thoughts, sense how they lie over greater reaches of awareness that are only partially verbal, and how the whole keeps changing, evolving, again and again turning different facets up.

What you have just been doing is bringing forward in your awareness one aspect, a part we all may experience as aware and conscious beings. We recognize an interface with the external world, while, at the same time, a great deal of other activity is continuing inside.

OBSERVATIONS ABOUT THE SUBJECTIVE REALM

Clinical practice offers an ideal position from which to make observations about the characteristics of human subjectivity. The sketches that follow were so derived. They need further study, confirmation or amendment, and articulation into a more embracing conceptual structure.

THE "RIVER" THAT IS THE SUBJECTIVE

Within each of us is a continually flowing process that we call awareness or consciousness and that, viewed in larger context, is our subjectivity. When I ask people how they know they are alive (rather than "on tape"), the almost unanimous answer is basically, "Because I feel things, have things going on inside of me." It is not too extreme to say that our lives, so far as we are aware of them, consist of exactly this internal river of awareness.

How incredible it is that psychologists and psychotherapists can try to dismiss or overlook the very core of our being alive!

Reflecting on the experience of attending to our inner process, this "river," it will be apparent that it usually takes at least a brief instant to translate into words what one discovers going on within. The subjective is prereflective, preverbal, preobjective. It is much larger than can ever be put into words. Attempting to do so requires that we make smaller what we can sense is immeasurably larger.

The subjective is the whole inner world of perceptions, ideas, emotions, impulses, anticipations and apprehensions, memories, fantasies and imaginings, bodily awareness, decision-making, associating, relating, planning, and much, much more.

Roger Walsh (1976), himself a psychologist and psychiatrist, wrote of his personal therapy and his discovery of his subjectivity:

One of the most wondrous discoveries of all was the slowly dawning awareness of the presence of a formerly subliminal, continuously changing stream of inner experience. The range, richness, Heraclitean, and awesome nature of this internal universe amazed and continues to amaze me. . . . Here was a previously unsuspected gold mine of information about myself and the meaning of my experiences. (pp. 122–123)

INTENTIONALITY

A major aspect of our subjectivity is intentionality, the capacity to have wishes, wants, and intentions and to carry them through or to change or even relinquish them. We therapists seek to enlist our clients' intentionality to help them discover more of what truly matters to them, to reexamine cherished attachments, to seek their ways out of seemingly hopeless circumstances, or to explore possible courses of action.

What is less familiar is the recognition that in all of these undertakings we are working with the most powerful force in our known world: *human intention.*

If the notion of intentionality being the most powerful force seems exaggerated, a reexamination of one's understanding of this power is in order. Our known world is the world we know because of human intentionality. There is no other. Consciousness is always consciousness of something, and the mode of our being conscious of anything is how we constitute the world. It is the world revealed by consciousness and interpreted by our subjectivity. What we can do with, or in, the "world out there" is limited by our subjective awareness.

Our lives are carried forward on the river of subjectivity. Indeed, as we have seen, our lives *are* our subjectivity. If we let ourselves become completely caught up in the world of objectivity, we come to treat ourselves as objects, as things. When that happens, we feel powerless to direct our own actions and experiences except in predetermined ways.

So, here it is directly in front of us—no, directly within us—even right now as I write and as you read. Here it is, one of the most profound of all the mysteries with which we are confronted: our own subjectivity. How little we know its nature, its limits and powers, its transformations and ultimate potentials.

SUBJECTIVE "CONTENTS" DIFFER FROM OBJECTIVE

The "contents" of the subjective are in important ways radically different from the contents of a book or of a computer file. Here are some of those differences:

- Subjective "contents" are epitomized in the dream. Thus they have many layers of meaning, shifting and multiple images, and ranging emotions that come into focus, then fade, and may return in changed form. They are expressive of much that is unavailable to usual consciousness. Of course, this is true whether we are awake or asleep—although we are less accustomed to recognizing how much of waking consciousness partakes of these same qualities that are familiar in dreaming.
- Only a small part of such "contents" exist in verbal form. Instead, so far as I can estimate, they are in preverbal constellations of cognitive, affective, and intentional elements that are continuously flowing and interacting.
- These constellations do not have clear boundaries but "bleed into" each other and are influenced by input from the outside so that the possible combinations and permutations approach infinity.
- The contents of the subjective may be infinitely "opened out" to bring into awareness materials previously unrecognized as related to the initial entry point. This is, of course, the basis of Freud's *free association*, of Gendlin's *focusing* (1978), of Welwood's *unfolding* (1982), and of what I prefer to call *searching* (1978, 1987).

There Is No "How-to" in the Subjective

- This is a point too often unrecognized by those who work with the subjective. As a result, many who seek to be helpful end up frustrated and relying on dubious substitutes. Specifiable procedures are possible only in the objective realm (or to the extent that subjective material has been reduced to objective or explicit form).
- There is no valid way to answer clients' questions, such as, "How can I get deeper into myself?" "How can I decide what I really want to do?" "How can I discover what made me so upset yesterday?" We can provide directions for turning on a machine, for following a street route, or for looking up a word in a dictionary, but no similar step-by-step recipe can be detailed for client questions about their inner processes.
- Intention is the source or basis of our subjective activity. While we cannot give clients answers to "how-to" questions, we can help them explore their aware and unaware impulses in relation to whatever matter they want to work on. Saying it differently, if one's subjective intention is single, unconflicted, and energized, one will find oneself already carrying out the desired subjective process.
- It is important to recognize that this is very different from the kind of mindless yielding to impulse with which it is sometimes confused. It is, rather, a mindful and demanding confrontation with one's intents and values. Only when hindering and conflicting impulses are confronted and worked out can one move into subjective action with the immediacy of focused subjectivity.

DEEP INTERCONNECTEDNESS OF SUBJECTIVITY

There is reason to believe that the subjectivities of separate persons may be interwoven at the deepest levels (Sterling, 1991). If further work lends support to this possibility, we may have taken a step toward increased understanding of those phenomena that we lump under the rubric of *transpersonal*.*

---

*I don't like the implication sometimes taken from the term *transpersonal* that these unusual experiences are something beyond the human. On the other hand, I am totally convinced that there is more to our being and to our relations with each other than our conventional outlook currently accepts.

ALL LANGUAGE IS METAPHOR

We can never exactly, directly, or completely put into words anything of true importance to our lives. It should be noted that this assertion is made without qualification, without limiting it to the subjective realm. This is in recognition of the fact that the objective is communicated only through our subjectivity and that that capacity grasps more of the objective's implications than can be reduced to words. Alfred North Whitehead (1954) made this explicit when he said:

In the study of ideas it is necessary to remember that insistence on hardheaded clarity issues from sentimental feeling, as it were a mist, cloaking the perplexities of fact. Insistence on clarity at all costs is based on sheer superstition as to the mode in which human intelligence functions.

There are no whole truths; all truths are half-truths. It's trying to treat them as whole truths that plays the devil. (p. 16)

THE SELF-AND-WORLD CONSTRUCT SYSTEM

In our subjective living, we are engaged in a lifelong task of creating the world and defining our place in it. From many sources, we assemble the materials for this monumental, life-structuring work. Our parents, siblings, relatives, friends, teachers, the media, and much else contribute materials, but each person alone weaves her or his own unique design for existence.

This design is the way we answer the crucial questions of existence:

- What is important in living?
- What will bring satisfaction?
- What will bring pain and frustration?
- What has power to make things happen or to change the way things are?
- What powers can I have to influence what happens to me?
- How can I be with the people I value and avoid those I fear?
- How can I change myself to bring more satisfactions and fewer disappointments?
- And so on and on.

These questions do not wait for us to research our responses; instead, we must act on tentative answers from our very first moments. Of course, this whole process is more implicit than verbalized, and much of it is only partially conscious or is even unconscious. Only as we get older and are impelled to reflection do we begin to recognize the life assignment on which we are engaged. By that time, many of our answers are so firmly established that they frame the very thoughts with which we seek to consider the issues.

This circumstance points to one of the central necessities for deep, life-changing psychotherapy: to support the client's reexamination of his or her way of being in the world and her or his efforts to revise or broaden the self-and-world constructs that have directed life.

THE POWER OF DESPAIR

The very word "despair" seems loaded solely with negative connotations. Yet life-changing psychotherapy teaches that this is not so. In *The Flies*, Sartre (1947) has Orestes say, "Human life begins on the far side of despair." How can this be?

When a client has fully confronted the failure of her or his way of being in the world (i.e., self-and-world construct system), the client faces what may be called a crisis of existence (an existential crisis). The very ground under one's feet seems to give way and there is desperation born of finding no way to continue to be (as one has been). This exhaustion of one's repertoire of responses when facing an intolerable situation can impel venturing into fresh paths. Sometimes these are truly constructive and creative; they also can be destructive and violent.

Manifestly, this is a time of particular urgency for therapists as well. Sometimes called "the dark night of the soul" and the setting for "the leap of faith," this crisis is not solely or intrinsically mystical. It is, rather, the very pragmatic moment in which one may recognize the ultimate autonomy of the subjective, the choicefulness that is always latent in our lives if we are aware and proactive.

The therapeutic alliance is an important support for this confrontation, and it can serve as a limited safeguard against destructive resolutions.

For example, when one of my clients gave up treating himself as an object and began deeply exploring within himself, he found he was in an apparently hopeless dilemma. He finally faced up to the fact that he could not continue to have an extramarital relationship with a woman who was demanding that he marry her and, at the same time, maintain his marriage. His wife promised a fight over a divorce and threatened that he would be compromised with their children. My client was desperate. He seriously considered running away from his work and his life and going to Mexico with his lover, but she was unwilling to accompany him. Next, he tried again to reconcile with his wife, but their divisions were too deep and too bitter. He then went rapidly through a half-dozen impulses: to live as a bachelor, to enter a religious order, to be so cruel to his wife that she would beg him for a divorce, to kill himself. Then he sank into a deep depression.

The depression, in my view, was grief work for the death of his old way of living. Rather abruptly, this phase ended when he arranged to be transferred by his employer to another city where he could restructure his life in new terms. Only a few months before, he had considered something similar and found it totally unacceptable. Now it seemed an opportunity with real promise.

The important point is how desperation may free the perceptual range and creative powers of the subjective. Familiar ways of defining ourselves impose limits that seem immutable; as a result, much that might seem possible to another person is not even conceivable to us. When we are in the midst of our struggles, we experience the world as shrunken and rigid. When we finally reach the despair of recognizing that there is no possibility that our usual repertoire of actions will serve us, our eyes discover new possibilities.

Contrast this scenario with those typical of therapies that try to teach new behaviors or offer fresh, therapist-proposed opportunities. In such cases, the most suitable alternatives may be discarded by clients blind to their potential benefits as they persist in trying to make old patterns work. Eric Berne's "game" of *Why Don't You; Yes But* (1964) is played out again and again in these circumstances. When clients still hope to avoid having to give up their familiar self-definitions and conceptions of the way the world is supposed to be, the best suggestions are futile.

FREEING OURSELVES FROM LIMITING PARADIGMS

The reluctance of clients to abandon their self-and-world construct systems is basically the same process that can be observed in groups of all sizes, including nations. For our present purposes, it is useful to note how the human sciences manifest the same pattern in their century-old clinging to guiding paradigms long since demonstrated to be futile and relatively impotent. I will describe four such instances:

1. Much of current psychology has had a distorting influence on our knowledge of ourselves. This comes about from its blind allegiance to 19th-century scientism—astonishingly, an allegiance that continues and is institutionalized, especially in American academic psychology. This is doubly astonishing since the physical sciences, the original models for this pattern, have long since abandoned it as unrealistic and counterproductive. From this outdated loyalty comes the blind dedication to objectivity as the prime value guiding method and interpretation.

2. A crippling heritage of this scientistic thinking is the myth that frequency equates to reality—one of the most revealing demonstrations of the poverty of our research products. Galileo did not have to drop weights 30 times to demonstrate that falling objects show the same responses to gravity whatever their size.

   When samples of 30 or 300 or even 3,000 are taken to reveal universal truths about 5 billion human beings, logic is lost in superstition. Still, statistical demonstrations are accorded the respect once reserved for Delphic oracles, despite their very similar records of ambiguous, contradictory, and even erroneous messages. (I've forgotten, is this the week in which those over 55 were advised to take an aspirin a day or is it the week in which that practice was proven to be harmful to the stomach?)

3. Psychology has tried to leap to the discovery of universal laws without having adequately fulfilled the first task of an effective science: amassing a coherent body of naturalistic description of the phenomena under study. We have been in the shaky position of people trying to move into the penthouse when the basement is still incomplete.

4. The confusion of experimental convenience with supposed discoveries of intrinsic reality demonstrates the ruthless determination to impose rigor at the expense of reason. The most striking example is the elevation of what has been called "Occam's Razor" or "Lloyd Morgan's Canon" to be "The Law of Parsimony." *Law*! This supposed law dictates that one always chooses the simplest explanation of observed phenomena, even if that means distorting the phenomena. Thus it is warranted that the contingencies of external reinforcement are more potent than the intentions of conscious human beings! While the canon may be useful to an advanced science with an abundance of uncontested observations to be processed, it is pernicious nonsense as a starting point— especially in the presence of a nature manifestly profligate in variation and multiplicity.

NATURALISTIC DESCRIPTION

I have several times referred to the great need in our field for the amassing of an extensive body of naturalistic description. The most meaningful aspects of being human have been much more thoroughly explored by literature than by formal psychology. A relatively small band of observers has dared to confront mystery by addressing genuinely meaningful topics. The following list is meant to be representative rather than inclusive.*

• Maslow's studies of the nature, range, and potentials of human life

---

*Each person named has published many times, so it would be unwieldy to provide specific references.

• Barron's investigations into creativity
• Kelly's and Anderson's setting forth of how we construct personal identity and social reality
• Moustakas's and Bakan's depiction of profound emotional states
• Giorgi and his associates' pioneering of a disciplined mode of phenomenological observation
• The ground-breaking descriptions of fundamental human experience by William James and Rollo May

As rich as the work of these investigators has been, there is vastly more to be done. One hopes that an existential crisis will disclose to our field the despair from which it hides. Only then will a new generation get on with the increasingly vital task of exploring such topics as the subjective aspects of conflict between individuals, between groups, and between individuals and groups; the possibilities for spiritual transcendence; the ways in which love and jealousy interact; the processes of awakening the latent sanity in those called "psychotic"; and the many more poignantly significant dimensions of the human experience.

CHANGING OUR IMAGES OF OURSELVES

We have seen above the importance to the individual of changing her or his self-concept. As a species, we have a similar need. Our currently regnant image of what is human is a confused and self-conflicted hand-me-down from such diverse sources as religious traditions, 18th- and 19th-century rationalism, primitive psychological observations, and literary depictions. Here are four needed changes:

1. We need to recognize that we are far more than passive receptacles for what is poured in from the outside. This destructive notion, so essential to the behaviorist-objective perspective, is directly and indirectly one of the main roots of much current personal and social distress.

2. We need to appreciate the fateful task of the human species—that we are cocreators of actuality. From the immense storehouse of

what is possible, we select some potentials that we seek to forward to become reality. Our sometimes partner, sometimes adversary in this enterprise is, of course, contingency, that which comes about by chance. So far as we know, only we humans bring consciousness and intention to this truly cosmic task.

What is the importance of this grandiose view? When we fully incorporate this reality, we may be able to reclaim the nobility and responsibility of the human condition from the desacralizing of the positivists who readily equate humans with rats, pigeons, or even machines. Our everyday concerns need to be seen, as Maslow (1971) so often said, in the light of eternity. What we do matters, and it matters for generations and centuries beyond our time. Consider the implications of our harnessing of atomic power, our voyages into space, or the recent war in the Persian Gulf.

3. We need to give more attention to the great power of reflexive awareness. It is not just that humans are aware; it is that we are aware that we are aware. This introduces "wild cards" into the course of events and of human experience.

Ask a computer 10 times, "Who are you (what version of software is operative)?" and one receives 10 identical answers. Ask a person the same question 10 times and one receives 10 different answers. Indeed, it would be impossible for a respondent to give the same answer 10 times except by rigid intention to suppress any other answers that might come to mind. Hearing one's own answer the first time changes the impact of the second question: thus, the "opening-out" process referred to above brings continual changes.

Unless one is determined to deny the evidence of common sense, actuality, and reason, human beings are very different from machines or rats. That difference has great significance for our lives. The endless opening of possibilities is an amazing potential that is far too little recognized and valued. Human life is, at least latently, continually self-renewing.

4. We need to appreciate and utilize the reality that our subjective life is a large, powerful, and rich source of possibilities, only some of which can be made actual in our objective lives. Out of this enlarged view of our nature can come the impetus to creative confrontations with the many problems and crises that confront our world at this time.

SUBJECTIVITY *AND* OBJECTIVITY, NOT *OR*

One of the most unexpected, but well-deserved, tributes to the power and pervasiveness of the subjective realm was accorded by the man who most often was viewed as its antagonist, B. F. Skinner. In his last years, he became bitter that his behaviorist perspective had not fully won over the human sciences. In 1987, in a paper in the basic journal of the American Psychological Association, the *American Psychologist*, he lamented the sad state of his perspective and indicted three influences that he believed had kept it limited: humanistic psychology, psychotherapy, and cognitive psychology. All three, of course, are concerned with human subjectivity!

It is worth noting that objective psychology has as its goal making its objects describable, predictable, and controllable. A subjective psychology, by its very nature, seeks to help persons become self-aware, innovative, and autonomous.

BALANCING SUBJECTIVITY AND OBJECTIVITY

In my first courses in psychology in the 1930s and 1940s, we were taught, "Psychology is the study of behavior and experience." *And experience!* Somehow, in the intervening years, those important last two words have been lost from our conception of our field.

It is time to recall our awareness and appreciation of this lost continent of the psychological world, which is in danger of being dismissed like Atlantis—as a quaint myth from the past. Our practice, our science, our species cannot afford to abandon its archaic home, its ultimate source of creativity and productivity.

Lest there be any misunderstanding, I do not urge that we abandon the objective dimension. It is essential. It is useful and productive. But, in all truth, it is also restrictive and destructive as it is carried into practice by some psychologists and therapists, as Skinner's lament evidenced.

We can adapt Aldous Huxley's (1990) observation and say we are amphibians, dwellers in the water world of the subjective and on the land world of the objective. Both are necessary to our lives; neither should be allowed to displace the other.

We need also to remember Paul Tillich's (1951) warning: "[The human] resists objectification, and if [the human's] resistance is broken, [the human itself] is broken" (p. 98).

CONCLUSION

Once the human was deemed the center of the universe. The gods dwelt among us, intruded into our lives, envied our mortality. Heroes and heroines moved through the world in pride, fought great battles, won glorious victories, died in terrible tragedies. Humankind was splendid in our own eyes (even as the average man and woman lived brutish lives).

Now much has changed. Expelled from the Eden of the center of the universe, we have repeatedly let ourselves be pushed toward the edge of the drama of the cosmos. Some of us seem to take a strange pleasure in recording our meanness and inconsequentiality. It is time to recall Pascal's (1966) words in 1670:

It is dangerous to show [humans] too often that [they are] equal to beasts, without showing [them their] greatness. It is also dangerous to show [them] too frequently [their] greatness without [their] baseness. It is yet more dangerous to leave [them] ignorant of both. But it is very desirable to show [them] the two together.

We live in a time of great pressures to make ourselves into objects, things. Not only mainstream human science, but many social and cultural influences press upon us to yield up our subjectivity, to deny our inner sover-

eignty, to go along with the popular and approved trend*—in Pascal's terms, to yield to our baseness and become but beasts. But we must recognize this: to do so is to betray our heritage, our potential, our very nature, and our species' future.

Tragically, psychology and psychiatry, which should be our first line of defense against objectification, have become persistent influences demeaning human nature. Too many psychotherapists see "subjective" as equivalent to "error." This equation derives, at least in part, from late 18th-century efforts (e.g., Wundt, Fechner) to make the subjective objective. Then, the main intent was to extricate psychology from philosophy and religion; subjectivity was not valued for itself.

Today we are coming back to philosophy. Can religion, or at least concern with the spiritual, be far behind?

What must be recognized (but is usually suppressed) is that the so-called "objective" is irrevocably a selection from the universe of the possible—*a selection made by subjective considerations*.

The same denial keeps us from realizing that all the world's macroproblems are, at root, problems of the subjective. They pose questions of human intention, motivation, values. The human sciences must address the subjective, accept that knowledge in that realm is always* ambiguous, incomplete, and uncertain, and still proceed with the tasks of saving our world. We can make *observations*, but not discover eternal *laws*.

AWE, DIGNITY, AND MYSTERY

James Gibson, one of the most creative psychological investigators of perception, said (as quoted in Reed, 1988):

Psychology, or at least American psychology, is a second rate discipline. The main reason is that it does not stand in awe of its subject matter. Psychologists have too little respect for psychology.

---

*Deikman (1990) presents a remarkable and thorough documentation of how we subvert our own being in this way.
*All knowledge is partial knowledge, is provisional. The "hardest" sciences are always in process, evolving, and never able to make the *final* statement on any matter.

To stand in awe of our subject matter is to accord respect to the dignity of the human, the dignity of each person's individuality, the dignity of the ultimate autonomy that is latent in being a person. The word respect is far too rare in psychology and psychotherapy. We need to recall Schweitzer's wise counsel (Bugental, 1989), "Only those who respect the personality of others can be of real use to them."

What is demonstrated so clearly by those who try to objectify and study by reduction is that too much of psychology and psychotherapy has lost the sense of awe, of respect, and of mystery. That loss confuses and enfeebles these once promising and important efforts to understand and help ourselves.

Those who try to objectify human experience dodge the hard questions to create simplistic psychologies. We must not be fooled. Word games are self-deception and shallow substitutes for living realities. Human life is a mystery set in the midst of boundless mystery.

The good news is, of course, that the humanness is seldom completely extinguished. It is latent in each of us, and it can be awakened to enliven and enrich our living.

REFERENCES

Berne, E. (1964). *Games people play*. New York: Grove Press.

Bugental, J. F. T. (1978). *Psychotherapy and process: The fundamentals of an existential-humanistic approach*. New York: McGraw-Hill (formerly Reading, MA: Addison-Wesley).

Bugental, J. F. T. (1987). *The art of the psychotherapist*. New York: Norton.

Bugental, J. F. T. (1989). [Copied from a maxim displayed in the birthplace museum of Albert Schweitzer in Kaisersburg, France, and there cited to his *Memories of childhood and youth*, p. 93. That book is no longer in print.]

Deikman, A. (1990). *The wrong way home: Uncovering the patterns of cult behavior in American society*. Boston: Beacon Press.

Gendlin, E. T. (1978). *Focusing*. New York: Everest House.

Huxley, A. (1990). *Tomorrow and tomorrow and tomorrow, and other essays*. New York: Harper & Row.

Maslow, A. H. (1971). *The farther reaches of human nature*. New York: Viking.

Pascal, B. (1966). *Pensées*. (A. J. Krailshaimer, Trans.) New York: Penguin. (Original date 1670).

Reed, E. S. (1988). *James J. Gibson and the psychology of perception*. New Haven, CT: Yale University Press.

Sartre, J.-P. (1947). *No exit and the flies*. New York: Knopf.

Schweitzer, A. [See Bugental, 1989, above].

Skinner, B. F. (1987). Whatever happened to psychology as the science of behavior? *American Psychologist, 42*, 780–786.

Sterling, M. M. (1991). *The experience of role-play during psychotherapeutic training: A phenomenological analysis*. Unpublished doctoral dissertation, Saybrook Institute, San Francisco.

Tillich, P. (1951). *Systematic theology*. Vol. 1. Chicago: University of Chicago Press.

Walsh, R. N. (1976). Reflections on psychotherapy. *Journal of Transpersonal Psychotherapy, 8*(2).

Welwood, J. (1982). The unfolding of experience: Psychotherapy and beyond. *Journal of Humanistic Psychology, 22*, 91–104.

Whitehead, A. N. (1954). *Dialogues of Alfred North Whitehead*. (As recorded by L. Price.) Boston: Little, Brown.

Youniss, J. (1991). Hermeneutics: Seeking meaning after positivism. [Review of M. J. Packer & R. B. Addison (Eds.), *Entering the circle: Hermeneutic investigation in psychology*.] *Contemporary Psychology, 36*, 17–18.

Discussion by Erving Polster, Ph.D.

◆

I have long regarded Jim Bugental as one of the sages of the psychotherapeutic community. His writings have given human flavor to therapeutic events, explicating with intelligence and depth, with warmth and responsibility, what many of us have in our hearts. His search for human flavor is evident in his discussion of subjectivity. His ideas summon three primary issues to mind.

The first is the difficulty of retaining simple qualities we all grow up with in the face of a complex therapeutic technology. Let us imagine that

I feel a touch of love when my patient, who has been chronically and bitterly ashamed, shows me a sweet side of himself. I wonder whether or not this sweetness can grow and dissolve his bitterness. The sweetness leaves, though, and he looks confused as he goes back, this time to tell me about growing up with his alcoholic father. Then, barely visible within the confusion, I see the fighter in him. Then, he tells me that when he was 9 years old, his father left him in the car while he pretended to be taking care of business, but was actually getting drunk. This 9-year-old boy finally got out of the car, walked into the bar, saw the lie, and told his father he was going to walk home, five miles away. When his father, caught, tried to drive him home, he refused and kept on walking through a heavy rain.

How do I measure such spunk and how do I allow the awe to register in me and in him? How do I register the courage of his resolve, which has now turned into madness when it makes him refuse to have sex with his criticizing wife? This bruised soul is making a fool of himself and destroying whatever benefits may exist in a marriage gone sour because he doesn't know how to yield. How sharp when I point out his stupidity. But this time he grins back, sweetly understanding that I mean him no harm and want only what he himself knows he also wants. How is it possible to include ordinary human qualities in therapy without mawkishness or untimely anger or self-centered purposes? That is a difficult task, and it is ours.

The second issue this presentation brings to mind is how therapists, absorbed with the very practical task of "curing" people, can see beyond into the larger-than-cure questions that can be posed by people and about such topics as religion, philosophy, and literature. Some of these questions seem sentimental, some seem unanswerable, but they are all part of the human concern and they insinuate themselves, welcome or not. Bugental beckons the mystery of existence—its meaning, its ambiguity, its origins, and its future. He welcomes the restoration of awe. He seeks a common ground and harmony among groups of people, ranging in size from the family to the nation. In calling for a change in our image of ourselves, he recognizes the natural effects of community and personal identity.

Perhaps the current surge to belong is a response to an individualistic society gone haywire. What will replace the easy identities that were provided by tightly knit families and homogeneous neighborhoods? Under these conditions, community pressures were an important part of the formation of self. The accompanying feeling that "I am what people say I am," or "I am what the people around me are," has created great personal distortions, which therapists try to correct. Yet, while trying to replace "I-am-what-people-say-I-am because my community says so" with "Who-am-I, because I have no community," do we not keep the problematics of selfhood as debilitating as ever? This vacuum of self calls out to be filled, and the community's contribution is being rekindled by the large numbers of people joining Alcoholics Anonymous, gangs, cults, ethnic alliances, fundamental religions, and the psychologically oriented groups with common clinical problems, such as sex abuse and codependency. A recent article by Richard Higgins in the *Boston Globe* reported that *each week* there are 200 types of "12-step" recovery programs drawing 15 million Americans to 500,000 meetings across the nation.

The third issue is the point–counterpoint character of subjectivity and objectivity. While Bugental speaks of subjectivity as the core factor in therapeutic work, he also quotes from Whitehead, who said that all truths are only half-truths, though we treat them as whole truths. I think we subjectivists need to increase our hospitality to objectivity, the other half-truth. In its honorable concern with what exists in the world outside, the world to which the person must inevitably attend, the objective calls for knowledge, accuracy, discipline, sensitivity, consequences, and other sobering ingredients of anything we subjectively do. Subjective or objective, we are, alas, all caught in the struggle between these paradoxically enmeshed guides.

QUESTIONS AND ANSWERS

Question: Dr. Polster, how do you see Bugental's existential psychology fitting into your brand of Gestalt psychology?

Polster: Gestalt therapy is one of the existential therapies, and so, generally speaking, we have a common frame of mind. I could fit right in with his ideas. But there are differences. For one thing, I think that in Gestalt therapy we create more of what we call experiments. I think that we are probably also more pointed conversationally.

Bugental: May I make one further comment? I don't know whether or not you really mean to imply it, but I am concerned about attempts to find how all of these approaches fit together, in the sense of trying to find the ultimate truth. Each of us stands in a particular position and looks at the mountain of mystery and describes what he or she sees from that position. Sometimes you can see totally different things, yet it's still the same mountain. As we hear each other, as in a conference, we can get a better sense of the whole, without ever really encompassing it all.

Question: Dr. Bugental, is there a sense in which emotional problems could be understood as part of the process of objectification?

Bugental: As we treat ourselves as objects, we lose the seed of power. We become backseat drivers, complaining about the route, but we don't get behind the wheel. Only as we get within our subjectivity are we at the steering wheel again. By making ourselves objects, we make ourselves victims. And to break free of that, we then look outside for ways to rectify the situation, rather than where we need to look.

Question: Dr. Bugental, Dr. Polster spoke of the objective half-truth. Is there a place for the objective within the field of psychotherapy, and what are some examples?

Bugental: Yes, we must have both the subjective and the objective. Perhaps I did not make that as explicit as I might have. I'm not arguing by any means that we should be solely into the subjective realm. However, I feel that in our field, we've had a disproportionate movement toward emphasizing objectivity and neglecting subjectivity, treating it as an error, as an aberrant phenomenon not to be seriously worried

about. By all means, it takes two legs to walk or two eyes to see, and it certainly takes both the objective and the subjective. We are indeed amphibians.

Question: There was a second part to my question. Could you give me an example of the use of objectivity in therapy?

Bugental: Talking is one. Making things explicit. There's an endless variety.

Question: Dr. Bugental, you said earlier that clients need a certain amount of ego strength to do this type of work. I would like you to be a little more concrete or objective about what ego strength would look like.

Bugental: I was referring to the fact that when we work deeply with people, we encourage them to loosen their dependence upon that self-and-world-construct system on which they've based their lives, because we know that only when they loosen that fixed grip does there emerge a possibility of significant life change. But if a person has weak ego functioning—I'm not going to try to get into all that that means right now—there is a looseness about self-identification and it can go on a runaway course. Thus one has to be cautious in encouraging loosening. As a practical example, with new patients with whom I feel uncertain about ego functioning, I would not put them on the couch or encourage freer exploration until we have done some work together and I feel the alliance could provide a sufficient container for safer exploration.

Question: Would you see any incompatibilities between your position and, say, that of Aaron Beck or of Don Meichenbaum?

Bugental: Yes, some, in that I feel that an orientation in which one imposes structure, even if that structure is supportive, is apt to heighten the sense of treating a person as an object. And certainly, the approach I am describing also has that tendency, though we are constantly trying to be aware of it.

Question: It seems that some therapies are easier to carry out than others. I don't know quite how to phrase this question, but I'll try. Dr. Bugental, how many therapists do you know who, to your satisfaction, can follow the kinds of things that you're suggesting and can enter into subjectivity?

Bugental: I do a lot of lecturing and teaching workshops around the country. One of the heartening things is how many people will say afterwards, "That was great. It's right in line with what I've been thinking, or doing, or hoping to get to." I seems to me that this particularly happens with people who have been out of training and in the field for a few years. (In some ways, you have to recover from the shock of graduate training.) As therapists get repeated exposure to living people, that kind of response seems to happen more frequently.

Polster: I think it is an important question because no matter how much and how eloquently and how accurately we may talk about what we are doing, if people cannot learn well *how* to do it, the theory will be misrepresented.

Carl Rogers started out with what seemed to be an incredibly easy therapy—if you think it calls for repeating what somebody said. The concept of clarification makes his method a little more complicated. In any case, the method, in unskilled hands, is reduced in impact. The paradoxical problem is how to make things easy—and yet to encompass the complexity of human beings. Often, teachers with magnetic quality make things seem easy, but if they do not get the complexity across, they will be misused.

Bugental: Carl Rogers evolved from what he did in his earliest years. Yet he was cruelly parodied in those early years as a kind of mechanical repeater. What he was trying to point to is akin to what I am trying to point to, and we're both using crude pointers. I am sure it's related to what Erv and Miriam Polster work with too—to try to get to that inner life and to give it an expression and power.

Question: Dr. Polster, Dr. Bugental commented about the necessity of ego strength in order to do existential therapy. I've read pros and cons with regard to doing Gestalt therapy with patients with schizophrenia. I would like to know your stance on this.

Polster: I don't experience what I do as excluding different levels of ego strength. I think there are certainly greater requirements for therapeutic sensitivity and precision, as in tuning in with a person whose system is ultraresponsive to words that would create alienation or excessive anxiety. I don't work much with seriously disturbed people, but I have no doubt that what I do would be relevant to working with people in a hospital, except that it would probably be more difficult to succeed.

Question: Dr. Bugental, would you comment on that?

Bugental: As I tried to indicate a bit ago, when I have a question about ego strength or "ego function" as I prefer to call it, I try to modify the work appropriately until such time as I feel an adequate container has developed. Too rapid an opening up of the subjective without good structuring can lead to panic and acting out. I've seen that happen and I don't want to bring that about.

Question: Dr. Bugental, I am a graduate student in counseling psychology and often in classes have found myself having to justify my appreciation for the subjective part of psychotherapy. Do you have any suggestions or comments on how to talk to faculty members who cling tenaciously to the objective?

Bugental: I don't know whether I do or not. Good question, though. Perhaps the best answer I can give you, and that's not going to be a very satisfying one, is to reduce the either/or quality. You can bring in the subjective not at the expense of recognizing that there is the objective, but to complement (that's with an "e," though maybe with "i" also) the views of the instructor.

SECTION IV

Psychoanalytic Therapies

The Vital Therapeutic Alliance with Borderline and Narcissistic Patients: A Developmental, Self and Object-Relations Approach

James F. Masterson, M.D.

James F. Masterson, M.D.
James F. Masterson (M.D., Jefferson Medical School, 1951) is Director of the Masterson Group and the Masterson Institute, which specialize in the treatment of adolescent and adult personality disorders. Masterson also is affiliated with Cornell University Medical College and New York Hospital, Payne Whitney Clinic. He has written or edited 10 professional books, serves on three editorial boards, and has received a William Schonfeld Award for outstanding achievement from the American Society for Adolescent Psychiatry. He is one of the most influential practitioners and teachers of contemporary psychoanalytic approaches.

James Masterson here provides a classification system for personality disorders and defines the differential psychodynamics of borderline and narcissistic patients. He indicates the course of treatment for each diagnostic category and emphasizes the need for therapeutic neutrality to avoid countertransference manifestations.

The therapeutic alliance, vital to successful psychotherapy of the borderline and narcissistic disorders, is achieved by two different therapeutic interventions. The advantage of viewing this issue from this theoretical approach is that it provides an architecture of the patient's inner emotional life, including self- and object-representations together with their linking affects and ego defense mechanisms and functions. This allows the therapist to identify and understand the ebb and flow of the patient's emotions—what emotional state is on center stage and must be dealt with and how to deal with it. Also, it provides a tool for evaluating the effects of the interventions.

THE THERAPEUTIC ALLIANCE

The therapeutic alliance can be defined as a real object relationship that is conscious and within which both patient and therapist agree to work together to help the patient improve through better understanding and control. As a real object relationship, it is based on the capacities of both the patient and therapist for what we call whole object relations: to be able to see each other as completely separate figures, whole objects with both positive and negative attributes. In other words, the patient must be able to see the therapist as he or she is, in reality, both good and bad aspects at the same time, as well as to see his or her projections upon the therapist.

WHY IS THE THERAPEUTIC ALLIANCE ESSENTIAL TO TREATMENT?

The therapeutic alliance, a precondition for classical psychoanalysis, represents a substantial achievement in these patients.

To understand why it is an achievement, we have to distinguish between the way a neurotic patient relates (i.e., transference) from the way borderline and narcissistic patients relate (i.e., transference acting out). The transference relationship is not conscious and the therapist is utilized not as a real object, but as a displaced object upon whom is projected unresolved infantile fantasies. The transference relationship also requires the capacity for whole object relations: How can a patient know he or she is displacing feelings onto an object unless the patient is able, at the same time, to recognize the independent reality existence of that object. In classical psychoanalysis, it is the therapeutic alliance that is operative at the beginning of treatment in the neurotic patient and forms the framework against which the fantasies, memories, and emotions evoked by the transference are measured, contrasted, interpreted, and worked through. The patient's awareness of the real object relationship—the therapeutic alliance—forms the essential background against which the patient can evaluate displaced, unresolved, infantile fantasies. The treatment starts out with the therapist's and patient's having a joint, united perspective in their study of the problem.

The borderline and narcissistic patient, however, relates not by transference, but by transference acting out, which is both the patient's style of relating to the therapist and his or her style of defense against the underlying anxiety and depression. There is no joint, united perspective and the patient's projec-

tions on the therapist usually make the therapist the problem. To understand the dynamics of transference acting out and its relationship to working through, we can refer to an article written in 1915 by Freud (see Freud, 1953). To adapt this brilliant discussion to borderline and narcissistic patients, we have only to substitute the words "transference acting out" for Freud's descriptive phrase "expressing what is forgotten in behavior" and "splitting" for "repression."

Freud highlighted the following: "The patient remembers nothing but expresses it in his actions, in his behavior." He reproduces it not in his feelings and memory, but in his behavior, that is, he repeats it in his transference acting out. These patients early in treatment seem to have a "poor memory" of their childhood. It is not that their memory is poor, it is that there is nothing to remember. It has been discharged (or defended against) by their transference acting out. The compulsion to repeat an action that defends against the impulse to feel and remember is activated in treatment. When it is curbed by therapeutic intervention, it is turned into a motive for remembering. The patient's repetitive reactions in the transference of affects, when not discharged by transference acting out, lead to the emergence of feeling and memories, which sets the stage for working through the underlying anxiety and depression.

The developmental arrests of the borderline and narcissistic disorders that produce the defensive style of transference acting out also result in a weak and fragile capacity for a therapeutic alliance. There is little basic trust and there is little capacity to use an observing ego to understand the differences between past and present, reality and fantasy, and mature and infantile aspects of mental life.

The initial, as well as continuing, goal of the psychotherapy is to establish, strengthen, and maintain a therapeutic alliance that will nonetheless routinely, inevitably, and repeatedly suffer transient breakdowns whenever the treatment impels the patient to give up defense and self-activate. However, these same breakdowns, properly managed, can lead many patients to an understanding and mastery of their emotional problem. A few words regarding diagnosis are in order before turning to the psychotherapy.

DIAGNOSIS: THE MASTERSON APPROACH

The advantage of the approach to the personality disorders delineated in the revised third edition of the *Diagnostic and Statistical Manual of Mental Disorders* (DSM-III-R) is that the system is descriptive and focuses on the most readily identifiable and most easily replicated phenomena—symptoms. In addition, since it is free of any theoretical bias, it can be used as a basis for studying any number of theories.

However, the Masterson approach to an understanding of the personality disorders views this diagnostic approach as having a number of limitations. Symptomatology is the most episodic and transitional of personality disorder phenomena. In point of fact, for a long time, our emphasis on symptoms prevented us from getting to the essence of these developmental disorders.

The great advantage of the Masterson approach to diagnosis is that it is developmental and psychodynamic, focusing on the least episodic, the most enduring of all personality disorder phenomena—the intrapsychic structure of self and object representations, ego defenses, and ego functions.

The clinical application of this perspective, or of this way of arranging the diagnostic categories, illustrates the guiding principle of the Masterson approach. We can reorganize the 11 categories of DSM-III-R from the perspective of the Masterson approach using an object-relations framework derived from many years of clinical experience, thus transcending the present limits of formal research.

The 11 categories of DSM-III-R could be divided into four categories, as follows:

1. Borderline personality disorder
   a. Histrionic
   b. Avoidant
   c. Dependent
   d. Passive-aggressive
   e. Compulsive
2. Narcissistic personality disorder
   a. Exhibitionistic
   b. Closet
3. Antisocial personality disorder

4. Paranoid and schizoid personality disorders
   a. Paranoid
   b. Schizoid
   c. Schizotypal

Thus, four basic diagnostic categories are borderline, narcissistic, antisocial, and schizoid. Within the borderline diagnosis, there are a number of subcategories, which reflect the same basic borderline conflict although with different styles of defense against the abandonment depression. The passive-aggressive emphasizes passivity, the dependent emphasizes dependency, and so forth. Underlying the different defensive structures are the abandonment depression and the same basic intrapsychic structure.

Within the diagnosis of the narcissistic personality disorder there are two subtypes, the exhibitionistic and the closet. The exhibitionistic exhibits grandiosity, whereas the one with the closet narcissistic disorder hides his or her grandiosity and idealizes the object (or other person).

The schizoid type comprises three subcategories: schizoid, schizotypal, and paranoid. Whether the schizotypal category belongs within the personality disorders or within the schizophrenia disease spectrum is not clear at this time.

The essential theme of this chapter is that different therapeutic interventions are required to establish the therapeutic alliance with these two disorders: confrontation with the borderline and interpretation of narcissistic vulnerability with the narcissistic personality disorder. It is the difference in the form and content of the intrapsychic structure in these two disorders that tells us why different interventions are necessary to establish a therapeutic alliance.

BORDERLINE PERSONALITY DISORDER

THE INTRAPSYCHIC STRUCTURE

Split Ego

The specific intrapsychic structure (see Figure 1) consists of the split ego and split object-relations unit. The ego structure itself is split

INTRAPSYCHIC STRUCTURE OF THE BORDERLINE PERSONALITY DISORDER

REWARDING OR LIBIDINAL PART-UNIT (RORU)

WITHDRAWING OR AGGRESSIVE PART-UNIT (WORU)

Part Object-Representation:

a maternal part object that offers approval for regressive and clinging behavior

Part Object-Representation:

a maternal part object that withdraws, is angry and critical of efforts toward separation-individuation

AFFECT

feeling good	being fed
being taken care of	gratifying the wish
being loved	for reunion

AFFECT

ABANDONMENT DEPRESSION

homicidal rage	hopelessness and helplessness
suicidal depression	emptiness and void
panic	guilt

Part Self-Representation:

a part self-representation of being the good, passive child — unique and special/grandiose.

Part Self-Representation:

a part self-representation of being inadequate, bad, ugly, an insect, etc

Splitting Defense

Developmental Arrest of the Ego:

Ego Defects — poor reality perception; frustration tolerance; impulse control; ego boundaries.

Primitive Ego Defense Mechanisms — splitting; acting out; clinging, avoidance, denial; projection; projective identification.

Split Ego — reality ego plus pathological (or pleasure) ego.

NORMAL DEVELOPMENT OF SELF- AND OBJECT-REPRESENTATIONS

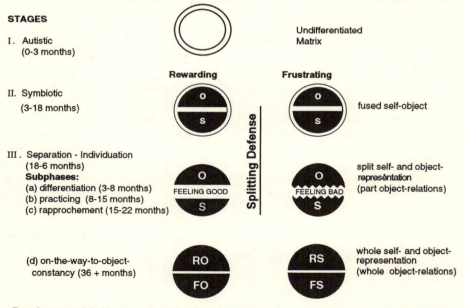

STAGES

I. Autistic (0-3 months) — Undifferentiated Matrix

II. Symbiotic (3-18 months) — Rewarding / Frustrating — fused self-object

III. Separation - Individuation (18-6 months)
Subphases:
(a) differentiation (3-8 months)
(b) practicing (8-15 months)
(c) rapprochement (15-22 months) — FEELING GOOD / FEELING BAD — split self- and object-representation (part object-relations)

(d) on-the-way-to-object-constancy (36 + months) — RO/FO / RS/FS — whole self- and object-representation (whole object-relations)

Splitting Defense

Developmental Achievements of the Ego: (1) no ego defects; (2) repression replaces splitting; (3) higher mechanisms of defense replace primitive mechanisms; (4) beginning of capacity for object constancy.

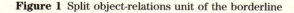

Figure 1 Split object-relations unit of the borderline

into two parts, one functioning according to the reality principle and the other according to the pleasure principle. The latter can be called the pathological ego. This contains defects in ego functioning, including poor reality perception, impulse control, frustration tolerance, and ego boundaries, plus primitive mechanisms of defense, such as splitting, avoidance, denial, clinging, acting out, projection, and projective identification.

Split Object-Relations Unit

The split object-relations unit consists of two split self- and object-representation part-units that I have called the rewarding object-relations part-unit (RORU) and the withdrawing object-relations part-unit (WORU), each having its own self- and object-representation and linking affect.

The rewarding object-relations part-unit part object provides reward or approval for regressive behavior; the self-representation is that of being a good passive child and the linking affect is that of feeling good. The withdrawn object-relations part-unit object representation is attacking or withdrawing at efforts to activate the self; the self-representation is of being bad, ugly, and inadequate, while the linking affect is the abandonment depression.

The Borderline Triad

The relation between the split ego and the split object-relations unit, a key to understanding the psychopathology, I have called the borderline triad: self-activation leads to anxiety and depression, which leads to defense. The clinical vicissitudes of this triad reflect the essence of this disorder.

An alliance is formed between either the rewarding or the withdrawing object-relations part-unit and the pathological ego that functions clinically as follows: Any later-life separation stresses or efforts at self-activation or improvement in treatment interrupt defenses and precipitate the withdrawing object-relations unit with its affect of abandonment depression. The patient then defends against these painful affects by activating the alliance with the pathological ego (either with the rewarding part-unit or the withdrawing part-unit or each unit alternately). If the alliance with the rewarding part-unit is activated, the patient begins to behave in a regressive maladaptive fashion. However, under the sway of the rewarding part-unit, the affective state is one of feeling good and the patient is able to deny his or her maladaptive behavior. If the alliance with the withdrawing part-unit is activated, he or she projects the withdrawing unit and does not feel the abandonment depression, but acts it out in a maladaptive manner that is also denied.

The defects in ego functioning and the primitive mechanisms of defense can be determined by history, as well as by observation in the session. The rewarding and withdrawing object-relations part-units can be observed in the history of relationships with the important people in the patient's life, as well as in the transference acting out with the therapist.

TREATMENT

The therapist's task can now be more defined: to help the patient convert transference acting out into therapeutic alliance and transference through the therapeutic technique of confrontation. Confrontation has several definitions. The first implies aggression, such as the eyeball-to-eyeball confrontations that have occurred between the United States and the Soviet Union. This definition is not what is meant. Rather, what is meant is the second definition, that is, empathically and intuitively, but firmly, bringing to the center of the patient's attention the denied self-destructive maladaptive aspect of this defensive behavior. As the therapist confronts, he or she is lending the reality perception capacity of his or her ego to the patient. The latter, through processes of identification and internalization, integrates the confrontation, repairing the defect in reality perception and controlling maladaptive defensive behavior, thereby interrupting the defense against the abandonment depression. The depression surfaces and, following the borderline triad, the patient then defends again and the therapist confronts again. This sequence eventually results in the strengthening of the ego through better reality perception, the overcoming of defense, and the containing of the depression.

The psychotherapy consists of three stages. In the first, the testing stage, the patient has relied on pathological defenses to provide security throughout life because he or she could deny their self-destructiveness. The patient is not about to turn this function over to the therapist until his or her questions are answered: Is the therapist competent? Is the therapist trustworthy? Only when these questions are answered positively will the patient allow a therapeutic alliance to be formed.

Eventually, the patient controls his or her defense continuously, establishes a therapeutic alliance, and experiences fully the abandonment depression, thus entering the second, or working-through, stage of the treatment. In this stage, much less attention has to be paid to confrontation, and the therapist can now use interpretation. It is vital to keep in mind that interpretation does not work unless there is a therapeutic alliance, unless the patient has that reality screen against which to contrast the interpretation.

The third stage is the separation stage, when the patient must work through the transference fantasies of the therapist as that object that provided support for self-activation.

CASE ILLUSTRATION OF CONFRONTATION

The clinical details in the treatment of an adolescent patient will be greatly condensed and summarized here in order to emphasize how the contents of the intrapsychic structure are manifested in the transference acting out, how they are confronted, and how they respond. Detailed clinical presentations are available in other publications (see Masterson, 1971–1987). The interventions described apply to adult patients, as well as to adolescents.

Frank, 16, had been battling with his parents since the age of 12, was doing poorly in school, and was taking drugs—pot, marijuana, LSD, and methedrine—for his depression. He was involved with a mildly antisocial gang and was occasionally picked up by the police. In his ear-

lier development, he had been overindulged, as well as overwhelmed, by his dominating mother, with whom he had complied. He had been ignored by his distant father. There was no history of overt symptoms before they flowered at age 12.

INTRAPSYCHIC STRUCTURE

Frank's rewarding object-relations part-unit consisted of a maternal object that was omnipotent, providing total approval and supplies for compliant and clinging behavior. The part self-representation was of being a good, passive child who was also omnipotent and quite unique and special. The affect was of feeling good and being loved.

The withdrawing object-relations part-unit consisted of a part object that was domineering, depriving, attacking, engulfing, and powerful. His part self-representation was of being a creep, an insect, a bug, a small and helpless victim with no aggression or self-assertion. The most important component of his profound abandonment depression was rage. The pathological ego's defense mechanisms consisted prominently of avoidance, denial, clinging, splitting, projection, projective identification, and severe acting out. The pathological ego formed alternate alliances with the rewarding and the withdrawing part-units. When the alliance was with the former, the abandonment depression was internalized and clinging was the principal defense. When it was the latter, the abandonment depression was externalized and projection and acting out were the principal defenses.

These alliances functioned as follows: First, in the rewarding-unit alliance, he would project the maternal part object onto his peers, who gave him supplies for meeting their standards of heavy drug usage. At the same time, he would spend a great deal of time fighting with the mother, and he also was able to project the rewarding object representation back onto her, and would have long, reunion-type conversations with her.

The major alliance seen clinically was with the withdrawing part-unit. He projected the withdrawing part object representation back on his mother, as well as on all authority figures in society. By acting out his rage at being deprived, he seemingly solved his problem from the past in the present. Instead of being the small, helpless victim of his mother's wishes, he was powerful, the victimizer, and others were his victims. In therapy, the first questions that would be asked by his testing behavior were: Would I, the therapist, resonate and respond with the rewarding-unit projection or with the withdrawing-unit projection or alternately with both? Or would I require him to face and work through his depression?

OUTPATIENT PSYCHOTHERAPY

I saw Frank three times a week and a social worker saw the mother and father once a week. In the fifth session, while denying his depression, Frank gleefully attacked his mother to see if I would resonate with his withdrawing object-relations part-unit projection and join him in attacking her. I immediately began the task of confrontation by casting grave doubts on his happy mood. I said that it certainly looked as if he were enjoying himself, but that I could not believe that he was enjoying it that much. I said that nobody in so much conflict with his mother could be so happy.

I went on to challenge him further by saying that underneath his superficial glee I suspected he was basically unhappy, but unable to admit it. I continued, "Perhaps you are expressing the anger at your mother this way, not only to get back at her as you say, but also to keep yourself from feeling bad." I elaborated that this unfortunately kept his feelings from coming to the surface in his interviews; as a result, their meaning remained elusive. I ventured to say that such expression might give him transitory relief, but certainly seemed to me to do him much more harm than good. It might be in his interest to air his feelings in the interviews and make an effort toward controlling them at home. Actually, I said, if his thesis that it was all his mother's fault were correct, then the answer would be for him to move away from home and he and I really had no business together. However, I added, I suspected that there was a good deal more to it.

Frank pushed his testing of the withdrawing-image projection further. He indicated how poorly he did in school: "It's to get back at my mother. I don't care." "That's too bad," I said. He was taken aback by this and said, "What do you mean?" I replied, "It's always very sad to see a bright person's potential for satisfaction and achievement thrown out the window in the service of a battle from which he cannot escape unwounded." This brought to Frank's attention the reality of the destructiveness of his behavior that he was denying.

Having failed with the withdrawing-image projection, Frank wanted to test if I would resonate with his rewarding-image projection. He said that if he should ever control his anger, he would feel so bad he would have to see me right away. I responded, "In addition, I'm afraid that you will have to maintain control over a period of time until you can get to see me; this is a long-term problem and emergency measures are not going to solve it."

Each time he verbalized his self-destructive acting out and attempted to make it a virtue, I quickly countered by pointing out the reality that he had denied (i.e., that he had harmed himself) and said that I wondered why. Each confrontation of the withdrawing-image projection caused him again to change his defense and go back to testing whether I would resonate with the rewarding-image projection.

This circular sequence of confrontation of both his rewarding and withdrawing unit projections continued for 12 sessions, at which point a therapeutic alliance began to be established and Frank turned, for the first time, from transference acting-out projections to take a look at what was bothering him, that is, his intrapsychic problem.

He expressed his feeling that he was too compliant with his mother, that he was actually a carbon copy of her wishes. He could not support himself or assert himself with her, and this made him feel extremely depressed, "like a creep." He took drugs mostly to blot out these feelings. He elaborated further: "I think something is missing inside me, I feel emasculated. I don't seem to be able to feel mad or strong and the drive to do things [i.e., to activate himself] is missing. I know I should face it, but I don't. I have no interest in girls and no competitive feelings. I can't say no. There doesn't seem to be anything I can do about it. I feel trapped and it makes me feel terrible."

A therapeutic alliance had been established and we were now no longer talking about his projections and acting out, but had begun to get to the conflicts that lay beneath these defenses. Of course, the treatment does not progress continuously in one direction from this point, since it follows the characteristics of the borderline triad—that is, self-activation leads to abandonment depression, which leads to defense. Therefore, when the patient confronted his depression, he retreated to defense projecting and acting out in the transference, which then had to be confronted to bring him back to considering the depression again. This sequence also has been described in great detail in other publications (see Masterson, 1971–1987).

FOLLOW-UP

The patient returned to see me when he was 24 because he needed psychiatric clearance in order to get a job as an economist with the Central Intelligence Agency (CIA), a job that involved keeping an eye on the Russian economy. He had left psychotherapy after graduating from high school, had gone to Israel and joined a kibbutz, and then had joined the Israeli army. He was a good soldier, but developed colitis and received a medical discharge. He then returned home and had been attending college for the past four years.

At school, he had experimented with a number of courses, finally deciding on economics as a major and Russian as a minor. He was now in his senior year, with a grade-point average of 3.4 and hoped to get this job with the CIA.

He said that he rarely had colitis symptoms, except when he was tense, and that he had no bouts of depression, had little or no conflict with authority, and was not taking drugs. When I was seeing him earlier, his aggression not only was antisocial, but his most athletic activity was stealing hubcaps. He now described his aggression as sublimated into more adaptive activities. He was able to be self-assertive without being destructive and he was interested in sports, characteristically, nonteam activities such as karate and jogging. He said that he was freer with his anger, but that he got angry less. As far as his object relations were concerned, he described his first relationship with a young woman, which lasted about a year and a half. She was 19 and also an economics major; he described her as "a young hippie" who thought he was too square. Their sexual relationship was good. The only problem was that she tended to be possessive and jealous, which he thought might interfere with his career. This is particularly noteworthy in view of the problem with the mother and with self-assertion and aggression described in his treatment. As for his relationship with his parents, he said, "When I left, they got scared that I would not return and they decided to leave me alone. When they let me do what I wanted to do, it turned out that what I wanted to do was what they wanted me to do after all."

At the time that I saw him, he rationalized his use of drugs by pointing out that everybody on the block was on drugs. I replied that I thought they would all come to a bad end. He then accused me of being a square and unaware of what was going on in the street. He now reported that every one of his drug-taking friends was dead, in prison, or in a state hospital. He described his self-image as, "I'm happy with myself, but things have been going pretty well for me—I don't know how I would be if they didn't." At this point in the session, my curiosity got the better of me and I asked, "What do you think now, in retrospect, about your treatment?" He replied, "Well, I don't want to put you down, Doc, but I just had a few growing pains." I said, "Right."

THE NARCISSISTIC PERSONALITY DISORDER

INTRAPSYCHIC STRUCTURE

The intrapsychic structure (Figure 2) of the narcissistic disorder contrasts with that of the borderline in both form and content. Rather

INTRAPSYCHIC STRUCTURE OF THE NARCISSISTIC PERSONALITY DISORDER

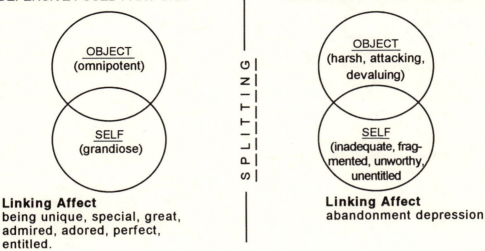

DEFENSIVE FUSED PART-UNIT

OBJECT
(omnipotent)

SELF
(grandiose)

AGGRESSIVE FUSED PART-UNIT

OBJECT
(harsh, attacking,
devaluing)

SELF
(inadequate, frag-
mented, unworthy,
unentitled

SPLITTING

Linking Affect
being unique, special, great,
admired, adored, perfect,
entitled.

Linking Affect
abandonment depression

Ego Functions
poor reality perception, impulse control, frustration tolerance, ego boundaries.

Ego Defense Mechanisms
splitting, avoidance, denial, acting out, clinging, projection, projective
identification.

Figure 2 Narcissistic personality disorder.

than having split self- and object representations, the patient has fused self-object representations. The content of these representations consists of a grandiose self-omnipotent object-defensive representation, with the linking affect of being perfect, adored, and admired. Underneath is a fused aggressive unit consisting of an extremely harsh attacking aggressive omnipotent object representation fused with a self-representation of being fragmented, inadequate, empty, and destroyed. These representations are linked by the affect of the abandonment depression. The ego structure of the narcissistic disorder is similar to the borderline in that it consists of a split ego with primitive mechanisms of defense. Clinically, the intrapsychic structure operates as described in the following.

The Exhibitionistic Narcissistic Personality Disorder

The patient's major emotional investment is in the grandiose self. He or she exhibits the grandiose self and seeks in transference acting out perfect empathy and responsiveness from the therapist, that is, to be adored, admired—the mirroring transference acting out. Failures to resonate and mirror the need for perfect responsiveness frustrate this grandiose self-defense and trigger the underlying aggressive fused unit. The object representation is projected onto the therapist, who is seen as disappointing and attacking. The patient experiences depression and a fragmented self and then defends against this, either by devaluing the therapist or by avoiding the therapist altogether.

The Closet Narcissistic Disorder

If the major emotional investment is in the fused omnipotent object representation rather than in the grandiose self, the patient does not present as grandiose and looking for mirroring responses. Rather, the patient idealizes the object, the therapist, and seeks the therapist's perfect responsiveness, basking in the glow of the perfect therapist—that is, the idealizing transference acting out.

An important and unusual characteristic of the defensive grandiose self of the narcissistic order that is in dramatic contrast to the borderline is its capacity to maintain continuous activation of the grandiose self and to coerce the environment into resonating with the grandiose self-projections. Where that is not possible to avoid, it denies or devalues any stimulus that interrupts the grandiose self-projections. As a consequence, the narcissistic disorder, unlike the borderline, is extremely intolerant of experiences of depression.

INTERPRETATIONS OF NARCISSISTIC VULNERABILITY

The patient begins therapy with either mirroring or idealizing transference acting out. The therapist cannot confront these projections since it would trigger the underlying aggressive unit and the patient would see them as an attack and respond as he or she would to any other kind of attack—that is, by projection, devaluation, or avoidance. The only way to gain entrance to this seemingly solipsistic system is through what I call the narcissistic window—mirroring interpretations of the patient's narcissistic vulnerability to the therapist's failures in perfect empathy in the relationship in the interview.

One does not confront a defense as in the borderline, but one interprets it as a defense against narcissistic pain. For example, one might confront a borderline patient who is late for a session with the fact that this is destructive to the patient's objective—that he or she is depriving himself or herself of time to do the work. In contrast, with a narcissistic personality disorder, one would interpret as follows: "It must be very painful for you to talk about yourself here and you must have felt the need to withdraw to deal with that pain." The goal of the psychotherapy is the same as with the borderline personality disorder, that is, using a therapeutic intervention to help the patient convert transference acting out into therapeutic alliance and transference. It is the type of therapeutic intervention that differs.

ESTABLISHING A THERAPEUTIC ALLIANCE WITH A NARCISSISTIC PERSONALITY DISORDER THROUGH INTERPRETATION OF NARCISSISTIC VULNERABILITY

A 16-year-old junior in high school was depressed, failing in school though he had a good IQ, being overweight, having difficulty with his plans for going to college, and being in conflict with his parents.

Intrapsychic Structure

This patient, a closet narcissist, had a grandiose-self/omnipotent-object defensive fused unit that consisted of an object representation that was omnipotent and idealized as the conveyor of all admiration and adoration. The grandiose self found perfection by maintaining the self-esteem and emotional equilibrium of this idealized object by mirroring its expectations and giving up activating the self. Underneath this defensive unit was the aggressive fused unit, consisting of an object representation that was terrifying, harsh, homicidally attacking. The self-representation was of being helpless, hopeless, empty, inadequate, with a linking affect of terror and depression underneath which lay homicidal rage.

Psychotherapy

The interventions described here apply to adults as well as to adolescents. The patient's intrapsychic structure operated in the following way. If he gave up individuation or real self-activation and instead mirrored the expectations of the idealized object—his parents, others, and the therapist—he fullfilled his grandiose mission. This was demonstrated in the transference acting out as follows: When I did not provide him with expectations and stimuli that he could mirror, such as questions, directions, or guidance, he felt angry at me, helpless to activate himself, as his underlying fused aggressive unit was triggered. I would then make a mirroring interpretation: "It seems that it is extremely painful for you to focus on yourself here and you turn to me to take over to relieve the pain. When I don't take over, you feel extremely disappointed and angry with me, which makes it more difficult for you to look at yourself." He would respond through the disappointment and anger that he could not activate himself and that he dealt with this by being motivated by the expectations of others. Thus, he complied with their expectations, received approval, and thereby restored not only his own sense of self-esteem, but also the emotional equilibrium of the object. This led him gradually and slowly to elaborate the quality of his need for approval—that it was not just approval, but actually adoration and admiration. He was actually like St. Francis of Assisi on a divine mission administering to the disequilibrium in the psyches of his objects, which he had this divine magical power to heal. On the other hand, when he would attempt to establish a relationship with a woman, he would feel with her exactly as he felt in the session with me. She had all the power, she was all perfection, and he was helpless, all he could try to do was give up his self-activation and attempt to mirror her.

Repetitive interpretations of his transference acting out to the effect that his wish to idealize and mirror me was his way of dealing with his pain and depression at having to face and activate himself gradually led him to contain this projection and begin to perceive me as I was, his therapist, and thereby he could establish a therapeutic alliance. This, of course, led him to begin to self-activate in the interviews and to focus on himself rather than on me. He also could self-activate in his outside life. This self-activation overcame his defenses and led to the abandonment depression; he then began to dream. In one dramatic dream, for example, he is talking to his father on the phone and the father suddenly comes right through the phone like a giant monster, attacks him, and tries to kill him; he is terrified. In other words, the aggressive fused unit that lay beneath his surface grandiose self-omnipotent object defense was now emerging, setting the conditions for working through in the interviews.

COUNTERTRANSFERENCE

One cannot consider psychotherapy of the narcissistic and borderline personality disorders without also saying a few words about countertransference. The reason countertransference is so prominent with these disorders, in my view, is a combination of the intensity of the patient's transference acted-out projections and the human vulnerability of a therapist.

These patients are not there at the beginning of treatment to get better since that would evoke depression. They are there to get the therapists to resonate with their projections. If it is the defensive projection, they feel better and treatment stops. If it is the underlying pathological rage and depressive projection, they get rid of all the rage they were unable to express as a child on the therapist and treatment stops. Thus, at the outset of treatment, the therapist is the problem. For this reason, it is vital that the therapist maintain therapeutic neutrality as a life preserver against the inundation of the treatment by the tidal wave of these projections. The therapeutic neutrality provides the framework for the development of a therapeutic alliance.

THE THERAPIST'S VULNERABILITY

Therapists' vulnerability to resonating with their patients' projections is partially due to the fact that one of their motivations for becoming a therapist is what I call a rescue fantasy. In other words, to the degree that the therapist's self was deprived in his or her own development, the therapist projects this deprived self onto the patient, and then does for this deprived self what he or she always wanted done for it as a child. If the therapist was smart in his choice of parents and his or her development was healthy and he or she has good self-and object differentiations, this particular dynamic will be the basis of a great deal of satisfaction in the work, since the therapist does in truth help the patient to remake the deprivations of his or her childhood. However, if the therapist was not so smart and the parents were not that healthy and the therapist's own development was extremely traumatic and he or she does not have good self- and object differentiation, the therapist ends up projecting the deprived self upon the patient and basically treats himself. The patient loves it because the patient then is not required to do treatment.

It is crucial for the therapist to be acutely aware of his or her own countertransference vulnerabilities. The therapist who is not able to control them, should either get supervisory assistance or, if necessary, not take into treatment those patients who will evoke countertransferences that cannot be controlled. This should be in no way viewed as a necessarily large defect in the therapist. Since we all are made of the same clay as our patients, it does not accord with the facts to think that we are necessarily free of countertransference.

In my view, it is unwise for a therapist to undergo an agonizing and long struggle with countertransference based on developmental vulnerabilities. On the other hand, if these vulnerabilities are so great that they cannot be controlled with supervision, they require treatment. If they cannot be controlled or overcome with treatment, then the question has to be raised as to whether this particular person is in the right line of work.

SUMMARY AND CONCLUSIONS

Different therapeutic techniques are required to establish the therapeutic alliance with these two disorders. Developmental self- and object-relations theory helps us to understand why the therapeutic alliance is crucial and how to go about establishing it: confrontation with the borderline personality disorder and interpretation of narcissistic vulnerability with the narcissistic personality disorder.

The difference in working with these two disorders goes beyond technique because the therapist also must shift his or her focus of observation and alertness to countertransference. With the borderline, the focus, in general, is on maladaptive behavior outside the session, with the emphasis on confrontation; countertransference vulnerabilities stress stepping into taking over for the patient or withdrawing or attacking the patient. In contrast with the narcissistic personality disorder, the focus is not on the behavior outside the session, but on narcissistic vulnerability inside the session in the relationship with the therapist. The therapeutic technique is interpretation, not confrontation, and the countertransference vulnerability con-

sists of failures in empathy, real or imagined. This difference in therapeutic atmosphere places a high premium on the therapist's flexibility and capacity to adapt his or her approach to these different disorders.

It is perhaps this requirement for both personal maturity and professional expertise that helps to explain the difficulties in psychotherapy of these disorders and some of the treatment failures. It is not necessarily that the patient is unable to do the work, but rather that therapists have such difficulty in creating the conditions to enable the patient to do the work. Not until we are able to master the latter, can we expect the patient to be able to master the former.

REFERENCES

Freud, S. (1953). Further recommendations in the technique of psychoanalysis: Recollection, repetition and working through. *Collected Papers*, Vol. II (pp. 366–376). London: Hogarth Press.

Masterson, J.F. (1971). Diagnosis and treatment of the borderline syndrome in adolescents (in French). *Confrontations Psychiatriques* (Paris), 7, 125–155.

Masterson, J.F. (1972a). *Treatment of the borderline adolescent—A developmental approach*. New York: Wiley.

Masterson, J.F. (1972b). Intensive psychotherapy of the adolescent with a borderline syndrome (in Spanish). *Cuaderno de la ASAPPIA, 3*, 15–50.

Masterson, J.F. (1976). *Psychotherapy of the borderline adult: A developmental approach*. New York: Brunner/Mazel.

Masterson, J.F. (1978). The borderline adult: Therapeutic alliance and transference. *American Journal of Psychiatry, 135*,(4), 437–441.

Masterson, J.F. (1980). *Psychotherapie Bei Borderline-Patienten*. Germany: CIP Kurztitelaufnahme der Deutschen Bibliothek.

Masterson, J.F. (1981). *Narcissistic and borderline disorders: An integrated developmental approach*. New York: Brunner/Mazel.

Masterson, J.F. (1983). *Countertransference and psychotherapeutic technique: Teaching seminars on psychotherapy of the borderline adult*. New York: Brunner/Mazel.

Masterson, J.F. (1985). *The real self—A developmental, self, and object relations approach*. New York: Brunner/Mazel.

Masterson, J.F. (1987). Borderline and narcissistic disorders—An integrated developmental object relations approach. In J.S. Grotstein, M.F. Solomon, & J.A. Lang (Eds.), *The borderline patient: Emerging concepts in diagnosis, psychodynamics, and treatment* (Vol. I, pp. 205–217). New Jersey: Analytic Press.

Masterson, J.F., & Rinsley, D. B. (1975). The borderline syndrome: The role of the mother in the genesis and psychic structure of the borderline personality. *International Journal of Psychoanalysis, 56* (II).

Discussion by Helen Singer Kaplan, M.D., Ph.D.

My position theoretically is quite different from Dr. Masterson's. I don't use ego-development theory or object-relations theory in my thinking. And I do not distinguish among borderline, narcissistic, and neurotic disorders. However, that's beside the point. This is not the place to discuss theoretical differences. I don't want to throw the baby out with the bathwater because of a theoretical difference, since Dr. Masterson is an absolutely brilliant, intuitive thinker, and I wish to focus on the excellent points that he raised.

You can see what a wonderful therapist Jim Masterson is by the way he talks about the patients. When I first read the chapter, I said to myself, "Oh, of course." But whenever one reads something and says, "Oh, of course," it means "Such a great innovation," because really creative new things often strike people as natural and obvious.

All of us have used confrontation to engage patients who are self-destructive outside of the therapy session and we use support with vulnerable patients. But I never gave the slightest thought to the criteria: "When do I use confrontation?" "When do I really continually try to mirror pain and be empathetic or excuse myself for not being perfectly empathetic?" Jim provides beautiful descriptions of the interventions of confrontation and mirroring. He has also articulated the importance of being careful to understand the characteristics of patients with whom one intervention works and of those for whom another works. So I thought about some of my cases. Of course, with certain patients, I confront and confront. I even interpret the content of dreams in a manner that confronts self-destructive behavior. Very often, I use dreams as a way of saying, "This is an early warning system, a message from your unconscious, that you are about to do something self-destructive." And that is confrontation, an engaging therapeutic maneuver with certain types of patients.

With other patients, I would never confront; I am constantly supportive. There are certain couples where I model, supporting the more vulnerable partner as a means of improving the relationship. For example, it is perfectly possible for someone to fall in love with a narcissistic person—even if he or she is a nonnarcissistic, perfectly healthy person. But that relationship, that sexual alliance, will never work unless the nonnarcissistic partner is constantly empathetic with and supportive of the vulnerable spouse. Such relationships can work beautifully, but continual support is essential for building a sexual alliance between such spouses.

Consider the use of the new penile injection method for impotence. Some of the women involved are very touchy about this. I don't know whether they meet all the criteria of the DSM-III for a borderline diagnosis, but there are certain rejection-sensitive, self-involved kinds of women who are insulted by these injections and who sabotage the sexuality of the the men who are using them. They seem to think, "If he can't get excited by me, this is a terrible insult." But when you work with such women in therapy and teach the husbands to be extremely empathic and supportive, it can work. One strategy is to have the husband wait for his narcissistic wife to ask him to use the injections and to indicate to her, "It is only for you so that I can make love to *you* that I want to use these injections." Then it can work.

That is by way of saying that I think Jim's contributions extend beyond engagement of the borderline and narcissistic patient in psychoanalytically, psychodynamically oriented treatment. Their usefulness and value extends to other kinds of patients and in other types of clinical situations.

Forming a therapeutic alliance is important in sex therapy. This is a very emotionally taxing treatment. We relentlessly strip the patients of their defenses against good sex and against intimacy by getting them to have therapeutic experiences of an intimate and erotic nature that they have previously avoided because they were too threatening. Most couples become extremely vulnerable during the treatment process. Unless you have a solid therapeutic alliance, it is not possible to do this. So we use techniques that rapidly induce therapeutic alliances with both partners at the very first session. By the second and third sessions, we should have a really firm alliance; otherwise, that case won't succeed.

Sex therapists must really be very empathic with both partners and strongly reinforce their right to have sexual pleasure. Coming from an authority figure, that "permission" can be very touching, and it is a powerful engagement technique. For example, we might comment when the patient reluctantly admits to self-stimulation, "Oh, you masturbate. That's wonderful!" Of course, in daily life, when sitting around the family table discussing what happened today, if the kid says, "I masturbated," the family doesn't say, "Isn't that wonderful!" We therapists give a different and more pleasure-reinforcing message. Often this is sufficient to engage people who are motivated to have their sexual dysfunctions treated. However, borderline, psychotic, and neurotic patients also develop sexual dysfunctions and we can improve the sexual functioning of some of those without trying to reconstruct the personality.

Patients with concomitant personality disorders are difficult to treat for sexual problems. Such patients provided a valuable learning experience for me because engagement techniques are so important. Also, you get an extra bonus of improving the couple's relationship, if you can get the partners to become sensitive to the same kinds of issues that come up in the therapy sessions and to use them in their daily lives.

QUESTIONS AND ANSWERS

Question: Can you discuss clinical features of decompensation as an impact of therapeutic alliance? And does the decompensated narcissist look different from the decompensated borderline personality disorder?

Masterson: Yes, according to the expected parameters. The effect depends on the stage of treatment. For example, with patients with a narcissistic disorder, you can expect them to shift from their wish to be adored and admired to an enormous anger and devaluation of you as the therapist, as they get further into their disappointment. With borderline patients, you often find extensive projection of withdrawing and attacking, but more than likely you'll get aggravation of the abandonment depression.

Years ago, it used to be said that you couldn't do any kind of intensive treatment with borderlines because you would get prolonged and difficult states of rage, but I have never seen that happen without there being an iatrogenic component to it. For example, some therapists have a rule that patients are supposed to identify what they feel and express it, whatever it is. If the patients are angry, they have to express the anger. If the patients are getting anger out, or they are working through their rage with their mother, the therapist thinks, "This is great." But what is really going on is, that they are transferring and acting out, and dumping the rage onto the therapist. If they can't be stopped, the treatment can't move beyond that point.

Question: Dr. Masterson, you mentioned that when working with borderlines, you can go in one of two directions: You can either work short-term, relatively speaking, meaning a couple of years, or you can do more intensive work to resolve the abandonment depression. Sometimes a person is willing to commit to treatment only once a week for a couple of years. During that time, there's been substantial improvement; this person is now much more highly functioning. The patient is able to work, to interact more effectively with the family, and so forth. However, the patient continues to say, "I still feel kind of empty inside, etc." But he or she is not willing to make the commitment to go beyond that and meet two or three times a week. Where do you go from there? Do you terminate?

Masterson: Very often, the patient's goals and our optimistic goals are not the same. And, unfortunately, the ones that are important are the patient's goals, not our goals. Here's the way I operate in this kind of a situation: If it were a patient who had come to me as a lower-level borderline patient whose adaptation had improved dramatically, but who still had some sense of emptiness and yet did not want to continue treatment, I would just agree and let the patient stop. I don't bring up the other option, because for many lower-level borderline patients, it is not possible to work through the abandonment depression. So what's the point of bringing it up?

If this happens with a higher-level borderline patient, I will bring up another option. But if the patient doesn't want to accept it, I say, "Okay. Maybe you'll change your mind." What you're banking on by saying that is that life is inevitably going to present the patient with another separation stress, and he or she may realize that there is more involved here than just a feeling of being empty, that he or she really hasn't overcome the developmental arrest. Then the patient will come back for that reason.

Question: Okay. I was thinking that you could go further with this. But the patient says, "Even though I have done good things and I've made adaptations, I still have this emptiness." When would you begin to move toward a termination? I still feel there is something I should do.

Masterson: If that's the case, you have to confront the patient. "There is more to do, why don't you want to do it?" By the way, there is another, prior consideration. Remember, as the termination phase comes up, the patient could be feeling empty just because it is the termination phase. Then you have to work that part through first before you can make the decision as to whether it is due to the termination phase or it is more underlying.

Question: If patients are not willing to make the commitment to the more intensive treatment of two or three times a week, then you just need to say, "Well. . . ." Is that the answer?

Masterson: First, you would explore it with them. The therapist is the only person in a position to make judgments about what is best for the patient. The patient cannot do it; the family can't do it. The therapist is the only person in a position to do it. That's what they're paying

you for. You have to put your nickel on the line, whether you like it or not or they like it or not. You have to confront them about it. "I think your reason for not wanting to go further is the same reason we talked about for several years; that is, you are anxious about facing this bad feeling. It offers you enormous dividends if you do face it."

Question: If you are dealing with a spouse or family members, what could you advise them to do to help these adult borderline and narcissistic patients?

Masterson: If they come in as a couple, we would start the treatment off as a couple. But if you have an adult come in for treatment, it is in the interest of the treatment to try to conduct it as much as possible through that individual and not become involved with the family. After all, one of our responsibilities as adults is to deal with all the others in our lives. When you have to bring the others in, what you're doing is taking over some of that function for the patient.

Sometimes you may have to do it. There are no blacks and whites in clinical work. An exception would be where pathological behavior is such that the patient cannot get a hold on it as he or she becomes more self-activated. Then you have to do more about it. What did you have in mind?

Question: If one of these people is making the spouse pretty crazy and the only alternative is to get out of the relationship, is there something that can be done to work with the spouse in such a way that would make it more likely that he or she would get into treatment?

Masterson: When I am working with patients, whether or not they stay with their spouses is really not an issue. I work mostly with the intrapsychic aspect of the patient. Now what happens? The patients begin treatment in a state where they are not very self-activated. If they are married, usually it reinforces this lack of self-activation; as they start to self-activate, it disturbs that balance. There then has to be a reestablishment of a new equilibrium. Sometimes the spouse is able to change and adapt to it, and sometimes not. My response is to bring to the patient's attention the consequences of this relationship. Then the decision as to what to do is up to the patient.

The degree to which a patient is in a life situation that is not supportive of his or her sense of self and self-activation ends up impairing the patient's ability to grow. How the individual wants to deal with that is then up to the individual.

Question: I know of a case in which marital therapy was tried with a narcissistic disorder. I am sure you would agree that it's pretty futile to try to do marital therapy because the person would feel attacked.

Masterson: Well, it is not futile. We have done it. In one of our books, *Psychotherapy of the Disorders of the Self,** we described an exhibitionistic–narcissistic disorder male and a closet narcissistic female who were a couple. Another therapist and I were seeing each individually. The two were having such battles that we decided to add joint interviews. Thus there were four of us in the joint session. We weren't very optimistic about the prospect at the beginning. In the classic Japanese movie *Rashomon,* four people who had undergone the same experience together relate it as if it were four different experiences. In a similar vein, we could never get these two patients to report the same experience in the same way. For a long time, we thought they were talking about two different experiences, not the same one. The reason for this eventually emerged. When the event happens in reality, it gets filtered through the participants' narcissistic perspectives, which can profoundly distort the reality event.

Actually, we did achieve a surprising amount of success with these two, enabling them to give up some of their narcissistic demands. When Dr. Kaplan mentioned a patient's falling in love with a narcissistic disorder, I agreed completely; of course, we do see that. But is it possible for a narcissistic disorder to fall in love with anybody else? That's the big question.

Question: Instead of separating them to work

---

*Masterson & Klein (1989). New York: Brunner/Mazel.

on individual issues, would you tend to see them together?

Masterson: No. The quicker you can get them to individual therapy, the better. What we do with couples is point out the partners' projections. With the narcissistic patient, we interpret, and with the borderline, we confront. At a certain point in this process, what tends to happen is that the patients begin to realize that all the emotion they were projecting on the spouse doesn't really belong there. It's in their head and it belongs with their past. When they get to that stage, we are able to shift to individual therapy. If both members of a couple are borderlines, consider yourself lucky, because you confront both of them and it's synergistic—and it works. When the couple includes a borderline and a narcissistic partner, it's a bumpy, rocky road.

Question: What about using group therapy with borderline and narcissistic patients?

Masterson: Group therapy works extremely well with borderline patients. It is very synergistic with individual therapy. We use it. The only important consideration is that the borderline patient relate from what we call a dyadic structure. There are only two representations in the psyche: self and object. The clinical significance of this is that the patient has a symbiotic possessive fantasy of you as a therapist; this is the carrot that makes the patient willing to endure the stick of the painful affects. Whenever you bring other people in, as in a group, the way the borderline patient deals with that is to reduce investment in you, because you have frustrated the symbiotic fantasy. The practical consequences are that, in marital or group therapy, you cannot possibly work through an abandonment depression. You don't have enough transference investment. But you can get all the results of confrontative therapy in those forms of treatment.

Question: What about using group therapy in conjunction with individual therapy with the borderline? Do you use the same therapist to do both?

Masterson: No, I don't think you should do

that. I've done a number of consultations where a therapist starts out with a borderline individual and then puts the patient in his or her group, and lo and behold, the borderline erupts in a rage and leaves, because he or she experiences it as an abandonment. The ideal way, if you can do it, is for you to do the individual work and have a friend do the group. Then you can do the group for your friend's patients in individual therapy.

Question: Dr. Masterson, could you talk a bit more on the difficult aspects of working with borderline people? What happens when the therapist goes away on vacation? What about the patient who is possibly suicidal, and while hospitalization may not be needed, daily contact could be beneficial? I am talking about a case of my own. Was I getting too wrapped up in caretaking when I thought that daily contact was necessary?

Masterson: The vacation is an issue, not just for patients, but for therapists as well. I think most therapists, when they go away, start to feel guilty. With borderline and narcissistic patients, you have to walk a kind of tightrope. Even as you recognize that separation stress is a crucial issue with them, you have to behave as if you are not aware of that fact. The reason is that your vacation is not the stress. It is merely a reinforcing precipitating stress to the original stress, which has to do with early life. So you want to provide a role model for them with regard to that. For example, you don't say to the patient, "Well, I know you have a separation problem and in six months I am going away for two weeks. I am giving you plenty of time to get used to the idea." If you do that, you are telegraphing your own anxiety about the separation. What I tend to do is tell the patient as much time in advance as I am going to be away. As soon as you tell patients that you are going away, they reduce their investment in the treatment. After you tell them, don't try anything heroic therapeutically; pull back a bit.

For example, once you have told patients, don't do a lot of investigation of their reactions. If they don't bring it up, you let it go. I tell patients, "I am going to be away," and I write

this down in my notes so as to be ready to deal with their denial. They come back two weeks later and say, "You never told me you were going away. How can you do this?" "Well, here is the note I made." It's not until later in their treatment that they are really ready to deal with the affects related to separation. There's no sense in pushing it too soon.

The same consideration applies when you return from vacation. What the patients have been doing is storing up what we call a "vacation present." The first day back in the office is the longest day of the week because they are going to dump all of the anger and depression they have been holding onto while you were away. You don't have to do anything about this except to listen and let them discharge it.

When you first come back, you also don't do anything heroic because you still don't have the reinvestment of transference. But very slowly—and it varies with every patient—patients will come back to the total reinvestment in the transference. Before you went away, they were working on a certain level about a certain issue, and that disappears from the therapeutic scene. When you return, you wait for it to reappear; it's almost as if they take up from the last sentence four months ago, and they are right back into it. Now you have the reinvestment and you can deal with it.

It's not a good idea when you are away to have daily phone contact. It sends the wrong message. The message you have to send to patients is that you have confidence in their capacity to activate themselves and manage things. Let them establish to you that they cannot do so and then deal with it. But your essential message has got to be a positive one of confidence.

If you have a patient you think might be suicidal, either have someone else see the patient while you are away or put the patient in the hospital. This clinical judgment itself is a measure of your confidence in the patient and he or she will interpret it that way. For example, when I go away, I think very carefully about whom I am going to tell what. I have somebody covering for me. If I have a higher-level patient, I am not going to tell the patient that somebody will be covering for me. I am going to assume that he or she assumes it, that if he or she calls, there will be somebody there. I don't want even to hint to patients that they may have that kind of trouble.

To others, I will say, "You must see So and So while I am away. I am worried about such and such happening, whether you are or not.' And to others, I will say, "I think you'll have to go to the hospital."

Now, once you get further along in analytic treatment, the vacations and separations become a great stimulus to growth, because they allow the patient to practice a newfound capacity for self-activation in the treatment.

The Essence of Dynamic Psychotherapy

Judd Marmor, M.D., Ph.D.

Judd Marmor, M.D., Ph.D.

Judd Marmor is Franz Alexander Professor Emeritus at the University of Southern California School of Medicine and Adjunct Professor of Psychiatry at the University of California School of Medicine in Los Angeles. He graduated from Columbia University College of Physicians and Surgeons in 1933. Marmor is a past president of the American Psychiatric Association, the American Academy of Psychoanalysis, and the Group for the Advancement of Psychiatry, and serves on numerous editorial boards. He has received a number of professional awards, including the Founders' Award from the American Psychiatric Association, the Ittleson Award from the American Orthopsychiatric Association, and the Pawlowski Peace Prize. Marmor is the author of five books and the coauthor of one. He has written or collaborated on more than 300 scientific papers, primarily on psychoanalysis and human sexuality.

Judd Marmor summarizes the evolution of contemporary dynamic approaches from the analytic process of Freud to more modern methods of short-term dynamic psychotherapy. The emphasis in psychodynamic psychotherapy over the past few decades has shifted from a focus on insight and the recovery of early memories to a recognition that the quality of the patient–therapist relationship is the quintessential factor upon which the success of therapy depends. This involves both the real relationship and transference–countertransference elements, all within a systems-theory orientation.

When one studies a gamut of psychotherapies, it becomes clear that patients can be helped by a variety of therapeutic techniques based on a diversity of theories. However, it is important to point out that a successful technique does not mean that the theory behind it is necessarily correct. The evolution of the theory and practice of dynamic psychotherapy over the years is an example of this. When I first went into psychotherapeutic practice more than 50 years ago, my approach was based on the classical psychoanalytic model in which I had been trained. In this model, the focus was primarily on the patient's intrapsychic processes and conflicts, as reflected in free associations, dreams, and fantasies.

As a result of increasing sophistication and research over the years, the focus of psychopathology is now sought not just within the individual's psyche, but also in the patient's total system, including relationships with family, with peers, and with the community and the society in which development has taken place. This does not mean that the essence of Freud's pioneering contributions has been totally discarded. Among the concepts that continue to be relevant are that human behavior is motivated; that the nature of this motivation is often largely concealed from awareness; that our personalities are shaped by both inherited and experiential vicissitudes; that disturbances in behavior, cognition, and affect are often the resultants of conflictual or deficient inputs; and that early developmental experiences are of particular significance in shaping perceptions and reactions later in life. Similarly, psychoanalytic constructs of the defensive and adaptive ways in which the human psyche deals with anxieties and conflicts, along with constructs such as rationalization, denial, identification, projection, and the meaningfulness of dreams and parapraxes continue to contribute significantly to our understanding both of ourselves and of our patients.

Nevertheless, the theoretical shift from an intrapsychic to a systems focus has led to important changes in the *practice* of contemporary dynamic psychotherapy. The assumption that the development of cognitive insight is the quintessential factor in cure and that the task of therapy, therefore, is to give the patient such insight has come to be increasingly questioned. Experience has shown that competent therapists using quite different explanatory theories for their patients' problems, and conveying diverse interpretations to their patients, all achieve essentially comparable results. Clearly, if the progress of patients were due specifically to the cognitive understanding that they receive, then only the "correct" interpretations would work, while others would not. The fact that this is not so indicates that there must be some common denominators, other than the insights given, in the psychotherapeutic process. Indeed, it is not uncommon to see patients who have improved tremendously under therapy and yet show little or no cognitive awareness of the psychodynamics involved in their former difficulties.

Without questioning the usefulness of understanding, therefore, it is clear that it is not a *sine qua non* for successful therapy. We have increasingly come to the conclusion that the critical foundation upon which the success or failure of treatment depends is not cognitive insight, but rather the nature and quality of the interpersonal interaction between patient and therapist. Thus therapy is not something a therapist does to or for a patient, but something that takes place between therapist and patient.

What takes place between them, however, is not a simple matter. It is a complex process involving not only unconscious elements, but also conscious and realistic ones. Therapists are not interchangeable units like razor blades. Their real attributes, their warmth, genuineness, empathy, knowledge, appearance, emotional maturity, and personal style, all play a significant role in the patient–therapist interaction, as do the conscious and unconscious emotional needs and value systems of both parties. This is not to say, however, that the relationship is the only basis of psychotherapy. In my remarks to the 1985 Evolution of Psychotherapy Conference, I tried to elaborate in depth what some of the other important factors were, and I shall merely recapitulate them briefly at this time.

ESSENTIAL ASPECTS OF PSYCHOTHERAPY

Psychotherapy is essentially a learning process. I have already referred to the insight that all dynamic psychotherapists endeavor to impart to their patients. Insight might be defined as a conceptual framework within which a therapist attempts to establish a meaningful relationship between events and feelings or experiences of which the patient is unaware. Insight is generally assumed to come in two forms: simple cognitive awareness, or "intellectual" insight; and cognitive awareness accompanied by a simultaneous release of emotion, so-called "emotional" insight. The latter is considered more effective in fostering change, but we have learned that even emotional insight does not necessarily result in change. There usually still remains the arduous task of helping patients to undo the previously deeply conditioned patterns of perception and behavior. That is where the quality of the relationship with the therapist in enabling patients to stay with the task and ultimately resolve their problems becomes crucial.

A number of other factors also are involved in contributing to this process. First, the fact that the help-seeking patient is able to confide in a person with help-giving potential and from whom help is desired and expected facilitates the reduction of anxiety and the release of emotional tension. This frequently produces a feeling of well-being, especially in the early phases of therapy. Second, a process of reparative operant conditioning takes place by virtue of covert and overt approval and disapproval cues from the therapist in response to what the patient is reporting. These cues are reflected not only in what the therapist interprets as "healthy" and "mature" behavior versus "neurotic" or "immature" behavior, but also in numerous subtle nonverbal facial reactions and empathic responses. Important operant conditioning also takes place by virtue of the different and more objective ways in which the therapist responds to the patient in contrast to the ways significant others did in the past. This is what Franz Alexander called "the corrective emotional experience," and it is apparent that it is not a matter of insight so much as it is one of *relationship*.

Third, another subtle but often quite significant process that occurs in the course of the patient–therapist relationship is the unconscious role-modeling that takes place by virtue of the patient's identifying with the therapist's implicit and explicit values and reactions. This is what James Strachey, Freud's translator, called, in the jargon of that time, the "dosed introjection of bits of the analyst's superego."

Fourth, in all psychotherapy, whether consciously intended or not, a certain amount of implicit or explicit suggestion and persuasion takes place. Although many therapists stoutly deny that this occurs in what they do, I have yet to see any psychotherapeutic process in which it could not be demonstrated, if only by virtue of the implicit promise that a favorable result will eventually ensue if the patient cooperates with the therapist's technique of treatment.

Finally, in the process of the learning that is involved in the psychotherapeutic process, a certain amount of repetition and rehearsal has to occur, so that the newly acquired adaptive reactions and healthier sense of self-confidence and self-worth can be successfully expressed and maintained in the total range of the patient's relationships.

THE EVOLUTION OF DYNAMIC PSYCHOTHERAPY

Let me now turn to a consideration of some of the other important technical changes that have taken place in the dynamic psychotherapeutic process during the past several decades. First, there has been a shift from the emphasis on the recovery of early memories to one in which the focus is on the here-and-now experiences of the patient in his or her current life-situation, particularly in the transference relationship with the therapist. This does not mean, however, that the patient's past history is now considered irrelevant. It remains an important basis for *understanding* how the patient's problems have developed and evolved, but the recovery of early memories no longer is regarded as the *basis* for therapeutic change.

Equally important, there has been a major change in how dynamic psychotherapists relate to their patients. In the 1930s, 1940s, and 1950s, the analytically oriented therapist was expected to sit impassively behind a couch and maintain, as much as possible, a personal incognito so as not to interfere with the patient's pristine associations and the process of uncovering what was going on in the patient's unconscious. Needless to say, no one questions the importance of a therapist's being a good listener, but the assumption that the therapist should be a kind of "neutral mirror," who does not interact with patients but merely reflects their feelings and thoughts back to them, is no longer considered to be the most desirable way of conducting psychotherapy. It should be remembered that Freud developed this guideline when he was essentially doing research on the previously unexplored territory of the subjective unconscious of his patients.

However, a good research technique is not necessarily an optimal psychotherapeutic technique. As a matter of fact, in psychotherapy, being relatively impassive and impersonal is not a "neutral" attitude at all, but an artificial one that always affects patients in some way. It can also be misconstrued as coldness, disinterest, or rejection. The concept of therapeutic neutrality *does* have a certain validity in the sense that it is indeed important to be nonjudgmental and not impose one's own value system on patients, but this should not be interpreted to mean that therapists are value-free. All therapists are products of their own cultural, religious, and ethnic backgrounds and inevitably acquire value systems shaped by these influences. Concepts about masculinity, femininity, emotional maturity, healthy and unhealthy aggression, "normal" sexuality, and the like all involve value judgments that are inevitably reflected to patients in what is interpreted as healthy or neurotic, mature or immature.

I shall return to the issue of the therapist's activity when I discuss the subject of short-term dynamic psychotherapy. At this point, I would like to move on to a totally different issue, that of planning the therapeutic approach.

THE THERAPEUTIC PLAN

How do therapists prepare their therapeutic plan? All too often, unfortunately, therapeutic planning does not take place at all. Many therapists have a procrustean bed that represents their particular technique of working, and they try to fit all of their patients into that bed. However, if the therapy is to be adapted to the *patients'* needs rather than the other way around, I believe it is imperative that the therapist take into consideration all of the systemic forces—biological, psychological, and social—that have played a role in producing patients' emotional distress or psychopathology.

In order to achieve that kind of understanding, it is essential, early in therapy, to obtain a comprehensive background history after having listened to the presenting problem. This does not negate the fact that there are often instances in which the presenting problem is so embedded in the current life situation or crisis that it can be dealt with directly and briefly, as we do in crisis therapy. If, however, as is often the case, we find ourselves dealing with a pattern that seems to go back many years, such as a personality disorder or persistent difficulties in interpersonal relationships, then a comprehensive developmental history provides an invaluable background for subsequent interactions with the patient.

It is also important to pay special attention to the history of the onset of the presenting problem. Was it acute or insidious? Were the precipitating factors massive or minimal? Were they crucial or trivial? Were the stress factors primarily intrapsychic, interpersonal, or environmental? A careful history also will tell us what strengths patients bring to the therapeutic process in terms of their adaptive capacities and of their environmental support systems, such as family, friends, financial resources, and employment. The best of therapies can run aground in the absence of some of these ancillary support elements in a patient's life.

TECHNICAL ECLECTICISM

Taking such a detailed history, then, enables the therapist flexibly to determine what kind of approach is apt to be most useful. Is the disturbance in the marriage? Then conjoint marital therapy may be the approach of choice. Is the disturbance in the dynamics of the family? Then family therapy may be indicated. Is it a matter of need for social skills training or for a particular behavioral therapy approach? Ideally, therapists ought to have at their disposal a multiplicity of technical capabilities that will enable them to apply whatever approach most effectively will modify the stresses in the patient's system of relationships. Arnold Lazarus was one of the first persons in the field of psychotherapy to espouse what he called a "multimodal" approach, and it is a tribute to his virtuosity that he is able to apply most of the diverse techniques himself. However, most therapists are trained in merely one or two approaches; when other techniques are indicated, they may have to refer the patient elsewhere for supplementary therapeutic assistance.

Incidentally, it is important in this regard to include pharmacotherapy as one of the supplementary possibilities for some patients, although I have never been one of those who assume that pharmacotherapy can ever be regarded as an adequate therapeutic approach in and of itself. In almost every case, individual, family, or group therapy, or some combination thereof, is essential fully to resolve the systemic disturbance involved in a patient's psychopathology, whether it be on a neurotic, characterologic, or psychotic level. However, you may recall the well-publicized case, just a few years ago, in which a severely depressed patient at a prestigious institution was treated only by psychotherapy for many months without improvement; when taken elsewhere, the patient improved rapidly on antidepressant medication and then sued the original institution for malpractice. This illustrates one of the dangers of ignoring the potential value of supplementary medication. We now live in an age of therapeutic accountability and it is important to keep such possibilities in mind.

By the same token, there are other conditions, such as phobias or obsessive-compulsive neuroses, where various forms of behavior therapy often will help more quickly than will dynamic psychotherapy. And these approaches, too, may be combined usefully at times with certain psychopharmacological medications.

This leads me to comment on the oft-debated issue of focusing on symptom removal as compared with dealing exclusively with the patient's underlying psychopathology. In the early days of dynamic psychotherapy, dealing with symptoms directly was considered an inappropriate thing to do. The prevailing myth was that if you removed the symptom without solving the underlying psychodynamic psychopathology, the symptom would inevitably recur. This reasoning was based on a closed "hydraulic system" conception of personality, as if the patient's symptom were a leak that had developed because of increased pressure within the system and would inevitably recur, if not in the same spot, then elsewhere, if the leak was sealed without reduction of the underlying pressure. However, experience has shown that this does not always jibe with clinical reality. When patients are relieved of symptoms, they not only feel better at the time, but often continue to feel better. The reason for this is that the human personality is part of an *open* biopsychosocial system, so that the removal of a symptom not only increases inner feelings of well-being, but also can produce improved interpersonal relationships, with the resultant positive feedback that can modify the entire system beneficially.

It is worth pointing out, also, that it is often feasible and desirable to supplement individual therapy with conjoint marital and/or family therapy. Here again, the point of view has changed substantially over the years. There was a time in the early days of psychoanalytic therapy when any contact with a relative or significant other, even over the telephone, was considered to be potentially detrimental to the therapeutic process and to be avoided at all costs. As a result, significant others who could have been helpful to the process were often antagonized or made suspicious and there was a negative impact on the patient's therapeutic progress. In contemporary psychotherapy, it is considered not only useful, but often therapeutic to have interviews with a spouse or significant other, or even to have conjoint or family sessions, always, of course, with the patient's approval. This is a form of multimodal therapy that all dynamic therapists should be equipped to employ.

THE TEMPORAL FACTOR

There are two other issues I would like to discuss: the frequency of interviews and the question of short-term dynamic psychotherapy. These are both issues demanding increasing attention in the face of shrinking financial resources and a growing emphasis on accountability.

What constitutes an optimal frequency for achieving satisfactory psychotherapeutic results? Despite the fact that most analytically trained psychotherapists were taught that a frequency of four or five visits a week was optimal for insight-oriented therapy, over the years, more and more of them have begun to see their patients less frequently. Indeed, recent studies of office-based practices among both psychiatrists and psychologists in the United States have shown that most of them see their patients fewer than 50 times a year, or an average of once a week.

Psychotherapeutic research in recent decades has shown again and again that patients who traditionally have been considered the best subjects for intensive psychoanalytic treatment, the so-called YAVIS (young, attractive, verbal, intelligent, and successful) patients are the very ones who do well also on a visit schedule of once or twice a week. This paradox is not as great as it initially appears. It should not be surprising that patients with the kind of adaptive strengths and ego resources that are required in order to cooperate in years of psychoanalytic exploration should be precisely the ones who are most able to benefit from less frequent therapeutic contacts.

Moreover, there is something to be said about the potential *negative* effects of seeing patients four or five times a week. Too great a frequency of visits has a tendency to make patients become excessively dependent on their therapists, thus working against the very autonomy and adaptive strength toward which the therapeutic process is aimed. I do not minimize the value of the intimacy and trust that can develop with frequent visits, but it is not in the best interest of patients to become so dependent on their treatment that they react as though they cannot function in life without their therapeutic hours.

I remember, in the early days of my work, when I used to see patients that frequently, that even a weekend interruption, to say nothing of one of a week or longer, was often regarded as abandonment and responded to with an intensification of symptoms and other regressive manifestations. In retrospect, this should have been predictable. When a relationship between a therapist and patient is set up that implicitly carries the message that it is essential for patients to be seen every day, the confidence of patients in their capacity to function without the therapist's support often tends to become impaired. Indeed, in the hothouse of dependency that sometimes develops in such a process, many patients act as if their whole life revolves around the therapeutic hours, while almost everything else becomes subordinate. It is difficult to believe that this constitutes a salutary development.

Too great a frequency tends to create an unconscious expectancy in patients that it is the therapist or the therapy that is going to resolve their problem, rather than their own efforts. When one superimposes on such a process the traditional analytic injunction against patients' making any changes in their lives as long as they are in treatment, one can see how this actually poses the danger of impeding rather than facilitating the therapeutic goal of autonomy and self-confidence.

What, then, should be the determinants in establishing the frequency with which patients are seen? Certainly, initial consideration should be given to the degree of psychopathology that the patient presents. If patients present in a state of intense anxiety, they may need a professional support system more frequently, at least at the outset, whereas patients with less anxiety can generally do better if not seen too frequently. I have found it useful at the beginning of therapy to see most patients at least twice a week. This enables the critical therapeutic alliance to be cemented more rapidly, and allows the therapist to arrive at a psychodynamic formulation so as to plan the therapeutic strategy more efficiently. Once this has been done and a working alliance established, it usually becomes possible to see most patients on a once-a-week basis.

Additionally, it is my feeling that the frequency of visits should not be permitted to become a fixed routine. Like medication, the frequency of sessions can be modulated and adjusted to the actual needs of patients in the course of therapy. As patients begin to feel more and more secure and their anxieties recede, it is often in their best interests that the frequency of sessions be reduced. In so doing, the therapist implicitly conveys the message to patients that they are becoming more capable of functioning on their own. The gradual reductions in the frequency of visits serve as tangible evidence of the patient's progress; such implicit encouragement is an important element in fostering the development of self-esteem and self-confidence. As progress is made, I have at times found it useful to space therapeutic visits over even longer periods, such as once every two weeks or on an irregular basis.

When patients are given the opportunity to develop and trust their own ego resources, experience shows that they make better therapeutic progress. That is why, with many patients, short-term dynamic psychotherapy is often remarkably effective despite the fact that the total number of visits may be relatively limited. Allowing more time between visits also gives patients an opportunity to apply the understanding and adaptive improvements that have been acquired in the psychotherapist's office to their other interpersonal relationships.

Unless such changes are generalized to their external life situations, no genuine progress has taken place.

SHORT-TERM DYNAMIC THERAPY

This brings us to the issue of short-term dynamic psychotherapy (STDP). One of the important things that we have learned during the past several decades is that many patients who were once seen as needing long-term therapy for two or more years are capable of changing more rapidly with more active techniques.

In a sense, STDP epitomizes the dramatic changes that have taken place in the practice of dynamic psychotherapy during the past 40 years. These are, with one important addition to which I shall allude later, face-to-face interaction, greater therapist activity, the maintenance of a consistent here-and-now focus on the central dynamic problem, and the diminished frequency of visits.

I have already mentioned the value of the face-to-face interaction versus sitting behind the couch. Sitting face-to-face creates a structure in which a more active transactional process can occur, while lessening the tendency toward transference regression. In so doing, it facilitates rather than retards the patient's path toward autonomy and emotional maturity.

The active interaction of the therapist with the patient has two other significant psychodynamic consequences. First, it is a direct reflection of the therapist's interest in and concern for the patient, in itself an important therapeutic factor. Second, by interaction and confrontation, the therapist is able to promote the patient's adherence to the central focus of their work together and is able to discourage the digressions that often conceal unconscious resistances. The activity thus serves to maintain a high level of therapeutic tension and interaction in each therapeutic session by persistent confrontations and interpretations of the patient's here-and-now behavior in relation to the central focus.

Active transference interpretations and the bringing out of negative feelings, as well as positive ones, also play an important role in STDP. It should be emphasized that the therapist's being active does not mean being directive. A directive approach constitutes what Sandor Rado called a "parentifying" relationship, which tends further to foster the infantilization of the patient. A nondirective relationship, on the other hand, encourages the patient's spontaneity and independent expression and demonstrates respect for the patient's own competence.

The additional element that sets STDP apart from long-term dynamic psychotherapy is the deliberate setting of a time limit. Three important consequences derive from this maneuver: First, the setting of a time limit places a central emphasis from the very beginning of the therapy on the issue of separation and individuation. This colors the entire therapeutic process and creates an entirely different set of expectations than in long-term therapy, where the patient is told at the outset that the length of therapy is open-ended, unpredictable, and likely to go on for a year or two or more. Second, not only is the issue of separation and individuation relevant, if not central, to the problem presented by most patients, but putting it in the forefront of the therapeutic technique reflects a basic respect for and encouragement of the patient's capacity to be autonomous. This counters the patient's impulse to see himself or herself as helpless, inadequate, and in need of dependent support. Third, the very process of termination constitutes a therapeutic act that tends to encourage the patient's independence and self-confidence. This is not to deny that the initial response of most patients to approaching termination is one of anxiety and, often, regression. Nevertheless, the firm and steady insistence on a termination date and the working through of separation anxieties are critical to the process of STDP.

Not all patients, of course, are suitable subjects for STDP. Suitability does not depend, however, on particular nosological categories, but on certain psychodynamic qualities. Most important among these are the following:

1. Evidences of ego strength (e.g., a satisfactory level of intelligence, education, sexual adjustment, type of work, and ability to accept responsibility).
2. A history of at least one meaningful interper-

sonal relationship in the past, indicating a capacity for basic trust (which is essential for the formation of a working alliance).

3. The ability to interact with the therapist (i.e., capacity to form a positive transference).
4. The ability to think in psychological terms.
5. The ability to experience feelings (i.e., to be in touch with inner emotions).
6. A strong motivation to change (i.e., not just a desire to get rid of symptoms, but a recognition that some change in adaptive patterns may be necessary).
7. The existence of a focal conflict around which most of the patients' difficulties revolve; this can be a dependence–independence conflict, an oedipal conflict, sibling-rivalry situation, or difficulty in coping with object loss.

These selection criteria in themselves are not necessarily indicative of the severity of the patient's psychopathology. Suitable patients can be relatively "sick," covering a wide range of personality disorders and psychoneuroses, as well as transitional crises. The critical issue is not the diagnosis according to the *Diagnostic and Statistical Manual of Mental Disorders* (DSM) so much as it is having the above-mentioned attributes. Nevertheless, I do not wish to give the impression that STDP is the method of choice for most patients. There still remain large numbers of patients, particularly those with long-standing character disorders and borderline disturbances, who need to be seen over longer periods.

"CURE" IN THERAPY

This brings me to one final point, namely, the overuse of the word "cure" with regard to psychotherapeutic results. Although it is true that there are symptomatic problems such as specific phobias or compulsions that can be totally removed by appropriate techniques, the assumption that the various personality disorders from which most of our contemporary patients suffer are "cured" by psychotherapy is one of the myths that grew out of the overoptimistic claims of the early psychoanalytic pioneers. It was as if there were a finite end point after which the patient would emerge certified as free of all inner psychological difficulties. Freud recognized that this was not so in one of his final papers, the famous 1936 paper on "Analysis—Terminable and Interminable." In truth, psychotherapy does not cure in that sense, but if successful, it does open the door to emotional growth—growth that can and should continue for the rest of the patient's life. If mental health means anything, it means precisely that capacity and ability to continue to learn and grow throughout the years of one's life.

SUMMARY

To summarize briefly, the techniques of individual dynamic psychotherapy have come a long way from their original roots in classical psychoanalysis. They are based on a biopsychosocial system orientation that sees patients' problems in the context of their total system of relationships. The emphasis is not on the recovery of memories, but on using the patient–therapist relationship as a dynamic framework within which the patient can learn to achieve greater feelings of self-worth and more effective techniques of adaptation. Within this framework, the therapist is an active participant-observer, while the focus is on the here-and-now experiences and interactions of the patient. Recovery of background information is helpful for understanding and for therapeutic planning, but does not in itself produce change. Patients are interviewed sitting up, as a rule, and therapeutic frequency is usually one or two visits per week.

The trend toward shorter-term approaches, together with an emphasis on flexibly adapting the therapeutic techniques multimodally to the specific needs of each patient, points to the direction in which the dynamic therapies of the future will be moving.

Discussion by Arnold A. Lazarus, Ph.D.

Many psychotherapists and perhaps most psychoanalysts are inclined to become so attached (dare we say cathected) to their favorite theories and techniques that they display an ossified and, at times, hostile defensiveness to any criticisms or suggestions of change. It is only the truly great thinkers, in my view, who have both the cognitive capacity and the affective courage to remain flexible and open to new ideas. Dr. Marmor, according to these and other criteria, stands out as an exceptional contributor to knowledge. Of course, anyone who pays tribute to my "virtuosity" is automatically a perspicacious and enlightened commentator of unquestioned distinction!

Apart from being an esteemed member of the psychoanalytic guild, Dr. Marmor, as a former president of the American Academy of Psychoanalysis, as well as of the American Psychiatric Association and other scientific groups and societies, has made noteworthy contributions and has profoundly influenced the course of mental health training for more than half a century. When a professional such as he states that "a successful technique does not mean that the theory behind it is necessarily a correct one," I would hope that those who remain wedded to particular theories are encouraged to reexamine their ideas. Our field is replete with theories that are wilting on the vine of anachronistic thought.

The fact that many methods may prove effective for reasons other than those that their originators ever considered has given rise to what is called *technical eclecticism*. The main tenor of Dr. Marmor's presentation appears to be extremely consonant with the essence of this view, namely, that decision making in psychotherapy needs to rest on empirical proof of specific and verifiable methods for addressing specified problems, particular conditions, and measurable patient–client variables. His caveats regarding the value and limitations of insight, still regarded by some as the *sine qua non* for successful therapy, are especially important.

Let me underscore that when an esteemed psychiatrist who was thoroughly steeped in psychoanalytic thought concludes that "unfortunately, even emotional insight does not necessarily result in change," professionals had better take note. What has this forward-looking thinker advocated in addition to, or in place of, insight? He advocates undoing "the previously deeply conditioned patterns of perception and behavior" and "the reparative use of operant conditioning," as well as the use of role modeling, rehearsal, and implicit or explicit suggestion. This takes us a long way from Allen Wheelis' discourse on psychoanalysis, in which he depicts the "psychoanalyst with the sad yellow face, shoulders stooped as if by an invisible weight" as he sits behind his couch analyzing his patient four times a week for how many years, the net result often being "insight to spare, but no change."

Dr. Marmor's advocacy of a "biopsychosocial system orientation," wherein the therapist serves as an active participant-observer and devotes time to here-and-now experiences and interactions, represents a broad-spectrum view that most progressive thinkers in our field will surely want to consider. I wonder wherein Judd Marmor and I would disagree, especially since he stresses the need flexibly to adapt "the therapeutic techniques multimodally to the specific needs of each patient." Perhaps we would differ over the value of the various short-term psychodynamic therapies. As Allen Fay and I had written in the book *Brief Therapy*, edited by Jeffrey Zeig and Stephen Gilligan (Brunner/Mazel, 1990), "Our personal reaction to brief psychodynamic therapy is that it is an attempt to make an archaic model work more efficiently, rather like hitting a nail harder and more rapidly instead of putting it in the right place and using power tools."

Let me say, in conclusion, that I have

learned a good deal from Marmor's writings over the years, that he was kind enough to come to my rescue a long time ago when I was under siege from my behavioral colleagues for deviating from the fold, and that kind and supportive words from such a preeminent scientist-clinician mean more than I can possibly convey.

QUESTIONS AND ANSWERS

Question: My question is on confidentiality. In your model, when you have an individual client, there might be an occasion where you might see the wife or family separate from the client. There is controversy about how to handle confidentiality in those situations. How would you handle it?

Marmor: I have already indicated that I would not see a significant other without the consent and understanding of the client. When I see the significant other, I say in advance that what is said to me is just between us; that I want his/her help in working with my primary client. If significant others want to tell me something they don't want the client to know, that's their decision and I respect it. I do not feel it is my job to tell a patient that his or her spouse/partner is having an affair if he or she doesn't know it and the partner doesn't want him or her to know it. But it might help me understand why the partner is behaving in certain ways. It gives me the opportunity to deal with the problem between them in a more understanding and helpful way. So anyone who speaks to me without initially telling me that anything he or she says to me can be reported to someone else has the guarantee of confidentiality. However, often a significant other will say, "Anything I am saying, you can tell to my other." Of course, that is something I prefer.

Question: Do you have, then, some concern about the withholding of secrets? You gave the example of being told of an affair, but not telling your patient. Then you become the holder of that secret. Does that interfere in the therapeutic work that you do?

Marmor: No, it doesn't. I've been able to do that over the years. It has made me more empathic to the patient's problem and more realistic about what I have to deal with. If I continue to see the significant other, I try to modify the situation toward truth and honesty, but I can keep a secret and not have it influence or impair my empathy and sensitivity to my patient's problems. I think most therapists are graveyards of secrets!

Question: I may be in somewhat of an unusual position in that I am starting a residency at the Menninger Clinic and am pretty much looking forward to starting a long-term analysis. Would you speak to some of the advantages of that process? Maybe I should be warned not to start it. I don't know.

Marmor: I think it is a useful thing if you can afford the time and the money. Over the years, I have seen many trainees and their families suffer because of the hardships caused by the demands on both time and money in analytic training. But if you can afford it, I think it is a very useful experience to undergo. More than a therapeutic experience, it is an experience into your own unconscious and into understanding your own dreams and fantasies. Also, it heightens your sensitivity and ability to understand the free associations, dreams, and parapraxes of others. However, I don't think it is absolutely essential to go into it if you want to be analytically oriented. I encourage those who feel they can do it to do so.

But there is a difference in the whole training climate of our time. In 1937, when I started my analytic training, there was no other way in which one could get any kind of dynamic understanding of what went on in the unconscious of people without going to a psychoanalytic institute. Today, people who are psychoanalytically and psychodynamically trained are teachers in almost every medical school and in most psychiatric training programs, so that trainees have access to these insights. However, whether or not you undergo analytic training, I do think it is very useful to undergo some kind of therapeutic experience yourself to see what it feels like to be on the other side of the process. You can heighten your own sensitivity to what it means to be a patient, and you can work on any blind spots you may have in your work with clients.

Psychotherapy is not a simple or easy thing to do. It is often stressful. Clients often make powerful demands on us. They may attack us; they may say things they wouldn't say to anyone else because they know they can say it to us. It is part of our therapeutic responsibility to tolerate and understand such negative reactions when they occur—as well as the idealized positive reactions!

One of the things I am distressed about is the fact that some of our colleagues, in the course of their work with clients, become involved in countertransference relationships that often involve the abuse of the client, particularly sexual abuse. I find that totally unacceptable and inexcusable no matter how it is rationalized. I see that as an untreated focus in the personality of the therapist that should have been addressed and worked with before he or she was turned loose on the community.

Question: Do you think that the regression you talked about occurring in analysis can have a damaging impact on the person's ability to function as a spouse or parent? If so, how would you suggest dealing with that as the marital or family therapist?

Marmor: Perhaps I didn't make it sufficiently clear that one of the other important differences in contemporary work, as compared with the classical model, is that regression is not encouraged. It is confronted and dealt with so that it becomes part of the dynamic process with which you work.

The theory behind the promotion of regression in classical analysis is based on the assumption that, as part of recovery, it is necessary for a client to undergo a repetition of the infantile neurosis in the course of the transference relationship. That regression is fostered by the silence of the analyst, by the analyst's studied "neutrality," by the use of the couch, and by the idealization by the client of the "voice behind the couch."

In contemporary dynamic psychotherapy, one deals with regressive behavior immediately; one confronts it. If a client is acting like a child,

you interpret it and say, "Have you noticed what you are doing here and now with me?" To a client who constantly asks, "What should I do?" I say, "Look at what you want me to do. You want me to tell you what to do? What do *you* think you should do?" That kind of process discourages regression, as does the wider spacing of visits and the flexible handling of the entire client–therapist relationship.

Question: I would be interested in your comments on the use of regression with adults who were abused as children. How appropriate is short-term psychodynamic therapy for those folks?

Marmor: Well, this brings me to a topic on which I may have unpopular views. I think we have a tendency to overemphasize the issue of sexual abuse in children. It has become a very popular issue among some members of the helping profession. Mind you, I *don't* condone the sexual abuse of children in *any* way. But I think we have to be careful that we don't create a kind of hysteria around an abuse experience that may give a person an alibi for the rest of his or her adult life. People say, "I was an abused child and that is why I am disabled at the present time." I think we must work with them, psychotherapeutically and behaviorally, to try to understand what role that incident has played.

However, over the years, I have found more patients who come to me because of *deprivation* in their childhood as a result of acts of *omission* rather than acts of *commission* by their parents. A lack of sufficient love, a lack of sufficient mothering, or absences, coldness, broken homes—those are the events that create serious problems in childhood and we must not assume that everything that causes psychopathology is a specific dramatic trauma. A specific traumatic event is important only if it has been part of a total climate of unhealthy relationships. Even a child who has been sexually abused can be comforted by loving parents and helped to overcome the traumatic experience. It is more difficult if the parents react as if that child has been ruined for life and heighten the sense of impairment the child feels and then must carry through life.

Question: I was interested also in whether or not you also use hypnotic regression.

Marmor: The rationale of hypnotic regression is that psychopathology derives from a single repressed traumatic event that has been repressed in the life of the individual. If you can uncover it, presumably there will be a remarkable cure. I just don't believe that. I haven't seen it work that way. Yes, I do think that abreaction often does cause temporary improvement. Freud began his career on the assumption that what made people sick were repressed traumatic memories. After working on that premise for a long time, he found that it wasn't enough. He had to do what he called the "working through" of the defenses and of the inhibitions and repressions that surround the traumatic memories. I don't share the assumption that therapy is merely recovering a traumatic memory with a great flood of emotion. I think that is a simplistic explanation. When patients respond to that kind of treatment, I think there is a powerful element of suggestion.

With time regression, you can have a patient presumably "remember" what she did in year 1250 when she was in a convent in a medieval monastery somewhere! That doesn't make it true. It simply is an adaptive response to what she feels is expected of her.

Question: Dr. Marmor, in the late 1940s, 1950s, and 1960s, Dr. Stanislav Grof and many other psychologists were using LSD in their psychotherapy. Would you comment on the ultimate impact as you can perceive it in that phase of psychotherapy?

Marmor: One of the things about living a long time is that you see new therapies come and go and you don't get as excited about them as do people who encounter them for the first time.

I lived through a phase in the history of psychotherapy when drugs, like LSD and its equivalents, were being hailed as miracle drugs. It was all based on the abreaction theory that if

you could get people to experience some kind of deeply repressed memory or pseudomemory, it would transform their personalities. Not only were a lot of people damaged by the use of LSD during that time, but those who were helped often ended up with recurrences. Actually, LSD is toxic. I took it once under experimental controls because I thought it might duplicate schizophrenia and I wanted to see what that experience was like. What I found was that it broke up my perceptual capacities. Under its influence, I saw people's faces the way Picasso pictured them, broken up into fragments. I saw trees moving. I saw the sky taking on different colors. I had what was called a wonderful "trip," but it was a toxic trip. I recognized at the time I was experiencing it that I was responding to a toxic effect on my cerebrum and my perceptual capacities. With individuals who are fragile, that kind of thing can be terrifying, and it often was terrifying. It often resulted in recurrent breakdowns after the drug no longer was being used.

I think there is much one can say about that, but I also think we must get away from the assumption that there is a single magical way of "curing" long-standing psychiatric problems. We don't "cure" most problems. We *can* open the way to understanding, growth, and maturation. We do that with certain techniques—behavioral, cognitive, or psychodynamic. But let us not be discouraged about this lack of "cure." In the field of medicine, doctors don't cure most of the patients they see. They are able to help a sore throat or an infection with antibiotics, but they can't replace—at least not yet—a rheumatic heart that was damaged early in life or joints that become severely disabled by arthritis. But they *can* help people feel better and deal with their disabilities better. That is what most medical practice is all about. We, too, have an equivalent responsibility to help our patients live better, more meaningfully, more adaptively, and more creatively. If we are able to open the door to such growth, we have served a useful purpose!

SECTION V

Mind–Body Approaches

Bioenergetic Analysis: A Mind–Body Therapy

Alexander Lowen, M.D.

Alexander Lowen, M.D.

Alexander Lowen, M.D., received his medical degree from the University of Geneva in 1951. He has published 12 books on his bioenergetic approach.

Lowen posits that engaging the body in the analytic and treatment process deepens a patient's self-understanding and provides powerful leverage to promote change. The body in its form and motility expresses the individual's personality as much as behavior and thinking do. If there is to be a change in personality, the body must reflect that change. To change bodily attitude, one should work directly with the energy dynamics of the body. By mobilizing a person's energy, one opens up deep feelings that are otherwise inaccessible. The history and background of Lowen's body-oriented therapy are examined; case histories demonstrate the value of his approach.

Lowen contrasts "understanding" with "knowledge." The former is a function of both mind and body, whereas the latter is merely intellectual. The goals of therapy are enlarged to include body values—namely, increased vitality, greater self-possession, and gracefulness.

I always have believed that the healing power of psychotherapy stems from the client's self-understanding, which is promoted by the therapeutic process. This view of psychotherapy is an outgrowth of psychoanalysis, which is similarly oriented. If my belief is valid, then the failure of psychotherapy or psychoanalysis to effect significant positive changes in a patient's emotional health is due to a lack of sufficient self-understanding by the patient. One reason for this lack is that a major aspect of the personality is usually not involved in the analytic or therapeutic process. That aspect is the body and its physical processes of breathing, movement, feeling, and the expression of emotion. When the analytic process focuses solely on mental events, thoughts, images, and

dreams, the insights that the analysand gains are relatively superficial.

ILLUSTRATIVE CASES

The advantage of engaging the body in the analytic process can be seen in Case 1.

CASE 1

A middle-aged man consulted me because he was suffering from a moderate elevation in his blood pressure that he thought could be related to some emotional problem. Apart from this complaint, he described himself as a happy man. One could believe it was true, as he smiled warmly whenever he looked at one. When I pointed this out to him, he said that it was an expression of his friendliness. He was just an agreeable person. I countered that he had no need to be agreeable or friendly with me. Could he look at me without smiling? Strangely, he could not. When our eyes met, the smile appeared. He had no control over it. He insisted, however, that the smile was genuine.

In bioenergetic analysis, this kind of smile is regarded as a mask. It is seen as covering up a deep sadness. One can remove the mask by preventing the smile. This is done by pressing lightly with two fingers on the risorius muscles alongside the bridge of the nose, which blocks the upward movement of the face. When I did this with my patient, I saw a very sad expression appear, which he, also, could see in the mirror. He still denied he was sad. However, when doing some breathing exercises, he spontaneously began to cry. In the course of two sessions, as I probed his background, he related that he had to be the emotional support of his mother and his family. If he broke down, he said, they would all drown in their sorrow. Keeping up a positive front was a hallmark of his family.

This patient kept himself "up" all the time, regardless of the situation. It was not just a mental attitude that he could change at will. The attitude was structured in his body. His chest was held in an overinflated position. His shoulders were elevated. His legs were tight and rigid to hold him up under any and all conditions. He could not let down. It was no surprise that his blood pressure also was up. In addition, he suffered from lower back pain. It is not difficult to drop the diastolic pressure with some simple bioenergetic exercises that induce a downward flow of excitation in the body.

But reducing the systolic pressure and maintaining a normal reading require a characterological change on a deep level that is dependent on a change in the energy dynamics of the body (Lowen, 1972).

THE ROOTS OF BIOENERGETICS

Disappointed with the results of psychoanalysis, two of Freud's students and colleagues adopted a more active role in the therapeutic process. Sandor Ferenczi (1953) used certain procedures involving the body in a process he called "analysis from below to mobilize the patient's response." Wilhelm Reich (1945) confronted his patients' behavior by imitating their bodily attitude and actions. In one case, that of a masochistic patient, Reich lay on the floor whining and complaining about the analysis, exaggerating the patient's behavior to make him see and understand the meaning of his actions. In another case, he pointed out to a patient how his overly polite behavior was a resistance to and defense against the analysis. This observation of a patient's physical attitude and behavior was a major advance in analytic practice. Reich published his ideas in *Character Analysis* (1945), which was, and still is, regarded as one of the most important contributions to analytic theory and practice.

Character analysis was also a breakthrough, however, in the understanding of "mental" or emotional problems through its recognition that these problems are correlated with certain bodily attitudes. Reich saw the relation between body and mind as a dialectic. On a superficial level, they are antithetical, each acting upon and influencing the other, but on a deeper level they are a unity. The person is one although he or she has two aspects or modes of expression—physical and mental—in actions or in words that would correspond to feelings and thoughts. This means that personality is reflected in the body as it is in the mind, in one's way of holding and moving as in one's thoughts and images. The functional identity of psychic and somatic processes is the basic premise of bioenergetic analysis. It enables a therapist to make a diagnosis of an individual's emotional problems by reading the body's expression. Just as one's character is shaped by one's life experience, so is one's body. In fact, every experience a person lives through is registered and, therefore, structured in the body, as well as in the mind, thus providing, I believe, the basis of memory. This principle underlies the ability of a forester to read the history of a tree from a study of its rings of growth. However, since a person is infinitely more complicated than a tree, only major experiences can be determined from the body's expression.

CORRELATING BODY SIGNS WITH PSYCHIC MANIFESTATIONS

The literature of bioenergetic analysis is replete with examples of the functional identity of one's physical expression in the form and motility of one's body with one's behavior and thinking. But looking at people to gain some understanding of who they are is not really unique to this therapy. All therapists pay some attention to the expression of the face, the look of the eyes, the set of the jaw, the posture, the quality of movement, and the tone of voice in their encounters with their clients. In bioenergetic analysis, this observation is raised to the level of an art through training and experience. Thus one can see that an individual is depressed, sad, frightened, or angry even when the person makes an effort to mask his or her feelings, as in the above case.

When a person is sad, the lines of the face are turned downward. If the person attempts to mask this expression by a fixed smile, one notices that the smile does not brighten the eyes, which have a sad look. In a depressed individual, all vital functions are reduced. Breathing is subdued, movements are diminished, the voice is lifeless. One can sense a person's fear by the way he or she holds himself or herself. The most common expression of fear is wide eyes and raised shoulders. In the startle or fright reaction, the breath is sucked in, the shoulders are elevated, and the eyes are opened wide.

ANGER

The most evident manifestation of suppressed anger is in the chronic tension of the muscles of the upper back. Since anger is most commonly expressed with blows, the muscles that carry out that action have to be contracted to block that impulse because its expression might invoke severe retaliation. The muscles involved would be the ones that attach the scapula to the spine and the shoulders to the scapula. The chronic tension that results curves the upper back. That curvature of the back is seen in dogs and cats as they prepare to attack or defend. We say of such persons that they "have their backs up," as if they, too, are ready to

attack or defend themselves. My back had such a configuration and I knew that I was an angry person. I was angry about the way people behaved: their selfishness, greed, and vulgarity and their insensitivity to the environment. Of course, this was not the real cause of my chronic anger. That stemmed from my childhood, but it was rationalized in these terms. Over the years, I worked to release the tension in my upper back with bioenergetic exercises, such as stretching and hitting a bed with my fists to get the anger out. One day, while having a massage, I told the masseur that I had marked tension in the muscles of my upper back related to my anger. Then, spontaneously, I said, "I don't have to be angry anymore." As I said this, I felt my back drop as if a burden had been lifted off. And I felt straighter. To judge from the tension in their upper backs, most people are angry, but few are aware of their anger, which sits like a monkey on their shoulders and back.

SCHIZOID BEHAVIOR

Not all persons who have suppressed anger manifest the body attitude described above. If the suppression occurred before the anger was fully conscious, in the first two years of life, the impulse did not activate the muscles that would carry through the action of hitting. The suppression takes place on a deeper level in the body. The whole body becomes rigid as an expression of the underlying terror of being killed or the fear of killing. The person is literally scared stiff. The stiffness does not persist because then it would be totally paralyzing, as in catatonia. It breaks down at the joints, leaving the body in a fragmented state that is typical of the schizoid or schizophrenic personality. The fragmentation splits the unity of the personality so that the limbs are not experienced as extensions of the trunk, but as separate appendages, and the head is not experienced as connected to the rest of the body.

Boadella (1990) describes the schizoid problem as follows: "In the schizoid person there is a specific disturbance in the neck area which involves tension in the deep muscles at the base of the skull. My patient felt this tension in the form of a noose drawn around his neck and pulled tight with the threat that he would have his head cut off from his body if he did not do what was expected of him. When his head felt all right, his body was wrong. When his body felt all right, his head felt wrong. His head was literally cut off, that is, dissociated from the body by the tensions" (p. 46). The effect is to split thinking from feeling, mind from body. By dissociating from the body, the schizoid person denies and suppresses the murderous rage that stems naturally from the experience of being terrorized.

There are specific body signs that characterize the schizoid personality and allow the diagnosis to be made from the body's expression. The head is not lined up with the neck and the trunk, but is carried slightly to one side. Similarly, the pelvis is askew. This is observable when the patient is put in the bow position, which places a small stress on the body and accentuates its disjointedness. The eyes do not focus on the person to whom the schizoid person is speaking or at whom the person is looking, with the result that there is little, if any, eye contact. Contact or connectedness is an issue for this personality. It was largely missing in the person's childhood relationship with his or her parents. The child did not have the feeling that he or she was seen or understood by the parents. Sensing their coldness and hostility, the child withdrew from any contact and retired into his or her head, living in fantasy.

Bioenergetic analysis, by its focus on the body, counteracts the tendency to dissociate from the body. The patient is seen as a physical being and his or her problems are immediately understood. The patient is allowed to reach out and make some physical contact with the therapist and is encouraged to express feelings verbally and physically. Thus the patient may be advised to twist a towel when sensing an impulse to strangle someone, to kick the bed to make a protest, or to hit out in anger by pounding a bed. These physical exercises are necessary if the patient is to feel his or her body, sense suppressed impulses, and release the severe muscular tensions that split the patient's body and personality.

These expressive actions should not be carried out, however, unless the therapist has personal experience with them and has been trained in their use. The patient must feel secure that the therapist knows what he or she is doing and can handle the destructive feelings that will arise. It has been my experience that most patients harbor a murderous rage that terrifies them and needs to be released through appropriate expression. I have worked with patients in this way in my office and in workshops for more than 40 years, and it has happened only once or twice that a patient has had to be temporarily restrained as a result of being out of control. Further, my office has many objects that easily could be broken, but there never has been any damage.

SADNESS

Just as we suppress our fear because it is paralyzing and our anger because it is destructive, so we suppress our sadness because it verges on despair. We do this by putting up a front, or facade, to hide our pain and sadness from the world, as well as from ourselves. We are taught very early that if we laugh, the world laughs with us, but if we cry, we cry alone. People come to therapy because they are hurting, yet it is often difficult to get them to release this pain and sadness through deep crying. Many will say that they have no difficulty crying, but all they can do is shed a few tears when touched by a sad story. Their own story, which is equally sad, evokes no more than the same few tears. The deep sadness is suppressed by chronic tensions in the throat and in the lower abdomen or belly. Deep crying is crying from one's gut. It corresponds to a deep belly laugh and has the same value in releasing tension. The individual who is incapable of belly crying is equally incapable of belly laughter—and is also incapable of feeling the sweet, melting sensation of sexual love, which also occurs in the belly and pelvis.

BIOENERGETIC METHODS

The overall effect of chronic muscular tensions is to deaden the body by decreasing its energetic level. Energy is produced through the metabolism of food, which requires an adequate supply of oxygen. Chronic tension restricts respiration, thereby decreasing oxygen intake and metabolic activity, which has the effect of reducing energy, movement, and feeling. Emotions are physical movements in the body that become our feelings as they are perceived. A reduction in energy, movement, and feeling is at the base of all depressive tendencies. If we are to help our patients feel and express more feeling, we need to help them breathe more fully and more deeply. Bioenergetic analysis has a number of techniques to bring this about, but these are effective only when used within the framework of the understanding of a patient's inner conflicts as they are expressed in bodily attitudes.

Using these techniques and others to effectuate the release of chronic muscular tensions does not mean that the verbal analysis is neglected or that transference issues are not fully explored and discussed. While we work with the body, we do not neglect the mind. There are many sessions in which physical activity is suspended while significant issues that come up in the patient's life are discussed. However, the body work is never neglected. Patients are encouraged to attend bioenergetic exercise classes and to do exercises at home. For personality change to be meaningful, it must be reflected in a corresponding change in the body. Following is an example.

CASE 2: A COLLEAGUE'S DEPRESSION

Some years ago I was consulted by a psychologist who was suffering from depression. He told me an interesting story about an experience he had had at Esalen in a workshop with Fritz Perls, the founder of Gestalt therapy. He had volunteered to work with Perls before the group on a recent dream. In the dream, he saw himself in a prison cell. At the time of the Esalen workshop, he was depressed.

Perls had him act out all the characters in the dream—himself as the prisoner, the jailer, and the bars of the cell that enclosed him. Acting each part in turn, in the Gestalt technique, he experienced intense feelings of sadness, which resulted in deep crying. The jailer was his super-ego and the cell bars were his inhibitions. Finally, the bars informed him that he was free,

that he did not have to constrain himself. He said that after this session he had a great feeling of joy that lasted for more than a month. Back at work in New York, he became depressed again.

As noted above, the bioenergetic approach sees depression as a loss of energy that underlies the loss of motivation. The loss of energy is due to a depressed respiratory function that significantly reduces the amount of oxygen to the body, accounting for the lack of vitality and inhibited expressiveness that characterize this condition.

There are also psychological aspects to the depressive reaction. The main one is the collapse of an illusion that had previously sustained the individual. In most cases, the illusion is that if one is good, or successful, or rich, one will be loved. These illusions are common in our culture and account for the endemic nature of depression in Western society. I did not point out to the patient the illusory aspect of his experience at Esalen, which consisted of the belief that giving himself permission to be free would change the dynamics of his personality. I looked at his body and his breathing as he lay over the bioenergetic stool. His breathing was shallow, his chest was inflated and showed little movement with respiration.

I offered the patient another interpretation of his dream. He was in a prison because his heart was locked up in a cage and he was unable to feel or express any love. I was referring to his rib cage, which was so rigid that it did not allow any feeling to come out. The feeling that was suppressed by the armoring of the chest was the pain of the loss of love in childhood, which is called heartbreak. That feeling is released by deep crying (that is, sobbing), which he had done at Esalen and which had temporarily set him free. However, since he had not dealt with those early experiences that had shaped his body and his personality, he was not free of his past. He needed to mourn the loss of love and to experience his grief, which could not be done in one session after so many years of holding in his desire for love and denying his pain. For there to be a sustained change in feeling and attitude, his chest had to become soft, his throat had to become open, and he had to regain the ability to reach out freely. That might take considerable work, but the change would be permanent because it would be structured in the body.

CASE 3: PERSONAL THERAPY WITH REICH

I had a somewhat similar experience in my therapy with Wilhelm Reich, which lasted three years. Very early in my therapy, I became aware of a tendency to hold back the expression of feeling and to hold my breath. Reich's therapy with me was based on the surrender to the body manifested in the ability to allow one's breathing to become free and deep. Reich had found that if one can let this happen, one cannot hold back feelings. They will arise spontaneously in the body and be expressed. In effect, one is surrendering ego control of the body in a setting that is safe and supportive.

I had some unusual experiences in the course of this therapy. On one occasion, I was lying on a bed, allowing my breathing to become free and deep, when suddenly my body began to bend forward and I found myself sitting up and then getting off the bed. Once off the bed, I turned around and began to beat the bed with my fists. As I did this, I saw the face of my father on the bed and I knew that I was beating him because he had given me a spanking. I had never remembered the spanking before. The amazing thing about this incident was the sense that I (my ego) was not directing my actions. I felt that some force inside me was moving me, doing it. When I spoke to my father later about the incident, he acknowledged that he had spanked me because I had come home late and my mother had been worried and upset.

During the course of the therapy, transference issues came up that Reich dealt with to the degree that I could openly express my need for his help and cry. The latter was not easy for me since I felt that I had to be independent and not needy. Apart from this, Reich did little analysis of my character or my history. Nevertheless, the therapy helped me make some important moves in my life and allowed me to surrender more fully to my body and my feelings. It was clear to me that my previous inability to do this was neurotic.

Full surrender was manifested by the development of a body movement that Reich called the orgasm reflex. When one's breathing is spontaneously deep and full, one's pelvis moves forward and back involuntarily in harmony with the respiratory waves—backward on inspiration, forward on expiration. This is called the orgasm reflex because the same movements occur in the course of sexual intercourse when one surrenders to the orgasm. In the act of intercourse, the movement is overpowering and ecstatic because of the strong sexual charge. When the movement happens during the therapy session, it is extremely pleasurable and releasing. Reich regarded this involuntary response as a sign that the therapy has reached a successful conclusion. It was his belief that the ability to surrender to the body, manifested in the therapy sessions by the orgasm reflex, would carry over into life so that the person would experience full orgastic satisfaction in sexual relations. I was, therefore, discharged from therapy as a healthy person. Unfortunately, this full satisfaction did not not occur. However, despite this failure, I felt that I had made significant progress in my therapy.

DEVELOPING BIOENERGETICS

In the next two years (from 1945 to 1947), I was a Reichian therapist, since I was one of the very few who had any firsthand experience of his therapy, which he called character analytic vegetotherapy. At the time that I was finishing my therapy with Reich, he was using his hands to release some of his patients' severe muscular tensions. In these two years, he obtained some remarkable results. He was able to have some patients give in to their bodies to the point where their breathing was fully free, with the development of the orgasm reflex as a sign of their surrender. But it did not hold up. Several of his patients consulted me after they had finished their therapy with Reich because they had lost this capacity and were back to where they were when they entered into therapy with him. Having been Reich's patient myself, I could understand what happened. His understanding of the human condition and of his patient's problems was deep and solid, which gave his patients a great sense of security. This, plus the charisma of his personality supporting the surrender to the bodily self, allowed them to give up their neurotic behavior. Unfortunately, they could not do it for themselves since his therapy had not worked through their problems.

I gave up my practice and went to the University of Geneva to study medicine. Following the completion of my medical studies and after I had obtained my license to practice medicine in 1953, I resumed work as a Reichian therapist. At this time, the process was called orgone therapy, denoting that its aim was to mobilize and free up a patient's energy, which Reich called "orgone." Breathing was still the main focus of this endeavor. While I agreed in principle with this approach, I saw that a lasting change could be realized only if the patient was fully in touch with himself or herself and had worked through major problems, *both* analytically and physically.

I was aware that this was not true of me. I still felt somewhat insecure despite an appearance of confidence, and I was more frightened and less courageous than I would have liked to have been. My orgastic potency (the ability to surrender fully to the sexual excitement in the climax) needed improvement. I did not believe that Reichian therapy as it was then practiced could address these issues successfully. Both personal and professional considerations led me to the conviction that I had to develop a new therapy, but one based, however, on such Reichian concepts as character analysis and the functional identity and antithesis of psychic and somatic functions. The new therapy would be much more active on the body level and more analytic psychologically. That therapy became bioenergetic analysis, so named to emphasize its focus on energetic processes such as breathing, integrated with the analysis of the patient's background as expressed in behavior, dreams, and transference phenomena.

I developed the principles and techniques of bioenergetic analysis by working on my problems with the assistance of an associate, John C. Pierrakos, who was 10 years my junior. I felt I needed some help, that I could not do it all by myself. I am deeply grateful to Dr. Pierrakos for the help he gave me, which extended over two years.

DEVELOPING SECURITY

How to become more secure? I had a bodily sense that the feeling of security was related to the legs and that courage was a gut phenomenon. Our language supports this view of courage. We say that a person with courage has guts. Since everyone has guts, it must mean that courage is connected to the feeling of the guts. The degree of courage varies with the amount of feeling, but some people do not feel their guts at all. They sense an emptiness in the lower abdomen.

The feeling of security stems from sensing the ground under one's feet. It is always there, but one can feel the ground only if there is an energetic charge in the legs. If our legs are like mechanical supports and means of locomotion, we do not sense the ground. This disturbance reflects the fact that the original ground of one's being, namely, one's mother, was not sufficiently "there" in a supporting role to give the child a feeling of security. Children in this situation have to hold themselves up (support themselves) by an effort of will that is reflected in the tension and rigidity of their legs.

My legs were tight and rigid because I have had to hold myself up, not trusting that anyone would be there for me if I fell. I was also aware that I had a fear of abandonment. Studying a person's legs and feet tells a lot about the person's early relationship to the mothering figure. Observing how an individual stands can inform about the person's role in life. The soldier has a special way of standing that differs greatly from the stance of a servant. However, this goes beyond the legs to the question of posture and carriage, which involves the whole body. Still, the base of one's postural attitude is the legs and feet.

How does one gain more courage or develop more security? Some help can be obtained through a verbal approach that helps a patient to understand the origin of any fears and insecurities. But I have never believed that talking alone can produce a significant characterological change. It did not do it for me. On the other hand, working directly with my body to get more feeling into my belly and an energetic charge into my legs has produced such a change in my personality.

THE GOALS OF BODY WORK

The aim of the exercises and other body work is to release the chronic muscular tension that binds the individual, reducing the person's energy and restricting his or her life. These muscular tensions stem from the suppression of impulses and feelings that could not be expressed. Each and every chronic tension represents a conflict between an impulse and its inhibition. One can describe the conflict as between the id and the superego. While some relief can be obtained from massage and relaxation techniques, that relief is only temporary. Lasting relief comes from resolving the conflict, which can be done only by understanding the conflict and expressing the impulse.

A good example is chronic jaw tension, which, when severe, creates the condition known as temperomandibular joint disease. This tension develops out of the suppression of such impulses as biting, crying, and defiance. The tense jaw says, in effect, "I will not give in to these impulses." Biting could lead to punishment, crying to humiliation, and defiance to rejection. Setting the jaw is an expression of determination, as we all know. But once the jaw is locked into that position, the attitude of determination becomes structured into the personality as second nature and cannot be released consciously. The attempt to do so results in the impossible position: "I am determined not to be determined." But such tension can be released by encouraging the patient to express the impulses by crying, biting a towel, or thrusting the jaw and saying, "I won't." Of course, the patient needs to understand the origin of the tension and of the role its persistence plays in present-day behavior.

Knowing is only part of understanding. We know with our heads, but we understand with our whole being. All therapists have patients who know what their problems are, even why they have these problems, but cannot change their behavior significantly because their understanding is inadequate. They lack the necessary feelings that would transform knowing into understanding.

CASE 4: THE ABUSED PATIENT

I had a patient who had been sexually abused by her father when she was very young. She realized that she was attracted to men who abused her. However, knowing this did not help because her attraction to these men made her vulnerable to their abuse. What she did not understand was that she was insecure as a person, dependent upon men, and unable to be adequately angry at the abuse. She lacked feelings in her legs that would give her the support and independence to be a woman. She was confused by her belief that her ability to earn money indicated that she was an independent adult. She lacked sufficient sexual charge in her pelvis to feel like a woman. On that level, she was still a child. Because of the abuse, she had withdrawn and dissociated from her sexuality. She could feel like a woman only through contact with a man's sexuality. Any intense feeling terrified her. After a mild expression of anger, she would curl up and whimper in fear. She was afraid of being overwhelmed by her anger or sexuality and feeling crazy. When a strong feeling arose in her, she lost the feeling of her body and depersonalized.

As she worked with her body over months, breathing, kicking, hitting, crying, screaming, and grounding, she was able to understand herself and her problems. She became very excited the day that she remarked, "I feel my legs." She even got to the point where she could scream without "going off." She lost much of her fear of going crazy when she could express her murderous rage at her father. As her feelings increased and the tension in her body diminished, she began to feel herself as a person and her sexual dependence on men dropped away.

These changes took considerable time and developed slowly because her body had to become used to the increased charge. It had to expand to tolerate the heightened excitement. She regularly attended a bioenergetic exercise class and did some exercises at home to promote this development. At the beginning, she could not finish the class. It was too much for her. She would curl up in a corner to hold onto herself and not be overwhelmed by her body's sensations. The most frightening sensation was the feeling in her pelvis of the sexual violation.

It was not a short-term therapy, but her improvement was steady, significant and solid.

All of this occurred in the context of an analysis and discussion of her history, her feelings, and her behavior. The talking went on together with the physical work, as much of it involved helping her understand her bodily reactions.

THE BIOENERGETIC PERSPECTIVE

Without words, feelings do not constitute understanding. A body without a head is as helpless to change as is a head without a body. We need both, and we need them to be integrated so that what one knows is connected to feelings and what one feels is connected to knowledge. In my work as a bioenergetic therapist, words are as important as the physical exercises I use. Often, there are many sessions in which there is no activity other than a discussion of the patient's present behavior and past history. Transference issues can be resolved only if they are discussed, but I do not believe they are ever fully resolved unless the patient understands their derivation from the physical dynamics of the body. An individual who does not feel his or her legs and feet firmly connected to the ground will necessarily transfer his or her dependent needs to the therapist and, at the same time, resent that dependency. Patients who are passive project their suppressed aggression onto the therapist.

Unfortunately, a patient often will discover some aspect of the personality of the therapist that will justify in his or her mind the feelings being projected. Therapists are not perfect, and few have worked through their own problems fully. I have seen too many therapies founder because transference and countertransference issues resulted in an irresolvable conflict between therapist and patient. In other cases, the therapy was unproductive because these issues were not faced honestly. Those problems can be avoided to some degree if it is recognized by both therapist and patient that they are structured in the body.

I always have believed that understanding is the key to health. Every patient's problem is directly connected to the fact that the patient was not understood by his or her parents. In terms of ego psychology, the patient was not "seen." The parents did not understand their child because they did not understand themselves. They were out of touch with many of their feelings and with a large part of their bodies. Since understanding is largely a process of feeling, one cannot feel for or understand another unless one feels one's self. We describe this process as empathy. Our bodies resonate with other bodies. But if our bodies are rigid, tight, frozen, or dead, our ability to resonate is severely limited or almost nonexistent. We do not see the other person, but only the image we want to have.

This is also true of the therapeutic situation. Therapists cannot have more feeling for patients or clients than they have in their own bodies. What we take for feeling is often pure sentimentality. How can we help a patient become graceful in his or her body if we do not feel the gracefulness of our own bodies? Can we even see the patient's lack of grace if we do not see our own?

I have a deep faith in the ability of the body to heal itself. If one has a cut, the body will heal the cut without any intervention from the mind. We get over our colds, our infections, our sprains without any conscious effort. And since every emotional problem is also a body problem, the same healing power should be operative here, too. Yet it does not happen because human beings do something to block the healing force. We do not trust the body because its impulses and feelings have gotten us into trouble as children. We do not trust the body because it is vulnerable, it is mortal, it is limited. We have been taught to trust our minds, which we can experience as powerful, immortal, and infinite.

In our minds, we can reach the stars, but in our bodies, we are extremely limited. We fight the surrender to our body with its feelings of sadness, fear, anger, and pain. How much easier it is to live in our minds! But who would call a life without feeling meaningful? Who would even call it living? Divorced from the body, there is no true life. Apart from pain, there can be no pleasure. Without sorrow, there is no joy. Without anger, there is no love, as true anger is a sign that one cares. In contrast with machines, humans are sentient beings whose lives revolve around feelings. The more feelings we can experience, the more alive we are. In death, there are no feelings and no movement.

tiful and graceful. It is manifested in a body that is vibrantly alive, eyes that are clear and bright, a manner that is gentle and gracious, and a love of one's self, of others, and of God's universe.

SUMMARY

The goal of therapy is to help a patient to be more alive, to feel more, to express more, and to have more of a self. Therapy aims first at self-awareness: to be in touch with ourselves not just psychologically, but with the whole body, from head to toe. That means, also, to be in touch with all one's feelings. The second aim is self-expression, which is the ability to express all one's feelings in words and/or action. The third aim, which includes the first two, is called self-possession. Self-possession means that one is in conscious control of one's behavior so that one's self-expression is appropriate and effective, promoting one's good feelings and joy in life. Being a body person, I see the goals of therapy in bodily terms, namely, a body that is beau-

REFERENCES

Boadella, D. (1990). The divided body. *Bioenergetic Analysis, 4*(1), 46.

Ferenczi, S. (1953). *The further development of an active therapy in psychoanalysis, the theory and techniques of psychoanalysis II*. New York: Basic Books.

Lowen, A. (1969). *The betrayal of the body*. New York: Macmillan.

Lowen, A. (1971). *The language of the body*. New York: Macmillan.

Lowen, A. (1972). *Depression and the body*. U.S.A.: Coward, McCann & Geoghegan. (Also published by Pelican Books, New York, in 1973).

Lowen, A. (1977). *The way to vibrant health*. New York: Harper & Row.

Lowen, A. (1988). *Love, sex and your heart*. New York: Macmillan.

Reich, W. (1945). *Character analysis*. New York: Orgone Institute Press. (This book is a translation of the German edition, which was published in 1993.)

Discussion by Miriam Polster, Ph.D.

◆

Much of our experience occurs when we are caught up in active response to the demands, surprises, disappointments, and pleasures of daily life. In this hustle and bustle, much of this experience is never translated into words. It is quickly deposited in our muscles, bones, and sinews; it echoes in our breathing, armors us in posture, and choreographs our gestures—all without ever reaching the level of articulation. Alexander Lowen deals with these deposits of human experience like an archaeologist of the individual.

However, there is much more to Lowen's skill than simple unearthing. He combines his search for the buried trauma with the knowledge of where to look—and how. From surface indications—a habitual smile, a skewed pelvis,

inhibited breathing—he draws his sense of where to search for the psychological bruises that underlie these behaviors. His technique is not simply to dig for them, however, but to endow them with the energy (long suppressed) to reveal and release themselves.

Lowen observes that "since a person is infinitely more complicated than a tree, only major experiences can be determined from the body's expression." The analogy is apt. Just as a tree registers its experience without words, there are two major influences that deprive the person of words to describe the source of conflict. Early on, of course, personal experience is registered preverbally because the infant has not yet acquired language. Later, when the child may have learned that open expression can result in pain or punishment, words may either be spoken silently to oneself or, in more dire circumstances, even be blotted out entirely.

Once the unmistakable experience of excitement and sensation has been brought into the open, Lowen points out, it is important to support it by a solid basis of "analysis and discussion." Lowen views talking as an essential step in understanding because it restores the severed connection between feeling and knowledge. Talking makes what was a private store of conflict into a shared human experience—and change thereby seems possible and desirable. Furthermore, adding the dimension of language makes experience recoverable. The individual, through adding words that make sense (an interesting way to put it) out of his or her physical experience, may not have to work laboriously through every step of the process every time.

Those of us who work primarily with words recognize that psychological conflict sometimes resembles a game of hide-and-seek. Hoping to be discovered, our patients nevertheless physically both conceal and reveal the struggles that have led them to our door. The figures of speech that patients use to describe their dilemma are metaphoric illuminations that often direct us to the physical expressions of psychological conflict.

I remember how often a patient's figure of speech incarnated a crucial struggle. One young woman, a dutiful daughter and subsequently a submissive wife, described herself as "not having a leg to stand on." She was a slender woman with short, stubby legs that she hated. Usually, whenever she sat down, her legs would not reach the floor. Another woman, who described herself as an "army brat," came in one morning complaining of a stiff neck. We experimented with her swiveling her head around and, as she did so, she asked me an idle question about my office. Amazed, she connected her simply curiosity when she let her head and eyes wander with the family admonition that she was just supposed to "take orders and not ask questions." Stiffening her neck obeyed that edict.

Lowen outlines a three-part goal of therapy: self-awareness, self-expression, and self-possession. It is clear that this triumvirate rests

confidently on its own two legs—the body and the mind.

QUESTIONS AND ANSWERS

Question: What is the role of body work in terms of your work? Do you do any hands-on therapy? I'm a practitioner of Tragor work and am now in analytic training at the Menninger Clinic, and I hope to combine those two schools of thought at some point. At Menninger's and in psychodynamic work, however, there's absolutely no touching of patients; that's firmly prohibited. Would you talk a little about that subject?

Lowen: To touch is to be in contact. And one of the main aspects of being alive is to be in contact. If you're afraid to touch a patient, then the patient is going to feel that there's something personally wrong, "I'm one of the untouchables. Maybe I give off a bad aroma or something." You can say, "Oh, we are not allowed to touch." But the patient wants to be touched. If they were touched enough as children, they wouldn't be patients. So touching is very important.

How you touch is the question. You have to make sure that when you touch patients, you don't violate boundaries. You don't just touch them. You have to sense that they are open to touch, that it's appropriate for the situation. And, it must be nonsexual. I think that Freud was frightened that people would misunderstand his whole work with sexuality, and the idea of no physical contact was so that nothing sexual would happen in a session.

When a man and a woman are in a room together, however, it's sexual. I don't care whether or not they touch. If you're not aware that it's sexual, then you're not aware that you're a man or that the other person is a woman. But being aware doesn't mean you act anything out.

Danger exists only when you cannot handle the feeling in the situation. There's no danger if you can handle it. And if you can't handle your touching a patient, you should go back into therapy yourself.

Question: Dr. Reich died, as I understand it, in a mental hospital.

Lowen: No, he died in a jail.

Question: Could you comment on his mental health and his later years?

Lowen: Well, he did suffer some emotional problems. We all do, though. And I am always sympathetic toward—not critical of—people who have emotional problems. I think that near the end of his life, Reich became somewhat psychotic. He always had a little paranoid tendency. He suffered very much as a young man. His own story is quite sad. On the other hand, he was a genius. And there's a belief that there's a little insanity in all geniuses. The way I look at it is that Reich certainly had emotional problems. He was an outsider. He felt himself to be an outsider. It's only the outsider who can criticize what's going on in the inside. The insider is too much a part of it. So the fact that he had emotional problems doesn't invalidate the greatness of his understanding.

Reich wasn't an easy person to get along with. He had his positive side and his negative side. Anyway, I am deeply grateful to Reich for what he gave me, and it's unfortunate that his life ended the way it did. I think he *was* persecuted. But it takes two to tango; there was something in his personality that allowed it to happen.

I have never felt persecuted because I speak openly about sexuality or recommend an active approach to a person, touching people somewhat undressed as they work with me. I think that if you can work through your own problems, you are much freer, and it's so much better for you. But that's the story about Reich, as far as I can tell you.

Question: Have you worked with psychotic patients at all? Has this experience been any different from your experience working with other, more normal people?

Lowen: I have worked with some psychotic patients, but I have never worked in a mental hospital as a resident. In answer to your question, what you do with a patient is in response to where the patient is at and what his or her needs are. If a man comes in who is narcissistic, a tough guy, and he has not much feeling, you take one approach. A schizophrenic comes in who is a little confused, and you take quite another approach. Your theory is one thing, but your practice is individualized.

I had a patient who was psychotic at times. This patient had been hospitalized for three years. She worked with one of my colleagues, and he couldn't help her much, so he asked her to see me. One day, her husband brought her to my office. She was out of contact. She was screaming. You couldn't talk to her. I held her in an embrace with my arms locked around her while she screamed; we rolled on the floor for 15 or 20 minutes. At the end of that time, she was quiet, and back to herself; she left, and everything was okay. Now that's done by others, too—holding a patient who is terrified and screaming. It is known to have a positive effect. But I don't do that with every patient who walks in screaming.

Question: It sounds as though both Dr. Lowen and Dr. Polster work on the mind–body connection, but from different directions. The question I have is about techniques like rebirthing and rolfing. How do you see them as fitting in with the type of work that you do, Dr. Lowen? Also, I would appreciate Dr. Polster's response.

Lowen: I find that all these body techniques have something to offer. I don't like to criticize them. I think that they differ from bioenergetic analysis in that I start the body work only after I have understood the person. After I look at people and at their bodies, I understand their problems. I talk to them before I touch them. I don't do body work before I've established some kind of a basic relationship.

M. Polster: I think we have to acknowledge that people who are determined to make sense out of experience can make sense out of almost any experience that they have. Rebirthing and rolfing, to the degree that the individual chooses to make meaning out of the experience for himself or herself, can be very valuable. I agree with Dr. Lowen. One of my rules of psychotherapy that might deal with bodily contact comes from that famous psychologist Lewis Carroll, who wrote *Through the Looking Glass.* If you remember, Alice goes over the chessboard and finally gets to the end and is made a queen, and they have a banquet in her honor. They introduce every course to her, and she is very hungry. They finally introduce the leg of mutton, or something, and she is ready to carve it. Then the Red Queen says to her, "You don't eat somebody you've just been introduced to."

Lowen: Let me say a word about the healing process as I see it. I am writing a book called *The Healing Spirit.* One of the basic principles that I work with is that the body heals itself. If you cut your finger, it heals. If you break a bone, it heals. We can facilitate the healing, but the body does the healing. Why doesn't the body heal itself from neurotic behavior? It's a physical disturbance just as much as any injury or sickness. The answer, in my understanding, is that we don't allow the body to heal. We do something to block the flow of feeling in our body, which is the healing spirit—the flow of the spirit. Therapy aims, in my opinion, not to change you, but to stop you from doing the things you do that are self-destructive. I believe that is a good way to put it.

The Wave Nature of Consciousness: A New Direction for the Evolution of Psychotherapy

♦

Ernest L. Rossi, Ph.D.

Ernest L. Rossi, Ph.D.

Ernest Rossi (Ph.D., 1962, Temple University) is in private practice in Malibu, Calif. Rossi has extensive experience as a Jungian Analyst; he is affiliated with the C. G. Jung Institute in Los Angeles and served as chairman of its certifying board. He is a recipient of a Lifetime Achievement Award from the Milton H. Erickson Foundation.

Rossi, the editor of Psychological Perspectives: A Semi-annual Review of Jungian Thought, *is a prolific author, having published books on dreams and on the psychobiology of mind–body healing. He also has written extensively on the hypnotic approach of Milton H. Erickson, and is the coauthor, with Erickson, of four books, the editor of four volumes of Erickson's collected papers, and the coeditor of four volumes of Erickson's early lectures, seminars and workshops.*

Ernest Rossi describes evidence that hourly and daily variations in consciousness are related to the wavelike flow of messenger molecules, operating on levels that may range from mind to gene. Stress, psychosomatic problems, and their resolution may be a function of how people manage the wave nature of their consciousness. Rossi reviews the history of these ideas from Charcot to Milton Erickson, including the most recent work of important contemporary researchers. Portions of this paper have been adapted from Rossi (1991).

What is the next step in the evolution of psychotherapy? What will be the origin of new ideas about the nature of mind and human consciousness? What will be the new database of a psychotherapy of the future? What will the psychotherapist of the future be able to do for people that we do not do today?

We will explore these questions in this chapter, extrapolating from the evolution of psychotherapy during the past 150 years. We will see that there has been a "hidden remnant," wherein many pioneers of psychotherapy have recognized the importance of time and rhythm as the essence of stress, illness, and healing.

Until recently, however, we have not understood these connections well enough to use them as a foundation for psychotherapy. We will explore current mind–body research that is leading to a new view of "the wave nature of consciousness" that can orient us to a psychotherapy of the future.

THE WAVE NATURE OF CONSCIOUSNESS

The "wave nature of consciousness" refers to the fact that virtually every aspect of our consciousness that we can measure is periodic.

Like the waves of the sea, our alertness, for example, has periodic peaks and troughs throughout the day.

The first real understanding of the wave nature of human consciousness began with the scientific research into dreams. Until fairly recently, it had been thought that sleep was simple rest. A profound revolution took place in 1953 when two researchers at the University of Chicago—Eugene Aserinsky and Nathaniel Kleitman (1953)—reported that approximately every 90 minutes throughout the night our sleep became an active process for about 10 to 30 minutes. The brain-wave pattern as measured by the electroencephalograph (EEG) was seen to be very similar to its active pattern when we are awake. In addition, it was noted that the sleeper's eyes moved rapidly under closed eyelids, as if a moving scene were being observed. Indeed, when people were awakened during these periods of rapid eye movement (REM sleep), they reported that they were dreaming.

The REM dream cycle immediately became the touchstone for evaluating all past and present theories of the meaning of dreams, as well as their role in mind–body performance, health, and behavior. During REM periods, oxygen consumption increases and more blood flows to the brain than when we are awake. Our breathing, heart rate, blood pressure, and gastrointestinal movements are more variable than during wakefulness. Clearly, sleep and dreaming could not be a simple, passive process of rest and recovery. The highly active periods of REM sleep must involve some adaptive processes that are important for survival, as well as for recuperation and rejuvenation. But exactly what are they? This remains a leading-edge question today, almost 40 years after Aserinsky and Kleitman reported their discovery of dream sleep.

The mystery only deepened when it was later discovered that the 90- to 120-minute dream rhythm apparently continues even during the day, when we are awake. Kleitman (1969) called this daytime rhythm the "basic rest–activity cycle" and originally described it as follows:

Manifestations of a basic rest–activity cycle (BRAC)

in the functioning of the nervous system were amply established by recording EEGs of sleepers. . . . The operation of the BRAC in wakefulness is not as obvious as it is in sleep; there are too many external influences that tend to disrupt or obscure the cycle. . . . [Nevertheless], everyday observations support the view that the BRAC operates during the waking hours as well as in sleep. The now common "coffee-break" at 10:30 A.M. divides the three-hour office stint from 9:00 A.M. to noon into two 90-minute fractions. The relief obtained by some individuals from brief 10-to-15-minute catnaps perhaps represents a "riding over" the low phase of a BRAC, and postprandial [after lunch] drowsiness may be an accentuation of the same phase. (pp. 34–37)

In a recent conversation with the 95-year-old Kleitman, who lives in retirement on the West Coast, I was surprised to learn that he thinks that our daytime experience of 90-minute rhythms is more important than the rhythm of our dreams every night! He believes this to be so because we can learn to recognize and use the profound effects that the basic rest–activity cycle has on our patterns of daily living in the areas of diet, sexuality, and general performance effectiveness. On the other hand, relatively few people know how to tune into their dreams to learn more about themselves as proposed by psychoanalysis.

In our conversations, Kleitman emphasized that the general public, as well as most professionals, has not yet grasped the deeper significance of these mind–body rhythms as a fundamental characteristic of the life process. He reflected this view in one of his recent research papers, "Basic Rest–Activity Cycle—22 Years Later" (Kleitman, 1982), where he stated, "The cycle involves gastric hunger contractions and sexual excitement—processes concerned with self-preservation and preservation of the species—which led to the designation of the cycle as basic" (p. 314).

Since Freud also believed that hunger and sex were the deepest motivations in life, I could not help but wonder whether Kleitman's view of the basic rest–activity cycle might eventually become recognized as the psychobiological basis of much that is of value in the insights of the depth psychology of Freud and Jung. My conversations with this brilliant, but somewhat

Stage One: A Daily Alternation of Being Awake and Asleep

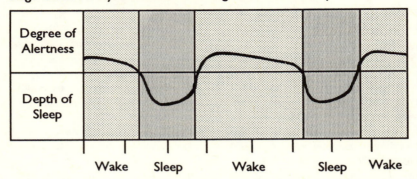

Stage Two: An Ultradian Rhythmn of Dream (REM) Sleep (Aserinsky, Kleitman, 1953)

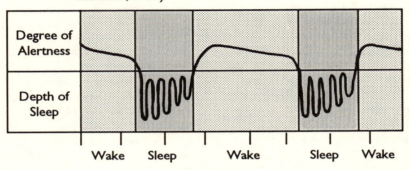

Stage Three: The New Model of The Wave Nature of Human Consciousness (Wever, 1985)

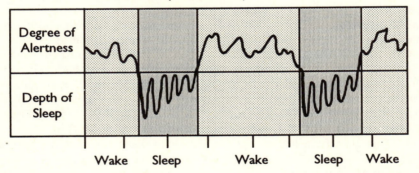

Figure 1 Three stages in the evolution of the current model of the wave nature of consciousness. (Adapted with permission from Rossi & Nimmons [1991]. *The 20-minute break: Using the new science of ultradian rhythms.* Los Angeles: Tarcher.)

forgotten, pioneer confirmed my conviction of the significance of the wave nature of consciousness for understanding and facilitating performance, healing, and well-being in every aspect of daily life.

There have been three stages in the evolu-

tion of this new model of the wave nature of consciousness, illustrated in Figure 1. The traditional view was that consciousness was a simple wave of increasing alertness, peaking around midday and disappearing into the deepest levels of sleep at night. This view was

updated when we recognized the nightly variations in consciousness and arousal in REM
dream sleep. A mathematical model of the wave
nature of human consciousness was then developed by Rutger Wever (1989) of the Max Planck
Institute in Germany.

Wever is another pioneer of chronobiology—the biology of time and mind–body
rhythms. For the past 30 years, he has made
detailed studies of *circadian* (daily rhythms,
such as our 24-hour rhythm of being asleep and
awake) and *ultradian* rhythms (faster rhythms
that take place many times a day, such as our
90-minute dream cycle) in human subjects living in a controlled environment. When I visited
him at the Max Planck Institute, he showed me
the lightproof and soundproof "bunker" in the
side of a sylvian hill where his subjects lived for
months at a time, isolated from all the normal
cues that influence our mind–body rhythms.
These cues from our environment—such as
daylight, temperature, sounds, and mealtimes—
are called *Zeitgebers* (the German *zeit* means
"time" and *geber* means "giver"). These are said
to "entrain" or "synchronize" our internal mind–
body "clocks" so that they can be continually
adjusted to the changing seasons and demands
of daily living.

When I objected that the idea of *Zeitgebers*
sounded like a rather rigid and mechanical way
of looking at life, Wever insisted that just the
opposite was the case. He emphasized that *personal relationships between people are actually
the most significant "time givers."* In a modern
society, we usually wake up and go to sleep, not
with the dawn of light and the setting of the sun,
but with the cues we give each other—such as
yawning, stretching, or showing other signs of
being sleepy. With the approach of his retirement, Wever had a beautifully traditional Bavar-
ian home and garden built, but with an important difference: he had oversized windows
constructed in the living room so that there
would be plenty of normal sunlight to cue his
daytime alertness. Even more important, he
claimed, were his plans to continue a balanced
schedule of personal and social interactions,
nicely paced throughout the day, to help him
maintain his consciousness at its optimum
level.

Although a great deal of research supports

Wever's ultradian model shown in Figure 1, it
is still theoretical in the sense that most of
the data were collected under carefully controlled laboratory conditions isolated from the
distracting influences of real life. If ultradian
rhythms are to be of practical significance as
a new approach for facilitating our consciousness, performance, and general health, it is
important to prove that people can recognize
them in ordinary, everyday life.

To explore this issue, I asked a pilot group
of seven people to keep diaries for two weeks
in which they would record those times
throughout their ordinary workday when they
felt a need to "take a break." I asked them to
record how long their restorative break lasted
and to write a few sentences about what they
actually experienced during this period.
Although this was a very small sample even for
a pilot study, the several hundred restorative
breaks recorded for the total group over the
two-week period were regarded as sufficient for
computer data analysis. (A more detailed analysis of these data compared with another group
of subjects doing self-hypnosis appears in Rossi,
1992, in press.)

The results as shown in Figure 2 are a striking confirmation of the top half of Wever's
ultradian model of the wave nature of human
consciousness. My original data appear as the
lighter, sharper line in the background. These
data were analyzed and illustrated by Helen
Sing, head statistician at the Department of
Behavioral Biology at the Walter Reed Army
Institute of Research. For over a generation, the
researchers at this laboratory had pioneered
many of the government's innovative studies of
the daily and hourly performance patterns of
pilots, radar operators, and military personnel
at all levels.

The Walter Reed researchers were particularly interested in some of the details of when
people tend to take a break. There appears to
be a tendency to take a break as early as 9 A.M.
or 10 A.M. The peak time when people take a
break in this early part of the workday is not
clear, however. It is probably spread uncertainly
over a few hours because the intense demands
of work in the morning hours do not allow most
people really to take their normal 10:30 break.
The first and longest break appears right after

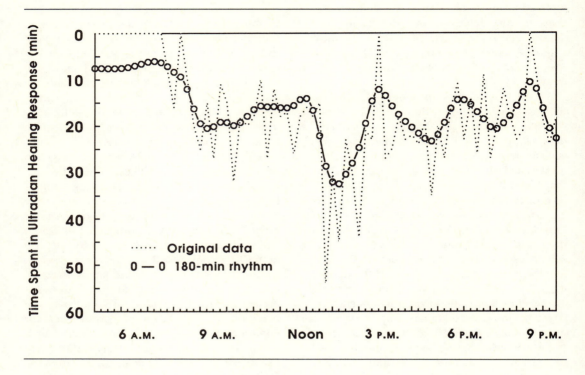

Noon
Ultradian Healing Response Rhythms

Figure 2 The wave nature of consciousness. (Reprinted with permission from Rossi [1991]. The wave nature of consciousness, *Psychological Perspectives, 24*, 1–10.)

noontime. This is consistent with most performance data from Walter Reed and other laboratories that show a "postlunch dip" in most activities.

Even when people begin to take breaks regularly throughout the rest of the afternoon and evening, they do not always follow the classic 90- to 120-minute basic rest–activity cycle as originally described by Kleitman. This rhythm may be an ideal; in everyday life, however, my data suggest that most people more typically take a break every two to three hours, or so.

Another significant detail illustrated in Figure 2 is that people usually break for about 20 minutes. Even if they are not obviously resting by sitting or lying down for that entire period, their level of alertness is reduced. Most workers typically "disguise" their

ultradian breaks by "doodling" around the office. They adjust papers on their desk, sharpen pencils, make a personal telephone call, chat at the water cooler, have a cigarette, go to the restroom, and so forth. These are all natural expressions of our need to take an ultradian break for about 15 to 20 minutes every few hours, even when it is not officially allowed or even recognized by us when we are doing it! Most of us are not entirely aware of these normal ultradian variations in our consciousness throughout the day.

An apparently odd aspect of Figure 2 is that it begins with a high plateau before 6 A.M. that extends to about 8 A.M. I frankly do not know if this is an artifact due to the fact that a few subjects woke up early in the morning (5 or 6 A.M.) when they apparently did not need to take ultradian breaks—or whether consciousness is really "higher and steadier" at this time. This type of early-morning plateau would certainly make sense in terms of the many meditative traditions that recommend awakening as early as 4 A.M. for the first meditation of the day because it is believed that this is when the mind is at its best. Further research is needed to validate this very interesting issue.

It is important to recognize that there is nothing rigid about the particular pattern of peaks and troughs of the waves of consciousness in Figure 2. I suspect that another sample of people in different life circumstances would have a different wave pattern. Although the idea of "biological clocks" is popular, it is actually somewhat misleading. Clocks are mechanical devices that are supposed to keep regular time. The more regular and accurate the clock is, the better. The natural waves of our mind–body rhythms are not accurate clocks in this rigid, mechanical sense, however.

Our natural rhythms are almost the opposite. They can shift their timekeeping by speeding up or slowing down or even skipping a few beats now and then. They are always altering their pace to adjust to the changing demands of our real world, as well as to our interest in what we are doing. In this sense, our waves of consciousness and mind–body rhythms are agents of adaptation and optimum performance in the outside world. They are like quality control engineers in that, under ideal conditions, they pace our activities to maximize our inner periods of rest, restoration, and rejuvenation, as well as our outer periods of performance efficiency.

But if these mind–body rhythms were really so important for adaptation and health, why had no one recognized them before? Or had they? The founders of depth psychology—the great 19th-century French neurologist Jean-Martin Charcot; Pierre Janet, an early pioneer of hypnosis; Sigmund Freud; and Carl Jung—all believed that conscious experience was rooted in our body. Unfortunately, the biology of their time was inadequate to understand the subtle relationships between mind and body. Yet, in much of their work, I was able to find a trail of clues that suggested that they understood some-

thing about the wave nature of consciousness, stress, and healing in everyday life as well as in the consulting room.

CHARCOT'S "HYPNOID" STATE, DREAMS AND HYSTERIA

Jean-Martin Charcot was a professor of neurology and psychiatry in Paris a century and a half ago (Ellenberger, 1970). He believed that there existed a state of consciousness that occurred periodically, somewhere between sleeping and waking. He called it "hypnoid" and identified it as a source of hysteria and many psychological problems. He believed that this state was something like hypnosis, but could appear spontaneously during everyday life. He did not know why it appeared, but hypothesized that it was much like the experience of being caught up in a dream at night. At such times, he believed, any strong emotional stimulus could become imprinted on the mind in an unhealthy or a neurotic fashion. Particularly when we cannot rest, we become prone to highly charged emotional states, anxiety, irritability, and depression. Charcot searched in vain to find a biological basis for such a hypnoid state. Another century of research was required before laboratory scientists coined the term *ultradian* and recognized that our nighttime dreams take place every 90 to 120 minutes when we sleep, while our daydreams follow the same rhythm when we are awake.

JANET'S "ABAISSEMENT"—A LOWERING OF MENTAL ENERGY

From Charcot, the trail led to one of his medical students, a brilliant physician named Pierre Janet who would go on to become one of the most profound theorists and practitioners of hypnosis. Janet noticed that, at various times through the day, we experience periodic daily fluctuations in our mental status that he termed *abaissement du niveau mental* (a lowering of mental level). During these periods of *abaissement,* Janet found, our psyche seems to lose some of its capacity to synthesize reality into a meaningful whole (Ellenberger, 1970; Rossi & Smith, 1990). If we encounter a traumatic or strong emotional event during these periods, the mind lacks its usual ability to make sense of it and to fit it properly into a meaningful, secure whole. During *abaissement*, we tend to be emotionally vulnerable and easily overwhelmed; we can register life experiences, but cannot "digest" them properly. The emotional experience floats in our unconscious, unassimilated, in effect, jamming the gears of the mind. Janet hypothesized that such unassimilated experiences could become the seed of psychological or psychosomatic illness, obsessive thought patterns, phobias—all sorts of behavioral problems. Many chronic problems, he believed, were the result of the mind–body's continuing, frustrated effort to make sense of the original disturbing experience.

Janet believed that there was an underlying physiological source of these *abaissements* during the day that were somehow associated with stress and exhaustion. Ellenberger (1970) summarized Janet's view:

We do not know the exact nature of psychological forces. Janet never doubted that they are of a physiological nature, and seems to have believed that the day would come when they could be measured. He considered that these forces were, to a great extent, connected with the condition of the brain and organs . . . and differ from one individual to another. These forces can obviously be reconstituted in some way. "I don't know where these reserves are, but I do know that they exist," said Janet. One of the main sources of this reconstitution is sleep; hence the importance for the therapist to teach his client about the best way of preparing himself for sleep. The same could be said about the various techniques of rest and relaxation, *the distribution of pauses throughout the day*, of rest days during the month, and of vacations during the year. . . . (p. 380)

Does not the phrase, "the distribution of pauses throughout the day," sound like Janet's anticipation of our new understanding of the wave nature of human consciousness? Many of Janet's ideas were adopted a generation later by Freud, when he formulated the foundations of psychoanalysis.

FREUD'S PSYCHOPATHOLOGY OF EVERYDAY LIFE

It was Freud's genius to recognize the essential connections between the sources of psychopathology and creativity in everyday life. In their early classic volume, *Studies on Hysteria*, Breuer and Freud (1895/1957) recognized that the *hypnoid* state was somehow related to "abnormal states of consciousness" as well as to the ordinary everyday "absence of mind" we all experience. They describe their puzzlement about these connections as follows:

The longer we have been occupied with these phenomena the more we have become convinced that *the splitting of consciousness which is so striking in the well-known classical cases under the form of "double conscience" is present to a rudimentary degree in every hysteria, and that a tendency to such a dissociation, and with it the emergence of abnormal states of consciousness (which we shall bring together under the term "hypnoid") is the basic phenomenon of this neurosis.* (p. 12)

Also:

. . . Are hypnoid states of this kind in existence before the patient falls ill, and how do they come about? I can say very little about this, for apart from the case of Anna O, we have no observations at our disposal which might throw light on the point. It seems certain that with her, the auto-hypnosis had the way paved for it by habitual reveries and that it was fully established by an affect of protracted anxiety, which, indeed, would itself be the basis for a hypnoid state. It seems not improbable that this process holds good fairly generally.

A great variety of states lead to "absence of mind" but only a few of them predispose to auto-hypnosis or pass over immediately into it. An investigator who is deep in a problem is also no doubt anesthetic to a certain degree, and he has large groups of sensations of which he forms no conscious perception; and the same is true of anyone who is using his creative imagination actively. . . . (pp. 217–218)

Here we find a basic question about the wave nature of consciousness posed with perfect clarity: "Are hypnoid states of this kind in existence before the patient falls ill, and how do they come about?" At that time, it was speculated that the hypnoid state was caused by a traumatic experience or a "hereditary taint," or perhaps a combination of both. It would take another 50 years before researchers would find that there is an entirely natural "absence of mind" that takes place for 10 to 20 minutes every 90 to 120 minutes or so throughout the day.

Freud's recognition that "a great variety of states lead to 'absence of mind' . . . and the same is true of anyone who is using his creative imagination actively . . ." was later elaborated by Carl Jung into a profoundly far-reaching theory of the evolution of mind and higher states of consciousness.

JUNG'S TRANSFORMATION OF CHARACTER AND CONSCIOUSNESS

The relationship between Janet's *abaissement* and the symptoms of ultradian stress, healing, creativity, and the transformation of character were described by Jung (1954) as follows:

The *abaissement du niveau mental*, the energy lost to consciousness, is a phenomenon which shows itself most drastically in the "loss of soul" among primitive peoples, who also have interesting psychotherapeutic methods for recapturing the soul that has gone astray. . . . Similar phenomena can be observed in civilized man. . . . He, too, is liable to a sudden loss of initiative for no apparent reason. . . . Carelessness of all kinds, neglected duties, tasks postponed, wilful outbursts of defiance, and so on, all these can dam up his vitality to such an extent that certain quanta of energy, no longer finding a conscious outlet, stream off into the unconscious, when they activate other, compensating contents, which in turn begin to exert a compulsive influence on the conscious mind. (Hence the very common combination of extreme neglect of duty and a compulsion neurosis!)

This is one way in which loss of energy may come about. The other way causes loss not through a malfunctioning of the conscious mind but through a "spontaneous" activation of unconscious contents, which react secondarily upon the conscious mind. These are moments in human life when a new page is turned. New interests and tendencies appear which have hitherto received no attention, or there is a sudden change of personality (a so-called mutation of character). During the incubation period of such a change we can often observe a loss of conscious energy: the new development has drawn off the energy it needs from consciousness. This lowering of energy can be seen most clearly before the onset of certain psychoses and also in the empty stillness which precedes creative work. (pp. 180–181)

Jung (1960) wrote what is probably the clearest description of the rhythmic or "wave-like character" of emotional complexes and imagery before the term ultradian came on the scene:

What then, scientifically speaking, is a "feeling-toned complex"? It is the *image* of a certain psychic situation which is strongly accentuated emotionally and is, moreover, incompatible with the habitual attitude of consciousness. This image has a powerful inner coherence, it has its own wholeness and, in addition, a relatively high degree of autonomy, so that it is subject to the control of the conscious mind to only a limited extent, and therefore behaves like an animated foreign body in the sphere of consciousness. The complex can usually be suppressed with an effort of will, but not argued out of existence, and at the first suitable opportunity, it reappears in all its original strength. Certain experimental investigations seem to indicate that *its intensity or activity curve has a wavelike character, with a "wave-length" of hours, days, or weeks. This very complicated question remains as yet unclarified.* (p. 96, italics added)

I would submit that Jung's "very complicated question" is answered, at least in part, by our developing understanding of the ultradian wave nature of consciousness in stress and healing. Jung later went on to elaborate these ideas into a new theory of how meditation and religious rituals could be used to facilitate heightened experiences of consciousness, which he described as "a supernormal degree of luminosity" (Jung, 1960, p. 436). In all of this, Jung went quite a bit further than anyone else in recognizing the rhythmic aspect of "higher consciousness" and healing.

We have come full circle, from the classrooms of 19th-century Paris and Vienna to our current exploration of the wave nature of consciousness, from the "hypnoid state" of Charcot and the *abaissement* of Janet as the source of psychopathology to Freud's and Jung's recognition of its role in healing, creativity, and the evolution of consciousness. Each of these pioneers seemed to describe much the same phenomenon: there are special periods of potential stress or healing that come on us naturally in daily life. Each described mind–body states when our balance of consciousness and capacities shifts, rises, and falls, leaving us not fully awake or quite asleep. All had glimpsed in it a "royal road" to our inner mind–body, holding the potential for pathology as well as for personal growth. What those 19th-century physicians could not know because of the limitations of the biological sciences, 20th-century researchers now explore in detail.

THE COMMON EVERYDAY TRANCE

One of the first healers to notice and actually utilize the wave nature of consciousness was Milton Erickson. While most therapists saw patients for a 50-minute session, Erickson preferred to meet for an hour and a half or more. In more than a half-century of treating people, Erickson noticed that the mental–emotional equilibrium of his patients naturally varied during the course of their sessions. He claimed that people in everyday life also quite naturally drift into distinct mind–body states. When he worked with patients for at least an hour and a half or two, he found, they were almost certain to go through a distinct changes in their consciousness (Rossi, 1982, 1986a,b,c).

During these lengthier sessions, for no apparent reason, the patient's head might start to nod rhythmically, the eyelids would blink slowly and then close over faraway-looking eyes. The body might become perfectly still, with fingers, hands, arms, or legs apparently frozen in an awkward position. Sometimes, there was a beatific smile on the person's face or, more often, the features were passive and slack—what Erickson described as "ironed out."

During his teaching sessions with me, he often pointed out patients' rapidly quivering eyelids, furrowed brows, trembling lips or chin,

and tears—the outward signs that they were intensely groping with private inner dramas. On some occasions, Erickson did nothing to direct people to go into trance; it just seemed to happen, sooner or later, all by itself. Erickson's sessions with patients seemed to be subtle and indirect forms of hypnotherapeutic encounters wherein nature came in as an equal partner in ways that most observers could not yet understand.

Erickson took advantage of the natural ebb and flow of consciousness that seemed to open and close like windows throughout his therapeutic sessions. Only after he observed that the patient's physical and mental processes were quieting down would Erickson "facilitate hypnotherapeutic trance." Years of treating patients had taught him that during these naturally inward-turning therapeutic periods, which usually lasted between 10 and 20 minutes, most people are able to gain better access to their emotions, intuitions, and deepest thoughts. Erickson would use these windows of inner access to help people learn to solve their own problems in their own way.

Erickson called these natural periods of healing "common everyday trance" because they appeared to be a normal feature of our daily lives, as well as occurring in the consulting room. All of us have such moments of inner preoccupation during the course of our day when we are in some in-between state of consciousness, neither fully awake nor quite asleep. The housewife staring vacantly over a cup of coffee in midmorning, the student with a faraway look in her eyes in the middle of a lecture, the truck driver who blinks in mild surprise as he suddenly reaches his destination without any memory of the last 20 minutes all are exhibiting the common everyday trance.

Although common, such brief periods of inner focus are clearly very special. During these quiet periods, we can be more open and introspective. Our focus turns inward as our dreams, fantasies, and reveries—the raw material of growth in everyday life, as well as in psychotherapy—become unusually vivid. Our natural common everyday trance seems to be when the window between our conscious and unconscious opens a bit. Because the inner mind is the source of our deepest intuitions, people may be at their most creative, and they may experience insights, fantasy, and intuitive leaps during these meditative moments.

The common everyday trance also can be a period of openness and vulnerability to outside influences; suggestions made during this time are sometimes more easily accepted. Erickson called his use of the common everyday trance the *naturalistic* or *utilization approach*, because he believed he was simply helping people to utilize their own natural inner resources to solve their own problems in their own ways during these periods.

This led me to speculate that Erickson's reputation for having an uncanny knack for facilitating deep hypnosis and resolving psychosomatic problems could be due, at least in part, to his unwitting utilization of our natural waves of consciousness—our natural circadian and ultradian mind–body rhythms. This became the seed in my mind for an entirely new theory of therapeutic hypnosis, as well as mind–body communication and healing: Excessive and chronic stress causes symptoms by distorting our normal ultradian/circadian rhythms; hypnosis could ameliorate these symptoms simply by providing an opportunity for these natural mind–body rhythms to normalize themselves. Hypnotic suggestion works because it *entrains* and *synchronizes* our natural ultradian processes of ultradian and circadian rest, restoration, and healing. The secret of transformation from illness to health to higher levels of performance and well-being lay in recognizing and facilitating a person's own creative resources during these natural windows of inner focus and rejuvenation that arise periodically for about 20 minutes every hour and a half or so throughout the day.

But precisely why were people so uncommonly accessible for therapeutic change during these special periods? In particular, how were they able to make curative connections between body and mind so readily? Term it the common everyday trance, hypnosis, relaxation, meditation, daydreaming, imagery, or whatever, just what was going on during these special periods? The questions led me to explore the psychobiological sources of the wave nature of our consciousness and their relationships to stress and healing.

STRESS, HEALING, AND THE WAVE NATURE OF CONSCIOUSNESS

There are four basic hypthoses at the heart of this new conception of stress, healing, and the wave nature of consciousness:

1. The timing and cyclic patterns of genetic processes at the molecular level are the ultimate source of all mind–body rhythms and the wave nature of consciousness.
2. All of the self-regulatory systems of the mind–body are coordinated by, and serve, these genetic sources.
3. Stress engendered when we chronically interfere with these natural mind–body rhythms is a major etiology for psychosomatic problems.
4. Most of the holistic approaches to mind–body healing unwittingly utilize the ultradian healing response to normalize our mind–body rhythms to optimize health.

Because I have already dealt in detail with the data that support these ideas (Rossi, 1986a, 1986b, 1987; 1990a, 1990b; Rossi & Cheek, 1988; Rossi & Ryan, 1986, 1992), I will cite only some of the most recent research from a wide variety of sources.

1. *The timing of genetic processes at the molecular level is the ultimate source of all mind–body rhythms and the wave nature of consciousness.*

All of the mind–body rhythms of life ultimately are related to the "cell cycle": this involves the replication, growth, and functioning of the cell, which is the basic unit of life. The life cycle of the cell is itself governed by an epigenetic clock.

The term *epigenetic* is central to my proposals about the genetic source of mind–body rhythms and the wave nature of consciousness. Epigenetic has been defined as the basic process of life on the molecular and cellular level by Lloyd and Edwards (1984) as follows:

Oscillations on the epigenetic time scale: The synthesis of macromolecules, their modification (processing), transport, and interaction, and their integration into membranes are all epigenetic processes. Broadly defined, these are the reactions involved in gene expression. The time domain occupied by these processes lies between the metabolic and the cell cycle domains. Thus, the cellular content of macromolecules changes slowly by comparison with the speed of metabolic interconversions that make up the metabolic map. Even so, the pace of this slow "adaptive" change is itself rapid by comparison with the time taken for a cell to double in volume and divide, the cell cycle time ... the epigenetic system is composed of reactions that have relaxation times lying within the range 10_2–10_4 sec (1.5 min to 3 hr), depending on the type of cell studied. (pp. 30–31)

The most dramatic demonstration of the genetic source of mind–body ultradian and circadian rhythms is recent research on how genetic mutations can modulate the expression of these rhythms (Dowse & Ringo, 1987; Hardin, Hall, & Rosbash, 1990).

Such research leads me to hypothesize that the epigenetic cycle on the molecular and cellular level sets and is served by all the other so-called "clocks" of the mind, brain, and body. By becoming more aware of the many obvious and subtle cues of our mind–body clocks (e.g., rest when we are tired, eat when we are hungry, create as we daydream, work when we are alert), we can optimize our daily performance and well-being right down to the molecular and genetic levels that are the final common path, the "bottom line," of all life, metabolism, and healing.

It is important to recognize how this hypothesis about the correspondence between the 90–120-minute ultradian epigenetic rhythms on the genetic level and our ordinary everyday experience can serve as a bridge between mind and matter. Many fundamental phenomenological processes of psychology, such as memory, learning, mood, and emotional complexes, are now known to be governed by the 90–120-minute ultradian mind–body rhythms that are in synchrony with the epigenetic processes at the molecular and cellular levels. I hypothesize that this is a two-way street. Just as the activity on the epigenetic level can serve as a source for the timing of mental and behavioral activities, so can mind and behavior modulate molecular activities at the epigenetic core of biological life

at the molecular level. I propose that this is the ultimate basis of all forms of mind–body healing wherein a mental process can modulate a biological process.

It takes 20 minutes for "cyclins" (a class of messenger molecules within our cells) to build up to signal the initiation of the process of mitosis whereby the genes separate themselves in cell division (Murray & Kirschner, 1989; Murray, Solomon, & Kirschner, 1989). I hypothesize that this is one basis of the wave nature of human consciousness and what I call "the ultradian healing response."

It takes between one and two hours for this critical phase of gene separation to take place. This so-called "M (mitosis) phase of the cell cycle" is just one example of an epigenetic clock that is related to many of the 90–120-minute ultradian mind–body rhythms discussed here. In rapidly proliferating (dividing) cells, this M phase usually takes place once every 16 to 24 hours. This is evidently related to our basic 24-hour circadian rhythm (Alberts et al., 1989; Edmunds, 1984, 1988; Lloyd & Rossi, 1992; Rapp, 1987).

2. *All self-regulatory systems of the mind–body are coordinated by and serve these genetic sources.*

My reading of the most recent literature leads me to hypothesize that all the major systems of mind–body self-regulation are in synchrony with their sources in the cellular epigenetic ultradian rhythms. The following four major mind–body systems of self-regulation are the familiar ones discussed in all medical textbooks.

The Central Nervous System

The Central Nervous System (CNS) regulates consciousness, sleep, and all our life activities and has a timing source in the pons area of the brain stem (called the reticular activating system). This part of the brain generates and sends out nerve impulses every 90 minutes while we sleep to initiate our ultradian dream rhythms (which last an average of 20 minutes). Jouvet (1962, 1973, Jouvet & Moruzzi, 1972), who discovered this CNS rhythm, believed that the purpose of dreams was to activate and exercise the basic genetic patterns of behavior of the organism.

We now know that this 90–120-minute ultradian rhythm is active throughout our daytime hours as well. This basic activity and rest cycle is the central pacemaker of our lives (Brown & Graeber, 1982; Kleitman, 1963, 1969, 1970).

The most recent research on how the nervous system works indicates that this 90–120-ultradian rhythm is the basic unit of time required to encode long-term memory and learning at the genetic level (Kandel, 1983, 1989). This ultradian rhythm is thus basic to all of our mental and emotional life.

The Endocrine System

The endocrine system, which regulates the hormones of the body, is commonly regarded as having its central time source in the suprachiasmatic nucleus of the hypothalamus of the brain. The hourly and daily pulses of hormones sent out by the hypothalamic-pituitary area synchronize everything from alertness, appetite, growth, and stress to sex and reproduction. These hormones function as signal or "messenger molecules" (the first signaling system) that travel through the blood to all cells of the body. Those cells that have the proper receptors pick up these hormone signals and convert them to "secondary messengers" (the second signaling system) inside the cell to regulate cellular metabolism by turning on certain genes.

Until recently, it was believed that purely physiological feedback was the primary regulatory mechanism of the endocrine system. We now know that is only part of the story. The current revolution in uncovering the ultradian and circadian release of most of our hormones that serve as messenger molecules among mind, body, and genes is typified by a number of representative researchers (Iranmanesh et al., 1989; Mejean et al., 1988; Veldhuis & Johnson, 1988; Veldhuis et al., 1987).

The Autonomic Nervous System

The autonomic nervous system regulates the basic patterns of stimulation (the sympathetic system) and relaxation (the parasympathetic system) of all the organs of the body. Recent research by Werntz and associates (Werntz, 1981; Werntz, et al., 1981, 1982) has confirmed the 5,000-year-old traditional system of yoga wherein a 90–120-minute nasal cycle has been used to regulate the autonomic nervous system to achieve the so-called miraculous feats of mind–body control. This ultradian nasal rhythm has now been found to have a contralateral relationship to the alternation in the activation of our left- and right-brain cerebral hemispheres, as well as an ultradian sympathetic and parasympathetic alternation of activation of the left and right sides of our body (Kennedy et al., 1986; Klein et al., 1986; Werntz, 1981; Werntz et al., 1981, 1982).

The Immune System

The immune system, which is made up of many different types of tissues throughout the body and white blood cells that protect us from all sorts of invaders from bacteria to viruses and cancer, also has many ultradian rhythms on the cellular level. The immune system has many molecular messengers (cytokines, immunotransmitters, etc.), which coordinate its activities with all of the other major mind–body systems of self-regulation cited above.

Altered ultradian and circadian rhythms have been found to be associated with the beginning stages of some cancers, as well as with many other psychosomatic illnesses, such as anxiety and depression (Crabtree, 1989; Green & Green, 1987; Klevecz et al., 1987; Todovov, 1990).

3. *Stress engendered by chronic interference with mind–body rhythms is a major etiology of psychosomatic problems.*

Stress is generated when we do not heed our natural mind–body signals for ultradian rest and recovery. I hypothesize that when we chronically push ourselves beyond our natural ultradian and circadian rhythms of self-regulation, we set the stage for a series of malfunctions that are ultimately expressed at the epigenetic level.

I outline four stages of what I call the

THE ULTRADIAN HEALING RESPONSE	THE ULTRADIAN STRESS SYNDROME
1. The Soft Sweet Signal: An acceptance of nature's call for your need to rest and recover your strength and well being leads you into an experience of comfort and thankfulness.	**1. The Stress and Fatigue Signal:** A rejection of nature's call for your need to rest and recover your strength and well being leads you into an experience of stress and fatigue.
2. The Deeper Breath: A spontaneous deeper breath comes all by itself after a few moments of rest as a signal that you are slipping into a deeper state of relaxation and healing. Explore the deepening feeling of comfort that comes spontaneously. Wonder about the possibilities of mind-gene communication and healing with an attitude of "dispassionate compassion."	**2. High on Your Own Hormones:** Continuing effort in the face of fatigue leads to the release of stress hormones that short circuits the need for ultradian rest. Performance goes up briefly at the expense of hidden wear and tear so that you fall into further stress and a need for artificial stimulants (caffeine, nicotine, alcohol, cocaine, etc.) leading to our addictive society.
3. Autonomous Inner Work: Spontaneous fantasy, memory, feeling-toned complexes, active imagination and numinous states of being are orchestrated for healing and life reframing.	**3. Malfunction Junction:** Many mistakes creep into your performance; memory, learning and emotional problems become manifest. You become irritable and abusive to yourself or others.
4. Rejuvenation and Rebirth: A natural awakening with feelings of serenity, clarity, and healing together with a sense of how you will enhance your performance and well being in the world.	**4. The Rebellious Body:** Classical psychosomatic symptoms now intrude so that you finally have to stop and rest. You are left with a nagging sense of failure, depression and illness.

Table 1. Four stages contrasting the ultradian healing and stress responses. We usually need a 20-minute rest and rejuvenation period every 90 to 120 minutes throughout the day to maintain excellence in performance, health, and well-being. (Adapted with permission from Rossi [1990a]. The new yoga of the west. *Psychological Perspectives, 22,* 146–161.)

ultradian stress syndrome in Table 1 and contrast this syndrome with the ultradian healing response. Whether or not we experience stress or healing during our natural 20-minute ultradian rest periods every two or three hours throughout the day depends on our attitude toward our mind–body signals for taking a break. If we reject nature's call for rest, we tend to fall into the ultradian stress syndrome, with feelings of failure, depression, and fatigue. If we heed nature's call for rest with the right attitude, we can experience it as a profoundly deep feeling of comfort, well-being, and rejuvenation.

Humans have about 100,000 genes. About a third (30,000) of these are called "housekeeping

genes" because they are active at every moment of our lives, regulating the basic metabolism of our cells. They are the bottom line of our life process. I have speculated that it is these housekeeping genes that we may be accessing and facilitating during the ultradian healing response.

I hypothesize that when we chronically disrupt our ultradian rhythms, we are interfering with the naturally coordinated activities of these housekeeping genes. I have previously detailed the theory and research for the hypothesis that this is the ultimate source of all mind–body mood and performance problems at the epigenetic level (Rossi, 1982, 1986a, 1986b,

1986c, 1990a, 1990b; Rossi & Cheek, 1988; Rossi & Nimmons, 1991)

4. Most holistic approaches to mind—body healing utilize the ultradian healing response.

The healing of psychosomatic disorders and the optimizing of all life activities (work, play, creativity, etc.) can be facilitated by our learning to recognize our natural ultradian mind—body signals. While there are common patterns we all share, each of us is unique in the way we experience them. This typically involves learning to recognize our personal signals of the ultradian stress response so that we can correct the stress conditions of our life that cause our problems. We can then learn to use the ultradian healing response to maximize our natural potentials for health and well-being.

Most of the currently existing holistic methods of mind—body healing, such as the relaxation response, therapeutic hypnosis, imagery, meditation, and prayer, utilize the ultradian healing response without realizing it. Since most people chronically experience an ultradian rest deficit, all the natural therapeutic benefits of the ultradian healing response immediately take place silently and autonomously just as soon as the person is given a moment to relax while the therapist performs a healing ritual that supposedly heals the person.

Healing rituals are important in many cultures because they help some believing patients to relax so that the so-called "therapy" can take place. It is this relaxation opportunity, however, that actually initiates the real healing factor; it allows patients to experience their own natural ultradian healing responses, which then facilitates healing right down to the epigenetic level.

SUMMARY

We have traced 150 years of the evolution of psychotherapy, from its origins in the in the 19th-century psychiatry of Charcot, Janet, Freud, and Jung to the 20th-century methods of Milton Erickson, to identify suggestions that there is a wave nature of human consciousness. Current research supports the view that a major

source of stress and psychosomatic illness may be found in the chronic abuse of our natural waves of consciousness and their associated mind—body rhythms of activity and rest. It is hypothesized that the source of these rhythms that modulate virtually all the self-regulating systems of mind and body (the CNS and the autonomic, endocrine, and immune systems) is at the molecular genetic level. It is speculated that most of our current approaches to holistic healing (hypnosis, meditation, imagery, ritual, prayer, biofeedback, etc.) share a common denominator in facilitating a natural ultradian healing response that coordinates all these systems of mind—body self-regulation every 90–120 minutes throughout the day. A major direction for the evolution of psychotherapy will be in tracing the pathways of mind—body communication whereby the phenomenological processes of mind (words, images, emotions, etc.) modulate molecular-genetic expression at the cellular level of the body and vice versa.

REFERENCES

Alberts, B., Bray, D., Lewis, J., Raff, M., Roberts, K., & Watson, J. (1989). *Molecular biology of the cell* (2nd ed.). New York: Garland.

Aserinsky, E., & Kleitman, N. (1953). Regularly occurring periods of eye motility and concomitant phenomena during sleep. *Science, 118,* 273–274.

Breuer, J., & Freud, S. (1895/1957). *Studies on Hysteria.* In J. Strachey (Ed., Trans.). New York: Basic Books.

Brown, F., & Graeber, R. (Eds.). (1982). *Rhythmic aspects of behavior.* Hillsdale, N.J.: Lawrence Erlbaum.

Crabtree, G. (1989). Contingent genetic regulatory vents in T lymphocyte activation. *Science, 243,*(20), 355–361.

Dowse, H., & Ringo, J. (1987). Further evidence that the circadian clock in Drosophila is a population of coupled ultradian oscillators. *Journal of Biological Rhythms,2*(1), 65–76.

Edmunds, L., Jr. (Ed.). (1984). *Cell cycle clocks.* New York: Marcel Dekker.

Edmunds, L., Jr. (1988). *Cellular and molecular bases of biological clocks.* New York: Springer-Verlag.

Ellenberger, H. (1970). *The discovery of the unconscious.* New York: Basic Books.

Erickson, M. (1980b). *The collected papers of Milton H. Erickson on hypnosis* (4 vols.). New York: Irvington.
Volume I: *The nature of hypnosis and suggestion*
Volume II: *Hypnotic alteration of sensory, perceptual, and psychophysical processes*
Volume III: *Hypnotic investigation of psychodynamic processes*
Volume IV: *Innovative hypnotherapy*

Erickson, M. (1986). *Mind—body communication in hypnosis. Vol. 3. The seminars, workshops, and lectures of*

Milton H. Erickson. E. Rossi & M. Ryan (Eds.). New York: Irvington.

Green, R., & Green, M. (1987). Relaxation increases salivary immunoglobulin A. *Psychological Reports, 61,* 623–629.

Hardin, P., Hall, J., & Rosbash, M. (1990). Feedback of the Drosophila period gene product on circadian cycling of its messenger RNA levels. *Nature, 343*(6258), 536–540.

Iranmanesh, A., Lizarradle, G., Johnson, M., & Veldhuis, J. (1989). Circadian, ultradian, and episodic release of B-endorphin in men, and its temporal coupling with cortisol. *Journal of Clinical Endocrinology and Metabolism, 68*(6), 1019–1025.

Jouvet, M. (1962). Recherches sur les structures nerveuses et les mechanismes responsables des différentes phases du sommeil physiologique. *Archives Italiennes de Biologie 100,* 125–206.

Jouvet, M. (1973). Telencephalic and rhonbencephalic sleep in the cat. In W. Webb (Ed.), *Sleep: An active process* (pp. 12–32). Glenview, IL: Scott Foresman.

Jouvet, M., & Moruzzi, G. (1972). *Neurophysiology and neurochemistry of sleep and wakefulness.* Heidelberg: Springer-Verlag.

Jung, C. (1954). *The practice of psychotherapy, Vol. XVI. The collected works of C. G. Jung.* (R. F. C. Hull, Trans.) Bollingen Series XX. Princeton, NJ: Princeton University Press.

Jung, C. (1960). *The structure and dynamics of the psyche. Vol. III. The collected works of C. G. Jung.* (R. F. C. Hull, Trans.) Bollingen Series XX. Princeton, NJ: Princeton University Press.

Kandel, E. (1983). From metapsychology to molecular biology: Explorations into the nature of anxiety. *American Journal of Psychiatry, 140*(10), 1277–1293.

Kandel, E. (1989). Genes, nerve cells, and the remembrance of things past. *Journal of Neuropsychiatry 1*(2), 103–125.

Kennedy, B., Ziegler, M., & Shannahoff-Khalsa, D. (1986). Alternating lateralization of plasma catecholamines and nasal patency in humans. *Life Sciences, 38,* 1203–1214.

Klein, R., Pilon, D., Prosser, S., & Shannahoff-Khalsa, D. (1986). Nasal airflow asymmeteries and human performance. *Biological Psychology, 23,* 127–137.

Kleitman, N. (1963). *Sleep and wakefulness as alternating phases in the cycle of existence.* Chicago, IL: University of Chicago Press.

Kleitman, N. (1969). Basic rest–activity cycle in relation to sleep and wakefulness. In A. Kales (Ed.), *Sleep: Physiology and pathology* (pp. 33–38). Philadelphia: Lippincott.

Kleitman, N. (1970). Implications of the rest–activity cycle: Implications for organizing activity. In E. Hartmann (Ed.), *Sleep and dreaming.* Boston: Little, Brown.

Kleitman, N., (1982). Basic rest–activity cycle—22 years later. *Sleep,* 5, 311–315.

Klevecz, R., Shymko, R., Blumenfeld, D., & Braly, P. (1987). Circadian gating of S phase in human ovarian cancer. *Cancer research,47,* 6267–6271.

Lloyd, D., & Edwards, S. (1984). Epigenetic oscillations during the cell cycles of lower eucaryotes are coupled to a clock: Life's slow dance to the music of time. In L. Edmunds (Ed.), *Cell cycle clocks.* New York: Marcel Dekker.

Lloyd, D., & Rossi, E. (Eds.). (1992). *Ultradian Rhythms in Life Processes: A Fundamental Inquiry into Chronobiology and Psychobiology.* New York: Springer-Verlag.

Mejean, L., Bicakova-Rocher, A., Kolopp, M., Villaume, C., Levi, F., Debry, G., Reinberg, A., & Drouin, P. (1988). Circadian and ultradian rhythms in blood glucose and plasma insulin of healthy adults. *Chronobiology International,* 5(3), 227–236.

Murray, A., & Kirschner, M. (1989). Cyclin synthesis drives the early embryonic cell cycle. *Nature, 339,* 275–280.

Murray, A., Solomon, M., & Kirschner, M. (1989). The role of cyclin synthesis and degradation in the control of maturation promoting factor activity. *Nature, 339,* 280–286.

Rapp, P. (1987). Why are so many biological systems periodic? *Progress in Neurobiology, 29,* 261–273.

Rossi, E. (1972/1985). *Dreams and the growth of personality.* New York: Brunner-Mazel.

Rossi, E. (1982). Hypnosis and ultradian cycles: A new state(s) theory of hypnosis? *American Journal of Clinical Hypnosis, 25*(1), 21–32.

Rossi, E. (1986a). Altered states of consciousness in everyday life: The ultradian rhythms. In B. Wolman & M. Ullman (Eds.), *Handbook of altered states of consciousness* (pp. 97–132). New York: Van Nostrand.

Rossi, E. (1986b). Hypnosis and ultradian rhythms. In B. Zilbergeld, M. Edelstien, & D. Araoz (Eds.), *Hypnosis: Questions and Answers* (pp. 17–21). New York: Norton.

Rossi, E. (1986c). *The psychobiology of mind-body healing: New Concepts of therapeutic hypnosis.* New York: Norton.

Rossi, E. (1987). From mind to molecule: A state-dependent memory, learning, and behavior theory of mind-body healing. *Advances,* 4(2), 46–60.

Rossi, E. (1990a). The eternal quest: Hidden rhythms of mind-body healing in everyday life. *Psychological Perspectives, 22,* 6–23.

Rossi, E. (1990b). The new yoga of the west. *Psychological Perspectives, 22,* 146–161.

Rossi, E. (1991). The wave nature of consciousness. *Psychological Perspectives, 24,* 1–10.

Rossi, E. (1992). A clinical-experimental assessment of the ultradian theory of therapeutic suggestion. Presented at the 32nd Annual Scientific Meeting and Workshops on Clinical Hypnosis. March 24–28, 1990, Orlando, Fl. (To be published in *Ericksonian Monographs.*)

Rossi, E., & Cheek, D. (1988). *Mind-body therapy: Ideodynamic healing in hypnosis.* New York: Norton.

Rossi, E., & Nimmons, D. (1991). *The 20-minute break: Using the new science of ultradian rhythms.* Los Angeles: Tarcher.

Rossi, E., & Ryan, M. (Eds.). (1986). *Mind-body communication in hypnosis. Vol. 3. The seminars, workshops, and lectures of Milton H. Erickson.* New York: Irvington.

Rossi, E., & Ryan, M. (Eds.). (1992). *Creative Choice in Hypnosis. Vol. 4. The Seminars, Workshops, and Lectures of Milton H. Erickson.* New York: Irvington.

Rossi, E., & Smith, M. (1990). The eternal guest: Hidden rhythms of stress and healing in everyday life. *Psychological Perspectives, 22,* 6–23.

Todorov, I. (1990). How cells maintain stability. *Scientific American, 263,* 66–75.

Veldhuis, J., & Johnson, M. (1988). Operating characteristics of the hypothalamo-pituitary-gonadal axis in men: Circadian, ultradian, and pulsatile release of prolactin and its temporal coupling with luteinizing hormone. *Journal of Clinical Endocrinology and Metabolism, 67*(1), 116–123.

Veldhuis, J., King, J., Urban, R., Rogol, A., Evans, W., Kolp, L., & Johnson, M. (1987). Operating characteristics of the male hypothalmo-pituitary-gonadal axis: Pulsatile release of testosterone and follicle-stimulating hormone and their temporal coupling with luteinizing hormone. *Journal of Clinical and Endocrinological Metabolism, 65,* 65–929.

Werntz, D. (1981). Cerebral hemispheric activity and autonomic nervous function. Doctoral thesis, University of California, San Diego.

Werntz, D., Bickford, R., Bloom, F., & Shannahoff-Khalsa, D. (1981). Selective cortical activation by alternating autonomic function. Presented at the Western EEG Society Meeting, February 12, Reno, Nev.

Werntz, D., Bickford, R., Bloom, F., & Shannahoff-Khalsa, D. (1982). Alternating cerebral hemispheric activity and lateralization of autonomic nervous function. *Human Neurobiology, 2,* 39–43.

Wever, R. (1985). Modes of interaction between ultradian and circadian rhythms: Toward a mathematical model of sleep. In H. Schulz & P. Lavie (Eds.), *Ultradian rhythms in physiology and behavior.* New York: Springer-Verlag.

Wever, R. (1989). Light effects on human circadian rhythms: A review of recent Andechs experiments. *Journal of Biological Rhythms, 4,* 161–185

Discussion by Carl Whitaker, M.D.

◆

The most important thing I got out of this presentation was the amazing tolerance of confusion that this man must have to move into the chaos of this kind of science. It takes the kind of guts I admire. About 20 years ago, I started reading *Scientific American.* I couldn't understand 90% of what I read because it was really far advanced. Looking back, it dawned on me that I had learned to tolerate reading things I did not understand. Something was happening to me, whether or not I understood it. Taking things in doesn't mean you have to understand them. It only means that you have guts enough to take them in. They may still be valuable. My old age has given me more courage. Now I read the *Science Newsletter.* It comes out every week and has about eight pages of summarizing science, from the cosmic to the subatomic. It's really very exciting. The practical tolerance of confusion to me is important. If you can tolerate confusion when you listen to patients, then you won't turn your back on them. You stay in your world with a tolerance of their living in their world. You can thereby respond and resonate even if you don't understand. You don't belong in their world, you don't know where they are, but you are able to help them with more courage as they expose their world to you.

There is a wonderful story. Alma Menn lives in San Francisco, where for 20 years she ran Soteria House for acute schizophrenics. The personnel here were chosen in a unique way. If you were going to find people who hadn't been sick before and who hadn't been on drugs to work with the acute schizophrenics, whom would you get? Obviously, it couldn't be professionals because they have theories. What the people at Soteria discovered is really amazing. They used the children of schizophrenic parents. The koan stuck me for awhile. Finally it dawned on me that those people know that craziness and love can coexist. They don't have to turn their backs on craziness because of panic. Alma Menn's motto for this place for 20 years was, "Don't just do something, stand there." I admire Dr. Rossi's guts for "standing there"—and I'll be listening.

QUESTIONS AND ANSWERS

Question: I am curious as to why you don't mention psychoimmunology or psychoneuroendocrinology as being a bridge between psychology and biology.

Rossi: Psychoimmunology and psychoneuro-immunology are both small parts of a bigger bridge—the general concept of mind–body communication. They are both examples of how the phenomenological experience of mind is in cybernetic communication with molecular messengers at all levels among mind, brain, and genes (Rossi, 1986, 1987, 1990a, 1990b, 1990c).

Question: You mentioned that you can get people to go into that ultradian rest period fairly easily because many of us experience a kind of ultradian deficit in the typical rush of modern life. I work with cancer patients. I find that they have a tremendous resistance against going into a healing ultradian state. It would seem to me that you would have to be quite conscious of when you are going into the 20-minute ultradian healing response. What if I suggest that they go into a meditation or into a relaxation or visualization at that time?

Rossi: I believe that all forms of meditation, visualization, and many other traditional approaches to holistic healing utilize the ultradian healing response as a common denominator without realizing it. I cannot help but wonder if there might not be a relationship between not being able to go into ultradian rest and having cancer. Since your cancer patients have a habitual stance of rejecting their natural mind–body signals for ultradian rest and rejuvenation, does a part of their mind–body compensate by going into hyperdrive? Are cancer patients somehow overactivating the molecular messenger systems that turn on genes that lead to cancer?

What is cancer? It is an excess of cell growth! When we trace the molecular biology of cancer, we usually find a growth factor, a growth gene, that has been turned on to excess. Could it be that some people don't know how to stop turning on excess growth? That they do not like to rest? This is only speculation, of course.

Question: So maybe the trick is to help them understand their ultradian rhythms?

Rossi: Yes. It is important to help people learn to recognize and respect their own mind–body cues. We have many mind–body cues for high performance; when we experience them, we should go for it! After every high-performance period, however, there is going to be a natural ultradian rest–rejuvenation period of 20 minutes or so when there are going to be body cues of hunger, relaxation, and restoration. These are just as important as the high-performance cues. These are the cues telling us we are entering a natural period of ultradian healing and rejuvenation.

Question: Is there anything definitely known about cancer and your speculations about a possible connection with mind–body rhythms?

Rossi: Yes. It has been pointed out that while there is a natural peak in cell division and growth for most people at around 10 P.M., in ovarian cancer, there is an extra peak at around 10 A.M. (Klevecz et al., 1987a, 1987b). That is why many cancer researchers are administering cancer drugs at certain times of the day. It would be interesting to determine whether or not mind–body approaches to cancer could be optimized by taking circadian and ultradian rhythms into account as well. At this point, the important thing is learning to recognize natural mind–body cues for ultradian rejuvenation. They are not just a cue to rest. So-called "rest" is actually a profound inner period of healing. Thus, all these people are going around with a high sense of virtue about their excessive activity. How tragic! They are victims of our culture's high-performance demands to the point where they are depriving themselves of the natural need for rest, rejuvenation, recovery. They are often victims of the stress-related illnesses when they do not heed their natural mind–body cues for ultradian recovery.

Question: I think people's resistance to getting into their healing ultradian rhythm has to do with repression and fear of pleasure. I wonder to what extent the high number of regions in the brain that are sensitive to sexual hormones are really a reflection of a need to understand and be able to read pleasure better in the body.

Rossi: I think you are absolutely right. This is the profundity of our new understanding of messenger molecules such as the sex hormones. Finally, we have a scientific basis, so to speak, for understanding much of the psychology of pleasure. It's not merely pleasure, it's the mind signal, "Hey, let me do my healing inner work. I'll let you feel good if you just sit down and rest on the outside so I can concentrate on doing the healing on the inside."

Question: Dr. Rossi, I have been aware of the brain–breath connection for a number of years, but I am quite ignorant of how it works. One of our clients said, "Well, that doesn't make sense because all the air goes into your lungs anyway." So I need to know how it works.

Rossi: We don't know everything about how it works, but I would recommend that you read my recent books in this area (Rossi & Cheek, 1988; Rossi & Nimmons, 1991), where I list much current research. Debra Werntz wrote her Ph.D. dissertation that started all this in 1981 (Werntz, 1981; Werntz et al., 1981, 1982). We believe that the brain–breath link is related to a nasal reflex, so it may have nothing to do with lungs.

Question: I am curious about the relationship between the nasal diagnostic test and the right–left-brain shift and the person's ultradian rhythms. Could you use one to try to get to the other?

Rossi: The nasal rhythm is an ultradian rhythm and it is related to cerebral hemisphere shift in brain dominance every few hours. That is the profound new insight that a lot of researchers are exploring. Yet, you can use your nasal rhythm to shift hemispheric dominance and gain access to certain autonomic nervous system controls, according to the yogis. When we look at the miraculous mind–body feats of the yogis, it is usually some aspect of their autonomic nervous system (the sympathetic and parasympathetic systems) that they can modulate via this breath–brain link.

Question: I am curious about what we commonly call "sleep disorders." Some people wake up specifically at 3 A.M., and the medical model usually tries to get them to stop that.

Rossi: I wonder if you are aware of the old psychiatry books published around 1900 that describe early-morning awakening as a sign of neurosis. Of course, I don't believe that is true. I believe that early-morning awakening means that the mind–body is overbusy, trying to deal with some emergency aspect of our lives. The mind–body allows you to get the basic, minimum sleep you can get by on and then wakes you up in those early-morning hours to deal with your problem. Asking people what is actually on their minds when they wake up at three, four, or five o'clock in the morning is the fastest way of accessing what these life emergencies are.

I believe that early-morning awakening is a psychodynamic issue, when people awaken out of a REM dream state. Dreams that come early in the morning, at 4 A.M. or 5 A.M., are usually more cognitive and reality oriented; they deal with issues that are related to the growing edge of a person's consciousness. This is an important indication of the way our consciousness and REM dream states are trying to solve inner problems. Early-morning awakening is not something annoying that should be stopped. It needs to be explored to facilitate the creative growing edge of the personality.

Question: What about the excess daytime sleepiness of narcolepsy?

Rossi: That is a psychobiological condition being researched by Dr. Dement and others in sleep clinics and laboratories. There is a valid medical model for studying narcolepsy that is very important. Narcolepsy is not simply psychodynamic, although it interacts with psychodynamic processes. Narcolepsy provides an opportunity for studying how an organic brain problem and psychodynamic issues can interact with each other to modulate behavior.

Whitaker: I would like to say something about the issue of waking up early in the morning. About 12 years ago, I frequently began to wake up at three or four o'clock in the morning. There was only a single word on my mind. I assumed it was a remnant of a dream I couldn't recall. Over a period of months, I gained the courage to get out of bed, turn on the light, and take that word fragment that came from somewhere within and expand it. This exploration has been continuing to grow until now I have about 18 inches of stuff written about it. But only twice in about 14 years has it come up during the day; it always comes up at night. It has now reached the point where it will be a whole conception, a whole pattern that I can write about for 20 minutes or so. I've never had the courage to do anything with it for publication. It is hard for me to do inner work during the day.

Rossi: My most profound personal experiences usually take place around three or four o'clock in the afternoon, which some Japanese researchers call the "breaking point" (Tsuji & Kobayashi, 1988). Their research suggests there is an arc of consciousness; from the time we are awake until around 3 P.M. or 4 P.M., there is an upward arc wherein we are oriented to the outer world. Around 3 P.M. or 4 P.M., the arc turns downward toward nutrient, self-care, sleep, dream, and inner-world rejuvenation.

Maybe this started in my work with Dr. Erickson because typically I would begin work with him at around 10 A.M. and we would work until around three or four o'clock in the afternoon. I would wheel him into the house and he would have lunch and take a nap while I would take a nap in the waiting room of his office. After being in that intense hypnotic atmosphere with him for about five hours, you can imagine (since he was usually beaming all kinds of indirect suggestions at me) how I would go into profound reveries during my nap time. I would frequently go into states of self-hypnosis, in which I would have visual hallucinations (with my eyes closed) and I would be able to experience all kinds of classical hypnotic phenomena. I really learned how to use that three or four o'clock breaking point in the afternoon for creative inner work, just when many people are tired, dragged out. That is the time of day when many people are so stressed that they feel they need a drink, and so forth.

Yet someone else, like Dr. Whitaker, may find early-morning awakening to be the best time for inner work. This is for all of us to explore: What is the time of the day when we can yield to the inner healing? I do actually turn

inward for ultradian healing three or four times a day. The afternoon period is just a special one.

Question: I picked up a book in London in 1974 written by a biologist who was taking measurements of the growth of trees. He was talking about a bioelectromagnetic current that also could measure hypnosis.

Rossi: You are probably referring to the work of Dr. Burr at Yale University in the 1940s and 1950s (Burr, 1972). Dr. Ravitz, who studied with Dr. Erickson, was the first person to have published an article about Burr's method of measuring hypnosis (Ravitz, 1950). I studied with Dr. Ravitz and used his apparatus to measure hypnosis in patients and myself for a time. These results are discussed in a book I wrote with Erickson (Erickson & Rossi, 1981). The problem with this research is that the electronic curve that purportedly measures hypnosis is the same as the curve you get when the person just goes to sleep. It is not really a marker for hypnosis alone. I call it a marker for letting go of your ego consciousness.

By the way, one day, with much trepidation, I attached the apparatus to Dr. Erickson himself and let him go into self-hypnosis to see what his curve would be like. In most people, the curve goes down if they go into self-hypnosis, but with Erickson the curve went up! I looked at the curve and said, "This man is going to blow the apparatus apart." Erickson apparently expressed more electronic energy (it is actually an electrodermal response) in a self-hypnosis state. The kind of self-hypnosis state he used to control pain was actually a kind of heightened concentration.

This validates Erickson's concept of what a therapeutic hypnotic state is. Is therapeutic hypnosis a state of passivity and deep relaxation? Or is it a state of heightened inner focus and activity? When I asked him that question, he said, "Of course, it is the more active inner state where you want a person to be." So with the Burr–Ravitz apparatus, we do not have a measure specific for hypnosis, but rather a measure of the intensity with which we are doing work within ourselves. There is certainly a lot of interesting clinical research to be done in this area on the nature of hypnosis and the wave nature of consciousness (Rossi, 1991).

REFERENCES

Burr, H. (1972). *Blueprint for immortality.* London: Neville Spearman.

Erickson, M., & Rossi, E. (1981). *Experiencing hypnosis: Therapeutic approaches to altered states.* New York: Irvington.

Klevecz, R., & Braly, P. (1987a). Circadian and ultradian rhythms of proliferation in human ovarian cancer. *Chronobiology International, 4,* 513–523.

Klevecz, R., Shymko, R., Blumenfield, D., & Braly, P. (1987b). Circadian gating of S phase in human ovarian cancer. *Cancer Research, 47,* 6267–6271.

Ravitz, L. (1950). Electrometric correlates of the hypnotic state. *Science, 112,* 341–342.

Rossi, E. (1986). *The psychobiology of mind-body healing: New concepts of therapeutic hypnosis.* New York: Norton.

Rossi, E. (1987). From mind to molecule: A state-dependent memory, learning, and behavior theory of mind-body healing. *Advances, 4*(2), 46–60.

Rossi, E. (1990a). The new yoga of the West: Natural rhythms of mind-body healing. *Psychological Perspectives, 22,* 146–161.

Rossi, E. (1990b). Mind-molecular communication: Can we really talk to our genes? *Hypnos, 17*(1), 3–14.

Rossi, E. (1990c). From mind to molecule: More than a metaphor. In J. Zeig & S. Gilligan (Eds.), *Brief therapy: Myths, methods, and metaphors.* New York: Brunner/Mazel.

Rossi, E. (1991). The wave nature of consciousness. *Psychological Perspectives 24,* 1–10.

Rossi, E., & Cheek, D. (1988). *Mind-body therapy: Ideodynamic healing in hypnosis.* New York: Norton.

Rossi, E., & Nimmons, D. (1991). *The twenty-minute break: Using the new science of ultradian rhythms.* Los Angeles: Tarcher.

Tsuji, Y., & Kobayshi, T. (1988). Short and long ultradian EEG components in daytime arousal. *Electroencephalography and Clinical Neurophysiology, 70,* 110–117.

Werntz, D. (1981). Cerebral hemispheric activity and autonomic nervous function. Doctoral thesis, University of California, San Diego.

Werntz, D., Bickford, R., Bloom, F., & Shannahoff-Khalsa, D. (1981). Selective cortical activation by alternating autonomic function. Presented at the Western EEG Society Meeting, February 12, Reno, Nev.

Werntz, D., Bickford, R., Bloom, F., & Shannahoff-Khalsa, D. (1982). Alternating cerebral hemispheric activity and lateralization of autonomic nervous function. *Human Neurobiology, 2,* 225–229.

SECTION VI

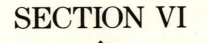

Contemporary Approaches

Short-Term Redecision Therapy in the Treatment of Clients Who Suffered Childhood Abuse

◆

Mary McClure Goulding, M.S.W.

Mary McClure Goulding, M.S.W.

Mary McClure Goulding is one of the leading exponents of Transactional Analysis. Along with her late husband, Robert Goulding, M.D., she developed an approach called Redecision therapy, which synthesizes Transactional Analysis and Gestalt. Together they founded and directed the Western Institute for Group and Family Therapy in Watsonville, Calif. The Gouldings have written two professional books about their approach, and there is an edited volume about the redecision model.

Mary Goulding has served as a member of the Board of Trustees of the International Transactional Analysis Association and is a Teaching Member of that organization. She has taught Transactional Analysis and Redecision therapy throughout Europe, South America, Japan, New Zealand, Australia, the United States, Canada, and Mexico. Her M.S.W. degree was granted in 1960 by the School of Social Welfare, University of California, Berkeley.

Mary Goulding outlines diagnostic considerations of her short-term approach to treatment, reviewing the treatment contract and diagnostic considerations, including the assessment of Ego States. She presents cases to illustrate her approach to treating childhood abuse: Change occurs when the client remembers, reenacts, uses therapeutically, and then discards early traumatic scenes.

Redecision therapy is a method that Bob Goulding and I developed from Transactional Analysis. The first transactional analyst, Eric Berne, often repeated to his trainees at meetings of the San Francisco Transactional Analysis seminar, "Each time before I begin a session, I ask myself how this person can be cured in this *one* session." Today, Berne's question is crucial. Incomes for most people are down. The cost of living is up. Therapy is expensive, and most medical plans and medical insurance pay for only a few sessions.

In this chapter, I am using as examples of our method of short-term therapy clients who were childhood victims of sexual, physical, or emotional abuse, because many therapists falsely believe that severe childhood trauma always requires long-term treatment.

DETERMINANTS OF TREATMENT LENGTH

Sometimes long-term therapy is needed, but often it is not. To estimate the length of therapy, I need to know three things:

239

1. Are both the client and therapist willing for the therapy to be brief?
2. What changes does the client want to make in his or her life?
3. What is the diagnosis?

HOW LONG DOES THE CLIENT WANT TO SPEND IN TREATMENT?

Obviously, if the therapist and client prefer long-term treatment and the client can afford it, they will be happy working together for years. I am an impatient person, and I also feel guilty if a client is spending money for treatment that could otherwise be used for a new car or a month in Hawaii, so I let all my clients know that I believe in short-term, effective treatment and that I expect every session to produce important changes for the client that the client will practice between sessions. If the client prefers a long-term approach, then a different therapist needs to be found.

THE TREATMENT CONTRACT

What do the client and therapist agree will be the therapeutic contract, or goal of treatment? Without a clear goal, therapy can wander forever through the client's past and present without personal change occurring. The specific goal, or contract, will affect the length of treatment. If the contract is the cure of a phobia, that can certainly be accomplished more quickly than curing a lifelong estrangement from other human beings. However, even when the contract suggests long-term treatment, intermittent therapy can be substituted, with perhaps three or four sessions in the beginning and then another dozen sessions spaced over a year's time. There is even an advantage to spacing sessions in this way: Clients recognize their own personal power to make life changes without the constant presence of the therapist.

THE DIAGNOSIS

What is the diagnosis? How well put together is the client? The standard diagnostic categories are helpful, particularly when the therapist is new at the therapy business, but if the standard diagnosis suggests lengthy treatment or lifetime supportive treatment without the expectation of growth or change, the very diagnosis may become a self-fulfilling prophecy. If this is true, throw out the diagnosis.

A more useful way of diagnosing clients is to assess the client's Ego States and early Child decisions. What Ego State strengths can the client muster to make the contractual changes and how well can the client sustain these changes once they are made? The following are the Ego State assessments that I find most important.

EGO STATE ASSESSMENTS

Nurturing Parent

Does the client nurture self well? Does the client's nurturing promote growth and change, or does the client tend to give self positive strokes only when sick, hurt, or abused by another person? If self-love is given primarily for unhappiness and pathology, it may take several sessions just to teach clients to nurture themselves more wisely. This self-nurturing should be learned before other issues are tackled, in order for therapeutic gains to be maintained.

To model positive nurturing, the therapist also must be willing to stroke for health rather than for pathology. This means that the therapist needs to learn to look for health in each client, recognize it, and build on it, while conveying the message that health is always more interesting and exciting than pathology.

Critical Parent

Does the client pay more attention to minor personal faults and flaws than to assets and successes? Destructive self-criticism will sabotage whatever gains a client makes in a therapy session, so clients need to learn to substitute nurturing for internal, negative diatribes.

If a client guards against self-change by using the Critical Parent to focus on the imperfections of others, therapy is impossible until this blaming is stopped. When a client is a blamer, the therapist must be perpetually on guard against becoming a judge rather than an expediter of change. Therapists can enjoy the process of shrinking the Critical Parent, both their own and their client's.

Adult Ego State

Is the Adult, or thinking part of the person, clear and uncontaminated by childhood fears and parental beliefs and prejudices? If contaminations stand in the way of achieving a contract, they need to be resolved. For example, beliefs—such as "Telling family secrets is disloyal," "All parents do the best they can," or "Children have to be beaten to keep them from becoming sinners"—obviously prevent recovery from child abuse. Child fears of revealing information, of showing vulnerability, or of "making the therapist angry" must be healed.

Natural Child

By definition, this is the healthy, happy, bright, competent core in each person that can form a base for success in therapy. In short-term therapy particularly, the therapist must make friends with this part of the client's personality and teach the client to use and strengthen whatever Child Ego State health the client possesses. For both therapist and client, an inventive Child and a keen Adult make short-term therapy both efficient and exciting.

Adapted Child

What early childhood decisions are causing problems today? Transactional analysts believe that each person makes important decisions during childhood in response to what are called injunctions. Injunctions originally are given by parents, others in the environment, or even by fate itself. Each child decides to accept or reject them. If they are accepted, the individual continues to reinforce them throughout life. In other words, adult clients still give themselves the injunctions that they once were given by others or by fate.

These are the primary injunctions that we have recognized in our work with clients: (1)

Don't exist. (2) Don't love yourself. (3) Don't be yourself. (4) Don't want or don't need. (5) Don't think. (6) Don't act. (7) Don't feel. (8) Don't grow. (9) Don't be successful. (10) Don't be a child. (11) Don't be important. (12) Don't be satisfied. (13) Don't trust. (14) Don't belong. (15) Don't be intimate. (16) Don't be well.

In Redecision therapy, the usual order of therapeutic progress is to begin with the establishment of the contract, which is the goal that the client wants but has not been able to achieve alone. When the contract is clear and agreed upon by both therapist and client, we look for early decisions that have kept the client from achieving this particular goal. Redecision therapy is a method by which clients return in fantasy to their own childhood scenes to repudiate the injunctions of childhood and make new decisions about themselves. Between sessions, clients practice carrying out the new decisions in their current lives.

SEXUAL ABUSE

EARLY WORK

The format I suggest will vary, of course, depending upon the contract, the diagnosis, and the needs and desires of the client. Sometimes the client comes in with a very clear request, which becomes the contract—for example, to recover from current effects of early abuse, such as lack of sexual responsiveness, phobias, fear of strangers or of men or women who love them. Today, particularly, because of the literature about the effects of sexual abuse, many clients already know that this is their problem and are not reluctant to deal with it. However, with other clients, sexual abuse is not mentioned or even remembered, but comes to light during the regressive work.

Child victims of sexual abuse usually believe themselves to be worthless. A first step in their recovery is to reclaim their own intrinsic worth. To use Redecision in this process, the therapist may ask the person to go back in time to some real or imagined scene before the abuse: "Pick a scene in which you are happy and worthwhile, a scene that begins and ends well. It doesn't have to be an important scene. Maybe you are playing in the sand or riding your tricycle or just lying on the floor watching the leaves make patterns on your bedroom window. Let it be a scene in which you make yourself happy, not one in which you think others make you happy." As the client tells the scene, the client and therapist together enjoy the happiness of the child.

The client then is encouraged to become a nurturing parent who holds the child and says, "You are worthwhile" and "I love you." The client alternates between being the child and being the kind, nurturing parent that every child needs. In this way, the client experiences both giving self-love and receiving that love.

Next, the client may imagine the scene of his or her own birth to assert, "This baby is worthwhile and I love this baby." The redecision is, "I am valuable, unique, and lovable, whether or not others in my childhood are capable of loving me. From now on, I will love and nurture me as the child I was and as the adult I am." Clients, of course, use whatever words are appropriate for them, rather than the therapist's words.

The abused client then may tackle difficulties in thinking, doing, and feeling. Victims of sexual abuse disown their natural abilities to think about what is happening to them, to do what is necessary to prevent recurrences, and to feel their own emotional responses. As children, they are powerless, and as adults, they may still tell themselves that they are powerless to think, feel, and do for themselves. To overcome these drastic early decisions, I suggest several fantasied returns to scenes of sexual abuse.

In order to feel safe with the process, the client may return first to the early trauma as an investigative reporter rather than as the victim. In this way, the person is free to think about what is going on without being overwhelmed by emotion. The client-reporter describes the scene, and both therapist and reporter discuss the scene until they are satisfied that all the facts are clear, including the psychological facts relevant to the child. For example: "This child seems to protect herself by not letting herself feel too much. Did you notice that, too?" Or, "I think a major rule in this house is 'See no evil.' Does that fit?" Or, "With Mother so ill, no wonder the child doesn't feel safe blowing the whistle on that bastard who's the abuser." Or, "In this household, it seems that sexual abuse is the only affection the child receives. I would expect the child to be confused about what is love and what is abuse. Does that seem true to you?" Or, "It's hard to watch this as a reporter. I kept wondering whether, when I was a child, I kept my eyes closed. I think so. Or maybe I just thought about other things."

Before the end of the session, it is important to encourage the client to become the abused child, not in the scene of the abuse, but sitting with the therapist and the investigative reporter. An empty chair is brought in for this imagined child. The client and the therapist ask the child to explain to them anything that they do not understand, while at the same time giving the imaginary child the support that they would give to any real child interviewed in this way: "We know that you are scared to talk about all this, but you are safe here in this room with us. We are taking care of you now." The therapist may ask, "Hey, is the reporter correct in believing that no one in the family knows what is going on? Or do they know and pretend not to know? I think you can answer that one better than a reporter can." The client-reporter may ask, "Is there anything I forgot to notice? Anything I didn't think about?"

As always in short-term therapy, time is left at the end of the treatment session for planning how today's therapy can be reinforced by the client between sessions. How was today's work in the childhood scenes relevant to the treatment contract? How will the client be different as a result of the work? What will the client do to nurture positive growth? While discussing this, it is important to focus on the happy scene, as well as the abusive one. In fact, an important assignment during the week would be one that involved bringing the happy, loved, worthwhile child into the client's current life.

SUBSEQUENT SESSIONS

At the beginning of each new session, the therapist asks for a report of what the client has felt, thought, and done to augment the work of the previous session, and gives positive strokes for gains that the client has made. If there are setbacks, the client and therapist explore these briefly.

In subsequent work, the client needs to return as the child victim to a scene of sexual abuse. To feel safe, clients sometimes imagine also bringing other adults into the scene to protect the child. They may choose to bring the police, a favorite teacher, or themselves as adults.

In the scene, the child must recognize, "I am not guilty." No matter what children do or do not do, they are not guilty of the abuse they are forced or seduced into enduring. Even if they enjoy the sexual acts, submit in order to get candy, or ask for a repeat of the abusive acts, they are not guilty. In the context of the scene, the client, as the child, must believe this. If the client maintains guilt, the therapist may come back to the present and discuss with the client whether or not "your own children" or "all children" are guilty if the same thing happens to them. Another method is for the client, as the child in the abusing scene, to take the position "I am guilty" and explore it until the client experiences that it simply is not true. The therapist needs to stay with this issue until it is resolved. If the client is a guilt collector, the therapist might ask how the client is guilty of his or her own conception and to deal with that guilt as well.

THE EMOTIONAL COMPONENT

Clients may enter an abusive scene in order to permit themselves emotional responses that were blocked during the actual experiences. Clients need to say, "I'm scared," and feel fear; "I'm sad," and feel the genuine sadness that is a natural reaction to being abused; and "I'm angry," and know their rage.

As in all therapy that involves experiencing feelings that were blocked, it is important for the person to be supported in whatever small degree of feeling is first expressed. The therapist will use whatever techniques are effective with a particular client to allow the client to experience emotion safely and to be pleased with the ability to express the emotion. Always encourage the client to express first the emotions that are easiest. The angry person will start with rage, and later know the underlying sadness. The sad per-

son will sob first, before learning rage without tears. The fearful client deals with fear before expressing either sadness or anger.

I support the client in learning to demonstrate feelings authentically. The expression of fear includes a tremulous voice and a trembling body, but not shouting, sobbing, or smiling. Sadness includes tears and a mournful expression, but not shouting, smiling, or trembling. Anger includes forceful gestures, loudness, and even tantrums, but does not include tears, smiles, or trembling. As a therapist, you can help your clients in all therapy work by teaching them to demonstrate their feelings unambiguously so that the whole body learns to experience rather than to repudiate emotion.

REDECISIONS

Clients need to return to scenes of sexual abuse to redecide any leftover early decisions. The client who is depressed or suicidal will have worked with this problem first, before tackling guilt, repressed emotions, or anything else. The client, as child, needs to recognize, "I didn't kill myself because of what you did to me, bad as it was, and I am not going to kill myself today." If the client does not experience suicidal thoughts or actions, this can be postponed, but I suggest that the scene be set up sometime before the end of therapy, so that the client can affirm the decision to stay alive. Every abused client can benefit from deciding, "I will take care of myself from now on, and I won't kill myself accidentally or on purpose."

Other redecisions include:

"From now on, I am going to find trustworthy people, and I will trust them. Everyone is not like you."

"From now on I am choosing my own sexual partners. I am grown now and am no longer a victim of sexual abuse."

"I can choose which sexual acts I enjoy, and enjoy them!"

"I enjoy sex today in spite of what you did to me. You are no longer in my bed."

"I can laugh and jump and dance because these actions are normal and not seductive. It was not my childlike fun that made you rape me! It was your perversity!"

After any piece of Redecision work, the client, as an adult, may imagine entering the scene to lead the child away. "Come with me. The abuse is over. From now on I will protect you."

After the Redecision work is finished, the client may decide what, if anything, to do about the abuser. This should be delayed until almost the conclusion of therapy, to avoid the danger that "changing the abuser" or "punishing the abuser" will substitute for true personal growth.

The client may decide to sue the abuser, to confront the abuser directly, to tell other family members about the childhood abuse, or to let it go. Of course, if it is possible that the abuser is currently abusing other children, local authorities must be notified immediately, without waiting for the "correct" therapeutic timing.

THE TERMINATION PHASE

The final step in the therapy is the realization that the early abuse is no longer relevant to the client's present life. When decisions about the past and present are completed, the client may want a final, fantasied confrontation with the abuser in the scene of the sexual abuse, to say good-bye to the abuser and to the scene. It is important that the client say in some way, "The abuse is over, and I am finished with it."

The client can complete all of this work in six to 12 sessions, depending on the abilities of the client and the therapist and how they work together.

PHYSICAL ABUSE

The physically abused often were painfully tortured throughout years of childhood, almost always by a parent or older sibling. Strangers or family members living outside the home are rarely involved. If a sibling or one parent was the abuser, a nonabusing parent may have cooperated in the torture by not stopping it. Physically abused clients have to come to grips with the terrible fact that they were hated by the abuser and not protected by those who professed to love them.

The work in early scenes as used for victims of sexual abuse is also relevant to the client who was physically abused during childhood. (The client may have been both physically and sexually abused or may have been the victim of one and an observer of the other. For example, in some abusing families, the boys are physically tortured and the girls are sexually abused.)

Like the client who was sexually abused, the physically abused client needs to find a happy, healthy core within the child to prove that "I am lovable even though unloved" and "I am worthy of loving treatment then and now."

The client may return to early scenes to collect facts, to experience the emotions that have been blocked, and to recognize that the abuser and the onlookers were guilty, but the victim was and is not. Just like the victim of sexual abuse, the physically abused child is never guilty. No matter what a child does that is wrong, no child instigates or deserves physically painful punishment.

It is important that the therapist focus on having the client decide to live, because many physically abused people have been silently suicidal during their entire lives. Even before they are 3 years old, they may, during beatings, have wished to be dead, and these tragic wishes remain "in their bones," even when their adult lives are rich and seemingly happy.

To decide to live, the client enters a fantasied scene in which the abuse is taking place, and says, "I will not kill myself no matter how much I am suffering." The child did not commit suicide in childhood in spite of the terrible fear, the pain, the humiliation, and the lack of love. The child did not commit suicide even though the loved, and sometimes worshipped, adult, the nonabuser, did nothing to stop the abuse. In the scene, the child needs to acknowledge this verbally, and recognize, "I am a survivor." Also, the client as a child decides, "I didn't kill myself over your torture, and I sure won't kill myself in the future." The client may enter the scene as an effective rescuer, saying, "Come away from this scene! I love you. From now on, I am taking care of you. I am going to fix our life so we won't have to tolerate any unnecessary suffering from now on."

The client, in other sessions, will redecide any other early decisions that still stand in the way of a healthy life, such as decisions never to feel, show feelings, be too successful, be less than perfect, love, trust, or be close to other human beings.

Before the therapy is ended, I ask the client to decide, "I will never under any circumstances abuse my own children or anyone else."

EMOTIONAL ABUSE

When a child is downgraded and left to feel humiliated and helpless, the child is the victim of emotional abuse. As in the treatment of the sexually and physically abused, the victim of emotional abuse needs help in developing a sense of self-worth and a functioning Nurturing Parent. Emotionally abused children grow into adults who belittle themselves and treat themselves with the same emotional cruelty that was used against them when they were children. The therapist needs to underline the lunacy and destructiveness of self-inflicted emotional torture. Humor, tenderness, and love all can be part of the therapists' tools in helping clients learn to stop harassing and to start loving themselves.

CASE EXAMPLE

Bob Goulding and I have a video (1986) that includes a one-session treatment of a man who suffered chronic emotional abuse from his ignorant, vindictive father. The man, who is about 40 years old, is successful in his work and his family life. He came to us to be cured of a minor speech phobia. When he has to make a speech, he overworks preparing for it and fears that it will not be well received. We ask him to remember a childhood scene in which he is being criticized, and to describe it. The client explains that his father was verbally abusive throughout the client's childhood. He chooses a scene in which his father is telling a neighbor, "My son is stupid. He'll never amount to a thing. He's lazy and no good . . ." As the father continues his verbal abuse, neither the neighbor nor the child respond.

Leaving the scene, the client explains, "In order to stand up for myself, I'd have to let them know what I feel. I will never do that. I just stay there and endure." He says that his childhood heroes were Indians, about whom he had learned in books. Whenever his father derided him, he

pretended to himself that he was a stoic Indian brave, enduring torture without letting anyone see his hurt. In this scene, as in many scenes with the father, he grits his teeth and shows no feeling. The client is asked how this scene might be connected to his speech phobia. He says, "If I am prepared enough, if I don't make a single mistake, if I do it so well, I defend against anybody who might criticize me and say I'm no good."

We hear three injunctions: Don't succeed. Don't feel. Endure. The first is given by the father to the son and the second and third are given by the son to himself. The client needs to repudiate them.

We suggest to the client that he return to the scene and tell his father that he is hurting. He does not want to do this. "I have such a reluctance to telling him I hurt!"

Bob and I do not believe in pushing against resistance when there are other options. In this case, there are several. He can return to the scene and tell his father, "I won't tell you that I am hurting. There is no way you can make me tell you I am hurting." And he can stay emphatically on that side until he finds a way to switch. Or he can say, "I have such a reluctance," to his father, and proceed from there. He can take his adult self with him to talk to the father. He can tell his feelings to someone else, such as the neighbor. We suggest that alternative.

After imagining that his father leaves the scene, he tells the neighbor, "I hurt." He speaks with true stoicism. I suggest that he repeat his words. After the third time, he says, "I really hurt! I feel so bad!" He lets himself cry and is no longer the brave Indian.

When he has completed that scene, we ask if he now will pick a way to confront his father. He does, choosing to begin with, "Back off. I am not you."

That is a most important statement. We suggest he expand on it by telling his father the ways in which he and his father are different. He says, "I can think! I don't humiliate people! Thank God, thank me, for all the books I read that showed me another kind of life! I am so glad I am not you!" He recognizes that his father was unintelligent, uneducated, and unappreciated. He acknowledges that he himself is successful in life. He is even, in spite of his fears, a successful public speaker.

He imagines that he is at the podium, lecturing to a large professional audience. We suggest that his father is entering the auditorium. The client realizes that his father would not even understand what he is saying: "My father wouldn't want to listen. He's jealous of me and always has been, but the others in the audience want to hear me. They came to hear me." The client discovers that he is no longer afraid.

We suggest that he imagine forgetting what to say next, losing his place, and then answering a trick question from a member of the audience. He handles these imagined situations without fear. The ultimate test, of course, is giving the speech to a real audience, which he does successfully later in the month.

SUMMARY

In summary, adults who were sexually, physically, or emotionally abused in childhood need therapists who believe that they can recover from past trauma and let the trauma go. The clients need to know that they do not have to be "scarred for life" because of terrible childhood experiences; they can heal themselves quite quickly and go on to happy and fulfilling lives.

REFERENCES

Goulding, R. L., & Goulding, M. (1986). *Redecision video.* San Francisco: International Transactional Analysis Association.

SUGGESTED READINGS

Goulding, R. L., & Goulding, M. (1978). *The power is in the patient.* San Francisco: TA Press.
Goulding, M. M., & Goulding, R. L. (1979). *Changing lives through Redecision therapy.* New York: Brunner/Mazel.
Goulding, M. M., & Goulding, R. L. (1989). *Not to worry.* New York: Morrow.

Discussion by Judd Marmor, M.D., Ph.D.

◆

It is a pleasure to have been invited to discuss the presentation of Mary Goulding. The work that she and Bob Goulding have done over the years in evolving their particular approach to therapy has received widespread and deserved recognition. What fascinates me as a student of the psychotherapeutic process, one who has devoted much of his professional life to trying to understand and recognize the common denominators that enable various forms of psychotherapy to be more or less equally effective with their patients, is trying to see how much of the Gouldings' method can be translated into terms that I have defined over the years as being essential ingredients in the psychotherapeutic process. My interest in the Gouldings' work is further enhanced by my own interest in shortening the length of the psycho-therapeutic process, and in the work I have done in recent years with short-term dynamic psychotherapy.

The first point that Ms. Goulding makes is one that other short-term therapists also have come to recognize—that the severity of the early trauma does not in itself preclude the possibility of a short-term psychotherapeutic approach. Her criteria for deciding what makes a client or patient suitable for a short-term approach are similar to those used by short-term dynamic psychotherapists. For example, the first point she makes is, "What does a client want to change in his or her life?" This deals with the motivation of the patient. Ms. Goulding's emphasis, as is the emphasis of others in the field, is on the strength of the client's willingness to change. As David Malan has emphasized in his book *The Frontiers of Short-Term Psychotherapy*, this motivation to change should imply not merely a wish to get rid of symptoms that are ego-dystonic, but rather a willingness to make fundamental changes in one's way of thinking, feeling, and acting in relation to life's challenges.

Ms. Goulding's second criterion is: "Are both the client and the therapist willing for the therapy to be brief?" This deals with the issue of mutual agreement to set a time limit for the therapy. This setting of a time limit, whether it be a specific number of sessions or simply the fact that it is going to be a limited therapeutic experience, is a critical factor in creating an ambiance that emphasizes autonomy and self-determination on the part of the patient.

Ms. Goulding's third criterion is one that she calls "the Ego State strengths" that the client must muster to achieve these changes. This is a factor that short-term dynamic psychotherapists emphasize in terms of "ego strengths," or, as I prefer to call them, "ego-adaptive capacities." Her concepts in this regard are essentially similar to those of other short-term therapists.

Then Ms. Goulding goes on to talk of the goal of treatment in terms of the "contract" that is set up between the therapist and the client. This is what more traditional therapists discuss in terms of the "focus of treatment." All short-term therapists agree that for the therapy to be successful, it must have a specific central focus, which becomes the agreed-upon target of the work. Although Ms. Goulding discusses this in terms of a contract, she is essentially talking about the same thing.

Further, as I listened to her, I found myself resonating positively to the spirit with which she works with her clients, with her emphasis on encouraging the client's autonomy and sense of his or her own responsibility, and on the therapist's abjuring the role of an authoritarian parent in the client–therapist interaction. Her focus is also on emphasizing the client's strengths rather than defects. I think this is a fundamental point. For too many years, there has been a tendency on the part of psychotherapists to focus on bringing to light—and by this I mean bringing into conscious awareness—the patient's unconscious defenses, anxieties, fears, and inhibitions, forgetting that the neurotic patient equally tends to repress and forget, or be unaware of, his or her strengths and positive attributes. The spirit of the Goulding relationship with the patient is one of constantly encouraging an awareness of these strengths and affirming the therapist's faith in the patient's ability to resolve his or her difficulties. Although Ms. Goulding talks of this in terms of the therapists not functioning as critical parents, she is essentially emphasizing the importance of the therapist being an accepting, nonjudgmental, and noncritical person. Her emphasis on helping to bring what she calls "the inventive exciting child" in the client's personality into functional awareness is a meaningful part of that interaction, emphasizing, as it does, the client's potential for bringing creativity to bear in resolving his or her adaptive challenges in life.

Where I would tend to take some issue with Ms. Goulding is with regard to her assumption that children consciously "decide" to accept or reject parental injunctions in their early childhood. Perhaps her reason for putting it this way is to emphasize the correct fact that it is possible for the "grown-up child" or client to reject these injunctions. However, that is not as easy or as simple as it seems, and indeed, this is really the critical core of the psychotherapeutic challenge that every psychotherapist faces. I do *not* think that children are able to make an independent choice or rational appraisal of parental behavior toward them. Because children are, in fact, dependent on their parents, they have a need to believe that their parents are all-knowing and all-powerful. Thus when parents treat children badly, children almost invariably conclude that they have done something wrong, that they have been bad children, and that that is why their all-wise and all-knowing parents are treating them that way. Indeed, the relationship of a helpless and young child to parents has often been compared to that of a patient under hypnosis. Whatever the parent says to the young child carries an enormous load of conviction for the child, and if that injunction or conviction is repeated over and over again over a period of years, it can become powerfully fixed in the child's mind. Children, in other words, become powerfully conditioned to believe in, and fully accept, the injunctions, convictions, taboos, and values that their parents have repetitively imposed upon them. In the language of psychoanalysis, we say that children tend to introject parental values and parental criticisms, and then carry the critical or judgmental parent around as a part of themselves, as a "critic within" or as a "tyrannical superego." Enabling the traumatized child to undo these patterns is the critical challenge of therapy, and it is not as easy as simply making the patient or client aware of the fact that the parental injunctions were unreasonable, unfair, or even harmful.

The way in which therapists accomplish this involves techniques that are quite common to most forms of therapy, even though different words are used in describing them. The patient is encouraged to recall, relive, and experience emotionally the pain and trauma of these early experiences. This is a form of *abreaction.* The therapist helps the client to understand cognitively how his or her psychopathology developed and, explicitly or implicitly, points in the direction in which the patient must move to overcome the early traumatic conditioning. In addition, the therapist, by explicit or implicit encouragement and approval or disapproval cues, is engaged in a form of powerful *operant conditioning* that is intended to move the client toward greater autonomy and self-acceptance. By enabling the client to reexperience the traumatic events in a new setting in a relationship with a kinder, more beneficent, and more understanding authority figure, the client also has a corrective emotional experience, which is a powerful form of operant conditioning in itself. In addition, in many ways, both subtle and overt, there are elements of suggestion, persuasion, and identification with the therapist; then, through a patient process of rehearsal and reeducation, the client is moved toward the constructive goals of greater autonomy and self-acceptance. Critical to all of this is the quality of the client–therapist relationship, because that is the matrix in which all of these other processes take place. It is clear from what we have heard that the particular emotional experience that Mary Goulding's clients have is one that tends to facilitate their moving relatively rapidly toward new adaptive potentials.

I would like to make one additional point about the rather popular trend these days to place enormous emphasis on early sexual abuse. I do not in any way wish to be misunderstood as implying that such things do not take place, but I do wish to emphasize the danger of creating an atmosphere, both in our society and in our psychotherapeutic milieu, in which we assume that every affectionate gesture from an older person toward a young child is a move in the direction of sexual abuse. With the McMartin school case, we recently went through a period in Southern California during which we saw the dangers of this kind of hysterical assumption mounting into a form of Salem witch-hunt, with many innocent people unjustly implicated as accused child abusers. Let us try to keep a cool head and to maintain an objective view toward all of this. Sexual abuse *does* take place, but not all of the physical affection between older people and younger children is necessarily a form of sexual abuse, and we should not create a kind of distrust in children toward older relatives that deprives them of the satisfaction of loving and warm relationships with these family members. Far more frequent than either sexual abuse or physical abuse, and far more deleterious in the long run for the growth of healthy personalities, is the *deprivation* of caring love and of genuine acceptance by parents and parent surrogates, and that is the cardinal issue that most of us have to deal with over and over again in our disturbed patients and clients.

QUESTIONS AND ANSWERS

Question: I am working with someone who is self-punitive. She has an eating disorder and it seems so difficult for her to make a redecision not to punish herself. I am struggling on how to help her with that.

Goulding: I work first with a no-suicide and no self-harm contract. If you can use humor, you can lighten it up. If all the strokes she gets are for punishing herself, she gets your attention and everybody else's for pathology. I might ask,

"If you were eating the way you need to eat, the way others think you ought to eat, what would you be doing for excitement?"

Question: I am working with a number of clients right now who have a strong sense that something happened. They have vague feelings, but no pictures. I am having a hard time having them access an actual memory. I also work with biofeedback. I noticed that when they start getting the sense and feelings of things, the meters jump. Yet they can't actually get a picture, and they doubt that something actually happened.

Goulding: There is a lot of controversy on this issue. It is very stylish these days to assume that if anyone has a vague memory of sexual mistreatment, you have to find it. They have to confront the family and do all that sort of stuff. First of all, why are they with you? What is the contract? What do they want to change? How does this vague feeling of being molested fit the person's present life? I would want to work with a client to find a redecision, such as, "I am going to live whether or not I was molested." "I am going to find partners who are trustworthy whether or not I was molested." Then the client could drop the issue.

Question: If the abuse was primarily a depreciation of love or understanding, is there a particular way you could work with that other than going into the past?

Goulding: Yes, and I am glad you mentioned that. I agree that most clients have a deprivation of love or a deprivation of understanding. You can have them return to an early scene and say, "What I need is . . ." After that, self-parenting is very important.

I know one woman who was raised in an efficient but loveless home. It was in a rural area and they worked on how to get the eggs and get them sold and how the corn was planted. She reparented herself. She read stories on parenting. She watched television to find signs of good parenting. In a fantasy, she then started when she was a newborn and spent 10 minutes every night reparenting herself. She took herself as a 10-year-old to get milk shakes: No one had ever

taken her to get milk shakes when she was growing.

Self-parenting is very helpful. You don't have to spend the rest of your life being deprived because you had deprivation, and you can also look for others to nurture and then find people to nurture you.

Question: If I understand Dr. Marmor correctly, he is skeptical that in just a few sessions a client can redecide his or her original reactions to basic parental injunctions. Is this the core of your theory and work? Would you comment further on this?

Goulding: I know that people can redecide in a very few sessions, and they have to practice what they redecided. If they redecide, for instance, to want, it will take a lot of practice. I see therapy as a wonderful, dramatic time when they redecide, which takes 20 minutes. Then there will be a lot of hard work putting it into practice. Here is why I like group. Clients can come back and say to the group, "This is what I've done." The group can discuss it, and the client gets a lot of strokes. If, for instance, the problem entails "never having said what you want," you know that right away because these clients don't make a contract worth a damn. They wait to see what you want for them. They need to practice saying what they want in simple sentences. They can tell store clerks what they want and buy what they want. Often, they are the type of people who go into the store to buy a pair of shoes and spend all day there because no pair of shoes is quite perfect. Or they buy and are disappointed. Then they need to give themselves permission to buy shoes and to throw them out if they don't want them, without hassling themselves. In other words, the practice counts, not just the redecision.

Marmor: I think that part of the confusion that exists in various mental health professions is in the concept of cure as a kind of end point. It is as though when patients leave us, they are supposed to be cured, to be all better. I think that is a profound misunderstanding. Good therapy and successful therapy open the door to growth and to change. They open the potential for growth and change. If we have done that, we have helped our clients. From then on, as Mary correctly says, we have to keep working on it. From time to time, it even may be helpful for patients to come back to get a sort of recharge. That is what therapy is all about. It is not a cure that makes somebody an AAA piece of government-inspected beef.

Ruth McClendon: I will exercise my moderator's license to comment on this: My experience has shown that, unfortunately, as a therapist, I am not privileged to experience most redecisions that have been made. The work gets started in my office and the "Aha" happens as the client is driving down the highway and realizes, when stopping at a stop sign, that other people have rights and privileges also. The "Aha" gets made while sitting at your desk or when preparing a meal. Many redecisions are reported to me—sometimes years later.

Question: One of the greatest obstacles to redecision is the loyalty that the client feels toward the abusing parent. He or she often needs approval from this abusing parent and this is an obstacle to putting the abuse to rest. Could you comment on that?

Goulding: Yes, loyalty to the abuser can be an obstacle. Find out if clients are treating their own children abusively. If they are, your first job is to stop the abuse. If they are not, you can congratulate them and say, "Good for you." You can also do a type of Greek chorus. As they talk to you, you can talk for them: "That really must have hurt." "That is a terrible thing." "That's a very sick woman you are talking about there." This can be more effective than confronting resistance head on.

Question: Could you give me a little guidance, or a few words, or clinical examples regarding trying to elicit a focal goal of therapy? I work with a military population in a relatively isolated area overseas. I see a tremendous number of young, unsophisticated individuals who had a deprived, stilted upbringing, during which self-expression was never reinforced. Although they are referred to me with vague intense feelings of distress, they find it difficult to come up with focal goals. They often express vague hopes

that will actually recreate an abusive situation in which I will admonish them into improving or they want me magically to hypnotize them. It is difficult for me to elicit a goal that will work in the therapy.

Goulding: You need to keep saying, "Hey, let's pretend that this therapy is the most successful experience you have ever had, and if it goes on for six months (or however long you have planned to see them), how are you going to be when it is all over? Whom do you know who has a life that is different from yours that you admire?" Just keep on asking those kinds of questions. Don't do regressive work until you and they have talked about this for awhile.

Question: Could you mention a few examples of focal goals that patients might have?

Goulding: One of the goals might be to know what you want. It could be to stand up for yourself, rather than to let your therapist pick your goals for you. I might ask, "When you were a little girl, who picked your dresses?" And then: "Aha, so you are waiting for me as your mother to pick your dresses."

Question: Many of my clients have been abused physically, sexually, and mentally. They come in and they are angry at everybody in the family. Where do you find is the best place to start in dealing with someone who is so angry that you can't find a focus?

Goulding: The best place to start is where the client wants to start. You can grant that the client has had a terrible life up to now, but, "What little piece would start making your life better?" Really, the place to start will be whatever the client can do for himself or herself. Granted that back then it was terrible, now clients need to find out what to do for themselves. It may be something basic, like discovering how to get child care.

Question: Many of these patients view themselves as the victim in the family. It is as though every time they try to do something independently, the family descends on them like a ton of bricks.

Goulding: The family often does. As soon as they make a little bit of money, the family often tries to borrow it. They need to learn how to say "No" to you and to the family, and then learn how to say "Yes." They are fun clients, by the way, if they have a little spark or a little fun in them. You can give them the ongoing thrust that they need. They need a good parent, and you can be it.

The Virtues of Our Faults: A Key Concept of Ericksonian Therapy

Jeffrey K. Zeig, Ph.D.

Jeffrey K. Zeig, Ph.D.

Jeffrey K. Zeig (Ph.D., 1977, Georgia State University) is the Founder and Director of The Milton H. Erickson Foundation in Phoenix, Ariz. He organized the International Congresses on Ericksonian Approaches to Hypnosis and Psychotherapy held in 1980, 1983, and 1986, as well as the Fourth International Congress on Ericksonian Approaches to Hypnosis and Psychotherapy entitled, "Brief Therapy: Myths, Methods, and Metaphors." Zeig is the architect of The Evolution of Psychotherapy Conferences.

Zeig received the Milton H. Erickson Award from the Netherlands Society of Clinical Hypnosis for outstanding contributions to the field of Clinical Hypnosis and the Milton H. Erickson Award of Scientific Excellence in Writing in Hypnosis from the American Society of Clinical Hypnosis. He has written one book and edited eight books on Ericksonian therapy, brief therapy, and eclectic approaches to psychotherapy. Additionally, a book about his work appears in Italian, and another in Spanish.

Zeig presents a key concept of Ericksonian therapy. Cornerstone principles of an Ericksonian approach that relate to this key concept also are presented and illustrated. Ericksonian methods can be incorporated into any psychotherapeutic discipline to enhance therapeutic effectiveness.

When we learn to become therapists, we learn particular ways of thinking as much as specific content. These ways of thinking become perceptual lenses. Lenses have advantages in that they focus us on important aspects of the patient. They have disadvantages because they also limit perspectives. Additionally, lenses act as filters to the degree that our perceptions circumscribe subsequent actions. In our early

training, perhaps in graduate school, lenses are "surgically implanted" by our teachers. They then become our heirlooms, to be carefully transmitted to patients and subsequent generations of students.

Having studied the hypnotic psychotherapy of Milton Erickson for more than 17 years, I have developed a particular way of thinking about therapy. I want to explore one "small" concept that has its roots in traditional hypnosis, but occupied a central place in Erickson's work. Indeed, it could be considered a wide-

The author is grateful to Margaret Ryan for her editorial assistance.

angle lens of Ericksonian methods. Although the concept is easy to understand, it is a difficult concept to master. To loosely paraphrase Jay Haley (1982): If I experientially understood this one idea, new worlds would open before me as far as doing psychotherapy is concerned.

In Ericksonian fashion, I will present the concept to you through a series of vignettes and scenes. This follows my commitment to the idea that dynamic experiences should precede dynamic understandings. Therefore, I would like you to react to the following situations and discover what they have in common. You should be able to describe the central theme in one word.

ILLUSTRATION OF THE CONCEPT

SITUATION 1

As you sit in your chair, you do not have to pay attention to the wall in front of you, to the darkness of the floor, to the color of your clothing, or to the changes in the blink of an eye. And yet you cannot help but pay attention to sounds outside the room, to sounds around you, to the sounds of your own breathing, to the sound changes that gradually occur to you. You can also pay attention to the sensation of your feet on the floor, to the pressure of your body being supported by the furniture, to the presence or absence of a head rest, back rest, arm rest, seat rest, foot rest.

And, in hypnosis, you merely limit the number of foci of your attention, and you allow yourself to attend to what is immediately relevant.

SITUATION 2

Recently, a couple requested hypnotherapy to stop smoking. He was in his 40s; she was in her 30s. Both were currently in therapy and were referred to me for habit control. As is my custom, I arranged to see them together. I suggested they dispose of their smoking material and put away their ashtrays the night before the session. They would have their last cigarette prior to going to bed, and they were to come in "uncomfortable" so that I could learn about their unique difficulties in order to individualize therapy.

When they arrived in my office, they reported that they had followed my suggestion, which I regarded as a positive prognostic indicator. In my interview, I asked if they had conquered other habits, and I learned that both of them had had extensive treatment for addictions: They were "working a program" in Alcoholics Anonymous and Narcotics Anonymous. I inquired about the husband's pattern of using alcohol and narcotics prior to treatment. He would say to his wife, "I just stopped for a beer," when actually he had imbibed hard liquor and drugs. His pattern of denial included bold lies.

I tried to ascertain the styles of the couple. They were both blue-collar workers. The man was superficially gregarious, but distant, avoiding intimacy. In fact, they had had some couples therapy at the wife's request in order to develop more closeness. The woman appeared tough, independent, rebellious, and sardonic. She had arthritis. "How do you deal with the discomfort?" I asked. She replied, "If I have pain, my body says, 'Take it easy,' and I take a bath or a nap." Her pain never caused her to miss work. The husband also had a high pain tolerance.

I switched abruptly from the topic of pain, knowing I would return to it shortly. I asked, "I know it is difficult to accurately describe the urge to smoke, but could you try to describe it?" As they struggled to articulate the components of the urge to smoke, I added, "I would like you to realize that you could think about the urge in many senses as being a 'pain.'" They could accept that the urge to smoke was a pain in many senses.

I then suggested they could have a private signal system that only would be used between the two of them. I reminded them that all couples have a private language that outsiders might not fully comprehend. If either one said the phrase, "that pain," as in "I am having *that pain*," it would be understood as indicating the experience of a discomforting urge, "which really is not an urge, but a pain." Once the signal was established, each could help the other.

I indicated to the husband: "Here's what you can do. Whenever you say to your wife, 'I am experiencing *that pain*,' she can touch you. She can give you a hug, or put her hand on your lap, or just gently take your hand. When you say, 'I am experiencing that pain,' she will immediately know to reach out." This idea cheered the wife, who openly desired a more intimate marriage. The husband blanched; his response was agreeable but muted.

I turned to the wife: "If you say to your husband, 'I am experiencing *that pain*,' he is to give you space. You are to have five minutes to yourself. During those five minutes, you can take a nap, you can do anything you want. But you must get time by yourself." The wife blanched; her response was agreeable but muted.

I explained to the husband that there was a second part of the therapy; he was to lie to and cheat on his wife on a regular basis. In fact, he should lie and cheat three times a day. He was compelled to lie and cheat. It would be a good idea if he did it at breakfast, lunch, and dinner, because then he would not forget. We agreed on what suitable lying and cheating would entail. The lies would have to be relatively minor and could not be about addictions. For example, he could say that he took out the garbage, when actually he had not. He could say that he did an errand, when actually he had not.

Her job was to catch him. At the end of the day, they would have an earnest conversation. She would say what she believed to be the incidents of lying and cheating. He would say what the lying and the cheating really entailed.

A third part of the therapy for the husband consisted of a simple thought-blocking technique, which could be used whenever he experienced *that pain*. The painful urge could be considered "an invader"; this was part of the "artillery" that he could use to bolster his lines of defense.

The technique is called "Visual–Auditory–Tactile 4, 3, 2, 1." He was to think to himself the sentence stem, "Now I am aware of ____," and silently say four visual things: "Now I am aware of the wall. Now I am aware of the darkness of the floor. Now I am aware of the color of my clothing. Now I am aware of changes in the blink of an eye." Then he would say four auditory things: "Now I am aware of the sounds outside the room. Now I am aware of the sounds around me. Now I am aware of the sound of my breathing. Now I am aware of the sound of

changes." Then he would describe four tactile things: "Now I am aware of the sensation of my feet on the floor. Now I am aware of the pressure of my body supported by the furniture." And so on.

After completing four sentence stems with visual, auditory, and tactile words, he was to complete three stems that were visual, auditory, and tactile; then two; and then one. He was told it was not so much a distraction technique as it was a method to "lose your mind and come to your senses." After finishing the exercise, he would have a heightened sensory awareness. He might even feel a bit "high."

I ended the session by saying that we had done enough. We would meet the next day for more therapy, which would entail formal hypnosis. I would meet individually with each for half an hour. My implication was that they would have no problem in maintaining a smoke-free environment until we next met for the "real" treatment.

The next day, I met with the wife first. She glibly said, "I have decided to stop smoking. I had no problem staying off cigarettes since I saw you last. It's just like alcohol—I decided to stop." I replied: "I would like you to be careful that you are not too cheerful about stopping smoking. If your husband sees that you are not struggling, he may have a problem. So, even if it is not true—*especially* if it is not true—tell him on a regular basis that you *are* having difficulty stopping smoking, because I think it is easier for you to stop smoking than it is for your husband. We both know truthfully that he is kind of a baby. And, I do not want him inadvertently to sabotage you."

The wife agreed that her husband could be "a baby" about difficulties, and we discussed ways in which he might inadvertently sabotage her if he were smoking and she was not. I conducted a "ceremonial" trance with her so that she would have something to discuss with her husband and he would know that she had received treatment. In the trance, I told her stories about adolescents who had learned to do things for their own benefit, even if authority required those things to be done. The therapy for her was complete.

The husband arrived and I met with him individually. He said, "I laughed all day yesterday about your ideas. Why did you tell me to cheat?" He added, "I did not say, 'I have *that pain,*' to my wife. I was comfortable." I admonished him, "You are really going to ruin the therapy. You *have to* tell your wife 'I have *that pain,*' " I continued: "You know, your wife really wants to be helpful. She has a veneer of being tough. She might be suffering more than she lets on through her veneer. Inside, she is much more sensitive than she discloses. In fact, it could be more difficult for her to stop smoking than it is for you." He agreed with my assertions. I added that because she also had a helpful side, he should say, "I have *that pain,*" as often as possible so that she could reach out to him, touch him, hug him, and feel useful to him in the process of their quitting smoking. If he only had a little discomfort, he could exaggerate it and say, "I have *that pain,*" Even if he was comfortable, he could bend the truth a little and say, "I have *that pain.*"

His trance consisted of learning self-hypnosis to "bolster his lines of defense." Similar to the "Visual–Auditory–Tactile 4, 3, 2, 1" technique, he would use self-hypnosis to abort any urge. I presented the method as a hypnotic *program* that he would *work.*

Five months after the sessions, I received a note from the husband, who indicated that they were both off cigarettes. They were grateful for my help, although they did not understand exactly why my methods had worked.

SITUATION 3

Here is another case with a similar theme. Consider the interaction between Jeff Zeig, an aspiring student of therapy, and Milton Erickson (Zeig, 1985). At the time, I was an avid pipe smoker. It was a hobby. I had a number of expensive pipes, custom tobacco blends, and other accoutrements. It fit with my image of being "the young psychologist."

Erickson saw me smoking my pipe in his backyard prior to our session. When we met, he began a long, lighthearted story about a friend of his who was a pipe smoker. The friend, he said, was awkward. He was awkward because he did not know where to place the pipe in his mouth. Should he place it in

the center of his mouth, a centimeter to the right of center, a centimeter to the left of center? He was awkward.

He was awkward because he did not know how to put the tobacco in the bowl. Should he use his pipe tool? Should he use his thumb? Should he use his forefinger? He was awkward.

The friend was awkward because he did not know how to light the pipe. Should he light the pipe by putting the flame in front of the bowl? In the back of the bowl? On the right side of the bowl? On the left side of the bowl? He was awkward.

All the time, I was thinking, "Why is he telling me this story? I don't look awkward smoking a pipe." Erickson continued. The friend was awkward when he held the pipe. Should he support the pipe with his left hand or with his right hand? Should he hold the bowl of the pipe or the stem? He was awkward.

The friend was awkward because he did not know how to blow the smoke out of his mouth. Should he blow the smoke up? Should he blow it down? Should he blow it to the side? He was awkward.

He was awkward because he did not know where to put the pipe down. Should he hold it in his hand? Should he put it on the table? He was awkward.

This story seemed to go on for an hour. I never knew there were so many ways of being awkward while smoking a pipe.

The day after that session, I left Phoenix to drive back to the San Francisco area, where I lived at the time. When I reached California, I said to myself, "I'm not smoking anymore." I put away my pipe forever. I did not want to smoke a pipe. I never smoked a pipe again. Never.

Part of Erickson's technique was pattern disruption. I became overly conscious of the process of smoking, which effectively *made* me awkward. Moreover, if there was anyone to whom I did not want to seem awkward, it was Milton Erickson. Subsequently, smoking a pipe did not seem appealing. But the credit for deciding to stop was all mine. The motive force came from me. Erickson did little. He did not tell me to stop smoking. He did not warn me about health hazards. He just told me a story. I was the one who did something constructive.

SITUATION 4

Consider a patient who described low self-esteem as follows: 1) He would wonder if he had the ability to cope adequately with the required task. 2) He would decide, "No, it's not present." 3) He would develop a heavy feeling in his stomach "like a stone."

My hypnotic induction with this man was the following sequence (Zeig, 1988):

Make yourself physically comfortable and then perhaps you can watch some spot and use that to focus your attention . . . all along just waiting, for a certain signal, a certain sensation, a certain sign in your body that you know will be there. A feeling I will name later.

(1) But first, mentally, the process can interest you. Because you can be thinking to yourself about the eye changes, and you can be wondering to yourself, "Will my eye behavior change? Will that fluttering sensation be there? Will there be an alteration in my blink reflex?"

(2) And then you can decide, "Yes, there can be that steadiness around the eye," and, "Yes, there can be that pleasant fluttery feeling," and "Yes, there can be that change in reflex."

(3) Then there is that physical sensation; for example, there is a feeling that can be described as a kind of numbness that can happen in the center . . . of your hands. And later there can be an uplifting movement. . . .(p. 372)

UTILIZATION REVISITED

Reflect on the four experiences I just presented, I have asked you to ascertain what these situations have in common. What theme can be found in each? The theme can be described in one word: *utilization.*

Utilization is a central principle in Ericksonian therapy. It is a hallmark of the Ericksonian approach (Zeig, 1988). Moreover, it is an important wellspring from which successful psychotherapy often proceeds. Erickson described the utilization method in this way (Erickson, 1965).

Therapists wishing to help their patients should never scorn, condemn, or reject any part of the patient's conduct simply because it is obstructive, unreasonable, or even irrational. The patient's behavior is part of the problem brought into the office. It constitutes the personal environment within which the therapy must take effect. It may constitute the dominant force in the total patient/doctor relationship. So whatever the patient brings into the office is in some way both a part of them and a part of their problem. The patient should be viewed with a sympathetic eye, appraising the totality which confronts the therapist. In so doing, therapists should not limit themselves to an appraisal of what is good and reasonable as offering a possible foundation for therapeutic procedures. Sometimes, in fact, many more times than is realized, therapy can be firmly established on a sound basis only by the utilization of silly, absurd, irrational and contradictory manifestations. One's professional dignity is not involved, but one's professional competence is. (p. 213, Collected Papers, Vol. IV)

In another article, Erickson (1952) augmented these ideas: Although he was specifically discussing the induction of deep hypnosis, the concepts also are applicable to psychotherapy.

Such recognition and concession to the needs of subjects and the utilization of their behavior do not constitute, as some authors have declared, "unorthodox techniques" based upon "clinical intuition," instead they constitute a simple recognition of existing conditions, based upon full respect for subjects as functioning personalities. (p. 155, Collected Papers, Vol. I)

What is utilization? It is the *readiness of the therapist to respond strategically to any and all aspects of the patient or the environment.* Utilization is the therapist's trance. Stephen Gilligan (personal communication) described the state of the hypnotherapist as an externally focused trance as compared with the internally directed trance of the patient. This externally focused trance is a state of response readiness—readiness to seize the moment by capturing and utilizing whatever happens.

Hypnosis can be defined objectively as a state of response readiness because the patient assumes a posture of responding to subtle cues presented by the therapist. In interactive terms, hypnosis can be defined as the response readiness of the patient as a function of the response readiness of the therapist.

If the therapist wants to promote a state of response readiness within the patient, the therapist should be willing to show the same kind of responsiveness. The therapist models a readiness to discern and utilize even minimal patient behaviors and previously unnoticed aspects of the environment. The four scenarios at the beginning of this chapter demonstrate the use of such unrecognized facets of experience.

An assortment of examples of utilization was provided: utilizing something from the environment, like the pressure of the back rest; utilizing something from the patient, such as idiosyncratic language, an appreciation of humor, avoidance of intimacy, the problem sequence, or the symptomatic behavior itself (as Erickson did in the case of my pipe smoking). Even the therapist's family can be used (see Zeig [1985] for cases in which Erickson used members of his own family to facilitate treatment). Whatever exists in the environment, in the patient, in the patient's history, in the patient's problem, in the therapist's office, can be utilized. In Ericksonian methods, we take things from the immediate situation and harness them in a constructive direction.

As Erickson would have admonished his students, one of the most important things to be utilized is the unconscious of the therapist. The therapist relies on a wealth of experience that is, in essence, convertible currency that can be used to reach the patient. Even the therapist's handicaps can be used. For example, Erickson explained that polio was one of the best teachers he ever had about human behavior. He used that infirmity constructively. I remember a time after a session when I tried to help him move his wheelchair up an incline. He looked back at me pointedly and explained, "No, there are some things a man needs to do for himself." I watched him struggle to complete the task. It was a way of punctuating the day's message of self-reliance for a young student and making it memorable. In the process, Erickson demonstrated that a therapist's limitations can be used.

Utilization signals that the therapist is an active participant in the process of cocreating patient-based change. He or she is a companion traveler—*not* a tour guide who metacomments on the inadequacies of patients who repeatedly step into ruts of inefficiency in the process of traversing the rocky paths of life. The therapist is actually *with* the patient for a few of the steps—not merely asking the patient to analyze and understand flaws. In essence, the therapist helps the patient to realize the virtues of his or her faults. A close examination of Erickson's cases indicates that they are studies in the application of the utilization principles.

THE HISTORY OF UTILIZATION

The concept of utilization appears in Erickson's early experimental work. Erickson (1958) dated the method to a 1943 investigation that used hypnotic age regression to effect therapy. A woman had developed a traumatic phobia of orange juice so that she could not tolerate the smell or sight of oranges. She imposed her problem on others by proscribing their behavior around orange juice. Although she wanted therapy, for some reason, she was ambivalent about accepting it. Erickson utilized the naturalistic social situation of a party to conduct a demonstration of hypnosis, using the phobic woman as a subject. During the demonstration, he regressed her to a time before the orange-juice trauma happened and arranged that she would be given a glass of orange juice, which she drank comfortably. He then gave her an amnesia for the experience. He reported a complete cure as a result of the procedure.

Ernest Rossi (Erickson & Rossi, 1977) dates the concept of utilization to Erickson's recovery from polio at the age of 17, during which time he was paralyzed and confined to bed. While recuperating, he made use of a concept we describe in hypnosis as *ideomotor* behavior*. He watched his young sisters learn how to walk in order to reteach himself. By observing them intently, his body remembered how to move the muscles.

The concept of utilization was so important that it appeared in a 1954 definition of hypnosis

---

*Ideodynamic activity involves thinking about something so intently that actual behavior follows. For example, if you think about a piece of fudge, you can begin to salivate (*ideosensory*); if you are on the passenger side of the car and you want the driver to stop, you might step on the nonexistent brake (*ideomotor*).

that Erickson wrote for the *Encyclopedia Britannica:*

Another essential consideration in the technique of investigative or therapeutic work is the *utilization* of the subject's own pattern of response and capacities, rather than an attempt to force upon the subject by suggestion the hypnotist's limited understanding of how and what the subject should do. The failures in hypnotic therapy and experimental work often derive from dealing with the subject as an automaton expected to execute commands in accordance with the hypnotist's understanding, to the exclusion of a recognition of the subject as a personality, with individual patterns of response and behavior. (see Erickson, 1980, *Collected Papers, Vol. III*, p. 22, italics added)

The principle of utilization has been developed and extended by a number of important thinkers, who have carried on traditions initiated by Erickson. References are so extensive that it is possible to mention only a few contemporary contributors.

Erickson and Rossi (1975) outlined the utilization theory of hypnotic suggestion; Haley (1973) described the importance of accepting the resistance; the Lanktons (1983) discussed Erickson's conception of utilizing resistance; Yapko (1984) further articulated the therapeutic utilization of the trance state; and Gilligan (1987) indicated how the client's individual pattern of expression constituted the basis of establishing trance. Also, Dolan (1985) explored the nature of Ericksonian utilization with resistant and chronic patients; de Shazer (1988) described how to utilize the patient's history of exceptions; O'Hanlon and Wilk (1987) outlined how utilization could be used to design and deliver therapeutic interventions; and O'Hanlon (1987) proposed the utilization approach as Erickson's most lasting contribution to therapy.

Suffice it to say that all of Erickson's followers have addressed the principle of utilization and incorporated it into their theories and methods. In fact, it can be said that utilization is to Ericksonian therapy as analysis is to dynamic approaches; as conditioning is to behavior therapy. Utilization is a central facet of the Ericksonian model and can be used in hypnosis as well as psychotherapy.

UTILIZATION IN HYPNOSIS

In practicing therapeutic hypnosis, even using traditional methods, therapists make use of utilization whether or not they realize it. For example, the traditional hypnotist might suggest, "With each breath you take, with every sound you hear, you will go deeper and deeper into trance." In this utilization technique, something from the environment is associated with the goal of going deeper into a trance.

In the Ericksonian approach, a therapist works to elicit resources from the patient, rather than authoritatively programming suggestions into a supposedly passive person. Rote hypnotic techniques are eschewed in favor of utilization methods that automatically individualize treatment. Following are six utilization techniques (see also Zeig, 1988).

RATIFICATION

The process of trance induction customarily involves two progressive steps: absorb and ratify. First, the patient's attention is absorbed in a sensation, a perception, a fantasy, a memory, and so on. Then this absorption is ratified: Changes that happen as the patient became absorbed are acknowledged through simple declarative sentences. For example, the therapist might reply, "As you have been listening to me, your pulse rate has changed; your breathing rate is different; your head is no longer in the same posture that it was before." The utilization method of ratification has the implicit meaning, "You are responding; you are showing desirable changes."

ATTRIBUTION

Attribution is an indirect form of utilization related to ratification. Ratification specifically implies hypnotic responsiveness; attribution assigns additional meanings that can be used for more general goals. Consider carefully this offering to the hypnotized patient who is slowly nodding his head: "You're nodding your head differently now *because your unconscious mind has its own way of agreeing.*" Here, the patient's emitted behavior is given an implied meaning—in this case, "Your unconscious mind is cooperating with me."

SYMPTOM PRESCRIPTION

Using symptom prescription, the therapist encourages symptomatic behavior and then subtly shapes it in a desired direction.

Here is an example from my own experience. As a master's degree student (prior to my first visit with Erickson), I had a psychiatrist supervisor for my practicum. I asked him if he would teach me hypnosis. He invited me to his office and motioned me to sit down. I was nervous. As I sat in his office chair, I unconsciously rolled my fingers on the arm of a chair. Picking up on that, he quickly suggested, "You can tap your fingers more quickly. And as you tap your fingers, notice the rhythm of the movement. As you notice the rhythm of the movement, notice how it changes. As the rhythm slows down, you can take a deep breath, close your eyes, and go into a trance."

This was my first personal experience with utilization. It was so interesting to me, as utilization experiences tend to be, that I remember that incident as vividly today as when it happened 18 years ago.

INCORPORATION

Incorporation is a variation of utilization technique, similar to ratification and attribution. One can incorporate disparate things from the reality situation into the induction patter. For example, if a door suddenly opens during an induction, the therapist can say, "You can constructively open new doors to the capacity of your inner mind to guide you." The therapist models a response style that he would like the patient to emulate. The therapist often has the therapeutic goal of helping the patient show a constructive response to outward events. If the therapist wants the patient to develop the ability, he or she can model it, for example, by utilizing incorporation.

HYPNOTIC REDEFINING

Another utilization technique is hypnotic redefining. If a person describes an aspect of the problem as being the experience of "pressure," in the induction of hypnosis, the therapist can begin orienting the patient to the *pressure* of the support of the chair, the back rest, arm rest, leg rest, and so on. Thereby, the concept of pressure is subtly redefined in more positive terms, and a symptom word is used as a solution word.

SYMBOLIC INJUNCTION

In traditional psychotherapy, the practitioner often interprets the symbolic behavior and idioms of the patient. If the patient states, "My neck hurts," the therapist might interpret the symbolism of the statement by asking the patient, "Who is being a pain in the neck to you?" Interpretations of this sort follow from the goal of traditional psychotherapy, which extols the importance of conscious understanding.

In Ericksonian fashion, therapists could apply the utilization method by thinking, "If a patient can communicate symbolically, then I can be equally intelligent and communicate symbolically to the patient. Instead of *interpreting* symbolism, I can *use* symbolic processes constructively and create therapeutic symbols."

For example, during an induction, Erickson placed a hypnotized woman's left hand on her right bicept (Zeig, 1980). Her posture then became one in which she seemed to be hugging herself. The symbolic message was "You can protect yourself; you can comfort yourself." Subsequently, Erickson used that reference experience.

Here is another example. In doing an ego-building induction, I suggested: "As you go into a trance, your head is aligned straight and can feel good on your shoulders. Your head can seem further away from your feet. Your left shoulder can seem further away from your right shoulder." Symbolically and idiomatically, having a "straight head," "a good head on your shoulders," feeling "tall," and being "broad-shouldered" are somatic aspects of positive self-esteem.

The hypnotic communication forms may seem primary process, but in trance, patients can be more literal in their response pattern. Also, indirection adds to the drama and thereby may enhance the effectiveness of the suggestions. An important proviso is in order here: In hypnotic utilization methods, as with all techniques, communication is judged by the response of the patient, not by the cleverness of the structure. If a positive response to the implication is not forthcoming, the therapist proceeds with a different technique.

Having examined some methods of utilization in hypnosis, discussion can proceed to the use of utilization in individual and family therapy.

UTILIZATION IN INDIVIDUAL AND FAMILY THERAPY

Utilization techniques can be extended from hypnotic induction to psychotherapy conducted without a formal induction. Here is a case example.

LEAVE NO STONE UNTURNED

I had a patient who suffered from what I thought was depression. She explained to me, however, that she had psychosomatic problems. I did not interpret her psychosomatic problems as masked depression. Instead, I asked her to carry around a rock. She could find a fist-sized rock, paint it black, and carry it around for 10 days. After I returned from traveling, she would see me in two weeks for the next appointment. This patient knew she could expect some seemingly unusual assignments from me, and she readily accepted the task.

At the second interview, she indicated she had done the assignment and had carried around the rock. I inquired what she had done with the rock after the 10 days. She replied, "I really didn't know what to do with the rock, so I put it in my husband's library." I said, "You know, I think it would be good idea if we did some couples therapy and got your husband involved in the next session."

I merely traded symbols. She gave me a symbol (her psychosomatic problem), and as a mat-ter of kindness, even as a matter of politeness, I returned a symbol: I suggested a black rock, which I thought would symbolize depression. Actually, the problem was not so much depression as it was a couples issue. She symbolically corrected my misinterpretation when she chose a place to put the rock.

Essentially, my intervention was to utilize a symbolic process. Then I could monitor the response to my symbolic task and appropriately adjust my method.

The following is an example of utilization in family therapy.

UTILIZING THE TOOTH OF THE TIGER

Fred, an obnoxious 10-year-old, was obstinate, attention-seeking, and negative. He would not sit up straight on the office chair. Rather, he reclined in odd postures or sat on the floor. Frequently, he was disruptive, and he was consistently argumentative when confronted. Fred was unpredictable; he would not anticipate the consequences of his actions or take personal responsibility for his behavior. His tantrums were "major league."

As I observed him interact with his parents in a family therapy session, three patterns of behavior were especially noticeable: (1) his use of distraction to get attention; (2) his oppositional behavior; and (3) his ability to find a flaw in anyone's argument.

Fred's stepmother told him that if he simply would sit in the chair and engage in conversation for 10 minutes, he would earn back one of the numerous toys he had lost at home as a result of infractions. Fred made a meager attempt to comply. I picked up on Mom's challenge and asked Fred if he could distract, say the opposite of what I said, and/or find a flaw in my position. He argued that he could. I had some doubts. I explained that if he could do these three things, he would earn one point. His father added that if he earned five points, he would get back a toy.

We conducted one trial to be certain that Fred clearly understood the rules: I would provide a stimulus sentence and he would respond with distraction, the opposite, or by finding a flaw. After a few stimulus sentences, it became clear that Fred was very good at finding flaws. In fact, he was better at finding flaws than he was at distracting or being oppositional. However, I insisted that he practice all three methods, and because he was so insistent on finding a flaw, I indicated that there would be a fourth technique, which would be to repeat the last technique, thereby demonstrating that he could stubbornly stay in a rut.

After a few trials, we changed the rules of the game so that he would do each of the four operations in order. First, he would distract, then he would say the opposite, then he would find a flaw, then he would stay in a rut. My stimulus sentences were primarily empathic in content because Fred demonstrated little ability to identify feelings. As the session progressed, I changed stimulus sentences. At a juncture, when Fred was required to be oppositional, I said to him, "You can't control your own behavior." He replied, "I'm sitting still now."

The game looked like fun, so Mom took a turn at giving stimulus sentences; then Dad took his turn. During the time that he was in the office, Fred redeemed 11 toys. At the end of the session, Fred looked up at me and offered a charming "Thank you." It was the first non-caustic communication he had directed to me.

Previously, Fred's patterns of behavior had served to alienate him from others. I utilized these behaviors to promote closeness. They became a game. In the process, Fred demonstrated that he could control his behavior—that, in fact, he had exquisite control. Moreover, the patterns became clearer to his parents, who began to feel as if they had some tools with which to proceed.

This "game" was merely one component of a comprehensive therapy with the family. In this case, the identified patient was addressed directly, using a modified symptom-prescription technique. The therapeutic intent was to establish some control and good will in a chaotic situation. Subsequently, these changes could be developed within the family.

Having examined utilization as a concept, having described its history, and having indicated examples of its use in hypnosis and therapy, next examined will be what I call the "principles of utilization."

THE PRINCIPLES OF UTILIZATION

Principle No. 1. The therapist's induction comes first.

The first step of treatment in an Ericksonian approach is *not* to induce the patient into hypnosis; rather, it is to "induce" the therapist to *utilize*. The therapist initiates therapy by assuming a mentality of utilization, by accessing within himself or herself a readiness to respond constructively to the patient's responses. This externally directed state was a central facet of Erickson's presence. He was alive to the intricacies of the moment and interested in harnessing them.

Principle No. 2. Whatever the patient brings can be utilized. Whatever exists in the therapy situation can be utilized.

Whatever the patient brings is *not* grist for the mill. *It is fuel to propel forward into new space.* The patient's values can be utilized; the patient's situation can be utilized; the patient's resistances can be utilized; the patient's symptom can be utilized. Examples of utilization methods in each of these cases were presented above.

It is also true that the *mechanism* by which the symptom is maintained can be utilized. It is axiomatic that although symptoms appear to occur automatically, actually the patient does something to maintain the symptom. For example, depressed people do something to maintain their depression. It is best to think of depression as something that one does, not something that just happens. The therapist can think, "How is the patient *doing* depression?" Once the mechanism that the patient uses to do the problem is discovered, it can be utilized. An example of utilizing such a mechanism was the sequence induction presented in Situation 4.

Principle No. 3. Whatever technique any patient uses to be a patient can be harnessed by a therapist.

Techniques do not come merely from a book; they can be developed from studying patients. For example, if a patient tells stories to be a patient, the therapist can tell stories to be a therapist. If a patient is confusing as a patient, the therapist can be confusing constructively (see Zeig, 1987).

Take the example of stammering: A patient might stammer as a problem. The therapist can stammer with any patient as a therapeutic maneuver. I have used a technique of stammering constructively in conducting hypnotic inductions with nonstammering patients. I suggested, "Hypnosis can be imagined and experienced as a present . . . uh . . . pleasant feeling. And as you go . . . uh . . . glow . . . uh . . . grow . . . uh . . . *go* inside, you can enjoy it in many ways." In this case, the patient can respond to any of the words on which I stammered. The experience can be pleasant or present; the feeling can be one of glowing, growing, or going inside. My stammer energizes the suggestion by making the key words stand out.

Principle No. 4. Whatever responses you get, develop them.

The following case illustrates a number of utilization principles and techniques. It also illustrates how to develop a response. Once the patient responds, it is the job of the therapist constructively to develop and harness the response. It is as if the therapist takes any bit of "gold" the patient provides and then helps to fashion it into something useful.

Erickson (Erickson & Rossi, 1979) made a house call on a patient who was dying of cancer. Her internist invited Erickson to consult with Kathy because she was in severe pain and unresponsive to conventional treatments of the day. When Erickson arrived, Kathy was lying on her left side in a fetal position, chanting, "Don't hurt me, don't scare me. Don't hurt me, don't scare me. Don't hurt me, don't scare me."

How might this patient be approached? Should the therapist disrupt the patient by saying, "Excuse me, I am your consultant. I'd like to talk with you. Could you please stop chanting?" Put yourself in Erickson's position: If you practiced hypnosis, would you say, "Excuse me, I know you are chanting, but would you please stare at a spot on the wall so that you can go into a trance?" In contradistinction, what would a therapist do who was wedded to the idea of utilization?

Erickson looked at Kathy and said, "I'm going to hurt you. I'm going to scare you. I'm going to hurt you. I'm going to scare you. I'm going to hurt you. I'm going to scare you. I'm going to hurt you. I'm going to scare you. I'm going to hurt you." Kathy replied, "But I don't want you to hurt me." Erickson continued, "But I've got to hurt you to help you. I've got to hurt you to help you. I've got to hurt you to help you."

Erickson then induced a trance by using an elegant technique of utilizing Kathy's memory. He told her, "Kathy, I cannot explain to you all of the things I am going to do, but I'd like you to remember what it was like when you turned over from your left side to your right side. Close your eyes, and really remember what it was like to turn over." Erickson utilized Kathy's memory of pain as an absorption device to facilitate hypnotic induction.

Kathy told Erickson, "I'm on my left side; I think I'm on my left side." Erickson continued, "Kathy, I'd like you to go inside and develop the most horrible, the most intolerable, the most awful itch that you can possibly develop in the base of your foot." Kathy tried and failed; "I'm sorry Dr. Erickson, I can't develop a horrible itch in the base of my foot. All that I can get is a sort of horrible numb feeling."

It was at this point in which Erickson *developed* her response: "Well, that's all right, Kathy. What I'd like you to do is to develop that numbness and allow the numbness to spread over your legs, across your hip, up your body, and into your arm, but not in that area where your left breast used to be." Kathy developed a generalized numbness.

Erickson was expectant and response ready. He would utilize whatever Kathy developed in reaction to his offering. If Kathy had developed tingling instead of numbness, he would have used that. If she developed "nothing," he could have used that; for example, "Kathy let the nothingness spread up your body." Erickson also used Kathy's psychology. He left an area of discomfort (one breast), knowing that patients must often take out feelings on themselves, and he left that possibility intact.

Utilization is an ongoing process. It is not something that the therapist starts and stops. The therapist's attitude of utilization is developed throughout the treatment and is integral to the process of therapy.

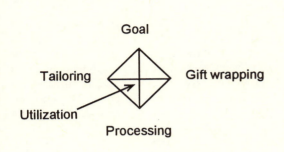

Figure 1 The Ericksonian Diamond.

UTILIZATION IN THE PROCESS OF THERAPY

The following metamodel is based on a structural communications approach. This approach uses social influence to harness structures existing in the present, including intrapsychic, interspersal, and environmental structures, in order to achieve future goals. It is a model that addresses *how* to elicit change, rather than *analyzing* why people are as they are.

Figure 1 shows a diagram of the model.

The major aspects of this model can be presented and examined only briefly here. In addition to the principle of utilization, there are four other components: (1) setting the goal; (2) gift wrapping, (3) tailoring, and (4) establishing a dynamic process.

SETTING THE GOAL

The therapist begins therapy by setting the goals and asking himself or herself: "What do I want to communicate to the patient?"

The particulars of establishing goals for any specific psychotherapy are numerous. There are two methods that I commonly use: making the problem into a process and dividing the solution into manageable bits.

1. *Making the problem into a process.* If one views the problem as a sequential process, often avenues for intervention become

immediately apparent. A goal of the therapy would be to help the patient modify the habitual sequential behavior that leads to the problem. Perhaps the therapist could accomplish this by adding a step to the sequence. For example, with a smoking problem, a patient can be asked to stroke his or her arm prior to inhaling, thereby adding a step to the habitual sequence. If the intervention is sufficient, systemic change can follow. An underlying premise is that patients will gravitate toward more healthful, effective patterns once a habitual sequence is modified.

2. *Dividing the solution into manageable bits.* This method of establishing goals requires the therapist to determine *how* the patient accomplishes the problem. For example, if the patient has been lowering his or her self-esteem, the therapist can wonder how that process is accomplished. Perhaps, among other things, the patient does not trust himself or herself, does not trust others, directs attention inward, and finds personal flaws that he or she exaggerates. These maneuvers can be conceived of as "sensible" things to do to achieve a goal; that is, if the intended outcome is lower self-esteem, it would be wise to distrust oneself, distrust others, be internally preoccupied, and find exaggerated flaws. The solution would be the reciprocal (opposite) of the problem strategy; namely, trust oneself; trust others; be aware, rather than withdrawn; and find internal strengths. Each of the components of the solution could be treated as a separate goal to be addressed and elicited. Once a patient trusts himself or herself, trusts others, enjoys awareness, and finds internal strengths, then overall self-esteem improves.

Once the therapist has a goal in mind, the next step is to find a way of presenting the goal to the patient. I call this process "gift wrapping."

GIFT WRAPPING

If the therapist has a component solution to present, a method is needed to offer the strategy to the patient so that the patient can retrieve that previously dissociated ability. For example, take external awareness as a goal. The therapist can *gift wrap* the idea "be external" in many ways. The therapist can direct the patient, "Open your eyes, look at the world, and be aware of and notice things around you." In my experience, however, patients resent paying an hourly fee for that kind of advice. Rather, the solution segment can be *gift wrapped* by presenting the theme within a technique rather than directly. One way of gift wrapping an idea is to present it under hypnosis.

A newspaper reporter interviewed me last December for an article on hypnosis. She inquired, "Dr. Zeig, what is hypnosis?" I replied, being seasonal, "Structurally, hypnosis is merely one way of gift wrapping ideas."

Solution components can be gift wrapped by using hypnosis, symbols, metaphors, symptom prescription, anecdotes, reframing, and so on. These techniques are powerful formats for offering simple ideas. The therapist wonders, "How can I present the goal?" and then decides upon a technique. As has been implied, techniques are selected by using methods to which the patient commonly or historically subscribes.

The process of linking solutions and gift wrapping can be considered psychotherapy by reciprocal association. The therapist's technique associates the patient to a solution component, which is elicited via the ideodynamic effect. Gift wrapping is selecting a technique with which to offer ideas.

It is not enough merely to gift wrap solution components. It is best to individualize the therapy. The process of addressing the unique style of the patient is referred to as "tailoring."

TAILORING

The therapist who is kind enough to gift wrap an idea for a patient can further improve the presentation by *tailoring*. It is nice to have a present, but if the present is individualized, it is even nicer. And it is more effective. Erickson emphasized the point by saying, "Psychotherapy for Patient A is not psychotherapy for Patient B."

To tailor, the therapist thinks, "What does the patient value? What is the position that the patient takes? What is the patient proud of?" Subsequently, the therapist individualizes the approach. For example, if the patient values adventure, therapeutic tasks can be done because they are adventurous. If the patient values slow understanding, the therapist can conduct slow therapy.

Let us go back to the goal of external awareness. If the patient is intropunitive (hard on himself or herself), the therapist could suggest, "I want you to be more aware because it will be really hard on you." If the patient is extropunitive (hard on others), the therapist can suggest to the patient, "I want you to be more aware because it will be hard on those around you." Thereby, the therapy is tailored to the patient's values and world view (c.f., Fisch, Weakland, & Segal, 1982). The therapy is filtered through the patient's inner lens. Sometimes the tailored therapeutic offering does not make logical sense. However, it may make emotional sense to the patient because it "fits" the patient's model of the world.

After determining a strategy for tailoring the technique, the therapist needs to create a method for presenting the offering over time. This method could be considered *processing*.

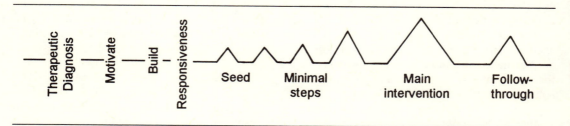

Figure 2 Time line of psychotherapy

PROCESSING

It is not sufficient to identify the goal and create a way to "gift wrap" or individualize it. In addition, the therapist works to create a *process*, a drama, through which the goal is offered. This process (Figure 2) involves a period of time, a time-line sequence of psychotherapy, that seeks optimally to evoke and utilize the patient's internal and social dynamics.

The therapist begins by evoking the patient's motivation, which is then "shaped" into responsiveness, especially to subtle cues. This is a way of "working the soil" so that it is fertile. The step of building responsiveness can also be thought of as conducting an induction.

Throughout the process, the therapist has in mind a tailored main intervention. This could be a symptom prescription, ordeal, or anecdote. Rather than moving directly to the "main course," however, the therapist "seeds" the main intervention by creating an indirect illusion to the technique that is to follow. Basically, this is a method of foreshadowing. (For more information on seeding, see Zeig, 1990.)

Next the therapist proceeds in small steps toward the main intervention, which is succeeded by a period of follow-through. This procedure has been named SIFT (Zeig, 1985). The therapist moves in *S*mall steps, *I*ntervenes, and then *F*ollows *T*hrough. Processing makes therapy into a *S*ignificant *E*motional *E*xperience, SEE (Massey, 1979), around which change can constellate.

WHY UTILIZE?

Utilization is a bridge between setting goals, gift wrapping, tailoring, and processing.* To set goals, the therapist can utilize the patient's

*Note: In the original model "utilization" was put in the center of an Ericksonian Diamond. Upon further examination it was realized that a more accurate formulation is to put "the posture of the therapist" in the center of the Diamond. Perhaps Dr. Masterson's confrontation about the place of countertransference in the Ericksonian model (in his discussion, which follows) was beneficial in increasing the scope of the metamodel. The posture of the thrapist now includes "utilization" among other technical and personal factors. Future publications will provide elaboration.

ability to divide the problem into component bits, so that the reciprocal of each becomes a "minigoal." To gift wrap, the therapist can utilize the technique that the patient uses to be a patient. To tailor, the therapist utilizes what the patient values as a motivator ("...because it would be hard on you"). To create the process, the therapist utilizes the sequence that the patient uses to create or experience a problem.

All good communicators in any field *utilize*. In the psychotherapy arena, utilization energizes therapy and makes it engaging. Utilization is respectful of the patient; it recognizes the patient's individuality. Utilization also encourages the patient to be alert and it keeps the therapist alive to the moment.

I remember when I first went to see Milton Erickson in 1973. At this point in his life, he was confined to a wheelchair and was in constant chronic pain. He had his own way of personalizing the philosophy of utilization. He said proudly, "I don't mind the pain. I don't like the alternative."

Erickson would start the day slowly speaking through his pain. I was energized and glad to be visiting him. I strained to catch his every word, his every nuance. I tried to classify in my mind all the different techniques he was using. I wondered to myself, "How is he effecting utilization now?"

As time went on, I got wearier. I could not cognitively fathom all the things that he was doing. As the hours passed, Erickson became further removed from his pain. Perhaps he was utilizing his interest in talking to me as a distraction technique. In any case, he became even more animated and alert. At the end of the day, I was worn out and Erickson was energized!

This leads me to posit the criteria for successful therapy. If the therapist feels better at the end of the session, probably it was a good one. And for the therapist to feel better, the concept of utilization is often central.

The metamodel has now been presented in its most general form. Treatment is based in the present and directed toward the future. The model's basic philosophy is that there are few new (profound) things to say to patients; there are, however, new (profound) ways to say what patients need to hear. To subscribe to this approach may require a modification in a therapist's definition of therapy.

REDEFINING THERAPY

Utilization requires a new definition of therapy in which it is no longer viewed as education or analysis of what is going on in the understructure of the patient's unconscious or family system.

To the practitioner of utilization, therapy becomes an *appeal*. Therapy is about appealing to the constructive history. Patients are seen as having what is needed to solve the problem in their experiential background. Every smoker knows how to be comfortable without a cigarette. Every schizophrenic knows how to communicate cogently. These talents exist in the patient's history. The therapist assumes that the patient has a history of functioning adequately and effectively. Therefore, the therapist does not have to teach the patient how to be adequate. Rather, the job of the therapist is to help the patient unlock the constructive history that is dormant. Therapy becomes a process of stimulating resources into play—resources that have been long closeted.

In Erickson's terms: "Psychotherapy is the reassociation of internal life."

REFERENCES

de Shazer, S. (1988). Utilization: The foundation of solutions. In J. K. Zeig & S. R. Lankton (Eds.), *Developing Ericksonian therapy: State of the art* (pp. 112–124). New York: Brunner/Mazel.

Dolan, Y. (1985). *A path with a heart: Utilization with resistant and chronic patients.* New York: Brunner/Mazel.

Erickson, M. H. (1952). Deep hypnosis and its induction. In L. M. LeCron (Ed.), *Experimental hypnosis* (pp. 70–114). New York: Macmillan.

Erickson, M. H. (1958). Naturalistic techniques of hypnosis. *The American Journal of Clinical Hypnosis, 1,* 3–8.

Erickson, M. H. (1965). The use of symptoms as an integral part of hypnotherapy. *The American Journal of Clinical Hypnosis, 8,* 57–65.

Erickson, M. H. (1980). *The collected papers of Milton H. Erickson on hypnosis, Vol. III: Hypnotic investigation of psychodynamic processes,* E. L. Rossi (Ed.). New York: Irvington.

Erickson, M. H., & Rossi, E. L. (1975). Varieties of double bind. *The American Journal of Clinical Hypnosis, 17,* 143–157.

Erickson, M. H., & Rossi, E. L. (1977). Autohypnotic experiences of Milton H. Erickson. *The American Journal of Clinical Hypnosis, 20,* 36–54.

Erickson, M. H., & Rossi, E. L. (1979). *Hypnotherapy: An exploratory casebook.* New York: Irvington.

Fisch, P., Weakland, J., & Segal, L. (1982). *The tactics of change: Doing therapy briefly.* San Francisco: Jossey-Bass.

Gilligan, S. (1987). *Therapeutic trances: The cooperation principle in Ericksonian hypnotherapy.* New York: Brunner/Mazel.

Haley, J. (1973). *Uncommon therapy: The psychiatric techniques of Milton H. Erickson, M.D.* New York: Norton.

Haley, J. (1982). The contributions to therapy of Milton H. Erickson, M.D. In J. K. Zeig (Ed.), *Ericksonian approaches to hypnosis and psychotherapy* (pp. 5–25). New York: Brunner/Mazel.

Lankton, S., & Lankton, C. (1983). *The answer within: A clinical framework of Ericksonian hypnotherapy.* New York: Brunner/Mazel.

Massey, M. (1979). *The people puzzle: Understanding yourself and others.* Reston, VA: Reston Publishing.

O'Hanlon, W. (1987). *Taproots: Underlying principles of Milton Erickson's therapy and hypnosis.* New York: Norton.

O'Hanlon, W., & Wilk, J. (1987). *Shifting contexts: The generation of effective psychotherapy.* New York: Guilford Press.

Yapko, M. (1984). *Trancework: An introduction to clinical hypnosis.* New York: Irvington.

Zeig, J. K. (Ed.). (1980). *A teaching seminar with Milton H. Erickson.* New York: Brunner/Mazel.

Zeig, J. K. (1985). *Experiencing Erickson: An introduction to the man and his work.* New York: Brunner/Mazel.

Zeig, J. K. (1987). Therapeutic patterns of Ericksonian influence communication. In J. K. Zeig (Ed.), *The evolution of psychotherapy* (pp. 392–409). New York: Brunner/Mazel.

Zeig, J. K. (1988). An Ericksonian phenomenological approach to therapeutic hypnotic induction and symptom utilization. In J. K. Zeig & S. R. Lankton (Eds.), *Developing Ericksonian therapy: State of the art* (pp. 353–375). New York: Brunner/Mazel.

Zeig, J. K. (1990). Seeding. In J. K. Zeig & S. Gilligan (Eds.), *Brief therapy: Myths, methods, and metaphors* (pp. 221–246). New York: Brunner/Mazel.

Discussion by James F. Masterson, M.D.

Dr. Zeig is indeed a very difficult act to follow. It reminds me of a story that was told by Adlai Stevenson. He was the after-dinner speaker at a political dinner and he was sitting at the banquet table with the noted humorist Fred Allen. Allen got up to introduce Stevenson, and within no time at all, he had the audience rolling in the aisles. Adlai Stevenson had to get up and compete with this performance. He said, "Ladies and gentlemen, Mr. Allen and I were sitting next to each other at dinner and actually we exchanged our papers. He has given you my paper and I have taken a look at his, and I don't think you would be very interested in it."

In trying to deal with this problem of him being a hard act to follow, I thought I might take a page from the Ericksonian technique. He mentioned that whatever a patient does to be a patient, a therapist can use with a patient, so whatever a speaker does to be a speaker, a discussant can use with the speaker. Did you notice how awkward he was? Did you notice how awkward his voice was? How awkward his mannerisms were? Well, I finally knew that wouldn't work because it's not my style. He has probably gotten over those anxieties anyway.

I can't really begin my discussion without first describing to you a little bit of my state of mind. Initially, I didn't really understand why Dr. Zeig wanted me to discuss his presentation since we have different lenses for what treatment is about. Clearly, I am not a hypnotherapist. Well, I didn't know why, but I decided to put the question on hold until I received his text. I thought it perhaps had had something to do with the ecumenical spirit of the conference.

Dr. Zeig, who was in charge of the conference, set the date for Invited Addresses to be received as of November 16, to which I looked forward eagerly. I knew him to be extremely well-organized. The paper didn't arrive by November 16. It hadn't arrived by December 3. My anxiety was mounting. What was he planning for me? I had to leave New York early to do some other things before I arrived at the conference, so I had my secretary call his secretary and say, "For God's sakes, send me that paper." Well, I gather that she sent it by Federal Express addressed to 60 Sutton Place South, but in Los Angeles, not in New York, as it should have been.

As a consequence, I finally received the paper at 9:30 Tuesday night at the faculty meeting. When I returned from the meeting, I noted two significant things: the manuscript was 48 pages long, and I was scheduled to spend the entire day on Wednesday working. If that wasn't bad enough, things are never so bad that they can't get worse. He was my host, and he was also going to be paying my bills. Needless to say, I felt in quite a bind. I figured I might as well again borrow from the Ericksonian method. I actually toyed with the idea of setting him a symptomatic task, as he had done with the woman with the black rock. I might suggest to him that at the next Evolution Conference, he would again procrastinate; he would not be able to set the date, to get his speakers on time, or to get a site, but I finally decided to discard that idea, again for the same reasons.

By this point, I figured, as he put it, that I had had the dynamic experience, but it hadn't yet led to the dynamic understanding. I hoped I would find my way to this understanding in the course of this discussion. So I screwed up my courage and I decided to use my capacity for utilization to see if I could tailor or gift wrap the discussion in such a way that it might effect some change in Dr. Zeig.

You will keep in mind that I am not a hypnotherapist; I am not qualified in any way to come in on the hypnotherapeutic aspects, and I have not had the time to give the presentation the serious study it deserves.

Dr. Zeig's goal was to describe and illustrate the five aspects of the Ericksonian diamond: utilization, setting the goal, gift wrapping, tailoring, and establishing a process. It seems to me, even though I am not a hypnotherapist, that he has clearly achieved that goal. Beyond that, I think he is to be commended for this effort at specifying the clinical approach so that it can be validated and researched by others, which is such a vital step in any scientific endeavor. I thought that what I could discuss were the many commonalities in attitude toward the patient and the work, and also note some of the differences. I hoped that this endeavor might lead me to the dynamic understanding I was looking for that follows the dynamic experience.

First, I was certainly struck by his view of Erickson's comments about pipe smoking. I could almost, from my perspective, interpret that what Erickson was doing was a confrontation: "I think what you are doing with the pipe is to deal with your anxiety about being a psychologist. And I think you ought to stop with the pipe and deal with the anxiety more directly." So that perspective would fit with mine pretty clearly.

There are so many of these attitudes that we share—for example, where he quotes from Erickson: "The therapist should never scorn, condemn or reject any part of the patient's conduct simply because it is obstructive, unreasonable or irrational. Whatever the patient brings into the office, is in some way both a part of the patient and a part of his problem."

"The patient should be viewed with a sympathetic eye, appraising the totality which confronts the therapist." Certainly I agree with this.

"In so doing, therapists should not limit themselves to an appraisal of what is good." I don't think that is the job of therapists, to make judgments about patients. And then he says, "To be good and reasonable." I would have an argument with that. I think reason is a very important part of our occupation.

In talking about utilization, he says, "It is the readiness of the therapist to strategically respond to any or all aspects of the patient's environment." There cannot be any argument about that. I might just change it to identify and include in his thinking all aspects. What he does about them is another issue.

Also, I agree with the idea of response readiness, "readiness to seize the moment by capturing and utilizing whatever happens." Also, "to whatever exists in the environment to the patient, the patient's history, the patient's problem, can be utilized, particularly if he emphasizes the conscious of the therapist." Certainly I agree with all that.

Utilization signals that there is an active participant in the process of the cocreating change. This participant is the companion traveler—not a tour guide. A tour guide is the bad guy, who comments on the "inadequacies of the patients who repeatedly step into the ruts of inefficiency in the process of traversing the rocky paths of life."

It seems to me that a straw man has been set up to be knocked down, because it seems as though this person is a poor therapist no matter what his or her perspective is. Again, this poor therapist raises his or her ugly head when we talk about failures in hypnotic therapy, as the therapist uses the patient as a automaton rather than taking his or her material from the patient. I certainly couldn't disagree with that.

Now we come to an area of disagreement. Dr. Zeig says, "It is a model. This model represents how to elicit change, rather than to analyze how people are, why people are as they are." From my perspective, the agent for eliciting change is the analysis of why people are the way they are, and some of this difference has to do with the kinds of patients we treat. Again he emphasizes this in redefining therapy, "It will not be seen as analysis of what is going on in the understructure of the patient's unconscious or family system." This is exactly what I do.

On the other hand, to show how complicated this matter is, I would agree with another aspect of this redefinition. "The therapist immediately assumes that the patient has a history of functioning adequately and effectively; therefore, the therapist does not have to teach the patient to be adequate. Rather, the job of the therapist is to help the patient unlock the constructive history that is dormant." Certainly I share that perspective.

Another that I share is, "All good communicators utilize. Utilization energizes therapy. Makes it engaging. Utilization is used because it is respectful to the patient. It recognizes the patient's individuality."

I have a qualification about his last statement, "If a therapist feels better at the end of the session, it probably was a good one." I think this depends a great deal on the therapist. You know the old saying, "If you're standing on the deck and everybody else is running around anxiously and wildly, and you're cool, calm, and collected, maybe you don't understand the situation."

Let me mention another difference. In the presentation, I missed concepts of diagnosis and differential diagnosis, which, in my perspective, are crucial to understanding what is wrong and what to do about it. I also sense an emphasis on symptom change, which is valid within itself; however, our focus is much more on changes in intrapsychic structure, which we see as more enduring. It is analysis of the past and how the patient got that way that is the agent that elicits and frees the patient up to activate change. I also miss emphasis on countertransference. I assume that hypnotherapists have the same problems with countertransference as we have in our work.

The use of suggestion or hypnosis is contraindicated for personality disorders. The reason is that the key pathology is the patient's defect within self—the difficulties with self-activation and self-assertion and the patient's defensive tendency to focus on others as a way of dealing with this difficulty. Thus in my view, the suggestion in hypnosis may take over for the patient's nonactivated self and so reinforce defense, which I would think inhibits change.

In conclusion, although obviously many of our attitudes toward the patient and toward the work are very similar, I have serious questions about the transfer of the techniques, particularly to personality disorder patients.

Now that I have finished the discussion, I think I've finally achieved the dynamic understanding that should follow the dynamic experience. I suspect that Dr. Zeig had slyly set me a task as he does his patients, such as the one to whom he gave the rock. He knows me pretty well, and I think he knows that my perspective places pretty heavy emphasis on the intellectual approach and reason.

I just wonder if he purposely allowed me so little time to prepare, in order to force me to bypass these types of intellectual resistances and to make me react spontaneously, which would overcome my intellectual views and defenses and open me up to input from his point of view.

In retrospect, like a good patient, I seemed to have responded in exactly that way, because what I have ended up doing is stressing the commonalities, rather than the differences, which represent my true intellectual position.

It has been a real learning experience—but it has made me really worried about posthypnotic suggestion. Am I going to have these thoughts bothering me on the long plane ride back to New York? If it continues, will I have to see a hypnotic therapist in New York to get it out of my system? Nevertheless, let me say, "Congratulations on a job well done."

Reality Therapy

◆

William Glasser, M.D.

William Glasser, M.D.
William Glasser who received his M.D. degree in 1953 from Case Western Reserve University, also was awarded an honorary doctorate in human letters by the University of San Francisco. Founder and Director of the Institute for Reality Therapy, he is author and editor of ten books on the topics of reality therapy and education.
William Glasser presents a brief history of reality therapy and explains that it is based on control theory. Reality therapy can be applied both to counseling and managing clients. Case examples are used to show that it has two major components: creating the counseling environment and the procedures that lead to change.

Although I can easily explain most of the process of reality therapy, it is difficult to describe how to create the therapeutic relationship that is necessary for its success. To do this well is an art gained only through constantly evaluating the progress of each client. This art, however, will not be acquired unless the therapist makes the effort to learn the control theory that is the foundation for all we do. The impetus for developing reality therapy was my dissatisfaction with what I was taught during my psychiatric residency at the Veterans Administration, West Los Angeles, and the University of California at Los Angeles from 1954 to 1957. Some specific points with which I disagreed were that:

1. Clients suffer from mental illnesses. Their only choice is to be the way they are, which means that they are not responsible for their present behavior.

2. The source of their present problem is almost always in the past and only can be corrected by working in the past.

3. It is important not to become friends with clients, but to remain aloof, uninvolved, and "objective."

4. The therapist should never advise clients, but, instead, work to create an environment in which clients eventually figure out what to do no matter how long this takes.

5. Other people and events are responsible for clients' behavior. Parents who did not raise their children "perfectly" are mainly responsible for their children's problems, even when the children become adults.

6. Therapy is a long, drawn-out process that must involve unconscious motivation or it will not succeed.

7. There are unconscious forces, such as the "id," that are so strong, mysterious, and deep that almost no one with problems can deal

with them successfully without the assistance of an expert therapist.

8. Self-destructive behaviors, such as alcoholism, compulsive gambling, and promiscuity, are components of mental diseases over which the sufferer has no control.

9. We can learn more about psychological problems by studying people suffering from these problems than by studying effective people who have been exposed to the same difficult situations, but who do not have these same problems.

There may be more, but this is a good cross section of what I was taught that I did not find to be true as I began to work with patients—and that I still do not believe. When I expressed this dissatisfaction to G. L. Harrington, M.D., my clinical supervisor in the third year of my residency, he reached across the desk, shook my hand, and said, "Join the club." I soon discovered that this was, and is, a very small club indeed. I was, however, fortunate to have Dr. Harrington as my mentor for the next seven years, during which I developed the ideas of reality therapy. He, along with Mary Perry, the first superintendent of the Ventura School for Girls (a California Youth Authority facility for delinquent girls), and her successor Beatrice Dolan, as well as Donald O'Donnell, a public school principal, were influential in the early development of these ideas.

In addition to my residency, much of which was in a psychiatric hospital, I have also worked in many institutional settings, such as public schools, youth custodial institutions, settings for the rehabilitation of drug addicts, and rehabilitation centers for the physically injured or handicapped, and with a large group of private patients, both adults and adolescents. I have used reality therapy in all of these situations, and I do not believe that there is any population for whom this method of counseling is not effective.

WHAT IS REALITY THERAPY?

Reality therapy is a method of counseling based on the idea that, in an effort to satisfy their innate needs, the people we call clients or patients make many destructive and self-destructive choices. The task of the reality therapist is to help them to make more effective choices. After I had worked out much of reality theory's basic practice, I discovered control theory, a biological theory that explains both our psychological and our physiological behavior. I am responsible for developing reality therapy, but I did not originate control theory. The person most responsible for doing so was William Powers (1973), but I have expanded and clarified his theoretical work (Glasser, 1984) to the point where it is now an integral part of reality therapy. Reality therapy can be used by practitioners who work with all human problems, psychological or medical, and control theory, as I have expanded it, can be used by anyone who wants to gain more effective control over his or her life.

Recently, I became aware of the fact that to say that counselors or psychotherapists counsel most of the people with whom they work is inaccurate. Counseling is only a part of what we do. When, for example, we work with addicts, child abusers, psychotics, criminals, school failures, sex deviants, and the many others who do not come for counseling voluntarily, it is much more accurate to say that our task is more to manage than to counsel. This is so because almost all of these people are sent to counselors by someone in authority (often legal authorities) with the charge that they be changed by counseling into what the authorities want them to be—for example, alcoholics will stop drinking, children will behave better, and spouses will change.

For these people, the counselor has an assigned counseling agenda, which is to get them to stop behaving as they have been behaving and to begin to lead what someone in authority calls a "normal" life. The counselor is an agent of someone other than the client, and, in accepting this role, he or she also accepts the management of the client. *Managing* is the process of working with someone so that this person will accept and work hard at someone else's agenda. Since counselors do so much managing, I have now incorporated into reality therapy the management ideas of W. Edwards Deming (1982), the world's leader in managing people so that they do quality work. I have done so because much of what Deming advocates for managers obviously is based on both control theory and reality therapy, even though Deming, himself, does not seem to be aware of these ideas.

Thus when the term "reality therapy" is used today, it means either a method of counseling based on control theory or a method of managing combined with counseling based on both control theory and Deming. Reality therapy is also taught to people who do not want to be counseled, but who do want to learn to lead a more effective life. For these people, reality therapy means that they are taught, or advised to learn, control theory and to put it to work in their lives. Therefore, it is important to understand that when the term reality therapy is employed in general usage, it may stand for one or more of at least three different applications.

TOTAL BEHAVIORS

Based on control theory, reality therapy contends that we are all responsible for how we behave and that all we do from birth to death is behave. For the practical purposes of counseling, managing, or living, all of our conscious behavior is both chosen and total. By total we mean that it is made up of some combination of four behavioral components: (1) acting, (2) thinking, (3) feeling, and (4) the physiology that accompanies our actions, thoughts, and feelings. Of these four components, only two, our actions and thoughts, are under our conscious, arbitrary control.

And so when I say that all of our behavior is chosen, I mean that all of our thoughts and actions are chosen. As we do not ordinarily choose the feelings and the physiologies that accompany our actions and thoughts, if we want to feel better or become healthier, we must improve our actions and thoughts, which will, in turn, change our total behavior. Keep in mind that the whole is the sum of the parts, and that, if we want to change the whole, we can do so by changing any part or parts. Therefore, in practicing reality therapy, we focus on helping people to choose to change the only parts of their behavior they can change—their *actions and thoughts*. It is not that we ignore or deny

feelings and/or physiology, but that we do not dwell on what no one can change directly. If we were to focus too much on these components, we would imply the impossible, which is that they can be directly changed.

For example, a client came into my office and told me that he was depressed. What he was describing was what most voluntary clients initially describe, which is the feeling component of the total behavior they are choosing. He wanted to feel better, but, short of giving him an addicting drug (which I would never do), there is nothing I, or anyone else, can do quickly or arbitrarily to "make" him feel better. And even if I were to give him a feel-good drug, it would still be as a result of his acting and thinking that he would take the drug. As he talked, he described how he had been sitting home for a week doing nothing but thinking obsessively about the fact that his wife had suddenly (he claimed) chosen to leave him and about how terribly he missed her. He also said that since she had left, he had no appetite and his stomach felt queasy.

He had now described all four components of his total behavior: (1) his action, *sitting home*; (2) his thoughts, *I miss her so*; (3) his feelings, *the depressing*; and (4) his physiology, *loss of appetite, queasy stomach*. We label any total behavior (and remember that all behaviors are total) by its most recognizable component, which was, in this case, the feeling component. We would call this total behavior the act of depressing, because all behavior is properly described by the use of verbs. We do not use the adjective depressed or the noun depression, because this would be misleading. All we can change is our behavior (always total), which means changing from one verb to another.

Thus on the basis of control theory, reality therapy uses gerunds or infinitives to describe the common psychological complaints. We say a client is *depressing* or *choosing to depress*, and as soon as we say this, we recognize that our job as counselor is to help the client choose a better total behavior. For example, we say that people are anxieting, phobicking, obsessing, compulsing, crazying, headaching, or sicking. Or we say that they are *choosing to* be anxious, be phobic, obsess, compulse, be crazy, have a headache, or be sick.

THE CAUSES OF BEHAVIOR

All Behavior is Caused By What Goes on Inside Our Brains

Misled by their "common sense," most people believe in stimulus-response theory—they believe that much of their behavior is caused by a stimulus or an event outside of themselves. When it comes to "mental illness," this belief approaches the 100% mark. Almost everyone believes that someone or something outside of "mentally ill" people is responsible for their pain or disability. They are believed to be the victims of a present or past outside event or events.

Following this belief, almost all people believe that they answer the telephone because it rings or that they stop at a corner because a traffic light turned red. In the case of my client, he believed that he was "depressed" because wife had left him, that it was she, not he, who was the problem. But if you examine even these simple events, you will see that you do not always answer the phone when it rings or stop at a red light. And not all men depress if their wives leave. In fact, if you have something better to do, you may choose not to answer the phone, and, in an emergency, you will run the red light. Control theory explains that you answer the phone, stop at a red light, depress when your spouse leaves, or do anything else that you do because it satisfies something inside you better to do this than to do anything else.

Therefore, what most people call a stimulus, we call *information*. Further, we claim that all we can get from outside ourselves is information, but this information, in itself, does not cause us to do anything. The ring does not make us answer the phone, but just tells us that there is someone on the other end who wants to talk to someone on this end. In the same way, the red light neither tells us about the traffic flow nor makes us stop. The fact that we usually act in a certain way given certain information does not make it a stimulus. It is just that given certain information, many people act in the same way. Whatever a client does is not a mental illness, but a choice. And the reasons for making that choice are always inside the person, not in the information that entered through the senses from the outside. The more information we

have, the better we may be able to decide what the best thing is to do. However, information itself does not *cause* us to do whatever we decide to do, including to act in ways that are called mental illness.

Control theory explains that all we do is act. We never react or respond, since only dead things or machines react or respond to outside events. The behavior of all living creatures, no matter how deviant it may be, is always an attempt to satisfy some purpose that exists within themselves.

All Human Behavior Is an Attempt to Satisfy Basic Needs That Are Built into Our Genetic Structure

Control theory contends that human beings are born with five basic needs that are built into their genetic structures: (1) love and belonging, (2) power, (3) freedom, (4) fun, and (5) survival. From birth, we will spend all of our lives trying to satisfy these five needs. It is this lifelong attempt that gives control theory its name, because what we are always attempting to do is *to control the world around us* so that we can best satisfy one or more of these needs. This means that we, more than all other living organisms, are always attempting to control our environment. We almost never settle for accepting it or, as it is commonly expressed, adjusting to it.

When I say "control our environment," I do not necessarily mean dominating it, although we may be the only species that does actually try to dominate the world around us. It is also necessary to understand that the only way we can do this is through our own total behavior. Therefore, what we actually do is control ourselves or, specifically, choose the total behaviors that we believe will best get us what we want from the world around us.

For example, driven by the need to love and belong, a small child may not want to stay home with a baby-sitter. The child may attempt to control the parents by choosing the total behavior of first sulking and then sobbing pitifully as they prepare to leave. The child hopes that what he or she is choosing will persuade the parents to choose to stay home. If they often do stay home, as a result the child will learn that choosing misery is a powerful, controlling choice and may sulk and depress as a major way to attempt to control people for the rest of his or her life. To gain control, many people are more than willing to choose to suffer.

Every client who comes for counseling—for example, the man whose wife left him or another who is sent because of drunk driving—is choosing whatever he or she is doing or complaining about as an attempt to satisfy one or more of these needs. Our job as reality therapists is to counsel these clients to choose a better total behavior than the one they are choosing. The fact that what we do is relatively clear-cut and understandable does not make it easy. It takes a skilled counselor to persuade clients that they are choosing what they are complaining about or doing and, further, to persuade them that it is to their benefit to choose a more effective total behavior.

What I have explained so far is the bare skeleton of control theory. For a more detailed explanation, I refer you to my book *Control Theory* (Glasser, 1984). Nevertheless, I believe that this brief explanation of a complex theory is basis enough for me to explain how we counsel people. Keep in mind that we do not diagnose people in the traditional way, because all people, whether they need counseling or managing, have the same underlying problem: *The total behavior they are choosing to satisfy one or more of their needs is painful or has led someone in authority to choose pain to deal with it.*

Clients' problems usually have their roots in the past, but their solution is always in the present, because the need or needs that are unsatisfied can only be satisfied in the present. It is not possible to satisfy needs retroactively. No matter how much the clients want to talk about the past, whatever happens in therapy that leads to change is always in the present. Let us take a look at the following case to see how this works out in practice.

AN EXAMPLE OF REALITY THERAPY COUNSELING

A young woman came for counseling because she was unable to sustain a love relationship and had become aware that she was fearful of men. She said that as soon as she got close to a man and began, or sometimes only contemplated, a sexual relationship, she would begin to suffer from severe anxiety and would figure out a way to end the relationship. But as soon as she did so, she would regret what she had done, and would choose to feel guilt and to hate herself. She then would try to establish another relationship, but, as soon as she again got close to intimacy, the process would repeat itself. Recently, a caring man, whom she had rejected, told her that she had a problem and that she should get some counseling.

In counseling, she made it clear that she wanted love and intimacy, but was unable to satisfy this need in an adult sexual way. The reality therapist was matter of fact with her. He explained that she, like all of us, had the need for love, but that she obviously did not trust men enough to satisfy it. She agreed. The counselor also told her that there must be a reason for her lack of trust. She was sophisticated enough to realize that as nothing frightening had occurred during her adolescence or adult life, the reason might be in her childhood. Early in her life, she either had had a bad experience with a man or she was fearful of having a bad experience because of something she saw, heard, or even imagined. It is also possible that she had misinterpreted as a bad experience something that went on in her childhood that is not usually seen as frightening. But whatever had happened, she claimed not to remember it.

Counseling, however, is not police work. It is not necessary to find the smoking gun of actual abuse and, in many cases, it will never be found. What was important here was for her to realize that she was living her life as if something had happened that frightened her. The fact that she could not actually remember such an event did not matter. She had to assume that she had a fear that was handicapping her life. If she did not get over this fear, she never would be able to satisfy her need for love and belonging in the adult way that she desired. If the counselor were to fall into the trap of thinking that "only if we uncover the actual trauma, will she be able to go on to adult sexuality," the woman might fail to get the help she needed. She might be more than willing to look for the trauma endlessly, because this quest would excuse her from the hard work of solving her problem.

The counselor knew that the woman could not undo what she had suffered or believed she had suffered in the past, and that what she had to do was to deal with her problem in the present. To do this, it was not necessary to go through all of her failed adult relationships or to talk a great deal about her anxiety or her guilt. She knew she had pushed men away. What the therapist had to teach her was that she was suffering because she did not have the love she wanted in her present life, not because of what she believed had happened to her in the past.

It was necessary to establish that the love she wanted was not extraordinary—it is what all people want. But she needed to be reminded that it is not that easy to find. Even people who had a loving and supportive childhood may find themselves inadequate when it comes to finding satisfying adult love. The reality therapist needed to be able to make her aware of the fact that she was choosing to fear men, not because of anything that actually happened, but because she did not have the skill to find the adult relationship she wanted.

To get started, the counselor asked her to talk in some detail about the best of her failed relationships. She told him that the latest one had been pretty good. She was able to be intimate with the man for several months, but then he disappointed her in what seemed, in retrospect, a small way. He had agreed to take her somewhere she had wanted desperately to go, but then found he had to work and had to break his promise. She said that although she believed him, she could not accept what she felt was a rejection. She provoked a fight and they broke up. It was then that he suggested that she seek counseling.

It became obvious that no matter what her past was, she had not yet learned how to relate to a man in a way that would lead to a trusting relationship. This is the tragedy of trauma, real or imagined. If we fail to learn to trust, we may be severely handicapped. Whatever the reason, this woman had failed to learn to trust men. If she could not learn to do this in counseling, she might never learn it. This was probably her best chance. But she had to have a counselor who would not fall into the trap of thinking that her

problem was in the past and that he had to focus on the past. Her problem was from the past, but its effect was in the present and *it had to be solved in the present.*

It was in the present that the counselor found the real resistance. If the counselor were to persist in focusing on the past, the woman's unsuccessful struggle to remember the trauma could be false resistance; it could even become a game that she would enjoy playing. In a sense, it would satisfy her need for power, as she said, "See what a big problem I have and how inadequate you are. You can't even help me get to the root of it." This might be a part of her life game, trying to hide her own inadequacy by showing that men are inadequate and she now included the counselor in this group.

But this is a game that reality therapists do not play. No matter what happened, and we would never deny that whether or not she could remember it, something might have happened, she had to deal with the fact that she did not have the adult behaviors to deal with men. She was attractive and would soon find another man, so it was necessary to help her plan to deal with this old situation more effectively, such as to learn some honest and sensible ways to determine whether a man is trustworthy. It would pay to talk to her about what she did with the man whom she had trusted that was effective and sensible—and also what she did to test him that was childish and foolish even before that weekend when they broke up.

Reality therapy is not general; it is specific. With gentleness, but firmness, she had to be asked to describe and evaluate the usual behaviors that she chose as she tried unsuccessfully to relate to men. But while what she actually did was important, it was equally important that she realize that she chose to do whatever it was. If she could accept that it was a choice, she then would have the opportunity to reject childish choices and try something that might work better.

The client had to be treated by the counselor as an adult, as someone who, even though she lacked adult behaviors, could learn them and begin to make more adult choices. It was she who might have been holding onto the childhood trauma, because she did not have the social and sexual skills to give it up, but one should accept her as the adult that she was in many ways. In our terms, we are more than willing to accept that she might not have had control over her life when she was a child, but also that she was no longer a child. She was in our office to learn to be an adult, and the question was, "Does she want to take effective control or not?" Was she ready to evaluate what she was doing then and commit herself, even if it was frightening, to discard some of her old childish behaviors and try something new? When she was ready to do this, the counseling would merge into coaching or teaching. She needed to plan what she was going to do as she embarked on a new relationship that was mature and sensible. If with this coaching she was able to get into an adult relationship, then counseling would have succeeded.

WHAT THE COUNSELOR DOES TO BRING THIS ABOUT

CREATING THE COUNSELING ENVIRONMENT

In practicing reality therapy, the counselor is taught to follow a basic set of guidelines that have been developed over the past 25 years with thousands of clients. These guidelines are best documented in two books of actual cases involving many skilled reality therapists working with the gamut of psychological problems, *What Are You Doing* (Glasser, 1983) and *Control Theory in the Practice of Reality Therapy* (Glasser, 1989). Basically, when dealing with a client, the counselor, whether counseling only or combining counseling with managing as previously explained, tries to accomplish two tasks with the client. First, and this continues throughout the counseling, the counselor creates and maintains the counseling environment. This environment is as need satisfying for the client as the counselor can make it. It is a warm, personal relationship and is best described as the counselor's attempt to become a friend to the client.

When this is done correctly, the client will believe that, no matter what he or she tells the counselor, the client is both safe and respected. The counselor is the client's advocate. He or she is always trying to help the client to find a better way to live. The counselor will plan with the client and will ask him or her to commit to the counselor to try to follow up on any plan that the client agrees is beneficial to progress. This means that it is important to the counselor that the client does what he or she says he or she will do. The counselor will be tough in that he or she will not excuse the failure to follow up on plans, even if the client tries to convince the counselor that the plan was too hard to follow.

Being tough enough not to accept excuses, however, does not mean that the counselor will ever be punitive or critical. There is no criticism or punishment in reality therapy. While no excuses are accepted, the counselor will always ask, "Do you want to make another plan?" Once the client makes a commitment to action to solve the problem, there must be a plan, but there is no single or perfect plan. If, after making a good attempt to follow it, a plan does not work, we do not waste time with excuses, but work together to come up with a different plan.

Above all, throughout the counseling experience, counselors, in all they do, send the strong message that the client's problem is solvable. If control therapy is correct, there is no such thing as an unsolvable psychological problem. It may take time and the solution may not be as good as the client wanted in the beginning, but choosing better total behaviors will lead to a more satisfying life. The client is constantly assured that the therapist will not give up and, in the beginning, all the client has to do is attend the therapy sessions. The rest is up to the skill of the therapist and how fast the client is able to learn to make more effective choices and to put them to work.

THE PROCEDURES THAT LEAD TO CHANGE

The only beliefs that lead human beings to change their behavior are embedded on the following control theory logic

1. The conviction that, in the long run, the total behavior or behaviors they are choosing will not get them what they want. Clients are always asked to tell the counselor what they want. (The counselor must help clients to

understand that they must keep what they want within their power to achieve it.)

2. The belief that there is another total behavior or behaviors that they can choose that will get them closer to what they want than whatever they are currently choosing.

This means that as soon as the counselor judges that the client is ready to focus on making a change, the counselor asks the client to take a good look at both (1) what the client wants and (2) what he or she is choosing to do with his or her life. This may mean that with many capable clients, the counselor will begin immediately to teach them enough control theory so that they understand that they are choosing the acting and thinking components of all they do. But whether or not clients are willing or able to learn the control theory that will accelerate this process, they are still taught that what they are complaining about is chosen through the counselor's asking of some form of the following crucial therapy question: *"Is what you are now choosing to do (your actions and thoughts) getting you what you want?"* If the counselor is not skillful enough to get clients to see that the acting and thinking that they are now choosing will not get them what they want, therapy will not work. In almost all cases, a well-trained reality therapist possesses these necessary skills.

MANAGING THE CLIENT WHO DOES NOT WANT TO CHANGE

While we are concerned with the resistance of all clients, many of whom do not want to change the way they are choosing to live their lives, we are most concerned with the resistance of clients we are asked to manage because they have to accept someone else's agenda, including ours. Most of the world's counseling is done with this kind of client, and most of these clients do not want to change. They find that it feels better to keep doing what they are doing than to change to what we want them to do. Our job is to convince them that what we are asking them to do is better for them, and *we cannot do this if we are coercive*. People resist coercion because it frustrates their basic need

for power. Therefore, the key to dealing effectively with people whom we are asked to manage is to understand that we cannot make them do what we want them to do. What we must do is convince them that they will be better off if they follow our agenda.

Basically, this means that they should accept us. Control theory explains that all of us have a special place in our brain where we store the knowledge of what we have discovered throughout life that feels good. While it is important for the counselor to find a way to get into this special place in the heads of all of their clients, it is absolutely essential that we do it with the clients we are asked to manage. Human beings will only give up what they find to be satisfying if they are convinced that there is another way to find the same satisfaction. And the only person who can convince us that this is worth looking for is someone whom we put into our brain as a need-satisfying person.

Since almost all management is coercive and based mostly on punishment, this kind of management has little chance to work with people who choose addictive, delinquent, or illegal total behaviors. It has been tried with them over and over, and all that has happened is that they reject the managers. But, in doing so, they have also separated themselves from the satisfying, responsible relationships they need. It is the task of the counselor to provide this kind of relationship, and what I have explained so far has a good chance of doing this if the counselor is careful to abstain from all coercion. Thus, when we manage people using reality therapy, we are never coercive. How to do this in public schools is the subject of my latest (Glasser, 1990) book on education. However, the same principles would apply to all the people we manage.

SUMMING UP

In my opinion, it is not possible for reality therapists to be successful with clients unless they have learned enough control theory to put it to work themselves. Just as the Freudians insist that every psychoanalyst in training be analyzed, we tell all those whom we train that they will not be successful at counseling, managing, or teaching unless they can utilize control theory in their personal lives. There is no other way. But we do not make this a requirement for becoming a reality therapist for two reasons. We do not coerce and we have no way to measure whether or not they have done so successfully. However, our training is designed to convince them that this is a necessary effort, and we have evidence that the people we have trained are doing this more and more as they gain the skills we teach.

REFERENCES

Deming, W. E. (1982). *Out of the crisis*. Cambridge, MA: Massachusetts Institute for Technology Press.
Glasser, N. J. (1980). *What are you doing?* New York: Harper & Collins.
Glasser, N. J. (1989). *Control theory in the practice of reality therapy*. New York: Harper & Collins.
Glasser, W. (1984). *Control theory*. New York: Harper & Collins.
Glasser, W. (1990). *The quality school, managing students without coercion*. New York: Harper & Collins.
Powers, W. (1973). *Behavior the control of perception*. Chicago: Aldus Press.

Discussion by Jeffrey K. Zeig, Ph.D.

◆

I found Dr. Glasser's words compelling and his logic impeccable. The understructure of "reality therapy" fits with my *weltanschauung*: effective therapies often proceed best when therapists assume the stance that Glasser offers.

In response to Dr. Glasser's brilliant induction, I decided to access a trance. Let me waste no time in telling you the end point of my very positive trance experience: I concluded that I am a reality theorist, but not a reality therapist. It is merely one of those cases where people use the same map and wind up in different territories. This should create no surprise. Using the same map to arrive at different locations happens on a daily basis in nearly every family.

Before getting to the central point (which, to me, is to enter the land of metaphor), I will examine the constitution of reality therapy and discuss points of agreement and disagreement.

There is much value in this approach, which seems to be based on four principles:

1. *We are the creators of our fate, not the victims*. This admirable concept of "responseability" surfaces in a number of important contemporary methods of psychotherapy, including the work of Albert Ellis and the Redecision model of Robert and Mary Goulding. Many outstanding therapies begin with this premise.

2. *Events should be considered "information" rather than stimuli (in the stimulus—response sense)*. Loosely translated, this proposition pours buckshot into the "make–feel" disposition to which many people cling tenaciously: No one can make another person feel sad, mad, or bad. We decide how to act; it is our choice. Events do not make us feel anything. Ultimately, we decide our reaction; we compose our affective responses.

Consequently, it is better to consider problems as dynamic processes than as static states. A grammatical shift can facilitate this conceptual shift. For example, it is more productive therapeutically to think in terms of a person's "depressing" (gerund) himself or herself than it is to grapple with "depression" (noun), because it is easier to conceive of modifying an active process of "depressing" than it is to conceive of changing a static "depression."

3. *People are driven by basic needs; one's behavior is one's best attempt to deal with the world in a manner that satisfies those needs*. In effect, reality therapists "teach

choice" by instructing clients how to satisfy needs in an adaptive manner. Reality therapists pose the catalyzing question, "Is what you're doing (choosing) getting you what you want?" (As will be seen, I believe therapists should keep this basic question in mind—literally.) A corollary to this question would be the understanding that patients hold mental images or expectations of an ideal that they can be taught to recognize and increasingly to achieve.

4. *The concept of "total behavior" comprises action, thought, feeling, and physiology.* Reality therapists focus on changing action and thought, which are "always voluntarily chosen," and which, in turn, will alter feeling and physiology. Problems are solved in the here-and-now, and it is the patient who does the work.

I am in general agreement with these assumptions. The epistemology is essentially strategic in the sense that Jay Haley (1973) defined therapy as being "strategic" if the clinician initiates what happens during the session and designs a particular approach for each problem. I am glad to think about my patients using reality therapy philosophy— which is why I am willing to describe myself as a reality *theorist*—although interventions that I would base on those propositions would be different than interventions a reality therapist would take. Moreover, although I agree with the philosophy, I do not necessarily agree with the idea of making the philosophy an overt aspect of therapy. Since most influence situations occur on a covert rather than an overt level, it may be better to keep one's philosophy commensurately covert.

In outlining the areas of disagreement between reality therapy and more experiential methods, I will begin by first examining the fourth principle of reality therapy, the concept of "total behavior." It seems to me that "total behavior" is comprised of more than action, thought, feeling, and physiology. Social factors also influence total behavior. Indeed, no behavior is independent of social determinants. For example, when I am driving alone in my car, my actions, thoughts, feelings, and physiology are different than when I am driving with

someone. I am unwilling to dismiss decades of work in social psychology and family systems theory.

The social psychology literature has demonstrated the effects of interpersonal factors. In one classic study, Regan (1971) invited two subjects to participate in an art-appreciation experiment in which they would be asked to rate the quality of several paintings. Being a social psychology experiment (which are often based in deception), one of the subjects was actually an experimental confederate. There were two conditions: In one, the stooge did a small favor for the experimental subject. (For example, he returned from a rest period with a drink, saying that since he had bought one for himself, he thought he would bring back an extra for his fellow subject.) In the second condition, the stooge took a break, but returned empty-handed. After the "experiment" had been conducted and the paintings rated, the stooge requested a favor from the subject. He asked the subject to buy raffle tickets for a good cause at 25 cents apiece. The major finding of the study was that subjects who were treated to a gift bought twice as many tickets as the subjects who weren't. Think about that the next time anyone hands you a flower at the airport and asks for a donation!

This example is merely one of many: Casual perusal of the social psychology and family therapy literatures points to the numerous social dynamics that affect behavior.

Reality therapy seems to extol the value of achieving an internal locus of control, which is good, but not to the point of neglecting interpersonal responsiveness. If we exclude social factors, we overlook potential avenues of effective intervention. For example, in many of Erickson's cases, patients discovered dormant strengths when they "found themselves" in new social settings. One cannot volitionally control social factors in the same manner as one can control actions. But one can make use of social factors to promote salutary change.

As far as the second principle is concerned, I like the hypothesis of reality therapy that views events as information rather than as stimuli that invariably cause responses. I even would extend the idea and consider events as "fuel" to be utilized. I described this idea in my

Invited Address at this conference and I can reiterate some of those points here.

As was mentioned earlier, it is important to turn problems into processes. However, the therapist can do more than turning a nominalized problem (e.g., "depression") into a gerund (e.g., "depressing"). For example, a therapist can wonder, "*How* is this patient depressing himself?"—and then seek to discover the patient's strategy for accomplishing the process of depression. The individual, for instance, could *do* depression by fixating attention internally, being inactive, thinking negatively, and living in the past. Then therapy could proceed by using such techniques as metaphorical communication, task assignments, or therapeutic hypnosis. Such approaches can trigger the patient's associations to previously dormant abilities to focus externally, be active, think positively, and live in the present. By considering *how* the patient is *doing* the problem and creating interventions to elicit solution components that are opposite to the problem components, the therapist extends the idea of turning the problem into a process.

The third central principle of reality therapy is that we are driven by basic needs. "Driven" implies autonomic functioning. Yet the contention of reality therapy is that actions and feelings are "*always* voluntarily chosen" (my italics). I do not think this is true: We exert little volitional control over our speaking, walking, or thinking. I have heard experts estimate that we have as many as 90 thoughts each minute. It would be impossible to control so many thoughts. There are *degrees* of control we can exert over actions, feelings, thoughts, and physiology. (Experiments in hypnosis have demonstrated control over peripheral blood flow, for example.) We even have some control over the regulation of basic needs.

We then arrive at the phenomenon of symptoms. One characteristic of symptoms is that they are experienced as *driving* us. They feel as if they happen automatically. I agree with Glasser that therapists should not commit the error of thinking that symptoms, in fact, function autonomously. Therapists should believe that patients have more control than they admit. However, therapists should not discount the fact that patients experience themselves as

being out of control. In my Invited Address, I contended that hypnotic induction demonstrates to patients that they can have a constructive dissociative response. This is the very nature of hypnotic induction: A patient can relinquish "control" for positive ends. The point is to meet the patient at the patient's frame of reference, rather than to ask the patient to fit into a preconceived template.

A related problem in reality therapy is that interventions are based on a model of teaching. I eschew the perspective of *teaching* as a therapeutic mainstay, preferring the concept of *eliciting*. I believe that every person has within himself or herself the resources necessary to achieve change. Depressed people already know how to be happy. I have never gotten much mileage out of teaching a patient the basic doctrine of reality therapy, which is, "You choose your own behavior." Rather, I structure therapeutic experiences via the use of hypnosis, metaphor, or task assignments so that, to their own credit, patients can rediscover their ability to change. It is the difference between instructing a person about the function of a tool and giving the person the direct experience of using it.

In working with patients, I might begin with a technique of reality therapy. (In hypnotic parlance, I would call this "direct suggestion.") A percentage of people would respond favorably to this approach. For those who did not respond well, I would not do *more* reality therapy by teaching control theory louder and longer, as though sheer volume and repetition would activate change. This approach treats the human system as if it were a physical object. Such an epistemology was summarized succinctly by Gregory Bateson, who, I believe, intoned: "You can kick a rock and compute its acceleration and trajectory. But if you kick a dog, it is a whole different story."

Bateson's "truism" provides an appropriate transition into the land of metaphor. I once listened to an audiotape of one of Erickson's lectures conducted for professionals in the 1950s. It seemed like one long induction of hypnosis; it did not resemble a content-based lecture, the kind of teaching to which I had been exposed during my formal education. I asked Erickson about his seminar. He replied that he didn't listen to tapes of his lectures, indicating, "I taught to motivate people, not to provide information." Erickson's therapy was similar: Elicit mood and perspective, do not merely provide content.

In one case, Erickson worked with an anorexic patient (Zeig, 1985). Let us examine one step in the elaborate treatment process. Anorexics often adhere to a particular kind of moral structure characterized by remarkably stubborn honesty. In response to Erickson, the girl agreed that he could be interested in her general well-being, not merely in aspects of her physical health. She further agreed that he could be interested in her dental health. Subsequently, Erickson effected a solemn promise that she would do whatever he suggested to ensure her dental health, as long as it did not entail swallowing anything. Then Erickson suggested that she should use cod liver oil as a mouthwash on a regular basis. The patient did as suggested, but conveniently "lost" the mouthwash in short order. In this way, she committed an offense that she agreed was punishable.

What would constitute adequate punishment? Erickson and the girl's mother decided that the consequence would be a scrambled egg. The patient's body thought it was nutrition. Psychologically, however, the patient was accepting her due punishment: She had morally agreed to do something, she had committed an offense, and she had been caught.

Another approach would have been to use reality therapy. Erickson could have reminded the girl of her goals, one of which had been good health. Then he could have shown her how anorexic behavior did not improve her chances of achieving the goal. Subsequently, he could have taught her "control." All of this would have been well and good, if it would have worked.

Here is a related example. I remember watching Carl Whitaker conduct a demonstration interview with the family of a hospitalized schizophrenic. This was a fishbowl setting for a master's class at the Philadelphia Child Guidance Clinic. Experienced students watched from the periphery as Whitaker sat with the family. Frequently during the interview, Whitaker fell asleep. I think he even reported a dream. His quips often seemed ambiguous and confusing, but upon closer examination,

they had deep and directed meaning. His method worked; by the end of the interview, the patient and family were talking directly and concretely.

Whitaker's technique was simple. He could be crazier than the family (although his craziness was constructive). Someone in the situation had to act sane. If it wasn't going to be the therapist, it would have to be the patient. In essence, a therapist can create a social vacuum so that patients can move forward independently.

These examples from Erickson's and Whitaker's works present therapy as a vehicle for providing mood- and motive-altering experiences. Therapy involves more than the imparting of information. The message in both examples (Erickson and Whitaker) is similar to the underlying theme of reality therapy that you can control your behavior. However, the message was experientially discovered; it was not just taught.

In summary, reality therapy teaches patients a method for meta-analyzing their own behavior. Patients can understand their situation and decide to behave differently. This is a great idea, as far as it goes. It is nice to give a person a tool, especially one that is very powerful. But it might be even better to provide many tools. A therapeutic philosophy should open up new avenues for intervention, not limit them. If a therapist wants patients to discover choices, the therapist should "*do* choice" in his or her interventions and model the desired outcome. Moreover, I believe therapy should provide more than information. Among other things, therapy should stimulate mood.

If people experience unwanted autonomous functionings, we should not confront them with the idea of "control." Rather, we should create experiences so that they can realize, from their own histories and to their own credit, "Yes, *I* can exert control." Therapy should provide experiences, not rules. Life is more experiential than cognitive. If a goal is for people to *think* about control in their lives, we should use reality therapy. If a goal is for people to *live* their lives more fully, then the approach should be more experiential.

A quote from Erickson (1965) illuminates this position:

The therapist's task should not be proselytizing the patient with his own beliefs and understandings. No patient can really understand the understandings of his therapist, nor does he need them. What is needed is the development of a therapeutic situation permitting patients to use their own thinking, their own understandings, and their own emotions in a way that best fits them in their scheme of life. [So that] in some peculiar way they can begin to unsnarl their lives in a fashion as inexplicable as was the fashion in which they had snarled their thinking and emotions. (p. 223)

REFERENCES

Haley, J. (1973). *Uncommon therapy, the psychiatric techniques of Milton H. Erickson, M.D.* New York: Norton.

Erickson, M. H. (1965). The use of symptoms as an integral part of hypnotherapy. *American Journal of Clinical Hypnosis, 8,* 57–65. Also in *Collected papers of Milton H. Erickson on hypnosis* (Vol. IV) (pp. 212–223).

Regan, D. T. (1971). Effects of a favor and liking on compliance. *Journal of Experimental Social Psychology, 7,* 627–639.

Zeig, J. K. (1985). *Experiencing Erickson.* New York: Brunner/Mazel.

RESPONSE BY DR. GLASSER

First, there's nothing that Dr. Zeig said in his critique, except for some very minor semantic differences, that I don't completely accept. I cannot include in one short chapter all the richnesses of reality therapy, but if he were to see me work, I think he would see that we are very close together.

I could clarify some things though. First of all, we don't push anything. Reality therapists are among the least pushy of all people. Also, I don't claim that the information that comes from the social milieu is not pertinent to the patient's choice. We are all part of the social milieu and the counselor is a very important part. And so everything we do is informative to the patient. It isn't the type of information you would get from the old program "Information Please." It has nothing to do with that.

Teaching is not necessarily confrontive; there are lots of other ways, and those are the skills I have, and I probably have 50 or 100 different skills. If you watch me role play, I'll show you all the skills I can come up with at the time. But I don't think you'll ever see me confront people in the sense that I am forcing them to admit that they are making a choice. That would hardly be skillful counseling.

I'll accept eliciting. I love eliciting. That's just wonderful with me. I agree completely with Gregory Bateson that it's different to kick a dog than to kick a rock. A rock doesn't care if it's kicked. Dogs have in their head a picture of themselves not being kicked, and when you kick them, they don't like it. So a rock is never going to bite you, but a dog might.

As far as Erickson and Whitaker are concerned, they're just using techniques, and they are all techniques with which I would agree. I worked with an anorexic one. I forget exactly what I did, but there was something very similar to what Erickson did. She said to me (she seemed to be a little more intelligent than Erickson's client), "Well, you're just trying to trick me into eating." I said, "Absolutely. Why in the world would you want a counselor who wasn't trying to trick you into eating when you are starving yourself to death?" She accepted that and said, "Yeah, that's a good idea. I think I'll start eating."

Thus, reality therapy is totally honest. We don't trick people. For example, I have used placebos with people, but I always told them it was a placebo. I explained what a placebo is, and, "A placebo can still be very good, it can help you." They liked their placebos, and the placebos often did help by giving them confidence.

As for Whitaker talking crazily so that the clients will talk sanely, if you know what you are doing, that's a skill—it's the thing that nobody can teach, although we try to. When Whitaker talked crazily, when Erickson said, "Rinse your mouth with cod liver oil," or anybody says anything, these are teaching skills. They are trying to teach the patient to do something better than he or she is doing: in Erickson's case, to start eating; in Whitaker's case, to start talking sanely. I've always wondered why people make such a big deal about working with crazy people and getting them to sound sane. I've never had any difficulty doing it. They want to sound sane. And unless they have been crazy from birth, they know how to talk in a sane manner. The reason they talk crazily is that they find it much more satisfying than talking sanely. To be able to talk to them in such a way that they begin to see that it's better to talk sanely than crazily is a skill. I think that many people possess that skill. It's not that hard to do.

So I appreciate Dr. Zeig's remarks, but I want to stress that we're just teaching. When I was working at the State University of New York in Plattsburg, a woman, who was in the Psychology Department, said, "I read your book *Control Theory*. And in the book, I discovered that you claimed that migraining is a choice."

I thought about her comment and I said to myself, "Well, I'm not choosing to have a painful head, but I am choosing certain total behaviors of which migraining is the physiological and feeling components as you explain." I've been doing it for 30 years. I decided to change my total behavior so that my acting and thinking would be much more satisfying. When I did, I stopped migraining. And that's what she did. When I saw her two years later, it had been two and a half years since she had had a migraine. I wasn't confrontive; I just wrote a book. She picked it out of the book and made the choice.

There's nothing necessarily confrontive about this at all. It's helping people learn something that is extremely useful in their lives. Our skill as counselors is to do it in any way we can. Certainly, if you used reality therapy, it would not be either in a confrontation or coercive way. But I like all the techniques of Milton Erickson. I especially like the one where he told the fat woman, "Gain weight." And she lost her appetite. Obviously, this was an absolutely marvelous bit of information that none of the people whom she had seen had ever offered her before.

SECTION VII

Social Issues

Eve's Daughters: The Forbidden Heroism of Women*

◆

Miriam Polster, Ph.D.

Miriam Polster, Ph.D.

Miriam Polster is Codirector of the Gestalt Training Center in San Diego, Calif., and Assistant Clinical Professor in the Department of Psychiatry, School of Medicine, at the University of California, San Diego. Along with her husband, Erving Polster, she is a coauthor of an important book on Gestalt therapy. Dr. Polster received her Ph.D. degree in Clinical Psychology from Case Western Reserve University in 1967.

Miriam Polster describes the importance of having heroic models. Our present ideals of heroism are dominated by unrealistic and larger-than-life stereotypes. Not only has this narrow view eliminated much of the heroism of women, but it has also provided men with simplistic solutions that are not only outmoded, but intimidating. Ultimately, it has deprived both sexes of a wide range of heroic examples and choices that could enrich their lives and the lives of those around them.

Polster proposes a redefinition of heroism that expands traditional images and suggests that recognizing the unhackneyed heroism that occurs in ordinary circumstances also may enrich therapeutic possibilities. She provides examples relevant to clinical practice, pointing out that "the heroic image becomes relevant to humble settings as well as to the grand stage."

Her contribution to the Evolution Conference was heroic in and of itself. Attendees' evaluations rated this Invited Address as one of the most highly valued events at the conference.

The myth of Eve is neither unintelligible nor irrelevant . . . Eve is very much alive, and every member of Western society is affected by her story. (Phillips, 1984)

For centuries, our hero tales have set forth, in dramatic and colorful terms, the cultural ideals and necessities of human times. These tales have provided countless generations of people with models of how to confront and deal effectively with hard times and personal challenges. They still do.

But along the way, and for reasons that make less sense than they once did, our images of heroism have endorsed a persistent model that has left us a legacy of ideals and behaviors that are admired in men, but mistrusted in women.

The predominant image of heroism, immortalized for centuries, has been active: bold, noisy, swift, and physically direct. Boys and men, often to their own discomfort, and sometimes even to their despair, are still admired for this kind of behavior. They have been encouraged to be tough, aggressive, self-confident, and independent—never mind whether or not this actually fits them or the times in which they live.

---

*Portions of this chapter are included in Miriam Polster's *Eve's Daughters*, published by Jossey-Bass, Inc., 1992, and have been used here with the permission of the publisher.

Correspondingly, girls and women were discouraged from exhibiting such classic heroic behaviors. They were admired for being unaggressive, gentle, submissive, and not self-confident or independent (Bardwick, 1971). Until recently, this is what most people considered normal and healthy behavior in women. Many still do, but ask yourself how healthy such behavior actually is.

The result? Heroism came to be considered an exclusively masculine attribute—one to which men could aspire—and women only if they acted like men. The image of heroism became a grand societal introjection, a massive "should" system. Under this influence, both sexes were provided with standards of "appropriateness."

It seems clear, however, that women (and men, as well) were thereby deprived of behavioral options that might actually be effective and sensible under the circumstances of their individual lives. Their sense of personal choice and competence was reduced. This is a dilemma with which we are only too familiar in psychotherapy.

HEROISM: THE FIRST DOUBLE STANDARD

Where the apple reddens
Never pry—
Lest we lose our Edens,
Eve and I.
(Robert Browning
"A Woman's Last Words")

The one-sided images that have dominated our ideas of heroism have their early expression in some of our culture's most treasured stories and legends—the Greek and Biblical accounts of the creation of the world. The oldest example of the difference in heroic recognition can be found in the stories of Prometheus and Eve. Both disobeyed the explicit commands of their gods. But although their behaviors were strikingly similar, Prometheus is regarded as a hero, whereas Eve has come down in most accounts as a classic villain.

According to Greek legend, Prometheus made the first man, fashioning him (like the God of Genesis) out of earth and water (Graves, 1982). Zeus, the lord of Mount Olympus, further empowered Prometheus to give his new creature a gift—any gift but fire, which was to remain the exclusive property of the gods.

Prometheus had a special fondness for his offspring and wanted to enrich him as much as he could. Fire seemed the perfect gift, and so Prometheus stole fire from the gods and gave it to the first man. For this, he was punished severely; Zeus had him chained to a rock where a vulture came daily to eat his liver, which, by the way, grew back nightly, thus extending his cruel (and certainly unusual) punishment even further (Bulfinch, 1979).

Prometheus' gift, as in most mythological themes, was a metaphor. His gift of fire was an assertion of his wish that his creature dominate all the other animals. It also symbolized one step along the way in humankind's increasing control of the dangerous natural elements that threatened human survival. Not only could fire create light in the darkness, but it also could transmute raw and unformed matter into a useful form. Prometheus' gift forged an ambitious connection between human aspiration and divine mastery. Although his gift proved to be a mixed blessing, generating its own burdens, his generosity was esteemed as a noble and beneficial act.

What about Eve?

One tradition tells us how the wily serpent nudged Eve against the forbidden tree and thereby proved to her that she would not die from just *touching* it (as Jehovah had warned). But this was just the opening salvo in his sales pitch. The serpent went further and argued that this proved that she could, therefore, also *eat* of the fruit of that tree—and not die (Graves & Patai, 1966). The benefit of that snack, the serpent promised, would be that the day she ate of the fruit of the tree, her eyes would "be opened" and she would be "as God, knowing good and evil." As with Prometheus, Eve aspired to a capacity that was explicitly limited to divinity. But this time the suggestion came from a disreputable source and was directed toward a gullible and naive subject.

Eve was enterprising. She found the serpent's message irresistible: Imagine, a privilege reserved for divinity also might be appropriate for human purposes. Like Prometheus, she was ambitious, and like Prometheus, she was punished for her defiance. But the similarity ends there.

Prometheus suffered in a "manly" fashion. He suffered alone, and he did not lie or try to pin the blame on anyone else. Once punished, he endured his agony admirably. He became the subject of poetry, music, and paintings, all of which extolled him. Eve, on the other hand, has been portrayed as evasive and unadmirable. She has been held responsible for evoking all the pain and toil that her descendants have endured ever since.

But let us take another look. Actually, Eve's act of disobedience admitted her—and all of us, whether or not we want it—into a previously forbidden territory of awareness, the knowledge of good and evil. Because of Eve, we all live in a world where personal consciousness underlies individual decision, where personal responsibility replaced docile obedience to divine authority. Like Prometheus' gift of energy and power, Eve's legacy ensured that, through our own energy, we are now to be held responsible for the consequences, happy as well as tragic, of our own actions.

Most parents welcome the development of curiosity, judgment, and conscience in their children. The curiosity of children and their increasing ability to ask useful questions mark their progress in becoming intelligent, reasonable, and self-determining members of society. The elementary questions of childhood, and the responses to these questions, serve as the basis for the moral and ethical standards of adulthood. As psychotherapists, we consider the development and support of these qualities essential to healthy self-governance.

Eve was unwilling to live innocently under protective restrictions, submissive to a divine but unexplained command that assured her status forever as the protected child of a benevolent but not-to-be-questioned father. Her surge into maturity grew naturally from her curiosity and liveliness of mind. She, like Prometheus, had aspirations that distinguished her from less complicated creatures—animals for whom knowledge and choice were dominated by instinctual species-specific needs and controlled, therefore, almost exclusively by instinct.

The knowledge of good and evil is a source of energy and power, like fire, and brings with it the inevitable need to develop judgment, deliberation, and conscience.

The legacy of Prometheus is still with us, even though our generation has gone far beyond the simple fire power of our mythological ancestors. We have escalated this energy into creative and life-supporting activities that Prometheus could not have dreamed of, but we have learned, to our dismay, that it also can carry within it a destructive power that our ancestors thought only gods possessed. The issue now is whether or not we can develop the wisdom to control this force.

The legacy of Eve is also still with us. Unwilling to live in a Paradise where she could not direct her own thoughts and behavior, her example has resounded throughout history in other troublesome human demands for appropriate participation and self-governance. The American colonists and the French peasantry made the same claim centuries later. Less than 100 years after that, woman suffragists asserted their right to vote on the laws and legislators that in large part determined their way of life. Eve's legacy reverberates in every woman's assertion that it is her birthright to make informed decisions about the conduct of her own life and of the world in which she lives.

Eve's dilemma also is repeated in the predicament that many modern women experience. Few women today would be willing to submit to an imposed innocence, nor would they believe that such a prerequisite would carry the promise of a Paradise in which it is worthwhile to live. Hungry for the full exercise of their intelligence and energy, modern women are asking disturbing questions and making troublesome demands. Their struggles lead women out of a distant and mythic Paradise into a real world of struggle—and achievement.

THE FUNCTIONS AND ATTRIBUTES OF HEROISM

Without heroes, we're all plain people and don't know how far we can go.

(Bernard Malamud,
The Natural)

The search for heroes begins in our child-hood and continues for a lifetime. As children, we knew pretty early who our heroes were; we found them in our families and in our fairy tales. Later, as adolescents and adults, we peered beyond the limits of our accustomed selves and found heroes in other times, other places, and sometimes other worlds. The concept of hero-ism nourished a constant and important hunger. It connected us with eternal and central human concerns.

The image of the hero endures because it serves a basic human need. It appears in differ-ent forms, with different voices and different actions. At its best, our admiration for heroes represents the human desire to resolve, even for a moment, the inconsistencies and injustices that every person experiences or witnesses. Heroism links the events and challenges of the commonplace actions, when behavior often seems dictated by reflex or habit, and reminds us of the lasting concerns and aspirations that have animated the human spirit for centuries. The hero dramatically transforms noble impulse into appropriate action, and for that moment, the kaleidoscopic pieces of human experience fall into place.

In its earliest form, the heroic image was a persuasive way to assure the continued survival of the community, be it family, clan, or tribe. In primitive times, a definition of heroism based on strength, speed, and the physical ability to overpower an adversary was essential to sur-vival. Introspection would be, at best, a leisure activity, not useful in dangerous conditions.

Today, however, thoughtful men and women are questioning whether or not the classic stereotype continues to offer a viable promise of survival in our complicated universe. Mark Gerzon (1982), for example, suggests that we now have a choice of heroes but that they must be heroes of a different kind, since today we *all* live on the battlefield. John Kegan (1987), too, eloquently points out the risks that inhere in our antiquated concept of heroic leadership. He argues that we live in a "postheroic" age, and that this is no time for our leaders to play Alex-ander the Great.

If we think of Eve as a hero like Prometheus, instead of as a disreputable sinner, her behavior becomes a challenging legacy instead of a taint.

Eve's Biblical name, Hahweh, means "the mother of us all" (Phillips, 1984). So we live in the world she left us—no Paradise to be sure. We pick up where she left off. Her struggles pre-ceded ours, but they still are relevant to ours, and even more important, her heroism adds a woman's dimension to the heroic image.

Once we move beyond the archaic heroic stereotypes, it is apparent that heroes are more numerous than we thought. Such an abundance of heroes, fully perceived and appreciated, pro-vides a range of heroic characteristics that are shared by women and men. The power of the heroic image to encourage and inspire is not lost; it is actually enlarged. For the individual, the sense of personal heroism can make the dif-ference between feeling like a victim of immu-table influences and feeling like a person who has a hand in shaping the events of her or his own life.

WOMEN'S HEROISM

What distinguishes the heroism of women in particular? Let us single out two elements, con-nection and fairness or responsibility, although there are more. These particular characteristics add breadth and dimension to the more tradi-tional images we have inherited. Perhaps, if we can assimilate them into our present images, it will make the heroic attitude more reachable for contemporary men, as well as for women.

CONNECTION

Gilligan, Lyons, and Hamner (1990) point out how the sense of connection shapes much of women's adolescence. Tannen (1990), too, has shown how the sense of connection pervades women's language. It is also a rich source of their heroism. Women's heroism is more likely to be marked by a sense of personal connection to other people with whom they feel a strong bond of kinship. This kinship may be familial, it may be neighborly, or it may be a link with other people with whom they feel they share a plight.

Much of women's heroism is directed by a strong sense of "the other." Their political involvement, for example, often begins in fighting for or opposing issues at a *grass-roots* level, in circumstances that move them or their loved ones personally, with characters with problems with which they can identify. From these beginnings, they move on. Many women who later worked for women's suffrage, for example, actually cut their political teeth on the abolitionist cause.

Remember the persistent vigil of the mothers and wives of political victims in South America? Under the windows of the dictators, they carried photographs of their husbands, sons, and daughters who had disappeared. These individual pictures cohered like tiles in a mosaic—each one adding its share of protest against the oppressor.

Sophia Bracy Harris and her sister were the first black children to go to an all-white high school in Wetumpka, Ala., in 1965. Her home was bombed, and she lived daily with the ostracism and scorn of both students and faculty. Years later, inspired by that early experience, she organized the Black Woman's Leadership and Economic Development Project to help black women get off of welfare and out of dead-end jobs. She remembered the anguish of her own high school days and wanted to help others to move beyond their pain. She said, "I'm not talking struggle. Struggle is OK. It's the pain that is wrong" (from *Mother Jones Magazine*, January 1988).

From their beginnings with personal projects, women moved on to founding local institutions to care for the sick, the needy, and those too young or too weak to care for themselves. Now women are moving on even further, to more global issues, generalizing from individual cases into powerful statements that dramatize larger concerns. The women who were active in political campaigns, either for specific causes or as workers for someone else's candidacy, have progressed in increasing numbers to become candidates themselves.

FAIRNESS OR RESPONSIBILITY

In a ground-breaking study, Carol Gilligan (1982) inquired into the basis on which women and men make their moral judgments. She observed that men seem more likely to base such judgments on a principle of "fairness," while the judgments of women more often rest on the basis of "responsibility."

"Fairness" implies a set of rules or a code (either articulated or implicit) that determines what behaviors may be justifiable under certain circumstances. Furthermore, it then establishes precedents that are to regulate subsequent interactions. The concept of fairness assumes the existence of a rational and orderly world.

The problem is that, all too often, fairness is an ethic that is invoked to govern the dealings between supposed equals. While this is admirable in theory, it may be a failure in practice, because this equality rests uneasily on an exclusionary system cf eligibility. Some individuals, although subject to a system's rules, have been powerless in formulating them. Continuing debates about the need for separate *but* equal criteria for school curricula, funds, and teaching staff, and about quota systems that some people posit create new ills to take the place of those they were set up to correct, are examples of the riddles that remain to be unraveled in the name of fairness.

How one woman combined a sense of fairness and a heroic sense of connection is exemplified by the legal battle of Beulah Mae Donald against the Mobile, Ala., Klansmen who murdered and lynched her son Michael. The trial was dramatic, with a tearful witness-stand apology from one of the defendants and a forgiving response from Ms. Donald. When the trial was over, the jury had awarded her a sum of money that led to the Klan's having to turn over to her the deed to its headquarters building. To her, the money was unimportant, as she had lived on little money all her life. What was important to her was that it had been proved that Michael had done no wrong (reported in the *New York Times*, November 1, 1987).

"Responsibility" is less devoted to calculating equality or regulating evenhanded transactions. Considerations about responsibility hinge instead on a scale of relationship, continuity, and circumstantial complexity. The dominant values here are interpersonal. They center around human costs rather than statistical values that are figured in percentages and precedents.

There is no doubt that the principle of fairness regulates many important human affairs. It seems clear, however, that these principles may not always be adequate to deal with much that matters deeply to many people. No sensible argument would try to establish which of the two values is superior. But moral judgments strongly influence the heroic response. *Heroism, after all, is idealism in action.*

The classic heroic images that have lasted throughout centuries still animate the heroic attitude. Cleared of traditional stereotypes, they can reflect the influence of women's heroism, enriching the heroic possibilities for men as well as women. Let us consider four basic attributes of heroism, essential values that animate the heroic attitude and that are served by heroes of either sex.

FOUR BASIC FUNCTIONS AND ATTRIBUTES OF HEROISM

FIRST: RESPECT FOR HUMAN LIFE

The single outstanding and lasting example of heroic behavior is when one person risks her or his life to save another's. And women are well represented in those efforts. Uli Dericksen, the purser on a plane that was involved in a 1985 hijacking, is credited with saving the lives of the plane's passengers. One survivor said, "She put her body between blows and took blows herself. I think there would have been many more killings, perhaps an entire planeload, if it had not been for Uli." And what did Ms. Dericksen herself say? "Fortunately or unfortunately, I was the purser on that flight, and I did my job" (from the *New York Times*, July 7, 1985).

Harriet Tubman, an ex-slave, risked her own life every time she went back to the pre–Civil War South to lead caravans of other slaves northward to freedom. Some people called her the Moses of her people; others compared her to Joan of Arc. One abolitionist said she deserved "to be placed first on the list of American heroines" (from the *New Yorker*, March 25, 1985).

Respect for human life takes other forms as well. Valuing life also can mean preserving or maintaining the dignity with which a life must be lived, often against overwhelming odds.

Many of the chores that women have performed through the years have been simple services that supported the dignity and welfare of the people in their care. Women often have been in the forefront of efforts to obtain humane treatment for undervalued or silent victims of an indifferent society. Feeding, clothing, and keeping people clean, and insuring them a decent place in which to sleep, are very humble tasks, but think of how quickly a life deteriorates when these basic needs go unattended.

Florence Nightingale, to use a familiar example, rebelled at the prospect of the conventional life that a genteel Englishwoman of her time was destined to lead. She chose instead to walk the grimy corridors of army hospitals miles away from her homeland. If you picture for a moment what that actually meant, you can get a measure of her heroism. She was much more than our image of her, prim in a lace collar. She challenged the appalling hospital care that was as devastating for injured soldiers as their experience on the battlefield. She established training standards for nurses that reformed the entire profession and, in doing so, reformed what had been a slatternly occupation and made it an acceptable way for respectable women to earn their living—thereby insuring the dignity of even more lives.

Less familiar, but chillingly instructive, if you have read any of the accounts of life in a German concentration camp, you will remember how dehumanizing and deadly it was to be deprived of the simple ability to keep clean (Des Pres, 1976). Even in less malevolent settings, research, for example, on the epidemic of foreclosures on farms that had been in a family for generations has suggested that the farm wife is the family bulwark: "If she remains strong," a journal article says, "the family stays together. If she crumbles, the family will probably dissolve" (APA, 1986).

Ultimately, respect for the dignity and value of a human life also rests on and enriches the respect for one's own worth. The ability to tolerate remarkable hardship, to persevere in the face of discouraging odds, to create and then take heart from dedication to a cause are often quietly personal behaviors. We are privileged as therapists to be admitted into the private world of heroic struggle and victory where the cast of characters may consist of only one person and a small group of intimates. But the heroic spirit is clearly there.

One woman, confronted with her imminent death, wrote notes from the bed she knew that she would never leave to all who were dear to her—acknowledging their importance in her life and her importance in theirs.

The story told by a social worker who works with AIDS patients provides us with another example. One afternoon, after a young patient had died, she and his brother shaved and dressed him neatly before his mother came to see him. To do this was not included in her job, but it was included in her sense of humanity. She spoke simply about her purposes in doing this. She felt that his mother had been through so much that she should be spared at least some last pain, and she wanted to insure for the young man some of the dignity he deserved.

SECOND: THE SENSE OF CHOICE AND PERSONAL EFFECTIVENESS

The hero sees herself as a potential force for change; an unhappy circumstance is not merely to be endured. She identifies a need to change and not only works toward that goal personally, but often mobilizes others to move against common problems.

Beverly Carl, a lawyer and a professor at Southern Methodist University, filed a class-action complaint against the university because of the bias she felt they exercised against all women in "hiring, promotion, retention, compensation and appointment to prestigious posts." In an out-of-court settlement, the school agreed to adjust the salaries of four women professors, complete an affirmative-action plan, and "correct some inequities in pay and working conditions for the custodial staff" (from *Dallas Life Magazine*, March 23, 1986). As a result, Ms. Carl received many phone calls from women in various other occupations who felt that they, too, were being discriminated against

and wanted to know what they could do for themselves.

Betty Washington singlehandedly recruited and organized her neighbors for a citizen's watch program to rid the neighborhood of drug dealing and crime. Her open opposition made her a prime target, vulnerable to reprisal from those whose income she was threatening. Here is how a modern hero talks, "Either you speak out and take the risk, or you die in the cesspool" (from *Newsweek*, July 6, 1987).

The sense of agency, of one's personal effectiveness at correcting a wrong or of supplementing an omission, is often awakened and supported in therapy. This sense of choice, restored in therapy, can make a crucial difference in whether or not people feel that they are living their own lives or merely following a well-worn path with no sense of individuality or appetite.

One young woman with whom I worked is a teacher at a nursing college. Dismayed at the insensitivity of the student nurses (and some more experienced nurses, as well), she challenged the standard curriculum that had not been changed for years. She organized a series of lectures during which people who had suffered from a debilitating injury or disease described their shame and anger at being treated as objects with no contribution to make to their own rehabilitative treatment. She designed these sessions to include dialogue between the nurses and the speakers, and these exchanges were found to make a visible difference in the nurses' attitudes toward and subsequent interactions with their patients.

THIRD: THE ORIGINAL PERSPECTIVE

The relationship between the hero and the established order of things is fluid; she perceives, within the established order of things-as-they-are, things-as-they-could-be. This can be a risky vision, since questioning the validity of well-established assumptions may result in scorn, isolation, and ostracism for the troublesome questioner.

Professor Robin West of the Law School of the University of Maryland, for example, suggested a drastic revision of some of the assumptions that underlie legal decision making. She defined what she called "gender injuries"; the pain felt "only by women from injuries experienced only by women," and presented the woman's perspective as crucially important in legal judgments (from the *Los Angeles Times*, October 7, 1988).

Anna Quindlen discussed the implications of having women serve in the armed forces. She saw beyond the image of women soldiers into women as-anything-they-can-be. She said, "But those of us who have been first woman something-or-other, who have done the jobs they said we couldn't do, know there's another way to move things along. Just do it. Just find a way to argue the case, to perform the surgery, to cover the war, and then everyone will know that it can be done" (from the *New York Times*, January 7, 1990).

I remember working with a woman who was chief administrator of a large church. As she sat in on organizational meetings over the years, she began to realize that what she wanted was not to be a member of the support staff, but to be the *minister*. For her, this was a revolutionary awareness, upsetting all the things she had learned as a girl, from her parents and from her ministers, about what her "proper place" was. It would involve years of study, taking her away from her husband and children and requiring *them* to assume many of the domestic responsibilities she had carried (along with her job). This was yet another separation from the familiar introjections about the responsibility of wives and mothers. She went through months of painful deliberation before she could even bring up the idea and her struggle with it to her family.

FOURTH: PHYSICAL AND MENTAL COURAGE

Heroic action requires courage, both physical and mental, and is not put off by the prospect of personal cost. The traditional hero almost inevitably risked death, injury, or humiliation. In our sensationalistic age, the defiance of these disasters remains the stereotypical hallmark of heroism.

But this is too easy. In disregarding personal conflict or welfare, the hero, it is true, may

appear to court death, when actually she either considers the risk of death or loss to be less important than her purpose, or she may be so intent that she overlooks it entirely.

Heroic courage is often more than simply physical strength. It involves persistence and focus and the stamina to tolerate demanding situations. The hero may calculate the personal cost of following a different drummer or of espousing an unpopular cause or opposing a popular one—she is not deterred.

In moments of crisis or opportunity, the mental courage of the hero is often stunningly efficient. Her perceptions are sharpened rather than dulled. Her behavior is on target, specific; she is aware of, but not restricted by, circumstance. She identifies the essentials and responds to them directly.

Carolina Maria de Jesus wrote about her life in a Brazilian slum. At one point, a reporter happened to overhear her berating the men who were beating some children, threatening to include them in her "book," the diary she was writing of life in the *favela*, the slums of Sao Paolo. The reporter asked her permission to publish excerpts of her diary in his newspaper—and they created a sensation. Maria wrote: "The politicians knew that I am a poetess. And that a poet will even face death when he sees his people oppressed" (Moffat & Painter, 1975).

An increased recognition of "female" heroism—rooted in human connection and responsibility, but sharing the timeless qualities that have been recognized for centuries—expands and enriches the heroic image. The heroic image becomes relevant to humble settings, as well as to the grand stage. Such recognition seems particularly valuable in an age when merely striving to be stronger or faster than one's adversary could be suicidal.

THE HEROIC ATTITUDE AND THERAPY

One must think like a hero to behave like a merely decent human being. (May Sarton)

Much has been written about the hero's journey and the significance that a personal sense of heroism could have in the lives of people who might not ordinarily think of themselves as heroes. Clearly, many people look to eternal heroic examples as a way of inspiring a perspective that they lack in the day-to-day practicalities of their lives. The books and articles that link contemporary life themes to the tales of ageless gods, goddesses, and heroes all are responding to people's need to make sense of the rush of experience that threatens to engulf them, like Alice in Wonderland, who finds herself, much to her surprise, swimming in a pool of her own tears.

The people who come to a therapist's office are often so embedded in their problems that nothing seems farther from their needs than a call to heroism. Even so, I would suggest that, among other complications, they are stuck with an archaic image of heroism that prevents them from seeing how a personal concept of heroism might be relevant to their dilemmas. The hackneyed image of heroism has disqualified what they *could* do, because it is not what they have been taught that they *should* do. They are stuck, unable to conceive of another course. To counter these unnourishing introjections, they must construe for themselves a new and individual definition of heroism. And often, in therapy, this is what happens.

Let me give you some examples from therapy of the heroic attitude: the hero's respect for the dignity and value of human life, the heroic sense of personal choice and effectiveness, the originality of the heroic perspective, and the physical and mental courage that supports heroic decision.

One woman agonized in therapy for a long time before she finally chose to become pregnant again after two devastating experiences. She had nursed an infant son through his illness until his death from a brain tumor. In her next pregnancy, she had had to have a painful late abortion because the fetus had died in utero. Nevertheless, after much anguish, she decided to try once again. Even after the birth of this healthy child, she still anxiously counted the days until the baby had lived beyond the short lifetime of her first child. But she said she was glad that she did it.

Another young woman suffered from a debilitating and chronic disease. While she was working toward her doctorate (a draining process under the best of conditions), she kept a detailed record of the phases of her disease and its response to the various prescribed medications she was taking to control it. Her hope was that such data, recorded properly by an informed person, might ultimately prove to be valuable in the eventual conquest of the disease. Refusing to be a victim, she hoped to seek a grant so that she herself might conduct research on her disease.

A well-established top executive in a national firm that had recently changed top management staff was dissatisfied with her life. She found the new style of management abrasive and inhumane. There was no doubt that she was well respected and could easily adopt, and even influence, the management philosophy. Unmarried, she had no financial support other than her own income. She had been reared in a conservative family that believed that once you had found your economic niche, you *stayed there*. As she talked, though, it became clear that she did not want to stay. She realized that she didn't want what she called "another career quest." She knew the routine; you complete one quest and right away you just start on another one. After considerable personal turmoil, she quit her job, set up a strict budget for herself, and took off with no guarantees to create a way of life she wanted to live and to find a place in which to live it.

The urge to heroism is natural, and to admit it honest. For everyone to admit it would probably release such pent-up force as to be devastating to societies as they are now. (Becker, 1973)

Although these examples from therapy all involved women, they represent *human* heroism, heroism that moves beyond the flamboyant images that crowd our newspapers, magazines, television news broadcasts, and movie screens. Such heroism is plentiful, but we have not accorded it proper notice, and thus the influence that it could have on our lives and on our communities.

CONCLUSIONS

These days, we must be less willing than our myth-making ancestors to picture our heroes as part-human, part-divine. Superman notwithstanding, we must make distinctions between fantasy and actuality. We must get smarter at looking for substantial heroes who are within our reach—heroes who live in the same world that we do and who share our vulnerabilities. In emphasizing the humanity of our heroes, we also emphasize their relevance to our own humanity. The heroic image is invaluable when our admiration inspires us to look at our own lives with an eye to the heroic possibilities.

Heroes are all around us, more numerous than we thought. Heroism is also more diverse. Not limited to the dramatic, quick-thinking, life-saving deed, human heroism also animates the active voices that are raised in schools, courtrooms, legislatures, and hospitals. It inspires the heroism that occurs at the negotiating table, as well as at the kitchen table; in the lawyer's office, as well as in the nursery; at the judge's bench, as well as at the bedside; in Congress, as well as at PTA meetings; and at the controls of powerful machinery, as well as at the stove. Women and men belong in all of these settings and more.

I remember a young woman, facing her own death, who clung tenaciously to life until she felt she had fulfilled her responsibilities to her young sons. I heard not a word of complaint about the debilitating treatment, about the monstrous surgery she underwent to get a few more months of life, about the implacable, discouraging progress of her disease. When someone called her "indomitable," she could accept it, but to be called a hero was hard for her to assimilate.

"What's in a name?" Shakespeare's Juliet asks. I think a name brings with it recognition, dignity, inspiration, and permanence, among other things. And all these are lost when heroes who differ from the familiar images are deprived of their rightful titles. A stereotyped view of heroism limits both women and men because they are arbitrarily compelled to surrender half of their potential range of actions in order to conform to archaic formulas.

There are essential qualities that pervade the range of heroic possibilities. As therapists, we have the opportunity, as well as the responsibility, to recognize heroism in its many everyday guises, and to call it by its proper name. Each individual, by seeing the substance of heroism in herself or himself, can develop a view of her or his own life, a heroic attitude, that can transform human hopes into human achievement.

REFERENCES

American Psychological Association. *Monitor*, June 1986.

Bardwick, J. (1971). *Psychology of women*. New York: Harper & Row.

Becker, E. (1973). *The denial of death*. New York: Free Press.

Bulfinch, T. (1979). *Myths of Greece and Rome*. Compiled by Bryan Holme. New York: Viking Penguin.

Des Pres, T. (1976). *The survivor*. New York: Oxford University Press.

Gerzon, M. (1982). *A choice of heroes*. Boston: Houghton Mifflin.

Gilligan, C. (1982). *In a different voice*. Cambridge, MA: Harvard University Press.

Gilligan, C., Lyons, N., & Hamner, T. J. (1990). *Making connections*. Cambridge, MA: Harvard University Press.

Graves, R. (1982). *The Greek myths 1*. Middlesex, England: Penguin.

Graves, R., & Patai, R. (1966). *Hebrew myths: The book of Genesis*. New York: McGraw-Hill.

Kegan, J. (1987). *The mask of command*. New York: Viking.

Moffat, M., & Painter, C. (Eds.). (1975). *Revelations: The diaries of women*. New York: Vintage.

Phillips, J. A. (1984). *Eve: The history of an idea*. San Francisco: Harper & Row.

Tannen, D. (1990). *You just don't understand*. New York: Morrow.

Discussion by James F. T. Bugental, Ph.D.

As I listened to Miriam Polster, I reflected that she has demonstrated her topic. To bring into a professional and scientific meeting so subjective a topic as heroism itself calls for a kind of heroism. Mine is a much less risky undertaking: I simply want to share some speculations that were triggered by this refreshing and confronting presentation.

Of the many things that might be said, I choose to underscore Miriam's basic observation—that heroism should be freed of the limitation of being considered a masculine trait. It is, and should be, a basic characteristic of human beings and not gender-specific. Certainly, to attempt to remake women in the outworn model of male heroism is not to liberate them, but to enslave them further.

The standards of heroism—like the standards of "success"—that have come down through history are becoming burdens that our species can no longer support, and that, indeed, threaten us with destruction. So long as such ways of conceiving values such as *heroism* or *success* dominate our thinking, we will have Persian Gulf crises and savings and loan disasters, and we will abandon the homeless, those in need of medical care, and the children of poverty.

The common element that I see in feminine heroism, as Miriam has portrayed it, is the bringing forward of those subjective qualities that we have traditionally associated with the feminine. It is time that such qualities be given more appreciation and validation when they are manifested by either women or men.

In commonplace usage, we have thought of the subjective as soft, sentimental, affect-governed, and "female"—thus devaluing both the gender and these important potentials in human nature. The subjective and the feminine are both also accessible, evolving, and creative. Robert Bly, in his description of the "wild man," makes clear that all of these same qualities are very much part of that masculine image. The

wild man is not some mindless, macho, Rambo-like destroyer. It is my hope—and, may I say, the hope for our species—that what we are here calling women's heroism will give recognition to the heroic potential in the inner living of both women and men.

When we label certain human qualities as "feminine" or "masculine" exclusively, we put needless limits on ourselves. A bit of lore I heard here from Gerard Haigh, a psychologist and a "birder," makes this point rather acutely. The story contrasts the hummingbird and the emperor penguin.

The male hummingbird flies elaborate aerobatics to attract a female to join him for 15 seconds of mating bliss conducted midair. The male then departs and may never again be seen by the female, who has to carry out alone the whole parenting task of gestation, hatching, feeding the young, and so on. "A typical male," according to some views.

But what about the emperor penguin? The male and the female go out on the ice to mate, and then, in due course, the female produces an egg. The male takes the egg into a flap in his foot and stands with the egg protected and warm for two months. The female returns to the sea to feed. In the meantime, the male endures storms and blizzards. Still he protects the egg—although in two months, he may lose 40 pounds.

When the female returns, she has gorged herself with food, and she regurgitates it to feed the newly hatched young. The male goes back to the sea to recover, a long trip, as now the ice has frozen further. Eventually, regaining his strength, he returns to share with the female the raising of the young.

Where are gender stereotypes? Both female and male are heroic, obviously.

In closing, I want to refer to a question that was asked when Erv Polster was speaking. The question had to do with the "sense of awe." This is a much neglected but important human subjective capacity and one that contrasts with macho values. It brings to mind a comment made some time ago by James J. Gibson, the preeminent psychologist of perception. Psychology, he said (quoted in Reed, 1988), "is a second-rate discipline because it does not stand in awe of its subject matter." We psychotherapists need always to approach our work with a sense of awe—to stand in awe of the human condition, the human spirit, the potential for heroism that resides in all humans, women or men.

REFERENCE

Reed, E. S. (1988). *James J. Gibson and the psychology of perception.* New Haven, CT: Yale University Press.

QUESTIONS AND ANSWERS

Question: This question is for both Erv and Miriam Polster, I see many bright highly functioning women in my practice, many of whom are struggling in relationships with men who are afraid to commit themselves to marriage. This seems to be a widespread problem. Are you seeing this in your practices, and would you comment on this phenomenon?

M. Polster: I see it in my practice, and I think it's tragic. I have seen so many fine women looking for some commitment, and yet settling for less. One of my patients told me of her realization that she will probably have men in her life, but only for short periods of time. She feels she's realistic to expect a series of short connections with different men. I think that is a very sad prospect. She regards it as the best she can do.

It's a difficult world in which to establish a sense of commitment, and I think that that's part of the damaging image of heroism that has been foisted on some men. It's an image whereby he moves on the next conquest, the next event, the next development, instead of seeing what it is that he can do now. I quoted Gerzon, who said that currently men have a choice of heroes. He also points out that some older men's heroes are either frontiersmen or soldiers. In this case, there is a sense of conquest, of moving, taking territory, either by

exploration or aggrandizement. That impetus can be very unsettling, and I wonder how much that influences this tragic situation.

I've also seen some young men who don't know how to find the women with whom they would like to settle down, so it is not just a one-sided question. They know quite well that they don't want to go to a bar because, as they've said to me, "The people you would meet at a bar are people who like to go to bars." That's not what they are looking for. I've also seen the situation tragically reflected in some men's existence.

E. Polster: I don't know the answer to the question, but I'll talk about it anyway. First of all, I think men have been raised to have poor taste. Second, men often retain a sense of superiority through distance rather than through their actual function.

Third, in psychotherapy and in the culture at large, we have taught people that they don't really need to have any frustration or any complexity—that they ought to get what they want and not work through the contradictions in what they want. Men, of course, are in a better position in society to behave this way; there is always something better around in the world. So we often don't want to commit to that which isn't all that we want because we might be able to get something else that we want more. It's the rabbit-at-the-dog-track phenomenon. The rabbit is perfect, and to chase it makes a great race, but the dog never does get the rabbit.

Bugental: I want to add one thing. I think that what's happened in our culture has been powerfully reinforced by some of our public leaders. I think of it as a "quarterly-report mentality": Don't think more than three months ahead. If you think about a year ahead, you may not be there then. This short-term outlook fosters much frustration for men and women in relationships. If it's got to work and work perfectly right from the start, it's doomed. There is enrichment that can result from struggle. The "enrichment struggle" can provide a partial antidote to the quarterly-report kind of mentality.

Question: Dr. Polster, I am wondering how you

might alter local newscasts. What would you do differently?

M. Polster: I would have more women reporting hard news and more men reporting PTA events, because the same observational skills apply to any event they are sent to cover. In this way, we would get a sense of the presence of women in some places and of men in others. The geography of heroism is very important.

It may be that an exchange of those roles can be a very important one. Dealing with particulars of everyday events needs to be much more merged into a common effort. I'm reminded of the standard joke about a husband and wife talking about who carries what responsibilities in the family, and the husband says, "Well, I make all the big decisions and my wife makes all the small ones. I decide whether the United States should join the United Nations in deciding whether we, let's say, should send more troops to the Middle East, and my wife decides where we will go on vacation and how we spend the family salary."

Question: Are there any further reflections you may have about what we as mental health professionals can take with us from this discussion back into our lives in terms of our own actions?

Also, how might we appropriately raise these issues and bring them into the consulting room in ways that do not impose our own thoughts and concerns on those of the patients and clients with whom we work?

M. Polster: Two things come readily to mind: First, there is the question of bringing issues into your consulting room. Often I have found it fruitful to compare the struggle that people are going through to a classic or famous struggle, especially if they have not seen the parallels before. It's surprising how often this can summon the heroic connection and hearten them to go out and do what they need to do.

Second, in reflection about your question, there are two qualities that distinguish women's heroism that I didn't mention in my chapter: A woman, upon listening to what I said, once told me, "You know, women's heroism is heroism in slow motion." That's a very interesting idea. Women's heroism is a step-by-step process, continued and persistent. Another quality that characterizes women's heroism is often the aggregate nature of heroic women. Women are frequently involved in activities that seek to include and bring in more and more members; they know that the more people you can get out there, the more weight your cause will carry.

The United States v. Drugs

◆

Thomas Szasz, M.D.

Thomas Szasz, M.D.

Thomas Szasz (M.D., University of Cincinnati, 1944) is Professor of Psychiatry, Emeritus at the State University of New York Upstate Medical Center in Syracuse. He has received numerous awards, including the Humanist of the Year Award from the American Humanist Association and the Distinguished Service Award from the American Institute for Public Service, as well as a number of honorary doctorates and lectureships, and he serves on the editorial board of many journals.

Szasz has written more than 400 articles, book chapters, reviews, letters to the editor, and columns. He also has more than 20 books to his credit.

Thomas Szasz presents a brief historical review of drug controls in the United States. He provides a critical analysis of the transformation of the trade in drugs from a free market at the beginning of the century to a tightly statist system of controls today. Also provided is a market-oriented analysis of the "drug problem." Szasz eschews paternalism and speaks to the ethics of self-determination.

The world is a perpetual caricature of itself; at every moment it is the mockery and the contradiction of what it is pretending to be.

(George Santayana)

For the better part of this century, America has waged a war on drugs. The hostilities began with minor skirmishes before World War I, grew into guerilla warfare after it, and now affect the daily lives of people not only in the United States, but in other countries as well.

Strange as it may seem today, there was a time when the United States was at peace with drugs. To retrace the route we took in our descent from a free market in drugs to chemical statism, we must begin our journey approximately a century ago, when the trade in drugs in America was as unregulated as the trade in diet books is today; when Americans did not view drugs as presenting the sort of danger that required the protection of the national government; and when, although virtually all the drugs of which we are now deathly afraid were freely available, there was nothing even remotely resembling a drug problem such as now plagues us.

Before 1907, all drugs could be sold and bought like any other consumer good. The manufacturers did not even have to disclose the contents of these concoctions. Hence we have the term "patent medicine," with the adjective alluding to the fact that the composition was a trade secret, protected by a patented name.

While there is no evidence that the American consumer ever complained about the free market in drugs, there is plenty of evidence that the consumer's self-appointed protectors complained bitterly and loudly. The first landmark event in the federal regulation of drugs (and foods) was the Food and Drugs Act of 1906. The aim of this legislation was "to assure the customer of the identity of the article purchased, not of its usefulness" (Temin, 1980, p. 33). It must be emphasized that Congress did not intend to abridge the drug manufacturer's freedom to make exaggerated, false, or even absurd therapeutic claims for products; or the consumer's freedom to purchase any drug desired and to enjoy the benefits, or the suffer of harms, of that choice. Accordingly, the government could not prosecute the drug maker for "misleading claims" about a product, as that was then still considered to fall within the realm of the seller's free speech and the buyer's responsibility to heed the warning, *caveat emptor* (U.S. v. Johnson, 1911). Correlatively, the buyer could not sue the drug manufacturer because the product he or she decided to buy and ingest caused an unpleasant reaction. Although, in some respects, this was a salutary piece of legislation that increased the consumer's power to make an informed choice in the market, with its enactment, the federal government entered an arena where the utmost vigilance was required to contain its power. Unfortunately, such a "paranoid" posture toward "therapeutic" state paternalism was, by that time, quite unfashionable.

Eight years later, Congress enacted another landmark antidrug legislation, the Harrison Anti-Narcotics Law (1914). Originally passed as a record-keeping law, the Harrison Act quickly became a prohibition statute. From these two pieces of legislation, the fire of "progressive" drug protectionism spread and soon enveloped the whole country, transforming the Harrison Act into the legislative embodiment of the "moral principle that taking narcotics for other than medicinal purposes was harmful and should be prevented" (Musto, 1973, p. 64). That threw the monkey wrench "medicinal purpose"—an undefined and undefinable concept

that has haunted us ever since—into the machinery of the trade in drugs. Finally, in 1920, the prohibitionists won a major victory: America was, at last, alcohol-free—if not *de facto*, then at least *de jure*. Since 1924, when Congress made it illegal to manufacture heroin, it has been free from heroin as well—if not in practice, at least in theory.

In retelling this tale, it is impossible to overemphasize that although the intent of the first drug laws was to protect people from being "abused" by drugs that others were eager to sell to them, this was soon replaced by the goal of protecting people from "abusing" drugs that they themselves were eager to buy. The government has thus succeeded in depriving us of our most elementary property right, namely, the right to introduce into our bodies whatever we choose. In the process—in which, fearful of the responsibility to choose freely in a free drug market, we crassly colluded—the government has also deprived us of our right to grow, manufacture, sell, and buy coca leaf, marijuana plants, and opium poppies, agricultural products used since ancient times. For a paltry pottage of "health care" rights, we have thus betrayed our Constitutional birthrights. The results of a *Washington Post*/ABC News poll taken in September 1989 are illustrative (Carpenter & Rouse, 1990):

[Sixty-two] percent of the respondents were willing to give up "a few" freedoms in order to curb drug use; 67 percent would allow police to stop cars at random to search for drugs; 52 percent would allow the police to search without court order the homes of people suspected of selling drugs, even if some homes were searched by mistake; 71 percent would make it against the law to show the use of illegal drugs in the movies. (p. 24)

These responses show us the unadorned visage of the current American *Zeitgeist*, and not merely with respect to drugs. Note that most of the respondents "would make it against the law to show the use of illegal drugs in the movies," a truly remarkable preference in view of the fact that nearly every American movie shows the use of guns, legal and illegal. This incongruity supports my conclusion that the American people are now more afraid of themselves than of others—ranking protection from empty syringes above protection from loaded guns, seeking to be shielded from their own temptations more than from the destructive acts of others (Szasz, 1976). For having thus yielded to the blandishments of the Therapeutic State, we are all paying dearly (Szasz, 1984).

Of course, we have long regarded our two most popular psychoactive drugs, alcohol and tobacco, with the utmost ambivalence. Throughout the 19th century, prohibition of alcohol, though not of tobacco, often was advocated and occasionally practiced on a local level. However, there was no question of the federal government's involvement in such an effort: that would have been seen as incompatible with the spirit and letter of the Constitution. Unlike today, most people then still appreciated the difference between temperance and prohibition; that is, between controls from within, or self-discipline, and controls from without, or external coercion.

After the turn of the century, respect for the right to acquire drugs began to drop precipitously. For example, in 1914, the Reverend Josiah Strong (Strong, 1914), an ardent alcohol-prohibitionist and coeditor of the magazine *The Gospel of the Kingdom*, smugly declared: "'Personal Liberty' is at last an uncrowned, dethroned king, with no one to do him reverence.... We are no longer frightened by that ancient bogy—'paternalism in government.' We affirm boldly, it is the business of government to be just that—paternal." Today, this credo is recited as if it articulated a scientific (medical) principle and hence as if none other were thinkable. Asserts Forest S. Tennant, medical adviser to the National Football League, as quoted in Breo (1986): "We use a strictly medical definition of drug addiction.... When human lives are at stake, a little totalitarianism is not such a bad thing." An observation by George Roche (1990), apropos of the government's war on a free market in higher education, applies to its war on a free market in drugs as well. "The only constitutional rule I can think of that is still fully observed," he remarked, "is electing two senators from each state."*

Clearly, we have come a long way since the government was, in principle at least, our servant rather than our master. For consumer advocates, this change is a necessary and welcome adaptation to an increasingly complex world with which the average citizen is no longer able to cope without the assistance of a corps of self-appointed Ralph Naders. In America today, the principle of *caveat emptor*, especially with respect to substances labeled "drugs," is a despised anachronism. Instead of appreciating this principle as the emblem of the consumer-citizen's personal responsibility, and hence independence, we disdain it as no longer socially appropriate, preferring instead to view certain personal choices as the symptoms of sickness.

Not only have we medicalized (mis)behavior and its coercive state control, but we have used that very medicalization as a mask to conceal our having naively relinquished real property rights in exchange for abstract political rights. No doubt, casting a ballot is an important act, emblematic of our roles as citizens and of our political liberties in society. But eating and drinking are surely much more important acts. If given a choice between the right to vote and the right to our bodily self-ownership—between the opportunity to choose one or another politician supposedly to represent our interests in a local, state, or federal bureaucracy, and the freedom to ingest, inhale, or inject into our bodies whatever we want—few, if any, would pick voting. Yet this is precisely the bargain we, the American people, have made with our government: fewer personal rights, but more political rights. The result is that the American people now consider self-government their blessed political right and self-medication their accursed medical malady.

In 1890, less than half of adult Americans had the right to vote. Since then, one class of previously ineligible persons after another has been granted the franchise. However, not only blacks and women have received that right, as

---

* Note in this connection, however, that we still consider the regulation of gambling to be a matter of states' rights. If we persist in viewing (pathological) gambling as a disease long enough, and persist in interpreting this metaphor literally, then, no doubt, we shall come to regard "gambling abuse" as also a health problem, for the solution of which we need the coercive-therapeutic apparatus of the federal government.

they deserved, but also others with questionable claims to the privilege, such as persons unable to speak or read English or to read and write any language, and even persons involuntarily confined as insane. During the same period, every one of us, regardless of age, education, or competence, has been deprived of the right to trade freely in substances the government decides to call "drugs." Yet, ironically, most Americans labor under the belief that they now enjoy many "civil rights" previously available only to a few, a belief true only for blacks and women, and for them only partially. At the same time, most Americans are completely unaware of the rights they have lost. They are aware only of the dread new diseases, such as "drug abuse," that they have acquired.

Consider, in this light, our escalating effort to curb personal desire and choice vis-à-vis drugs. At the beginning of the century, our principal drug problem was that people drank too much, for which the solution was seen as alcohol prohibition. Then Prohibition became the problem, which was solved by repealing that law. Then the problem was that people bought many drugs, not because they *needed* them to become healthier, but because they *wanted* them to feel better. This was defined as a medical problem to justify solving it by giving physicians (and pharmacists) monopolistic control over the trade in certain drugs (that were deemed ineffective or habit-forming). This led to a host of new problems and remedies, such as prescription-drug abuse, triplicate prescriptions for certain "controlled substances," monitoring and prosecuting doctors for "overprescribing," and an orgy of escalating quasi-therapeutic repressions. "Fanaticism," George Santayana sagely observed, "consists in redoubling your effort when you have forgotten your aim." Exactly so: The more desperate our drug problem becomes, the more stubbornly we cling to the myth that drugs pose a threat to every man, woman, and child in the world, and the more certain we are of our duty to combat drug abuse.

Fanatics, it seems, not only redouble their efforts after they have forgotten their aims, but they redouble their efforts once again after they have forgotten the rhetoric justifying the fanaticism. Although the term "drug abuse" was never clearly defined, antidrug activists typically claimed that it referred to the intemperate use of addictive or dangerous drugs. The trouble, for the antidrug fanatic, is that not all illicit drug use is addictive, dangerous, or in any way harmful. Nevertheless, in actual practice, the term drug abuse has come to be attached to self-medication with virtually any illegal or socially disapproved substance. But why is drug abuse (self-medication) considered to be a problem? It is for the same reason that, for more than a century, self-abuse (masturbation) was considered to be a problem (Szasz, 1970). Or, to put it in the succinct words of former drug czar William Bennett (1990), because "the simple fact is that drug use is wrong." This ludicrous assertion illustrates once again that persecutory myths are social fictions we are supposed to support, not scrutinize. Although the wrongful use of drugs neither is a fact nor is it simple, it is a judgment powerful enough to sustain a multibillion-dollar, federally funded bureaucracy. In the current fiscal year, the federal government "is spending about $1.3 billion on drug treatment programs . . . and more than twice that amount on law enforcement" (Hilts, 1990). The distinction between "drug treatment" and "law enforcement" is, of course, another fiction, as drug czar Bennett proudly acknowledges. In a White Paper issued in June 1990, Bennett's Office of National Drug Control Policy (ONDCP) praised punitive drug laws as intrinsic to effective drug treatment programs, since "as many as 90 percent of the people undergoing treatment did not seek it on their own . . . but were compelled to do so by family, legal, or employment pressures" (ONDCP, 1990). All drug-treatment advocates seem proud of blackmailing their victims. "The threat of prison," explains Muskegon County (Mich.) prosecutor Tony Tague, "is sometimes the only way to get pregnant addicts to seek treatment" (Lacayo, 1990).

But exactly wherein lies our "drug problem"? I believe it lies in two simple facts. One is that most of the psychoactive drugs Americans want are illegal: literally, like cocaine and heroin, or medically (being unobtainable without a physician's prescription), like Seconal or Valium. The other is that, having been placed under medical tutelage nearly a century ago, we have failed to develop the sort of self-reliance and self-discipline with respect to drugs that we have developed with respect to the countless complex artifacts of our modern age. Unfortunately, few people are aware of, or care about, prescription drug prohibitions as social symbols legitimatizing tutelary-statist arbitrariness: for example, it is legal to sell 200-mg tablets of Motrin (an antiarthritis drug), but not (without a prescription) 400- and 600-mg tablets of it; 25-mg capsules of Benadryl (an antihistamine), but not 50-mg capsules of it.

Inevitably, drug prohibition (criminal and medical alike) generates a black market in illegal and prescription drugs, creates a criminal underclass, and corrupts the medical profession. It is then concluded that these unintended but predictable consequences of the laws protecting us from dangerous drugs are so destructive to the nation's health and welfare that they require a domestic and indeed worldwide war on drugs to combat them. Now, many critics of the war on drugs, even former supporters of it, declare that the war is "not working." What are we to do?

Actually, we do not have many options. One is to maintain our present course and escalate the intensity of the war on drugs by increasing the penalties for using as well as for making and selling illegal drugs. Another is selectively to "decriminalize" or "legalize" certain currently illegal drugs, with government bureaucrats and/or doctors dispensing drugs according to some poorly thought out but clearly harebrained scheme. There remains one option so simple and old-fashioned that it is dismissed out of hand as too radical and impractical— namely, repealing drug prohibitions and returning to a free market in drugs, such as prevailed in the United States from 1776 until 1914.

To understand what such a recapture of our original constitutional rights to drugs would require and entail, let us suspend our customary concerns with the drug user's motivations, society's judgments of drug use, and the pharmacological effects of particular drugs, and focus instead on the various ways an American who wants to use drugs now gains access to them. Categorizing drugs according to their availability or mode of distribution yields three categories:

1. No special government controls limiting sales: for example, coffee, aspirin, laxatives. Produced by private entrepreneurs, distributed through the free market. Product called "food," "beverage," or "over-the-counter drug"; seller, "merchant"; buyer, "customer."

2. Government controls limiting sales:
   a. To adults: for example, alcohol and tobacco. Produced by private entrepreneurs, distributed through the free or state-licensed market. Product called "beer," "wine," "cigarette"; seller, "merchant"; buyer, "customer."
   b. To patients: for example, digitalis, penicillin, steroids, Valium. Produced by government-regulated pharmaceutical manufacturers, distributed through state-controlled physicians' prescriptions and pharmacies. Product called "prescription drug"; seller, "pharmacist"; buyer, "patient."
   c. To addicts: for example, methadone. Produced by government-regulated pharmaceutical manufacturers, distributed through special federally approved dispensers. No legal sellers or buyers. Product called "drug (abuse) treatment"; distributor, "drug (treatment) program"; recipient, "(certified) addict."

3. Government controls prohibiting sales to everyone: for example, marijuana, heroin, or cocaine. Produced illegally by private entrepreneurs, distributed illegally through the black market. Product called "dangerous drug" or "illegal drug"; seller, "pusher" or "trafficker"; buyer, "addict" or "drug abuser."

As such a market-oriented perspective on our so-called drug problem shows, we have nothing even remotely resembling a free market in drugs in America. Nevertheless, most people mistakenly think of prescription drugs, and even of specifically restricted drugs such as methadone, as "legal." This situation must be contrasted with the genuinely free market in drugs that prevailed in the United States less than 100 years ago, when opium, morphine, cocaine, hashish, and other "dangerous drugs" such as bromides and chloral hydrate were freely available.

Since virtually all criticisms of drug controls are now aimed at the way particular drugs are distributed, proposals for reform correspond to the categories described above. I shall summarize each posture vis-à-vis drug controls by identifying the characteristic strategies of its proponents.

1. Criminalizers ("Do you want more crack babies?"): Keep type 3 substances in category 3; expand categories 3, 2b, and 2c, and constrict categories 1 and 2a; drug offenders are criminals who should be punished as well as patients who should be (coercively) treated.
2. Legalizers ("The war on drugs cannot be won"): Remove certain type 3 substances, such as heroin, from category 3 and transfer them to category 2b or 2c (for example, make the manufacture and sale of heretofore prohibited substances a government monopoly); drug abusers are sick and should be (coercively) treated in government-funded programs.
3. Free marketeers ("Self-medication is a right"): Abolish categories 2b, 2c, and 3, and place all currently restricted substances in category 2a. Drug use is a personal choice, neither crime nor illness.

I disagree with both the drug criminalizers and the drug legalizers. I disagree with the former because I believe that the criminal law ought to be used to protect us from others, not ourselves. I disagree with the latter because I believe that behavior, even if it is actually or potentially injurious or self-injurious, is not a disease, and that no behavior should be regulated by sanctions called "treatment" (Ebeling, 1990; Mitchell, 1990).

I realize, of course, that the laissez-faire posture vis-à-vis drugs I propose is now anathema, beyond the pale of intellectually respectable debate in America. In fact, after lecturing and writing about drug-using and drug-prohibiting behaviors for several decades, and after many private discussions of this subject with colleagues and friends, I have been compelled to conclude that even many libertarians and supporters of the free market recoil from the idea of a free market in drugs. A typical conversation with such a hypothetical Libertarian Friend (LF) might go like this.

LF: The war on drugs is a dismal failure. We should legalize cocaine and heroin. They should be sold like gin and whisky are sold today.

I: That's fine, but why do you ignore prescription drugs? I believe we cannot address our so-called drug problem without acknowledging the role prescription laws play in it. It is absurd to want to "legalize" heroin but not Valium. I think we ought to have a free market in all drugs.

LF: Tom, you know that's impractical. No politician would hear of it.

I: I am not interested in talking to politicians who care only about getting reelected. To paraphrase a familiar saying, I'd rather be right than be listened to by politicians. I can't accept the scheme you propose because it is incompatible with our present prescription laws: How could you sell heroin like alcohol so long as physicians cannot even prescribe heroin? There can be no sound solution of the "drug problem" without coming to grips with the fundamentally unconstitutional nature of prescription laws.

It is plainly foolish to believe that people need the help of the state to protect them from chemicals we call "drugs," when all they need to refrain from introducing them into their bodies is their own free will. The opposite situation prevails with respect to chemicals we do not call drugs, which are introduced, typically without our knowledge or consent, into the air we breathe, the water we drink, and the food we eat, thus posing a danger from which we cannot so easily protect ourselves. Nevertheless, we wage real wars against so-called drug pushers, but mount only mock battles against the worst polluters in the world, the great nation states and their government-protected industries. Why? Among many reasons, I can here mention only one, namely, that we have lost sight of the distinction between vices and crimes.

"*Vices,*" wrote Lysander Spooner (1977), the great 19th-century American libertarian, "are those acts by which a man harms himself or his property. *Crimes* are those acts by which one man harms the person or property of another."

It follows that for protection from vice, no responsible adult needs the help of the government; it is something one can, indeed must, do for oneself. Contrariwise, for protection from crime, everyone needs, and must have, the help of the government, lest the law of the jungle replace the rule of law. With disarming simplicity, Spooner emphasized that:

No one ever practices a vice with any ... criminal intent. He practices his vice for his own happiness solely, and not from any malice toward others. Unless this clear distinction between vices and crimes be made and recognized by the laws, there can be on earth no such thing as individual right, liberty, or property; no such things as the right of one man to the control of his own person and property, and the corresponding and co-equal rights of another man to the control of his own person and property. (p. 1)

More than 100 years earlier, in his epoch-making work, *The Fable of the Bees: Or Private Vices, Publick Benefits*, Bernard de Mandeville (1988) had actually gone much further, positing "private vices" as the very foundations of the public interest conceived as the free market. By cannily characterizing the market as a mechanism for turning *private vices into public virtues* (benefits, as he put it), Mandeville (1670–1733), a Dutch-born British physician-satirist, succeeded not only in giving a satisfactory account of the free market's psychosocial underpinnings, but also in making it morally acceptable.

Not surprisingly, abolishing or prohibiting market relations reverses the process Mandeville described. By replacing *personal* self-control with *impersonal* legal coercions, Communist antiproperty laws and American antidrug laws transform (what ought to be) *private virtues* into (what are in fact) *public vices*. This is precisely the lesson we draw from what market controls on goods and services have wrought in the Soviet Union, and ought to draw, but stubbornly refuse to draw, from what market controls on medicinal and recreational drugs have wrought in the United States.

REFERENCES

Bennett, W. (1990, March). Should drugs be legalized? *Readers Digest*, pp. 90–94.

Breo, D. L. (1986, October 24–31). NFL medical advisor fights relentlessly against drugs. *American Medical News*, pp. 18–19.

Carpenter, T. G., & Rouse, R. C. (1990, February 15). Perilous panacea: The military in the drug war. *CATO Institute Policy Analysis*, p. 24.

Ebeling, R. M. (1990, April). The economics of the drug war. *Freedom Daily*, *1*, 6–10.

Food and Drugs Act. (1906). 34 Stat. 768, Chap. 3915.

Harrison Anti-Narcotics Law. (1914). 38 Stat. 785.

Hilts, P. J. (1990, September). Experts call for U.S. to expand drug treatment; Bush aides are receptive. *New York Times*, p. 20.

Lacayo, R. (1990, Fall). Do the unborn have rights? *Time*, p. 22.

Mandeville, B. (1988). *The fable of the bees: Or private vices, publick benefits* [1732]. In F. B. Kaye Edition (two vols.). Indianapolis: Liberty Press. See also Hunter, R., & Macalpine, I. (Eds.), *Three hundred years of psychiatry, 1535–1860* (p. 296). London: Oxford University Press.

Mitchell, C. N. (1990). *The drug solution*. Ottawa: Carlton University Press.

Musto, D. F. (1973). *The American disease: Origins of narcotic control*. New Haven, CT: Yale University Press.

Office of National Drug Control Policy. (1990). *Understanding drug treatment* (quoted in National Drug Strategy Network, *News Briefs* (1990, August 1, p. 1). Washington, DC: Government Printing Office. See also U.S. Department of Justice, (1988). *Treatment alternatives to street crime: TASC programs*. Washington, DC: Bureau of Justice Assistance.

Roche, G. (1990, October). The Hillsdale idea. *Imprimis* (Hillsdale College), *19*, 2.

Spooner, L. (1977). *Vices are not crimes: A vindication of moral liberty [1875]*. Cupertino, CA: Tanstaafl.

Strong, J. (1914, July). Editorial remarks. *The Gospel of the Kingdom*, *8*, 97–98. Quoted in J. H. Timberlake, *Prohibition and the progressive movement, 1900–1920* (p. 27). New York: Atheneum, 1970.

Szasz, T. S. (1970). *The manufacture of madness: A comparative study of the inquisition and the mental health movement*. New York: Harper & Row.

Szasz, T. S. (1976). *Heresies*. Garden City, NY: Doubleday/Anchor.

Szasz, T. S. (1984). *The therapeutic state: Psychiatry in the mirror of current events*. Buffalo, NY: Prometheus Books.

Szasz, T. S. (1989). *Law, liberty, and psychiatry: An inquiry into the social uses of mental health practices* [1963]. Syracuse, NY: Syracuse University Press.

Temin, P. (1980) *Taking your medicine: Drug regulation in the United States*. Cambridge, MA: Harvard University Press.

United States v. Johnson. (1911). 221 U.S. 488.

Discussion by Rollo May, Ph.D.

◆

About 2,400 years ago, there lived a man in ancient Athens who continually interrupted the Athenians in their street discussions. Why did he persist in asking people if they were really wise, and then demonstrating that they weren't wise by pointing out the contradictions in their statements? When they asked him what his role was, he said that he had been sent to be "a saddle burr for the state. "The gods sent me to Athens," he said, "in order to disrupt your quiet complacency and to show you, by asking questions, what really is the truth. My role is to make you think."

Inevitably, the people of Athens began to hate this man, and ultimately, they executed him by making him drink hemlock. The man was Socrates.

I think that Dr. Szasz is a Socrates to us. Over the three decades or so that I have known him, he has been pointing out, like Socrates, the absurdity of people's rules, customs, and beliefs. He makes our Athenians mad. But he says that he does it for their own good. I hope, however, that they do not execute him!

I have followed Dr. Szasz, as a friend and a professional, for about 30 years. I remember the complacency that underlay our relations to medicine, particularly the American Medical Association (AMA), and to the various legislatures around the country. In New York State, the AMA would direct the legislators, "We want this such and such law," and the legislators would pass the law without any real consideration of its meaning. The legislators seemed to hold the conviction that doctors are noble; if they wanted a law, the law would be passed.

Dr. Szasz is the "saddle burr" for New York State as Socrates was for Athens. I remember when he was hired by the state's Department of Psychiatry. Shortly after his hiring, the department came across his book entitled the *Myth of Mental Illness*. Horrified, his employers tried to fire him. But he sued—and, thank God, he won.

Since then, he has always been to me a kind of "saddle burr," a light thrown on our absurdities, particularly the absurdities of medical psychiatry. Soon he also attacked the absurdities of psychology, because we seemed to be aping the medics as fast and hard as we could (which I think, incidentally, is a very bad idea).

The main thing I have heard Dr. Szasz say— and I've heard him say a good many things—is the word myth used in the sense of an anachronism, meaning falsehood. I am scheduled to make a presentation in which I describe the fact that the term myth has a positive meaning, and I believe that using it in its negative sense is itself false. However, that is a minor problem, and that is the way medics think of myth anyway; the probably will continue to use the word as meaning "falsehood" regardless of what I say or anyone else says.

When Dr. Szasz reads my new book, he will see that he also has been using the word wrongly, because I think the word myth has a positive meaning. I am amused by his attack on the misuse of myth, but because he is on the side of the angels, I forgive him.

I always will follow Dr. Szasz with great interest and humor because he is so good at putting his finger immediately on the point where our culture is absurd. Our society is foolishly destroying itself. Dr. Szasz points this out with a little sense of humor. That is why you laugh from time to time, and very rightly so. I welcome him as our modern Socrates.

QUESTIONS AND ANSWERS

Question: Dr. Szasz, I want to ask you a question that troubles me, because I can't reconcile these two issues: freedom and state control. Suppose there were free trade in drugs and that, at some future time, someone would develop a drug that would make people more open and positive—make people feel powerful, as with cocaine; free of anxiety, as with Valium; have interesting experiences, as with LSD. Or that a drug might be developed that would diminish a person's will, so that the person would become compliant to the will of the drug giver. Or a drug would appear that would create a superrace of human beings. What should the State or human beings do? I am interested in the question because I think the theoretical possibility exists that such drugs can be manufactured.

Szasz: Before I answer your question, I should like to take a moment and thank Rollo May for his generous remarks. Rollo, you were most kind and I want you to know that I appreciate it.

Now, the question asked is challenging and I shall try to answer it, though perhaps not head-on. I believe we have enough problems with drugs without conjuring up such an Aldous Huxley-ish scenario. But since I have been asked this sort of question before, I have a ready-made answer in mind. Posing a problem such as you describe is like asking, before one knows how to add or subtract, how to do calculus. First, one has to learn algebra. So far as drugs go, we, as a people, haven't mastered algebra. Instead of being knowledgeable about drugs, we are either phobic or gullible about them. Let me explain.

Before we try to grapple with more difficult questions, we must get two basic ideas clear in our heads. The first is that a drug on the shelf is an inert substance. It can't be dangerous. It can become dangerous only if it gets into your body. And it can get into your body in only one of two ways. One way is that you decide to take a drug, in which case you engage in an act similar to eating or drinking—which ought to be viewed as an elementary human right. The other way is that someone else decides to give you a drug, and introduces it into your body by force or fraud, in which case you are being poisoned—which we ought to view as a crime even if the poisoner is a doctor and the ostensible motive is "therapeutic." Throughout history, until the 20th century, taking a drug was considered to be an elementary right, like eating. Now we regard self-medication, unless it is

permitted by doctors and the State, as a crime. From that premise, only intellectual confusion and social mischief can result.

The second thing we must keep in mind is that the fact that we can buy X does not mean that we should buy it, much less use it. Whatever X is—cocaine, alcohol, fatty foods, lottery tickets, racist literature, a motorcycle—it may or may not be good for us. Again, this is like algebra; it's pretty elementary. It follows, then, that we need the government to protect us from other people, who want to injure us, such as muggers and thugs, but we don't need it to protect us from ourselves, from our own choices. We can protect ourselves from heroin by self-control. Yet we talk about drug users, especially if they are poor inner-city people, as if they were victims, done in by "pushers" and "drug lords." But tempting someone is not a crime: advertisers do it all the time. Selling someone a product is not a crime: merchants do it all the time. On the other hand, aggression is. Yet we bomb the coca fields in Columbia and I don't hear anyone in the mental health professions protesting against *that*.

You raise an important question, however, and I thank you for it. No doubt, with the inexorable march of science, chemists will develop novel psychoactive drugs. What we will then need is more, not less, emphasis on personal self-control and on the classic maxim *caveat emptor* (buyer beware). Of course, if we don't control ourselves, the State will control us. Many people, unfortunately, prefer that.

Question: Yes, the war on drugs has a long history. When, at the end of the 16th century, Raleigh brought tobacco to England, he was immediately persecuted by King James, who wrote the first major antitobacco tract in the English language. The mercantile problem has been with us because we took sacred substances with which we were not familiar, such as tobacco, marijuana, and cocaine, and made them commercial. In colonial America, tobacco was used as currency. We ruined the land with the way we grew it. Then we made it a part of our drug war with the Indians. We gave them alcohol and destroyed them with it, reducing their population from 15 million to 1 million. Ever since, they have been getting back to us with 350,000 tobacco-related deaths a year. This seems to be their revenge, and we don't seem to be addressing those issues at all. I think you discussed this some time ago in your book *Ceremonial Chemistry*, and I would like to know what you think about our having to examine those major cultural differences in trying to work out this so-called "new world" we are in and its old drugs.

Szasz: Thank you for bringing up the history of drug use and drug controls. This is a very important subject. Our educational establishment commits a crime against our young people by teaching them all sorts of nonsense and outright falsehoods and calling it "drug education." As a result, everyone now knows what ain't so, as Josh Billings put it. For example, suppose you mentioned the first Opium War. Every red-blooded American youngster would *know* that the term must refer to some sort of government effort to prohibit the use of opium. Actually, it refers to the British government's waging war on China, in the 19th century, to make China lift its prohibition on importing opium from India. In other words, it was a war against trade barriers; it was a war to keep the market in opium free.

Our present policies supporting the exportation of tobacco products are similar. The U.S. government says cigarettes are bad for us and it discourages the domestic consumption of tobacco. But it encourages the exportation of tobacco, especially to Japan, Korea, and other Asian countries. After leaving government service, some of President Reagan's closest advisors became international tobacco lobbyists, using their influence to make foreign countries accept imported American cigarettes. It's simply hypocrisy and conceit: My drug, tobacco, is okay; yours, cocaine, is poison. My religious beliefs are God-given truths; yours are Satanic heresies.

The most important thing to understand about the war on drugs is that the drugs we prohibit are scapegoats. In the past, we had other scapegoats, for example, Japanese-Americans. After Pearl Harbor, we locked up Americans, whom we decided to *call* Japanese, in concentration camps. Now we scapegoat the drugs we love to hate. We call humankind's oldest and most useful plants, the coca leaf and the opium poppy, "dangerous drugs."

May: The only way we are ever going to deal with these problems is by making a world that is worth living in. It is very doubtful whether what has been going on in the past 10 or 15 years has made our world better. I think that, frankly, it has made it worse. The suicide rate for young people has been going up, as has depression. If you were born after 1950, your chances of having a deep depression are 10 times what they are if you were born before 1950. This does not look like a world getting better. But what is required? In some way, we must construct a world that people will not have to get drunk in order to avoid living in, a world that could be so beautiful.

Question: I just have a simple request. I want to know where I can get a copy of your presentation.

Szasz: I'll give you a copy. But if you are interested in the subject, I would like to suggest that you look at my book *Ceremonial Chemistry* (New York: Doubleday, 1974; rev. ed., Holmes Beach, FL: Learning Publications, 1985).

Question: Dr. Szasz, I've read your work, I've listened to you, and I agree. What frustrates me is, what do I do? What can I do to help make more real the kinds of things you are talking about? How can I help change the thinking processes, or lack of thinking processes, in this country on the subject?

Szasz: It may sound old-fashioned, but I think there is a good deal you can do, by starting at home, so to speak. Charity begins at home. Or it should. And so should drug controls. And so should decent, responsible behavior. And with that goes, in my mind, rejecting paternalism, especially coercive, therapeutic paternalism. Where would psychiatry be without coercion? Nowhere. Where would our "drug treatment programs" be without coercion? Nowhere. The belief that the government can legitimately exercise *power* to protect us from ourselves lies at the root of our drug problems—and much else besides. Look how much interest and money we now waste on the imbecility we call "suicide prevention," and *that* in a country with the highest homicide rate in the world.

Question: Dr. Szasz, I was pleased that you brought out the point regarding prescription drugs, because they pose a much more pervasive problem than a lot of people in our society and our field realize. Also, how do we reconcile the fact that nicotine is available and legal and that more people die per day from that than from so-called "street drugs"? And if we were to make other drugs more available or legal, how do we reconcile that? In other words, would you consider yourself a proponent of natural selection?

Szasz: I don't know what relevance natural selection has to what we are discussing. I am afraid you may be using the term as a code word, conjuring up an image of something you had better be against if you don't want people to say bad things about you, such as that you lack compassion, or worse. I see life as a continuous succession of choices: whether you smoke, eat scrambled eggs, go to Las Vegas to gamble, marry or don't marry, and so on. Choices. Choices. Forgive me for saying this, but your language implies a paternalistic outlook on human relations. Who, in your question, "is making drugs more available"? To whom? Why? Your question implies that the State is like the family—the government/parents permitting the people/children to do what is good for them, and prohibiting them from doing what is bad for them. For parents, you can substitute therapists, and then you have psychiatry; or you can substitute the State, and then you have the Totalitarian State or the Therapeutic State. It's an old idea that goes back to Plato. Ironically, the United States was explicitly founded on the opposite principle—on the principle that the government should be our servant, not our master. We have come a long way from that image. People now expect the government to protect them from dangerous drugs. We have forgotten the old Roman warning: Who shall guard the guardians?

Question: Dr. Szasz, you spoke briefly about drug treatment and I was wondering if you could share your view on organizations that are self-supporting, such as Alcoholics Anonymous, where 99% of the people are not coerced and the government has nothing to do with it and they manage to quit drinking. However, they are based on the disease model. How do you feel about organizations like that?

Szasz: I am in favor of any organization that is noncoercive and uses only private funds. If they want to help people to smoke or stop smoking, or to gamble or stop gambling, and so forth, that should be only their business. We are talking about learning various behaviors, about acquiring habits and breaking habits. Some people can do these things alone; they prefer to do these things by themselves. They decide to stop smoking, and they stop. Others prefer to do it with the help of books, or friends, or hypnotists, or acupuncturists, or priests. Still others may want to do it in the company of former "victims," which seems to me a typically American phenomenon. What is wrong with any of it? Nothing. In fact, that is my idea of freedom. The trouble is that people usually decide that *their* particular way or group has the solution to the problem and that only their methods should be allowed. Take drinking alcohol. Some people who don't want to drink simply decide to stop drinking. Others may prefer to take Antabuse or go to Alcoholics Anonymous. Why shouldn't they?

Question: That's okay, even though they are based on the disease model?

Szasz: I look on your question as addressing a practical problem, not an ideological or linguistic controversy. And that is the sense in which I answered it. The "disease model" as a concept is both too vague and too complicated for me to address here. If a person wants to think of drinking as a disease—or a genetic defect, or God's will, or free choice—that is his or her business. For me, the crucial issues with respect to drug-using and drug-avoiding behaviors are freedom versus coercion and paying for the help one wants or getting it "free" (using tax-supported, government services). I regard self-harm and self-help as elementary human rights. And I believe in the maxim that people pay for what they value and value what they pay for. I think it is silly that awe expect people who want to smoke or drink to pay for their cigarettes and booze, but don't expect people who want to stop smoking or drinking to pay for the help they supposedly want. Why do we always hear about drug addicts mugging people to get money for drugs, but never about them mugging people to get money to pay for drug treatment? It is because drug treatment is a silly euphemism for coercing people to behave as we want them to behave.

Now, if what you mean by the "medical model" is that it is something that somehow *morally justifies* mental health professionals' depriving certain people of liberty (involuntary hospitalization and treatment) or giving them a "service" they don't want (coerced treatment), then we are talking about the operation of the Therapeutic State, a subject I have considered in several of my books.

Question: Dr. Szasz, I thought your analogy between drug treatment programs and concentration camps was pretty interesting. I agree that people often choose drug treatment as opposed to incarceration, and in that case, the concentration-camp analogy would be adequate. However, I think there are folks who choose to exercise their right to become drug-free, and that is the other side of the coin of drug treatment. My question is, how do you view addiction? Does it exist? And how does your view fit into the use of prescription drugs, or street drugs, and the freedom to use of them?

Szasz: It is essential that we be clear about what we mean when we use the word addiction. Actually, the term has two distinct meanings, one physiological and the other behavioral. There are certain drugs to which the human body becomes adapted in such a way that a person who suddenly stops taking the drug may become ill and even die. Barbiturates are the classic example. If you take phenobarbital regularly, day after day, it will lower your seizure threshold, so that when you stop taking it, you will have convulsions. That's physiological addiction. That is a fact that exists regardless of what anyone says about you or your body.

We also use the word addiction to refer to a habit, typically, a drug habit of which we disapprove, such as smoking. We speak of people being addicted to food or gambling or sex. A reading aid program for children, advertised on the radio, is called "Hooked on Phonics." These are metaphorical uses of the term.

Addiction as a habit also exists, but its existence depends in part on what people say about "it." For example, whether a person who habitually smokes cigarettes is *considered to be* an addict is not a fact, but an opinion. You all know that only a few years ago it was abnormal for a psychiatrist not to smoke. For analysts, smoking a cigar was almost as important as putting a patient on the couch. My point is that smoking cigarettes or marijuana is something a person *does*; it is the way that particular person behaves. The person who wants to change a behavior can change it. Where there is a will, there is a way. There is more to it than that, of course. But this is a fair summary of my view of addiction as behavior.

You also ask about prescriptions and prescription drugs. The policy that we need a prescription to obtain certain drugs again reflects a paternalistic organization of that part of the drug market. At the same time, it should be clear that if we can buy something without legal restrictions, for example, an automobile or a washing machine, then it is our responsibility to familiarize ourselves with these things before we buy or use them. If we don't, we are likely to be victimized by the seller and hurt by the product, or, more precisely, we will be victimized and hurt by our own ignorance and lack of responsibility. The same goes for drugs. If we don't know enough about how our bodies work and about what various drugs do, then we cannot intelligently decide what drug to use or not use. We have prescription laws because people are too ignorant and too lazy to rely on themselves and familiarize themselves with basic physiology and pharmacology. Instead, people prefer to rely on doctors, and they believe that if a doctor prescribes a drug for you, it will be good for you; and if the doctor does not prescribe it, then it is bad for you, and the State should not let you have it. If we abolished prescription laws, laypersons could still rely on doctors, could still consult them and get their advice on what drug to take or avoid. But people would not be forbidden to buy and use substances we now call "prescription drugs." Ironically, some prescription drugs—for example, Nicorette, the nicotine chewing gum—are now advertised to the public. This is like advertising certain cereals on children's TV programs to encourage children to pressure their parents to buy the advertised breakfast foods. Prescription laws parentify doctors and infantilize the population. For a people who aspire to be politically free, it is a dangerous habit to fall into.

One Hundred Years of Solitude, or Can the Soul Ever Get Out of Analysis?

James Hillman, Ph.D.

James Hillman, Ph.D.
James Hillman, who received his Ph.D. degree from the University of Zurich, has served as honorary secretary of the International Association for Analytical Psychology and for 10 years was Director of Studies at the C. G. Jung Institute in Zurich. He has written 12 books and was nominated for a Pulitzer Prize.

James Hillman raises fundamental questions concerning the place of psychotherapy in today's world. In his erudite and witty chapter, he presents a social overview and examines failures of individual psychotherapies. Psyche has been located wholly intrapersonally (within the individual) or interpersonally (between persons, families, groups), but never is it conceived of also extrapersonally as a component of the world, as a world soul or anima mundi *in the classical sense.*

INDIVIDUALISM

It is always fun to begin with a profound statement from one of the founding dignitaries. This time I'll cite Sigmund Freud, the bearded patriarchal pro-founder. He wrote: "There is nothing for it but to summon help from the Witch—the witch metapsychology. Without metapsychological speculation and theorizing—I had almost said 'fantasy'—we shall not get a step further" (Freud, 1937, p. 326).

This quotation comes from one of Freud's last papers, "Analysis Terminable or Interminable." That paper shows that the topic of this chapter,—"Can the soul ever get out of analysis?"—bothered him too. It seems a root question of therapy. The solution he offered is

bewitching: to move at all, we must speculate, theorize, and fantasize.

As I begin to speculate now, I shall try to draw the line between analysis or therapy as a system of basic ideas and the practice of therapy that varies according to the clinician. Therefore, when I find fault with therapy, that does not mean that I am trying to find fault with its practitioners. Rather, I would attest to the sincerity of our work despite what I believe to be faulty, and even pernicious, ideas within that work. My criticism is of thought, not of people. Therefore, what I say should not be taken personally by therapists, but it should be taken to heart.

First, I would draw your attention to a curious—no, desperate—theoretical fact: the soul or psyche remains locked up within individualism. In all our work, the psyche is conceived of either *intra*personally (what goes on inside one's skin) or *inter*personally (what goes on between people in transference, and relationships, or among them in groups, families, offices, and other systems). Never in our theories of therapy does the soul have any place in the world of trees and rocks, whales and spiders, buildings and highways, ashtrays and toasters, or political and social institutions.

Psychotherapy omits the *anima mundi*, the soul in the world—although the psyche of nature and of things, as far back as Plato, in our tradition has been considered inseparable from the psyche of the individual person. This sense of an ensouled world is also true, of course, of tribal and pagan cultures, where what we call "animism" attests to a soul quality in places, objects, times, animals, tools, and vessels. In therapy, however, soul is to be found only in the person in the chair, never in the chair itself. For psychotherapy, in general, these nonhuman, nonpersonal objects are mere decor. The world impinges on the psyche as a kind of background noise; the world of animals, vegetables and minerals, and especially politics is beyond the concern of the analytical session.

Example: For many years I have been engaged in selecting, teaching, analyzing, supervising, and examining candidates in Jungian training for the profession of analytical psychotherapy. In the intense examination of these candidates, from the time of their first application and interviews through supervision sessions and case reports, there has been an outstanding omission—an omission in our methods of examination that I came to recognize only in recent years, when my own metapsychological speculations bewitched me.

The omission? We never inquired into the political life, history, opinions, and activities of the candidates, nor was the political life of the patient whose case was being supervised in extensive detail ever brought into the discussion. To what party does the patient belong, if any? What are the patient's political leanings with regard to daily issues, such as Vietnam, race, animal rights, or abortion? What causes does the patient espouse and how do politics play a role in family fights? What was the polit-ical atmosphere during childhood? Were the grandparents anarchists, socialists, fundamentalists, Naderites, knee-jerk liberals, Archie Bunker bigots, protesters, or red, white and blue (*i.e.*, redneck, white skin, blue collar)? In other words, what kind of citizen is the patient?

Omission, whatever the reason, represents a lacuna in consciousness, indicative of a repression. Or, to put it more vigorously, does this omission indicate the presence of a denial, a defense mechanism against the political? Let us consider the denial of the political to be a symptom, and as such, necessary to the economy of psychotherapy, inasmuch as symptoms always play a necessary, even if unsatisfactory, role in the picture as a whole. So what does the absence of the political serve? What is the presence in the absence?

I suggest that we read the denial of the political as an immunological defense, protecting therapy from invasion by the passions of the passing parade, keeping the bell jar sealed so that the psycho-patho-phenomena of the individualized personal client may bud, bloom, and flourish in dream and mood, fantasy and feeling, projection, memory, symbol, body, free association, and transference within the confines of the consulting room. Actualities of today's world shall be banned so as to nourish the deep world, the past world, the private world. This is the job of psychotherapy—the articulation of the inner life. The outside world stays on the other side of the wall.

Psyche is conceived of wholly as an interior phenomenon, even if Freud (1914) insisted on an "object libido" that reaches into the world and without which the psyche remains narcissistic. And Jung (1921a; 1985) insisted that we are in the psyche, not the psyche in us, thereby placing the human being within the larger *anima mundi* or world soul.

The fear of the soul's leaking through the walls is manifest in the ever narrower framework that therapy sets up as its immunological defense. Therapists are not supposed to see lovers or relatives of their patients; they do not socialize with them or attend their seminars, exhibitions, or performances. The lines between life and psyche are strictly defined, even policed, by new codes and committees of professional ethics unimagined by Freud, or by

Jung, Adler, Reich, Ferenczi, et al. One therapist told me that recently she relaxed the usual constraints; she and her patient talked of political events, about which they both have strong feelings. The patient, at the end, thanked my colleague for the "chat," as if the current international crisis and a new hazardous-dump ruling were not a serious part of psychological discussion.

Clearly, here the metapsychological witch is at work, for this barrier between life and psyche conceals ontological assumptions about the nature of the human being:

1. That human being can be sectioned off from wider being;
2. That the conscious will can maintain this division without seepage;
3. That segmentation improves concentration and, therefore, psychological awareness;
4. That the psychological and the political can be conceived as two distinct discourses; or
5. Finally to put it as an extreme contradiction so as for greater emphasis—that the political is not psychological and the psychological is not political.

For simplicity's sake, I am using the term "individualism" for this person-enclosed idea of psyche. And, I want to point out that individualism was a 19th-century modernist notion of the human being that dominated thought and action in the late Victorian period, whether in industrialism, colonialism, capitalism, or in depth psychology (Cf. Sampson, 1989). If psychotherapy is to evolve in the next decade, or even exist as a viable activity rather than a yuppie anachronism, a white suburban ghetto, a romantic nest of intimacy, a playroom for the hapless child, a ventilator of spleen against phantom parents of the past, or a narcissistic chamber of mirrors and self-referent body sensations, then we shall have to deconstruct, destabilize, and displace individualism.

Neither Freud nor Jung offers a way out of individualism nor do they seem to want to. Freud (1921) confronts the question directly, admitting that man "passes his life" as a *zoon politikon* (Aristotle's phrase), by examining Trotter's theory of a herd instinct "that impels individuals to come together in larger commu-

nities" (p. 84). Freud, however, contradicted Trotter, saying, "Even if the social instinct [and here he is also taking on Adler] is innate, it may be traced back to . . . the childhood of the individual . . . (1922, p. 134). "Let us venture to correct the pronouncement that man is a herd animal and assert that he is rather a horde animal, and individual creature led by a chief"(1922b, p. 89).

Jung (1934) attacks self-centered egotistical individuality; nonetheless, he named the innate process of the psyche's course toward death "individuation," by which he meant becoming ever more distinctly unique (Jung, 1921b). Moreover, again and again, Jung (1916) praises the individual over "the collective," a term that indiscriminately covers s"the group, the crowd, and the mob. Jung uses an analogy with the fractions we learned in the sixth grade: the larger the common denominator, the smaller is the value and the power of the numerator, the individual. Freud's horde and Jung's collective are both put down in favor of a romantic individualism.

The dilemmas of individual/collective, private/public, interiority/world, personal soul/world soul that I am casting as a dilemma of therapy/politics, this agonized dilemma that releases my own desire to return the soul to the world from its encapsulation in therapy, recapitulate one of the long-standing conflicts in our culture: the conflict between affirmation of the political community by the polytheistic Greeks and Romans and the affirmation by Christians of the private, personal, monocentric individual.

For the Greek Aristotle, to quote one of his most famous phrases, "man is by nature a political animal" (*anthropos physei politikon zoon*). Marcus Aurelius, the most philosophical of the Roman emperors, wrote:

In what I do, I do in the service of mankind; in what happens to me, I accept from the Gods. . . . , My own nature is civic [or political]: I have a city, and I have a country . . . and consequently what benefits these communities is the only good for me. . . . Bear in mind that to perform social duties is to obey the laws of human nature and your own constitution. . . . You help complete the social whole; therefore your every action should help complete the life of society.

Jesus denied these assumptions that placed the human so firmly in the world. "My kingdom is not of this world" (John 18:36). Christianity as promulgated and exemplified by Paul and Jerome, and particularly by Augustine, gave the individual overriding importance. The human task was to follow the interior voice, the vocation, away from the world even if it led to the desert wilderness or crucified martyrdom. Intense individualism, guided by the God within and the unique spark of the interior soul, was the path of freedom.

As Elaine Pagels (1988) writes: "The idea that each individual has intrinsic, God-given value and is of infinite worth quite apart from social contribution . . . pagans would have rejected as absurd"(p. 81). Anyone who withdraws to the privacy of the consulting room, the meditation chamber or the isolated vision quest in the wilderness, from the pagan viewpoint, is nothing other than an idiot. The Greek term literally referred "to a person concerned totally with personal or private matters [*idios*, 'one's own'] instead of the public and social life of the larger community" (p. 80). *Idios* also means "apart"—apart from, not a part of. *Idios* was often contrasted with *demosios*—of the people; *demos*; democracy.

From this civic, communal, and pagan viewpoint, therapy is a recrudescence of Christianism's emphasis on the solitary person whose life is a constant compulsive search for brethren and sisters, intimacy and relationship, over which looms the isolated cross of suffering (hence our term "patient," from passion, *passio Christi*), a suffering from which therapy offers surcease, and yet can only perpetuate by its apolitical separation from the world and its pagan animation.

Even worse: From the civic and pagan viewpoint, therapy, for all its virtues in shaping, sophisticating, and affirming the patient's interior being, the ownership of his or her own life and soul, in actuality produces, *idiotes*, political idiocy. Self-focus yields idiocy.

I intend this to sound exaggerated. As Ortega y Gasset said, "What's the use of talking to make a point if you don't exaggerate?" My claim that therapy may be turning us all into political idiots even as it makes us more sensitive individuals makes me believe that we are no longer

tracking the unconscious. The unconscious does not stand still. We are always unconscious anew with each step of consciousness. Where and what is the unconscious today? It is certainly not in childhood, family, sexuality, feelings, relationships, arcane symbols, altered states—that stuff is on every talk show, in every self-help manual. Kids of 12 who dutifully clock in their 18 hours a week of TV time know as much as professionals about codependency, multiple personalities, channeling, violence, addiction, and bulimia. The classical unconscious that used to appear as a slip of the tongue is now on the tip of the tongue. Where we are least able, however—and against which most people anesthetize themselves with earplugs, alcohol and aspirin, jogging, Walkman radios, sleeping tablets, sugar, shopping, and flipping through magazines and catalogs—is in the world out there, the *polis*, the political communal city. Therapy removes psyche from it and remains unconscious with regard to it; it is the great unanalyzed. So the equation becomes: the polis equals the unconscious. We have become superconscious patients and analysts, very aware and very subtle interiorized individuals, and at the same time less and less conscious as citizens, passive-aggressive in our complaints, stimulus-blocking of the tragedies among which we live and the horrors our nation officially perpetrates, imagining redemption through intimacy and personal understanding, rather than through political awareness and communal activity.

PATIENT AS CITIZEN

I would like to return to Aristotle in order to expand on the four terms of his sentence: "Man is by nature a political animal."

1. *Anthropos*: means "man" but also "mankind," "human being," and "the completely realized human being." For Aristotle, the final goal, that for the sake of which we exist, is the realization of our formal essence, of what we are, and what we are is political.

2. *Physei*: the basic stuff, essence, original nature of human being.

3. *Politikon*: this word, from which come our

words "political" and "police," refers to the Greek word for city, *polis*. *Polis* in its roots and cognates means "throng," "crowd," "runny," "pour," "flow," "fill," "flood," "overflow," "swim"—it is essentially plural, *poly*, as in its Latin cognates *plenus*, *plerus*, *plebs*, *plus*, meaning many, more, full. *Polis*, therefore, refers less to established civic institutions than to the flow of life through a throng, a community or *demos* (meaning populace), from which comes our *democracy*; incidentally, Dionysus, the God of the wet flow of life, was the favorite divinity of the populace.

4. *Zoon*: from which come our zoo and zoology, the animal force of life, an organic vitality. Here, too, we find Dionysus, since *zoe* was one of his nicknames.

What would therapy be like were we to imagine the patient as citizen? What would be the nature of psychotherapeutic discourse? Could psychotherapy evolve toward a postanalytic therapy, a post–self-centered therapy, a therapy that dissolves rather than reinforces individual identity? Here I am joining with recent deconstructionism, which has shown the invalidity of such identities as gender, family role, and historical continuity of the person, let alone its development. And I am joining with recent social theory that states, "there are no subjects who can be defined apart from the world" (Sampson, 1989, p. 918) and "understanding the individual as individual is no longer relevant to understanding human life" (Sampson, 1989, p. 916). I am imagining a future of therapy whose language no longer relies on self-enclosing terms such as unity, centeredness, wholeness, and especially that wicked witch of the West's favorite term, Self. Though I am represented at this conference as a Jungian, I wish to deconstruct the basic idealization and literalization of Jungian psychology, the Self.

Suppose we were to reimagine this term. Suppose we were no longer to conceive of self as a homeostatic interior *dynamis* of a biological organism, or as the moral spark of an unknowable transcendent, or as the simply given, reflexive activity of consciousness or the integrative processor of experience (whatever that is), or as the auton, or autonomy, of any distinctly defined system. Suppose we set aside our usual notions of self and instead imagine another definition neither biological, theological, or metapsychological, but political—self as the interiorization of community.

Then, to ask in a therapeutic session about the political is also to ask about self. Then, to pursue self-development requires community pursuits. Then, to turn for confirmation of one's self-steering course—"Am I on track or off"; "Am I repressing"; "Am I centered"—one looks less to the dynamics of psyche and body, or the voices and visions of transcendent epiphanies, inner feelings, inner child, inner guru, than to the actual community of one's actual life. Then the pursuit of insight necessitates an objective correlative, the place where insight arises, the community rather than the transference.

By interiorization, I am avoiding literalizing community into some actual political program, some idea of community, as this produces fanaticism. Rather, I am tending toward Alfred Adler's (1988) *Gemeinschaftsgefühl*, a social feeling of commonality that fictionalizes many goals, many political activities, where a feeling of fellowship or *Gemeinschaftsgefühl*, can be intensified, differentiated, and manifested. One imagines oneself a citizen, with discourse about self conceived within a context of communal feeling. I am "really" as I am perceived and responded to, not apart and hidden behind my mask. I am my effects in the world of people and animals, ideas and objects, places and atmospheres. And this community shifts all day long—now with neighbors and then with my plants and dog at home, or with the author and ideas of a book I am reading, or the dead who have come in my dream. But always, whatever is "me" is less apart *from* them than a part *of* them.

If self is given a communal definition, to find "myself," my attention will turn from introspection to noticing simply where I am among the events of the day, what the day asks of me, how it is proceeding and what is occurring in the actual ecological situation—the animals, food, furniture, sounds, and smell—all the visibles and invisibles with which the day is shared. Then to work on my unconscious, foster my growth and self-understanding, and cure my dysfunctions, my lucidity will turn less toward my dreams, and I will be less likely to shut myself away to meditate or to analyze my childhood, expecting something inside my skull or skin to reveal itself and guide me. I turn to what is simply there as it is there, my rooms and their trash, my acquaintances and their reactions, my job associates and their concerns, for these represent my self since it is of community that I am constituted. My definition is always precisely where I am now and, therefore, I am always codependent on others and always contoured by fluctuating permeable borderlines. By definition, I can never be wholly in control, or alone. Interiorization of community means sensing, noticing, attending to what actually engages me and enrages me. The environment is now the mirror of self-reflection and insight now rises from grief over the world; outrage over hypocrisy, exploitation, and corruption; shame at injustice and stupidity; pain for the world's suffering and fear for its future.

Emotions remain dominant, but no longer are they considered to be literally interior. Instead, an emotion may be imagined as a "divine influx," as William Blake said—not mine, but belonging to the soul of the world, which is deprived of its messages and its feelings, deadened when I claim emotions as mine own. My longings for intimacy, my anxiety at solitude, and my paranoid suspicions reflect the world soul's isolation from humans whose love focuses exclusively on one another. Of course, I feel depressed, for this is the appropriate response to the dying of the world, and the world's soul mourns in me beyond my ability to comprehend.

THERAPY AS SYMPTOM

Now we are coming to the actual practice of therapy and the seeds of its potential evolution. As I shall be suggesting, these seeds reside hidden inside therapy's own symptomatic disorders.

First: The evolution of psychotherapy has always followed the symptom. Therapy does not just cook up ideas and then apply them to people. Its theories are responses to symptoms. The symptom leads the way. The urgency and

the enigma of the symptom steer the evolution of the psychotherapeutic endeavor, pressing its inquiries into new unknowns.

Charcot in Paris followed the hysterical paresthesias of girls in his Tuesday demonstrations, which Freud attended; and Freud followed the hypnotic trances and hysterical amnesias, thereby inventing the idea of sexual repression and the unconscious. Jung followed the symptoms of his deeply psychotic patients at the Burghölzli asylum, thereby leading to the idea of the dissociability of the psyche, schizophrenia, the complexes' thematic contents, and the archetypes. More recently, the symptoms called "narcissistic" and descriptive of borderline personality disorders have led Kohut and others to evolve further ideas of the self and models for engaging this self. Therapy follows the symptoms. Pathologizing derails the soul off its fixed tracks, announcing its immediately present complaint.

Contemporary symptoms fall into two classes. First, those symptoms that therapy addresses directly—addictions, traumatic neuroses of veterans and victims, dysfunctions, and social, physical, and psychological inferiorities. These are imagined to be external to therapy, exclusively in the client, and for which therapy provides palliative, even curative measures.

The second class of symptoms lies within therapy itself, such as countertransference abuse. This, therapy addresses by means of tightening of the frame against personal erotic involvement, such as I mentioned earlier.

There are at least three other symptoms occurring in therapy that rate our close attention. The first of these complaints runs like this: "I believe I have a slight narcolepsy; I fall asleep, dozed right off in the middle of a session, and can't seem to control it." The second: "I wish I really could cut down, I'm doing 28, or 36, or 45 or more hours a week, sometimes seeing 60 or 70 different people, and it's just too much. I can't seem to get my schedule under control." The third refers to support and recovery groups. Let us look at the first two before turning to the third.

What is the psyche doing in these symptoms that afflict therapy, perhaps because of therapy? One thing is clear: in these therapy-induced symptoms, including the countertransference abuse of sexual acting out, some desire wants to prevent therapy from going on, to bring it to a close.

For example, falling asleep during the session puts closure to consciousness itself, if we define consciousness, as it is usually defined in our textbooks, by such terms as "attention," "wakefulness," "cortical activation," "apperceptive alertness," "intentionality," "continuity of awareness." Suddenly, in the midst of a therapeutic conversation, consciousness absents itself; it enters the dream state, that very condition that requires analysis. And, curiously, the overpowering drowsiness occurs only in these analytical sessions, never at home watching the tube, or when driving the car, or during other conversations, lectures, committee meetings. The narcolepsy seems to be specifically "therapeugenic," as if therapy in the consciousness of the analyst were not merely deconstructing itself, but was hell-bent on destruction of consciousness itself.

The language of the other complaint—"I wish I could cut down"; "Do less"; "Get away more"; "Rearrange my schedule"—takes us into the realm of addiction. The addiction to my schedule of regular client hours each week, month, and even into the next year, literalizes and substantiates time as exact blocks in an appointment book. To mislay or lose the agenda is utterly destabilizing: the therapist, agenda-dependent, looks forward to September or January each year to opening the new blank-paged schedule book.

Although I have usually set this schedule myself, I am not its master. I have become a slave of therapeutic time. Schedule has become a Golem, robot, Frankenstein monster from which our desire fantasies freedom. Desire imagines libidinal objects other than therapeutic sessions—rafting in Idaho, pineapple in Hawaii, long sleeps in a wide bed—but the schedule book does not allow it. "I must check my schedule." I have become dependent on the autonomy of substantiated time. It is my most significant Other with which I am codependent; I am abused and victimized by it, even more than by my clients.

These first two symptoms seem to cancel each other out, whereas they actually reinforce each other in a vicious circle. The more manic the addiction to schedule, the more likely will be the narcoleptic denial. The more narcoleptic drowsiness that defeats the schedule's intention, the more I intensify my therapeutic activities: keeping up, needed, packing the hours back to back, only to fall asleep in the middle of them. Therapy self-destructs from within.

As for the third symptom of therapy, I believe we need to look at it a bit more closely, because in it lies a clue to the resolution of the problem we have been struggling with: the relation between therapy and politics, between personal soul and world soul. So let us follow the witch and speculate about support and recovery groups. Monday nights, I meet with fellow alcoholics; Tuesday nights, it is fat friends at our overeaters' group; Wednesdays, it is adult children victims recovering from early abuses or partners of spouses who were abused, Thursdays, it is battered wives or codependent husbands or divorced fathers raising children alone; and Fridays, it is exhibitionists. Then a weekend retreat recovering from other catastrophes and finding support for other afflictions. "So much going on; I can't even get to the movies, let alone attend a tiring, drawn-out political meeting to select candidates for the school board or state offices. I can't attend hearings on the planned high-rise that will cut off all afternoon sun from my street, or the cleanup of the local river, the tax revolt, the violence at the abortion clinic, or school-book censorship."

If we look closely, the support and recovery groups of Monday through Friday display the main signs of single-issue political groups. Instead of constellating, however, around abortion, censorship, or nuclear energy, their single focus is alcohol, obesity, childhood sexuality. What joins us in these new communities of recovery is no longer the political ward or our ethnic heritage, as in older politics, but our symptoms. No longer am I an Irish-American Democrat or a Swedish-American Farm Laborite. Rather, I am attending this or that meeting because I'm a heavy smoker, a drinker, a flasher. We meet together and fiercely and loyally help one another because of one sole issue: our common symptom, and nothing else, *basta*.

Why do I call these groups a symptom? Their origin and purpose, of course, arise from a symptom, but are they themselves symptoms?

Yes, because they support the individual person. They remain within therapy's old model of the individualized self. The community is not the focus. The community is there for the sake of each individual's psychological problem. I and my symptoms remain in the center. But does the bell toll only for me?

Before we go too far in condemning these groups for maintaining modernist individualism, let us recall Freud's and Jung's sense of symptoms in general. They are necessary compromises. They defend against, and yet offer a roundabout way of satisfying, what the psyche really needs. The symptom attempts to redress a basic psychic dysfunction and points the way to the cure of this dysfunction.

Therefore, these groups are both substitutes for community action and feeling-charged cells of community. On the one hand, they do keep the individual locked into his or her subjective complaint, but on the other hand, they are functioning psychological communities, hampered only by their person-centered subjectivism.

The pathology around which the group gathers remains mainly within the person, for instance, as an eating disorder, rather than also in the world, as a food disorder. In that case, the group might focus less on why I eat, how I eat, when I eat, and what I eat, and the causes of these patterns in childhood and my "problems," but might also, even mainly, focus on school lunches, fast food, food storage and subsidies, agribusiness and land use, price supports and food conglomerates, TV ads, sugar addiction, food stamps, packaging and distribution, global effects on fishing, grazing, fertilizing, pesticides, and the deepest prejudices and symbols in the culture regarding what is good, what is healthy, and what is impure, disgusting, and taboo. An obese person is already in the food business and can apply psychological insights into the gross distortions, the obesity, in the world soul's food disorders of which our eating disorders are but reflections.

The corporation, the very basis and bulwark of capitalism, is itself a corporate body, imagining itself as a predator, following its motto of "grow or die," ever struggling to keep lean by trimming excess fat.

I have used overeating as one example, but we could similarly speculate on how a support group might consider addictions, molestation, battering, and exhibitionism, and what political actions might then ensue from these psychological speculations. Members might soon discover victimizations and abuses taking place in the cultural psychology of their daily lives that far exceed in significance the reconstructed abuses of childhood long ago and far away. Therapy would then be moving into the arena of the world, and clients, patients, analysands would bring the acute sensitivity of their psychological hearts to the neglected and unconscious political life that cries for the attention of the awakened adult.

The awakened adult continues to be the aim of soul work ever since Socrates. Another term for this awakened adult is simply "citizen." And this awakened adult, this citizen, cannot get out of therapy so long as he or she remains lulled in the comforting lap of therapies that sing lullabies to the inner child, whether idealized or damaged, whether a source of hope and glory or a traumatized survivor. The appeal to that figure, the nurturing of it, longing for it, and imagining of it as redeemer of my present predicament, not only serves nostalgic sentimentalism for a lost paradise and a fairy-tale transformation, not only concentrates the awakening mind and its tender feelings on a past that is gone, or never was, and the isolated subjectivity of loneliness, abandonment, and powerlessness, but also the appeal to the inner child puts blame on others, and especially on the slow and painfully built institutions of civilization: family, education, government, and culture.

Worse yet, the child archetype, this imaginary inner child that is both so frail and so divine, so full of promise and ever incapable of achieving this promise, captured by the omnipotence fantasy of endless inner growth and addicted to ideas of independence, empowerment, and control as well as narcissistically obsessed with its hurts, sores, and failures, and what it deserves, this archetypal figure who now monomaniacally rules the models of therapeutic thought is wholly apolitical. The child does not, cannot vote. The child feels itself a victim of forces greater than and outside of itself; it is fickle; it rebels and complies. The child is passive with its aggression, and paranoid with its insights, feeling itself always "dis'd": disempowered, disaffected, disrespected. The child's complaint cripples the body politic: What can I do? I'm only one vote. And in this way, therapy, despite its honorable intentions, sincere practitioners, and notable results, works hand-in-glove with the cynical nonparticipation that marks our political system, keeping the awakening adult citizen harnessed to this archetypal child, the inner monster that therapy has invented and fostered, thereby depriving the city and our culture of their most sensitive citizens.

The evolution of therapy translates to mean the end of individualism, the patient become citizen, the abandonment of the child, and the return to the world of the soul as the place of its making. As the English poet John Keats (1819) said not long before his death at 25, "Call the world . . . 'the vale of soul-making,' then you will find out the use of the world . . ." (p. 326).

REFERENCES

Aristotle. *Politics*, 1253 a2 and elsewhere.

Aurelius, Marcus. *Meditations*, Books 8:12 & 23 and 9: 23.

Freud, S. (1914). On narcissism: An introduction. In *Collected papers, Vol. IV*. London: Hogarth.

Freud, S. (1922a). The libido theory. In *Collected papers, Vol. V*, (p. 134). London: Hogarth Press.

Freud, S. (1922b). *Group psychology and the analysis of the ego* (pp. 84, 89). London: Hogarth Press.

Hillman, J. (1983). *Healing fiction*. Barrytown, NY: Station Hill Press.

Hillman, J. (1988). Power and Gemeinschaftsgefühl. *Individual Psychology: The Journal of Adlerian Theory, Research and Practice, 44*, (1), 3–12.

John. (Bible). *New Testament, 18*, 36.

Jung, C. G. (1916). Adaptation, individuation, collectivity. In *Collected works, Vol. 18*. Princeton, NJ: Princeton University Press.

Jung, C. G. (1921a). Psychological types. In *Collected works, Vol. 6*. Princeton, NJ: Princeton University Press.

Jung, C. G. (1921b). Definitions. In *Collected Works, Vol. 6*. Princeton, NJ: Princeton University Press.

Jung, C. G. (1934). The development of personality. In *Collected works, Vol. 17*. Princeton, NJ: Princeton University Press.

Jung, C. G. (1963). Memories, dreams, reflections, (Glossary) p. 352. London: Collins.

Jung, C. G. (1985). In Hillman, J. *Anima: An anatomy of a personified notion*. Dallas: Spring Publications.

Keats, John. (1895). Letter 1819. In H. B. Foreman (Ed.). *The letters*, (p. 326). London: Reeves & Turner.

Pagels, E. (1988). *Adam, Eve, and the serpent*. New York: Random House.

Sampson, E. E. (1989). The challenge of social change for psychology. *American Psychologist, 44*, (6), 914–922.

Discussion by Alexander Lowen, M.D.

◆

First, I compliment Dr. Hillman on bringing to our attention some of the major flaws in the therapeutic approach. On the other hand, I have much to criticize concerning his remarks.

Dr. Hillman argues that therapy has failed because it has been too strongly or completely focused on the individual. As proof of this failure, he cites the increasing chaos in the world. I will agree with Dr. Hillman that our society has become increasingly dysfunctional in this century, the same period that has seen the increasing interest in and need for psychotherapy. Obviously, psychotherapy has been unable to prevent this social deterioration. To blame this state of affairs upon the fact that the ther-

apeutic process is primarily concerned with the welfare of the individual is shortsighted. To think that individuals in therapy are not seriously concerned with the social situation is erroneous. To believe that if therapy were more focused on the individual's relationship with and responsibility for the community, both individual and social welfare would improve is naive.

To say that people today are self-centered is wrong. They are narcissistic, which means that they are ego-centered and that their sense of self is weak. And they are not individuals in the true sense of the word. They should properly be described as mass individuals, subject to mass advertising, influenced, and, therefore, controlled to some degree, by mass media, and overwhelmed by mass movements, massive noise, and massive litter. A true individual tries to hold himself or herself apart from the mass to preserve his or her sense of self. This does not mean that such a person is isolated. That person is, in fact, more sensitive to the communal condition and the communal problem because he or she is not engulfed in or overwhelmed by the mass culture. Unfortunately, there are too few such individuals in our society.

Just as a mass individual is not a true individual, so a mass society is not a true community. Only true individuals can create a true community—one that respects the individuality of its members, who return that respect by taking responsibility in preserving the human values that make community life possible. I have personally assumed that responsibility in my work and in my life, in my writings and in my practice. One cannot separate private behavior from public behavior, personal values from community values, individual responsibility from community responsibility. We are the community and how we live determines what goes on in the community.

I believe that our values have become distorted. We have abandoned the values associated with a sense of self for ego values. For example, dignity is a word one rarely hears today. Dignity is associated with the self, not with the ego. Narcissistic individuals who are identified with their ego image do not think or function in terms of dignity. Their values are power, success, acclaim, status, and so on. Gentleness is another value that is missing from today's culture of violence and sex. Its absence is reflected in the fact that there are few true gentlemen in today's world. Another value is gracefulness that, on the psychological level, would be represented by graciousness. These are body values, not ego values. Individuals who are identified with their bodies have an understanding of these values. Most people in the modern world try to shape their bodies to conform to an image in the mind, rather than to use their minds to understand and appreciate the majesty and magnificence of the human body.

Without an identification with the body, we cannot identify with nature or the earth. We exploit these realms for profit and power. Since we are also dependent on them for survival, we are self-destructive.

Many psychoanalysts, including Reich and Bettelheim were political activists in the period before Hitler. They believed that it was necessary to change the social system to produce healthy individuals. Both Reich and Bettelheim gave up that approach because it was not possible to implement, and they came to the conclusion that one could not build a healthy society if one did not have healthy individuals. It is like trying to build a house with warped timber. I see my role as a therapist to be one of helping some individuals, albeit a very few, to become more fully true individuals who know the joy of living and can share that joy with others. I feel good when I can achieve that goal with some persons. More may be necessary, but more than that I cannot do.

But to do that I have to return the individual to his or her body. The individual has lost full touch with the body as he or she has lost touch with nature and the earth. That cannot be done, I believe, through a purely verbal therapy of any kind. If we are to become identified with our bodies, we can only do so by understanding and feeling the body. In my view, that means engaging the body directly in the therapeutic process.

DISCUSSION BETWEEN DR. HILLMAN AND DR. LOWEN

Hillman: I am very glad that I had the honor of your response, because in those few words, you have summed up so well the current reality of therapeutic philosophy: that we must make better, healthier, stronger-defined individual people, with a living spirit and a strong self and a living body. When that occurs, we shall then be able to have a better society.

Lowen: When and *if* that occurs.

Hillman: We are still waiting for that. And in the last 50 years, we have had more and more therapy, and the world has got worse.

Lowen: But it is not the problem of therapy; it's

the problem of television, the automobile, the overactivity.

Hillman: The problem here is that again we are back into the box of "we are good and they are bad." We are good, the politicians are bad. Television is bad, the world is dysfunctional, but what *we* are doing is okay, and I am trying to say that won't go anymore. We have got to self-criticize; we've got to move from being smugly sure that what we are doing is the right thing, because there is perhaps a correlation between the increased sensitivity of our class of people, therapists and clients, who have become more sensitive through all of our work. We have become more sensitive, and at the same time, we have become more anesthetized. It is what Robert J. Lifton calls, "psychic numbing," so that we don't want to hear what is going on in the street and in the piles of garbage, and so on and so forth. We have become more personally and privately sensitive and more politically numb.

This problem of separation, of imagining the individual as still something that can enter, depart from, be different from, the community, sets the problem of community always as something other than or outside of. I am trying to reimagine self so that it includes community *by its very definition*, and that one doesn't retire to find self, but enters to find self.

I have to admit that what I have been trying to say is "wonkey," because it has not been very well established. I can only imagine; I don't how it will be or how it could be. I understand what you are saying, because that is what we are doing, and what therapy has been believing in, but I do not think it is viable any longer. I think it's got a shadow. I think what has been the virtue has become a vice. I think we have to take what you call the dysfunction of our political world (I mean community world—I don't mean politicians) as a correlate of our increased concern with therapy. We think we have become better and better. We think therapy has done all the good things you mention; and it has. But what's the correlation with the decline of the world?

Lowen: Well, I don't agree with you about some of those things. For example, I don't think therapy has made much of an impact. The prob-

lems of people have become worse during the last 40 years. Therapy hasn't caused that. On the contrary, therapy is struggling against that problem. In Freud's time, the outstanding problem that he struggled with was hysteria. I haven't seen a hysterical patient in 40 years, and I have been practicing for 50 years. What I see are narcissistic individuals who have no feelings. At least the hysterical patients in Freud's time had some passion, even though they could not handle it. Our problem is that we have lost passion.

I do not agree that we are trying to isolate ourselves. When I work with patients, we talk about their daily lives. We don't talk about their daily life in a narrow sense of the word, but we talk about them as human beings in the world, in contact with people.

Hillman: What about toasters and ashtrays and subway tickets, and their whole world?

Lowen: You want to get rid of them? I would applaud you.

Hillman: No, I *don't* want to get rid of them! I want to reensoul the world or promote the reenchantment of the world. That is the world in which we live. That is the world that abuses us. If we don't recognize its claims on us, and its screaming for attention, then we only find soul among people. And then we are living in the Cartesian world—the world out there is dead; that's where litter.... Descartes invented litter: "Everything out there is dead," and the soul is only inside human beings or in relationships. I think that is the major problem with our theory—that soul does not extend into the animals, trees, rocks, roads, institutions, things, ashtrays, toasters, a plastic jar.

Lowen: Well, let me go a step further. I would say that the problem with psychotherapy is that it is too damn psychic. There is too much concern with thinking, there is too much concern with ideas, and when you are concerned with ideas, you have separated yourself from the *anima mundi*, which is concerned with feelings, movement, and being. We are one-sided in our basic therapeutic approach. We focus on words. Our whole way of intervening is through ideas and words. That is half-sided. We have to get more into the body itself directly. We can make it come alive, and that is where the soul of human beings will contact the soul of the universe.

Hillman: That has been your great contribution. The work with enlivening the body has been a marvelous thing that you have done in your writing and in your practice. What about the body of the world? The decrepit, corrupted, composting body of the world?

Audience Member: We are the body of the world.

Hillman: No, the body of the world is also the chair upon which you are sitting.

Lowen: Yes, but it's also the amount of paper that is littered around us. There are the automobiles and the emissions that destroy the air. Somebody said years ago that the greatest tragedy that befell humankind was the automobile. I believe that.

Hillman: I am not going to stay with nostalgia for the preautomobile time. That won't do it. We have got to find a way to work the automobile so that its form and its beauty enhance the world. We can't think that we are going to sit behind a horse and watch its backside move like that.

Robert Bly once said, "Do you realize how courting used to be? You used to get the buckboard and you would sit behind the horse and you and your girl would sit there and watch that horse's ass going like that for about two hours."

Lowen: Well, it is a sad day when we don't see any movement like that in people either. Let me say, Dr. Hillman, that I wish you success, and you have the promise of my sincere effort in trying to change that sick soul out there. If there is any way that you could show me how I can do it, I will gladly cooperate.

QUESTIONS AND ANSWERS

Question: My name is Sal Minuchin and I live in New York. Dr. Lowen also lives in New York,

and I want to tell you what you can do in New York. There are a lot of poor dispossessed people in New York whom one can join. There are people on the corner of where you live whom one can join. There are ways of working politically from the point of view of being a psychiatrist. I think that your dichotomy is a way of avoiding that.

Question: Dr. Hillman, I wanted to address the whole concept of abandoning the inner child. It has surprised me that you would say that because it seems like it is abandoning some of the psychic, that has validity, as all parts do. It seems that it's only been society that has disempowered that child. That child is very powerful in all aspects, and I expect that many of our political leaders need more child.

Hillman: I should have said abandon the *exclusive worship* of the inner child, not abandon the inner child.

Question: I am wondering what Dr. Hillman feels we might do to nurture a world community, earth soul, a collective soul. . . .

Hillman: I have not used inflating ideas like "world community" or "global something-or-other." I said the idea of community shifts all day long from where you immediately are. Whatever the community is—whether you are at home with your dog and your plants, or you are talking to your neighbors about the broken elevator, or having Thanksgiving dinner with family members you haven't seen for 12 years—that self is always communal. It isn't a matter of talking of the "whole earth" and giant ideas that don't immediately and actually involve us. As Dr. Minuchin said, "You can join with what is immediately on the corner of your street"; I'll add, "You *are* what is immediately on the corner of your street."

Question: As I heard someone say in another workshop, I think you two need each other. It seems to me that what you are saying, Dr. Hillman, about our needing to focus our attention on the outer world is absolutely correct. But Dr. Lowen is giving us the mechanism for perceiving that external world. If you are dead to yourself, you can't watch your cat and understand that there is a little soul in there. You can't feel the cat stretching. You can't be with the world you're in if you haven't the basis within yourself and I think . . .

Hillman: Very, very true. My question is: Why must we wait until we are somewhat healed? Is it the case that the wounded can't be active? One of the assumptions of therapy is that we must cure or fix the wounded so that they can be active. Throughout history, we have had wounded, and the wounded always have been able to be active to the limits of their wounds.

Question: A preface to my question: I just want to state that I felt that Dr. Lowen and Dr. Hillman demonstrated, despite their differences, a communal action, and in their handshake, I saw that symbolized.

Dr. Hillman, I'd like to ask you how you would see individual, excuse the term, "psychotherapy," proceeding with your premise about *anima mundi*? Any sense of that?

Hillman: In another five years, at another one of these meetings, maybe I can answer that. But I think it has a lot to do with defocusing on the "me." However, I don't quite know yet what that means, defocusing on me.

Question: It seems we are still stuck with analysis and individual sessions.

Hillman: Before we look for what we should do, we have to realize the extent of where we are. One of our difficulties is that we want to keep moving West. But you can't move now: you've had it when you finally get to Los Angeles. Americans always ask: "What should we now do?" Before we can *do*, we need to understand the depths of where we *are* and how that baggage weighs on us; the baggage of individualism.

SECTION VIII

Benediction

In the Days of the Giants—The Steps in Therapy to the Present Day

Rollo May, Ph.D.

Rollo R. May, Ph.D.

In 1949, Rollo May received the first Ph.D. degree in Clinical Psychology granted by Columbia University. Eleven years earlier, he received a Master's of Divinity degree from Union Theological Seminary. Currently, he lives in Tiburon, Calif. Rollo May is the author or coauthor of 15 books and the recipient of many awards and honors for distinguished contributions and humanitarian work, and has received 16 honorary doctoral degrees. He is one of the main proponents of humanistic and existential approaches to psychotherapy.

Rollo May traces the roots of psychotherapy into antiquity. The need for psychotherapeutic ministrations can be found in classical writers, including Shakespeare, Nietzsche, and Ibsen. May describes his interaction with, and perspectives on, four presenters at the 1985 Evolution of Psychotherapy Conference who died prior to the 1990 meeting, and he orients us to their legacy.

Since the 1985 first Evolution of Psychotherapy Conference, a number of our "giants" have died. Virginia Satir, with her high spirits, is no longer with us. Carl Rogers, with his great integrity, is gone. Bruno Bettelheim, with his charming fairy tales, has left us. And Ronnie Laing, a close friend of many of us, also is gone.* When I was talking to the organizers of this conference, I asked, "But our chief heroes have now left us. What shall we do?" One cannot imagine that there could be four persons who were more central to

our work, our aims, and our hopes than those I mentioned who are now gone.

I discovered when I arrived at the conference that there are many other heroes who will arise to take the place of those who have departed. But because I have been thinking about these friends who no longer are with us, I put together some ideas that are partly a remembrance of them and partly a eulogy.

ANCIENT ROOTS

As I was thinking about our loss of these great therapists, I looked through some of my notes to see how far back I could trace psycho-

* *Editor's Note*: Lewis Wolberg, M.D., and Murray Bowen, M.D., were also members of the 1985 faculty who died prior to the 1990 conference. Bob Goulding, another member of the 1985 faculty, could not attend in 1990 because of ill health. Dr. Goulding died in early 1992

therapy in human history. The essence of being human, I found, is the conviction that we are part of one another. In this sense, a kind of psychotherapy is present through all of the past centuries. When we look back, for example, to the Second Century B.C., we find the following: "Epicuras saw that all that was wanted to meet human beings' vital needs was already at their disposal." Yes, this also applies to our own time; we are a rich nation. We have all the mechanical devices at our disposal.

The writer continues: "Epicuras saw men in full enjoyment of riches and reputation, happy in the fair fame of their children. Yet for all that, he found aching hearts in every home, racked incessantly by pangs the mind was powerless to assuage and forced to vent themselves in recalcitrant repenting."* Throughout human evolution, we encounter such passages, in which people beg for some kind of psychotherapy.

Centuries later, we find another scene that is very much like that we experience today. This is from Shakespeare's *Macbeth*. With his doctor, Macbeth is hiding behind the drapes to listen to the ranting of Lady Macbeth in her psychosis. She walks back and forth in her sleep, trying to rub what she thinks is blood from her hands, as she moans in her hysterical guilt. Macbeth whispers to the physician as they stand behind the curtain,

Canst thou not minister to a mind
   diseas'd,
Pluck from the memory a rooted sorrow?
Raze out the written troubles of the brain?

And, with some sweet oblivious antidote,
Cleanse the stuff'd bosom of that perilous stuff
   Which weighs upon the heart. (Act 5, Scene 3)

This is an amazing description of psychotic melancholy in Lady Macbeth. But the doctor answers, "Therein the patient must minister to himself." Macbeth then angrily retorts, "Throw physics to the dogs! I'll have none of it." For no matter what medicine we may develop, no matter how many forms of pills like Valium or

---

*Lucretius, (1951), p. 217. *The Nature of the Universe*. London: Penguin Books.

Librium, we will not basically confront the rooted sorrow or raze out the written troubles of the brain.

NINETEENTH-CENTURY EXPLICATIONS

In the last century, we find another reference to a great need for psychotherapy. I now quote Frederick Nietzsche. He proclaimed that science in the late 19th century was becoming a factory and he feared advances in technology and techniques without a parallel advance in ethics. Then Nietzsche uttered his prophetic warnings about what would happen in the 20th century in a parable called, "The Death of God."

It is a haunting story of a mad man who ran into the village square shouting, "Where is God?" The people in the village square did not believe in God. They laughed and said, "Perhaps God has gone on a vacation" or "Perhaps God has emigrated."

But the mad man continued to shout, "Where is God?" Then he proclaimed:

I shall tell you. We have killed him—you and I. Yet how have we done this? Who gave us the sponge to wipe away the whole horizon? What did we do when we unchained this earth from its sun? Whither do we move now? Away from our suns? Do we not fall backwards, incessantly sidewards, forwards in all directions? Is there yet any up or down? Do we not err as though we were in an infant not? Do we not feel the breath of empty space? Has it yet not become colder? Is not night and more night coming on all the while?

"God is dead!" continues this mad man. "God remains dead and we have killed him."

Here, the mad man became silent and looked around at his listeners. They too remained silent and looked at him. Then he said, "I come too early. This tremendous event is still on its way." (Kaufmann, 1950, p. 75)

This was written 100 years ago, and one can ponder for hours on the question: Has our great progress in technology led us to a development without the ethical parallel that has caused the death of God?

Nietzsche was not calling for a return in the old belief in God. He was, rather, pointing out what happens when the society loses its center of values. That the tremendous event did become true became only too obvious to us in World War I, Hitler, World War II, and almost continuous wars since. What Nietzsche is describing is that we live in a world where there are no directions, no north or south, no up or down. This event was "too early" when he wrote it; but there is a real probability that this is what we will experience in our own day. This question is what psychotherapy tries to answer.

Just 15 years after Nietzsche wrote the above words, Ibsen (1963) produced *Peer Gynt*. In this drama, he has Peer Gynt traveling back to Norway. Gynt, who pretends he is a great blustering hero, turns out to be like everybody else, a lost human being. He is on his way back to find the one person who really loved him, Solveig. As he stands at the railing of the ship in a storm, another ship is sinking nearby. A character on the ship whom Ibsen has called the "Strange Passenger" stands by Peer at the railing. (Remember, this was written 10 years before Freud and about the same length of time after Nietzsche.) The Strange Passenger says, "When a man stands with one foot in the grave, he sometimes tends to be generous." Peer becomes disgusted with the Strange Passenger and he expostulates, "Go away!" The Strange Passenger answers, "But, my dear sir, consider: I'll open you up and let in the light. I want to discover the source of your dreams. I want to find out how you are put together." The angry Peer Gynt cries out, "Go away from me!" And he runs from the railing, calling back to the Strange Passenger, "Blasphemous man!"

Now this Strange Passenger is a psychotherapist 20 years before Freud, put in place by Ibsen's poetic imagination. This illustrates the opening that Freud so voluminously filled, which he called "psychoanalysis."

When we think of mankind all the way down from the time of the cavemen, we realize that we have needed people like the psychotherapist through the centuries. We can find in the history of different centuries these cries for help—for an understanding of the inner person, an understanding of the soul where we think our most serious thoughts, and what we experience when we feel our greatest joy.

CONTEMPORARY GIANTS

When we think of understanding the soul, we think of those four people who were so central to our 1985 conference. One was Virginia Satir. All of us who knew her were captivated by her enthusiasm, by her joy, by the fact that she could take everybody in and not forget anybody. This was a strange power. When she was in New York at one time, she stayed at our house, and my wife asked her what she would like to do that evening. Did she want to go to the opera or to a drama? And all Virginia answered was, "I want to go to the circus," which was then appearing at Madison Square Garden. So I obediently got tickets and we had a very jolly time.

One of the things about Virginia Satir is that she was always exuberant. I never saw her depressed. This exuberance could take in everybody around her. This was the secret of her success as a family therapist. She was like Bruno Bettelheim in that sense: When you were with her, you had the feeling of having found an old friend. I did not know her very well, but I did feel, when I was around her, the spirit of friendship, or the spirit of love, as she would say.

No longer with us from the first conference is the unforgettable Carl Rogers. The strange thing about Carl Rogers was that you had the feeling that he penetrated you. I never could be around him without feeling, "I'm understood." How this developed, I am not entirely sure. It came as part of Rogers' heart, a part of the fact that he never seemed to condemn anybody, but always was open. I can see how a session with Carl Rogers would bring a great deal of good because his heart was so big. Once when I was in Madison, I stayed at his house. At that time, he was doing an experiment in psychotherapy with psychotics in the veterans hospital near Madison. When he and his students finished their sessions after some six months with these psychotics, he sent the tapes to 12 selected people around the country, asking their judgment of what went on. I was one of the 12. When I listened to these tapes by Rogers and his students, I realized that this was something that would do anybody a great deal of good. But my main criticism was that Rogerian therapy has no place for evil and destructiveness. Hence, he was not successful with many of the inmates. However, whether or not Rogers understood the problem was not the issue. He was always devoted to what he believed was true.

He once said to me, "I would walk 20 miles in my bare feet to see my worst enemy if I could learn something from him." Now Rogers could learn a great deal because some of these tapes were not great psychotherapy. But I am sure that they were good for the patient to whom he happened to be seeing at the time.

When I was in New York almost 40 years ago in the early 1950s, we psychotherapists who were psychologists were very much threatened by the bills that were being continually introduced in the legislature to make psychotherapy a branch of medicine. I was appointed chairman of the joint council, which brought together all of the groups that were nonmedical. Though there were not very many therapists, only five or six in the entire state of New York, we were doing our best to get legislation for psychologists. In the course of that work, I telephoned Rogers, who was then in Chicago. I had never met him, but I did know a great deal about him.

I told him of our predicament, and asked him, "Will you back us up?" He said, "I'm not at all sure that psychologists should be licensed." Now I differed sharply with him, but I knew that this was not an enemy speaking. This was a man who wanted psychology to retain the kind of purity it would not have if we were licensed and had all sorts of exams to pass. Today we realize the complex problems that licensure can bring us.

Then there was Bruno Bettelheim, who also was prominent in the conference of five years ago. He was a neighbor of mine in California. His beautiful book on *Fairy Tales* remains here as his legacy to us. He firmly believed that the opening of the imagination of children with fairy tales was essential in the development of these children. And he railed vehemently against those who believed that myths and fairy tales, and that whole aspect of life ought to be thrown out the window, and we ought to live only by technology. I agreed with him completely on this and so did Aristotle. He quoted Aristotle, "He who would know wisdom must know and understand the first tales and the myths for this is where wisdom begins."

Finally, we come to the last of these four friends and teachers who have now left us, Ronnie Laing. It is difficult for me to talk about Laing because he was a very dear friend of mine. I met him in Europe, and he later stayed at our home in San Francisco. He had a fantastic capacity to pierce into the center of another person's mind and to say in a word what the problem was. This came out of a kind of living on the borderline of a psychosis. I don't mean that Laing was psychotic, but I mean that he kept his mind open so that, at each point, he could do therapy by using only a few words. He and I walked in the Muir Woods, the place where the great trees grow to such surprising heights. He would look at these trees and not speak, but one could see how deeply he felt.

CONCLUSION

I want to draw together in this presentation our feeling of loss of these four people, and to state that they are a part of us so long as we are conscious. Whether they live or die is not so relevant. What is relevant is that we take into ourselves the sensitivity of Ronnie Laing, the enthusiasm of Virginia Satir, the spirit of Bruno Bettelheim, and the integrity of Carl Rogers— that we take into our own hearts characteristics like those that made them great. When I was asked to be a part of this conference, I rhetorically asked, "Will it be possible to have a conference without these four persons who meant so much to us?" I knew it was possible, but I wanted to do homage to those who had passed on. We have had an excellent conference, one built upon the integrity of these persons who have been with us and are now gone. I think this is one of the reasons why the conference reflects a real evolution from the ancient men and women who painted signs on their wall, from the ancient Greeks, from the Hebrews, and from the giants in our own age. We all know that our best way of doing honor to these four people is to carry on in their fields; to use what they have taught us, which is to make of psychotherapy a way of life that will be a blessing to all humankind.

REFERENCES

Ibsen, H. (1963). *Peer Gynt* (p. 29). Tran. M. Meyer. New York: Doubleday, Anchor Books.

Kaufmann, W. (1950) *Nietzsche: Philosopher, psychologist, anti-Christ.* Princeton, NJ: Princeton University Press.

Discussion by: James Hillman, Ph.D.

◆

This rare presentation expresses the deep existential vision of Rollo May, who reminds us that the work of psychotherapy is soul searching and not technique. There are many things to learn, but why we are learning them has to do with the soul. To begin, as Rollo May did, with an invocation of the dead seems to me appropriate, because every tradition has to have its ancestors. To ask about the evolution of a field is not merely to look at the process of its history and of its ideas, but also to recollect its lore.

In fact, that may be the very reason many come to see us crazy old men and women on the podiums of this conference—to see what we look like, to hear our voices, not only read our words in books. Our presence is part of the physical lore of tradition. Rollo reminded us that the ancestors are with us—as a source and also as a baggage. We don't leave our baggage behind as the field evolves. We carry it all with us. The tradition builds through time, and we go back to feed from it and be nourished by it, back to Freud, back to Jung, back to Adler, and back to those whom Rollo May invoked.

What I gathered from you, Rollo, is that when we examine the *evolution of psychotherapy*, we have to go backward. This backward look conforms to an old Renaissance idea—in order to move forward, you have to look back. Why? Because that baggage is continually weighing us down, and at the same time it is nourishment. The baggage provides the models and the exemplars that keep us on track.

I also was reminded about what therapy truly is, and I thought that the word itself helps tell us this. The root of the word *therapeia*, the Greek word, meant service, or attendance at an altar. The altar to which we therapists submit remains as a kind of humanist altar—what some today call "secular humanism," a term that is actually quite accurate. The Greek idea of therapy, however, meant an attendant at an altar of the gods, a service to something invisible—present in the world, but invisible, not personal relationships, not humanism. And I think that somehow the invocation of the dead reminds us that the work of therapy attends to the invisible parts of the soul—a presence, an existence of powers that cannot be framed or formulated, but are felt in every therapeutic hour.

Let me tie this idea of *therapeia* to another part of Rollo May's remarks with reference to Nietzsche and the "God is dead" idea, a theme that has been dominant in our culture for the past 50 years, especially in postholocaust theology. I wonder about therapy in relation to Nietzsche's "God is dead." Is therapy practicing in the vacant realm where God is dead? And how does therapy practice without the gods? It seems to me that Nietzsche may have been right. God is dead in one sense: the old God (what feminists would call "the patriarchal,") is less prominent. But there is a tremendous recrudescence of Greek mythology and a new interest in the myths. The revival of the tales and stories and images of pagan gods and goddesses suggests that perhaps God is dead, as Nietzsche said, but the old gods may not be altogether dead. Maybe we are still engaged in that ancient struggle between what was once called

Christianity and paganism, or between mono-theism and polytheism, and, the gods are still around somewhere. But whether it is God or the gods, or whatever, I do not believe therapy can go on in a vacuum, merely discovering new modes of defining the self and what to do about personal relationships, interventions, transfer-ence, frames, cures, adjustments, and so on and so forth.

Therapy, in the vacuum left by God's exclu-sion, becomes what the critics call secular humanism, which is definitely not the deep, and beautiful, existentialism to which Rollo May has been devoted in a long and important career that has been extremely valuable to all in the field.

QUESTIONS AND ANSWERS

Question: Dr. May, you spoke of Nietzsche and how without ethics there would be annihilation. How do you see, in the evolution of the 1990s, the role of psychotherapy in our ethical milieu?

May: I can speak a bit about how therapy evolved from a milieu. I was trained originally as a minister, as Carl Rogers was. Rogers grad-uated from Union Theological Seminary three or four years before I did. A number of psycho-therapists were originally members of the clergy. I wonder how that influences our work. Perhaps there was an effect on Freud. Freud attacked narrow-minded religion very strongly, but his therapy uses the spitting image of Cath-olic confession. He had the patient lie on a couch, and he sat behind, separated from the patient. Who could ever forget he was there? That is exactly what happens in Catholic con-fession. You don't know who the confessor is. You are alone with your confession; the con-fessor is there, but behind a screen, and so somewhat separated from you. His presence is not supposed to interfere with your own rela-tionship to your own heart, your own self. Freud developed something similar in the use of the couch, which he, Father Confessor, sat behind.

I was on the couch for some three or four years in my analysis, and there is a real value

in it. You tend to forget that anybody is there. It's a kind of half-dreamlike state. Your free associations have a kind of depth, a kind of real-ity, and a kind of beauty about them precisely because they are half-dreams. You lie there on the couch and you let yourself go, and some of the material that comes up is fantastic.

Question: Dr. May, you spoke of Carl Rogers and his questioning of licensing. What might that do to us as therapists? I reflected on the struggle that has gone on for years in the Amer-ican Psychological Association between scien-tific and academic endeavors and psychother-apy. That struggle has taken many forms, including, at times, psychotherapists' willing to withdraw from the association. Do you have any comments on that?

May: New York was the first state that gave any legal status to psychologists. Representa-tives of the American Psychological Association came up from Washington, D.C., and helped a great deal. They did so because, they said, New York is not just another state and what goes on in New York will have repercussions all over the country. I then realized that Eric Fromm was right and Carl Rogers was right: There are great dangers to being licensed. You become part of a factory, like machinery, and you have sold your soul in various ways. Once you have licensing, you get all kinds of cheating. A whole system of dishonesty develops. This is caused precisely by the endeavor to be honest through licensing. I used to say in New York, "I am for licensing on the even days of the week and against licensing on the odd days of the week."

I had a great deal to do with establishing licensing in New York State. My conclusion was that it was absolutely necessary; otherwise we would not have had a profession at all. But we have to be humble and careful about our pro-fession because of licensing. In preparing for this conference, the faculty had to write ques-tions so continuing-education attendees could get credit for licensing. That is one of the values and problems associated with licensing. I'm 51 percent in favor of licensing and 49 percent against it. We have to have it—there is no doubt about that. But it also creates problems that have to be faced.